A Practical Approach to Family Law

Third Edition

Jill M. Black BA (Dunelm)
of the Inner Temple and the North-Eastern Circuit, Barrister

and

A. Jane Bridge LLB
of Gray's Inn and the South-Eastern Circuit, Barrister

BLACKSTONE PRESS LIMITED

This edition published in Great Britain 1992 by Blackstone Press Limited,
9-15 Aldine Street, London W12 8AW. Telephone 081-740 1173

First edition 1986
Second edition 1989
Third edition 1992

ISBN: 1 85431 205 7

British Library Cataloguing in Publication Data
A CIP catalogue record for this book is available from the British Library

Typeset by Style Photosetting Ltd, Mayfield, East Sussex
Printed by Redwood Press Ltd, Melksham, Wiltshire

Contents

1 General points   2 Matters to be covered when taking instructions   3 Taking action on the client's behalf   4 Preparing a statement and proof of evidence

1 Introduction   2 The solicitor's duty to advise his client on legal aid   3 Legal aid not retrospective   A: The green form scheme: Part III, Legal Aid Act 1988 and Legal Advice and Assistance Regulations 1989   4 The scope of the green form scheme   5 Financial limits on the work that can be done under the green form scheme   6 Financial eligibility   7 Filling in the green form   8 Repeated advice under the green form scheme   9 Collection of the client's contribution (reg. 28)   10 Representation in court under the green form scheme   B: Full Legal Aid: Part IV, Legal Aid Act 1988 and the Civil Legal Aid (General) Regulations 1989   11 Proceedings for which full legal aid is available   12 Determining eligibility for legal aid   13 Making the legal aid application   14 The issue of a full legal aid certificate   15 Notification of issue of certificate   16 Effect of issue of legal aid certificate   C: Reimbursement of the legal aid fund and the statutory charge   17 Reimbursement of the legal aid fund   18 Solicitor to receive moneys due to assisted person   19 The statutory charge under s. 16(6), Legal Aid Act 1988   20 Where green form advice only is given   21 The duty to make the client fully aware of the potential impact of the charge   22 Minimising the effect of the charge

D: Method by which solicitor obtains payment in legal aid cases   E: Legal aid and the Children Act 1989   23 Legal aid under the Children Act 1989

Contents vii

orders under s. 6   8 Orders to continue payments made during voluntary separation (s. 7)   9 Miscellaneous provisions relating to periodical payments and lump sum orders (duration, orders for children, etc.)   10 Effect of living together on financial orders under DPMCA 1978: s. 25 DPMCA 1978   11 Procedure   12 Enforcement of orders   13 Variation

1 Grounds for application   2 Jurisdiction   3 Orders that can be made   4 Factors to be considered on an application under s. 27   5 Procedure   6 Interim orders 7 Variation of s. 27 orders   8 Section 27 compared with Domestic Proceedings and Magistrates' Courts Act 1978 (DPMCA 1978)

1 The difference between separation and maintenance agreements   2 Likely contents of separation agreements   3 What a separation agreement cannot do 4 The form of a separation or maintenance agreement   5 Effect of a separation agreement   6 Advantages of a separation or maintenance agreement   7 Enforcement   8 Impact of subsisting separation agreement or maintenance agreement on financial arrangements after divorce, etc.   9 The provisions of ss. 34–36, Matrimonial Causes Act 1973 as to maintenance agreements   10 Alteration of maintenance agreements relating to children under the Children Act 1989

1 Introduction   2 The basic provision   3 Possible applicants   4 What property is covered?   5 What orders can be made?   6 Ordinary trust principles generally apply in determining disputes   7 Disputes over land   8 The ownership of cash and assets other than land   9 Fixing the size of each party's share in the disputed property 10 Orders for sale   11 Procedure   12 Practical importance of s. 17

1 Introduction   A: Income support   2 Income support and family credit compared 3 Who can claim?   4 Entitlement to income support   5 Amount of income support 6 Rates of benefit   7 The social fund   8 How to claim   9 Appeal and review 10 Statutory duty to maintain other members of the family   11 The diversion procedure   B: Family credit   12 Who qualifies?   13 Entitlement to family credit 14 Amount of family credit   15 Current rates of family credit   16 Period for which family credit is payable   C: Housing benefit   17 Who qualifies?   18 What payments will be made?   19 Amount of housing benefit   D: Child benefit and one-parent benefit   20 Child benefit   21 One-parent benefit   E: State benefits and marriage breakdown   22 Relevance of state benefits in determining appropriate maintenance 23 Maintenance versus state benefits: pros and cons for the recipient   24 Lump sums and income support

1 The homeless   2 Secure tenants

Preface

Once again, I have endeavoured to ensure that the new edition of this book contains information that is as up to date as possible whilst trying to maintain Jill's clarity of exposition. It has been a hard act to follow!

14 October 1991, bringing with it the implementation of the Children Act 1989 (not to mention its 'supporters', the Family Proceedings Rules 1991 and the concisely-named Family Proceedings Courts (Children Act 1989) Rules 1991), will remain a long-remembered date in the mind of every family law practitioner! It has brought about far-reaching radical changes to the public law and the private law relating to all children. One of the most important features of the new legislation is that the law is now contained in one relatively streamlined statute. However, as the practitioner struggles his way through the ever-increasing mounds of Rules, regulations and dreaded transitional provisions that accompany the Act, he can be forgiven for taking some time to master the new law and its terminology. It is hoped that this book will go some way towards helping that process.

Just as we start to recover from the shock waves of the Children Act 1989 other pieces of legislation are looming on the horizon. The Maintenance Enforcement Act 1991 came into force on 1 April 1992. It provides new methods whereby the courts can attempt to enforce maintenance orders: at the same time it improves the efficiency of existing methods of enforcement.

Finally, the Child Support Act 1991, which received its Royal Assent on 25 July 1991, is due to come into force early in 1993 over a phased three-year period. It will introduce a formula for calculating children's maintenance based upon income support rates and will implement a system for the collection and enforcement of such payments. A Child Support Agency will be set up within the Department of Social Security which will take over from the courts the responsibility for the calculation, collection and enforcement of most child maintenance payments. The courts will, however, retain jurisdiction in limited circumstances.

There are many people who have helped me with this edition. In particular, I would like to thank District Judge John Sennitt for his help in explaining, inter alia, the new procedures for considering the arrangements for children in the context of divorce proceedings. Rosemary Sands of Miller and Co. has also been an unstinting source of helpful advice as to the practicalities involved in implementing the Children Act 1989. Hazel Clark, one of my long-suffering room-mates in chambers, unhesitatingly accepted the challenge of updating the last two chapters of the book, thereby contributing her undoubted expertise on the intricacies of welfare law. I hope that my supply of chocolate cakes to the members of Fenners Chambers to celebrate the finishing of this manuscript went some way towards thanking them for putting up with me whilst I monopolized the library, photocopier and printing facilities for several weeks. Finally, I would like to thank my husband, Stuart, for his help with the book and for remaining a continuing source of moral support throughout its preparation.

The Green Form and Key Card have been reproduced by courtesy of the Legal Aid Board. Form M4 in respect of Arrangements for Children on Divorce is reproduced with the permission of the Controller of Her Majesty's Stationery Office.

I have attempted to state the law as at May 1992.

A. Jane Bridge
Fenners Chambers
Cambridge

Preface to the Second Edition

It has been my task to edit this book and bring it up to date, although Jill Black has maintained an overview of its progress and content. I hope that while inserting new material I have managed to retain the clarity and practicality of approach achieved by Jill in the first edition.

The Children Bill currently before Parliament will prove to be a landmark in the development of the law relating to children in family, matrimonial and care proceedings. I have endeavoured to point out the likely effects of the Bill upon the law at relevant intervals throughout the book. It should be borne in mind that once the Children Act 1989 has received its Royal Assent it will not actually come into force for some twelve to eighteen months thereafter. Thus it will not have any immediate effect upon the present law. For a full picture of the changes to be brought about the reader should refer to Blackstone's Guide to the Children Act 1989.

The Legal Aid Act 1988 has come into effect and transfers the administration of legal aid from the Law Society to the Legal Aid Board. A number of new regulations have been made in its wake.

The Family Law Act 1986 is now almost entirely in force. It makes relatively few alterations to substantive family law, and is mainly a private international law measure laying down a new statutory code for the recognition and enforcement by courts within the United Kingdom of custody orders and foreign divorces, annulments and judicial separations.

The Family Law Reform Act 1987 is now mostly in force and brings the law in relation to illegitimate children more into line with that relating to legitimate children.

I would like, in particular, to thank Mrs Mavis Pilkington and Mrs Margaret Richards for their invaluable assistance with the chapters on taxation and welfare law respectively. Finally, I would extend thanks to my husband Stuart for his enormous assistance, patience and support throughout the preparation of this second edition.

The Green Form and Key Card has been reproduced by courtesy of the Legal Aid Board.

I have attempted to state the law as at July 1989.

A. Jane Bridge
25 Park Square
Leeds

Preface to the First Edition

The student preparing for the Law Society's final examinations is faced with a mammoth task. In the course of one year, he is expected to leave behind the academic approach to law and get to grips with what really happens in practice. How is he to do this when he may never even have been inside a solicitor's office and has no idea what is meant by 'filing', 'service' or 'the green form', let alone how to draft a divorce petition or what to do when a client needs an injunction in an emergency?

This book aims to provide a clear picture of the workings of those aspects of matrimonial law that are most likely to concern not only the student but also the practitioner. It is hoped that sufficient information has been provided, in the text and in the numerous examples, to enable the reader to deal confidently with most matrimonial problems on paper in his final examination or in practice.

Obviously, in writing this book I have had to draw to a large extent on my own experience in practice. However, practice and procedure in matrimonial cases does vary in different parts of the country and the reader should not be surprised if he finds that one or two things are done slightly differently in his local court.

I would like to thank my family, colleagues and friends, all of whom have endured the writing of this book with me and assisted in every way they could. I am also most grateful to the many other people who have given me the benefit of their valuable experience in the matrimonial field.

I should like to acknowledge the kind permission given by the Lord Chancellor's Department and the Law Society to reproduce certain documents.

I have endeavoured to state the law as at November 1985.

Jill M. Black
32 Park Square
Leeds

Table of Cases

Table of Statutes

Table of Statutory Instruments

List of Abbreviations

CAA 1984	Child Abduction Act 1984
CCA 1980	Child Care Act 1980
CCR	County Court Rules
CTTA 1984	Capital Transfer Tax Act 1984
CYPA 1969	Children and Young Persons Act 1969
DPMCA 1978	Domestic Proceedings and Magistrates' Court Act 1978
DVMPA 1976	Domestic Violence and Matrimonial Proceedings Act 1976
FLRA 1987	Family Law Reform Act 1987
GMA 1971	Guardianship of Minors Act 1971
ICTA 1988	Income and Corporation Taxes Act 1988
IHTA 1984	Inheritance Tax Act 1984
LPA 1925	Law of Property Act 1925
MCA 1973	Matrimonial Causes Act 1973
MHA 1983	Matrimonial Homes Act 1983
MWPA 1882	Married Women's Property Act 1882
RSC	Rules of the Supreme Court
TCGA 1992	Taxation of Chargeable Gains Act 1992

PART I
GENERAL MATTERS

1 The first interview

1 GENERAL POINTS

The first interview with any client is extremely important. Matrimonial cases are no exception. This is the opportunity for the solicitor to gain his client's confidence and to equip himself with much of the information that he will need in the course of the case.

The client will no doubt have made an appointment to see the solicitor about a particular problem, for example, because she has separated from her husband and is not receiving any maintenance or because she is being subjected to violence. It is up to the solicitor to ascertain the client's views not only on her immediate problem but on related matters as well so that he can advise her properly. To take the client with maintenance problems as an example, there would clearly be a number of ways in which she might secure a maintenance order against her husband. In order to decide on the appropriate course of action, the solicitor needs to know whether the client envisages getting divorced and whether there is any basis on which she can file a petition. It would be a waste of time to seek periodical payments in the magistrates' courts if the client's instructions were to commence divorce proceedings — the right thing to do would be to file the divorce petition forthwith and seek maintenance pending suit and long term ancillary relief.

If the client is undecided about what she wants for the future, unless she has a problem that requires urgent action, there is no harm in putting the options to her and suggesting that she go away and think things over for a few days, arranging another interview, for instance, for the following week.

2 MATTERS TO BE COVERED WHEN TAKING INSTRUCTIONS

2.1 The basics

2.1.1 Name, address and telephone number

The client's full name and address must, of course, always be noted, as should her telephone number at home and at work so that she can be contacted urgently if necessary. Every firm has its own system for noting routine information of this sort, often on the file itself or on a printed label attached to it. The client should be reminded to keep her solicitor up to date with any changes of address. If her address does change, the new address should be noted and the old address deleted from the file so that there is no danger of letters and documents being sent to the wrong address.

If the case is one where the client's address is to be kept secret from her spouse (for example, because it is feared that otherwise there will be violence), this should be noted clearly on the file with the address so that no member of the solicitor's firm inadvertently discloses the address.

2.1.2   Green form

The solicitor should find out whether the client is eligible for legal advice and assistance under the green form scheme. Eligibility is determined by filling in the green form and comparing it with the key card. This should be done in the presence of the client at the first interview. Before the client decides to accept green form advice, the solicitor should explain the Legal Aid Board's statutory charge to her clearly. If the client decides to accept green form advice, she must sign the green form. Any contribution which she is liable to pay towards her green form assistance should be collected from her forthwith or arrangements should be made as to when it will be paid.

The full details of the green form scheme and the means of assessment are set out in Chapter 2 paragraphs 4 to 10. Note that there is an obligation on the solicitor to advise his client as to her eligibility for legal aid generally whether or not his firm undertakes this work (see Chapter 2 paragraph 2).

The limits for financial eligibility for legal aid are set out in the regulations produced each year by the Lord Chancellor's Department pursuant to the Legal Aid Act 1988.

2.1.3   Assistance by way of representation and full legal aid

The green form scheme does not cover taking any steps in court proceedings (although, of course, it does cover the cost of the solicitor dealing with an undefended divorce case; see Chapter 2 paragraph 4.2). It is therefore usually necessary at some stage to consider applying for legal aid or, in the case of the magistrates' courts, for assistance by way of representation. The full details of the legal aid scheme and the system of assistance by way of representation are given in Chapter 2 paragraphs 10 to 16.

Although the solicitor may be able to deal with the case initially on the basis of the green form scheme, he should nevertheless consider at the outset whether legal aid or assistance by way of representation is likely to become necessary later on. He should bear in mind that full legal aid, in particular, can take some weeks to come through. This means that in an urgent case he may need to seek an emergency certificate and, even in a routine case, it may well be desirable to send off a normal application fairly promptly so that things are not held up later whilst waiting for a certificate to come through.

2.1.4   Clients who are not eligible for green form or legal aid

If the client is not eligible for green form advice and assistance or legal aid, she should be advised, if possible, of the likely cost of her solicitor's services. A precise estimate is unlikely to be feasible as the ultimate costs will depend on what problems are encountered in the course of the case. A rough guide should, however, be given so that the client can decide whether she can afford to pay for legal help. If an estimate is given, the solicitor should take care to make a note of it in the file so that he can refer to it when rendering his bill. The client is not likely to be happy, for instance, if the solicitor quotes a figure for a straightforward undefended divorce and then bills her for twice as much even though there have been no problems associated with the case. A payment on account can be required from the client if the solicitor feels it would be prudent to do so.

2.1.5 Further general information

The solicitor may find it helpful to use a checklist during the interview to ensure that all relevant matters are covered. The checklist below is merely a suggestion. No doubt the solicitor will need to add other matters which he regularly wishes to cover with clients.

Checklist: General information required from matrimonial clients

1. Name

2. Current address

3. Telephone   Home
     Work

4. Eligible for green form?

5. Legal Aid Board's charge explained?

6. Legal aid applied for?

7. Marital status; if married, date of marriage

8. Name and address of spouse/cohabitee

9. Spouse/cohabitee's solicitors

10. Children (names and dates of birth)

11. With whom do children live?

12. Previous proceedings   Nature
     Outcome
     Solicitors who acted

13.	Nature of problem
14.	Wants divorce
15.	Reconciliation discussed?
16.	Any agreement with spouse/cohabitee?
17.	Conciliation service involved

2.2 Reconciliation

The solicitor should always find out from the client whether there is any prospect of a reconciliation. He should be alive to the possibility that the purpose of the visit to the solicitor may not actually be the stated purpose, for example, to obtain a divorce. The real claim may be, for instance, to encourage the other party to mend his ways by forcing upon him the realisation of what will happen if he does not.

The solicitor is not expected to offer practical assistance in bringing about a reconciliation, nor is he qualified to do so. However, there are numerous agencies that do offer such assistance and the solicitor should be in a position to advise on some of the agencies available and how to contact them should the client be interested in pursuing the possibility of a reconciliation. The largest national organisation offering help with marital problems is:

Relate
National Marriage Guidance
Herbert Gray College
Little Church Street
Rugby
Warwickshire CV21 3AP
Telephone 0788 573241

Relate has local counselling centres, the addresses and telephone numbers of which appear in the telephone directory. They do not only deal with reconciliation; they are also prepared to help people who are in the process of getting divorces come to terms with the divorce and make decisions about the future.

There are various religious organisations offering counselling, for example, the Jewish Marriage Council and the Catholic Marriage Advisory Council. The local Citizens' Advice Bureau should have a file listing other organisations offering help and support, particularly those with branches in the area.

Where proceedings are brought for divorce or judicial separation or for an order under s. 2, Domestic Proceedings and Magistrates' Courts Act 1978 (periodical payments and lump sum orders), the court has a duty to consider whether there is any prospect of a reconciliation (see s. 6(2) and s. 17(3), Matrimonial Causes Act 1973, and s. 26, Domestic Proceedings and Magistrates' Courts Act 1978). If there appears to be a reasonable prospect of reconciliation, the court may adjourn to enable attempts at reconciliation to be made. There is machinery whereby the case can be referred to a court welfare officer or a probation officer or some other suitable person for help in effecting a reconciliation.

2.3 Conciliation

Reconciliation is concerned with helping the parties to overcome their difficulties and make a fresh start together. Conciliation becomes important once it is accepted that the marriage has finally broken down. The more bitter and protracted the aftermath of a broken marriage, the more difficult it is likely to be for the spouses and the children to put the marriage behind them and start to build a new life. Conciliation aims to make the breakdown of a marriage as painless as possible by assisting the parties to reach agreement over matters such as the matrimonial home and other property, finances, residence orders and contact orders, thus reducing the areas of conflict to a minimum.

The solicitor has a distinct role to play in conciliation. His own attitude to the case will, to some extent, condition that of his client. If he treats the case as a personal vendetta against the other spouse or his solicitor, this will encourage his own client to dig in her heels and refuse to negotiate or to reach agreement over contested matters unless her precise demands are met. On the other hand, if the solicitor remains objective about the matter, he can encourage his client to give careful consideration to any proposals made by the other spouse and it is much more likely that agreement will be reached.

In addition to the solicitor's own role in conciliation, there is an increasing number of local conciliation services being established to offer mediation and counselling. The exact nature of the facilities offered varies from service to service. The solicitor should be able to find out the addresses and telephone numbers of any services operating in his area through the local divorce court. If he feels that a conciliation service may be able to help he should encourage the client to contact them as soon as possible before 'battle lines' are drawn up.

As well as the independent conciliation services, there is machinery enabling ancillary relief disputes in divorce cases to be referred by the court itself with a view to conciliation by a court welfare officer, probation officer or other suitable person. There is also currently an experimental procedure in the Family Division in contested residence and contact cases whereby the first hearing of the case is an appointment for conciliation with a court welfare officer available to assist in resolving the dispute. The procedure also applies to certain cases where a problem arises over the district judge giving his certificate of satisfaction in relation to the children under s. 41, Matrimonial Causes Act 1973 (as substituted by sch. 12, paragraph 31 of the Children Act 1989) and to contested applications for care and control in certain wardship proceedings.

3 TAKING ACTION ON THE CLIENT'S BEHALF

3.1 Possible courses of action

The matters covered in the checklist on pages 3–4 are fairly general. This general information should enable the solicitor to decide what course of action might be appropriate. The table below is designed as a reminder of the principal remedies available for most of the problems commonly encountered in matrimonial work.

Principal remedies available	
Client's problem	*Remedies to be considered*
Wants divorce	Divorce proceedings (though bear in mind that very occasionally, nullity proceedings may be more appropriate)
Maintenance problems — self (married client)	Welfare benefits Maintenance pending suit and periodical payments under MCA 1973 if intending to seek divorce/nullity If not intending to seek divorce/nullity, consider judicial separation (same ancillary relief as divorce) *or* magistrates' court proceedings under ss. 2, 6 and 7 DPMCA 1978 *or* s. 27 MCA 1973
Maintenance problems — self (unmarried client)	Welfare benefits No court procedure for obtaining maintenance for self
Maintenance problems — children (married client)	Welfare benefits can include a sum in respect of children Maintenance for child can be ordered in the course of divorce /nullity or judicial separation proceedings or under ss. 2, 6 and 7 DPMCA 1978 as it can for a spouse *alternatively* maintenance can be ordered in proceedings under the Children Act 1989 *or* in wardship proceedings

Maintenance problems — Children (unmarried client)	Welfare benefits Maintenance orders can be made under sch. 1 Children Act 1989 and in wardship proceedings
Dispute over property (married client)	Ancillary relief under MCA 1973 if divorce/nullity being sought S. 17 MWPA 1882 if divorce not intended Lump sums can be ordered under DPMCA 1978 and s. 27 MCA 1973 Where children are involved, sch. 1 Children Act 1989 enables the court to make periodical payments, lump sum orders and property adjustment orders
Dispute over property (unmarried client)	Normal principles of contract, tort, trusts and property law apply, e.g., proceedings under s. 30 LPA 1925 for order for sale of real property, proceedings for declaration of trusts, etc. Where children are involved, sch. 1 Children Act 1989 enables the court to make periodical payments, lump sum orders and property adjustment orders
Residence and contact (married client)	Can be resolved in course of proceedings for divorce/nullity or judicial separation proceedings If financial order sought under DPMCA 1978, the court can exercise its powers under Children Act 1989 with respect to child *Alternatively* Children Act 1989 *or* wardship

Residence and contact (unmarried client)	Children Act 1989 *or* wardship
Violence (married client)	Non-molestation injunction ancillary to divorce/nullity or judicial separation DVMPA 1976 DPMCA 1978 s. 16
Violence (unmarried client)	Injunction under DVMPA 1976 *or* injunction in ordinary tort proceedings for trespass to the person, etc. *or* if there are children, an injunction ancillary to a residence order (i.e. make application for residence order under s. 8, Children Act 1989 and then seek injunction under ss. 38 and 39, County Courts Act 1984 or, if High Court, under Supreme Court Act 1981)
Difficulties over occupation of home (married client)	Order under MHA 1983 *or* injunction under DVMPA 1976
Difficulties over occupation of home (unmarried client)	Injunction under DVMPA 1976 *or* ordinary tort proceedings for trespass, etc.

Note:

If there is agreement between the parties, the solicitor should not overlook the possibility of a separation/maintenance agreement as an alternative to proceedings. There is no reason why an unmarried couple should not make a binding agreement on matters such as maintenance, property, etc. in just the same way as a married couple. (See Chapter 33).

3.2 Preparing to commence proceedings

In some cases, the solicitor will have to commence proceedings without delay, for example, where the client has been subjected to serious physical violence and requires an injunction to prevent a repeat performance.

The solicitor should ensure that he takes down all the further information from the client that he needs to start proceedings. One good way of ensuring that nothing is missed is for the solicitor to have in front of him at the interview a precedent of each of the documents required to commence proceedings. He then works through each document asking the client for the particulars required to draft each paragraph. So, for example, if divorce proceedings are to be commenced, the solicitor will work through a blank form of divorce petition and a blank statement of arrangements form with the client.

The solicitor should also bear in mind what additional documents he will need to file when commencing proceedings so that he can ask the client for any required documents that may be in her possession. For example, in divorce cases the client must be asked for a copy of the marriage certificate, and in wardship proceedings for a copy of the child's birth certificate.

3.3 Negotiating

Although it is sometimes necessary to issue proceedings without delay (for example, in a domestic violence case), it will not always be desirable to launch proceedings straight away. It is often a good idea to attempt to negotiate a settlement of disputed matters without proceedings first. Obviously some remedies, such as divorce, can only be obtained through the courts. With other matters, such as maintenance, the solicitor may be open to criticism if he embarks upon proceedings without first seeing whether agreement can be reached. In the first place, the proceedings might place added strain on relations between the parties concerned and reduce the chances of settling things amicably. Secondly, the party commencing proceedings may find herself responsible for extra costs (of her own and possibly of the other side) as a result of her precipitate action.

The solicitor is free to write to the other party, or to his solicitor if he is already represented, asking whether he is willing to consent to a particular course (for example, to give his consent to a divorce decree based on two years' separation and consent) or to make his own proposals for settlement (for example, an offer of maintenance) or indeed, asking the other party to desist from a particular course of action (for example, from harassing the client). However, if the other party is not represented, it is good practice to suggest in the letter that he might like to seek independent legal advice, particularly if the issue is complex.

3.4 Writing letters

Apart from writing to the other party or his solicitor, there may also be other letters to be written. For example, if the client is being pressed for payment of gas and elctricity bills or of mortgage instalments it can be helpful for the solicitor to write a letter on her behalf explaining the matrimonial difficulties and asking for forbearance until matters are resolved. There may be witnesses to contact (for example, in support of an application for an injunction) and reports to request (for example, a medical report in relation to a child of the family who is disabled for the purposes of considering the arrangements for the children under s. 41, Matrimonial Causes Act 1973, as substituted by sch. 12, para. 31, Children Act 1989).

3.5   Advising the client

The client will no doubt be anxious about matters and have her own questions to ask. In particular she will want to know what is going to happen next. In addition to giving the client the information she requests, the solicitor should be alive to other matters of which the client will not be aware but of which she should be informed or warned. For example, a client seeking a divorce should be warned of the dangers of prolonged cohabitation in the run-up to the divorce (for example, more than six months' cohabitation after discovering the respondent's adultery will debar the petitioner from relying on the adultery).

3.6   Miscellaneous other steps

Depending on the nature of the case, the solicitor will find there are a number of other jobs to do. For example:

(a)   If the matrimonial home is in the sole name of the other spouse, he should register a Class F land charge or a notice to protect his client's interest in it.

(b)   He should consider whether to serve a notice of severance of joint tenancy if the parties are joint owners of the matrimonial home.

(c)   He should consider the question of the client's will.

4   PREPARING A STATEMENT AND PROOF OF EVIDENCE

After the first interview with the client, it is customary to prepare a statement setting out all the relevant information she has provided about the case in a readable manner for future reference.

Should it ever become necessary for the client to give oral evidence in court, it is good practice to prepare a proof of evidence from the client's statement, setting out the matters that are relevant to the particular proceedings in a convenient order. The proof can then be used as an *aide-mémoire* when taking the client through her evidence in chief.

2 Legal advice and assistance and legal aid

The statutes and regulations dealing with legal advice and assistance and legal aid and the legal aid forms work on the basis that the applicant for legal aid is male. As this chapter makes extensive reference to these provisions and forms, in order to avoid confusion the same approach is adopted although this is contrary to the practice used in the rest of the book.

1 INTRODUCTION

1.1 General

This chapter cannot cover all aspects of legal work that may arise in practice. The Legal Aid Board produces the *Legal Aid Handbook* which is regularly updated. It includes the relevant statutory provisions and regulations together with information and guidance for solicitors on legal aid matters and is invaluable as a reference work for legal aid problems.

The idea of legal aid is that the services of a solicitor (and where necessary a barrister) should be made available not only to those of substantial means who can afford to meet the cost themselves but also to others who cannot manage to do so or who can only afford to pay a limited amount towards their legal costs.

1.2 The three types of legal aid

There are three forms of legal aid:

    (a)   legal advice and assistance;
    (b)   civil legal aid;
    (c)   criminal legal aid.

The practitioner dealing with matrimonial matters must be familiar with the first two forms of legal aid.

Legal advice and assistance (generally referred to as 'the green for scheme') covers preliminary advice and help with legal problems falling short of taking court proceedings on the client's behalf. However, there is an extended form of legal advice and assistance known as *assistance by way of representation* which does cover the solicitor going to court in certain cases.

Civil legal aid covers all the work leading up to and including court proceedings and representation by a solicitor and, if necessary, a barrister.

1.3 Legal aid system derived from Legal Aid Act 1988

The Legal Aid Act 1988 came into force on 1 April 1989. The Act created the Legal Aid Board as the body to be responsible for administering the legal aid scheme and at the same time removed the duties formerly enjoyed in this area by the Law Society. A new series of regulations dealing with the practical workings of the scheme was promulgated to coincide with the coming into force of the new Act.

1.4   The machinery

England and Wales are divided into 15 legal aid areas, each with a legal aid office. The addresses and telephone numbers of the offices are listed at the back of the *Legal Aid Handbook*. Solicitors should generally direct enquiries to their local legal aid office or to the office for the area where their client lives and all legal aid applications and claims for payment, etc. should be directed to that office. Each office has a full-time staff and is run by an Area Director (otherwise known as a secretary). Each area has an area committee appointed from practising solicitors and barristers who sit on the committees part-time.

The Area Director has power to grant and refuse applications for legal aid. In most cases where he refuses legal aid, there is a right of appeal to the area committee which also has a number of other functions such as dealing with complaints about practitioners and questions of remuneration of practitioners in legally aided cases.

2   THE SOLICITOR'S DUTY TO ADVISE HIS CLIENT ON LEGAL AID

There is no obligation on solicitors to do legal aid work and some prefer not to do so. However, every solicitor must consider as soon as possible after he has been consulted by a client whether the client would be likely to benefit from any form of legal aid and advise the client accordingly, even if he does not undertake legal aid work himself and his advice would therefore involve counselling the client to seek the help of another firm of solicitors. If a solicitor persistently neglects to advise clients of their rights to legal aid after his oversight has been pointed out to him, he may find himself disciplined by the Law Society for professional misconduct. Furthermore, if a client suffers financially as a result of the solicitor's failure to advise him as to legal aid (as may be the case, for example, where he has to meet legal fees from his own pocket that could have been met from the legal aid fund), the solicitor may find himself sued successfully for negligence by the client.

3   LEGAL AID NOT RETROSPECTIVE

Costs incurred before the completion of the green form or, in the case of full legal aid, before the issue of the legal aid certificate, cannot be recovered by the solicitor from the legal aid fund. It is vital, therefore, that the solicitor should attend to the question of legal aid as soon as possible. It is hardly an exaggeration to suggest that the solicitor should be reaching for the green form with one hand whilst shaking hands with the new client in introductory greeting with the other!

A: THE GREEN FORM SCHEME: PART III, LEGAL AID ACT 1988 AND LEGAL ADVICE AND ASSISTANCE REGULATIONS 1989

All references to regulations in this part of the chapter are references to the Legal Advice and Assistance Regulations 1989.

4   THE SCOPE OF THE GREEN FORM SCHEME

4.1   Generally

Subject to a limit on the costs that can be incurred (see paragraph 5 below), under the green form scheme the solicitor can advise on the application of English law to his client's problem (whatever the nature of that problem) and as to any step that the client might appropriately take, such as bringing or defending proceedings, making an agreement or will, seeking full legal aid, etc.

The solicitor can help the client to take the appropriate steps or can take the appropriate steps for the client except for the very important limitation that the solicitor cannot himself take any step in the institution or conduct of court proceedings under the scheme (s. 2, Legal Aid Act 1988).

The following are examples of the type of work that can be handled under the green form scheme:

(a)   The solicitor can consider the client's problem and advise him on its legal implications and as to any practical steps that can be taken to sort it out.

Example. The solicitor is consulted by a woman who complains that her husband is persistently violent towards her. Under the green form scheme, the solicitor advises her that she is entitled to the protection of an order from the magistrates' court under the Domestic Proceedings and Magistrates' Courts Act 1978, that proceedings will have to commence in the magistrates' court and that meanwhile she is not obliged to continue to live with her husband if she would prefer not to do so. He might also suggest that she could take refuge temporarily in a hostel for battered wives if there is one locally. He cannot commence the magistrates' court proceedings under the ordinary green form scheme. Before doing this he would have to make an application for assistance by way of representation for the client. This is a specially extended form of green form assistance; it is fully described at paragraph 10.1 below.

(b)   The solicitor can enter into correspondence on the client's behalf.

Example. The solicitor is consulted by a woman who has got into difficulties with the mortgage instalments and other household bills relating to the matrimonial home since her husband left her. He advises her to write to the building society and other creditors explaining what has happened and asking them not to take any action yet as she will be seeking maintenance from her husband and therefore expects that her problems will be short-lived. He helps her with the terms of the letters. If necessary he could write the letters for her.

(c)   The solicitor can negotiate for the client.

Example. The solicitor writes on behalf of the woman in the previous example to her husband asking what proposals he makes for her maintenance and that of the children. If the husband makes an offer he can advise the wife as to whether she should accept it, and in the event of the husband's proposals being unacceptable, he can negotiate with the husband (or his solicitor if he has one) to obtain a better offer. If an agreement is reached, he can advise the wife as to the best method of putting it into practice. If no agreement is reached he can advise the wife as to her rights to take the matter to court but he cannot commence proceedings for her until he has obtained assistance by way of representation or full legal aid (whichever is appropriate) on her behalf.

(d)   The solicitor can draft documents for the client.

Example. The solicitor drafts a new will on behalf of a husband to prevent the husband's assets passing to his estranged wife by will in the event of his death before they are divorced.

(e)   The solicitor can make an application for full legal aid or for assistance by way of representation on the client's behalf if it is clear to him that he will need to take steps which are not covered by the green form scheme.

4.2   In relation to divorce and judicial separation

The green form scheme has assumed particular importance in undefended divorce and judicial separation cases in relation to the actual decree proceedings (as opposed to proceedings in relation to ancillary matters such as residence orders and finance). Full legal aid used to be available for divorce and judicial separation decree proceedings but was withdrawn in 1977 (Legal Aid (Matrimonial Proceedings) Regulations 1977) except in a very limited class of case. For the client who cannot afford to pay privately for his solicitor's services, therefore, help under the green form scheme is generally the only form of legal assistance available for obtaining a decree. The present law as to legal aid and decree proceedings is set out in Chapter 6 and examples are given of the type of work that the solicitor may be expected to carry out for a client in relation to decree proceedings under the green form scheme.

5   FINANCIAL LIMITS ON THE WORK THAT CAN BE DONE UNDER THE GREEN FORM SCHEME

5.1   Normal limit

In the first instance, the solicitor can normally incur up to £84 costs (in respect of two hours' work) and disbursements exclusive of VAT (reg. 4(1)).

Where the solicitor is instructed on behalf of a petitioner in a divorce or judicial separation case and prepares the petition, there is a higher limit of £126 (representing three hours' work).

The financial limits are raised periodically by statutory instrument.

5.2   Extensions of the normal limit

5.2.1   When extension is appropriate

If the client needs further help beyond the relevant financial limit, the solicitor will have to seek authority to exceed the limit ('an extension') before incurring any more costs and disbursements (reg. 21). It is important to consider carefully whether it is appropriate to apply for an extension or whether full legal aid or authority for assistance by way of respresentation should be sought instead. An extension simply enables the solicitor to incur greater than normal costs whilst carrying out work within the scope of the ordinary green form scheme, whereas full legal aid and assistance by way of representation authorise the solicitor to go outside the scope of the ordinary scheme and act for the client in court proceedings (normally with no financial limit on costs); see paragraphs 10 to 16 below.

5.2.2 Method of seeking extension

The solicitor should seek an extension by completing form GF3 which should be sent to the Area Director. If the client urgently needs further help, an extension can be requested over the telephone. In this case, the solicitor should be ready to give orally the information he would normally have provided on the written application form.

6 FINANCIAL ELIGIBILITY

6.1 Financial limits

Eligibility for green form advice and assistance is dependent upon the client being within the financial limits of the scheme. He must qualify in terms of both capital and income.

6.2 Means of assessment

The client's eligibility for green form advice is assessed by the solicitor himself using the green form and the green form key card. Both the green form and the current key card are reproduced on pp. 44–7. New key cards are issued whenever the capital and income limits for eligibility change.

The key card gives advice as to the details that should be inserted on the green form and tells the solicitor whether, in the light of these details, the client is eligible for legal advice and assistance and, if so, what financial contribution he should be required to make. The reverse of the key card provides useful explanatory notes on various aspects of the green form scheme. Additional notes on filling in the green form can be found at paragraph 7 below.

6.3 Calculating the client's capital and income

It is *disposable* capital and income that matter. These are calculated in accordance with sch.2, Legal Advice and Assistance Regulations 1989. The following rules apply:

(a) To arrive at disposable capital and income the solicitor starts by ascertaining:

(i) all the client's capital resources at the date of assessment (i.e. when the green form is completed); *and*

(ii) the total income from all sources which the client has received or may reasonably expect to receive in respect of the seven days up to and including the date of assessment.

Note that the value of the subject matter of the claim in respect of which the client is seeking advice and assistance is always left out of account.

(b) To these capital and income figures, the general rule is that the solicitor must add the capital and income resources of the client's spouse. (Unmarried couples living together are to be treated for financial assessment purposes as spouses.) However, this will not normally be necessary in the case of a client seeking advice about his matrimonial affairs, because sch.2 provides that the spouse's resources shall be left out of account:

(i)   if the spouse has a contrary interest in the matter in respect of which advice and assistance is being sought; *or*

(ii)   if the client and his spouse are living separate and apart; *or*

(iii)   if, in all the circumstances of the case, it would be inequitable or impractical to treat the spouse's resources as those of the client.

(c)   Various sums should be left out of account or deducted when calculating disposable capital and income as follows:

Capital

(i)   the value of the main or only dwelling house where the client resides;

(ii)   the value of his household furniture and effects, personal clothing and tools or implements of his trade;

(iii)   the subject matter of the problem with regard to which the client seeks advice and assistance;

(iv)   where the client has living with him a spouse whose resources are aggregated with his or a dependant child or dependant relative whom he maintains wholly or substantially, a deduction is made from his capital (presently £335 for the first such person, £200 for the second and £100 for each further person). These deductions are not mentioned specifically on the key card; allowance is made for them by specifying different maximum capital limits for financial eligibility according to whether the client has dependants or not. As we noted earlier, the client's spouse's resources will hardly ever be aggregated with his in a matrimonial case, therefore a client with no children will count as a client with no dependants on the key card, a client with one child whom he maintains wholly will count as having one dependant, etc.

Income

(i)   income tax on the client's income;

(ii)   national insurance contributions for the seven days up to and including the date of assessment;

(iii)   actual maintenance payments for the same seven-day period for a spouse who is living apart, a former spouse, a child or a relative who is not a member of the client's household;

(iv)   if the client and his spouse are living together (regardless of whether her resources are aggregated with his or left out of account) a fixed allowance is made to take account of the maintenance of the spouse. Similarly if the client has a dependant child or relative who is a member of his household, a fixed allowance is made to take account of his maintenance. The amount of the allowance is raised regularly and can be ascertained from the key card.

6.4   Determining capital eligibility

The solicitor compares the client's total disposable capital calculated in accordance with the rules set out in paragraph 6.3 above with the maximum disposable capital for financial eligibility shown on the current key card (at the time of writing £935).

If the client's capital exceeds the limit he is not entitled to green form advice however small his income. He may, however, be entitled to full legal aid, in respect of which the financial limits are slightly different (see paragraph 12.1 below).

If the client's capital is within the limit the solicitor should then consider his income eligibility. The amount of capital can thereafter be ignored.

6.5 Determining income eligibility

If the client is receiving income support or family credit and his capital is within the limit of the scheme he is automatically entitled to green form advice.

In all other cases the solicitor compares the client's weekly disposable income calculated by the above rules with the 'client's contribution' figures on the key card. At the rates of contribution in force at the time of writing, if the client has a disposable income exceeding £135 per week he is not entitled to green form advice and assistance (though he may be entitled to full legal aid, see paragraph 11 et seq.). At the other extreme a client with a disposable income not exceeding £70 per week will receive free green form advice. A client with an income in between these two extremes must make a contribution towards the cost of his green form advice. The maximum contribution is presently £75 and applies to those with an income over £130 per week but not exceeding £135.

7 FILLING IN THE GREEN FORM

7.1 Attendance of the client

Applications for green form advice and assistance have generally to be made to the solicitor by the client in person (reg. 9). However, if the client has a good reason why he cannot see the solicitor himself he can provide someone else with all the relevant information about his financial circumstances and the problem on which he wants advice and authorise that person to attend for him (reg. 10).

7.2 The form itself

There should be no difficulty in filling in the green form if the notes on the green form key card are followed. Note that the form asks whether the client has received green form help previously in relation to the same matter from another solicitor. If so, it will be necessary to seek authority before further assistance can be given (see paragraph 8 below).

The solicitor must ensure that the client reads the entire passage headed 'To be completed and signed by the client'. This makes brief reference to the statutory charge on property recovered or preserved in respect of unpaid legal costs (see paragraph 17 et seq. below). The solicitor should explain the charge fully to the client, taking care that the client understands how it may affect him in practice. The client should then sign the green form.

8 REPEATED ADVICE UNDER THE GREEN FORM SCHEME

8.1 Further advice from the same solicitor (reg. 17)

It may be that the client has already received advice and assistance from the solicitor in the past under the green form scheme.

If the problem on which he has already received help can be classed as a 'separate matter', a fresh green form can be used to offer him further advice and assistance.

Example. A client who received advice under the green form scheme two weeks ago about some defective goods which he had purchased can receive further advice this week under a fresh green form in relation to his matrimonial problems.

However, where the client's problems are all connected with or arise from proceedings for divorce or judicial separation (actual or prospective) between himself and his spouse, they canot be treated as separate matters. Only one green form can therefore be used. If there are a number of problems and the work appears likely to exceed the green form limit on expenditure, the solicitor should consider applying for an extension (see paragraph 5 above).

8.2   Previous advice from another solicitor (reg. 16)

The client may already have consulted another solicitor under the green form scheme about the same matter, for example, he may have been to another firm or to a neighbourhood law centre. In this case, the solicitor must satisfy himself that it is reasonable to give further advice and assistance and must seek authority from the Area Director before he can give further green form help. There is no application form for seeking such authority; the solicitor should apply by letter or over the telephone in urgent cases. A solicitor who fails to take these steps may find that he cannot recover his green form costs.

9   COLLECTION OF THE CLIENT'S CONTRIBUTION (REG.28)

Where the client is required to make a contribution, it is up to the solicitor to collect it. Various points arise:

(a)   Whatever the client's maximum contribution as assessed on the green form, the solicitor should not collect more by way of an initial contribution than is likely to cover the actual cost of advice and assistance. If one simple interview is all that is likely to be required, therefore, the solicitor may need to collect only a small proportion of the client's potential contribution. If it subsequently turns out that more work is required, the solicitor can then collect the balance of the contribution from the client.

(b)   Where the £84 limit (as opposed to the £126 limit) on expenditure applies, the solicitor should never collect more than £84 by way of contribution from the client at the outset even though the client may, in theory, have a maximum contribution of up to £90. This is because the solicitor is not, of course, authorised to incur costs of more than £84 without applying for an extension of the green form. He should, however, make it clear to the client that the small balance over £84 may become payable at a later date if more than £84 worth of work is needed and the solicitor is granted an extension or if assistance by way of representation is authorised. If the £126 limit applies, the full contribution can be collected at the outset provided it is justified in the terms of the work that is to be carried out, which it almost certainly will be.

(c)   It is a matter for the solicitor how he collects the appropriate contribution from the client. The counsel of perfection is that he should safeguard his position by collecting the client's initial contribution before doing any work at all. However, in many cases it is impractical and unfair to insist upon this. The client frequently turns up with a problem that needs immediate attention but with nothing more than his return bus fare in his pocket. Most solicitors finding themselves with a matrimonial client in this situation would probably arrange with the client that the contribution will be paid at the next interview or by way of instalments and meanwhile would get on with whatever needed doing. The drawback is that if payment is not forthcoming from the client the solicitor will not be able to recover from the legal aid fund the amount that the client should have contributed towards his legal costs, although he can recover the difference (if any) between the client's maximum contribution and the actual cost of the work carried out under the green form. It will rarely be worth taking proceedings against the client for the outstanding sum, so the solicitor may be out of pocket to this extent.

(d)   If costs turn out to be less than the amount collected from the client by way of contribution, the solicitor should refund the difference to the client (reg. 28(2)).

10   REPRESENTATION IN COURT UNDER THE GREEN FORM SCHEME

As we have seen at paragraph 4 above, the general rule is that the green form scheme does not permit the solicitor to take any step in court proceedings. However, there are two situations in which the solicitor can represent his client in court under the scheme.

10.1   Assistance by way of representation

Where domestic proceedings are to be taken against or on behalf of the client in the magistrates' courts (for example, proceedings for an order under the Domestic Proceedings and Magistrates' Courts Act 1978, or for an order under the Children Act 1989), the solicitor can apply to have the green form extended to cover full representation in the court proceedings. In its extended form the scheme is known as assistance by way of representation and has largely replaced legal aid for domestic proceedings in the magistrates' courts. It is now derived from s. 8(2), Legal Aid Act 1988.

10.1.1   The scope of assistance by way of representation
Once assistance by way of representation has been authorised by the Area Director, the solicitor can undertake all necessary work in relation to the court proceedings including representing the client in court himself. There normally ceases to be any financial limit on the costs and disbursements that can be incurred although, of course, the solicitor must still act reasonably and not extravagantly or he may find he cannot recover his costs and disbursements from the legal aid fund. If the solicitor needs to instruct counsel, to incur expenditure on an unusual item or of any unusually large amount or to obtain an expert's report or the attendance of an expert at court, he must get permission from the Area Director before doing so (regs 22 and 23).

10.1.2   Method of application
(a)   The green form should be completed to assess the client's financial eligibility. The capital limit for assistance by way of representation is £3000 whereas the limit for the green form is £935. Otherwise the financial eligibility

limits are the same as for ordinary green form advice and assistance. If the solicitor has already assessed the client for the green form, this assessment will indicate whether he is eligible for assistance by way of representation and no further green form need be completed.

(b) If the client is financially eligible, the solicitor should complete an application for assistance by way of representation on Form ABWOR 1A. The form has been revised to take into account the changes made by the Children Act 1989. There may be some degree of overlap with form CLA2A which also extends to proceedings in the magistrates' courts. (See further paragraph 13.1 below.). The form is simple and self-explanatory. It requires the solicitor to state in relation to what sort of proceedings the assistance is required. A signed statement from the client is required on the reverse of the form. The purpose of this statement is to enable the Area Director to decide whether assistance by way of representation is appropriate and the solicitor must therefore be careful to provide a fairly detailed statement from the client. The criteria for granting assistance by way of representation are the same as for granting legal aid (see paragraph 12.2). Thus the application will generally only be granted if there are reasonable grounds for taking, defending or being a party to the proceedings concerned, and can be refused if it appears unreasonable that approval should be granted in the particular circumstances of the case (reg. 22). In particular, the Area Director will need to be satisfied that it is in the client's best interests to proceed in the magistrates' courts rather than seeking some other form of relief, for example, a divorce.

(c) The form should be sent to the area legal aid office. In urgent cases it may be possible to obtain approval for assistance by way of representation over the telephone.

(d) The solicitor will be notified as to whether the application has been successful. Once he receives approval for assistance by way of representation he can act for his client in the court proceedings.

10.1.3   Notification of approval to court and other party (reg. 24)
Once assistance by way of representation is approved, the solicitor has a duty to notify the other party to the proceedings and the court of this fact as soon as practicable. If the proceedings to which the client is a party have already been commenced by the time approval is given, this will mean giving notification at once. If the client does not become a party to proceedings until after approval is given, notification must be given as soon as practicable after the client becomes a party. There is no prescribed form for giving notice, so a letter should suffice.

10.1.4   The relationship between assistance by way of representation and full legal aid
The approval of the area secretary is required for both assistance by way of representation and full legal aid. However, assistance by way of representation does have a considerable advantage over legal aid in that the assessment of the client's means is carried out by the solicitor on the green form whereas with full legal aid it is necessary for the application to be referred to the Department of Social Security for an assessment of the client's financial circumstances, which can take some time to carry out. This means that as a general rule it takes

considerably less time to obtain approval for assistance by way of representation than to obtain a legal aid certificate.

Where the client is eligible for assistance by way of representation, full legal aid will not be granted. However, legal aid is still available for domestic proceedings in the magistrates' courts in cases where the client is outside the financial limits of the green form, the financial limits for legal aid being somewhat higher than those applicable to the green form scheme. A client may fall just outside the green form limits but just within the legal aid limits. Where it appears to the solicitor that this is likely to be the case, he should make an application for legal aid on his client's behalf (see below at paragraph 11 et seq.). The application form used in relation to magistrates' court proceedings is CLA2A.

10.2 Green form in court

10.2.1 When applicable

By virtue of regs 7 and 8, Legal Advice and Assistance (Scope) Regulations 1989, a magistrates' court or county court can authorise a solicitor to represent a party to proceedings in court under the ordinary green form scheme provided that the party concerned is financially eligible under the scheme. There are two ways in which this can arise:

(a)   At or after the beginning of proceedings *the court* can request a solicitor who is present within the precincts of the court to give assistance by way of representation to a party to the proceedings. In this case it is likely that the solicitor will not have had any prior contact with the party concerned before attending court that day, probably on a totally unrelated matter.

(b)   The *solicitor* can request the court to approve the giving of assistance by way of representation to a party to proceedings and the court does so at or after the beginning of the proceedings when the solicitor is present within the precincts of the court. In this case the solicitor will probably have been consulted by the person concerned about the court proceedings but only a very short time before the hearing.

This procedure cannot be used when a legal aid certificate is in force in connection with the proceedings, or where a party has already been refused representation in the proceedings concerned.

10.2.2 Practical significance

In practice the solicitor will find that he rarely relies upon the above procedure in domestic matters for the following reasons:

(a)   The normal expenditure limit of the green form applies (£84/£26, see paragraph 5.1 above). Payment in excess of this limit for steps taken in court proceedings *cannot* be authorised.

(b)   Note 4 of the 'Notes for Guidance' issued by the Legal Aid Board indicates that it is not appropriate to use regs 7 and 8 to avoid the need to make a full legal aid application or to seek authority for assistance by way of representation.

(c)   An emergency legal aid certificate or approval of assistance by way of representation can, if necessary, be obtained with very little delay. In cases of extreme urgency the matter can be dealt with instantly over the telephone provided it is within the hours of the legal aid office.

Nevertheless, from time to time, the procedure can be useful.

Example. Mrs Smith consults a solicitor at 5.30 p.m. on Friday afternoon. She is being subjected to serious violence by her husband and needs a personal protection order from the magistrates' court forthwith. The magistrates can deal with the application on Saturday morning but the legal aid office is closed and Mrs Smith's application for assistance by way of representation cannot be processed until Monday morning at the earliest. The solicitor fills in the green form and establishes that Mrs Smith is financially eligible for help under the scheme. When he attends court on Saturday morning to request an expedited personal protection order, the solicitor's first job at the beginning of the case will be to ask the court to approve his proposal that he represent Mrs Smith in court under reg. 7. By the time he leaves court on Saturday the £84 green form expenditure limit will almost certainly have been reached. He will have to seek approval for assistance by way of representation for Mrs Smith in the normal way in order to proceed, in due course, to obtain a non-expedited personal protection order for her.

B: FULL LEGAL AID: PART IV, LEGAL AID ACT 1988 AND THE CIVIL LEGAL AID (GENERAL) REGULATIONS 1989

Notes: (a) All references to regulations in this part of the chapter are references to the Civil Legal Aid (General) Regulations 1989 except where otherwise stated.

(b) It is important always to bear in mind the potential impact of the Legal Aid Board's statutory charge. This is dealt with fully in paragraphs 17 et seq. below. When mention is made of 'free legal aid' and the applicant's 'maximum contribution' and 'actual contribution' this does not take into account the fact that, because of the statutory charge, the applicant may ultimately also have to put some part of money or property recovered or preserved in the proceedings towards his outstanding legal aid costs.

11   PROCEEDINGS FOR WHICH FULL LEGAL AID IS AVAILABLE

Legal aid is generally available for matrimonial proceedings, for example, ancillary proceedings following a divorce, injunction proceedings, nullity proceedings, residence order applications and wardship. There are, however, a number of classes of case where legal aid is not available. The most notable are:

(a) The vast majority of undefended proceedings for a decree of divorce or judicial separation (see paragraph 4.2 above and Chapter 6).

(b) Domestic proceedings in the magistrates' courts where assistance by way of representation is available (i.e. majority of such proceedings, see paragraph 10.1 above).

However, legal aid is now available for all proceedings under the Children Act 1989 (see s. 15, Legal Aid Act 1988, as amended, and the Civil Legal Aid (General) Regulations 1989, as amended). Where a Children Act 1989 order is sought in proceedings other than under the Children Act 1989, e.g. in matrimonial proceedings or in proceedings under the Domestic Violence and

Matrimonial Proceedings Act 1976 or the Domestic Proceedings and Magistrates' Courts Act 1978, Form CLA2A is to be used.

12 DETERMINING ELIGIBILITY FOR LEGAL AID

Except in the case of some applicants in certain Children Act 1989 proceedings (as to which see paragraph 23 below) the grant of legal aid in a particular case will depend upon:

(a) the applicant being financially eligible; *and*
(b) the Area Director being satisfied that it is proper for him to have legal aid.

12.1 Financial eligibility (s. 15, Legal Aid Act 1988)

12.1.1 The limits
As with the green form, the client must qualify in terms of both disposable capital and disposable income (except in the case of some applicants in certain Children Act 1989 proceedings). The limits for eligibility are prescribed by regulations and are periodically amended.

The disposable income limit (above which the applicant is ineligible for legal aid) is an absolute limit and is currently £6,350 a year.

As far as capital is concerned, if the client has disposable capital of over £6,310 he *may* be refused legal aid on financial grounds even though he qualifies in terms of income, if it appears that he could afford to proceed without legal aid. Thus although the client's disposable capital exceeds the limit he may still be granted legal aid, for example, where his case is likely to prove expensive and his capital is only slightly above the limit.

If the applicant's disposable income and capital are at or below a certain level (presently set at £2,860 for income and £3,000 for capital) he will be entitled to free legal aid provided, of course, the Area Director considers his case is a proper one for legal aid.

If the applicant's disposable income or capital is above the free legal aid limits but he is nevertheless financially eligible for legal aid, he will be offered legal aid on condition that he pays a contribution towards his own legal costs.

12.1.2 Means of financial assessment
Whereas financial eligibility for the green form scheme is determined by the solicitor himself on the spot, the question of financial eligibility for legal aid has to be referred for determination by an assessment officer of the Department of Social Security in accordance with the Civil Legal Aid (Assessment of Resources) Regulations 1989.

The assessment officer will usually arrange an interview with the applicant to determine whether the applicant's finances are such that he is eligible for legal aid and if so, how much his maximum contribution to his own legal costs should be.

The regulations as to assessment are not set out here because the solicitor can normally leave the detailed assessment of his client's means entirely to the assessment officer. However, it is worth noting that the applicant's disposable income and capital will not necessarily be the same for legal aid purposes as they are for the green form scheme as the assessment rules differ. Unless the client is clearly of small means, for example, where he is on income support, the solicitor will not necessarily know for certain at the outset whether he will be financially eligible for legal aid. He should therefore make an application if, on the information he has about his client's circumstances, he feels that the client *may* be eligible.

12.1.3 Contribution

12.1.3.1 Maximum contribution The applicant's maximum contribution as determined by the assessment officer is the most he will have to pay by way of contribution to his legal costs. He will not necessarily have to pay the full amount of his maximum contribution — what he actually has to contribute is determined not by the assessment officer but by the Area Director when he considers his application for legal aid.

12.1.3.2 Actual contribution The applicant's actual contribution will be fixed by the Area Director to tie in with the probable costs of the proceedings (reg. 31). The Legal Aid Board provides guidance as to the average cost of cases of particular kinds.

If the costs of the proceedings are likely to be equal to or in excess of the applicant's maximum contribution, he will be required to pay the full amount of his maximum contribution. If the costs are likely to be less than his maximum contribution, he will only be required to contribute, in the first instance, such smaller amount as is equal to the probable cost. However, if the case turns out to be more expensive than expected, the assisted person's actual contribution can subsequently be increased provided his maximum contribution is not exceeded (reg. 52(2)). The solicitor has a duty to advise the Area Director as soon as it becomes clear that the costs are likely to exceed the amount of the assisted person's actual contribution. He should also warn his client, at the outset, of the possibility of an increase in his contribution.

12.1.3.3 Payment of contribution (reg. 43) The applicant will be notified of the terms as to payment of his contribution when he receives his legal aid offer. If he is required to make a contribution from his capital, immediate payment of the whole contribution will be required if the sum is readily available and, if not, payment within such time as the Area Director finds to be reasonable in all the circumstances. A contribution from income will usually be required to be paid in monthly instalments.

Whereas contributions payable under the green form scheme are collected by the solicitor, contributions due in relation to legal aid are payable to the secretary.

12.2 The merits of the application

Except in the case of some applicants in certain Children Act 1989 proceedings (as to which see paragraph 23, below), when deciding whether to grant legal aid, the Area Director must consider all questions of fact or law arising out of the action, cause or matter to which the legal aid application relates and the circumstances in which the application was made (reg. 28). Legal aid will not be granted unless the Area Director considers that the case is a proper one for legal aid. The grounds on which he can refuse legal aid are set out in the Legal Aid Act 1988 and the regulations:

(a) A person shall not be given legal aid in connection with any proceedings unless he shows that he has reasonable grounds for taking, defending or being a party to those proceedings (s. 15(2), Legal Aid Act 1988). This does not mean that the applicant must show the Area Director that he will necessarily win — it is not the Director's function to try the case. In practice, all that is required in a matrimonial case is that the applicant satisfies the Director that he has a case which he should have a chance to put before the court.

> **Example 1.** The applicant was divorced some years ago. His wife has been harassing him by shouting abuse at him in the street. He seeks legal aid to bring proceedings for nuisance. Nuisance is an action based upon interference with the plaintiff's enjoyment of his own land. As the trouble has arisen in the street, the applicant has no cause of action in nuisance and he does not therefore have reasonable grounds for taking proceedings in nuisance. His application will be refused.

> **Example 2.** The applicant is a father who wishes to seek a residence order in respect of his daughter who is presently living with her mother and has been for some months. The applicant is unlikely to succeed in obtaining a residence order but he has a number of worries about the way in which the child is being cared for and, as her father, he has reasonable grounds for making a residence application and he will probably be granted legal aid.

(b) Legal aid can also be refused if, in the particular circumstances of the case, it appears unreasonable that the applicant should receive legal aid or more appropriate that he should receive assistance by way of representation (s. 15(3), Legal Aid Act 1988). This provision gives the Area Director a fairly wide discretion. Thus, for example, legal aid may be refused for injunction proceedings in the county court under the Domestic Violence and Matrimonial Proceedings Act 1976 on the basis that it would be better (and cheaper) to take proceedings in the magistrates' courts for a personal protection order under the Domestic Proceedings and Magistrates' Court Act 1978, and that therefore it would be more appropriate for the applicant to receive assistance by way of representation.

Two further situations in which the Area Director may consider it unreasonable to grant legal aid are set out in reg. 29. This specifically provides that the Director may refuse legal aid if he considers that, although the applicant may have a good case in law, the benefit that would be achieved by successful proceedings would be trivial or if the proceedings are of such a simple nature that a solicitor would not normally be employed. For example, there is a tendency for legal aid (and assistance by way of representation) to be refused for applications in the magistrates' courts for the variation of a periodical payments order on the basis that the proceedings are too straightforward to justify the employment of a solicitor. This is likely to be the case where all that is required is a mathematical calculation to take account of an increase in the payer's salary, for instance.

There is a particularly heavy burden on an applicant seeking legal aid to defend a divorce to show that his case is a proper one for legal aid. The question of legal aid and defended divorce is dealt with separately at paragraph 2 of Chapter 10.

13 MAKING THE LEGAL AID APPLICATION

13.1 The normal method

A legal aid application is normally made on one of the forms produced by the Legal Aid Board for the purpose. The forms now in use under the new Legal Aid Act 1988 are:

CLA1 — General Form of Application for Legal Aid (appropriate, for example, when seeking legal aid on behalf of a cohabitee).

CLA2A — Application for Legal Aid in Matrimonial Proceedings. (This is the form normally used for matrimonial work and/or where a Children Act 1989 application is being made within those matrimonial proceedings, including magistrates' courts proceedings. The appropriate means form must be submitted with Form CLA2A.)

CLA3 — Application for an Emergency Certificate (see paragraph 13.2 below).

CLA5 — Application for legal aid for means tested Children Act 1989 applications and for all other free-standing Children Act 1989 applications not made within matrimonial proceedings. This form is also to be used for wardship and adoption proceedings. It must be accompanied by the appropriate means form.

CLA5A — Application for legal aid for special Children Act 1989 proceedings (see paragraph 23 below). This form enables the solicitor to certify that he is acting for a client entitled to non means, non merits tested legal aid (referred to as 'free legal aid'). The form must be received by the area office within three working days of instruction to act. It will be submitted alone without any other supporting documentation or means form. The CLA5A form must be filled in correctly to ensure remuneration from the date of instruction to act, otherwise the solicitor's costs will be covered from the date of issue of the certificate only.

Although the application forms are basically simple and self-explanatory, it will normally save a lot of time and trouble if the solicitor fills in the appropriate form on behalf of the client rather than leaving the client to muddle through himself. Payment for this chore can be claimed by the solicitor under the green form scheme.

The applicant is required to state for what purpose legal aid is sought, for example, to be heard on financial provision/property adjustment or to take/defend proceedings under the Domestic Violence and Matrimonial Proceedings Act 1976. Background information is also required both in answer to specific questions that appear on the form and in the form of a rather longer statement of case. The solicitor should always take care to give sufficient detail of his client's case on the form, bearing in mind that legal aid will only be granted if the Area Director is satisfied that the applicant has reasonable grounds for taking, defending or being a party to the proceedings.

It may be necessary for the solicitor to forward with the application copies of documents connected with the case to support and explain the application. For example, where legal aid is sought for matrimonial proceedings, the applicant is required to give details of previous matrimonial proceedings and send with the application any court orders that he has. In addition, if a divorce petition is already in existence, a copy of this should also be enclosed with the application as should any other pleadings which are relevant to the application (originating application, supporting affidavit, originating summons in wardship, etc.).

The solicitor or applicant should also complete Forms CLA4A, B or C (statement of applicant's circumstances), and Form L17 should be completed by the employer where the applicant and/or his/her partner is in employment. The forms should be sent to the area office which will decide whether it is reasonable for the applicant to receive legal aid. Assessment officers of the Department of Social Security who specialise in civil legal aid cases carry out the assessment of means. The assessment officer will assess the applicant's disposable income and capital, and the maximum contribution, if any.

13.2   Emergency application (reg. 19)

13.2.1   When appropriate
It can take upwards of six weeks for a legal aid application to be processed. In some cases, the solicitor and his client will simply have to put up with this delay, for example, where legal aid is being sought for financial relief and property adjustment proceedings after divorce — if prompt application has been made for legal aid the client's case should not suffer by waiting. Sometimes, however, the client's problem requires urgent attention and it is not practical to wait for legal aid to come through in the normal way.

> **Example.** Mrs James consults the solicitor on Monday because she is in matrimonial difficulties. She has a black eye and a cut on her arm which she tells the solicitor were caused by her husband when he returned from the pub on Saturday night, drunk. She is afraid that this will happen again, particularly as her husband has issued threats of violence towards her. The solicitor takes the view that Mrs James should seek a non-molestation injunction as a matter of urgency. Clearly she cannot wait for weeks whilst a full legal aid application is processed. He decides to seek emergency legal aid.

An emergency certificate will be granted if:

(a)   the applicant is likely to satisfy the usual criteria for the granting of legal aid (i.e. he is likely to be financially eligible and it is likely to turn out to be a proper case for legal aid; see paragraph 12 above); *and*

(b)   it is in the interests of justice that the applicant should be granted legal aid as a matter of urgency (reg. 19).

13.2.2   Method of application

13.2.2.1   On Form CLA3   Normally an application for an emergency certificate should be made on Form CLA3 which sets out the steps that are proposed on the client's behalf (for example, taking proceedings for an ex parte non-molestation injunction) and the reason why legal aid is required as a matter of urgency (for example, because the client has already been assaulted on one occasion and other assaults have been threatened).

Form CLA3 should be submitted to the legal aid office together with a completed application (on Form CLA1 or CLA2A as appropriate) for full legal aid which will ultimately replace any emergency certificate issued.

13.2.2.2   By telephone   In cases of extreme urgency an emergency certificate can be obtained by telephone. Where a telephone application is made, the solicitor must be in a position to provide the Area Director, over the telephone, with the information he would otherwise have provided on the form. The solicitor will also be required to undertake to forward written applications for emergency and full legal aid and the necessary supporting papers forthwith. The telephone procedure should only be used where absolutely necessary. The Area Director will not normally grant a telephone application if the call is made late in the day and there has been ample time during the day to submit the application forms duly signed by the client.

13.2.3   *Effect of emergency certificate*

An emergency certificate is very much a temporary measure. It tides the client over until his full legal aid application has been considered at which stage, if legal aid is granted, it will be replaced by a full legal aid certificate. The emergency certificate will usually cover only a limited period and authorise only those steps that are necessary to deal with the emergency that has arisen. If the emergency certificate looks likely to expire before a full legal aid certificate is granted, the solicitor should make application to the area secretary for an extension of the time limit on the emergency certificate.

Before application is made for an emergency certificate, the solicitor must make clear to the client:

(a)   that, having sought an emergency certificate, he will be obliged (as and when required) to provide further information or documents or to attend for interview so that his means can be assessed and his legal aid contribution determined. If he fails to do so, he will not be granted full legal aid and his emergency certificate may be revoked;

(b)   that if he turns out to be financially ineligible for legal aid once his means have been assessed, he will not be granted full legal aid and his emergency certificate may be revoked;

(c)   that if an offer of legal aid is made to the client, he will be told the basis on which he will be granted full legal aid (i.e. what his contribution must be) and given the opportunity to accept or reject the offer. If he wants to accept the offer, he must do so promptly. If he fails to accept the offer, not only will he not get full legal aid, his emergency certificate may also be revoked.

The client must not be left in any doubt as to the effect of revocation of the emergency certificate. The results of revocation are that the client will be deemed never to have been an assisted person at all and he will become liable to repay to the Legal Aid Board all the costs paid out of the legal aid fund on his behalf in connection with the work done under the emergency certificate. Furthermore, he will be liable to pay direct to his solicitor the difference between the legal aid costs the solicitor will be able to claim from the legal aid fund and the costs he would have been entitled to charge had the client always been a private client.

14   THE ISSUE OF A FULL LEGAL AID CERTIFICATE

14.1   Mechanics of issue where no contribution payable

Where there is no contribution to be paid by the applicant or the application relates to special Children Act 1989 proceedings (as to which see paragraph 23 below), a legal aid certificate will be issued forthwith. The actual certificate will be sent to the solicitor and a copy to the applicant himself (reg. 42).

14.2 Mechanics of issue where contribution is payable

If the applicant is liable to pay a contribution, he will first be notified of the terms on which legal aid is offered to him (i.e., what his maximum and actual contributions would be, the terms for payment, etc.) (reg. 43). If these terms are acceptable to the applicant, within 28 days of being notified he must:

(a) complete the acceptance form (and a form of undertaking to pay the contribution required) and return them as directed; *and*

(b) if the contribution or any part of it is required to be paid before the certificate is issued (as is normally the case, for example, where a contribution from capital is required), make that payment accordingly (reg. 45).

When he has complied with these requirements, a certificate will be issued and sent to the solicitor.

15 NOTIFICATION OF ISSUE OF CERTIFICATE

If proceedings to which the client is a party have already been commenced by the time a legal aid certificate is granted, the solicitor should:

(a) serve all other parties to the proceedings straight away with notice of the issue of the certificate; *and*

(b) if any other person later becomes a party, serve him with a notice of issue also; *and*

(c) send a copy of the certificate to the appropriate court office or registry (reg. 50).

If the client is not yet a party to proceedings when he is granted legal aid, the solicitor's duty to notify other parties and to provide the court with a copy of the certificate arises as soon as his client does become a party to proceedings (reg. 50). It is not necessary (except in relation to appeals) to notify the other parties of any limitation on the legal aid certificate. The provisions as to notification and filing apply to both emergency and full legal aid certificates. The solicitor is also required by the regulations (reg. 54) to notify other parties of any amendment (other than financial) of the certificate, of the extension of an emergency certificate or its replacement with a full certificate and of the revocation or discharge of a certificate. In addition he must send a copy of the amendment, notice of discharge, etc. to the court.

16 EFFECT OF ISSUE OF LEGAL AID CERTIFICATE

16.1 Generally

Once a legal aid certificate is issued, the assisted person's legal expenses will be met from the legal aid fund. Generally speaking, this means that he can be represented by a solicitor (and, if necessary, counsel) and given all such assistance as is usually given by a solicitor or counsel in the steps preliminary and incidental to any proceedings or in arriving at or giving effect to a compromise to avoid or bring to an end any proceedings (s. 2(4), Legal Aid Act 1988).

The exact nature of what can be done for the client under this particular certificate depends on two things:

(a)   the terms of the certificate itself;
(b)   the provisions of the regulations which require special authorisation to be obtained before certain steps are taken.

16.2   The terms of the particular certificate

The certificate will state what proceedings it covers and will set out any condition or limitation imposed by the committee.

> **Example 1.** Mrs Green is granted a legal aid certificate 'to take proceedings under s. 17, Married Women's Property Act 1882'. Before proceedings are commenced, she decides that she would like to get divorced after all. Clearly it would therefore be more appropriate for questions of property to be dealt with in ancillary relief proceedings. The existing certificate does not cover ancillary relief proceedings. The solicitor will have to seek to have it amended accordingly before any further steps are taken on Mrs Green's behalf.

> **Example 2.** Miss Woolworth lived for some years with Mr Wadham. They separated about a year ago because of Mr Wadham's violent behaviour. Some weeks later Mr Wadham was sent to prison for assault on Miss Woolworth. She has heard that he is coming out in two months' time and she is afraid that he will come and assault her again as he has threatened to do. She cannot seek an injunction under the Domestic Violence and Matrimonial Proceedings Act 1976 because she is not cohabiting with Mr Wadham. Her only course of action is to start civil proceedings for trespass to the person and to seek an injunction in the course of those proceedings. She cannot, however, limit her claim to an injunction only. To give the court jurisdiction she must also claim damages. Obviously, Mr Wadham has no means to pay damages. Therefore she is granted legal aid to take proceedings for trespass limited to obtaining an injunction. If she wishes to pursue a judgment for damages, she will have to seek to have the limitation lifted before doing so.

The solicitor should always be careful to note the terms of the legal aid certificate and particularly so in matrimonial cases where it is routine practice to impose quite a number of special restrictions on the scope of the certificate. Thus, for example, legal aid certificates issued in relation to *ancillary relief* in connection with divorce, nullity and judicial separation are normally expressed to cover an application for all forms of ancillary relief except an order for the avoidance of a disposition or for variation. All ancillary relief certificates are limited, in the first instance, to the securing of one substantive order only. Note that legal aid for ancillary relief does not cover taking enforcement proceedings should the ancillary relief order not be complied with. A separate application (for amendment or for a fresh certificate as appropriate) must be made if this becomes necessary.

16.3   Limitations imposed by the regulations

The regulations impose an obligation on the solicitor to obtain prior approval from the Area Director before taking certain steps in relation to proceedings, for example:

(a)   before instructing Queen's counsel or more than one junior counsel (reg. 59) (there is no need to obtain special authority to instruct one junior counsel save for certain domestic proceedings in magistrates' courts for which assistance by way of representation is available (see regs 59(1)(a) and 3(1));

(b)   before obtaining an expert report or opinion or tendering the evidence of an expert (reg. 61) unless the Legal Aid Board has given general authority in cases of that particular class for an expert to be engaged (reg. 60);

(c)   before performing an act which is unusual in its nature or unusually expensive (reg. 61).

The reason why specific authority is required is, of course, that the steps concerned are particularly costly. The solicitor should remember that, in view of the Legal Aid Board's statutory charge, the client may ultimately have to bear the additional cost himself. He should therefore warn the client of what he proposes to do and of the probable cost and obtain his agreement as well as authority from the secretary (*Re Solicitors, Re Taxation of Costs* [1982] 2 All ER 683, [1982] 1 WLR 745).

If the solicitor does not obtain authority from the Area Director when he should have done, he may find the costs relating to this matter disallowed on taxation of his costs and he will therefore be out of pocket (reg. 63).

16.4   Duty to act reasonably

The solicitor must remember that a legal aid certificate does not give him a free hand in relation to his client's case. Apart from the need to obtain specific authority before taking certain steps (see paragraph 16.3 above):

(a)   He must act with reasonable competence and expedition. If he wastes costs by not doing so, these costs may be reduced or even disallowed completely on taxation (reg. 109).

(b)   He has an obligation to report to the Area Director if he has reason to believe his client has required his case to be conducted unreasonably so as to incur unjustifiable expense to the legal aid fund or has required unreasonably that the case be continued (for example, when he has been competently advised that the only proper course is to settle on the terms offered and he refuses to do so) (reg. 67). The secretary has power to discharge the certificate in cases such as this (reg. 78).

16.5   Solicitor not to accept payment other than from fund

Once a legal aid certificate has been granted, the solicitor must not take any payment from the client himself (or indeed from any other person) in respect of the client's legal costs. He must look only to the legal aid fund for payment (s. 15(6), Legal Aid Act 1988 and reg. 64).

16.6   Costs in legal aid cases

The fact that one of the parties to the proceedings is legally aided can affect the court's order for costs as follows:

(a)   Order for costs *against* a legally aided party: the court can only order a legally aided party to pay the costs of the proceedings to the extent that it is reasonable to expect him to pay having regard to all the circumstances including the financial resources of all the parties and their conduct in the course of the dispute (s. 17(1), Legal Aid Act 1988). In practice, the court will often use the legally aided person's maximum contribution as a guide to what it is fair to expect him to pay, i.e. he should not be expected to pay more towards the costs of the other parties to the proceedings than he could have been required to pay towards his own costs. Where the legally aided person has a nil contribution, this often means that the court will decline to make any order for costs against him. It is worth noting, however, that money recovered by the assisted person in the proceedings can be considered part of his financial resources (for example, a lump sum payable recovered in ancillary proceedings, *McDonnell* v *McDonnell* [1977] 1 All ER 766, [1977] 1 WLR 34). This may even justify the court making an order for costs against a legally aided party with a nil contribution.

(b)   Order for costs *in favour* of legally aided party: the solicitor must not fall into the trap of thinking that, because his client is legally aided, there is no need to pursue an order for costs with any great enthusiasm. Firstly, he has a duty to the legal aid fund to apply for costs in the same situations as he would apply for costs on behalf of a private client. Secondly, he clearly has a duty to his client to seek costs in order to reduce the effect of the statutory charge (see paragraph 17 et seq. below). The more of the client's costs that are paid by the other party to the proceedings, the less the deficit to the legal aid fund that the client will have to make up from his own pocket.

(c)   Order for costs against the legal aid fund: where an unassisted person is successful against an assisted person, the court has power to award the unassisted person costs out of the legal aid fund to the extent to which they are not paid by the assisted person himself (s. 18, Legal Aid Act 1988). The court can only make an order if it is satisfied:

(i)   an order for costs would have been made in the proceedings were the 1988 Act not applicable: *and*

(ii)   (as respects costs of a first instance hearing, i.e., not an appeal) the proceedings were instituted by the assisted party and the unassisted party would suffer severe financial hardship unless the order was made; *and*

(iii)   it is just and equitable in all the circumstances that provision be made for costs out of public funds.

C: REIMBURSEMENT OF THE LEGAL AID FUND AND THE STATUTORY CHARGE

Paragraphs 17 and 19 deal particularly with the situation in relation to legal aid. Paragraph 20 deals with the situation in relation to the green form.

17   REIMBURSEMENT OF THE LEGAL AID FUND

Where legal aid has been granted, the legal aid fund will assume responsibility for paying the legal costs of the assisted person. The Legal Aid Board has a statutory duty to recoup for the legal aid fund whatever this costs. It does so as follows:

(a)   From any payment made in the assisted person's favour under any order or agreement for costs with respect to the proceedings (s. 16(5), Legal Aid Act 1988).

Example 1. Mr and Mrs Robinson are divorced. Mrs Robinson is granted legal aid to be heard in ancillary proceedings. It is agreed that Mr Robinson will transfer the house to Mrs Robinson and, in return, she will forego all her remaining ancillary relief claims. Mr Robinson agrees to pay Mrs Robinson's legal costs in relation to ancillary matters. The agreement is embodied in a consent order.

Mr Robinson will pay an amount equal to his wife's legal costs to her solicitor who will pay it on to the Legal Aid Board. The Board will use it to reimburse the legal aid fund partially or wholly for the cost of Mrs Robinson's legal aid.

(b)   If the costs recovered for the assisted person are not enough to cover the cost of the assisted person's legal aid, the Legal Aid Board will also put the assisted person's legal aid contribution towards the costs (s. 16, Legal Aid Act 1988).

Example 2. Mr Robinson pays £700 of his wife's costs by agreement. Her costs are in fact £1,000. The legal aid fund therefore remains out of pocket in relation to Mrs Robinson's legal costs. Mrs Robinson has paid a contribution towards her legal aid. This contribution is retained by the Legal Aid Board and put towards discharging the deficiency.

Note that if the total contribution made by an assisted person to the legal aid fund is more than is required to make up the deficiency in the fund the balance will be repaid to the assisted person (s. 16(4), Legal Aid Act 1988).

Example 3. Mrs Robinson's contribution towards her legal aid was £400. The deficit to the legal aid fund after Mr Robinson has paid his share of her costs is only £300. She is entitled to have £100 repaid to her by the Legal Aid Board in respect of her unused contribution.

(c)   If the deficit to the legal aid fund has still not been made good, subject to certain exceptions, the Legal Aid Board will look to any money or property recovered or preserved for the assisted person in the proceedings to which the certificate relates to recoup the balance (s. 16(6), Legal Aid Act 1988). This is commonly called the Legal Aid Board's statutory charge and is more fully described below at paragraph 19.

Example. In ancillary relief proceedings after divorce, Mr Sidebottom is ordered to pay his wife the sum of £5,000. Mrs Sidebottom is legally aided with a nil contribution. No order of costs is obtained against Mr Sidebottom. At the end of the proceedings, therefore, the legal aid fund is out of pocket to the tune of the entire cost of Mrs Sidebottom's legal aid, some £1,500. £1,500 of Mrs Sidebottom's lump sum will therefore be applied in discharging the cost of her legal aid.

If the total of (a), (b) and (c) above still does not make good the legal aid fund's deficit, the legal aid fund will bear the balance of the deficit. If there is no order for costs, no property recovered or preserved and no contribution paid by the assisted person, the legal aid fund will, therefore, bear the entire costs of the proceedings.

18   SOLICITOR TO RECEIVE MONEYS DUE TO ASSISTED PERSON

Regulation 87 of the Civil Legal Aid (General) Regulations 1989 requires that all moneys payable to an assisted person by virtue of any agreement or order made in connection with the action, cause or matter to which his certificate relates (whether made before or after proceedings were taken) must be paid to the assisted person's solicitor. This includes sums due in respect of costs as well as sums due in settlement of the assisted person's claim.

The solicitor is obliged forthwith:

(a)   to pay all moneys received by him by virtue of such an order or agreement to the Legal Aid Board (though note the power of the Area Director where the legal aid fund would be sufficiently safeguarded by payment of a lesser sum to direct that only part of the moneys received by the solicitor should be paid to the Board and the balance to the assisted person himself); *and*

(b)   to inform the area committee of any property recovered or preserved for the assisted person (reg. 90 ibid).

The purpose of reg. 90 is, of course, to ensure that the question of reimbursement of the legal aid fund can be dealt with before the assisted person has a chance to spend any part of the money that may be required to reimburse the fund.

19   THE STATUTORY CHARGE UNDER S. 16(6), LEGAL AID ACT 1988

19.1   Generally

As we saw in paragraph 17 above, the effect of s. 16(6), Legal Aid Act 1988 is that if the amount of costs recovered for an assisted person together with his own contribution towards his legal aid is not sufficient to cover the cost to the legal aid fund of his legal expenses, the Legal Aid Board can look to any property recovered or preserved for him in the proceedings to recoup the balance. Section 16(6) gives the Legal Aid Board a first charge for the benefit of the legal aid fund on any such property — this is commonly referred to as 'the Legal Aid Board's charge' or 'the statutory charge'.

Regulation 90 obliges the solicitor to notify the area committee of any property recovered or preserved (see paragraph 18 above) and it is the area committee which then decides whether or not a charge arises. The considerations to be borne in mind in reaching such a decision are set out in the following sub-paragraphs of paragraph 19. In practice the question will normally arise in connection with ancillary relief proceedings following divorce, nullity or judicial separation and the remainder of paragraph 19 is therefore written with this in mind.

19.2   'Property' includes money

Although s. 16(6) refers only to property, this does include money. Therefore the statutory charge can attach, for example, to a lump sum received by the assisted person just as it can to a house recovered or preserved for him.

19.3   Has any property been recovered or preserved?

This can be a very vexed question. The leading case is *Hanlon* v *The Law Society* [1981] AC 124, [1980] 2 All ER 199. In this case the House of Lords held that property is 'recovered or preserved' if it was *in issue* in the proceedings and either the assisted person made a successful claim in respect of it (in which case the property is recovered for him) or successfully defended a claim in respect of it (in which case the property is preserved for him). The fact that the court has a general discretion over all property and money belonging to the parties in ancillary proceedings following a decree of divorce, nullity or judicial separation can be disregarded. What is important is whether the particular item that may be the subject of the charge has actually been in issue or not and this is a matter to be decided on the facts of each case by looking at the pleadings, the evidence and the court's judgment or order.

> **Example.** (The facts of the *Hanlon* case.) The husband and wife were married in 1957. In 1963 a matrimonial home was purchased in the husband's name with a mortgage. Both parties contributed equally in money and work to the family and the marriage. The wife got legal aid to petition for divorce (this was in 1971 when full legal aid was still generally available for divorce), to apply for ouster and non-molestation injunctions and to take proceedings under s. 17, Married Women's Property Act 1882. She made a small contribution towards her legal aid.
>
> The wife was granted a divorce, given custody of the two children of the marriage and granted a property adjustment order requiring the husband to transfer the matrimonial home to the wife absolutely. The equity in the home was worth about £10,000.
>
> The wife's legal costs were £8,025 (£925 for the divorce and applications for an injunction, £1,150 for custody and access applications and £5,950 in respect of the property adjustment order). The husband was legally aided also and no order for costs was made against him. Clearly therefore the legal aid fund was substantially out of pocket in relation to the wife's legal costs and the question arose as to whether the Law Society had a charge on the house in respect of the wife's costs.
>
> The House of Lords held that the whole house had been in issue. It was pointed out that, if the husband had agreed at the outset that the wife had at least a half share in the house, then only the husband's half share would have been in issue (and therefore recovered by the wife and subject to the charge). However, in this case in the original pleadings each spouse was claiming the transfer of the other's interest in the house to himself and this position was never altered by agreement or concession that the wife was entitled to at least part of the house. Thus the entire house was property recovered by the wife (the husband's interest) or preserved for her (her own interest) and therefore (apart from the first £2,500 of the house's value which was excepted from the charge by regulation; see paragraph 19.5 below) the whole house was subject to the charge.

The *Hanlon* case concerned an issue over *title* to property. The case of *Curling* v *Law Society* [1985] 1 All ER 705, carries the charge a stage further. In that case a matrimonial home was bought in joint names. The husband petitioned for divorce and sought a property adjustment order in respect of the home. The wife was legally aided. She sought an order that the house be sold. The husband did not dispute the wife's entitlement to a half share in the property (so her title to half the house was never in issue). However, he did wish to remain in the house and negotiations led to an agreement whereby the husband would buy out the wife's interest in the house. The wife argued that as the title to the house had never been in issue in the proceedings, the sum she received for her interest in it could not be regarded as property recovered or preserved and therefore could not be the subject of the statutory charge. The Court of Appeal held that the ownership of the house could not be looked at in isolation when considering whether the wife had recovered or preserved property in the proceedings. The fact that a party recovers in the proceedings that to which he is already entitled in law does not by itself prevent the attachment of the statutory charge. The property has been in issue in the proceedings if the party's right to realise his share in the property is contested just as much as if his rights of ownership had been disputed. Thus, because the parties had been in dispute over whether the house should be sold forthwith enabling the wife to realise her share in it, her interest in the property had been in issue and the sum paid by the husband in respect of her interest was therefore property recovered by her and subject to the charge.

In summary, the following propositions are tentatively put forward on the question of whether property has been recovered or preserved:

(a)   Property can only have been recovered or preserved if it has been in issue in the proceedings (*Hanlon*).

(b)   Whether particular property has been in issue must be determined as a matter of fact from the pleadings, the evidence, the court's judgment/order (*Hanlon*) and, as in *Curling*, the correspondence.

(c)   If there has been an argument over ownership of the property, the property has been in issue (*Hanlon*).

(d)   However, it is necessary to look specifically to see whether the whole title to the property was in dispute or just part. If the person defending the claim conceded from the outset that part of the property belonged to the claimant as a matter of prior entitlement, the title to that part of the property was never in issue (*Hanlon*).

(e)   The mere fact that a claim was made by the petitioner in her divorce, nullity or judicial separation petition (or presumably by the respondent in Form 11 or in his answer) in relation to particular property is not sufficient, by itself, to put that property in issue (*Curling* commenting on the case of *Jones* v *Law Society* (1983) 4 FLR 733).

(f)   Although there has been no dispute over ownership of the property in question, that property can still have been in issue if there has been conflict over whether a party should be allowed to realise his share in the property within a certain time or not (*Curling*). Thus, if the parties agree that the matrimonial home is owned, say equally, but one party seeks a prompt sale and equal division of the proceeds (or a lump sum payment from the other party in respect of his interest) and the other seeks a Mesher order, the property has been in issue.

19.4   Charge applicable to property recovered/preserved as a result of a compromise

Section 16(7) makes it quite clear that property recovered or preserved includes any property paid to the assisted person by way of a compromise arrived at to avoid or bring to an end the proceedings as well as property recovered or preserved as a result of a judgment or order of the court. Thus the assisted person cannot avoid the charge by settling a claim out of court even if he does so before proceedings are commenced.

19.5 Exemptions from the charge

Regulation 94 of the Civil Legal Aid (General) Regulations 1989 provides that certain property is exempt from the charge. The exemptions include:

(a) periodical payments of maintenance for a spouse, former spouse, or child;

(b) the first £2,500 of any money or of the value of any property recovered or preserved by virtue (*inter alia*) of:

(i) a lump sum order made in accordance with the Matrimonial Causes Act 1973 (for example, after divorce or on a s. 27 application) or on an application under the Domestic Proceedings and Magistrates' Courts Act 1978;

(ii) a property adjustment order made after divorce, etc.;

(iii) an order made under s. 17, Married Women's Property Act 1882;

(iv) a lump sum order made under the Children Act 1989. (In practice this exempts the first £2,500 of any lump sum or property that the solicitor is likely to come across in a matrimonial case.)

19.6 Charge only attaches to property recovered or preserved for the assisted person

It is important to note that the charge only attaches to property recovered or preserved for the assisted person himself or for his benefit. Thus, if, for example, a wife applies on divorce for a lump sum or transfer of property order on behalf of her child and an order is made, any lump sum paid or property transferred will escape the charge entirely.

19.7 What costs form part of the charge?

It is the outstanding cost of 'the proceedings' that is the subject of the charge. This means that the charge is not confined to the cost of the part of the proceedings which resulted in the recovery or preservation of the property in question. It extends to the cost of the whole cause, action or matter covered by the legal aid certificate (*Hanlon* v *The Law Society*; see paragraph 19.3 above). The facts of the *Hanlon* case illustrate this principle. There, the wife's certificate covered the divorce suit and the ancillary proceedings arising out of it in relation to property adjustment and custody of and access to the children. The charge on the matrimonial home therefore comprised not only the cost of the property adjustment proceedings themselves but also the cost of the divorce proceedings and the custody and access proceedings.

Where the client first receives green form advice and then goes on to obtain full legal aid in relation to the same proceedings, the cost of the green form advice will be added to the cost of the assisted person's legal aid in determining the cost to the legal aid fund of the case (s. 16(9), Legal Aid Act 1988).

Example. Mrs Wetherby petitions for divorce. Her solicitor advises her under the green form scheme in relation to the divorce and drafts the petition. She then obtains full legal aid for ancillary proceedings. She has a nil contribution. Her husband is ordered to pay her £7,500 in the ancillary relief proceedings but no order for costs is obtained against him in relation to ancillary relief or the divorce itself. The Legal Aid Board will look to

Mrs Wetherby's lump sum for payment of all the costs incurred under the green form and on full legal aid.

Sometimes the certificate covers two separate proceedings (for example, proceedings under s. 17, Married Women's Property Act 1882 may occasionally be authorised in the same certificate as proceedings for ancillary relief after divorce). In such cases the charge will only relate to the costs of the cause, action or matter in which the property is recovered or preserved. However, where a certificate has been discharged because the Area Director is satisfied that the proceedings to which it related have been disposed of, then the statutory charge on any property recovered or preserved in subsequent proceedings under a fresh certificate will not extend to the costs of previous proceedings in respect of which the earlier certificate was discharged (*Watkinson* v *Legal Aid Board* [1991] 2 All ER 953, CA). Thus where, as often happens in matrimonial proceedings, there is a likelihood of having to make successive applications e.g. to vary an order for periodical payments (as in the case of *Watkinson*) wherever possible previous certificates should be discharged and fresh certificates obtained if a fresh certificate will avoid the impact of a statutory charge.

19.8   Enforcement of the charge

The charge vests in the Legal Aid Board who are entitled to enforce it in just the same way as anyone else entitled to a charge. If the charge affects land, it can be registered as a charge against the property (reg. 95, Civil Legal Aid (General) Regulations 1989). If both cash and a dwelling house are recovered or preserved, the charge will first be enforced against the cash and the balance only against the property. However, it would appear that the assisted person is entitled to set the £2,500 exemption against the first £2,500 of his cash and this may mean that the charge has to be registered against the dwelling house.

Example. Mr and Mrs Lock get divorced. They have two houses, both in joint names and free of mortgage and some capital in Mr Lock's name in the building society. They fight tooth and nail in ancillary proceedings over who is entitled to the property. Therefore the entire property is in issue. Ultimately, Mr Lock is ordered to transfer his share in one dwelling house (10 Acacia Avenue) to Mrs Lock and to pay her £2,900 (the entire building society account balance). Mrs Lock, is ordered to transfer her share in the other dwelling house (50 Wood Lane) to Mr Lock. Mrs Lock is legally aided with a nil contribution. Mr Lock is also legally aided. Neither party is ordered to pay the other's costs. Mrs Lock's legal costs amount to £1,000. The first £2,500 of her lump sum is exempt from the charge. She will lose the remaining £400 immediately towards the Legal Aid Board's charge. The balance of her legal costs (a further £600) will be the subject of a charge registered against 10 Acacia Avenue. Mr Lock's legal costs are also £1,000. The first £,2500 of the value of the Wood Lane house is exempt from the charge but there is ample equity in the property in excess of this figure. Because Mr Lock has not recovered or preserved any cash, the full amount of his legal costs will be a charge on 50 Wood Lane.

The Legal Aid Board can agree to postpone the charge in appropriate cases. In practice this means that, if the charge relates to the assisted person's home, the Board will accept a registered charge over the property. Thus the assisted person will not be forced to sell the property straight away to repay the Board's charge. However, when he does decide to sell of his own accord he will be bound to repay the Board out of the proceeds of the sale and the Board may agree to transfer the charge to his next house. If the assisted person wishes the charge to be transferred in this way, application should be made to the Board. The Board will only agree to swop if:

(a)   the Area Director is satisfied that there is sufficient equity in the new home to cover the amount of the charge; *and*
(b)   the assisted person agrees that the new house will be subject to a new charge (interest being payable in certain circumstances) (reg. 98).

Where the only property recovered or preserved is a sum of money which by order of the court or under the terms of the agreement reached is to be used for the purpose of purchasing a home for himself or his dependants, then the Board may agree to defer enforcing its charge over the sum if:

(a)   the assisted person wishes to purchase a home in accordance with the order or agreement, and agrees that the new home will itself be subject to a charge; *and*
(b)   the Area Director is satisfied that the new property will provide adequate security for the amount in question (reg. 96).

If the provisions of reg. 96 (which overruled the effect of *Simpson* v *The Law Society* [1987] 2 FLR 497) are not satisfied in any given case, then the Board will have no discretion to postpone the enforcement of the charge. It would appear from the case of *Scallon* v *Scallon* [1990] 1 FLR 194, [1990] Fam Law 92, CA, that the court has jurisdiction to impose a condition in its order that a sum of money which by its order is to be paid to a party shall be used for the purchase of a house for that party. *Scallon* also holds that the court is entitled to assume that the Legal Aid Board will use its powers to postpone its charge over that sum of money so as not to frustrate the order of the court.

20   WHERE GREEN FORM ADVICE ONLY IS GIVEN

The provisions set out in paragraph 19 relate to cases where a legal aid certificate is granted. Occasionally it may be possible to deal with a client's case on the basis of the green form alone. Where this happens, there is a similar system for the reimbursement of the cost to the legal aid fund but, this time, instead of the Legal Aid Board administering the system, it falls mainly to the solicitor to do so in the course of obtaining payment of his own costs.

Thus s. 11, Legal Aid Act 1988 provides that the solicitor should obtain payment of his green form costs:

(a)   first from any sum paid to the solicitor on behalf of the client as party and party costs;
(b)   then from the client's own contribution;
(c)   then from the charge imposed by s. 11(2), Legal Aid Act 1988 in the solicitor's favour on any costs payable to the legally assisted person by any other person (e.g., the opponent in the proceedings concerned) and on any property recovered or preserved for the client in connection with the matter except such property as is set out in sch. 4 of the Legal Advice and Assistance Regulations

1989 (the property exempted is the same as for legal aid; see paragraph 19.5 above). The solicitor is unlikely to take much comfort from a charge for his costs over, say, the client's dwelling house. He can therefore assign the benefit of his charge to the Board who will pay him the costs due to him instead. Alternatively he can apply to the area committee for authority not to enforce the charge in certain circumstances (reg. 33, Legal Advice and Assistance Regulations 1989), in which case the deficiency in his costs will be met by the legal aid fund (note that there is no equivalent power to waive the charge in legal aid cases);

(d)   and only then from the legal aid fund.

21   THE DUTY TO MAKE THE CLIENT FULLY AWARE OF THE POTENTIAL IMPACT OF THE CHARGE

It is imperative that the client is made fully aware of the existence of the statutory charge and of its potential impact in his particular case. The client can hardly be reminded of the charge too frequently. It is suggested that, at minimum, the solicitor should explain it to him comprehensively:

(a)   when the green form is completed; *and*
(b)   when application is made for full legal aid; *and*
(c)   when any settlement is being considered which would produce cash or property which might be affected by the charge; *and*
(d)   if the cost of proceedings is mounting particularly high for any reason.

Clients have a knack, as all solicitors are aware, of forgetting that unpalatable advice has ever been given. It is not unknown, therefore, for a client to turn round when, for example, a large part of his lump sum is eaten up by the statutory charge and say that he was never warned that this would happen. It is therefore suggested that, in addition to explaining the charge to the client orally, the solicitor should also write to the client giving a further brief explanation so there is a record of his advice.

Solicitors should be aware that, in order for the client to appreciate properly how the charge may affect him in practice, he will probably have to be given a rough estimate of the likely costs of the proceedings in just the same way as a private client.

22   MINIMISING THE EFFECT OF THE CHARGE

The best way to minimise the effect of the charge is to seek to recover the client's costs from the other party to the proceedings. However, this is often not possible in matrimonial cases as there is a tendency in such cases for no order to be made as to costs.

As we have seen at paragraph 19.3 above, the charge will only attach to property that has been in issue. Another way in which to minimise the charge is therefore for the issues involved in the proceedings to be narrowed down as far as possible *at the outset*.

Example. Mrs Hill consults her solicitor with a view to a divorce. The matrimonial home is in joint names and Mrs Hill thinks that her husband accepts that she is entitled to half of it. She wishes to claim the entire house (in which there is an equity of about £6,000) in ancillary proceedings. She then proposes to sell the house and buy a smaller property. The solicitor writes to Mr Hill's solicitor asking him to confirm that Mr Hill accepts his wife's entitlement to half the house and that the dispute between the parties is only over the other half share. Mr Hill's solicitor confirms this. Mrs Hill files a divorce petition making a comprehensive claim for financial relief and property adjustment and, in particular, claiming the transfer of the house to her. She obtains legal aid for ancillary relief proceedings. The district judge ultimately orders that the house should be transferred to her.

Mrs Hill's half of the house was never in issue. The statutory charge in relation to her costs will only attach to the half share in the house which she has recovered from her husband in the proceedings. Mrs Hill does sell the house immediately after the proceedings are over. The Legal Aid Board are not prepared to take a charge over her new house — they require immediate repayment of their charge. Broadly speaking, her debt to the Board will be as follows:

Equity in house	£6,000
Property recovered by Mrs Hill in the proceedings is therefore half this figure	£3,000
Less exemption from charge	£2,500
Property subject to the charge	£500

Mrs Hill's costs amounted to £1,000. She paid no contribution to her legal aid and no order for costs was obtained against Mr Hill. The legal aid fund is therefore out of pocket by £1,000. Mrs Hill will be required to pay £500 towards this but the balance will have to be borne by the Legal Aid Board.

Note that, had the whole of the house been in issue in the proceedings, Mrs Hill would have recovered half of it and preserved the remainder. Thus the entire equity of £6,000 less the £2,500 exemption (i.e. £3,500) would have been open to the charge and Mrs Hill would therefore have lost £1,000 to the legal aid fund instead of £500.

If possible, not only the correspondence but also the pleadings themselves should make clear what property is and what property is not in dispute.

D: METHOD BY WHICH SOLICITOR OBTAINS PAYMENT IN LEGAL AID CASES

The solicitor looks to the legal aid fund for payment of his bill in legal aid cases. It is not the province of this book to go into detail about the procedure for obtaining payment. Briefly, however, what happens is that the solicitor's costs will have to be taxed or assessed. The costs will be assessed where the case is settled before proceedings are even commenced and can also be assessed, *inter alia*, where the sums found due to the solicitor and counsel on taxation would not, in the opinion of the solicitor, be more than £500. Assessment is carried out by the Area Director (reg. 105, Civil Legal Aid (General) Regulations 1989). In other cases (i.e. the majority of cases where proceedings have been commenced), the solicitor's costs will be taxed in accordance with any direction or order given or made in the proceedings (reg. 107 ibid.). To facilitate taxation, the solicitor (or counsel, if he is involved) should be careful to ensure that the court gives a direction that the assisted person's legal aid costs be taxed when it makes a final order in proceedings.

E: LEGAL AID AND THE CHILDREN ACT 1989

23   LEGAL AID UNDER THE CHILDREN ACT 1989

The introduction of the Children Act 1989 has necessitated amendments to the Legal Aid Act 1988. Civil legal aid under part IV of the Legal Aid Act 1988 is now available for all proceedings under the Children Act 1989 (s. 15, Legal Aid Act 1988, as amended). The relevant regulations which implement those changes are as follows: The Civil Legal Aid (General) (Amendment No. 2) Regulations 1991; the Legal Aid in Criminal and Care Proceedings (General) (Amendment No. 2) Regulations 1991; the Legal Aid in Family Proceedings (Remuneration) Regulations 1991; the Legal Aid Act 1988 (Children Act 1989) Order 1991; the Legal Aid in Criminal and Care Proceedings (Costs) (Amendment No. 3) Regulations 1991.

There are now three categories of legal aid for Children Act 1989 proceedings:

(a)   special Children Act proceedings;
(b)   means test only proceedings;
(c)   means and merits test proceedings.

The appropriate category will depend upon the exact nature of the proceedings and/or the status of the client. The proceedings which attract non means and non merits tested, or means only tested legal aid are governed by the Children (Allocation of Proceedings) Order 1991. Where the solicitor represents more than one child then *each child* must have a separate legal aid certificate. If, however, the solicitor represents a party other than a child in proceedings involving more than one child, then only one legal aid certificate is necessary.

23.1   Special Children Act proceedings

Under the new provisions set out in the Legal Aid Act 1988 (Children Act 1989) Order 1991, non means, non merits tested legal aid, sometimes referred to as 'free legal aid' is available to:

(a)   parents;
(b)   children;
(c)   persons with parental responsibility.

The proceedings for which 'free' legal aid is available are as follows:

(a)   proceedings for care orders and supervision orders (s. 31);
(b)   proceedings for child assessment orders (s. 43);
(c)   proceedings for emergency protection orders (s. 44);
(d)   proceedings relating to the duration and discharge of emergency protection orders (s. 45).

Finally, 'free legal aid' will be available to the *child only* in proceedings brought pursuant to section 25 of the Children Act 1989 (the use of secure accommodation).

23.2 Means test only proceedings

Legal aid granted only upon a means test (i.e. no merits test necessary) will be available to other parties applying to be joined, or required to be joined by the Rules of Court, in the proceedings listed in paragraph 23.1, above.

23.3 Means and merits test proceedings

Legal aid will also be available for Children Act 1989 proceedings upon the normal basis whereby the applicant undergoes a test both of his means and of the merits of his case.

23.4 New legal aid forms

New legal aid forms have been issued as a consequence of the amendments to the Legal Aid Act 1988. Further details of those forms will be found in paragraph 13.1, above.

23.5 When will an amendment to the certificate be necessary?

The certificate will cover all of the normal steps involved in the conduct of the case. It will also cover proceedings which are commenced in respect of one of the specified orders set out in paragraph 23.1, above, but which are concluded with a different type of order, e.g. where care proceedings are concluded with a section 8 residence order or where an application for a child assessment order is treated as an application for an emergency protection order.

However, specifically stated cover or an amendment to the certificate will be necessary for the following:

(a) to make (but not to oppose) an application for a section 8 order in care or supervision proceedings; or
(b) to appeal against the making of a care or supervision order.

23.5.1 'Related proceedings'

A certificate granted in respect of 'free' legal aid can be extended to cover 'related proceedings'. Such an extension will be neither means nor merits tested. However, 'related proceedings' are not defined in the Legal Aid Act 1988 or in the regulations, and therefore the decision as to which proceedings are 'related' will lie with the area office. An appeal against the decision of the area office will lie to the area committee. Examples of proceedings which will *not* be considered as 'related' are applications between individuals for ancillary relief or applications for injunctions under the Domestic Violence and Matrimonial Proceedings Act 1978; these would require a separate application for another certificate.

23.5.2 Appeals

The prohibition against amending an existing certificate in order to appeal from a magistrates' court decision is now removed in respect of 'special Children Act proceedings'. It will now be possible to amend a certificate to cover an appeal from a magistrates' court decision but a merits test will apply. In all other cases the prohibition continues. It is possible to amend the certificate in relation to appeals from the High Court or the county court to the Court of Appeal.

GF 1

LEGAL AID BOARD
LEGAL AID ACT 1988

GREEN FORM

Key Card

	PLEASE USE BLOCK CAPITALS		
Surname	Forenames	Male·Female	AREA REF. No.
Address			

CAPITAL		CLIENT	£
TOTAL SAVINGS and OTHER CAPITAL		SPOUSE OR COHABITEE	£
		TOTAL	£

Ⓐ

INCOME

State whether in receipt of Income Support or Family Credit

YES NO   If the answer if YES ignore the rest of this Section.

Ⓑ

NOTES FOR SOLICITORS

1. Advice and assistance may only be given in relation to the making of **wills** in the circumstances set out in The Legal Advice and Assistance (Scope) Regulations 1989. In such circumstances your client must complete **Form GF 4**

2. Where advice and assistance are being given in respect of **divorce or judicial separation proceedings** and the work to be carried out includes the preparation of a petition, the solicitor will be entitled to ask for his claim for costs and disbursements to be assessed up to an amount referred to in The Legal Advice and Assistance Regulations 1989.

Total weekly Gross Income

Client	£
Spouse or Cohabitee	£
TOTAL	£

Allowances and Deductions from Income

Income tax	£
National Insurance Contributions, etc.	£
Spouse	£

Ⓒ
Ⓓ
Ⓔ

Dependent children and/or other dependants	Number	
Under 5		£
5 but under 11		£
11 .. 13		£
13 .. 16		£
16 .. 18		£
18 and over		£

Ⓕ

LESS TOTAL DEDUCTIONS →	£
TOTAL WEEKLY DISPOSABLE INCOME	£

TO BE COMPLETED AND SIGNED BY CLIENT

I am over the compulsory school-leaving age.

I have have not previously received help from a solicitor about this matter under the Legal Aid and Advice Schemes.

I am liable to pay a contribution not exceeding .... £

Ⓖ

I understand that any money or property which is recovered or preserved for me may be subject to a deduction if my contribution (if any) is less than my Solicitor's charges.

The information on this page is to the best of my knowledge correct and complete. I understand that I may be prosecuted for giving false information.

Date   Signature

CLAIM FOR PAYMENT TO ACCOMPANY FORM G F 2

Name of Client

Has a Legal Aid Order been made?   Yes/No.
If so, give date ....

PLEASE ATTACH ANY AUTHORITIES GIVEN BY THE AREA OFFICE.

TICK THE APPROPRIATE LETTER TO INDICATE THE NATURE OF THE PROBLEM

A. Divorce or judicial separation (see note on page 1)

B. Other family matters (Specify in Summary)   G. Accident injuries

C. Crime   H. Welfare benefits/tribunals

D. Landlord/tenant/housing   J. Immigration/Nationality

E. H.P. and Debt   K. Consumer problems

F. Employment   L. Other matters (Specify in Summary)

Has any money or property been recovered?
If so, give details.

No. of letters written

No. of telephone calls
  Made
  Received

Time otherwise spent:
  Specify in
  Summary

Has a legal aid certificate or order been granted?
                                        Yes/No.

If not, is one being applied for?   Yes/No.

Certificate or Order No.
if appropriate:

Summary of work done:

PARTICULARS OF COSTS

£   £

1. Profit costs   Details of disbursements: -

2. Disbursements (including Counsel's fees)   Counsel's fees (if any)

3. Add VAT as appropriate   Other disbursements (listed)

      TOTAL CLAIM

4. Deduct maximum contribution (if any)

      NET CLAIM

Have you previously made a claim for legal advice and assistance for your client in respect of divorce or judicial separation
proceedings or matters connected therewith.   YES/NO   If Yes, how much was allowed   £

Signed	Solicitor Date	Solicitor's ref.
Firm name (in full)		
Address		

Date   NOTICE OF ASSESSMENT

   The Area Director has assessed your costs in this matter as set out below. In view of the fact that the sum assessed is less than that
claimed, you may appeal in writing to the Area Committee in support of your claim as originally submitted or on any item in it, if you wish.
These representations must be received within 14 days of the date hereof. I have deleted this matter from the consolidated claim form G.F.2
with which it was sent and I should be obliged if you would do the same. If you accept the assessment, please include this matter on your
next consolidated claim form as assessed below AND RE-SUBMIT THIS FORM WITH IT.

                                        Authorised Signatory Legal Aid Area No.

                                                                  £

1. Profit costs

2. Disbursements

3. Add VAT as appropriate

      TOTAL CLAIM

4. Deduct maximum contribution (if any)

      NET CLAIM

NOTE. –You are advised to keep a copy of this page because if in the same matter your client obtains a L.A. Certificate or Order, you
may on taxation of your costs and disbursements be required to produce to the Taxing Officer a copy of this form indicating work done
and quantum of payment. You may also require a copy of this page if after submitting your claim for payment you apply to the Area Office
for a financial extension to enable you to give further advice and assistance to your Client.

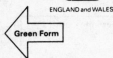
ENGLAND and WALES

GREEN FORM KEY CARD
(NO. 23)
Effective from 8th April 1991

Green Form

Please see over for
further explanatory notes.

N.B. The green form (GF 1) should not
be used for advice to suspects at police
stations. Such cases are covered by
forms DSPS 1 and DSPS 2.

CAPITAL means the amount or value of every resource of a capital nature
In computing Disposable Capital disregard
(i) the value of the main or only dwelling house in which the client resides, and
(ii) the value of household furniture and effects, articles of personal clothing and tools or
implements of the client's trade, and
(iii) the subject matter of the advice and assistance.

Maximum Disposable Capital for Financial Eligibility (dependant = partner, child or relative)

Advice and Assistance*	ABWOR**
£935 – client with no dependants	£3000 – client with no dependants
£1270 – client with 1 dependant	£3335 – client with 1 dependant
£1470 – client with 2 dependants	£3535 – client with 2 dependants
Add £100 for each additional dependant	

*Capital must be assessed for advice
and assistance even if client is on
income support or family credit. See
note 3.

**All capital is disregarded if client is on
income support. See note 3.

B INCOME means the total income from all sources which the client received or became entitled to during
or in respect of the seven days up to and including the date of this application.

The capital and weekly income of both
partners must be taken into account
unless:
(a) they have a contrary interest
(b) they live apart
(c) it is inequitable or impractical to
aggregate their means

Some types of income are ignored. See
note 3.

In computing Disposable Income deduct:-

C (i) Income Tax

D (ii) Contributions paid under the Social Security Acts 1975-88

E (iii) £39.06 in respect of the client's partner (if living together) whether or not their means
are aggregated. Where they are separated or divorced, the allowance will be the
actual maintenance paid by the client in respect of the previous 7 days.

These deductions also apply to the
partner's income if there is aggregation.

F (iv) £16.69 for each dependent child or dependent relative of the household under 11
years of age
£24.69 for each dependent child or dependent relative of the household of 11 but
under 16 years of age
£29.56 for each dependent child or dependent relative of the household of 16 or
17 years of age
£38.94 for each dependent child or dependent relative of the household of 18 years
of age or over

Where the child or dependent relative is not a member of the household the allowance will
be the actual maintenance paid by the client in respect of the previous 7 days.

There is no deduction in relation to a
foster child.

Client's Contributions

Disposable Income	Maximum Contribution	Disposable Income	Maximum Contribution
Not exceeding £70 a week	nil	Not exceeding £102 a week	£38
„ £74 „	£5	„ £108 „	£45
„ £78 „	£12	„ £114 „	£51
„ £84 „	£19	„ £120 „	£58
„ £90 „	£25	„ £125 „	£64
„ £96 „	£32	„ £130 „	£70
		„ £135 „	£75

G Where the initial green form limit is two hours' worth of work (the green form rate is currently £42.00
per hour or £44.50 in London), a client's contribution in excess of this amount can only be called
for if a financial extension has been obtained from the legal aid area office.

Note

The green form must be signed by the client at the initial interview as soon as his her eligibility has been
determined except in the case of an authorised postal application.

GREEN FORM KEY CARD (NO. 23)
EXPLANATORY NOTES

1. General
Your attention is particularly drawn to *The Legal Advice and Assistance Regulations 1989* ("the regulations") and to *The Legal Advice and Assistance (Scope) Regulations 1989* ("the scope regulations").

2. Conveyancing and Wills
You should note that it is not permitted to give advice and assistance in respect of conveyancing matters or the making of a will except in those circumstances set out in *regulations 3* and *4* of the scope regulations. Form GF4 must be signed by the client in respect of advice and assistance in the making of a will.

3. Financial Eligibility
(a) The responsibility for determining eligibility is placed upon the solicitor under *Schedule 2* of the regulations.

(b) *Schedule 2* of the regulations sets out the method of assessment of resources of the client. The only deductions and allowances which can be made are those referred to in *Schedule 2*. Built-in deductions have already been made for miscellaneous expenditure such as rent, mortgage repayments and hire-purchase repayments etc.

(c) When considering a client's means it may be useful to have the following points in mind:-

(i) If part of the main dwelling is let and the client lives in the remaining part, although the capital value of the main dwelling house should be left out of account in computing capital, the rent should be included in computing income.

(ii) Capital means the amount or value of every resource of a capital nature so that capital derived from a bank loan or borrowing facilities should be taken into account.

(iii) There is no power to disregard income in self-employed cases merely because the client may have incurred unspecified expenses at an earlier date.

(iv) A cohabitee should be included within the definitions of a spouse.

(v) Income means the total income from all sources which the client received or became entitled to during or in respect of the seven days up to and including the date of application. It will include child benefit.

(vi) Fostering allowances received in respect of fostered children should not be taken into account in assessing the financial eligibility of the client.

(vii) Mobility Allowance should be disregarded when computing income.

(viii) Because different capital limits apply for advice and assistance and ABWOR, clients may be eligible for ABWOR when not eligible for advice and assistance.

(ix) Clients in receipt of income support (but not family credit) will always be eligible for ABWOR regardless of capital but not necessarily for advice and assistance.

4. Solicitor and Client relationship
(a) A solicitor may, for reasonable cause, either refuse to accept an application for legal advice and assistance or, having accepted it, decline to give advice and assistance without giving reasons to the client. He may however be required to give reasons to the legal aid area office.

(b) Once financial eligibility has been established, a client should be told the amount of the contribution due (if any), and arrangements should be made for payment either outright or by instalments. Any contribution paid should be retained on client account until the matter for which advice and assistance has been given has been concluded.

(c) If the contribution exceeds the costs payable and VAT, the excess should be returned to the client.

5. Remuneration
(a) The initial financial limit of expenditure (at present two hours' worth of work, or three hours' worth of work in the case of an undefended divorce or judicial separation petition) is exclusive of VAT as is any financial extension granted.

(b) The financial limit of three hours' worth of work in undefended divorce or judicial separation cases is only applicable where a petition has been drafted. It need not, however, have been filed.

(c) The legal aid fund is only responsible for paying to solicitor and counsel such of their costs as are not covered by the client's contribution (if any), party and party costs awarded and the charge which arises in the solicitor's favour on any property recovered or preserved. *Schedule 4* of the regulations sets out the circumstances when the charge does not apply. Application may be made to the area committee for authority not to enforce the charge where (a) it would cause grave hardship or distress to the client, or (b) it could be enforced only with unreasonable difficulty.

(d) Costs for work done under *regulation 7(1)(b)* or *regulation 8* of the scope regulations, should not exceed the usual financial limit.

6. Court Proceedings
A solicitor may not take steps in court proceedings unless either approval is given by the legal aid area office for ABWOR in a magistrates' court or a solicitor is acting according to the other conditions detailed in *regulation 7* and *regulation 8* of the scope regulations.

7. Authorities
(a) The authority of the legal aid area office is required before accepting an application from a child, a person on behalf of a child or a patient (in the case of such person not falling within the categories referred to in *regulation 14* of the regulations) a person residing outside England and Wales, or a person who has already received advice and assistance from another solicitor on the same matter.

(b) Where approval of the legal aid area office is required for ABWOR even if approval is given, the prior permission of the legal aid area office is required to obtain a report or opinion of an expert, to tender expert evidence or to perform an act which is either unusual in its nature or involves unusually large expenditure. Thus the prior permission of the legal aid area office would be required before obtaining a blood test even if it was ordered by the court.

Printed by Oakley Press Plc

PART II
DIVORCE, NULLITY AND JUDICIAL
SEPARATION: THE DECREE

3   The ground for divorce and the five facts

1   THE GROUND FOR DIVORCE

There is only one ground for divorce, that is that the marriage has irretrievably broken down; s. 1(1), Matrimonial Causes Act 1973.

2   THE FIVE FACTS

The court cannot hold that the marriage has irretrievably broken down unless the petitioner satisfies the court of one or more of the five facts set out in s. 1(2), Matrimonial Causes Act 1973. These are:

(a)   that the respondent has committed adultery and the petitioner finds it intolerable to live with the respondent;

(b)   that the respondent has behaved in such a way that the petitioner cannot reasonably be expected to live with the respondent;

(c)   that the respondent has deserted the petitioner for a continuous period of at least two years immediately preceding the presentation of the petition;

(d)   that the parties to the marriage have lived apart for a continuous period of at least two years immediately preceding the presentation of the petition and the respondent consents to a decree being granted (two years' separation and consent);

(e)   that the parties to the marriage have lived apart for a continuous period of at least five years immediately preceding the presentation of the petition (five years' separation).

Because of the requirement that one of the five facts should be proved, it is possible for a situation to arise where the marriage has undoubtedly broken down irretrievably but no divorce can yet be granted because neither party can establish any of the five facts.

Example. A couple separate by mutual consent simply because they have found that they are incompatible. Neither has committed adultery or behaved in such a way that the other cannot reasonably be expected to live with him. Although the marriage has irretrievably broken down, they are not able to obtain a divorce during the first two years of their separation as none of the five facts can be established. When two years are up, assuming they both wish to be divorced, it will be possible to establish two years' separation and consent (s. 1(2)(d)) and one or other party will be able to seek a decree.

3 IRRETRIEVABLE BREAKDOWN

3.1 No link necessary between s. 1(2) fact and irretrievable breakdown

It is not necessary for the petitioner to show that the irretrievable breakdown of the marriage has been caused by the s. 1(2) fact on which she relies (*Stevens* v *Stevens* [1979] 1 WLR 885; *Buffery* v *Buffery* [1988] FCR 465, [1988] 2 FLR 365, CA).

Example. (The facts of *Stevens* v *Stevens*.) The petitioner established that the respondent's behaviour was such that she could not reasonably be expected to live with him: s. 1(2)(b). The marriage had irretrievably broken down but in fact it was established that it was the petitioner's own behaviour that had caused the breakdown.
The petitioner was nevertheless entitled to a decree.

3.2 Proving irretrievable breakdown

Section 1(4), Matrimonial Causes Act 1973 provides that if the court is satisfied that one of the s. 1(2) facts is proved, unless it is satisfied on all the evidence that the marriage has not broken down irretrievably it shall grant a decree of divorce (subject to the provisions of s. 5, Matrimonial Causes Act 1973, see Chapter 11). In other words, once one of the facts is established, a presumption of irretrievable breakdown is raised. In an undefended case, there is not normally any evidence to displace the presumption and the court therefore accepts the petitioner's statement in her petition that the marriage has irretrievably broken down without further enquiry.

However, it is open to the respondent to challenge the petitioner's assertion of irretrievable breakdown by filing an answer denying that the marriage has irretrievably broken down. In this event, the suit will become defended and it will be up to the court to determine on the basis of all the evidence at the hearing whether or not the marriage has irretrievably broken down by that date (see *Ash* v *Ash* [1972] Fam 135, [1972] 1 All ER 582; *Pheasant* v *Pheasant* [1972] Fam 202, [1972] 1 All ER 587).

3.3 Adjournment with a view to reconciliation

If at any stage in the divorce proceedings the court feels that there is a reasonable possibility of a reconciliation between the parties, the court may adjourn the proceedings for whatever period it thinks fit to enable attempts at reconciliation to take place: s. 6(2), Matrimonial Causes Act 1973.

4 ADULTERY: S. 1(2)(a)

4.1 Two separate elements to prove:

There are two matters that the petitioner must prove:

(a) that the respondent has committed adultery; *and*
(b) that she finds it intolerable to live with him.

The adultery may be the reason why the petitioner finds it intolerable to live with the respondent but it is not necessary for there to be any link between the two matters (*Cleary* v *Cleary* [1974] 1 All ER 498, [1974] 1 WLR 73 followed in *Carr* v *Carr* [1974] 1 All ER 1193, [1974] 1 WLR 1534).

Example. (The facts of *Cleary* v *Cleary*.) The respondent wife committed adultery. The petitioner husband took her back afterwards but things did not work out because the wife corresponded with the other man, went out at night and then went to live at her mother's and did not return. The petitioner said that he could no longer live with the respondent because there was no future for the marriage. Although it was the respondent's conduct after the adultery and not the adultery itself that had made it intolerable for the petitioner to live with her, he had satisfied both limbs of s. 1(2)(a) and was entitled to a decree.

4.2 Intolerability

Normally, at least in an undefended case, the petitioner's statement in her petition that she finds it intolerable to live with the respondent will be accepted at face value.

However, further evidence may be required in support of her contention if either:

(a)   the information supplied by the petitioner in the petition itself and in support of the petition raises doubts in the mind of the court (usually in the person of the district judge who considers the case under the special procedure) as to whether the petitioner finds it intolerable to live with the respondent: *or*

(b)   the respondent files an answer challenging the petitioner's assertion, in which case the divorce will become defended and the court will hear evidence from both parties on the issue.

The test to be applied when an issue arises over whether the petitioner finds it intolerable to live with the respondent is a subjective one (*Goodrich* v *Goodrich* [1971] 2 All ER 1340, [1971] WLR 1142) i.e., 'does *this petitioner* find it intolerable to live with the respondent' and not 'would *a reasonable petitioner* find it intolerable to live with the respondent?'

4.3 Meaning of adultery

Adultery is voluntary sexual intercourse between a man and woman who are not married to each other but one of whom at least is a married person (*Clarkson* v *Clarkson* (1930) 143 LT 775, 46 TLR 623).

4.4 Proof of adultery

It would be quite extraordinary if the petitioner were able to produce a witness who had actually *seen* the respondent committing adultery. Proof is therefore normally indirect.

Examples of the type of evidence commonly used are set-out in the following paragraphs.

4.4.1 Confessions and admissions

It used to be routine practice for a confession statement to be obtained from the respondent (and if possible the co-respondent as well) admitting adultery and setting out briefly the circumstances in which it took place.

Nowadays, the acknowledgment of service forms used by respondents and co-respondents in adultery cases ask the question 'Do you admit the adultery alleged in the petition?' If the respondent answers this question in the affirmative and signs the form, the court can accept this as sufficient evidence of adultery (see the prescribed form of acknowledgment of service in the Family Proceedings Rules 1991, Appendix 1, Form M6). Depending on the nature of the case and the practice of the particular court in which proceedings are pending, it may or may not still be necessary for the old style of confession statement or other evidence of adultery (see paragraphs 4.4.2 and 4.4.3) to be obtained as well. The only case in which it is safe to say that most district judges will probably be satisfied on the basis of admissions in the acknowledgment of service alone is where the respondent and co-respondent both return acknowledgment of service forms admitting adultery and disclosing that they live at the same address. If the respondent denies adultery and proceeds to file an answer, the case will be defended and the court will have to consider whether, on all the evidence available at the hearing, adultery is proved.

If the respondent does not admit (or even denies) adultery in the acknowledgment of service but does not go so far as to file an answer, his non-cooperation will not necessarily be fatal to the petitioner's case. She will simply have to attempt to prove adultery by other evidence.

4.4.2 Circumstantial evidence
The following are examples of the type of evidence from which the court can be asked to infer adultery:

(a) Evidence that the respondent and another woman are living together as man and wife. The petitioner may be able to state this from her own observations. Alternatively she may be able to produce an independent witness of her own to the fact (for example, the next door neighbour of the respondent and his cohabitee). If necessary an enquiry agent can be instructed to watch the respondent and collect evidence of cohabitation.

(b) Evidence that the respondent and another woman had the inclination and the opportunity to commit adultery, for example that they had formed an intimate relationship (they may have been seen kissing or holding hands in public, for example, or the petitioner may have obtained copies of 'love letters' passing between them) and had spent the night together in the same bedroom or alone together in the same house. Again, the petitioner may be able to supply this evidence herself but if not, an enquiry agent may be able to help. Indeed in the case of evidence of the type set out in both (a) and (b), the court may *require* independent evidence before it is satisfied of adultery.

(c) Evidence that the wife has given birth to a child of which the husband is not the father. Normally it is presumed that a child born during the marriage is legitimate. However, this presumption can be displaced, for example, by evidence that the parties did not have any contact with each other during the time in which conception must have taken place (for example, where the husband has been working overseas continuously for a prolonged period). A birth certificate can be admitted as prima facie evidence of the facts required to be entered on it. This can be useful where the wife has registered the birth and named someone other than the husband as the father of the child. However, it would appear that the fact that a birth certificate names a husband as father does not prevent a rebuttal of the presumption where the mother and the putative father agree that the child is theirs, or the putative father admits that it is his child (see *King's Lynn Magistrates' Court, ex parte M* [1988] FCR 436, [1988] 2 FLR 79).

4.4.3   Findings in other proceedings

If the husband has been found to be the father of a child in affiliation proceedings or a finding of adultery has been made against either party in matrimonial proceedings, that finding is admissible as evidence of adultery by the party against whom the finding has been made.

A conviction of rape against the husband would also be evidence that he had committed adultery.

If the petitioner has already been granted a decree of judicial separation on the basis of the same adultery on which she relies in the divorce proceedings, the court may treat the judicial separation decree as sufficient proof of the adultery (s. 4(2), Matrimonial Causes Act 1973, see Chapter 12 post).

4.4.4   The co-respondent

A person with whom it is alleged the respondent has committed adultery must be made a party to the suit unless he is not named in the petition or the court otherwise directs (see Family Proceedings Rules 1991, r. 2.7(1)). As to whether it is necessary to name a co-respondent, see Chapter 7 paragraph 3.13 post.

Where a co-respondent is named, in most cases if there is no admission of adultery by the co-respondent, the co-respondent will be dismissed from the suit. This does not mean that the petitioner will be denied her decree of divorce. Provided that, by other evidence, she has proved to the satisfaction of the court that the respondent has committed adultery, the court can find adultery with a person against whom adultery has not been proved.

4.5   Living together

In some cases the petitioner can be prevented from relying on adultery because she has lived with the respondent after she discovered his adultery. This matter is dealt with at paragraph 10.1 below.

5   BEHAVIOUR: S. 1(2)(b)

5.1   The test for behaviour

The test as to whether the respondent has behaved in such a way that the petitioner cannot reasonably be expected to live with him is a cross between a subjective and an objective test. The formula used in the case of *Livingstone-Stallard* v *Livingstone-Stallard* [1974] Fam 47, [1974] 2 All ER 766, seems to have been accepted (see *O'Neill* v *O'Neill* [1975] 3 All ER 289, [1975] 1 WLR 1118 and *Buffery* v *Buffery* [1988] 2 FLR 365) i.e.:

Would any right-thinking person come to the conclusion that this husband has behaved in such a way that his wife cannot reasonably be expected to live with him, taking into account the whole of the circumstances and the characters and personalities of the parties?

Thus, not only must the court look at the respondent's behaviour but also at the petitioner's behaviour (asking, for example, whether she provoked the respondent deliberately or simply by her own anti-social conduct). Consideration must also be given to what type of people the petitioner and respondent are (asking, for example, whether the petitioner is particularly sensitive and vulnerable) and to the whole history of the marriage. The court must then evaluate all this evidence and decide objectively whether, in these particular circumstances, it is reasonable to expect the petitioner to go on living with the respondent.

5.2   Examples of behaviour

5.2.1   Violent behaviour

It is quite common for petitioners to rely on violent behaviour on the part of the respondent. One serious violent incident may entitle the petitioner to a decree (for example an unprovoked attack upon the petitioner causing her an unpleasant injury for which she required medical treatment). If the violence used is relatively minor (for example, the occasional push and shove), more than one incident will be required or it will be necessary for the petitioner to show that there was other behaviour as well as the violence.

5.2.2   Other behaviour

The respondent's behaviour need not be violent to entitle the petitioner to a decree. All sorts of other anti-social behaviour can be sufficient as the following examples show. Incidents which are relatively trivial in isolation can amount to sufficient behaviour when looked at as a whole, particularly if the petitioner is especially sensitive to the respondent's behaviour for some reason.

Example 1. (The facts of O'Neill v O'Neill supra.) The parties' marriage had never been entirely satisfactory. The husband was withdrawn and relations between the parties lacked warmth. They bought a flat and the husband began an extensive programme of renovations to remedy damp. He was determined to do all the work himself without advice. He raised floorboards, removed rubble and deposited it in the garden and mixed cement on the living room floor and in other rooms from time to time. He took off the lavatory door and left it off for eight months. It was embarrassing to have visitors to the flat and the lack of a lavatory door particularly embarrassed the wife and the parties' teenage daughter. After two years of renovation the wife left home. The husband then wrote to the wife's solicitor casting doubt on the paternity of the two children of the family. During the cohabitation the wife had suffered increasingly from abdominal pain and had required sleeping pills. After she left her husband her condition greatly improved.

The wife was entitled to a decree.

Example 2. (The facts of Livingstone-Stallard v Livingstone-Stallard supra.) The husband was 56, the wife 24. The marriage was unsatisfactory from the start. The wife's complaints about her husband's behaviour included the following matters. The husband criticised the wife over petty things — her behaviour, her friends, her way of life, her cooking, her dancing — and was abusive to her, called her names and, on one occasion, spat at her. Once he tried to kick her out of bed. On one occasion he criticised her for leaving her underclothes soaking in the sink overnight (although he did the same himself) and said that it was indicative of the way she had been brought up. He made a fuss when she drank sherry with a photographer who had brought round their wedding photographs, forbidding her to give refreshment to 'tradespeople' again (on the basis that if she drank sherry with a tradesman it might impair her faculties so that the tradesman might make an indecent approach to her). The wife left after the husband had bundled her out of the house on a cold evening and locked her out, throwing water over her when she tried to get back in. She suffered bruising and was in a very nervous state for six weeks, needing sedation.

Although many of these complaints were trivial themselves, the wife was entitled to a decree.

Note that although Examples 1 and 2 are taken from the facts of decided cases they are not intended to be looked on *as precedents* of what is and is not sufficient behaviour; every case is different and must be decided on its own facts. The examples are only intended to show the sort of conduct which is relevant in establishing behaviour.

Other matters which can constitute behaviour include excessive drinking leading to unpleasant behaviour, unreasonably refusing to have sexual intercourse or making excessive sexual demands, having an intimate relationship (falling short of adultery) with another person, committing serious criminal offences, and keeping the other party unreasonably short of money.

5.2.3   Where the respondent is mentally ill
The fact that the respondent's behaviour is the result of his mental illness does not necessarily prevent it from being sufficient to entitle the petitioner to a decree. However, the fact that he is mentally ill will be a factor for the court to take into account in determining whether s. 1(2)(b) is satisfied (*Katz* v *Katz* [1972] 3 All ER 219, [1972] 1 WLR 955 and see also *Richards* v *Richards* [1972] 3 All ER 695, [1972] 1 WLR 1073 and *Thurlow* v *Thurlow* [1976] Fam 32, [1975] 2 All ER 979).

5.2.4   Behaviour which is not sufficient
Section 1(2)(b) will not be satisfied if all that is proved is that the petitioner became disenchanted with the respondent or bored with marriage.

Simple desertion cannot amount to behaviour; the petitioner must wait for two years to elapse from the date of desertion and petition on the basis of s. 1(2)(c) (*Stringfellow* v *Stringfellow* [1976] 2 All ER 539, [1976] 1 WLR 645).

5.3   The relevance of living together despite the behaviour

In some cases the petitioner may not be able to prove sufficient behaviour because she and the respondent have continued to live together, see paragraph 10.2 below.

6   ESTABLISHING AS A MATTER OF FACT THAT THE PARTIES ARE LIVING APART

The facts set out in s. 1(2)(c) to (e) all require cohabitation to have ceased and the parties to have lived apart for a period of time.

6.1   Living apart for the purposes of s. 1(2)(d) and (e)

'Living apart' is defined for the purposes of s. 1(2)(d) and (e) (the two year and five year separation facts) in s. 2(6), Matrimonial Causes Act 1973. This provides that a husband and wife shall be treated as living apart unless they are living with each other in the same household.

It is usually possible to pinpoint a time at which the spouses began to live apart in the sense required by the Act. This is normally the time when one or the other moves out of the matrimonial home to live in his own accommodation elsewhere and the parties start to lead separate lives. However, difficulties can arise:

(a)   When the parties have been living separately in any event, not because the marriage has broken down but for some reason, for example because one spouse has gone to look after his or her invalid parents or because they are working in different cities or because one is working abroad. Although as a matter of fact they are living separately, this physical separation is not sufficient; they will not be counted as living apart within the meaning of the Matrimonial Causes Act until at least one of them has decided that the marriage is at an end (*Santos* v *Santos* [1972] Fam 247, [1972] 2 All ER 246). It is not necessary for that spouse to communicate this decision to the other spouse. Of course, it is easier to prove that the requisite state of mind did exist if something was said to the other spouse but in other cases, a decision that the marriage is at an end can be inferred from conduct, for example, where the party living away ceases to write or to telephone the other party or to return home for holidays or sets up home with someone else.

Example 1. The husband is posted abroad. To begin with, he and his wife correspond frequently and he spends his periods of leave at home with her and the children. After he has been abroad for a year, contact between him and his wife ceases and he does not answer her letters. In 1985 he writes to his mother saying that he does not see any future in the marriage and does not intend to come home when his posting is over. Two years later the wife wishes to petition for divorce; the husband consents to a decree. She can rely on s. 1(2)(d). It can be seen from the husband's conduct and his letter to his mother that he had decided in 1985 that the marriage was over. The two-year separation period therefore began to run from that date.

Example 2. The husband is sentenced to a period of six years' imprisonment. To begin with the wife intends to stand by him. However, after six months she meets another man whom she wishes, ultimately, to marry and with whom she starts to live. The parties will be treated as having separated at this point.

(b)   When the parties continue to live under the same roof but contend that they are actually living there separately. Whether or not the court will accept in these circumstances that there has been a sufficient degree of separation will depend on the living arrangements. To establish that the parties have been living apart it must be shown that the normal relationship of husband and wife has ceased and that they have been leading separate existences. The position is best illustrated by an example.

Example. (The facts of *Mouncer* v *Mouncer* [1972] 1 All ER 289, [1972] 1 WLR 321.) The husband and wife slept in separate bedrooms in the matrimonial home. They shared the rest of the house. They continued to take meals (cooked by the wife) together and shared the cleaning of the house making no distinction between one part of the house or the other. The wife no longer did any washing for the husband. The only reason the husband went on living in the house was his wish to live with and help look after the children.
    The parties had not been living apart.

If the parties in *Mouncer* had lived in separate parts of the house, had not shared cleaning and had taken meals separately, no doubt the court would have found that they were not living in the same household, albeit that they were living under the same roof, and would have accepted therefore that they were living apart.

6.2   Living apart in desertion cases

Section 2(6) applies only to s. 1(2)(d) and (e). However, if a question were to arise in a desertion case as to whether cohabitation had ceased, there is no doubt that similar principles would be applied (see *Smith* v *Smith* [1940] P 49, [1939] 4 All ER 533).

7   DESERTION: S.1(2)(c)

Under s. 1(2)(c), the petitioner must show not only that the respondent has deserted her but also that this state of affairs has gone on for a continuous period of at least two years immediately preceding the presentation of the petition.

7.1   Desertion rarely pleaded

It is rare these days for a petitioner to rely on desertion. No doubt the reason for this is that if the respondent has seen fit to desert the petitioner, he is usually sufficiently disenchanted with the marriage to consent to a decree of divorce being granted. Thus the petitioner need not struggle with the technicalities of desertion but can base her petition much more conveniently on two years' separation and consent (s. 1(2)(d)). Furthermore, if the respondent has committed adultery, the petitioner need not even wait for two years' separation; she can petition directly on the basis of the adultery.

It should never be necessary to rely on *constructive* desertion (i.e. behaviour by the respondent causing the petitioner to withdraw from cohabitation). In such cases, the petition should be based on behaviour under s. 1(2)(b). Apart from being more straightforward than desertion, the behaviour fact has the marked advantage that the petitioner need not wait for two years' separation to have elapsed before petitioning as she must with desertion.

Desertion is thus only likely to be used where adultery and behaviour cannot be made out and where, despite having walked out in the first place, the respondent is not prepared to consent to a decree being granted or where he has simply disappeared and cannot therefore be asked to consent to a decree.

7.2   What is desertion?

The law relating to desertion is detailed and rather technical. This book outlines the main provisions; it does not deal with the intricacies. A fuller picture of the law can be found in the standard practitioners' work on divorce.

The essentials of desertion are as follows:

(a)   The respondent must have withdrawn from cohabitation with the intention of bringing cohabitation permanently to an end.

(i)   *Cessation of cohabitation*: it is vital that cohabitation should have ceased. The petitioner cannot say that the respondent has deserted her if he is, in fact, still living with her, even if he contributes virtually nothing to family life. See paragraph 6 above as to when the parties will be taken to be living apart.

(ii) *Intention*: The respondent must intend to bring cohabitation permanently to an end.

> **Example 1.** As far as the wife is concerned, she and her husband have been living together in the matrimonial home perfectly happily. One day, the husband packs his suitcase and departs to live in his own flat, saying that the wife has done nothing wrong but that he needs his freedom and does not intend to live with her ever again. The husband has thus withdrawn from cohabitation with the intention of bringing it permanently to an end. He has, in fact, deserted the wife.

This example deals with a couple who are living in the same house at the time that the desertion occurs. Whilst this is the normal situation, it is not always the case. It is quite possible for one party to desert the other at a time when they are living in different places anyway (*Pardy* v *Pardy* [1939] P 288, [1939] 3 All ER 779). It is not the actual packing up and leaving that is important. What is important is the change in the respondent's state of mind so that he no longer regards himself as a married man with all the normal obligations of married life (including, ultimately, returning to live with the petitioner), but decides that he will never resume cohabitation with the petitioner and therefore regards himself as a free agent.

> **Example 2.** The husband and wife live together at 10 Acacia Avenue. The husband gets a job in Saudi Arabia and, with the wife's consent, he goes off for a year's contract. Just before he is due to come home, he decides that he is not going to return to live with the wife and he telephones to tell her so. The physical separation of the parties would, up to now, have had no consequence as far as divorce proceedings were concerned. At this point, however, the husband starts to be in desertion. If this state of affairs continues for two years, the wife will be able to petition for divorce on the basis of this desertion.

It does seem, however, that where the original separation was consensual, a party cannot be in desertion simply because he subsequently makes up his mind privately not to resume cohabitation at the end of the agreed period as originally planned. He will not be in desertion until he communicates this to the other party or until the agreed period of separation expires and he does not return (*Nutley* v *Nutley* [1970] 1 All ER 410, [1970] 1 WLR 217).

In other cases, there is no need for an express statement by the respondent of his intentions. It can be inferred from his conduct that he intends to bring cohabitation permanently to an end. In Example 1, therefore, the husband would have been just as much in desertion if he had said nothing to the wife but had merely departed with all his belongings to live in his own flat, with no intention of resuming cohabitation.

Because the respondent's state of mind is the essence of desertion, he will not be in desertion if he is forced to live separately from his wife against his will, for example if he is imprisoned. However, if he is already in desertion when the involuntary separation supervenes (for example, he is sentenced to a period of imprisonment after he has deserted the wife), the desertion will be presumed to continue throughout the period of involuntary separation (*Williams* v *Williams* [1938] 4 All ER 445). The court may treat the respondent as having been in desertion during a period which he was excluded from the matrimonial home by a court order (i.e., an order made under the Matrimonial Homes Act 1983, an ouster injunction granted by the High Court or county court or an exclusion order made by a magistrates' court under the Domestic Proceedings and Magistrates' Courts Act 1978) (s. 4(4), Matrimonial Causes Act 1973).

(b)   The petitioner does not consent to the respondent's withdrawal from cohabitation.

If the petitioner consented to the respondent's withdrawal from cohabitation, she cannot allege that he has deserted her. Consent can be expressed (for example, where a separation agreement is drawn up providing for immediate separation) or can be implied from what the petitioner says or does.

> **Example.** (The facts of *Spence* v *Spence* [1939] 1 All ER 52.) For a fortnight before she left home, the wife engaged in open preparations for her departure. Her husband was perfectly aware of her intentions and they discussed the division of their household goods. The husband did not make the smallest attempt to deter his wife from going or to delay her departure.
> The husband was held tacitly to have consented to his wife's departure.

However, the mere fact that the petitioner breathes a sigh of relief when the respondent has gone does not mean that she has consented to his departure (*Harriman* v *Harriman* [1909] P 123).

The following situations may arise:

(i)   Consent can pre-date the respondent's departure, in which case desertion never begins.

(ii)   On the other hand, the petitioner may decide to consent to the separation after the event, in which case her consent can bring the respondent's desertion to an end (*Pizey* v *Pizey* [1961] P 101, [1961] 2 All ER 658).

(iii)   Consent may be to a limited period of separation (for example whilst the respondent works abroad). Such consent comes to an end when that period ends; thereafter, the respondent can be in desertion (*Shaw* v *Shaw* [1939] P 139, [1939] 2 All ER 381).

(iv)   If consent is given to an unlimited period of separation, it can be withdrawn and either party can seek a resumption of cohabitation. If the other party, without just cause, refuses to resume cohabitation, he will be in desertion (*Fraser* v *Fraser* [1969] 3 All ER 654, [1969] 1 WLR 1787). Furthermore, if the parties originally separate contemplating that they will get back together eventually (even though no time may be fixed) and one of them then decides he will never go back to live with the other and communicates this to the other, he will be in desertion from that point unless, of course, the other spouse is agreeable to the permanent separation (*Nutley* v *Nutley* supra).

(c)   The respondent must not have any reasonable cause to withdraw from cohabitation.

Normally, if the respondent has reasonable cause to leave, this will arise from the behaviour of the petitioner although there would seem to be no reason, in principle, why some cause unconnected with the petitioner should not be sufficient justification for the respondent going (for example, where it is shown that it is imperative for his health that he should leave the petitioner permanently). Where the petitioner's conduct is relied on, it must be shown to be 'grave and weighty' and not merely part of the ordinary wear and tear of married life (*Dyson* v *Dyson* [1954] P 198, [1953] 2 All ER 1511).

There are no recent authorities on the point but it would seem logical to suggest that the sort of behaviour that would form the basis of a petition under s. 1(2)(b) would also constitute reasonable cause in a desertion case. Furthermore, a reasonable belief that the petitioner has committed adultery will give the respondent reasonable cause to leave even though the adultery cannot be proved (*Glenister* v *Glenister* [1945] P 30, [1945] 1 All ER 513).

7.3 Termination of desertion

The ways in which desertion can be brought to an end include the following:

(a) By the parties subsequently agreeing to live apart (*Pizey* v *Pizey* supra).

(b) By the granting of a decree of judicial separation. Once a decree of judicial separation has been granted, neither party has any further obligation to live with the other and cannot therefore be in desertion by failing to do so (*Harriman* v *Harriman* [1909] P 123). However, if the decree of judicial separation was based on two years' desertion, the petitioner can subsequently issue a divorce petition based on the same desertion (s. 4(1), Matrimonial Causes Act 1973). The desertion will be deemed to have taken place immediately prior to the issue of the divorce petition if the parties have not resumed cohabitation since the judicial separation decree was granted and the decree of judicial separation has continued in force since it was granted (s. 4(3)). Furthermore, the court may treat the decree as sufficient proof of desertion in the divorce proceedings: s. 4(2) (see further, Chapter 12 paragraph 8).

(c) By the resumption of cohabitation for a prolonged period (certain periods of cohabitation are disregarded, however, in determining whether there has been a continuous period of desertion; see paragraph 10.3 below).

(d) By the deserting spouse making a genuine offer to resume cohabitation which the deserted spouse unreasonably refuses (*Ware* v *Ware* [1942] P 49, [1942] 1 All ER 50).

(e) By the deserted spouse subsequently providing the deserter with reasonable cause to stay away, for example, where she commits adultery which comes to the notice of the deserter.

7.4 Living together during a period of desertion

In determining whether the period of desertion is continuous, certain periods of cohabitation can be ignored, see 10.3 below.

8 TWO YEARS' SEPARATION AND CONSENT: S. 1(2)(d)

8.1 Two separate matters to prove

There are two matters which the petitioner must prove:

(a) that she and the respondent have lived apart for a continuous period of at least two years immediately preceding the presentation of the petition; *and*

(b) that the respondent consents to a decree being granted.

8.2 Living apart

As to what is meant by living apart, see paragraph 6 above. Certain periods of cohabitation can be disregarded in considering whether the parties have lived apart *continuously*, see paragraph 10.3 below.

8.3 Respondent's consent

The respondent normally signifies his consent to the court on the acknowledgment of service form (which must be signed by him personally and, if he is represented by a solicitor, his solicitor; see Family Proceedings Rules 1991, r. 2.10(1)), see Chapter 8, paragraph 7.

The respondent can make his consent conditional, for example, giving his consent provided that the petitioner does not seek an order for costs of the divorce (*Beales* v *Beales* [1972] 2 WLR 972, [1972] 2 All ER 667).

Whether his consent is unqualified or conditional, the respondent can withdraw it at any stage before the decree is pronounced (*Beales* v *Beales* supra). If s. 1(2)(d) is the only basis for the petition, the petition will then have to be stayed (Family Proceedings Rules 1991, r. 2.10(2)).

If decree nisi is granted solely on the basis of two years' separation and consent, the respondent can apply at any time before the decree is made absolute to have the decree rescinded if he has been misled by the petitioner (intentionally or unintentionally) about any matter which he took into account in deciding to give his consent (s. 10(1), Matrimonial Causes Act 1973).

8.4 Section 10(2), Matrimonial Causes Act 1973

Under s. 10(2), the respondent may seek to hold up decree absolute until his financial position after the divorce has been considered by the court, see Chapter 11 paragraph 2.

9 FIVE YEARS' SEPARATION: S. 1(2)(e)

9.1 Establishing the five years' separation

If the petitioner can establish that she and the respondent have been living apart for a continuous period of at least five years immediately preceding the presentation of the petition, she is entitled to a decree whether or not the respondent consents to a divorce (subject only to the respondent's right to raise a defence under s. 5, Matrimonial Causes Act 1973 of grave financial or other hardship, see Chapter 11 paragraph 1).

9.2 Cohabitation during the five-year period

Certain periods of cohabitation can be disregarded in determining whether the five-year period is continuous, see paragraph 10.3 below.

9.3 Section 10(2), Matrimonial Causes Act 1973

As with section 1(2)(d), the respondent can seek to hold up decree absolute by an application under s. 10(2) to have his financial position considered, see Chapter 11, paragraph 2.

10 THE EFFECT OF LIVING TOGETHER IN RELATION TO THE FIVE FACTS: S. 2

Section 2 deals with the relevance of the parties having lived with each other when considering whether any of the five facts have been made out. Section 2(6) provides that the parties are to be treated as living apart unless they are living together in the same household, see paragraph 6 above.

10.1 Cohabitation after adultery

10.1.1 Cohabitation exceeding six months is a total bar
Section 2(1) provides that the petitioner cannot rely for the purpose of s. 1(2)(a) on adultery committed by the respondent if the parties have lived with each other for a period exceeding or periods together exceeding six months after the petitioner learnt that the respondent had committed adultery.

> **Example 1.** Mr Brown commits adultery on one occasion only in June 1986. On 1 July 1986 Mrs Brown learns of this. She and her husband continue to live together as man and wife as before although they bicker constantly. In March 1987 Mrs Brown decides that the marriage is doomed and consults a solicitor with a view to petitioning for divorce on the basis of her husband's adultery. She cannot do so. She has cohabited for a period exceeding six months since she learnt of the adultery on 1 July 1986.

If the respondent commits adultery on more than one occasion, time will not begin to run until after the petitioner learns of the last act of adultery.

> **Example 2.** Mrs Green begins an affair with his secretary at the office party at Christmas 1986. He first commits adultery with her on 23 December 1986. The affair continues until April 1987. Mrs Green learns almost straight away of the adultery on 23 December 1986 but thinks that that is the only occasion on which adultery took place. She discovers the true facts about the continuing adultery on 1 August 1987. She continues to live with her husband until 1 September 1987 when she leaves him because relations have become so strained. Mrs Green will be able to petition for divorce on the basis of her husband's adultery. The last act of adultery was in April 1987, she learnt of it on 1 August 1987 and she only cohabited with her husband for one month thereafter.

10.1.2 Cohabitation of six months or under to be disregarded
Section 2(2) provides that where parties have lived together for a period or periods not exceeding six months in total after it became known to the petitioner that the respondent had committed adultery, the cohabitation is to be disregarded in determining whether the petitioner finds it intolerable to live with the respondent. Thus, in Example 2 above, it could not be said against Mrs Green that she did not find it intolerable to live with her husband because she had in fact lived with him for a month after finding out about his last act of adultery. This period of cohabitation would be disregarded in determining the question of intolerability.

10.2 Cohabitation and behaviour

10.2.1 Cohabitation of six months and under to be disregarded
Section 2(3) provides that the fact that the petitioner and the respondent have lived with each other for a period or periods not exceeding six months in total

after the last incident of behaviour proved, is to be disregarded in determining whether the petitioner cannot reasonably be expected to live with the respondent.

Example 1. The last incident of behaviour proved by the petitioner was on 3 January 1987 when the respondent beat her over the head with a snow shovel. She did not leave the respondent until the middle of February 1987. The period of cohabitation from 3 January 1987 until mid-February 1987 will be disregarded.

The behaviour on which the petitioner relies may be continuous in which case time will only start to run against the petitioner if she cohabits with the respondent after the particular behaviour ceases.

Examples 2. The petitioner makes several allegations of violence on the part of the respondent during 1985. She continues to live with the respondent until shortly before decree nisi is pronounced. No specific incidents are detailed in relation to the period after 1985. However, the petitioner alleges generally that the respondent continually criticises and belittles her, keeps her short of money and prevents her from having any contact with her friends and family. Her cohabitation for more than six months since the last specific incidents in 1985 will not prejudice her entitlement to a divorce because the other behaviour of which she complains continued right up to the day when she left and time therefore never started to run against her.

10.2.2   Cohabitation of more than six months

If the petitioner continues to live with the respondent for a period or periods exceeding six months in total, the cohabitation will be taken into account in determining whether the petitioner can reasonably be expected to live with the respondent. The longer the petitioner goes on living with the respondent after the last incident of behaviour, the less likely the court is to find that it is not reasonable to expect her to live with the respondent unless she can give a convincing reason for her continued cohabitation. However, cohabitation for more than six months is not an absolute bar in a behaviour case as it is in a case of adultery (*Bradley* v *Bradley* [1973] 3 All ER 750, [1973] 1 WLR 1291).

Example. (The facts of *Bradley* v *Bradley* supra.) The wife petitioned on the basis of the husband's behaviour, alleging many incidents of violence. She was still living with the husband. The parties lived in a council house with four bedrooms with seven of their children. The wife said she had no alternative but to continue to sleep with the husband, cook his meals, etc. because she was too frightened of him to do anything else. She could not be rehoused by the council whilst she was still married. The wife was not prevented from relying on s. 1(2)(b) by reason of her continued cohabitation. She was entitled to have her case investigated on its merits and to call evidence to show that, although she was still living with her husband, she could not reasonably be expected to continue to do so.

10.3   Cohabitation and s. 1(2)(c) to (e)

Section 2(5) provides that in considering whether a period of desertion or living apart has been continuous, no account is to be taken of a period or periods not exceeding six months in total during which the parties resumed living with each other. However, no period or periods during which the parties lived with each other can be counted as part of the period of desertion or separation.

Example. Husband and wife started living apart exactly two years ago. However, they have lived with each other for two periods of a month during this time. Neither can petition for a divorce therefore until two years and two months have elapsed since the initial separation.

It should be noted that s. 2(5) is dealing with the question of *continuity* of the period of separation. It does not say that the periods of cohabitation should be disregarded for other purposes. A short period of cohabitation (six months or less) may therefore be relevant in determining, for example, whether desertion has been terminated or whether, in the case of either separation ground, there has been the sort of decision required by *Santos* v *Santos* supra, that the marriage is at an end.

Although the statute does not say so expressly, it must be the case that a period or periods of cohabitation in excess of six months *will* automatically break the continuity of the separation.

4 Bar on presentation of divorce petitions within one year of marriage

1 ABSOLUTE ONE-YEAR BAR

Proceedings for divorce cannot be commenced within the first year of marriage (s. 3(1), Matrimonial Causes Act 1973 as amended by s. 1, Matrimonial and Family Proceedings Act 1984).

Before the 1984 amendment, proceedings for divorce could not normally be commenced within the first *three* years of marriage. The new law therefore represents a substantial reduction in the restricted period. However, it used to be possible to apply for leave to present a petition within the three-year period (even within the first year of marriage) in cases of exceptional depravity on the part of the respondent or of exceptional hardship on the part of the petitioner. In contrast, the new bar is absolute so this option is no longer open. However grave the petitioner's situation, she must sit it out for at least a year before she can seek a divorce.

2 BAR NOT APPLICABLE TO NULLITY PETITIONS

It is important to remember that the one-year bar does not apply to nullity petitions. Indeed, in the case of certain voidable marriages, far from there being a time bar which prevents the petitioner from presenting a petition too *soon* after the marriage, there is a bar which prevents her from petitioning if she leaves it too *long* after the marriage (in these cases, the petition must usually be presented within three years of marriage, see Chapter 13, paragraph 4.2.1). If there are grounds on which the marriage is void or voidable (see Chapter 13) a petition for nullity can therefore be presented without delay, even within days of the wedding in an appropriate case.

3 ALTERNATIVE COURSES OF ACTION FOR THE FIRST YEAR OF MARRIAGE

The wish to remarry is of course one of the reasons why people seek divorces. Unless there are grounds for seeking a nullity decree, the absolute bar on divorce within the first year of marriage means that there is nothing the solicitor can do to enable a client to remarry during that period. However, a desire to remarry is not, in fact, what usually motivates people to seek advice on divorce. Far more commonly they seek divorce because they see it as the only way to escape from an intolerable home life or to resolve other problems that have arisen as a result of the failure of their marriage, for instance, financial problems, difficulties over property, problems over the children. Even though divorce is temporarily out of the question, the chances are that something can be done to help a client with problems of this sort. The main options are as follows:

(a)   The client can be advised that she is free to look for alternative accommodation if things are not working out — although she must remain married, no one can force her to cohabit with her spouse.

(b)   Judicial separation (see further at Chapter 12): there is no restriction on the presentation of petitions for judicial separation in the first year of marriage. However, now that the bar on divorce proceedings is so short it is questionable whether it is worth petitioning for judicial separation on behalf of a client who has made up her mind that she wants a divorce and is only prevented from seeking one by the one-year bar. Bearing in mind that it will take at least several weeks to obtain a decree of judicial separation, unless the solicitor is consulted only a short time after marriage, he may well find that no sooner has he obtained a decree of judicial separation than the one year is up and proceedings have to be commenced all over again to obtain the decree of divorce that the client really wants. Consideration should therefore be given to whether, whilst waiting for the year to elapse, time would be better spent in concentrating on alleviating the client's immediate problems by means of other proceedings in the magistrates' courts or county court.

(c)   Section 27, Matrimonial Causes Act 1973 (see further at Chapter 32).

(d)   Domestic Proceedings and Magistrates' Courts Act 1978 (see further at Chapter 31).

(e)   Children Act 1989 (see further at Chapters 25 and 26).

(f)   Wardship proceedings (see further at Chapter 27).

(g)   Proceedings under s. 16, Domestic Proceedings and Magistrates' Courts Act 1978 for a personal protection order or under Domestic Violence and Matrimonial Proceedings Act 1976 for a non-molestation injunction (see further at Chapter 21).

(h)   Proceedings under s. 16, Domestic Proceedings and Magistrates' Courts Act 1978 for exclusion order or under Domestic Violence and Matrimonial Proceedings Act 1976 for an ouster injunction or under Matrimonial Homes Act 1983 for an order regulating occupation of the matrimonial home (see further at Chapter 21).

(i)   Section 17, Married Women's Property Act 1882 proceedings (see further at Chapter 34): it should be noted that under s. 17, the court only has power to declare existing property rights and not to vary them. Should a divorce subsequently take place it will be open to the court to override any declaration already made under s. 17 and adjust the parties' rights in the property under s. 24, Matrimonial Causes Act 1973. Therefore, in the case of a client who intends to petition for divorce as soon as she is allowed to do so, careful consideration should be given to whether a s. 17 application is worth while. It may well be better to advise the client to wait to have any property disputes determined in the aftermath of the divorce.

4 WHEN THE FIRST YEAR IS UP

As soon as the first year of marriage is up it is open season for divorce. In practice, only petitions based on adultery (s. 1(2)(a), Matrimonial Causes Act 1973) and behaviour (s. 1(2)(b) ibid.) will be feasible for at least another year as the other s. 1(2) facts depend on there having been at least two years' separation.

Even though the temptation is to shelve the question of divorce entirely until the first year has elapsed, in fact there is no reason why the case should not be prepared (marriage certificate obtained, divorce petition drafted, etc.) before the end of the year so that the petition can be filed at the earliest possible opportunity.

Section 3(2), Matrimonial Causes Act 1973 as amended by s. 1, Matrimonial and Family Proceedings Act 1984, makes it clear that a divorce petition may be based wholly or partly on matters which occurred during the first year of marriage even though it cannot be presented during that year. Thus, for example, once the year is over a decree could be sought on the basis of adultery that occurred during the year and a period of separation upon which reliance is placed under s. 1(2)(c) to (e) can start to run during the first year.

5 Jurisdiction in divorce, nullity and judicial separation suits

1 JURISDICTION FOR DIVORCE, NULLITY AND JUDICIAL SEPARATION, S. 5, DOMICILE AND MATRIMONIAL PROCEEDINGS ACT 1973

The court has jurisdiction to entertain proceedings for divorce, nullity or judicial separation if either party:

(a) is domiciled in England and Wales when the proceedings are begun, or
(b) was habitually resident in England and Wales throughout the period of one year ending with the date on which proceedings are begun (s. 5, Domicile and Matrimonial Proceedings Act 1973).

2 DOMICILE

Determining a person's domicile can be very tricky. This book provides only a very broad outline of the law of domicile. Should a problem over domicile be encountered, reference should be made to the standard practitioner's works on family law and also to textbooks on private international law.

2.1 What is domicile?

Domicile is essentially a legal concept used to link an individual with a particular legal system. The concept of domicile is primarily used to determine which country's law should govern questions of an individual's personal status. Domicile and nationality are two quite separate matters; it is not possible to find out where a person is domiciled merely by finding out his nationality. Nor is it possible to ascertain a person's domicile simply by finding out where he lives; residence and domicile are not the same thing.

> **Example.** Mr Handel is a German national. He came to England as a child and has always looked upon himself as English although he has never sought British nationality. He is temporarily working in Scotland and lives in a flat there but he still regards England as his home country. He is having problems with his marriage and wishes to seek a divorce in the English courts.
> Mr Handel is domiciled in England. The English courts would have jurisdiction to entertain his petition for divorce.

2.2   Key points

(a)   A person must be domiciled in a place which has only one legal system. This means that it is not possible to be domiciled in the British Isles — one is domiciled in England and Wales or in Scotland or in Northern Ireland.

(b)   Every person has a domicile.

(c)   It is not possible to have more than one domicile at one time.

(d)   However, it is possible for an individual's place of domicile to change as his personal circumstances alter throughout his life.

2.3   Determining where a person is domiciled

There are three types of domicile: domicile of origin, domicile of dependence and domicile of choice.

2.3.1   Domicile of origin

The law attributes a domicile to every new-born baby. This is his domicile of origin.

Normally a legitimate child receives the domicile that his father has at the time of his birth and an illegitimate child receives that of his mother.

An individual must never be without a domicile. Therefore, he retains his domicile of origin throughout his life. At times it may be overtaken by a different domicile of dependence or domicile of choice but in the absence of any other domicile it will always revive.

2.3.2   Domicile of choice

2.3.2.1   Residence and intention   Once an individual reaches the age of 16, he will be able to acquire a domicile of choice. An individual acquires a domicile of choice by living in a country other than the country of his domicile of origin with the intention of continuing to reside there permanently or at least indefinitely. Where a person has a residence in his domicile of origin and a residence in another country, then acquisition of a domicile of choice in that other country will be difficult to prove unless his chief residence is in that other country (see *Plummer* v *IRC* [1988] 1 All ER 97, [1988] 1 WLR 992).

(a)   *Residence*: for a domicile of choice to be acquired in a country, the individual must actually take up residence there. It is not enough for him to make up his mind in his freezing flat in North London that he will emigrate to Australia or even for him to buy his airline ticket or board his plane. He must actually arrive in the country.

(b)   *Intention*: an individual cannot acquire a domicile of choice in a country until he decides to live there permanently or at least indefinitely. Thus a domicile of choice will not be acquired in Saudi Arabia by someone simply posted there by his employers or spending some time there on holiday. See also *Cramer* v *Cramer* [1987] 1 FLR 116.

2.3.2.2   Examples of domicile of choice

Example 1. Mr Maynard has always lived in England as had his father before him. His domicile of origin is English (taken from that of his father when he was born). He becomes a famous writer and decides to investigate the possibility of going to live in

Switzerland. He goes to stay in Switzerland to look at property. At this stage, his domicile of origin is still operative as he has not yet made up his mind whether to live in Switzerland. He returns home and decides that he will move permanently to Switzerland. He has still not acquired a domicile of choice there as he has not taken up residence there. He sells his house and winds up his business in England and travels to Switzerland. He has now acquired a domicile of choice in Switzerland.

Example 2. Mr Connor, a man of 35, has always lived in the United States. He has a domicile of origin in Texas. He comes to England to work for an English company. He buys a house in England and moves his family over. However, he intends to return to the United States when he retires. He does not acquire a domicile of choice in England because he lacks the required intention to live here at least indefinitely.

2.3.2.3 Loss of domicile of choice In contrast with the domicile of origin, a domicile of choice can be lost forever. Although there is a question mark over the exact nature of the intention required, it would seem that a domicile of choice will be lost if the individual gives up residence in the country in question and ceases to have the intention to reside there permanently or at least indefinitely. Both elements must be present. Intention to leave the country without actually leaving is not sufficient, nor is leaving without any change in the original intention to live there permanently or indefinitely.

An individual may acquire a new domicile of choice immediately the old one is abandoned. However, if he does not do so, for example, if he gives up his home in one country and then travels around whilst making up his mind where to settle for the future, his domicile of origin will revive to fill the gap.

2.3.2.4 Proof of intention The individual concerned may not have formulated his intentions as to the future explicitly. His intention can, however, be inferred from all the circumstances of the case — what he did, what he said, etc.

2.3.3 Domicile of dependence
Until a child is 16 and can acquire an independent domicile of choice, he has a domicile of dependence on one or other of his parents. To begin with, this is the same as his domicile of origin, but if the domicile of his parent changes, so will the child's domicile of dependence.

Thus a legitimate child's domicile will normally change with that of his father, or, if his father dies, with that of his mother. If however the child's parents are separated and he is living with his mother, his domicile will change with that of his mother: s. 4, Domicile and Matrimonial Proceedings Act 1973. An illegitimate child will have a domicile of dependence on his mother.

When the child becomes capable of acquiring an independent domicile at 16, he will retain his domicile of dependence until he acquires a domicile of choice.

Example. Mr and Mrs Hall are happily married. Mrs Hall gives birth to a baby daughter, Sarah. Sarah takes her domicile of origin from her father who is domiciled in England at this time. Subsequently, Mr and Mrs Hall decide to go and live in France and take up residence there. They therefore acquire domiciles of choice in France and Sarah thus has a domicile of dependence in France. Mr and Mrs Hall then encounter marital problems and separate. Mrs Hall goes to live with her mother in Scotland, intending to stay there permanently and taking Sarah with her. Sarah's domicile is now dependent on her mother as her parents are living apart and she has her home with her mother. She is therefore domiciled in Scotland. This is still the case after her sixteenth birthday until, at the age of 23 she marries and goes to live permanently in Northern Ireland. She now has a domicile of choice in Northern Ireland.

3 HABITUAL RESIDENCE

Until quite recently, habitual residence had not been defined for the purposes of s. 5, Domicile and Matrimonial Proceedings Act 1973. However, in the case of *Kapur* v *Kapur* [1985] 15 Fam Law 22, Bush J held that habitual residence is essentially the same as ordinary residence (a concept with which the courts are familiar in other areas of the law). He therefore held that habitual residence means voluntary residence with a degree of settled purpose.

Example. (The facts of *Kapur* v *Kapur* supra.) The husband and wife were Indian nationals. The marriage had broken down in India and the wife remained there when the husband came over in August 1981 to England to study for the Bar examinations wanting to practise in England eventually. He was granted restricted leave to remain in the United Kingdom which was extended annually during his stay in England. The Home Office had power to refuse to renew his right to remain. On 1 October 1982 the husband petitioned for divorce in England.

It was held that a limited purpose such as education could be a settled purpose and the husband was held to have satisfied the requirement of 12 months' habitual residence.

There are numerous cases on the meaning of ordinary residence in various contexts. For a case on ordinary residence decided by the House of Lords the reader is referred to *Shah* v *Barnet London Borough Council and other appeals* [1983] 2 AC 309, [1983] 1 All ER 226.

It is suggested that, in summary, the practical position as to habitual residence is as follows:

(a)   There should not normally be any difficulty in establishing jurisdiction on the basis of 12 months' habitual residence if one or the other party has been living in England and Wales for, for example, business, education, family reasons, health or even simply love of the country, throughout the whole year preceding the presentation of the petition.

(b)   Temporary or occasional short absences, for example, on holiday abroad, will not prevent an individual from establishing habitual residence.

(c)   Even rather more prolonged absences will not necessarily disrupt an individual's habitual residence if the case of *Oundjian* v *Oundjian* (1979) 10 Fam Law 90, (1979) 124 SJ 63, is followed. In that case, French J found that there was jurisdiction to entertain a divorce petition based on the habitual residence of a wife who had spent 216 out of the relevant 365 days out of the country (mainly in a holiday villa in Spain). The House of Lords held recently in the case of *C* v *S* ([1990] 2 All ER 961, [1990] 3 WLR 492) that habitual residence in one country ceased when the party concerned left that country with the settled intention not to return. The question was one of fact to be decided with reference to all of the other circumstances in the case.

(d)   It is irrelevant that the individual's real home is outside England or that he intends or expects to live outside England in the future.

4 RECOGNITION OF FOREIGN DECREES

4.1 Recognition of divorce and separation decrees

There are detailed statutory rules as to the recognition of foreign decrees of divorce and separation. These are set out in the Family Law Act 1986.

A distinction is made between decrees granted under the law of any part of the British Isles and divorces and separations obtained overseas. Note that a decree of divorce or judicial separation granted under the law of any part of the British Isles must be recognised throughout the United Kingdom: s. 44(2) Family Law Act 1986.

4.2 Recognition of nullity decrees

The recognition of foreign nullity decrees is governed by the Family Law Act 1986, sections 45 to 48.

4.3 Entitlement to ancillary relief in English courts after foreign divorce, nullity or legal separation

Part III of the Matrimonial and Family Proceedings Act 1984 gives the English courts jurisdiction to grant financial relief after an overseas divorce, annulment or legal separation which is recognised in this country as valid. Such an application for ancillary relief can be made whether the decree in a foreign country was made before or after the 1984 Act came into force (*Chebaro* v *Chebaro* [1987] 2 FLR 456). Leave of the court is required before such a financial relief application can be made.

6 Legal aid and undefended divorces

1 LEGAL AID NOT GENERALLY AVAILABLE

Since 1 April 1977, legal aid has not been available for undefended divorce or judicial separation decree proceedings save in exceptional cases (see Part I, paragraph 5A of Schedule 2 to the Legal Aid Act 1988).

2 LEGAL AID AVAILABLE FOR DEFENDED CASES

Legal aid can be granted for defended divorce or judicial separation proceedings (either to the respondent to defend the proceedings or to the petitioner to continue the proceedings after an answer has been filed). Legal aid for defended proceedings is dealt with in more detail in Chapter 10 at paragraph 2.

3 LEGAL AID EXCEPTIONALLY AVAILABLE FOR UNDEFENDED CASES

Legal aid can be granted for an undefended case:

(a) if the district judge directs that the petition shall be heard in open court (for example, where he is not satisfied that the petitioner has made out her case for a decree, see Chapter 8 paragraph 10.2.2); *or*

(b) if by reason of physical or mental incapacity, it is impracticable for the applicant to proceed without legal aid.

4 LEGAL AID AVAILABLE FOR PROCEEDINGS IN CONNECTION WITH DIVORCE OR JUDICIAL SEPARATION OTHER THAN DECREE PROCEEDINGS

The restriction on legal aid applies only to the proceedings for obtaining the decree itself. There is no restriction therefore on the granting of legal aid to make or oppose, for example:

(a) an application for an injunction ancillary to the divorce or judicial separation proceedings;

(b) an application for ancillary relief;

(c) an application under the Children Act 1989 e.g. for residence or contact orders. (Following the implementation of the Children Act 1989 on 14 October 1991, civil legal aid under Part IV of the Legal Aid Act 1988 is available for all proceedings under the Children Act 1989: see further Chapter 2, paragraph 23).

There is a residual power to grant legal aid for the purposes of making or opposing any other application or satisfying the court on any other matter which raises a substantial question for determination by the court. This provision covers, for example, applications under s. 10, Matrimonial Causes Act 1973 (for consideration of the respondent's financial position after divorce, see Chapter 11).

5 GREEN FORM HELP AVAILABLE FOR DECREE PROCEEDINGS

In view of the fact that legal aid is not usually available for decree proceedings the green form scheme has assumed a particular importance in undefended divorce and judicial separation cases. Provided the client is financially eligible for green form assistance (see Chapter 2 paragraph 6), the solicitor will be able to give her considerable help with the decree proceedings under the scheme. The following are examples of the work that a solicitor may be expected to carry out under the scheme:

(a) preliminary advice on the grounds for divorce or judicial separation, the effects of a decree on status, the future arrangements for the children, the income and assets of the family and matters relating to housing and the matrimonial home;

(b) drafting the petition and the statement of the arrangements for the children and where necessary typing or writing the entries on the forms;

(c) advising on filing the documents at court and the consequential procedure, including service if no acknowledgment of service is filed;

(d) advising a client when the acknowledgment of service is received as to the procedure for applying for directions for trial, and typing or writing the entries on the form of affidavit of evidence;

(e) advising as to any attendance before the district judge to explain the arrangements for the children and as to what, if any, evidence will be required by the judge other than that of the petitioner, but not attending court;

(f) advising on obtaining decree absolute.

The solicitor can also negotiate with the other party (for example, he can write to the proposed respondent asking him for his consent to a divorce on the basis of two years' separation: s. 1(2)(d), Matrimonial Causes Act 1973).

Boiled down to essentials, this means that the solicitor can give the client all the help he could reasonably expect in relation to his divorce except that he cannot accompany him to court on any children's appointment that might be requested by the district judge (pursuant to s. 41, Matrimonial Causes Act 1973, as substituted by sch. 12, para. 31, Children Act 1989) unless he agrees to do so as a favour without payment. If the client is worried about the children's appointment, the solicitor should take care to explain fully to him what will happen. If necessary, the solicitor can write to the court or telephone in advance of the appointment, explaining any matters which are complex or may be of particular concern to the district judge. For further details as to the circumstances in which the district judge may decide to hold a children's appointment under the new procedures, see Chapter 8, paragraph 13.

The examples of work given above (which are taken from the Legal Aid Board's 'Notes for Guidance', Notes 2–22, *Legal Aid Handbook*, 1991) contemplate that the solicitor is acting for a petitioner. There is a specially increased expenditure limit on the amount of work a solicitor can do under the green form scheme when he acts for a petitioner and prepares the petition, presently set at £126 including disbursements and excluding VAT (see Chapter 2 paragraph 5 for further details on the green form expenditure limits).

The solicitor may just as easily find himself acting for a respondent under the green form scheme. In such a case, he would be able to advise on the same matters as he would advise a petitioner on, help with filing documents and drafting (for example, with filling in the acknowledgment of service), advise on dealing with the court (for example, advising the respondent on returning the acknowledgment of service and how to obtain decree absolute if the petitioner has not done so, etc.). The solicitor must, however, be aware that the normal green form expenditure limit of £84 applies to advice and help given to a respondent.

Should it become necessary to exceed the expenditure limit in the case of a petitioner or a respondent (for example, if there are problems over service and it becomes necessary to instruct an enquiry agent to serve the petition), the solicitor should bear in mind the possibility of applying for an extension (see Chapter 2 paragraph 5.2).

7 Drafting a divorce petition

1 GENERAL

Every divorce suit is commenced by petition (Family Proceedings Rules 1991, r. 2.2(1)). The petition is the central document in the case. It is filed by the spouse seeking the divorce ('the petitioner') and served on the other spouse ('the respondent').

The petition informs the respondent and the court of the basis on which the petitioner claims to be entitled to a decree and of the other orders that she will be seeking as part of the divorce process, for example, in relation to periodical payments, property and the children.

The solicitor normally prepares the petition on behalf of the client. If the client is receiving green form advice, the solicitor will be entitled to payment for doing this under the green form scheme. The private client must meet the cost personally. In some cases it may be possible to recover at least part of the cost of the proceedings from the respondent or co-respondent if there is one (see Chapter 8 paragraph 10.2.1).

2 THE CONTENTS OF THE PETITION

Rule 2.3 and Appendix 2 of the Family Proceedings Rules 1991 stipulate what information shall be contained in the petition. Every petition for divorce shall contain:

(a) the names of the parties to the marriage and the date and place of the marriage;

(b) the last address at which the parties to the marriage have lived together as man and wife;

(c) where it is alleged that the court has jurisdiction based on domicile:

(i) the country in which the petitioner is domiciled, and

(ii) if that country is not England and Wales, the country in which the respondent is domiciled;

(d) where it is alleged that the court has jurisdiction based on habitual residence:

(i) the country in which the petitioner has been habitually resident throughout the period of one year ending with the date of the presentation of the petition, or

(ii)   if the petitioner has not been habitually resident in England and Wales, the country in which the respondent has been habitually resident during that period,
with details in either case, including the addresses of the places of residence and the length of residence at each place;

(e)   the occupation and residence of the petitioner and the respondent;

(f)   whether there are any living children of the family and, if so;

(i)   the number of such children and the full names (including surname) of each and his date of birth or (if it be the case) that he is over 18, and

(ii)   in the case of each minor child over the age of 16, whether he is receiving instruction at an educational establishment or undergoing training for a trade, profession or vocation;

(g)   whether (to the knowledge of the petitioner in the case of a husband's petition) any other child now living has been born to the wife during the marriage and, if so, the full names (including surname) of the child and his date of birth or, if it be the case, that he is over 18;

(h)   if it be the case, that there is a dispute as to whether a living child is a child of the family;

(i)   whether or not there are or have been any other proceedings in any court in England and Wales or elsewhere with reference to the marriage or to any children of the family or between the petitioner and the respondent with reference to any property of either or both of them and, if so:

(i)   the nature of the proceedings,

(ii)   the date and effect of any decree or order, and

(iii)   in the case of proceedings with reference to the marriage, whether there has been any resumption of cohabitation since the making of the decree or order;

(j)   whether there are any proceedings continuing in any country outside England and Wales which relate to the marriage or are capable of affecting its validity or substance and, if so:

(i)   particulars of the proceedings, including the court in or tribunal or authority before which they were begun,

(ii)   the date when they were begun,

(iii)   the names of the parties,

(iv)   the date or expected date of any trial in the proceedings, and such other facts as may be relevant to the question whether the proceedings on the petition should be stayed under Schedule 1 to the Domicile and Matrimonial Proceedings Act 1973;
and such proceedings shall include any which are not instituted in a court of law in that country, if they are instituted before a tribunal or other authority having power under the law having effect there to determine questions of status, and shall be treated as continuing if they have been begun and have not finally been disposed of;

(k)   where the fact on which the petition is based is five years' separation, whether any, and if so what, agreement or arrangement has been made or is proposed to be made between the parties for the support of the respondent or, as the case may be, the petitioner or any child of the family;

(l)   in the case of a petition for divorce, a statement that the marriage has broken down irretrievably;

(m)   the fact alleged by the petitioner for the purposes of section 1(2), Matrimonial Causes Act 1973 or, where the petition is not for divorce or judicial separation, the ground on which relief is sought, together with brief particulars of the individual facts relied on but not the evidence by which they are to be proved.

Every petition for divorce shall conclude with:

(a)   a prayer setting out particulars of the relief claimed, including any application for an order under any provision of Part I or Part II of the Children Act 1989 with respect to a child of the family (NB where no such application is sought the appropriate clause in the prayer should be crossed out; where an application is sought it will assist the court greatly for the prayer to make clear the exact nature of the order requested e.g. a residence or contact order). The prayer should also set out any claim for costs and any application for ancillary relief which it is intended to claim;

(b)   the names and addresses of the persons who are to be served with the petition indicating if any of them is a person under a disability;

(c)   the petitioner's address for service, which, where the petitioner sues by a solicitor, shall be the solicitor's name or firm and address. Where the petitioner, although suing in person, is receiving legal advice from a solicitor, the solicitor's name or firm and address may be given as the address for service if he agrees. In any other case, the petitioner's address for service shall be the address of any place in England and Wales at or to which documents for the petitioner may be delivered or sent.

No form of petition is set out in the rules but printed forms of petition on which the relevant information can be typed or written can be obtained from law stationers or from the offices of divorce county courts. Not all printed petition forms are exactly the same; one of the forms commonly in use is reprinted at pp. 88–90.

A carefully drafted petition will go a long way towards ensuring that a decree of divorce is obtained swiftly and smoothly. The solicitor should therefore bear in mind the following notes when drafting the petition. However, it is a comforting thought for an inexperienced practitioner struggling to draft his first divorce petition that, since the withdrawal of legal aid for undefended divorces, petitioners have not infrequently succeeded in drafting their own petitions without any legal help whatsoever and have gone on to obtain the decree of divorce which they were seeking with no problems. Whilst it is sensible therefore to observe conventions that have grown up within the profession in relation to the drafting of petitions, as long as the petition contains the required information it would be a mistake to spend hours worrying, for example, over whether to say that the respondent threw the turkey on the floor on Christmas Day 1984 whilst drunk or whether it would be better to say that, on the twenty-fifth day of December 1984, having partaken of an excess of alcohol, the respondent deposited the Christmas repast on the floor causing the petitioner great distress and annoyance.

3   NOTES ON DRAFTING THE PETITION

These notes refer to the printed petition form reproduced on pp. 88–90. They should, however, be equally useful to the solicitor when he is using an alternative printed form or drafting a petition from scratch.

3.1   'In the County Court'

The solicitor can decide in which divorce county court he will commence proceedings; alternatively he can commence proceedings in the Divorce Registry in London (see Chapter 8 paragraph 2). He should complete the divorce petition accordingly.

3.2   'No'

This refers to the number of the cause which is allocated by the divorce court office when the petition is filed. It will be inserted on the original of the petition and on the copy(ies) for service on the respondent (and co-respondent) by the court staff. The solicitor will be informed of the number and should take care to record it on his file copy of the petition as it must be quoted on all subsequent documents relating to the divorce and ancillary matters.

3.3   Paragraph 1

The details of the marriage should be taken exactly from the marriage certificate. The place of marriage should be fully stated, including the county in which it took place. The full names of the parties should be given including their surnames. In the case of a wife there is no need to give her maiden name as well as her married name.

3.4   Paragraph 2

The full address of the place where the parties last lived together as husband and wife should be given, including the county.

3.5   Paragraph 3

This paragraph is concerned with the basis for the court's jurisdiction. Jurisdiction can be based either on domicile of either of the parties in England and Wales or on habitual residence of either party in England and Wales for one year preceding the presentation of the petition (see Chapter 5). Jurisdiction is normally based on domicile of the petitioner in England and Wales in which case the only statement required as to domicile is already printed on the form. If the petitioner is not domiciled in England and Wales, the alternative grounds of jurisdiction should be considered:

(a)   Domicile of the respondent in England and Wales: if jurisdiction is claimed on this basis, the petition should state where the petitioner is domiciled and state that the respondent is domiciled in England and Wales. The printed petition form could still be used with the petitioner's domicile corrected and the respondent's domicile stated at the end of the paragraph.

(b) Habitual residence of either party: if reliance is placed on habitual residence it will no doubt be more convenient to abandon the printed petition form and arrange for the petition to be typed in full. Paragraph 3 should then state that the petitioner (or if the petitioner does not qualify, the respondent) has been habitually resident in England and Wales throughout the period of one year ending with the presentation of the petition and details of that residence should be given including the addresses where the petitioner (or respondent) has lived and the periods of residence in each place.

Paragraph 3 also requires the present residence of the petitioner and the respondent to be given. The addresses should be stated in full including the county but if either address is the same as that already stated in Paragraph 2 (as it will be if either party has stayed in the matrimonial home), the address can be given in shorthand form by stating simply the first line followed by the word 'aforesaid' (for example, '10 Acacia Avenue aforesaid').

The occupation of both parties must also be given. It is acceptable to state that a wife who does not work by choice is a housewife by occupation. Where the party concerned is out of work involuntarily it would be more suitable to state that he is 'unemployed'.

3.6 Omitting the petitioner's address from the petition

In some cases the petitioner does not wish the respondent to know her address. Where the petitioner is receiving green form help (or where the solicitor is acting privately or on full legal aid) the soliticor's address can be given for service but the rules still require a statement of the petitioner's address in the body of the petition. The district judge has a general power under the Family Proceedings Rules 1991, r. 2.3 to direct that information that would otherwise be required in the petition can be omitted and, where it is necessary for the protection of the petitioner, he can use this power to allow the petition to stand without the petitioner's address. It must be stressed, however, that this is for the *protection* of the petitioner. Therefore, although it is understandable that the petitioner may want to start a new life with the security that the respondent does not know where she is living, this in itself will not be sufficient to justify the omission of the address. The district judge will normally look for evidence (often provided by the respondent's own past conduct) that if the address is given the petitioner will be in physical danger or will be subjected to serious molestation by the respondent. It should be borne in mind that an alternative method of dealing with problems of molestation is to apply for an injunction against the respondent, see Chapter 21.

If the solicitor wishes to omit the petitioner's address from the petition the procedure laid down in the Practice Direction of 8 May 1975 [1975] 2 All ER 384, [1975] 1 WLR 787 should be followed:

(a) The petition should be drawn up and filed omitting the petitioner's address from the body of the petition and giving the solicitor's address as her address for service.

(b) An ex parte application should be made to the district judge before the petition is served for leave for the petition to stand notwithstanding the omission of the address. It would be good practice to support the application with an affidavit although it is up to the district judge whether he is prepared to deal with the application without one. If an affidavit is filed the petitioner's address should be stated in it; if the district judge deals with the matter without an affadavit, the address should be given in a letter to the court.

(c)   If the district judge gives leave:

(i)   the petition and a copy of the district judge's order will be served on the respondent;

(ii)   the petitioner's solicitor should take care not to disclose her where-abouts directly or indirectly in other documents required for the divorce proceedings, for example, by the information given in the statement as to arrangements for the children about where the children are to live and about their schools or in affidavits required later in the proceedings. If there is a danger that the statement as to arrangements will give away too much information, the information in question should be omitted and by way of explanation it should be stated that the petitioner has applied for leave to permit the petition to stand notwithstanding the omission of her address. It should still be possible for the petitioner to give sufficient information in the statement as to arrangements by simply stating the nature of the accommodation where the children will live and the type of school they attend, omitting any reference to names and addresses. Affidavits (for example, in connection with ancillary relief) should omit any reference to the petitioner's address and commence with a statement that the petitioner has been given leave not to disclose her address in the petition. If there is any objection to the affidavit in this form, leave for it to be accepted can be sought at the hearing for which it is intended.

(d)   If the district judge does not grant leave, he will make an order that the petition be amended by inserting the petitioner's address.

3.7   Paragraph 4

This paragraph requires the details of all living children of the family to be given.

'Child of the family' in relation to the parties to a marriage is defined in s. 52, Matrimonial Causes Act 1973 (as amended by the Children Act 1989, s. 108(4), sch. 12, para. 33) as:

(a)   a child of both of those parties; and

(b)   any other child, not being a child who is placed with those parties as foster parents by a local authority or voluntary organisation, who has been treated by both of those parties as a child of their family.

A child will qualify as a child of the family on the basis that he is a child of both parties to the marriage even if he was born to them before the marriage took place or after it broke down or was adopted by them rather than being their natural child.

A child can become a child of the family by virtue of the second limb of the definition even though he is the child of only one party to the marriage or indeed where he is the child of neither of the parties. It is not always easy to determine whether a child has become a child of the family by virtue of treatment. It is a broad question of fact which must be decided by the court looking at all the circumstances of the case. The test is objective. It is the view that the independent outside observer takes of the facts that is important rather than the view taken by the parties to the marriage of the child's status (*D* v *D* (*child of the family*) (1980) 2 FLR 93). What the parties thought about the position of the child in their family will no doubt be one of the relevant factors in determining whether the child has been treated as a child of the family. However, a number of other factors are likely to be taken into account by the court as well, for example, where the child lives, who pays for the child, who exercises discipline and whether the step-parent has in fact exercised or claimed any of the responsibilities of a parent.

The following points should also be borne in mind:

(a)   The exclusion of children boarded out with the parties automatically prevents children such as foster children becoming children of the family.

(b)   A child can only be treated as a child of the family once it is born so a generous attitude towards a forthcoming baby on the part of a husband during his wife's pregnancy by another man will not lead to the baby becoming a child of the family. It is only if he continues to treat the child as a child of the family once it is born that it will achieve the status of a child of the family (*A* v *A* (*family: unborn child*) [1974] Fam 6, [1974] 1 All ER 755).

(c)   The family can cease to exist before a divorce takes place if the parties to the marriage separate permanently. Where this happens and the wife gives birth to a child by another man after the separation, it is not possible for that child to be treated as a child of the family (*M* v *M* (1980) 2 FLR 39).

(d)   If a child has been treated as a child of the family, the fact that the husband only behaved in this way towards the child because he believed, mistakenly as it turns out, that the child was his own will not prevent the child being classed as a child of the family (*W(RJ)* v *W(SJ)* [1972] Fam 152, [1971] 3 All ER 303).

Example 1. Susan is the natural child of Mr and Mrs Smith born whilst they were living together before they got married. She is automatically a child of their family.

Example 2. Mr and Mrs Smith get divorced. Mrs Smith subsequently remarries. Susan lives with Mrs Smith and her new husband, Mr Jones. Mr Jones welcomes Susan as his own daughter and takes an interest in all that she does. For example, he regularly attends parents' evenings at Susan's school with Mrs Smith, he supports Mrs Smith in matters of discipline and he provides Susan with pocket money. Although Susan's natural father does pay £7 per week towards her maintenance, the housekeeping that Mr Jones gives to Mrs Smith is used to feed the family as a whole including Susan. Susan addresses Mr Jones as John. There is little doubt that Susan is a child of the family of Mrs Smith and Mr Jones.

Example 3. The wife has a child by her first marriage. The child goes to live with her grandparents when the first marriage breaks down. The wife remarries. The child visits the wife and her new husband to stay at weekends and for substantial periods during the school holidays (about 50/60 days a year in all). She has her own room at their house and the new husband buys her a pony which he expects her to groom and keep clean. He also reproves her if she does not keep her bedroom clean.

In the case of *D* v *D* supra, a child in this situation was held not to be a child of the family — her home was with her grandparents and the husband's behaviour towards her did not amount to treating her as a child of his and the mother's family.

Example 4. Mrs Brown remarries after the death of her first husband. Her son Sam is at boarding school. He spends the holidays living with Mrs Brown, her new husband and the new husband's two children by his previous marriage who live with their father permanently. He has his own room at their house and all three children are treated in exactly the same way by both Mrs Brown and her new husband. It is likely that all three children are children of the family.

The petition should state the full names (including surnames) of all living children whom the petitioner alleges are children of the family. If the child is not the natural or adopted child of both parents it is good practice to state his paternity and that he has been treated as a child of the family. It is open to the respondent subsequently to deny that a child is a child of the family. It may be necessary for him to do this, for example, in order that he should be excused from any financial liability for the child.

If the children are 18 or over this should be stated. The court has a duty under s. 41, Matrimonial Causes Act 1973 (as susbstituted by the Children Act 1989, sch. 12, para. 31) to look after the interests not only of minor children but also of those children over 18 who have special needs. (See Chapter 8 paragraph 13). Therefore if there is a child of the family who is over 18 but is still dependent on his parents and unable to look after his own interests, for example, because of mental handicap, brief details should also be given of his circumstances to enable the court to decide whether it needs to look more closely at the arrangements for him in accordance with s. 41. If the children are not over 18, their dates of birth should be given. Where there are children of 16 and 17 the petition should state whether they are receiving instruction at an educational establishment (school, technical college, etc.) or training for a trade, profession or vocation (e.g. an apprenticeship, day-release, etc.). There is no need to go into detail here; a simple statement that the child is receiving education/training will suffice. Further details will, however, be required for the statement as to arrangements for children (see Chapter 8 paragraph 1.3).

3.8 Paragraph 5

The full names and dates of birth (or a statement that the child is over 18 if that is the case) of any other children now living who have been born to the wife during the marriage should be given. If the husband is the petitioner, he may only be able to state the position to the best of his knowledge but this is quite sufficient. If there is a dispute as to whether a child mentioned is a child of the family, this should be stated. Therefore if, for example, the husband is the petitioner and he denies that one of the children that his wife has had during the marriage is a child of the family, that child's name will be omitted from the list of the children of the family in paragraph 4 and particulars of the child will be given instead in paragraph 5. Paragraph 5 will go on to state that the petitioner denies that the child is a child of the family and to state whom the petitioner alleges is the father.

3.9 Paragraph 6

In this paragraph details must be given of *all* court proceedings in relation to the marriage or the children of the family or between the petitioner and respondent in relation to their property (see paragraph 2 above at (i) for exactly what details of the proceedings are required). This means that proceedings which were dismissed or adjourned must be included as well as those in which an order was made. Proceedings such as complaints to a magistrates' court under the Domestic Proceedings and Magistrates' Courts Act 1978, applications for non-molestation injunctions, and s. 17, Married Women's Property Act 1882 proceedings must obviously be mentioned. It is sometimes overlooked that if any of the children of the family have been adopted, details of the adoption proceedings must be given.

3.10   Paragraph 7

It is less common for there to be any proceedings which are relevant to this paragraph. An example of the type of proceedings to which reference should be made would be foreign divorce proceedings. Full particulars of the proceedings should be given (see paragraph 2 above at (j)). The court would have to consider in the light of these particulars whether the English proceedings should be stayed under the Domicile and Matrimonial Proceedings Act 1973, sch. 1.

3.11   Paragraph 8

It is only necessary for this paragraph to be included in a petition based on five years' separation. In all other cases it can be deleted and the subsequent paragraphs renumbered. If an agreement or arrangement has been made (for example, for the payment of periodical payments or the transfer of the matrimonial home), concise details should be given.

3.12   Paragraph 9

This paragraph can be left to stand just as it appears on the printed form.

3.13   Paragraph 10

The s. 1(2), Matrimonial Causes Act 1973 fact upon which the petition is based must be stated and brief particulars given of the individual facts relied upon. The statement of the s. 1(2) fact normally follows the wording of the section closely. For example, in a s. 1(2)(b) case, the fact will be stated thus:

> The respondent has behaved in such a way that the petitioner cannot reasonably be expected to live with him.

Brief particulars of the supporting facts relied on must be given but not the evidence by which they are to be proved. It can be difficult to decide how much detail should be given. The standard practitioners' textbooks give precedents of petitions and the following guidelines should also help:

(a)   Adultery cases: if possible, give the date(s) and place(s) of the adultery (or, where adultery has taken place frequently over a period of time, the dates between which it was committed) and the identity of the other party (who will thereafter become the co-respondent). If the respondent and the other party to the adultery have been cohabiting, the dates and place of cohabitation should be given. If there has been a child as a result of the adultery, this should be stated. Sometimes the petitioner is reluctant/unable to name the other party to the adultery or to give particulars of when and where it was committed. It is quite possible to file a petition stating simply that the respondent committed adultery with a man/woman whose identity is not known to the petitioner at times and places unknown to the petitioner. However, there is a risk that the district judge will not then be satisfied that adultery has taken place and will refuse to grant his certificate that the petitoner is entitled to a decree until further information is forthcoming. Furthermore, it is clearly inappropriate to state that identity/ details are unknown where the petitioner does in fact know more but prefers not to disclose the information (see *Bradley* v *Bradley* [1986] 1 FLR 128).

(b)   Behaviour cases: as a rule of thumb, where the petitioner's statement clearly discloses sufficient evidence of behaviour and there is no reason to believe that the petition will be defended, it should be sufficient to select about six allegations/incidents by way of particulars. Generally it is appropriate to include the first, the worst and the last incident of behaviour during the marriage. Incidents should be described in chronological order wherever possible. A long narrative is not required. The date of the incident should be given as precisely as possible together with sufficient information to identify the incident the petitioner has in mind and to see why it is alleged to constitute behaviour. If the petitioner suffered an injury to health as a result of the incident, this should be stated. It is quite common to include a general paragraph summarising the characteristics of the respondent's behaviour.

(c)   Desertion cases: the date and circumstances of the respondent's departure should be given in sufficient detail to show that the respondent intended to bring cohabitation to an end permanently. The particulars should also state that the petitioner did not consent to the respondent's departure and gave him no cause to leave.

(d)   Consensual separation cases: the date and brief circumstances of the separation should be given. Care must be taken in cases where the parties have continued to live in the same house to give sufficient information to establish that they did maintain separate households under the same roof.

(e)   Five years' separation cases: particulars should be given as in consensual separation cases.

It should be made clear in all cases in the particulars whether the petitioner and respondent have ceased to cohabit and, if so, when. The provisions of s. 2, Matrimonial Causes Act 1973 as to cohabitation (see Chapter 3 paragraph 10) should be borne in mind when drafting the particulars and any relevant periods of cohabitation should be referred to.

Example. The petitioner and respondent separated on 4 May 1980. The petition alleges five years' separation. The parties have, in fact, resumed living together for two periods, from 1 August 1984 until 22 September 1984 and from 3 February 1985 until 8 April 1985. These periods do not together exceed six months therefore they will be disregarded in determining whether the petitioner should get a decree. However, they should be referred to in the particulars of separation thus:

The petitioner and the respondent have lived apart for a continuous period of at least 5 years immediately preceding the presentation of this petition, namely from 4 May 1980 when the petitioner left the respondent, save that the petitioner and the respondent have resumed living together for 2 periods not exceeding six months in all, namely from . . . In the premises, no account should be taken of the said periods.

3.14 The prayer

(1) *Prayer for dissolution of marriage*: this is a standard prayer which takes the same form in all divorce petitions.

(2) *Prayer for an order under Part I of Part II of the Children Act 1989*: the full names of any children in respect of whom the petitioner seeks an order should be given. (N.B. Where no such application is sought the appropriate clause in the prayer should be crossed out; where an application *is* sought it will assist the court greatly if the prayer makes it quite clear which type of order is requested e.g. residence or contact order.)

(3) *Prayer for costs*: careful consideration should be given to whether the costs of obtaining a decree should be claimed from the respondent or the co-respondent. A claim for costs will normally be included where the petitioner is receiving full legal aid or is paying privately for the services of her solicitor. Whether costs will be ordered is a matter within the discretion of the court (see Chapter 8, paragraph 10.2.1). The general view is that costs should *not* normally be claimed where the petitioner is receiving advice and assistance under the green form scheme. There seem to be two reasons for this. Firstly, the financial benefit of a claim for costs will inevitably be small as the petitioner will only be entitled to costs as a litigant in person in any event. Secondly, the prayer for costs can sometimes prove to be the last straw that decides the respondent not only to contest the issue of costs but also to oppose the granting of a divorce. It must be said, however, that quite a number of practitioners do nevertheless claim costs in green form cases and some district judges continue to grant costs although practice seems to vary around the country. It may be that the reason for solicitors continuing to claim costs is to save the trouble of amending the petition later to claim costs should the case be defended. It is suggested that unless it is clear from the outset that the case will be defended this practice is ill-advised and unnecessary bearing in mind that only a small proportion of cases are defended and that leave to amend to add a prayer for costs will be granted as a matter of course if the case should unexpectedly become defended (see Chapter 9 for the procedure for seeking leave to amend).

If a prayer for costs is included, it is open to the respondent/co-respondent to contest his liability to pay. He will do this initially by notifying the court of his objection on the acknowledgment of service form. For the subsequent procedure, see Chapter 8 paragraph 10.2.1.

(4) *Prayer for ancillary relief*: it will normally be advisable to include a prayer for all available forms of ancillary relief. This is because the petitioner is obliged to make any claims that she wishes to make on her own behalf for maintenance pending suit, financial provision orders and property adjustment orders in the petition (Family Proceedings Rules 1991, r. 2.53(1)); Chapter 14, paragraph 2.4). If she fails to include all her claims in the petition at the outset, she will not be able to make them at all unless either:

(a) if the omission is discovered before a decree is granted, the petition is amended to include the appropriate claims. The petition can be amended without leave before it is served but thereafter leave is required for amendments (Family Proceedings Rules 1991, r. 2.11(1)); as to amendment, see further Chapter 9; *or*

(b)   if the omission is not discovered until after a decree has been granted, then leave of the court to make the application is necessary. The only exception to this is that if the parties are agreed as to the terms of the order, the petitioner can make an application for the agreed order without leave (Family Proceedings Rules 1991, r. 2.53(2)).

If the omission is not discovered until after the petitioner has remarried, she will be debarred from making any claim at all (whereas a lump sum or property adjustment claim made before remarriage can be pursued after remarriage).

> **Example.** Mr and Mrs Williams have been married for many years. They have always lived in a council house and, as far as Mrs Williams is aware, they have no savings. Mrs Williams leaves her husband and seeks a divorce. She obtains a flat from a housing association so she does not want a transfer of the council house nor does she want any of the contents of the house which have had their day. She does not even want maintenance because she has met someone she intends to marry. When her petition is filed, all the claims for ancillary relief are struck out of the prayer. After decree absolute comes through, Mrs Williams remarries. She then discovers that her husband had been saving a worthwhile sum from his earnings throughout the marriage without telling her. He has amassed savings of over £15,000 over the years. Mrs Williams consults her solicitor with a view to claim a share. She cannot do so because no claim for a lump sum or property adjustment order was included in her petition and she is debarred from making one now by her remarriage. Had her petition included a comprehensive prayer for ancillary relief, she could have proceeded with a claim in relation to the savings despite her remarriage.

Although claims for ancillary relief for children can be made at any time, it will generally be convenient to include full claims on their behalf in the petition as well.

3.15   Signature

Where the petitioner is receiving help under the green form scheme, she should sign the petition herself.

If the solicitor is acting for the petitioner on full legal aid or on a private basis, the petition should be signed by counsel if settled by him or otherwise by the solicitor in his own or the firm's name (Family Proceedings Rules 1991, r. 2.5).

3.16   When is there a co-respondent?

Section 49, Matrimonial Causes Act 1973 and Family Proceedings Rules 1991, r. 2.7 provide that:

(a)   Where the petition alleges that the respondent has committed adultery with a named person or persons, each such person must be made a co-respondent unless:

(i)   it is alleged that she has been raped by the respondent in which case she will not normally be made a co-respondent; *or*

(ii)   the court otherwise directs.

(b)   Where the petition alleges that the respondent has committed adultery with a person whose identity is not known to the petitioner there will be no co-respondent.

(c)   Where the petition includes an allegation that the respondent formed an improper association falling short of adultery with a named person (this will normally arise in a petition based on s. 1(2)(b), Matrimonial Causes Act 1973), the court may direct that that person be made a co-respondent.

If a person is made a co-respondent, that person is entitled to be served with a copy of the petition (and such of the accompanying documents as are appropriate) and to defend the allegations and/or any claim for costs made against him in the petition.

3.17   Addresses for service

The respondent's address for service (and that of the co-respondent if there is one) must be given. This will be the address of the last-known residence of the respondent (and co-respondent) unless the petitioner's solicitors have been notified that the respondent (or co-respondent) is represented by solicitors who will accept service of the petition on his behalf.

The petitioner's address for service will be care of her solicitors if the solicitor is acting for the petitioner on full legal aid or on a private basis or, where the petitioner is receiving help under the green form scheme, if (as is likely) the solicitor has agreed that his address should be given for service.

Before completing this form, read carefully the attached *NOTES FOR GUIDANCE*

IN THE   COUNTY COURT

IN THE DIVORCE REGISTRY*   No.

(1)   On the   day of   19   the petitioner
                                                               was lawfully married to
                                                               (hereinafter called "the
respondent") at

(2)   The petitioner and respondent last lived together at

(3)   The petitioner is domiciled in England and Wales, and is by occupation a

                              and resides at

                                                    and the respondent

is by occupation a

                              and resides at

(4)   There are no children of the family now living *except*

(5)   No other child, now living has been born to the petitioner/respondent
during the marriage (so far as is known to the petitioner) *except*

(6)   There are or have been no other proceedings in any court in England and
Wales or elsewhere with reference to the marriage (or to any child of the family)
or between the petitioner and respondent with reference to any property of either
or both of them *except*

(7)   There are no proceedings continuing in any country outside England or Wales which are in respect of the marriage or are capable of affecting its validity or subsistence *except*

(8)   (This paragraph should be completed only if the petition is based on five years' separation.) No agreement or arrangement has been made or is proposed to be made between the parties for the support of the petitioner/respondent (and any child of the family) *except*

(9)   The said marriage has broken down irretrievably.

(10)

(11)   <u>PARTICULARS</u>

<u>PRAYER</u>

The petitioner therefore prays:

(1)   That the said marriage be dissolved.

(2)   That the petitioner may be granted [e.g. a residence order, contact order. N.B. If no orders sought in relation to the children then cross out this clause (2)]

(3)   That the   may be ordered to pay the costs of this suit.

(4)   That the petitioner may be granted the following ancillary relief:
  (a)   an order for maintenance pending suit
      a periodical payments order
      a secured provision order
      a lump sum order

  (b)   a periodical payments order
      a secured provision order   } for the children of the family
      a lump sum order

  (c)   a property adjustment order

Signed

The names and addresses of the person to be served with this petition are:—

Respondent:—

Co-Respondent (adultery case only):—

The petitioner's address for service is:—

Dated this   day of   19

Address all communications for the court to: The Chief Clerk, County Court,

The Court }
office at

is open from 10 a.m. to 4 p.m. (4.30 p.m. at the Divorce Registry) on Mondays to Fridays.

*Delete as
appropriate

IN THE

COUNTY COURT*

No.

IN THE DIVORCE REGISTRY*

BETWEEN:—

Petitioner

and

Respondent

DIVORCE PETITION

Full names and address of the petitioner or of
solicitors if they are acting for the petitioner.

8 Undefended divorce: procedure for obtaining the decree

1 DOCUMENTS REQUIRED

The following documents should be prepared/assembled for presentation to the court. A copy should be kept for the solicitor's own file of all documents that are to be filed at court.

1.1 The petition

For notes on drafting the petition see Chapter 7.

Every divorce suit is commenced by petition (Family Proceedings Rules 1991, r. 2.2). The court will require the petitioner to provide the original petition plus one copy for each party who is to be served. Therefore the solicitor must always have ready the original petition plus one copy for the respondent. Where there is a co-respondent, a further copy will be required. It is possible for there to be more than one co-respondent if the petition makes several allegations of adultery. In this event one further copy of the petition will be required for each additional co-respondent.

1.2 The marriage certificate

The marriage certificate must be filed with the petition (Family Proceedings Rules 1991, r. 2.6(2)). If the client does not have a marriage certificate one can be obtained by post or by personal attendance from the office of the Superintendent Registrar of Marriages for the district where the marriage took place. A standard fee is payable, presently of £5.50. Alternatively a copy can be obtained from The Registrar General, General Register Office, St Catherine's House, 10 Kingsway, London WC2B 6JP. In this case the fee varies depending on whether the certificate is collected in person (£5.50) or sent by post (£15).

If the client is receiving green form assistance, the cost of obtaining the certificate can be met under the green form scheme. However, the financial limit on green form advice is often little enough as it is and some solicitors request the client to obtain a copy of the certificate herself. If it is necessary for the solicitor to obtain the certificate for the client the possibility of seeking an extension of the green form limit should be borne in mind if costs are nearing the normal limit.

Only one copy of the marriage certificate is required. It is kept on the court file. The respondent is not served with a copy (nor, of course, is any co-respondent).

1.3   The statement as to arrangements for children (Form M4)

1.3.1   Generally

Where there is a child of the family who is:

(a)   under 16; or
(b)   between 16 and 18 and receiving instruction at an educational establishment or undergoing training for a trade or profession,

then the Family Proceedings Rules 1991, r. 2.2 require the petitioner to file a Form M4 setting out the arrangements for those children. In 'exceptional circumstances' the district judge can direct that a decree not be made absolute until matters in respect of the children have been resolved (s. 41(2), Matrimonial Causes Act 1973, as substituted by Children Act 1989, sch. 12, para. 31).

Rule 2.2 requires that 'if possible' the statement of arrangements for children be agreed with the respondent (and provision is made for this in Part IV of the new statement or arrangements Form M4). If this is not possible, then it would appear that the petitioner cannot be compelled to comply with the requirement. If the respondent's agreement has not been, or cannot be obtained, then it would be good practice to provide a letter of explanation for the court when the Form M4 is filed (see also Family Proceedings Rules 1991, r. 2.38 which deals with the respondent's statement in response to the petitioner's statement).

So far as legal aid is concerned, any extra work involved in obtaining the respondent's agreement to the statement of arrangements, in drafting the much more extensive Form M4, or in doing any other work to provide the court with information as to the arrangements for the children, should attract an extension under regulation 21(1) of the Legal Advice and Assistance Regulations 1989 to cover the extra work necessary. An application should be made to the Legal Aid Board for any such extension.

The statement of arrangements should be signed by the petitioner personally (even where a solicitor is acting for her), giving background information about each child, for example, where he is to live after the divorce, details of his school, health etc. (Family Proceedings Rules 1991, r. 2.2(2)). This statement is the core of the information available to the district judge when he considers the arrangements for the children.

Form M4 can be obtained from the offices of divorce county courts or from law stationers. Where there is more than one child to whom r. 2.2(2) applies, then details in relation to all the children can be given on one form. See paragraph 13 below for a more detailed analysis of the way in which the new procedures for s. 41, Matrimonial Causes Act 1973 will operate.

1.3.2   Completing Form M4

Completing Form M4 is a relatively straightforward matter. The margin notes on the form indicate what information is required. A blank copy of Form M4 appears on pp. 94–101. The solicitor should take care to give as much information as possible on the form. The court will require the original statement as to arrangements plus one copy for service on the respondent, together with the original and a copy of any medical report that is attached to Form M4. The arrangements for the children are of no concern to the co-respondent and he is not provided with a copy of Form M4.

1.3.3 Medical Reports

If a child has a long-standing illness or suffers from a disability, this must be stated in Form M4. If there is an up-to-date medical report, it should be attached to Form M4. If there is not, consideration should be given as to whether a report or at least a letter should be obtained from the doctor responsible for the child. In a relatively straightforward case (for example, where a child was born with a disability, such as the lack of a finger on one hand, which does not need treatment and with which the child has learned to cope) no report or letter may be required. In more complex cases, for example, where the child is currently receiving regular treatment of more than a routine nature (as where the child is undergoing a series of surgical operations), a report will be necessary in order that the district judge is sufficiently well informed about the child to decide whether he can grant a s. 41 declaration.

If no report is provided and the district judge decides when giving directions for trial that a report is necessary, he can give a direction to that effect: see Family Proceedings Rules 1991, r. 2.39(3) (see paragraph 13.1 below).

The cost of obtaining a medical report is covered by the green form scheme. However, as this will increase the petitioner's costs of obtaining the divorce, the solicitor should bear in mind that it may become necessary to apply for an extension at some stage.

1.3.4 Where children are not living with petitioner

Where the children are not living with the petitioner, she may not be able to give all the information required by Form M4. It would be good practice for the respondent in such a case to file a statement in Form M4 together with his acknowledgment without any prompting. However, this is not always done.

Where the petitioner is not able to give the necessary information and the respondent has not supplied it voluntarily, it is likely that the court will ask the respondent to file a statement giving information about the children in the form of a letter or in Form M4 (see Family Proceedings Rules 1991, r. 2.38). However, there does not appear to be any power to require the respondent to provide information and, if he fails to do so by the time the district judge considers the arrangements for the children, the proper course would appear to be for the district judge to direct that a court welfare officer's report be prepared giving details of the respondent's arrangements for the children (see paragraph 13, below).

1.4 Legal aid certificate

Full legal aid is not normally granted for the decree proceedings as opposed to proceedings in relation to ancillary matters such as applications made under the Children Act 1989 and property (see Chapter 6). If legal aid is granted, however, the solicitor has a number of duties under reg. 50, Civil Legal Aid (General) Regulations 1989 to fulfil in connection with it (for further details, see Chapter 2 paragraph 15). These duties include:

Rule 2.2(2)   **Form M4**

Statement of Arrangements for Children

In the	County Court
Petitioner	

Respondent		
	No of matter *(always quote this)*	

To the Petitioner

You must complete this form
if you or the respondent have any children • under 16
or • over 16 but under 18 if they are at school
or college or are training for a trade,
profession or vocation.

Please use black ink.
Please complete Parts I, II and III.

Before you issue a petition for divorce try to reach agreement with your husband/wife over the proposals for the children's future. There is space for him/her to sign at the end of this form if agreement is reached.

If your husband/wife does not agree with the proposals he/she will have the opportunity at a later stage to state why he/she does not agree and will be able to make his/her own proposals.

You should take or send the completed form, signed by you (and, if agreement is reached, by your husband/wife) together with a copy to the court when you issue your petition.

Please refer to the explanatory notes issued regarding completion of the prayer of the petition if you are asking the court to make any order regarding the children.

The Court will only make an order if it considers that an order will be better for the child(ren) than no order.

If you wish to apply for any of the orders which may be available to you under Part I or II of the Children Act 1989 you are advised to see a solicitor.

You should obtain legal advice from a solicitor or, alternatively, from an advice agency. The Law Society administers a national panel of solicitors to represent children and other parties involved in proceedings relating to children. Addresses of solicitors (including panel members) and advice agencies can be obtained from the Yellow Pages and the Solicitors Regional Directory which can be found at Citizens Advice Bureaux, Law Centres and any local library.

To the Respondent

The petitioner has completed Part I, II and III of this form
which will be sent to the Court at the same time that the divorce petition is filed.

Please read all parts of the form carefully.

If you agree with the arrangements and proposals for the children you should sign Part IV of the form.
Please use black ink. You should return the form to the petitioner, or his/her solicitor.

If you do not agree with all or some of the arrangements or proposals you will be given the opportunity of saying so when the divorce petition is served on you.

Part I–Details of the children

Please read the instructions for boxes 1, 2 and 3 before you complete this section

---

1. **Children of both parties** *(Give details only of any children born to you and the Respondent or adopted by you both)*

Forenames	Surname	Date of birth
(i)		
(ii)		
(iii)		
(iv)		
(v)		

---

2. **Other children of the family** *(Give details of any other children treated by both of you as children of the family: for example your own or the Respondent's)*

Forenames	Surname	Date of birth	Relationship to Yourself	Respondent
(i)				
(ii)				
(iii)				
(iv)				
(v)				

---

3. **Other children who are not children of the family** *(Give details of any children born to you or the Respondent that have not been treated as children of the family) or adopted by you both)*

Forenames	Surname	Date of birth
(i)		
(ii)		
(iii)		
(iv)		
(v)		

Part II–Arrangements for the children of the family

This part of the form must be completed. Give details for each child if arrangements are different. If necessary, continue on another sheet and attach it to this form

4.	Home details	*(please tick the appropriate boxes)*
(a)	The addresses at which the children now live	
(b)	Give details of the number of living rooms, bedrooms, etc. at the addresses in (a)	
(c)	Is the house rented or owned and by whom? Is the rent or any mortgage being regularly paid?	☐ No ☐ Yes
(d)	Give the names of all other persons living with the children including your husband/wife if he/she lives there. State their relationship to the children.	
(e)	Will there be any change in these arrangements?	☐ No ☐ Yes *(please give details)*

| 5. | **Education and training details** | *(please tick the appropriate boxes)* |

| (a) | Give the names of the school, college or place of training attended by each child. | |

| (b) | Do the children have any special educational needs? | ☐ No ☐ Yes *(please give details)* |

| (c) | Is the school, college or place of training, fee-paying? | ☐ No ☐ Yes (please give details of how much the fees are per term/year) |
| | Are fees being regularly paid? | ☐ No ☐ Yes *(please give details)* |

| (d) | Will there be any change in these arrangements? | ☐ No ☐ Yes *(please give details)* |

6.	**Childcare details**	*(please tick the appropriate boxes)*

(a)	Which parent looks after the children from day to day? If responsibility is shared, please give details	
(b)	Does that parent go out to work?	☐ No ☐ Yes *(please give details of his/her hours of work)*
(c)	Does someone look after the children when the parent is not there?	☐ No ☐ Yes *(please give details)*
(d)	Who looks after the children during school holidays?	
(e)	Will there be any change in these arrangements?	☐ No ☐ Yes *(please give details)*

7.	**Maintenance**	*(please tick the appropriate boxes)*

(a)	Does your husband/wife pay towards the upkeep of the children? If there is another source of maintenance, please specify.	☐ No ☐ Yes *(please give details of how much)*
(b)	Is the payment made under a court order?	☐ No ☐ Yes *(please give details, including the name of the court and case number)*
(c)	Has maintenance for the children been agreed?	☐ No ☐ Yes
	If not, will you be applying for a maintenance order for the children?	☐ No ☐ Yes *(please give details)*

8.	**Details for contact with the children**	*(please tick the appropriate boxes)*

(a) Do the children see your husband/wife?	☐ No ☐ Yes *(please give details of how often and where)*

(b) Do the children ever stay with your husband/wife?	☐ No ☐ Yes *(please give details of how much)*

(c) Will there be any change to these arrangements? Please give details of the proposed arrangements for contact and residence.	☐ No ☐ Yes *(please give details of how much)*

9. **Details of health**   *(please tick the appropriate boxes)*

(a) Are the children generally in good health?	☐ Yes ☐ No *(please give details of any serious disability or chronic illness)*
(b) Do the children have any special health needs?	☐ No ☐ Yes *(please give details of the care needed and how it is to be provided)*

10. **Details of care and other court proceedings**   *(please tick the appropriate boxes)*

(a) Are the children in the care of a local authority, or under the supervision of a social worker or probation officer?	☐ No ☐ Yes *(please give details including any court proceedings)*
(b) Are any of the children on the Child Protection Register?	☐ No ☐ Yes *(please give details of the local authority and the date of registration)*
(c) Are there or have there been any proceedings in any court involving the children, for example adoption, custody/residence, access/contact wardship, care, supervision or maintenance?	☐ No ☐ Yes *(please give details and send a copy of any order to the court)*

Part III–To the Petitioner

Conciliation

If you and your husband/wife do not agree about the arrangements for the child(ren), would you agree to discuss the matter with a Conciliator and your husband/wife?

☐ No ☐ Yes

Declaration

I declare that the information I have given is correct and complete to the best of my knowledge.

Signed .... (Petitioner)

Date: ....

Part IV–To the Respondent

I agree with the arrangements and proposals contained in Part I and II of this form.

Signed .... (Respondent)

Date: ....

(a) Filing the legal aid certificate at court as soon as divorce proceedings are commenced or, if proceedings have already begun when the certificate comes through, as soon as he receives it.

(b) Filing a notice of issue of the legal aid certificate with the court for the court file.

(c) Serving notice of issue of the legal aid certificate on all other parties to the proceedings. Where legal aid has been granted before the divorce proceedings are commenced, the notice of issue to be served on the respondent (and co-respondent) should be filed at court with the petition. It will then be annexed to the petition and served with it. Where legal aid is granted after proceedings have been commenced, the solicitor bears the responsibility for serving the appropriate notices.

2   COMMENCEMENT OF PROCEEDINGS

Divorce proceedings are commenced by the presentation of the divorce petition and supporting documents at court. The petition may be presented to any divorce county court (Family Proceedings Rules 1991, r. 2.6), or to the Divorce Registry in London (the principal registry of the Family Division of the High Court which is treated in many respects as another divorce county court (see r. 1.4, Family Proceedings Rules 1991 and s. 42, Matrimonial and Family Proceedings Act 1984). Not all county courts are divorce county courts. They must be designated as such by the Lord Chancellor.

The solicitor will normally find it most convenient to commence the divorce proceedings in his local divorce county court or the divorce county court nearest to where the petitioner lives. The petition and supporting documents listed in paragraph 1 above must be filed at the court office of the chosen county court (or at the Divorce Registry). They can be handed in personally over the counter in the court office or sent by post.

3   FEE

There is a court fee of £40 payable when the petition is filed. If the petitioner is in receipt of green form advice and assistance or is receiving income support or family credit (providing, in the latter two cases, that she is not also receiving full legal aid), she is entitled to exemption from the fee. A form applying for exemption is obtainable from the court and should be completed on the petitioner's behalf. The fee will almost certainly be payable when the petitioner is paying privately for her solicitor's services or is receiving full legal aid (although in the latter case it will constitute a disbursement covered by legal aid so the petitioner will not have to provide the money herself). However, there is a residual power in the Lord Chancellor to reduce or remit the fee in cases of undue hardship.

4   ADDITIONAL MATTERS WHERE THE SOLICITOR IS ACTING

4.1   When is the solicitor acting?

The solicitor *is not* acting in the decree proceedings if his client is receiving only green form advice and assistance in relation to them. Such a client is looked upon as a litigant in person for the purposes of the decree proceedings. This is unaffected by any legal aid certificate that may have been granted in the client's favour in relation to ancillary matters. The solicitor *is* acting in the decree proceedings if his client is paying privately for his services or if full legal aid has been granted in relation to these proceedings.

4.2 Additional duties

The solicitor must file a certificate in Form M3 (one copy only required) with the petition (Family Proceedings Rules 1991, r. 2.6(3)). This states whether or not he has discussed with the petitioner the possibility of a reconciliation and given her the names and addresses of persons qualified to help effect a reconciliation (see Chapter 1 paragraph 2.2 for further details of such persons). There is not, in fact, any requirement that the solicitor *must* discuss reconciliation with the client. However, the fact that he must file Form M3 ensures that he will at least turn his mind to the question and, unless it is clearly inappropriate in the client's particular circumstances, it will usually be good practice to discuss the possibility of reconciliation with the client.

5 ENTRY IN COURT BOOKS

When the court receives the petition, it enters the cause in the books of the court and a file number is allocated to it. The solicitor will be notified of the number. This is the official identity tag for the case and must be quoted on all correspondence with the court and used on all pleadings connected with the divorce and with ancillary matters.

6 SERVICE OF THE PETITION

Before the divorce can go any further the petition must be served on the respondent and any co-respondent (Family Proceedings Rules 1991, r. 2.9(1) and 2.24) or, in exceptional circumstances, service may be dispensed with (r. 2.9(11)).

6.1 Tracing a missing respondent

The petitioner may have lost touch with the respondent and be unable to provide an address for him. Efforts will have to be made to trace him in order that the petition can be served either by post or personally. Apart from the normal enquiries that can be made of the respondent's former employers, his relations and friends, his clubs and trade union, there are various special ways of tracing a missing respondent. These are set out fully in a Practice Direction of 13 February 1989 [1989] 1 All ER 765, [1989] 1 WLR 219. In summary, if the petition is filed by a wife and includes a claim for maintenance for her or the children or there is an existing maintenance order in favour of the petitioner or children which the petitioner is seeking to enforce, the court can request a search to be made on behalf of the petitioner for the respondent's address from the records of the Department of Social Security or, failing that, of the passport office. Application should be made to the district judge for a search to be requested. If the respondent is known to be serving or to have served recently in the Armed Forces, the petitioner's solicitor can request an address for service on the respondent from the appropriate service department.

It is also useful to know that if the petitioner is making or seeking to enforce a maintenance claim, the Department of Social Security is often willing to provide the petitioner's solicitor with an address for the respondent when requested to do so simply by a letter from the solicitor. This should be tried before asking the district judge to request this information. The Department of Social Security will also forward a letter to a party's last known address in all cases. The respondent's bank may well be prepared to do the same.

6.2　Court normally responsible for service

Normally the court sees to the service of the petition and accompanying documents. The administrative procedure followed by the court office is as follows:

(1)　Each copy of the petition for service has annexed to it:

(a)　a notice of proceedings (Form M5) which explains to the respondent that a petition for divorce has been presented and instructs him to complete the acknowledgment of service. It also contains notes on completing the acknowledgment of service;

(b)　a form of acknowledgment of service (Form M6);

(c)　if there is a legal aid certificate, notice of issue of the legal aid certificate.

(2)　The respondent's copy of the petition also has annexed to it a copy of the statement as to arrangements for the children if there is one plus a copy of any medical report attached to it.

(3)　A copy of the petition and the documents annexed to it is served on the respondent by the court. Normally service is effected by the court simply by posting the documents to the respondent at the address given for him by the petitioner at the foot of the petition (known as 'postal service').

(4)　If the acknowledgment of service is then completed and signed by the respondent (or his solicitor on his behalf if this is appropriate) and returned to the court, the petition is taken to have been duly served (Family Proceedings Rules 1991, r. 2.9(5)).

6.3　Alternatives to postal service by the court

6.3.1　General

Postal service through the court is not always successful or appropriate. All sorts of problems can arise over service, for example the petitioner may not be able to provide an address for service on the respondent or the respondent may fail to return the acknowledgment of service after the documents have been posted to him.

There are various alternatives to postal service by the court. What is appropriate depends on the nature of the problem that has arisen. The various methods of service are described in paragraph 6.3.2. Common problems and suggested solutions are dealt with in paragraph 6.3.3.

6.3.2 Alternative methods of service

6.3.2.1 Personal service by the court bailiff The district judge can direct bailiff service on the petitioner's request made in writing on the appropriate form. There is an extra fee payable for this service (currently £5).

The petitioner must provide some means whereby the bailiff can identify the respondent, normally a photograph. Where the petitioner is represented by a solicitor it will be necessary to show why service by bailiff is requested instead of personal service by a process server (Practice Direction of 7 March 1977 [1977] 1 All ER 845). This does not, of course, apply in green form cases.

Service is effected by the bailiff delivering a copy of the petition to the respondent personally. He will attempt to get the respondent to sign for the papers.

Once the bailiff has served the respondent personally he files a certificate to this effect, stating how he identified the respondent. If the respondent returns the acknowledgment of service to the court, this will prove service. Where the acknowledgment of service is not returned it will be necessary for the petitioner in her affidavit in support of the petition to identify the respondent's signature for the documents or to identify the respondent in the photograph used by the bailiff. Together with the bailiff's certificate, this will be sufficient proof of service.

6.3.2.2 Service through the petitioner The petitioner can request that service be carried out through her (Family Proceedings Rules 1991, r. 2.9(2)(b)). The petitioner herself must never effect personal service of the documents (r. 2.9(3)) but her solicitor can serve the respondent or an enquiry agent can be instructed to do so. Some means of identification must be provided by the petitioner as with bailiff service, usually a photograph.

Personal service through the petitioner has an advantage over bailiff service in that the bailiff cannot be expected to search for the respondent if the petitioner cannot supply a definite address or if the respondent is not at his address when the bailiff calls whereas an enquiry agent can be instructed to do so.

Where personal service through the petitioner is required, the solicitor will probably need to obtain an extension of the green form financial limit to cover the cost of service (see Chapter 2 paragraph 5). The person serving the petition should attempt to get the respondent to sign for the documents. If no acknowledgment of service is returned to the court office, the server will be required to file an affidavit of service stating that he has served the petition and stating how he identified the respondent (Family Proceedings Rules 1991, r. 2.9(7)). In her affidavit in support of the petition, the petitioner will then identify the respondent's signature for the documents or identify the photograph used by the server as a photograph of the respondent, as with bailiff service.

6.3.2.3 Deemed service Where the acknowledgment of service has not been returned to the court but the district judge is nevertheless satisfied that the petition has been received by the respondent, he can direct that service is deemed to have been effected (Family Proceedings Rules 1991, r. 2.9(6)).

A letter should be sent to the district judge with the petitioner's request for directions for trial (see paragraph 9 below) asking for service to be deemed. The district judge will need some evidence that the respondent has received the petition; an affidavit should therefore be filed from someone who can give evidence to this effect exhibiting documentary evidence that the respondent has received the petition. The person who can give evidence that the respondent has received the petition is often the petitioner herself. However, to deem service effective on the basis of the petitioner's evidence alone does carry an obvious danger in that an unscrupulous petitioner could, by giving false evidence on this point, ensure that the respondent knew nothing of the divorce proceedings. Some district judges may therefore be reluctant to agree on the basis of the petitioner's uncorroborated evidence that service should be deemed.

Example 1. The petitioner and respondent continue to live in the same house even after divorce proceedings have been commenced. The petitioner is present when the respondent picks up the divorce papers which have arrived in the post, opens the envelope, glances at the contents and deposits them in the dustbin. The petitioner's affidavit to this effect *may* be sufficient to satisfy the district judge that the respondent has received the documents.

Example 2. After receiving the petition the respondent consults a firm of solicitors who write to the petitioner's solicitors concerning the petition but the respondent then fails to return the acknowledgment of service, terminates his instructions to his solicitors and disappears into thin air. The district judge deems service to have been effected in view of the letter from his ex-solicitors.

6.3.2.4 Substituted service Where all the petitioner's efforts to trace the respondent have failed, the petitioner will have to ask either for an order for substituted service or for service to be dispensed with (see paragraph 6.3.2.5 below).

An order for substituted service directs that the petition be served in some way other than postal or personal service. It will only be permitted where the petitioner has made proper attempts to trace and serve the respondent by post or personally. The alternative method of service permitted will be clearly specified in the order.

Example. The respondent is known to visit a relative regularly but efforts to effect personal service at that address have failed. Substituted service by posting the documents to that address could be authorised.

One method of substituted service is by advertisement. However, no order for service by advertisement will be given unless it appears to the district judge that there is a reasonable possibility that the advertisement will come to the knowledge of the person concerned (Family Proceedings Rules 1991, r. 2.9(9)). Indeed, in practice, the district judge is unlikely to permit any form of substituted service unless he is satisfied that it has a reasonable chance of bringing the proceedings to the knowledge of the person concerned. If service by advertisement is permitted, the district judge will settle the advertisement (r. 2.9(9)) and may well arrange himself for it to be inserted in the appropriate publication on payment of the required fees to him. If the court authorises someone else to insert the advertisement, that person shall file copies of the newspapers containing the advertisement at court (r. 10.5(3)).

Application for substituted services should be made to the district judge ex parte by lodging an affidavit setting out the grounds on which the application is made (r. 2.9(9)).

6.3.2.5 Dispensing with service If all else fails, the district judge may be asked to make an order dispensing with service of the petition. He will do this where in his opinion it is impracticable to serve the petition or for other reasons it is necessary or expedient to dispense with service (Family Proceedings Rules 1991, r. 2.9(11)).

Clearly it can be a serious matter for the district judge to dispense with service as it means that the respondent may be divorced without even knowing that divorce proceedings have been commenced. The district judge will therefore have to be satisfied that exhaustive enquiries have been made to trace the respondent (see paragraph 6.1 above) and that substituted service would not be appropriate.

> **Example.** The petitioner has no idea where the respondent is. Enquiries of his relatives suggest that he has gone to work abroad but no one knows where. Enquiries of his past employers, past landlady, the Department of Social Security, the passport office, etc. draw a blank. The district judge may well be inclined to dispense with service.

The district judge can make an order dispensing with service altogether or dispensing with further service once one final method of service is tried.

An application for service to be dispensed with should be made, in the first place, ex parte by affidavit setting out the grounds of the application (the attempts made to serve the respondent, the enquiries made as to his whereabouts and so on) but the district judge can require the attendance of the petitioner to support the application (r. 2.9(11)).

6.3.3 Common problems and solutions

Problem 1 From the outset the petitioner is not able to give a definite address for service for the respondent. The court cannot attempt to effect service.
Solution: (a) Check that enquiries of the nature outlined in paragraph 6.1 above have been made. If they have not, they should be set in motion; they may produce an address at which postal service can be effected.

(b) If the petitioner is able to provide information as to where the respondent may be found (although she cannot provide an address as such), it may well be appropriate to request *personal service through the petitioner* so that an enquiry agent can be instructed to trace the respondent and serve him with the petition personally.

(c) If an address or information as to the respondent's whereabouts is still not forthcoming, apply for *substituted service* or for *service to be dispensed with*. Personal service by the court bailiff or through the petitioner will be impossible as the respondent cannot be traced. Deemed service is obviously inappropriate as the petitioner cannot even attempt to serve the petition on the respondent so he clearly cannot be deemed to have received it.

Problem 2 The petitioner thinks she knows where the respondent is and provides an address for service. The acknowledgment of service is not returned.
Solution: (a) If the court office have not received the acknowledgment after 7 days from the date they posted the petition to the respondent they may automatically inform the petitioner's solicitor that the acknowledgment of service has not been returned and invite an application for bailiff service. On the

other hand some courts do not automatically inform the petitioner's solicitors of non-receipt of the acknowledgment, so the petitioner's solicitor should remember (he would be well advised to make a diary note to remind himself) to review the case after the respondent has had a reasonable period to return the acknowledgment (which will probably not be less than two weeks from the date of filing the petition). If at this stage no copy acknowledgment has been received from the court, the solicitor should confirm with the court office that nothing has been received by them and should then take the appropriate steps to deal with service.

(b) If the petitioner still reasonably believes that the respondent is resident at the address given or can give another address, *bailiff service* should be requested.

(c) If the petitioner is no longer confident about the respondent's address but still thinks she knows where he can be found (e.g., he regularly visits a certain public house), *personal service through the petitioner* should be requested.

(d) If the petitioner no longer has any idea where the respondent is, an application should be made for *substituted service* or for *service to be dispensed with*.

(e) Should the petitioner be able to provide evidence that despite his silence the respondent has received the petition, an application should be made for *service to be deemed* as an alternative to substituted service or dispensing with service.

Problem 3   Bailiff service is attempted and fails.
Solution: If the petitioner has any real idea of the whereabouts of the respondent and there is a prospect of him being traced by an enquiry agent, *personal service through the petitioner* should be requested. Otherwise, application should be made for *substituted service* or for *service to be dispensed with*. *Deemed service* is an alternative where appropriate as in Problem 2.

Problem 4   Personal service is attempted and fails.
Solution: Apply for *substituted service* or for *service to be dispensed with*. *Deemed service* is an alternative.

6.4   Service on a party under a disability

The court does not carry out service where the party to be served is under a disability, i.e. he is under 18 or a mental patient (Family Proceedings Rules 1991, r. 9.3). Service must be through the petitioner (r. 2.9(2)(a)) and there are special rules as to the method of service and as to procedure generally (r. 9.2 and r. 9.3).

6.5   Service on a co-respondent

The procedure for serving a co-respondent with the petition is the same as for the respondent. The routine practice is for the court to attempt postal service. The copy of the petition for service has annexed to it a notice of proceedings in Form M5 and a form of acknowledgment of service in Form M6 and, if there is a legal aid certificate, a notice of issue of the legal aid certificate. The co-respondent does not, however, receive a copy of the statement as to arrangements for the children.

If postal service fails, bailiff service or personal service through the petitioner will normally be tried. Application can be made for service to be deemed or dispensed with or substituted service ordered as in the case of service on the respondent. As the divorce will not affect the status of the co-respondent, it may be rather easier to persuade the court to dispense with service where difficulty is experienced than it is in relation to service on a respondent.

6.6   Service ouside England and Wales

The Family Proceedings Rules 1991, r. 10.6, allow any document in family proceedings (including a divorce petition) to be served outside England and Wales *without leave* either in accordance with the FPR 1991 (i.e. by prepaid first class post, or personally or by substituted service), or:

(a)   in a High Court case, in accordance with RSC Order 11, rules 5 and 6; or
(b)   in a county court case, in accordance with CCR Order 8, rules 8 to 10.

'Family proceedings' for the purposes of the FPR 1991 are defined by r. 1.2 which gives the phrase the same meaning as that contained in the Matrimonial and Family Proceedings Act 1984. (N.B. This is different from the meaning of 'family proceedings' as defined for Children Act 1989 purposes by s. 8(3) of the Children Act 1989.)

7   RETURN OF THE ACKNOWLEDGMENT OF SERVICE

7.1   Filling in the acknowledgment of service

The acknowledgment of service is straightforward. It is in question and answer form and the respondent is given extra guidance as to how to fill it in in Form M5 (notice of proceedings).

The solicitor can sign the acknowledgment for the respondent unless either:

(a)   in adultery cases, the acknowledgment contains an admission of adultery;
or
(b)   in cases of two years' separation and consent, the acknowledgment is used to signify the respondent's consent to the decree (Family Proceedings Rules 1991 r. 2.10(1)).

In both these cases, the respondent must sign the acknowledgment personally as well as the solicitor.

Note that the fact that the respondent states in the acknowledgment that he intends to defend the divorce does not amount to a formal step towards defending. The respondent's statement merely ensures that the divorce will be held up to give him time to file an answer (see paragraph 7.2). However, if he fails to do so within the proper time, the case will proceed undefended as if he had never raised any objection.

Note also that what the respondent says about his intention when filling in the acknowledgment of service in no way binds him. He may, for example, indicate that he intends to defend and then do nothing about it, or indicate that he has no intention of seeking a Children Act 1989 order in respect of the children and then change his mind and make an application.

7.2   Returning the acknowledgment of service

The acknowledgment of service must be returned (normally by post) to reach the court within seven days after the respondent received the divorce papers (Family Proceedings Rules 1991, r. 10.8(2)(a)).

The respondent and co-respondent can normally be relied upon to return the acknowledgment of service at least with a little prompting from the court, who may well send a reminder and a new copy of the acknowledgment of service if the first one is not returned within a reasonable period.

If the acknowledgment of service is returned:

(a)   The court sends a photocopy of it to the petitioner's solicitor (r. 2.9(8)).

(b)   If the respondent or co-respondent indicates in the acknowledgment of service that he or she intends to defend the case matters will automatically be held up for a period of 28 days from the date he received the divorce petition to give him the opportunity to file an answer (r. 2.12(1)) (see Chapter 10 for further details concerning the filing of an answer). If neither the respondent nor the co-respondent files an answer within this period, the case will proceed as an undefended matter unless, at any time, the respondent or co-respondent gets leave to file an answer out of time (see Chapter 10 paragraph 3).

(c)   If, as is more likely, the respondent and co-respondent indicate that they do not intend to defend the case, the next step will usually be for the petitioner's solicitors to request the district judge to give directions for trial.

If the acknowledgment of service is not returned, the petitioner's solicitor will have to decide what further steps are to be taken in relation to service of the petition (see paragraph 6 above).

8   WHEN DIRECTIONS FOR TRIAL CAN BE GIVEN

The district judge can give directions for trial if he is satisfied of the following matters:

(a)   *Due service*   The district judge must be satisfied that a copy of the petition has been duly served on every party required to be served (Family Proceedings Rules 1991, r. 2.24(1)(a)). Where there is a respondent and a co-respondent service on both will be required. Where the acknowledgment of service has been returned by a respondent or co-respondent, this will be taken as proof of due service of the petition on that party provided:

(i)   that it is signed by that party or by a solicitor on his behalf; *and*

(ii)   where the form purports to be signed by the respondent, the signature is proved to be that of the respondent — this is usually proved by the petitioner identifying the signature as the respondent's in her Form M7 ((a) to (e)) affidavit which she files in support of the petition when directions are requested (see paragraph 9, below) (r. 2.9(5)). *And*

(b) *Case undefended* The district judge must be satisfied that the case can be classed as undefended, i.e. either:

(i) the respondent and co-respondent have informed the court (almost certainly in the acknowledgment of service) that they do not intend to defend the case; *or*

(ii) no notice of intention to defend has been given by either the respondent or any co-respondent and the time for giving such a notice has expired; *or*

(iii) if notice of intention to defend has been given by any party, the time allowed him for filing an answer has expired, i.e. 28 days from the date on which the respondent or co-respondent received the petition inclusive of the day of receipt (r. 2.12(1) and r. 2.24(1)). *And*

(c) *Consent given if s. 1(2)(d) case* Where the petition is based on two years' separation and consent, the district judge must be satisfied that the respondent has given notice to the district judge that he consents to the decree being granted (r. 2.24(3)). This consent is normally given in the acknowledgment of service.

9 REQUESTING DIRECTIONS FOR TRIAL

The district judge will not give directions for trial automatically. It is up to the petitioner's solicitor to make a written request that he should do so (Family Proceedings Rules 1991, r. 2.24(1)). This is done by filing:

(a) A standard form of request for directions for trial signed personally by the petitioner (this form can be obtained from the court office if necessary). *And*

(b) An affidavit from the petitioner in support of the petition. There is a standard printed form of affidavit suited to each of the s. 1(2), Matrimonial Causes Act 1973 facts (Form M7(a) to (e); Appendix I, Family Proceedings Rules 1991). These affidavits are in question and answer form and although use of the standard printed form is not obligatory, it is usually convenient. Even if for some reason the standard form is not used, the information required to answer the questions it contains must still be incorporated in the petitioner's affidavit as near as may be in the order set out in the printed affidavit form (r. 2.24(3)). Great care should be taken in completing the affidavit. The following points should be borne in mind:

(i) The affidavit requires the petitioner to swear that everything stated in the petition is true. If there are errors in the petition something must be done about them before the affidavit is sworn. If the corrections or amendments required are minor (for example, the date of birth of one of the children of the family if wrongly stated or the middle name of one of the parties has been omitted), they can be set out in the relevant paragraph of the affidavit. The district judge will then, in most cases, treat the petition as amended in these respects without any requirement that it should be re-served in its amended form on the respondent or co-respondent. However, if the alterations required are more serious (for example, if the petitioner wishes to add an allegation of behaviour in a petition based on s. 1(2)(b), Matrimonial Causes Act 1973), the proper course will be to apply to the district judge for leave to amend the petition which will then have to be re-served on the respondent (and co-respondent if there is one) before the petitioner will be able to request directions and file her affidavit in support of the petition. See Chapter 9 for further details as to amendment of the petition.

(ii)   It is this affidavit that provides the district judge with evidence of the fact relied on in the petition and of irretrievable breakdown of the marriage. There are five different versions of Form M7 because each is tailored to one of the facts in s. 1(2) so that the petitioner is prompted to provide information relevant to the fact on which she relies. The solicitor has a great advantage over a petitioner filling in the affidavit without legal help because he knows the case law on the subject and he can therefore give an informed answer to each question ensuring that all the information that the petitioner can give in support of her case is given. It is most important for the solicitor to keep the substantive law as to divorce (set out in Chapter 3) in mind, so that this advantage is not thrown away.

(iii)   Where the petitioner and respondent have lived in the same household since the matters complained of, care should be taken in stating the period(s) of this cohabitation and the reason why it occurred. Certain periods of cohabitation can be disregarded in considering whether the petitioner is entitled to a decree (see Chapter 3 paragraph 10); cohabitation in excess of this may bar the petitioner from obtaining a decree unless she is able to give a good reason for it. If the petitioner and the respondent are still living together at the time the affidavit is completed, it would be prudent to give a reason for this in case it raises doubts in the district judge's mind as to whether the marriage has truly broken down.

(iv)   Where the petitioner is relying on s. 1(2)(c) to (e) (all facts where a period of separation is required) and it is alleged that the parties have been living apart under the same roof, great pains should be taken to show that the parties were indeed maintaining two separate households (giving details of which rooms were used by which party, whether meals were shared, washing done by one for the other, etc.). *And*

(c)   Any corroborative evidence on which the petitioner intends to rely (Family Proceedings Rules 1991, r. 2.24(3)). It is not always easy to decide when the district judge will be satisfied with the petitioner's evidence alone and when further independent evidence will be required. There are no rules about this; it depends on the standards of the district judge who considers the case and the best guide is therefore experience of the practice of the local district judges. However, the following points may be helpful:

(i)   The object of the exercise is, of course, to satisfy the district judge that the petitioner is entitled to a decree. The district judge has a two-part decision to make when considering whether he is satisfied with the petitioner's case; firstly, he must decide whether the details contained in the petition, *if true*, would entitle the petitioner to a decree; and secondly, whether the details contained in the petition *are in fact true*. The first stage is a question of law and, if the district judge is not satisfied on the law no amount of evidence provided by the petitioner to corroborate what she says in the petition will change his mind — the case will have to be removed from the special procedure list (see paragraph 10.2.2 below).

The second stage is a question of fact and corroborative evidence can help the district judge to be satisfied as to the truth of the petition.

(ii)   The majority of the facts stated in the petition do not need any further support than the evidence of the petitioner in her Form M7 affidavit. However, corroboration may be required of the s. 1(2), Matrimonial Causes Act 1973 fact alleged and the particulars given in relation to it:

(iii)   Adultery cases:

Example 1. The petitioner names the other party involved in the adultery and both the respondent and the co-respondent admit the adultery (in the acknowledgment of service which has a further question specifically directed to the issue or in a separate confession statement). Further corroboration of the adultery may not be required.

Example 2. The petitioner names the other party involved and the respondent admits the adultery but the co-respondent makes no comment as to whether the allegation is true or false (or vice versa). Some district judges may accept the petitioner's evidence coupled with the respondent's admission as sufficient, others would require further corroboration, for example the affidavit of an enquiry agent who watched the house where they spent the night on their own together.

Example 3. The petitioner names the other party involved but neither the respondent nor the co-respondent make any admission as to the adultery. Corroborative evidence would almost certainly be required here.

(iv)   Behaviour cases:

Example 1. The behaviour described in the petition amounts to a strong case, for example, there have been repeated incidents of violence by the respondent towards the petitioner. Corroborative evidence is unlikely to be required although if it is readily available it should be provided, for instance, in the form of a doctor's letter describing bruises and cuts seen on the petitioner or of an affidavit from a neighbour who witnessed an occasion when the respondent was violent towards the petitioner.

Example 2. The behaviour alleged is rather weaker, for example, the petitioner relies upon the fact that the respondent failed to take baths for weeks on end or to change his clothes, belittled her in front of friends and tried to turn the children against her. Corroborative evidence may well be required (for instance, in the form of an affidavit from the petitioner's mother who states that she often saw the respondent looking dirty and untidy and heard him speak rudely to the petitioner in public). It is not necessary to corroborate every incident described, merely to give sufficient corroboration to confirm that basically the petitioner appears to be speaking the truth.

(v)   Separation cases generally:

Example 1. The petitioner alleges that the parties have lived separately under the same roof. Corroborative evidence of this fact is virtually indispensable (for instance from someone who has stayed with the parties or visited them). Indeed, some district judges remove all cases of this type from the special procedure list and refer them to a judge for hearing in open court.

Example 2. The petitioner alleges that the parties have lived in separate houses. Corroboration is unlikely to be necessary.

(vi)   Corroborative evidence need not necessarily be in the form of an independent affidavit. For example, the district judge would probably be prepared to accept as corroboration a letter from a doctor speaking of injuries he witnessed on the petitioner's body or a letter from the respondent apologising to the petitioner for his wholly unreasonable behaviour. Letters such as these could be exhibited to the petitioner's own affidavit in support of the petition.

(d) Costs: it often happens that a petitioner claims costs against the respondent in her divorce petition without giving much thought as to whether she really wishes to pursue that claim. The respondent often files an acknowledgment of service objecting to the payment of costs, sometimes giving reasons and sometimes not. When the petitioner then goes on to file her M7 affidavit it will be of great assistance to the court if she makes it clear whether she still wishes to claim costs in spite of the respondent's objections. It will also assist if she can give any specific reasons to support her claim and to refute any of the objections made by the respondent. It may well save delay in the processing of the petition, since it will save the district judge from having to seek information from the parties as to whether or not they really wish to pursue the claim.

(e) It should be noted that the new Form M7 differs slightly from its predecessor in that it contains three additional clauses at the end which ask the petitioner whether she has read the Statement of Arrangements and whether she wishes to alter anything contained in that statement or in the petition itself. It also requires the petitioner to identify the signature at the bottom of Part IV of the Statement of Arrangements and to confirm that it is that of the respondent.

10   DIRECTIONS FOR TRIAL

10.1   Entering the cause in the special procedure list

The district judge gives direction for trial firstly by entering the cause in the special procedure list (Family Proceedings Rules 1991, r. 2.24(3)).

The special procedure was introduced in the early 1970s as an alternative to what was then the normal procedure for undefended divorces which involved a hearing in open court in front of a judge at which the petitioner was required to give oral evidence in support of her petition. In contrast, the special procedure made obtaining a divorce largely a matter of paperwork and cut out the need for the petitioner to attend court at all in relation to the decree. At the outset, the special procedure was applicable only to petitions based on s. 1(2)(d), Matrimonial Causes Act 1973 (two years' separation and consent), hence the label 'special'. Gradually the procedure was extended to all undefended petitions and the label 'special procedure' has become a misnomer — it has taken over as the regular procedure.

10.2   Consideration by the district judge of the evidence (Family Proceedings Rules 1991, r. 2.36)

The entry of the cause on the special procedure list does not, of itself, entitle the petitioner to a decree. As soon as practicable after the cause is entered in the special procedure list, the district judge must consider the evidence filed by the petitioner (i.e. the petition, the petitioner's supporting affidavit and any corroborative evidence she has filed). In practice, the district judge will normally enter the cause on the special procedure list and consider the evidence at one and the same time. Only if he is satisfied on the evidence that the petitioner has sufficiently proved the contents of her petition and is entitled to a decree will the cause proceed to the pronouncement of a decree.

10.2.1 District judge satisfied

If the district judge is satisfied that the petitioner has sufficiently proved the contents of the petition and is entitled to a decree:

(a) He makes and files a certificate to that effect.

(b) A day is fixed for the district judge or the judge to pronounce decree nisi in open court (see Family Proceedings Rules 1991, r. 2.36(2) which extends this power to district judges).

(c) Notice of the date and place fixed for pronouncement of decree nisi and a copy of the certificate are sent to each party.

(d) If the petitioner claims costs in her petition the district judge considers her claim and, if he is satisfied that she is entitled to the costs of obtaining the divorce, he includes in his certificate a statement to that effect. Whether costs are ordered is a matter within the discretion of the court. If there are any general rules, they are as follows:

(i) behaviour and desertion cases — respondent pays the costs;

(ii) adultery cases — respondent and/or co-respondent pay the costs unless they show that this would be unjust because the adultery took place after the breakdown of the marriage or was brought about by the petitioner's own conduct or, in the case of the co-respondent, because he/she did not know and could not have been expected to know that the respondent was married;

(iii) consensual separation cases — petitioner and respondent pay half the costs each. However, it is open to the respondent to prevent this by refusing to give his consent to the decree unless the entire costs are borne by the petitioner;

(iv) five years' separation cases — no order as to costs. This means that the respondent's solicitor's bill is likely to be noticeably less than that of the petitioner's solicitor.

Costs can be awarded even though the petitioner is receiving only green form assistance and is therefore looked upon as a litigant in person: Litigants in Person (Costs and Expenses) Act 1975. In practice, where costs are granted to a green form petitioner what she is likely to recover is simply the amount of her contribution under the scheme.

The respondent and co-respondent are entitled to make representations on the question of costs (Family Proceedings Rules 1991, r. 2.37). If they do not inform the court at any stage of any objection to paying the costs, many district judges will grant the petitioner costs without question. If, on the other hand, they do wish to object to a claim for costs, the appropriate place is normally in the acknowledgment of service. The district judge will then bear in mind their objections in deciding the question of costs. If the district judge does not feel that he has sufficient information as to why the respondent or co-respondent objects to paying the costs, he can require either of them to make a written statement setting out the reasons for the objection (r. 2.37(1)) in the hope that this will enable him to make his decision. A copy of the statement will be sent to the petitioner. She is free to withdraw her claim for costs at any stage, for example, because she reaches agreement with the respondent that he will not defend the case if she does not pursue her claim to costs or in the light of what the respondent says in his statement to the district judge. If she decides to withdraw her claim before she files her Form M7 affidavit, she can indicate this to the court in the affidavit. If she only decides after directions have been sought, she can withdraw her claim to costs simply by writing a letter to the court.

The district judge will not finally rule out the petitioner's claim for costs. If he is not satisfied that she is entitled to her costs, he will refer the question to the judge who is to pronounce decree nisi. Notice will be given to any party who objects to paying the costs that he must attend before the court on the date fixed for pronouncement of decree nisi to argue his case. If the party concerned fails to turn up on the day, it will be taken that he does not wish to proceed with his objection to paying the costs and an order will almost certainly be made in the petitioner's favour. The petitioner may attend to support her claim for costs to the judge or district judge but need not do so (see further at paragraph 11).

(e)   If the parties have reached agreement over finances, an order in relation to financial provision for the petitioner or respondent can be made by the judge or district judge when he pronounces decree nisi. The procedure laid down in the Family Proceedings Rules 1991, r. 2.61 should be observed (see Chapter 15, paragraph 11), application being made at any time before the district judge gives directions for trial. The district judge will then include in his certificate a statement that the petitioner/respondent (whichever is appropriate) is entitled to an order as agreed. The draft order then becomes an order of the court on pronouncement of decree nisi by the judge or district judge in accordance with the district judge's certificate. However, the order itself will not become effective until after decree absolute. Alternatively, the parties' agreement as to financial provision can be made a rule of court; the district judge can give a direction to this effect.

Further details of the law and procedure in relation to financial matters are given in Part III.

10.2.2   District judge not satisfied

If the district judge is not satisfied that the petitioner is entitled to a decree he can do one of two things:

(a)   He can give the petitioner the opportunity to file further evidence: in this case, the petitioner will receive a notice from the court stating that the district judge is not satisfied and giving the reason for this. The district judge may tell the petitioner in the notice what further evidence he requires or he may leave it up to the petitioner to produce what further evidence she can. The district judge will direct the petitioner as to the way in which further evidence should be given. Normally this will be by way of further affidavits but the district judge has power to request the petitioner to attend to give oral evidence before him.

Example. The petitioner does not name the co-respondent in her adultery petition. The district judge is not satisfied as to the adultery on the basis of the petition and supporting affidavit and he feels that it should be possible to identify the other party to the adultery. He directs that the petitioner should make all reasonable enquiries to trace and identify the person with whom the respondent has committed adultery and, if successful, should apply for leave to file an amended petition naming that person as co-respondent or, if unsuccessful, should file a further affidavit setting out the efforts she had made to trace and identify that person.

Once the petitioner has complied with the district judge's direction he will reconsider the case and decide whether to grant his certificate or to remove the case from the special procedure list with the result that a hearing before a judge in open court will be necessary (see (b) below).

(b) He can remove the case from the special procedure list: if the district judge does this he will normally refer the case for hearing by a judge in open court (see paragraph 12 below). If he does not fix a date for a hearing before a judge automatically, the petitioner can seek a hearing date in front of a judge by applying for directions for trial in the ordinary way.

It is important to realise that no order that the district judge makes can amount to a final refusal of a decree. It is only the judge who can finally dismiss the petition and in practice he will rarely find it necessary to do this.

11 PRONOUNCEMENT OF DECREE NISI

If the district judge has certified that the petitioner is entitled to a decree, decree nisi will be pronounced by a judge or district judge in open court on the day fixed by the district judge.

The pronouncement of the decree is unexciting. It is quite likely that all that will happen is that the clerk of the court or the judge or district judge himself will read out a list of cases and ask if there are any applications in these cases (for example, objections as to costs or attempts by respondents to prevent the pronouncement of the decree by having the district judge's certificate set aside and seeking leave to file an answer). Once any applications are dealt with, the judge or district judge will then announce that decrees are pronounced in all the cases listed and that other relief is granted in accordance with the district judge's certificate. When the judge or district judge grants other relief in accordance with the district judge's certificate, this means that if the district judge has certified that the petitioner is entitled to costs or that the petitioner or respondent is entitled to agreed financial provision (see paragraph 10.2.1) an order of the court is automatically made to that effect. This saves the judge or district judge the trouble of going through all the cases on his list ordering costs here and financial provision there as appropriate.

Both parties can attend the pronouncement of the decree if they wish but it is not normally necessary for either to attend. However, if the respondent is making an objection to a claim by the petitioner for costs and the district judge has referred the question to the judge or district judge who is to pronounce decree nisi, it will be necessary for the respondent to attend the hearing to put his arguments on costs to the court if he wishes to pursue his objection to the bitter end (see paragraph 10.2.1). The petitioner will be aware that the question of costs has been referred to the judge or district judge from the notice she received from the court when the case was placed on the special procedure list and the district judge's certificate granted. She has no need to attend to argue her side of the costs question but she can do so if she wishes, for example, she may well wish to do so if the case was defended at some stage and her costs are therefore high.

12   CASES REFERRED TO THE JUDGE

It can happen that the district judge is not satisfied with the petitioner's case and refers it for hearing in front of the judge (see paragraph 10.2.2 above). The hearing will take place in open court and the petitioner must attend as she will be required to give oral evidence on oath in support of her petition. Legal aid is available for such hearings (see Chapter 6 paragraph 3), so the petitioner will normally be represented by her solicitor or by counsel.

The judge will consider the evidence and decide whether to grant the petitioner a decree nisi. If he decides to do so, decree nisi will be pronounced there and then and the judge will make whatever order as to costs he thinks fit. He will normally refer all ancillary matters to chambers for determination. Once decree nisi has been pronounced, the case will proceed in exactly the same way as a case dealt with under the special procedure.

If the judge decides that the petitioner is not entitled to a decree (for example, in a s. 1(2)(b) case he may take the view that the behaviour of which the petitioner complains is not such that she cannot reasonably be expected to live with the respondent), he will dismiss her petition and will make whatever order as to costs he thinks fit. Apart from the possibility of an appeal against the judge's order, this is the end of the petition as far as the petitioner is concerned.

13   CONSIDERATION OF ARRANGEMENTS FOR THE CHILDREN OF THE FAMILY

The Children Act 1989 has brought significant procedural changes to the method by which the court considers and approves arrangements for the children on divorce. The Family Proceedings Rules 1991, r. 2.39 now place the main burden of 'considering' those arrangements upon the district judge, whereas under the old law the judge used to hear the 'children's appointments'.

The new version of s. 41 of the Matrimonial Causes Act 1973 (as substituted by sch. 12, para. 31 of the Children Act 1989), requires that in any proceedings for divorce, judicial separation or nullity the court must *consider*, at the date on which the court considers the arrangements:

(a)   whether there is any child of the family who has not reached the age of 16; and

(b)   whether there is a child who has reached 16 in respect of whom it should direct that s. 41 should apply.

In practice this duty will usually be carried out by the district judge in special procedure cases where there is no application for an order under Part I or Part II of the Children Act 1989 pending in respect of a child of the family.

13.1   Where there is no application for an order under Part I or Part II of the Children Act 1989 pending

The district judge will consider the arrangements that are proposed for the upbringing and welfare of the children immediately after making his certificate of decree nisi under the Family Proceedings Rules 1991, r. 2.36(1). He will then consider whether he should exercise any of his powers under the Children Act 1989 with respect to any of the children of the family. He will do this by a close examination of the Form M4 which has been filed with the divorce petition. Usually it is the petitioner who has submitted it. The respondent is perfectly entitled to file a Form M4 if he wishes, but it is rare to find this in practice.

In examining the Form M4 the district judge will look for anything in the proposed arrangements which may be unsatisfactory so far as the children are concerned. He will look to see that there is, for example, adequate accommodation, education, health care and financial provision for the child.

If the district judge considers, pursuant to s. 41(2), Matrimonial Causes Act 1973 (as substituted), that:

(a)   the exercise of his powers is, or is likely to be, necessary but the court is not in a position to exercise them without further consideration, *and*

(b)   there are *exceptional* circumstances which make it desirable in the interests of the child to do so,

then he may direct that a decree of divorce or nullity be not made absolute, or a decree of judicial separation be not granted, until the court orders otherwise.

If, however, the court is satisfied, pursuant to the Family Proceedings Rules 1991, r. 2.39(2), that either:

(a)   there are no children of the family to whom s. 41 applies, or

(b)   there are such children, but that the court need not exercise its powers or make a direction under s. 41,

then the district judge will certify accordingly.

13.1.1   What happens if the district judge is not satisfied with the proposed arrangements?

If the district judge is not satisfied with the proposed arrangements for the children then he may give one of the following directions, pursuant to the Family Proceedings Rules 1991, r. 2.39(3):

(a)   that the parties, or any of them, shall file further evidence as to the arrangements for the children (the exact nature of the information required may be specified e.g. a medical report);

(b)   that a welfare report be prepared;

(c)   that the parties, or any of them, shall attend before him. (N.B. Legal aid: under the old law practitioners acting for petitioners under the green form scheme have rarely attended s. 41 appointments. However, where a direction for attendance is made under r. 2.39(3)(c) it might well be prudent to seek a representation certificate: see para. 5A of Part II of s. 2, Legal Aid Act 1988 – imported by reg. 2 of the Civil Legal Aid (Matrimonial Proceedings) Regulations 1989.)

Example 1: The Form M4 filed by Mrs Plum revealed that the three year old child of the family, Tracy, was living with Mrs Plum and was suffering from leukaemia.

However, the form gave no information as to whether the child was still being treated for the illness or not. The district judge then asked the petitioner to file a medical report in relation to the child. The medical report showed that the child's treatment was being satisfactorily undertaken by the health authorities and that the parents were cooperating with the treatment programme. The district judge decided there was no need to look any further into the matter.

Example 2: The facts are as in example 1 above but Mrs Plum failed to file any medical report. The district judge asked Mr and Mrs Plum to attend at court for an appointment with him so that he could find out from them the reasons for their failure to give the information requested. The parties failed to attend the appointment. The district judge decided to order a court welfare officer's report in respect of Tracy. He was reluctant to take this step unless it was absolutely necessary because he knew that generally it took two or three months for such a report to be compiled. However, there appeared to be no other way of obtaining proper information about Tracy.

Example 3: The facts are as in example 2 above. The court welfare officer tried to make an appointment with Mr and Mrs Plum on many occasions but they refused to see her on any basis. The court welfare officer reported the difficulties to the court. The district judge applied the cumulative test in s. 41(2), Matrimonial Causes Act 1973 and found that the circumstances of the case might well require the court to exercise some of its powers under the Children Act 1989: s. 41(2)(a) (1973 Act) (e.g. to ask the local authority to investigate the case and to report to the court as to whether it wished to take any action in relation to the child: s. 37 Children Act 1989). Applying the next limb of the test (s. 41(2)(b) (1973 Act)), the district judge considered that he was not in a position to exercise that power without giving further consideration to the case. He wished to extend to the parties a final invitation to attend court for an appointment with him, along with a clear warning as to the consequences that might follow if they refused. He then applied the third, cumulative, part of the test in s. 41(2) and considered that there were 'exceptional circumstances' in this case which made it desirable in the interests of Tracy that he should direct that the decree was not to be made absolute until the outstanding problems had been resolved.

It seems clear from the wording of s. 41(2) that the intention of Parliament was that decree absolute should not be withheld lightly. The cumulative requirements of s. 41(2) make it clear that it should be a power used only in 'exceptional circumstances'. What will constitute 'exceptional circumstances' in this context only time and the evolution of caselaw will tell.

General examples of matters which might cause the district judge to consider whether the court is, or is likely to be, required to exercise any of its powers under the Children Act 1989 are as follows:

13.1.1.1   Accommodation   Where the parties are living in cramped accommodation (for example, three children with the petitioner and her parents and brother in a two-bedroomed flat), or in unsuitable accommodation (for example, a rented flat with no bathroom over a nightclub), or where there is doubt as to the petitioner's security of tenure over the accommodation (for example, where she has been served with notice to quit). In such circumstances the district judge may want the court welfare officer to look at the accommodation, or he may require documentary evidence that the petitioner will soon be able to provide suitable accommodation, for example, a letter from the council promising her accommodation within a limited period of time.

13.1.1.2 Financial provision Provided that the petitioner has sufficient money to look after the children the fact that it comes from social security payments rather than from the respondent will not usually cause the district judge concern. If, however, the district judge does take the view that the interests of the children require the respondent to make a contribution, or an increased contribution, to their maintenance then he could probably exercise his powers under s. 15 and sch. 1, Children Act 1989 to ensure that an appropriate order for financial provision in respect of the children is made.

13.1.1.3 Disputes over residence of and contact with the child If it is clear that the parents are in dispute as to where the child should live and how much contact, if any, he should have with the parent with whom he is not residing, then it is likely that one or other of the parties will apply for a section 8 order. If no application has yet been made for a section 8 order by the time the district judge comes to consider the arrangements for the children then the district judge may well arrange an appointment for the parties to come to court and see him. He might well point out to them the relevant applications they might make to resolve the issue. If a section 8 application is then made, the issue will automatically fall to be determined by the judge in any event, and the district judge need not consider the issue further.

If, however, the parties do not take any steps to seek a section 8 order it is not clear to what extent the district judge will inquire further into the matter. If, in due course, the parents make it clear that neither of them wishes to make an application, and all of the other circumstances relating to the child appear satisfactory, then the authors would tentatively submit that the court is unlikely to take the view that it should interfere further. In that case, the court will certify under the Family Proceedings Rules 1991, r. 2.39(2)(b) that there is no need for the court to exercise any of its powers under the Children Act 1989 or to give any direction under s. 41(2), Matrimonial Causes Act 1973. However, practice will no doubt vary from court to court and only time will tell how these new provisions will develop and evolve.

13.2 Where an application for an order under Part I or Part II of the Children Act 1989 is pending

Where an application for an order under Part I or Part II of the Children Act 1989 is pending then it will not be necessary for the district judge to consider the arrangements for the children because they will be fully considered in due course by the court which disposes of the application. The fact that an application, for example, for a residence or contact order, is merely contained in the prayer of the petition would not be sufficient to relieve the district judge of the duty to consider the arrangements for the children. There must be an actual notice of application before the district judge is no longer required to consider the arrangements.

Where an application for an order under Part I or Part II of the Children Act 1989 is pending in the magistrates' court prior to the commencement of the cause then the usual practice would be for the magistrates to transfer the application to the county court so that all matters could be heard together. In that case the district judge would not be required to consider the arrangements for the children, since they would be dealt with in the disposal of the application.

If an application were to be made to the magistrates' court *after* the commencement of the cause then the Family Proceedings Rules 1991, r. 2.40, require that the application be made within the cause.

14   DECREE ABSOLUTE

14.1   The need for decree absolute

The first divorce granted to a petitioner is a decree nisi. This does not free the petitioner or the respondent from the marriage. The marriage is ony dissolved once decree absolute is obtained.

14.2   Application for decree absolute

A decree nisi may normally not be made absolute before the expiration of six weeks from the date on which it is granted (s. 1(5), Matrimonial Causes Act 1973 as varied). There is power to expedite decree absolute but it is rarely used (see paragraph 14.5).

As soon as the six-week period expires, the petitioner can apply for decree absolute by lodging with the district judge a notice in Form M8 (Family Proceedings Rules 1991, r. 2.49(1) and Appendix 1). There is no need to give the respondent notice of the application.

When he receives Form M8, the district judge searches the court minutes in relation to the case. He has to satisfy himself on various matters which are set out in full in the Family Proceedings Rules 1991, r. 2.49(2). In a nutshell, he must be sure:

(a)   that the court has complied with the duty to consider the arrangements for the children under s. 41, Matrimonial Caues Act 1973 and has not given any direction under s. 41(2) that requires the decree not to be made absolute;

(b)   that no-one is trying to upset the decree nisi by means of an appeal or an application for re-hearing;

(c)   that no intervention is pending by the Queen's Proctor or by any other person to show why the decree should not be made absolute;

(d)   that the provisions of s. 10(2) to (4), Matrimonial Causes Act 1973 (consideration of the respondent's financial position after the divorce) either do not apply or have been complied with.

If the district judge is satisfied as to the matters set out in r. 2.49(2), he will make the decree absolute.

Both the petitioner and the respondent will be sent a certificate in Form M9 (Family Proceedings Rules 1991, Appendix 1) certifying that the decree nisi has been made final and absolute and giving the date on which this was done.

As soon as the decree is made absolute, the petitioner and respondent are both released from the marriage and are free to remarry should they wish to do so.

14.3   Application by respondent

If the petitioner does not apply to have the decree made absolute, once three months have elapsed from the earliest date on which the petitioner could have applied for decree absolute, the respondent may make application for decree absolute (s. 9(2), Matrimonial Causes Act 1973). The earliest that the respondent can apply is therefore three months and six weeks after the pronouncement of decree nisi.

The respondent's application may be made to a judge or to a district judge. Notice of the application must be served on the petitioner not less than four clear days before the day on which the application is heard (Family Proceedings Rules 1991, r. 2.50(2)).

14.4 District judge can require affidavit

If application is not made to have the decree made absolute until after 12 months have elapsed after decree nisi was granted, the notice in Form M8 must be accompanied by a written explanation giving reasons for the delay, stating whether the parties have lived together since decree nisi and, if so, between what dates, and stating (if the wife is the applicant) whether the wife has given birth to any child since the decree or (if the husband is the applicant) whether the husband has reason to believe that the wife has given birth to such a child and, in either case, if so, stating the relevant facts and whether it is alleged that the child is or may be a child of the family. The district judge may require the explanation to be verified by an affidavit from the applicant and may make such order on the application as he thinks fit. In particular he must ensure that s. 41, Matrimonial Causes Act 1973 has been complied with where it appears that there is, or may be, a child of the family born since decree nisi (Family Proceedings Rules 1991, r. 2.49(2)).

14.5 Expediting decree absolute

If there is some urgency about obtaining decree absolute, it is possible to apply for a special order giving leave to expedite decree absolute. However, the normal six-week waiting period between decree nisi and decree absolute is so short that it should very rarely be necessary to do so (Practice Direction [1977] 2 All ER 714, [1977] 1 WLR 759).

It is suggested that, in urgent cases, rather than attacking the problem after decree nisi, the solicitor should make efforts to speed things up at an earlier stage. Naturally this means him dealing with his own part of the case (drafting the petition, etc.) expeditiously. It is also suggested that the solicitor should write a letter to the court to accompany the petitioner's Form M7 affidavit explaining the urgency and asking the court to ensure that the district judge gives directions as soon as possible and fixes an early date for the pronouncement of decree nisi. This is the proper practice in cases proceeding under the ordinary procedure (Practice Direction [1964] 3 All ER 775, [1964] 1 WLR 1473) and there is no reason why it should not apply also to special procedure cases.

9 Amended, supplemental and new petitions

1 AMENDMENT, SUPPLEMENTAL PETITION OR FRESH PETITION?

It is important to recognise which matters can be the subject of an amendment of the petition and which necessitate the filing of a supplemental petition or of a completely fresh petition.

1.1 Addition of s. 1(2), Matrimonial Causes Act 1973 facts

(a)   Where the new facts arose before the date of the petition: if the petitioner wishes to add to the petition an additional s. 1(2) fact which arose before the date of the original petition, she may do so by means of a straightforward amendment.

> **Example 1.** In January 1987 the wife discovers that her husband has committed adultery at Christmas. His behaviour towards her has been violent and unpleasant since the beginning of the marriage and this is the last straw. She leaves him immediately and files a petition based on his adultery. Contrary to expectations the respondent indicates that he intends to deny the allegation of adultery and the petitioner's solicitors decide that it would be prudent to add an allegation of behaviour under s. 1(2)(b). This can be done by amendment of the original petition because the behaviour alleged occurred before the date of the original petition.

(b)   Where the new fact arose after the date of the petition: a petition cannot be amended to add new s. 1(2) facts that have arisen after the date of the original petition. This rules out not only straightforward amendments to the original petition but also the filing of a supplemental petition which (although a separate document) is, in effect, another means of amending the original petition. The petitioner wishing to add a s. 1(2) fact that has arisen (or, in the case of a separation fact, has been completed) since the date of the original petition must therefore file a fresh petition.

> **Example 2.** In January 1985 the petitioner leaves the respondent and files a petition based on his adultery. The respondent defends the petition and the matter drags on into 1987. By this time the parties have been separated for two years and the respondent is prepared to consent to a decree. The petitioner now wishes to seek a decree on the basis of s. 1(2)(d) (two years' separation and consent). She cannot do this by amendment of the original petition because the two years' separation were not complete at the date of the original petition nor, for the same reason, can she file a supplemental petition. She must file a fresh petition based on s. 1(2)(d).

1.2 Addition or amendment other than the addition of new s. 1(2) facts

(a)   To take account of matters arising before the date of the petition: this can be done by means of a straightforward amendment to the original petition or, in the case of very minor corrections in special procedure cases, through the petitioner's Form M7 affidavit.

Example 1. The petitioner files a petition based on s. 1(2)(b) without first consulting a solicitor. She then seeks legal advice before obtaining decree nisi. It is clear to her solicitor that her petition is inadequate as it stands and that there are other allegations of behaviour on the part of the respondent before the date of the petition which should properly be added. This can be done by amendment of the petition.

Example 2. In the petition the date of birth of one of the children is given incorrectly as 1 June 1975. It should be 2 June 1975. This is a minor correction and can be dealt with by means of the petitioner's Form M7 affidavit.

(b) To take account of matters arising after the date of the petition: certain matters arising after the date of the petition can be dealt with by means of a straightforward amendment, for example, the petition can be amended to add details of a child born after the date of the petition.

However, if the petitioner wishes to add further allegations to the particulars of the s. 1(2) fact on which the petition is based in respect of incidents which arose after the date of the petition, she will have to file a supplemental petition.

Example. In January 1985 the petitioner files a petition based on the respondent's behaviour (s. 1(2)(b)). The parties continue to live together after the petition is filed and nothing is done about the divorce. However, in 1987 the petitioner leaves the respondent because of his unpleasant and violent behaviour which has continued since the date of the divorce petiton. She wishes to proceed with the divorce. If the petitioner attempts to proceed on the basis of the petition as it stands she will find herself in difficulty in view of the long period of cohabitation that has followed the last incident of behaviour alleged (well in excess of the six-month period that s. 2(3) says should be disregarded). She cannot amend the petition to add further incidents of behaviour that have arisen between 1985 and 1987 as these post-date the petition. She will have to file a supplemental petition alleging further incidents of behaviour during this period.

2 PROCEDURE FOR AMENDMENT

In theory amendments can be made up until the date of decree absolute. In practice it will rarely be necessary or appropriate to make amendments after decree nisi.

The standard procedure for amendment is set out in the Family Proceedings Rules 1991, r. 2.11. The solicitor should prepare an amended petition with the amendments clearly shown in red:

(a) Where an answer has not yet been filed a petition may be amended without leave (Family Proceedings Rules 1991, r. 2.11(1)(b)).

The amended petition should then be filed at court together with the appropriate number of copies for service (see Chapter 8 paragraph 1.1). It will be served on the respondent (and co-respondent) in the normal way.

(b) Once an answer has been filed, leave is required and, whether an answer has been filed or not, once directions for trial have been given no pleading may be filed or amended without leave (Family Proceedings Rules 1991, r. 2.14). A copy of the amended petition should first be sent to the respondent (and co-respondent) with a covering letter asking whether he would be prepared to consent to the proposed amendment. If he is prepared to consent in writing to the amendment an application for leave should be made ex parte to the district judge. If either the respondent or the co-respondent is not prepared to consent to the amendment, an application for leave will have to be made on notice to the district judge. If the district judge grants leave the amended petition must be filed at the court office with a copy for re-service on the respondent (and co-respondent). The district judge will make any further directions that have become necessary as a result of leave being granted, for example, where the respondent (or co-respondent) has given notice that he wishes to defend he will need time to amend his answer if he has already filed one or to file an answer to the amended petition if not, so the district judge will fix the time within which he must do this.

Where only a minor amendment to the petition is required (for example, the date of birth of a child of the family has been wrongly stated), it is not likely to be necessary to go through the standard procedure for amendment. It will usually be acceptable if the amendment is detailed in the petitioner's Form M7 affidavit. The district judge will almost certainly give leave for the petition to stand corrected as outlined in the affidavit without the need for re-service on the respondent or co-respondent. He will then proceed to consider the case as if the petition had originally been filed as corrected.

3 SUPPLEMENTAL PETITIONS

A supplemental petition is a separate document filed at some stage after the petition itself. It is not a new petition; it is part of the original petition and is used to make amendments to this where it is inappropriate to do so by means of a straightforward amendment in red of the original document. As we have seen (paragraph 1 above) a supplemental petition should always be used where the petitioner wishes to add to the particulars of the s. 1(2) fact on which her petition is based further allegations in respect of matters that arose *after* the date of the petition. If a supplemental petition is being prepared for this purpose and other amendments are required to the petition as well, the other amendments can conveniently be dealt with in the supplemental petition too, even though, had no supplemental petition been filed, they would have been made by means of a straightforward amendment.

A supplemental petition may be filed without leave at any time before an answer is filed, but thereafter only with leave (Family Proceedings Rules 1991, r. 2.11(1)(a)).

4 FRESH PETITIONS

As we have seen at paragraph 1 above, where alterations required to the original petition cannot be accomplished by means of amendment or supplemental petition, a fresh petition will be required. The most frequent use of a fresh petition is probably where the petitioner wishes to rely on a new s. 1(2) fact that has only arisen since the date of the original petition.

The procedure for filing a fresh petition depends on whether the original petition is still extant.

If the original petition has been dismissed (either because it has been discontinued by the petitioner before service (Family Proceedings Rules 1991, r. 2.8) or dismissed after service on the petitioner's application or after adjudication, or otherwise disposed of by final order, a fresh petition can be filed in the normal way without leave of the court.

It is quite likely, however, that the petitioner will not want to burn her boats by seeking to discontinue the first petition or to have it dismissed and will prefer to file a fresh petition whilst the original petition still stands. To do this she will require leave of the court (r. 2.6(4)). She will have to show good reason why two petitions should be on the go at the same time.

Example. Reference should be made to Example 2 given in paragraph 1.1 above. The petitioner in that example may well wish to preserve the first adultery petition until after she has obtained decree nisi on the s. 1(2)(d) petition just in case the respondent should decide to withdraw his consent to the decree before decree nisi. If the s. 1(2)(d) decree is granted without difficulty, the first petition should be dismissed at the same time. However, should the respondent withdraw his consent, the petitioner could resurrect the adultery petition and go on to attempt to prove adultery and obtain a decree on that basis.

10 Defended divorces

1 GENERAL

Gone are the days of the sensational divorce suit reported in detail on the front page of the national papers and attended by everyone who was anyone. Nowadays it is rare to see a divorce contested to the bitter end at all.

Partly this is due to the shift in emphasis in matrimonial law from looking for a culprit when a marriage breaks down to enabling the parties to extricate themselves from their unfortunate situation with the minimum of distress. There is no doubt, however, that it is also due to financial considerations (the cost of a defended suit can be enormous) and to the attitudes of judges and district judges concerned with divorce cases who will encourage the parties time and again to look for alternative ways of resolving their differences.

This book aims to deal with the routine matrimonial practice. Therefore, whilst the procedure for an undefended divorce is described in great detail in Chapter 8, the procedure in relation to defended divorce suits will be described in outline only in this chapter. The practitioner involved in a defended suit is referred to the specialist family law textbooks for further information.

2 LEGAL AID FOR DEFENDED DIVORCES

2.1 For the respondent

The respondent who consults a solicitor wishing to contest a divorce petition will find that the first hurdle he must overcome is the cost of the whole affair.

If the respondent is not financially eligible for legal aid his decision on cost is simple — can he afford to defend the case bearing in mind that he may not recover his costs, even if he is successful in having the petition dismissed?

The fact that the respondent *is* financially eligible for legal aid does not mean he can ignore the cost of the divorce:

(a) Despite the respondent's financial eligibility, legal aid will only be granted to him to defend the case if he satisfies the legal aid committee that he has reasonable grounds for defending the proceedings and it is not unreasonable for him to be granted legal aid (see Chapter 2 paragraph 12.2).

(b) If he is granted legal aid to defend, it will be limited to all steps up to and including discovery of documents and thereafter obtaining counsel's opinion on the merits of the cause continuing as a contested cause. This means that he can only go so far on his initial certificate. If he wants to go on from discovery of documents to a full contested hearing of the case, the papers will have to be sent to counsel for an opinion on the merits. Application will then have to be made to the committee to have the limitation on the certificate removed. The committee is only likely to agree to this if counsel's opinion is favourable.

(c)   Even if he is granted legal aid to cover the entire proceedings, a large part of the ultimate bill is likely to be met by the respondent himself out of his share of the family property because of the Legal Aid Board's statutory charge (see Chapter 2 paragraph 17 et seq.).

2.2   For the petitioner

The petitioner will not have had legal aid when she filed her petition; at most, she will have received advice and assistance under the green form scheme (see Chapter 6). If the respondent files an answer and the petitioner wishes to proceed with the petition, she will have to consider the cost of a defended suit just as the respondent must.

As soon as an answer is filed, the cause is looked upon as defended and legal aid is, therefore, theoretically available. However, if the petitioner is to be granted legal aid, she must satisfy the legal aid committee that it is reasonable for her to continue with the proceedings.

The Legal Aid Board's statutory charge will also affect the petitioner. Thus if she loses (i.e. her petition is dismissed) or if she otains a decree but fails to recover her costs, she too may find herself footing a large part of the legal aid bill from her share in the family property.

2.3   Is it reasonable to defend/proceed with the case?

Whether the legal aid committee will be prepared to accept that it is reasonable for the respondent or the petitioner to defend the petition or to proceed with the petition after an answer has been filed will depend on the particular facts of the case. Legal aid will not, however, be granted/continued if there is a suitable alternative way of proceeding with the case.

> **Example.** A petition is filed based on behaviour (s. 1(2)(b), Matrimonial Causes Act 1973). The petitioner is not legally aided. The respondent is legally aided. He obtains legal aid to file an answer denying the behaviour and cross-petition on the basis of the petitioner's adultery. The petitioner denies the adultery. Although it is clear that both parties want a divorce, the case drags on with both parties maintaining their positions.
>
> Eventually two years elapse, during which the parties have lived apart. It would therefore be possible for one or the other party to obtain a decree on the non-contentious basis of two years' separation and consent. Both parties are willing to present a petition based on s. 1(2)(d) but neither party is willing to give consent to the other party obtaining the decree — each wants to obtain the decree *himself*. At this point, it is necessary for the respondent to seek counsel's opinion as discovery of documents has taken place and he needs to have the limitation on his legal aid certificate lifted before he can go any further with the case. Counsel advises that the only reasonable course is for a decree to be obtained on the basis of s. 1(2)(d). In all probability, therefore, the respondent's legal aid certificate will be terminated and he will be forced, by financial considerations, to agree to a divorce on the basis of s. 1(2)(d).

3   OUTLINE OF PROCEDURE IN A DEFENDED CAUSE

(a)   Notice of intention to defend: the respondent/co-respondent returns the acknowledgment of service giving notice of his intention to defend. The time for giving notice of intention to defend is seven days from service of the petition, inclusive of the day of service (Family Proceedings Rules 1991, r. 10.8(2)(a)).

(b)   Filing an answer — the normal procedure: a respondent/co-respondent who wishes to defend the petition or dispute any of the facts alleged in it, or a respondent who wishes to make in the proceedings any charge against the petitioner in respect of which the respondent prays for relief, or to oppose the grant of a decree on the basis of s. 5(1), Matrimonial Causes Act 1973 (grave financial or other hardship), shall file an answer within 21 days after the expiration of the time limit for giving notice of intention to defend, i.e. within 28 days after service of the petition inclusive of the day of service (Family Proceedings Rules 1991, r. 2.12(1)).

Note: (i)   An answer may be filed even though the party concerned has not given notice of his intention to defend (r. 2.12(2)).

(ii)   No answer is necessary merely to contest the petitioner's claim for costs (for the procedure for contesting costs, see Chapter 8 paragraph 10.2.1), or to contest the petitioner's claim for an order under Part I or Part II of the Children Act 1989 or in relation to ancillary relief.

(c)   Filing an answer — after directions for trial given: it is not unknown for the respondent/co-respondent to make up his mind that he wants to defend only after directions for trial have been given. The case will normally have proceeded under the special procedure up to this point and the chances are that the district judge will therefore have granted his certificate that the petitioner is entitled to a decree (see Chapter 8 paragraph 10.2.1). The district judge's certificate is tantamount to decree nisi (*Day* v *Day* [1980] Fam 29, [1979] 2 All ER 187). To enable the respondent/co-respondent to defend, it will therefore be necessary for him to:

(i)   apply to the district judge before decree nisi is pronounced to have his certificate set aside; *and*

(ii)   in accordance with Family Proceedings Rules 1991, r. 2.14 seek leave from the district judge to file an answer out of time.

It may be an uphill battle to persuade the district judge to make the necessary orders to permit the respondent/co-respondent to defend.

Should the respondent/co-respondent only decide to defend immediately before decree nisi is pronounced, a last ditch attempt can be made to enable him to do so. The respondent/co-respondent should attend court for the pronouncement of decree nisi and should notify the court clerk before the day's list begins that he wishes to make an application in relation to the case. He should then ask the judge or district judge (see r. 2.36(2)) to adjourn the case for a limited period to enable him to make the necessary applications to the district judge. If there is time, the solicitor can contact the court himself by letter or telephone to explain the situation. If he is advising his client under the green form scheme, he cannot, of course, attend court to deal with the matter for the client unless he does so without payment.

(d)   Transfer to High Court: when the answer is filed, the district judge may order that the cause be transferred to the High Court (s. 39, Matrimonial and

Family Proceedings Act 1984). Transfer to the High Court is no longer mandatory.

(e) Subsequent procedure: a reply to the answer may be filed. Thereafter, once pleadings are closed, discovery and inspection will take place, directions for trial will be given and the cause will proceed ultimately to a full hearing at which the judge will examine the evidence given by both parties and decide whether a decree should be granted. This gives the impression that a defended divorce will be resolved one way or the other speedily and clinically. The chances are, on the contrary, that the proceedings will be fraught with emotion and protracted over a long period of time.

11 Protection of respondents in separation cases, ss. 5 and 10, Matrimonial Causes Act 1973

Applications under ss. 5 and 10, Matrimonial Causes Act 1973 are normally made by wives. Therefore this chapter departs from the practice adopted in much of the rest of the book and assumes that the wife is the respondent.

1 SECTION 5, MATRIMONIAL CAUSES ACT 1973 — GRAVE FINANCIAL OR OTHER HARDSHIP

1.1 Provisions of s. 5(1)

Where a divorce petition is based on five years' separation (s. 1(2)(e), Matrimonial Causes Act 1973), the respondent may oppose the granting of a decree on the ground that the dissolution of the marriage will result in grave financial or other hardship to her and that it would in all the circumstances be wrong to dissolve the marriage (s. 5(1)).

1.2 Effect of s. 5 defence

Where the only fact on which the petitioner is entitled to rely is s. 1(2)(e), the court will have to dismiss the petition if it finds that the respondent's s. 5 defence is made out (s. 5(2)). There is no point, however, in the respondent raising a defence under s. 5 where the petitioner relies on and can establish alternative s. 1(2) facts as well. The s. 5 defence only operates in relation to s. 1(2)(e); therefore the petitioner would be able to go on to obtain a decree on the basis of one of the alternative facts despite the respondent's objection.

1.3 Hardship

1.3.1 Generally
Whether the respondent relies on financial hardship or some other form of hardship, she must show:

    (a) that it would be grave: divorce almost inevitably causes a certain amount of hardship — the hardship must be very serious; *and*

    (b) that it would result from the dissolution of the marriage: if the respondent's hardship arises, in fact, from the breakdown of the marriage rather than from the divorce, she will not be able to establish a s. 5 defence.

Section 5(3) specifically provides that hardship shall include the loss of the chance of acquiring any benefit which the respondent might acquire if the marriage were not dissolved (for example, widow's pension benefits).

1.3.2 Financial hardship

In deciding whether the respondent will suffer grave financial hardship, the court is entitled to look not only at what the respondent will lose as a result of the divorce (for example, possible pension rights) but also at what she will gain (for example, income support) (*Reiterbund* v *Reiterbund* [1974] 2 All ER 455, [1974] 1 WLR 788 affirmed by Court of Appeal [1975] Fam 99, [1975] 1 All ER 280).

Where the respondent sets up a prima facie case of hardship, the petitioner will usually seek to put forward proposals (for example, the provision of an annuity to replace lost pension rights) to alleviate the hardship and the court will then decide whether the proposals are sufficient. If the petitioner's best proposals are not sufficient to remove the hardship, the petition will be dismissed (see, for example, *Le Marchant* v *Le Marchant* [1977] 3 All ER 610, [1977] 1 WLR 559).

1.3.3 Other hardship

Most reported cases on 'other hardship' have concerned foreign wives who have claimed hardship on social and religious grounds (see, for example, *Banik* v *Banik* [1973] 3 All ER 45, [1973] 1 WLR 860). Their efforts to defend on this basis have generally met with failure.

1.4 Wrong in all the circumstances to dissolve the marriage

It is possible for the court to grant a decree despite the fact that the respondent has established grave hardship. This is because the court will only dismiss the petition if it considers it would be wrong in all the circumstances to dissolve the marriage.

Section 5(2) provides that the circumstances the court must consider include the conduct of the parties to the marriage and the interests of those parties and of any children or other persons concerned. The court can also consider any other relevant circumstances, for example, that the petitioner intends to remarry, and can consider the broader aspect of the case, i.e. whether a marriage which has hopelessly broken down long ago should be preserved or whether it is not right in the public interest to terminate it (see, for example, *Mathias* v *Mathias* [1972] Fam 287, [1972] 3 All ER 1, and *Brickell* v *Brickell* [1974] Fam 31, [1973] 3 All ER 508).

1.5 Procedure

If the respondent wishes to raise a s. 5 defence, she must do so by filing an answer setting out her contentions.

She would be well advised to make a claim under s. 10(2), Matrimonial Causes Act 1973 (a less radical provision) as an alternative (see paragraph 2.1 below).

2 SECTION 10, MATRIMONIAL CAUSES ACT 1973

2.1 Section 10(2): prevention of decree absolute pending consideration of respondent's financial position

2.1.1 When can s. 10(2) be used?

Where the petition is based on two years' separation and consent or on five years' separation, the respondent is entitled to apply to the court for consideration of her financial position after the divorce (s. 10(2)). The court will not consider the respondent's position under s. 10 where a finding has been made as to any other fact mentioned in s. 1(2), Matrimonial Causes Act 1973 (i.e. adultery, behaviour or desertion) as well as a finding under s. 1(2)(d) or (e).

The time for consideration of the respondent's position is between decree nisi and decree absolute.

2.1.2   Section 10(3) and (4)

Section 10(3) provides that, where the respondent makes an application under s. 10(2), the court shall not make the decree absolute unless it is satisfied:

(a)   that the petitioner should not be required to make any financial provision for the respondent; *or*

(b)   that the financial provision made by the petitioner for the respondent is reasonable and fair or the best that can be made in the circumstances.

Section 10(4) relaxes the provisions of s. 10(3) slightly by providing that the court can make the decree absolute notwithstanding the requirements of s. 10(3) if:

(a)   it appears to the court that there are circumstances making it desirable that the decree should be made absolute without delay; *and*

(b)   the court has obtained a satisfactory undertaking from the petitioner that he will make such financial provisions for the respondent as the court may approve.

2.1.3   Circumstances to be considered

The court hearing a s. 10(2) application must consider all the circumstances including the age, health, conduct, earning capacity, financial resources and financial obligations of each of the parties and the financial position of the respondent as, having regard to the divorce, it is likely to be after the death of the petitioner, should the petitioner die first (s. 10(3)).

2.1.4   Section 10(2) — a delaying tactic, not a defence

The respondent cannot prevent a divorce being granted by making an application under s. 10(2). What she can do is substantially delay the granting of decree absolute, thus, assuming that the petitioner is anxious to have the divorce made final as soon as possible (for example, so that he can remarry), putting pressure on the petitioner to make acceptable financial arrangements for her.

> **Example.** The husband, who wishes to remarry, issues a petition based on five years' separation. He is a wealthy man. The wife has very little in her own right. The parties are unable to reach any agreement over property and finance. The wife makes an application under s. 10(2) for consideration of her financial position after the divorce. Decree nisi is granted on the basis of five years' separation. The husband cannot obtain decree absolute until after the question of the wife's finances is sorted out. Therefore, in view of his wish to remarry, he is put under pressure to come up with a sensible offer of a settlement.

In a sense, of course, in a s. 1(2)(d) case (two years' separation and consent), s. 10(2) merely reinforces the bargaining power which the respondent already has in that she can withhold her consent until financial matters are sorted out to her satisfaction. In a s. 1(2)(e) case, however, the respondent has no bargaining power and s. 10(2) can be used to give her a valuable lever over the petitioner.

2.1.5   Procedure

A s. 10(2) application must be made by notice in Form M12 (Family Proceedings Rules 1991, r. 2.45(1)).

The considerations taken into account by the court are very similar to those listed in s. 25, Matrimonial Causes Act 1973 for consideration on ancillary relief applications. In practice, the respondent will usually make her s. 10(2) application together with a comprehensive application for ancillary relief under ss. 23 and 24, Matrimonial Causes Act 1973 and the two applications will normally be heard at the same time. It is convenient for one affidavit to be filed in support of both applications.

It would seem that the same approach should be adopted in respect of both applications (see, for example, *Krystman* v *Krystman* [1973] 3 All ER 247, [1973] 1 WLR 927, and *Lombardi* v *Lombardi* [1973] 3 All ER 625, [1973] 1 WLR 1276). Thus it is likely that the hearing of the applications will be virtually indistinguishable from a normal ancillary relief hearing except that, as well as making ancillary relief orders, the court will be asked to make an order under s. 10(3) approving the financial provision so as to enable the petitioner to go on to obtain decree absolute.

2.2   Section 10(1): rescission of decree nisi under s. 1(2)(d)

By virtue of s. 10(1), where the court has granted a decree nisi of divorce on the basis only of two years' separation and consent, the court may rescind the decree on the respondent's application if it is satisfied that the petitioner misled the respondent (whether intentionally or unintentionally) about any matter which the respondent took into account in deciding to give his consent.

The respondent must apply before the decree is made absolute.

12   *Judicial separation*

1   THE GROUNDS FOR JUDICIAL SEPARATION: S. 17, MATRIMONIAL CAUSES ACT 1973

A petition for judicial separation may be presented to the court by either party to a marriage on the ground that any of the facts mentioned in s. 1(2), Matrimonial Causes Act 1973 exists (see Chapter 3 for a full discussion of the law concerning the s. 1(2) facts).

The provisions of s. 2, Matrimonial Causes Act 1973 concerning the effect of cohabitation in relation to the s. 1(2) facts apply as they do in the case of divorce (see Chapter 3 paragraph 10).

The court is not concerned to decide whether the marriage has broken down irretrievably. It merely has a duty to inquire, so far as it reasonably can, into the facts alleged by the petitioner (and the respondent if he files an answer).

2   THE APPLICATION OF SS. 6 AND 7, MATRIMONIAL CAUSES ACT 1973 TO JUDICIAL SEPARATION

By virtue of s. 17(3), the provision of ss. 6 and 7, Matrimonial Causes Act 1973 apply as they do with divorce.

Section 6(1) provides that rules of court shall be made requiring a solicitor *acting* for a petitioner to file a certificate as to whether he has discussed the possibility of a reconciliation with the petitioner. Family Proceedings Rules 1991, r. 2.6(3) provides that such a certificate shall be filed in Form M3 (see Chapter 8 paragraph 4.2).

Section 6(2) enables the court to adjourn the proceedings at any stage for reconciliation attempts if there appears to be a reasonable possibility of a reconciliation (see Chapter 1 paragraph 2.2).

Section 7 permits rules of court to be made to enable the parties to refer any agreement or arrangement that they have made or propose to make in connection with judicial separation for the court's opinion as to its reasonableness. No rules of court have yet been made so s. 7 remains a dead letter.

3   NO TIME RESTRICTION ON PETITION

Section 3, Matrimonial Causes Act 1973 (the one-year bar on divorce petitions) does not apply to judicial separation petitions. There is therefore no restriction on when a petition for judicial separation can be presented — if one of the s. 1(2) facts can be made out, a petition can be presented the day after the wedding.

4 SECTION 5, MATRIMONIAL CAUSES ACT 1973 NOT APPLICABLE

Section 5 (see Chapter 11) does not apply to petitions for judicial separation. It is therefore not possible for the respondent to defend the proceedings on the basis that a decree would result in grave financial or other hardship to him. The best that he can do if he is worried about his financial position is to make an application for ancillary relief under ss. 23 and 24, Matrimonial Causes Act 1973.

5 SECTION 10, MATRIMONIAL CAUSES ACT 1973 NOT APPLICABLE

Section 10 (see Chapter 11) does not apply either. The respondent cannot therefore seek to have the judicial separation decree granted on the ground of s. 1(2)(d) (two years' separation and consent) rescinded on the basis that the petitioner misled the respondent into giving his consent. Nor can the respondent in a case based on s. 1(2)(d) or s. 1(2)(e) (five years' separation) hold up the granting of a decree, as he can in divorce proceedings, by applying to have his financial position considered by the court.

6 THE PROCEDURE FOR SEEKING A DECREE OF JUDICIAL SEPARATION

The procedure for seeking a decree of judicial separation is virtually the same as the procedure for seeking a decree of divorce: see Chapter 8. The following points should be noted, however:

(a) There is only *one* decree of judicial separation as opposed to the two decrees (decree nisi and decree absolute) in divorce proceedings. There is therefore no need to apply to have the decree of judicial separation made absolute.

(b) The special procedure applies where appropriate. Doubtful cases can be referred for hearing in open court in front of a judge as they can with divorce. Judicial separation petitions can, of course, be defended in the same way as divorces but because a judicial separation decree does not finally dissolve the marriage, the incentive to do this may be rather weaker. If the petition is defended, the procedure for trial is the same as with a divorce although, as we have seen, the court will only be looking to see if the s. 1(2) fact is made out and will not be concerned with irretrievable breakdown.

(c) Although the petition in a judicial separation case will look almost the same as a divorce petition, irretrievable breakdown of the marriage will not be alleged and the prayer will be for judicial separation instead of dissolution of the marriage. Other documents such as the petitioner's Form M7 affidavit will also be amended accordingly.

(d) Whereas, with divorce, decree nisi will not be made absolute until the district judge has considered the proposed arrangements for any relevant child of the family, in the case of judicial separation no decree will be granted at all until the district judge has considered the s. 41 arrangements.

(e) The legal aid position is the same as it is with divorce cases; see Chapter 6. Legal aid is therefore only available in a limited class of judicial separation cases; the majority of cases will be dealt with under the green form scheme.

7   THE EFFECT OF THE DECREE: S. 18, MATRIMONIAL CAUSES ACT 1973

Where a decree of judicial separation is granted it does not terminate the marriage but it does have the following important consequences:

(a)   The petitioner is no longer bound to cohabit with the respondent (s. 18(1)). Of course, no one can force the petitioner to cohabit with the respondent even when there is no decree of judicial separation, so at first sight s. 18(1) seems to be stating the obvious. However, what it is designed to do is make it clear that neither the petitioner nor the respondent can be in desertion after the decree is granted by virtue of the fact that she or he declines thereafter to live with the other party.

(b)   If either party dies intestate whilst the decree is in force and the separation is continuing, his or her property devolves as if the other party to the marriage had been dead (s. 18(2)). Note, however, that, in contrast with the position on divorce, wills are unaffected by a decree of judicial separation. If the client has made a will leaving property to her spouse, she should therefore be advised that he will benefit under the will despite the judicial separation. If she does not wish this to happen, a new will should be made.

(c)   The court can make ancillary orders as to finances and property under ss. 23 and 24, Matrimonial Causes Act 1973. Note that, as with divorce, the court can also make orders for maintenance pending suit in respect of the period between the filing of the petition and pronouncement of the decree. See Chapter 14 for full details of the court's powers in relation to these matters.

(d)   Orders under Part I and Part II of the Children Act 1989 can be made by the court, pursuant to s. 41 of the Matrimonial Causes Act 1973, as substituted by the Children Act 1989, sch. 12, para. 31; see Chapter 26.

8   SUBSEQUENT DIVORCE: S. 4, MATRIMONIAL CAUSES ACT 1973

8.1   Judicial separation no bar to divorce

The parties are free to petition for divorce even after they have been granted a decree of judicial separation (s. 4(1)).

8.2   Procedure for seeking subsequent divorce

The most convenient way in which a subsequent divorce can be sought is for the divorce petition to be presented by the spouse who petitioned for the decree of judicial separation on the basis of the same facts. The court may then treat the decree of judicial separation as sufficient proof of the fact by reference to which it was granted.

The petitioner will have to establish irretrievable breakdown of the marriage which would not, of course, have been established at the time of the judicial separation decree. In practice, however, irretrievable breakdown is normally presumed once a s. 1(2) fact is proved so this should not present a problem (see Chapter 3 paragraph 3).

The petitioner must give evidence in support of her divorce petition in the normal way (usually in her Form M7 affidavit in support of her petition) even where the petition follows an earlier judicial separation (s. 4(2)).

One situation to watch out for is where the parties have resumed cohabitation since the date of the judicial separation decree. Where this has happened, the provisions of s. 2, Matrimonial Causes Act 1973 must be borne in mind. Note that it will not necessarily be only the period(s) of cohabitation that has/have taken place since the date of the decree that will be relevant. Reference must be had to the terms of the section in order to ascertain which period of cohabitation is relevant in relation to which s. 1(2) fact.

In some cases it will not be possible or desirable for the divorce petition to be put on the same basis as the judicial separation petition, for instance it may now be the other party who wishes to petition. In such situations the right approach is to examine the facts in the normal way to see whether any of the s. 1(2) facts can be made out independently of the judicial separation decree. The only bearing that the judicial separation decree has on this is that it prevents either party being in desertion after it has been granted.

Example. In 1990 the wife obtains a decree of judicial separation on the basis of her husband's adultery. The reason why the husband had committed adultery was, in fact, that the marriage had broken down owing to the wife's thoroughly unpleasant behaviour. In 1991 the husband decides that he wishes to petition for divorce. He cannot petition on the basis of his own adultery but he can file a petition based on his wife's behaviour (s. 1(2)(b)).

9 REASONS FOR SEEKING JUDICIAL SEPARATION

Although judicial separations are fairly rare these days, from time to time a case will arise in which it is appropriate to seek a decree of judicial separation. Judicial separation does have the following advantages over divorce:

(a)   There is no restriction as to when the petition can be presented. Judicial separation may therefore be useful during the first year of marriage when divorce is not permitted. However, the lack of restriction is clearly far less of an advantage than it was, now that the restriction on divorce has been reduced from three years to one year by s. 1, Matrimonial and Family Proceedings Act 1984. If the client really wishes to be divorced and is contemplating judicial separation as second-best, it will often be better for her to wait patiently until the first year of marriage is up rather than devote several months of that year to obtaining a decree of judicial separation only to spend more time the next year having it converted into a decree of divorce.

(b)   There are less likely to be religious objections on the part of either party to judicial separation than to divorce.

(c)   Some people find it less traumatic to accept the half-way house of a judicial separation than to sever their ties with their spouse completely by a divorce. Judicial separation enables them to have their cake and eat it — the fact that judicial separation does not enable them to remarry is of no consequence to them because they are in no state of mind to do so anyway and they *are* able to take advantage of the same wide powers of the court in relation to ancillary relief as they could after a divorce.

(d)   If the choice is between judicial separation and other methods of seeking financial relief during the marriage, for example, an application under s. 27,

Matrimonial Causes Act 1973 (see Chapter 32) or under the Domestic Proceedings and Magistrates' Courts Act 1978 (see Chapter 31), judicial separation has the advantage that the court's powers in relation to finances and property are more comprehensive. For example, the court can make orders for sale of the matrimonial home or transfer of specific assets from one party to the other after a judicial separation, whereas under s. 27 of the 1978 Act the court can only grant periodical payments and lump sum orders. However, for most clients seeking financial relief during the marriage, judicial separation will not fit the bill either because they are unable to make out any of the s. 1(2) facts and therefore cannot petition anyway, or because judicial separation seems too drastic a step. By far the majority of these clients will be advised to make an application to a magistrates' court under the Domestic Proceedings and Magistrates' Courts Act 1978. Insoluble problems over property can be dealt with during the marriage by an application under s. 17, Married Women's Property Act 1882 (see Chapter 34), although in practice such applications are avoided where possible.

13 Nullity

In the eyes of the law some marriages suffer from impediments which lead to them being either void or voidable. In relation to marriages celebrated after 31 July 1971 the grounds on which a marriage is void or voidable are contained in ss. 11 and 12, Matrimonial Causes Act 1973. The solicitor will rarely be called upon to deal with a marriage celebrated before this date.

1 THE NEED FOR A NULLITY DECREE

1.1 Void marriages

A void marriage is void *ab initio* and can, in theory, be treated by both parties as never having taken place without the need for a decree of nullity. However, it is almost always advisable to seek a decree even where the marriage clearly appears to be void. One reason for this is that most clients will wish to take advantage of the court's powers under the Matrimonial Causes Act 1973 to grant ancillary relief in relation to finance and property. These powers are only exercisable if a decree of nullity is sought. Another reason is that possession of a nullity decree puts the status of both parties beyond doubt (which is particularly important where one party does not agree that the marriage is void), thus avoiding complications that could arise, for example, when one party seeks to remarry.

1.2 Voidable marriages

Because a voidable marriage is valid unless and until a decree of nullity has been granted, a decree is essential.

2 VOID MARRIAGES: S. 11

A marriage shall be void on the following grounds only:

(a)   That it is not a valid marriage under the provisions of the Marriage Acts 1949 to 1983, i.e. where:

(i)   the parties are within the prohibited degrees of relationship (which can be relationship by blood or by marriage), for example, where they are father and daughter, brother and sister, son and step-mother; *or*
(ii)   either party is under the age of 16; *or*
(iii)   the parties have intermarried in disregard of certain requirements as to the formation of marriage, for example, where they marry according to the rites of the Church of England in a place which is not a church or other building

in which banns may be published or without observing the requirements as to banns, licences, etc., both being aware of the irregularity at the time of the marriage.

(b)   That at the time of the marriage either of the parties was already lawfully married.

(c)   That the parties are not respectively male and female.

(d)   In the case of polygamous marriage entered into outside England and Wales, that either party was at the time of the marriage domiciled in England and Wales.

3   VOIDABLE MARRIAGES: S. 12

A marriage shall be voidable on the following grounds only:

(a)   That it has not been consummated owing to the incapacity of either party to consummate it.

(b)   That it has not been consummated owing to the wilful refusal of the respondent to consummate it.

(c)   That either party to the marriage did not validly consent to it whether in consequence of duress, mistake, unsoundness of mind or otherwise.

(d)   That at the time of the marriage either party, though capable of giving a valid consent, was suffering (whether continuously or intermittently) from mental disorder within the meaning of the Mental Health Act 1983 of such a kind or to such an extent as to be unfitted for marriage.

(e)   That at the time of the marriage the respondent was suffering from venereal disease in a communicable form.

(f)   That at the time of the marriage the respondent was pregnant by someone other than the petitioner.

4   BARS TO RELIEF WHERE THE MARRIAGE IS VOIDABLE: S. 13, MATRIMONIAL CAUSES ACT 1973

4.1   Absolute bar applicable to all voidable marriages

The court shall not grant a nullity decree on the grounds that the marriage is voidable if the respondent satisfies the court:

(a)   that the petitioner, knowing that she could have the marriage voided, so conducted herself in relation to the respondent as to lead the respondent reasonably to believe that she would not seek to do so; *and*

(b)   that it would be unjust to the respondent to grant the decree (s. 13(1)).

4.2   Bars applicable only to certain voidable marriages

4.2.1   Limitation period

There is a 'limitation period' for the institution of proceedings for a decree on the grounds set out in s. 12(c), (d), (e) and (f) (see paragraph 3 above), i.e. lack of consent, mental disorder, venereal disease and pregnancy by someone else. The court shall not grant a decree on any of these grounds unless it is satisfied that proceedings were instituted within three years from the date of the marriage

(s. 13(2)). However, there is an exception to this rule: by virtue of an amendment to s. 13 made by s. 2, Matrimonial and Family Proceedings Act 1984, a judge may grant leave to institute proceedings on any of these grounds after the three-year period if:

(a)   he is satisfied that the petitioner has at some time during the three-year period suffered from a mental disorder within the meaning of the Mental Health Act 1983; *and*

(b)   he considers that in all the circumstances of the case it would be just to grant leave for the institution of proceedings (see s. 13(2) and (4)).

An application for leave can be made even if the three-year period has already expired (s. 13(5)).

4.2.2   Knowledge of petitioner
The court shall not grant a decree on the grounds set out in s. 12(e) and (f) (venereal disease and pregnancy) unless if is satisfied that at the time of the marriage the petitioner was ignorant of the fact alleged (s. 13(3)). This is an absolute bar.

5   PROCEDURE

(a)   The special procedure does not apply. The petition will therefore be heard in open court by a judge in the same way as a divorce that is removed from the special procedure list (see Chapter 8 paragraph 12).

(b)   Legal aid is available for nullity proceedings.

(c)   There are two decrees, decree nisi and decree absolute, as there are with divorce.

(d)   Section 41, Matrimonial Causes Act 1973 (arrangements for children of the family) applies as it does in divorce cases (see Chapter 8, paragraph 13).

6   EFFECT OF A DECREE OF NULLITY

6.1   On status

6.1.1   Voidable marriages
A decree of nullity granted in respect of a voidable marriage operates to annul the marriage only from after the date of decree absolute. The marriage is treated as if it had existed up to that time (s. 16 Matrimonial Causes Act 1973). Because the marriage existed until the decree, children of the union are automatically legitimate. Remarriage can take place after the decree absolute. Provision in a will by one spouse for the other will lapse (Wills Act 1837, s. 18A, added by the Administration of Justice Act 1982, s. 18(2)). Neither spouse will be able to claim on the other's intestacy.

6.1.2   Void marriages
A void marriage is a nullity from the very start and the nullity decree simply declares this fact. Children of a void marriage are treated as legitimate by virtue of the Legitimacy Act 1976 if, at the time of conception, (or the celebration of the marriage if this is later) both or either of the parents reasonably believed the

marriage was valid and the father was domiciled in England and Wales at the time of the birth or, if he died before the birth, was so domiciled immediately before his death.

6.2   Other effects

The full range of ancillary relief orders under the Matrimonial Causes Act 1973 in relation to children, property and finance are available in connection with a suit for nullity just as they are with a divorce.

PART III
ANCILLARY RELIEF AFTER DIVORCE, NULLITY AND JUDICIAL SEPARATION

Part III deals with ancillary relief after divorce, nullity and judicial separation. The first three chapters deal with routine ancillary relief applications as follows:

Chapter 14 sets out the financial provision and property adjustment orders available in connection with divorce, nullity and judicial separation.

Chapter 15 sets out the procedure for seeking ancillary relief orders.

Chapter 16 deals with the considerations that the court will bear in mind in deciding what orders to make and gives examples of the sort of orders that might be expected in particular circumstances.

Chapter 17 deals with a rather less routine matter — the preventing and setting aside of dispositions under s. 37, Matrimonial Causes Act 1973.

Chapter 18 covers enforcement of ancillary relief orders.

Chapter 19 deals with variation of orders.

Reference should also be made to Part IV of the book, which deals with taxation — a matter which is of vital importance in connection with ancillary relief.

The practitioner must be aware of three important pieces of new legislation:

(a)   The Social Security Act 1986, ss. 24A and 24B which came into force on 15 October 1990 (see Chapter 14, paragraph 5).

(b)   The Maintenance Enforcement Act 1991 which came into force on 1 April 1992 (see Chapter 14, paragraph 6).

(c)   The Child Support Act 1991 which received its Royal Assent on 25 July 1991 and is due to come into force early in 1993 over a phased three-year period. It will make sweeping changes to the assessment, collection and enforcement of child maintenance (see Chapter 14, paragraph 7).

14   Ancillary relief orders available

All the orders described in this section can be made in connection with proceedings for divorce, nullity or judicial separation. Where the principles in relation to the orders differ depending on whether the order is made after divorce, nullity or judicial separation this is stated. The reader is specifically referred to paragraphs 5, 6 and 7 of this chapter which deal with three important pieces of legislation:

(a)   the Child Support Act 1991 which will make sweeping changes to the assessment, collection and enforcement of child maintenance;

(b)   the Maintenance Enforcement Act 1991 which improves the methods of collecting and enforcing all maintenance payments;

(c)   the Social Security Act 1986, ss. 24A and 24B, which together with the new Income Support (Liable Relatives) Regulations 1990 provide for the Department of Social Security (DSS) to recover from a liable relative a contribution towards the benefit being paid for a spouse or child even after decree absolute.

1   MAINTENANCE PENDING SUIT: S. 22, MATRIMONIAL CAUSES ACT 1973

1.1   The nature of maintenance pending suit

An order for periodical payments in favour of a party to a marriage can only become effective once a final decree has been granted in the suit, be it a suit for divorce, nullity or judicial separation. However, it is quite likely that one or other spouse will be in financial difficulties as a result of the breakdown of the marriage and will not be able to wait for money until after a final decree has been granted. Maintenance pending suit exists therefore to bridge the gap between the commencement of the proceedings and final determination of the suit and is essentially a temporary measure. The order will be for the regular payment of a sum of money by one spouse to the other normally at weekly or monthly intervals.

1.2   Who can apply

Either party to the marriage can apply. It is immaterial whether they are the petitioner or the respondent in the suit.

Applications cannot be made by or on behalf of children. This is because they are not necessary — in contrast to the position in relation to periodical payments for the parties, periodical payments can be granted to or for a child of the family at any time after the petition is filed to become effective immediately.

1.3 When available

The court can make an order for maintenance pending suit at any time after the petition has been filed until a final decree has been granted (i.e. decree absolute in a divorce or nullity suit or the one and only decree in the case of judicial separation).

1.4 Duration of order

An order for maintenance pending suit can be made for such term as the court thinks reasonable beginning not earlier than the date of the presentation of the petition and ending with the determination of the suit (i.e. the decree of judicial separation or decree absolute of divorce or nullity or, in all cases, the dismissal of the suit). Orders for maintenance pending suit can therefore be back-dated from the date on which they are made as far as the date of presentation of the petition if the court thinks fit. Reference should be made to Chapter 15 paragraph 9.3 for the guidelines as to when the court will decide to back-date an order.

1.5 Maintenance pending suit distinguished from interim periodical payments

There is often confusion between maintenance pending suit and interim periodical payments. Whereas the former is ordered to tide a spouse over until such time as the court has power to make a periodical payments order and is only effective up to decree absolute, the latter is essentially a temporary periodical payments order in favour of a spouse or a child made at a time when the court *has* power to order periodical payments but is not yet in a position to make a final decision on the appropriate rate (for example, because the respondent's accounts are still in the course of preparation or the court does not have an appointment available for a full ancillary relief hearing). Interim periodical payments are dealt with more fully at paragraph 4.

2 LONG-TERM ORDERS: SS. 23 AND 24, MATRIMONIAL CAUSES ACT 1973

2.1 Orders available

The following long-term ancillary relief orders are available:

(a) financial provision orders (s. 23), i.e. periodical payments, secured periodical payments, and lump sums;

(b) property adjustment orders (s. 24), i.e. transfer of property, settlement of property, and variation of settlement.

2.2 In whose favour

2.2.1 Parties to the marriage
The court can make any of the orders listed at 2.1 above in favour of a party to the marriage.

2.2.2 Children of the family
Subject to certain age limits, the court can also make any of the orders listed at 2.1 in favour of a child of the family (defined in Chapter 7 paragraph 3.7). This

does not necessarily mean that the child will receive money or property directly into his own hands. The court can order the payment of money or transfer of property to someone else for the benefit of the child. Note that in early 1993 the Child Support Act 1991 will come into force over a phased three-year period. To a large extent this will transfer to the Child Support Agency the responsibility for assessing, collecting and enforcing child maintenance. See further paragraph 7 below.

The age limits on orders for children are set out in s. 29, Matrimonial Causes Act 1973. The general rule is that no financial provision or transfer of property order shall be made in favour of a child who has attained the age of 18 (s. 29(1)). However, by virtue of s. 29(3) orders can be made for children who are 18 or over if either:

(a)   The child is or will be (or if a financial provision order or transfer of property order were made would be) receiving instruction at an educational establishment or undergoing training for a trade, profession or vocation whether or not he is also (or will also be) in gainful employment

Example. The parents of a child are divorced. At the age of 18 the child goes to university. She is eligible for a minimum grant only. She will require her income to be topped up by her parents. A periodical payments order can be made in her favour as she is receiving instruction at an educational establishment.

(b)   There are special circumstances justifying the making of an order.

Example. Bernard is a child of the family. He is 20 but he suffers from Down's syndrome and he has a mental age of about 6. He lives with his mother, the petitioner. The court can order the respondent to make financial provision for Bernard or to transfer property to him on the basis that there are special circumstances.

Note that there is no age limit on the making of orders requiring a settlement of property to be made for the benefit of a child or varying a settlement for the benefit of a child.

2.3   The nature of the orders

2.3.1   Periodical payments (s. 23(1)(a) and (d), Matrimonial Causes Act 1973)
An order for periodical payments will be for the payment of a regular sum of money by one spouse to the other or to or for a child of the family, normally at weekly or monthly intervals. See paragraph 7 below for the changes in the assessment, collection and enforcement of child maintenance which will be implemented by the Child Support Act 1991 when it comes into force in early 1993.

2.3.2   Secured periodical payments (s. 23(1)(b) and (e), Matrimonial Causes Act 1973)
Having decided that a spouse or a child of the family is entitled to periodical payments, the court may feel that it is necessary to take steps in advance to ensure that he will actually receive the sum ordered and will not be burdened with problems over enforcement. This can be done by means of a secured periodical payments order.

The way in which a secured order operates varies from case to case depending on the exact terms of the order and the assets used as security. In some cases, the assets serving as security produce an income which is used to pay the periodical payments ordered. In other cases, assets which do not produce an income are used as security. The idea in cases of the second type is that the spouse against whom the order is made, let us say the husband, makes the periodical payments from his own income in the normal way, but if he defaults the assets stand charged with the amount of the unpaid periodical payments which the wife can therefore be sure of recovering by enforcing her charge.

Example 1 (income-producing assets). The court orders the husband to secure to the wife the annual sum of £500 upon his entire shareholding in three companies. The income by way of dividends from the shares is used to provide the wife with the annual sum of £500.

Example 2 (assets which do not produce income). The court orders the husband to secure to the wife the annual sum of £1,000 to be charged upon the freehold property Rose Cottage, Lake View, Gullswater (the husband's holiday cottage). As long as the husband pays the wife the annual sum of £1,000, the holiday property will be unaffected. Should he default at any stage, the amount of the arrears will form a charge over the property which the wife can seek to realise by forcing a sale of the property.

Whilst the order for secured periodical payments is in force, the husband cannot dispose of the assets forming the security. Indeed, in a case such as Example 1, he may feel that the court might as well have ordered him to transfer the assets to the wife outright as he may be deprived of all the benefits of owning the property whilst the order is in force if the entire income is required for the payment of the secured order. However, secured periodical payments do have the important advantage for the husband that once the secured order comes to an end the assets revert to him to do with as he pleases.

2.3.3 Lump sums (s. 23(1)(c) and (f), Matrimonial Causes Act 1973)
A lump sum order is, as its name suggests, an order for the payment of a specified sum of money. Payment of the whole sum at once may be required or the payment of the lump sum can be extended over a period of time as the court has the power to provide for payment by way of instalments (s. 23(3)(c)). The court can order that the payment of the instalments be secured to the satisfaction of the court (s. 23(3)(c)). Security will be provided in the same way as with secured periodical payments (see paragraph 2.3.2). If the lump sum is not to be paid in full immediately (for example, where it is to be paid in instalments or where the payer is given a period of time to raise it), the court can order that the amount deferred or the instalments shall bear interest at a rate specified by the court and for a period specified by the court not commencing earlier than the date of the order (s. 23(6)).

2.3.4 Transfer of property (s. 24(1)(a), Matrimonial Causes Act 1973)
The court can order one spouse to transfer to the other spouse or to or for the benefit of the children any property to which he is entitled either in possession or reversion. Transfer of property orders are most commonly used in relation to the title to the matrimonial home, for example, where the court orders the husband to transfer the house from his sole name into the wife's name or, where the house

is in joint names, to transfer his share in it to the wife. However, there are all sorts of other property which can also be made the subject of an order, for example, a car, furniture, a holiday cottage, a tenancy, title to a building held by one spouse as an investment and presently let, shares, etc.

2.3.5   Settlement of property (s. 24(1)(b), Matrimonial Causes Act 1973)

The court can order one spouse to settle property to which he is entitled for the benefit of the other spouse or the children. One example of the use of this power is the making of a Mesher type of order ordering that the matrimonial home be held on trust for sale, the house not to be sold until the youngest child reaches 17. The power could also be used, for example, to order one spouse to set up a trust fund out of capital perhaps to benefit the wife for life or until remarriage and thereafter for the children or alternatively for the wife for life and thereafter to revert to the husband.

2.3.6   Variation of settlement (s. 24(1)(c) and (d), Matrimonial Causes Act 1973)

The court can vary for the benefit of the parties or of the children of the family any ante-nuptial or post-nuptial settlement made on the parties to the marriage (including such settlement made by will or codicil). Furthermore, the interest of either spouse in such a settlement can be extinguished or reduced.

2.4   When available

2.4.1   In favour of a spouse

2.4.1.1   *The basic rules*   All the orders set out in 2.1 above can be made in favour of a spouse on granting a decree nisi of divorce or nullity or a decree of judicial separation or at any time thereafter (s. 23(1) and s. 24(1)). It is important to observe that where a consent order was drawn up by the district judge prior to the decree nisi, the Court of Appeal held that it had been made without jurisdiction and that it could not subsequently be revived after decree nisi by the operation of the slip rule or the exercise of the inherent jurisdiction of the court (*Board (Board intervening)* v *Checkland* [1987] 2 FLR 257, [1987] AC 861, [1987] 2 All ER 481, [1987] 2 WLR 1390). Note that the fact that orders can be made at any time after granting a decree means that there are no time-limits on the making of an application for ancillary relief. Therefore a spouse could, at least in theory, make an application for ancillary relief out of the blue 10 years after the divorce or could suddenly decide to pursue an application made in the initial stages of the divorce which has been allowed to go to sleep for years. In practice there are a number of reasons why this is unlikely to be profitable and may indeed be impossible:

(a)   Family Proceedings Rules 1991, r. 2.53(1) dictates that all the petitioner's applications for ancillary relief must be made in her petition and all the respondent's applications in his answer if he files one (see Chapter 15 paragraph 3). If an application is not made as required by r. 2.53(1), leave will be needed before it can be made and the passage of time between the beginning of the suit and the application for leave will increasingly influence the court against granting leave.

(b)   If the court first comes to consider an application for ancillary relief an unusually long time after the parties have been granted a final decree, it will be influenced adversely by the lapse of time in exercising its discretion as to what orders to make; see Chapter 16 paragraph 5.1.

(c)   Repeat applications for ancillary relief are not possible (see below at 2.4.1.2).

Orders made on or after granting a decree nisi of divorce or nullity cannot take effect until the decree is made absolute (s. 23(5) and s. 24(3)). The gap between the commencement of the suit and the final decree is filled by maintenance pending suit (see paragraph 1 above). Orders made on or after granting a decree of judicial separation can become effective immediately.

2.4.1.2   Repeat applications   Once the court has dealt with an application for ancillary relief on its merits (i.e. by making an order of the type sought or by dismissing the application), it has no future jurisdiction to entertain applications by that spouse for the same sort of ancillary relief. The most that the court can do is to vary or discharge the original order under s. 31, Matrimonial Causes Act 1973 if it is an order which is capable of variation (see, for example, *Minton* v *Minton* [1979] AC 593, [1979] 1 All ER 79, [1979] 2 WLR 31). The principles governing variation of orders are set out in Chapter 19.

Example 1. The petitioner makes a comprehensive prayer for ancillary relief in her petition. After the divorce the court orders that the matrimonial home should be transferred to her absolutely and that all her other claims to ancillary relief should be dismissed. The petitioner cannot come back to the court in two years' time when she has lost her job and is short of money asking for periodical payments or indeed for any other form of ancillary relief against the respondent. The court dealt with her application for all forms of ancillary relief on its merits after the divorce; she cannot revive the claims that were then dismissed and the one order that she was granted, being a transfer of property order, is not variable.

Example 2. The petitioner makes a comprehensive prayer for ancillary relief in her petition. After the divorce the court orders that the respondent should make periodical payments at the rate of £30 per week for the petitioner. As the respondent has no capital assets whatsoever the petitioner's other claims for ancillary relief are dismissed. A year after the order the respondent has a substantial win on the football pools and the petitioner wishes to claim a share. She cannot do so as her claims for a lump sum and for property adjustment orders have been dismissed. The best she can do is to seek an increase in the rate of the periodical payments order to reflect the respondent's improved circumstances.

The fact that the court's original order was made by consent does not affect the principles governing repeat applications (see, for example, *Minton* v *Minton* supra).

There are two ways round the rule about repeat applications:

(a)   If it appears that one spouse may come into a worthwhile sum of money (as yet of an uncertain amount) in the not-too-distant future, instead of the court pressing on to deal with the other spouse's application for ancillary relief immediately after the divorce, it would be possible (at her suggestion) for the court to adjourn some or all of her ancillary relief applications to be heard at a later date when the position is clearer. Note though that in *Roberts* v *Roberts* [1986] 2 All ER 483, [1986] 1 WLR 437, [1986] 2 FLR 152 the view was expressed that it would be wrong to adjourn a lump sum application for more than four or five years.

> **Example.** The petitioner makes a comprehensive claim for ancillary relief in her petition. At present the respondent has very little capital although he has a reasonable income. However, he is likely to benefit substantially under the will of an ancient, sick relative whose demise will almost inevitably occur during the next year. The court can make an order for periodical payments in favour of the petitioner immediately after the divorce and adjourn her other claims so that the position with regard to the respondent's inheritance will be known. When the court ultimately considers the adjourned claims, it will have a free hand to make whatever orders it thinks fit and, as the order for periodical payments is variable under s. 31, it can adjust that order also in the light of the changed circumstances.

(b)   Where one spouse, say the petitioner, seeks periodical payments against the other but a periodical payments order is not appropriate in the light of the parties' financial circumstances at the date of the hearing, instead of permanently debarring the petitioner from seeking periodical payments against the respondent by dismissing her claim, the court can preserve her entitlement to periodical payments in the future by making a nominal order for periodical payments against the respondent. This is an order for the payment of a minimal sum (5 pence/50 pence/£1 per annum) to the petitioner by way of periodical payments which the petitioner can seek to have varied under s. 31 to a worthwhile sum should circumstances change in the future.

> **Example.** When the petitioner's application for periodical payments is considered the respondent is out of work through no fault of his own. The petitioner is tied to the house with young children and cannot work. If the respondent were working, a periodical payments order would clearly be appropriate. The court can make an order for nominal periodical payments to the petitioner which she can seek to have increased when the respondent gets a job.

Nominal orders used to be made almost as a matter of course not only where the respondent was presently unable to make periodical payments because of his financial circumstances but also where the petitioner was not presently in need of periodical payments because of her circumstances, for example, where she was working. In recent years the courts have come to think more in terms of a clean break between the parties where both spouses can work and this attitude will undoubtedly have been reinforced by the provisions of s. 25A, Matrimonial Causes Act 1973 as added by s. 3, Matrimonial and Family Proceedings Act 1984 (see Chapter 16 paragraph 2.4). It may be that the courts will therefore be more reluctant to grant nominal orders in the future.

2.4.2   *In favour of a child of the family*

(a)   *Financial provision orders*   These can be made in favour of a child of the family at any stage after the commencement of the suit (s. 23(1) coupled with s. 23(2)(a)). Section 23(4) expressly provides that the power to make financial provision orders for a child can be exercised from time to time. Unlike the position with regard to spouses, therefore, an application for financial provision for a child can never be finally dismissed and repeat applications for financial provision orders can be made provided that the child concerned is still within the age limits for the order sought (see paragraph 2.2.2 above).

Example 1. An application is made against the respondent in the divorce petition for periodical payments for Alicia, a child of the family aged 8. Alicia is one of the potential beneficiaries of a discretionary trust set up by her grandfather. Since her birth the trustees have provided sufficient income from the trust each year for her maintenance. There is every indication that they will continue to do this so no order for periodical payments for Alicia is made when ancillary relief is dealt with after the divorce. However, when Alicia is 10, one of the other potential beneficiaries under the trust gets into serious financial difficulties and the trustees have to use the trust income to help him so payments can no longer be made for Alicia. There is nothing to prevent periodical payments being sought again for Alicia at this stage.

Example 2. As part of the long-term resolution of finances and property after the divorce, the respondent is ordered to make a lump sum payment of £1,000 to Samantha, a child of the family. An application for a further lump sum for Samantha can be made in the future.

Even if the main suit is dismissed, provided that this happens after the beginning of the trial, the court can make financial provision orders in relation to a child of the family on dismissing the suit or within a reasonable period after dismissal (s. 23(2)(b)). This is not possible in the case of an application for an order in favour of a spouse. Note, however, that whereas there is normally no time-limit on the making of applications for ancillary relief, if no order is made for financial provision within a reasonable time after the suit is dismissed the power to make such an order will be lost for ever. On the other hand, if the court does make an order for the benefit of a child of the family on or after dismissing a suit (whether it be for periodical payments, secured periodical payments or a lump sum), it is empowered by s. 23(4) to make further financial provision orders (which need not be of the same type as the original order) from time to time thereafter for the benefit of that child of the family. Note that the Child Support Act 1991 will come into force in early 1993 over a phased three-year period. To a large extent this will place the responsibility for assessing, collecting and enforcing child maintenance payments on the Child Support Agency. However, the court will retain jurisdiction in certain circumstances. For further details of the changes see paragraph 7 below.

(b) *Property adjustment orders* These can be made for the benefit of a child of the family on granting a decree nisi of divorce or nullity or a decree of judicial separation or at any time thereafter. As there is no express power to make such orders from time to time, it would appear that the child is in the same position as a spouse in relation to repeat applications — once the child's application has been dealt with on its merits no further application for an order of the same type can be made.

Orders made on or after a decree of judicial separation become effective immediately. Orders made on or after granting a decree nisi of nullity or divorce do not take effect until the decree is made absolute (s. 24(3)).

2.5   Who can make the application

2.5.1   Parties to the marriage

Either party to the marriage can apply for any of the orders listed in paragraph 2.1 above on behalf of himself or herself or on behalf of a child of the family. After the decision of the House of Lords in the case of *Sherdley* v *Sherdley* [1987] 2 WLR 1071, [1987] 2 All ER 54, it became clear that a parent with custody of a child of the family could apply for a periodical payments order for the child against himself. The motive behind this was to save tax, since the custodial parent obtained tax relief for provision for the child by way of periodical payments and the child was not taxed on the money unless his income exceeded his personal allowance. The case of *Sherdley* v *Sherdley* enabled a father to get tax relief on his children's school fees. The principle was extended by the case of *Simister* v *Simister* [1987] 1 All ER 233, [1986] 1 WLR 1463 so that a party to a marriage could seek against himself an order that he pay periodical payments to the other party.

However, the 1988 Budget made sweeping changes to the availability of tax relief upon periodical payments (see Chapter 20 for a full explanation). Any such orders as those discussed above which were made prior to 15 March 1988 will remain tax effective until they end. However, any parent paying school fees under an order made after 15 March 1988 does not get tax relief, except to the extent that they may be part of the maintenance paid by one spouse to the other.

Prior to the 1988 Budget, maintenance payments were subject to the deduction of income tax at basic rate by the payer unless they were small maintenance payments. However, as from 15 March 1988 maintenance payments are only subject to the regime if embodied in a court order or written agreement made before 15 March 1988. Any such orders made after 15 March 1988 are paid gross and are not deductible by the payer or taxable in the hands of the recipient.

2.5.2   Children of the family

Where he has been given leave to intervene in the cause for the purpose of applying for ancillary relief, the child himself can apply for any of the orders listed in 2.1 (r. 2.54(1)(f) of the Family Proceedings Rules 1991.

> **Example.** (The facts of *Downing* v *Downing* [1976] Fam 288, [1976] 3 All ER 474.) The parents of the child are divorced. At the age of 18 the child goes to university. Her parents fail to make the parental contribution to her grant assessed by the local education authority. Because she is receiving instruction at an educational establishment she is eligible for ancillary relief (s. 29, Matrimonial Causes Act 1973). Either parent can apply for an order for ancillary relief for her against the other but, if neither chooses to do so, the child herself is entitled to apply.

2.5.3   Others on behalf of a child

Apart from the parties to the marriage and the child himself, there are various other people empowered by r. 2.54(1), Family Proceedings Rules 1991 to apply for ancillary relief in respect of a child of the family, for example, the child's guardian or any person in whose favour a residence order has been made with respect to a child of the family.

2.6 Duration of periodical payments and secured periodical payments order (ss. 28 and 29, Matrimonial Causes Act 1973)

2.6.1 In favour of a spouse

Subject to s. 25A(2) (duty of court to consider making order for fixed term only, see below in this paragraph and also Chapter 16 paragraph 2.4), an order for periodical payments or secured periodical payments for a spouse can last for whatever period the court thinks fit with these limitations:

(a) Commencement of the term: the term shall not begin earlier than the date of the making of an application for the order (s. 28(1)(a)). This provision enables the court, if it sees fit, to back-date its order for periodical payments or secured periodical payments to the date of the making of the application (see Chapter 15 paragraph 9.3 for guidelines in relation to back-dating of orders). A petitioner's application will normally have been made in her petition and the court therefore has the power to back-date an order in her favour to the date of the presentation of the petition. If the respondent files an answer he will normally make his claim for periodical payments in his answer. The Family Proceedings Rules 1991 do not lay down rules as to when a respondent who does not file an answer should make his application for ancillary relief (see Chapter 15 paragraph 3.3.2). His application will be made at whatever stage in the proceedings his solicitor sees fit by filing a notice of application in Form M11 (Appendix 1, Family Proceedings Rules 1991) and an order for periodical payments or secured periodical payments can be back-dated to the date on which this notice was filed.

(b) End of the term: the court cannot make an order for a term defined so as to extend beyond:

(i) The remarriage of the party in whose favour the order is made (this provision applies only, of course, to cases of divorce and nullity as remarriage is clearly out of the question in a case of judicial separation). Note that remarriage of the paying spouse will not have any direct effect on the periodical payments or secured periodical payments order. However, where the paying spouse remarries this may constitute a change in his circumstances that would justify his making an application for a reduction in the rate of the order (see Chapter 19 with regard to variation). or

(ii) In the case of a secured periodical payments order, the death of either of the parties to the marriage, or, in the case of a secured periodical payments order, the death of the spouse in whose favour the order is made. (Note that in contrast to a straightforward order for periodical payments, a secured order can continue beyond the death of the paying spouse.)

Subject to these limitations the court can leave the periodical payments order open-ended if it thinks fit. On the other hand, the court can make the order for a limited period of time. The court has always been able to do this but the new s. 25A, Matrimonial Causes Act 1973 (added by s. 3, Matrimonial and Family Proceedings Act 1984) draws particular attention to this power by directing the court, when exercising its power to make periodical payments orders in favour of a spouse, to consider whether it would be appropriate to make the order only for a limited period such as would be sufficient to enable the payee to adjust to being self-supporting. Where the court makes such an order in favour of a party

to the marriage, it may direct that that party shall not be entitled to apply under
s. 31 for the order to be varied by extending the term (s. 28(1A)).

> **Example.** ('Open-ended' order.) 'It is ordered that the respondent do make periodical
> payments to the petitioner for herself during their joint lives until she shall remarry or
> until further order at the rate of £x per week payable weekly in advance.'

> **Example.** ('Fixed term' order.) 'It is ordered that the respondent do make periodical
> payments to the petitioner for herself at the rate of £x per month payable monthly in
> advance for a period of one year from the date of this order or during their joint lives
> or until the petitioner shall remarry or until further order whichever period shall be the
> shortest.'

2.6.2   Special provisions with regard to children

Section 29(2) provides that the term specified in a periodical payments or secured
periodical payments order in favour of a child may begin with the date of the
making of the application or at any later date (so back-dating is possible), but:

(a)   shall not extend, in the first instance, beyond the child's next birthday
after he attains school-leaving age unless the court considers that in the
circumstances of the case the welfare of the child requires that it should extend
to a later date. As the present school-leaving age is 16 this means that when first
granted most periodical payments orders will be expressed to be 'until the said
child shall attain the age of 17 years or further order'. If it is clear that the child
will not be leaving education at the first possible opportunity, for example, where
it is certain that the children will be staying on at school to do A-levels, the court
should be asked specifically to grant the order to last until the child is 18 instead.
And

(b)   shall not in any event extend beyond the date of the child's 18th birthday
unless s. 29(3) applies. Reference should be made to paragraph 2.2.2 above for
the full provisions of s. 29(3). Basically it enables the court to make orders in
favour of children who are over 18 if they are being educated or there are special
circumstances.

The death of the paying spouse will bring a periodical payments order in
favour of a child to an end unless it is secured (s. 29(4)). Remarriage of either
spouse will not affect orders in favour of a child.

3   ORDERS FOR SALE: S. 24A, MATRIMONIAL CAUSES ACT 1973

This section was added to the Matrimonial Causes Act 1973 by s. 7, Matrimonial
Homes and Property Act 1981.

3.1   The power to order sale

Where the court makes: (a) a secured periodical payments order; (b) a lump sum
order; (c) a property adjustment order, on making the order or at any time
thereafter the court may make a further order for the sale of property in which
or in the proceeds of sale of which either or both of the parties to the marriage
has or have a beneficial interest either in possession or reversion.

3.2 Consequential and supplementary provisions

The sale order may contain whatever consequential or supplementary provisions the court thinks fit (s. 24A(2)). Two forms of consequential or supplementary provision are specially mentioned in the subsection:

(a) A requirement that a payment be made out of the proceeds of sale (s. 24A(2)(a) (for an example of this, see Example 2 at paragraph 3.4 below); *and*

(b) A requirement that the property be offered for sale to a particular person or class of persons specified in the order (s. 24A(2)(b)).

Directions as to the conduct of the sale (for example, as to whose solicitor should be in charge of the conveyancing and how the sale price is to be fixed) can be given under the s. 24A(2) power and will usually be necessary.

3.3 When effective

(a) Not before decree absolute: if an order for sale is made before decree absolute, it will not become effective until after the decree is made absolute (s. 24A(3)).

(b) Suspended orders: the court can specifically direct that the order (or a particular provision of it) shall not take effect until a particular event has occurred or a specified period has elapsed.

3.4 Examples

(a) Order for sale enabling capital provision to be made: the order for sale may be made at the same time as the secured periodical payments, lump sum or property adjustment order, timed to take effect before it as an enabling measure.

Example 1. The court orders that the matrimonial home which is in the respondent's name be sold (the s. 24A(1) order) and a sum equal to half the net proceeds of sale be paid by the respondent to the petitioner (a lump sum order).

(b) Order for sale as enforcement measure: alternatively the spouse in whose favour a secured periodical payments, lump sum or property adjustment order has been made already may need to return to court for an order for sale as a means of enforcement if the original order has not been complied with.

Example 2. The court orders the respondent to pay to the petitioner a lump sum of £10,000 within three months of the date of the order. The respondent fails to comply within the three-month period. The petitioner applies for an order for sale of certain of the respondent's assets and payment of £10,000 from the proceeds to her.

(c) Not available as a means of varying a property adjustment order: the power to order a sale cannot, however, be used to vary a property adjustment order (*Norman* v *Norman* [1983] 1 All ER 486, [1983] 1 WLR 295).

Example 3. (The facts of *Norman* v *Norman*.) In 1979 in ancillary relief proceedings after a divorce, the registrar made a property adjustment order under s. 24(1)(b) settling the matrimonial home on trust for sale on the husband and wife equally, the sale to be postponed until the youngest child ceased to receive full-time education or training, whereupon the property would be sold and the proceeds divided equally between the husband and wife. In 1982, when one child still remained in full-time education, the husband applied for an order for immediate sale of the house so that he could buy himself a mobile home. The court held that there was no jurisdiction under s. 24A(1) to grant the order for sale which would in effect vary the original property adjustment order by substituting an earlier sale date.

4   INTERIM ORDERS

Pending the final determination of an ancillary relief application, the district judge has power to make an interim order upon such terms as he thinks just (Family Proceedings Rules 1991, r. 2.64(2)).

By far the most common form of interim order is an interim periodical payments order:

(a)   Interim periodical payments for children: whilst the court does have power to make a final order for periodical payments for children at any time after the commencement of the suit, it is likely that only interim periodical payments will be ordered until the full hearing of the ancillary relief application takes place. This leaves the way open for the court to adjust the rate of payments in the light of the provision made for the spouses without the need for a variation application to be made in respect of the children.

(b)   Interim periodical payments for a spouse: interim periodical payments for a spouse can be ordered in divorce and nullity cases at any time on or after granting decree nisi to become effective after decree absolute (in judicial separation, interim periodical payments can be ordered and become effective as soon as the single decree is granted). An interim order should be sought when ancillary relief matters cannot be finally resolved until some time after decree absolute. The gap between commencement of the suit and decree of judicial separation/decree absolute can be filled by maintenance pending suit.

5   THE SOCIAL SECURITY ACT 1986, SS. 24A AND 24B

Section 8 of the Social Security Act 1990 inserted ss. 24A and 24B into the Social Security Act 1986 on 15 October 1990. This, when taken in conjunction with the new Income Support (Liable Relatives) Regulations 1990, provides for the Department of Social Security to recover from a liable relative a contribution towards the benefit being paid for a spouse or child even after decree absolute (N.B. under the old regulations the liability ended on decree absolute). However, a liable relative will not be required to contribute towards a child of whom he or she is not the natural parent.

6   THE MAINTENANCE ENFORCEMENT ACT 1991

The Maintenance Enforcement Act 1991 came into force on 1 April 1992. It improves the methods of collecting and enforcing maintenance payments for spouses and children. The Act provides for the High Court or county court to specify that payments of maintenance be made by standing order or some other method, or by attachment of earnings. It provides that the magistrates' court must specify that payments be made directly from debtor to creditor, through the court, by standing order or some similar method, or by attachment of earnings. As the law stood prior to the Act there was no provision for the courts to order payment of maintenance by standing order, and an attachment of earnings order could only be made if the debtor consented or if he had defaulted on the payments by wilful refusal to pay or by culpable neglect. The Act is an interim measure to improve the mechanics of maintenance collection and enforcement pending the coming into force of the Child Support Act 1991. However, it will continue to be of use after the Child Support Act 1991 comes into force because it deals with *all* maintenance payments and not simply child maintenance payments.

7 THE CHILD SUPPORT ACT 1991

The Child Support Act 1991 received its Royal Assent on 25 July 1991 and is due to come into force over a phased three year period, commencing early in 1993. It will, to a large extent, remove the task of assessing child maintenance from the courts and will transfer that responsibility to the Child Support Agency. The Child Support Agency will be set up within the Department of Social Security and where it has been involved in the assessment of the level of child maintenance it will also take over from the courts the responsibilities of collection and enforcement of the payments.

The Act defines those persons who are entitled to apply to the Secretary of State for a maintenance assessment under the Act. Applicants who are not in receipt of state benefits have a choice as to whether or not to apply. However, a potential applicant who is in receipt of state benefits *must*, if so required by the Secretary of State, authorise the Secretary of State to take action to recover child support maintenance. The Act gives the child support officer extensive powers to obtain the necessary information as to the financial means of the parties. When he has collected the information the officer will make his assessment based upon the formula contained in Part I of Schedule I. The formula contains no element of discretion and is said to provide for all possibilities! There will be an appeals system, firstly by way of review carried out by another child support officer and then, if the person concerned is still aggrieved, by way of appeal to a Child Support Appeal Tribunal. Appeal from there will be to a Child Support Commissioner and thence, on points of law, to the Court of Appeal.

The courts will retain jurisdiction in respect of children not covered by the Act. These include the following:

(a) step-children;
(b) cases where one party is abroad;
(c) children over the age of 18;
(d) children who are or have been married.

Furthermore, the court will retain jurisdiction in the following types of cases:

(a) 'top up' cases where the formula 'ceiling' has been reached and the person with care of the child seeks more maintenance for the child;

(b)   'school fee' cases – to meet some of the expenses incurred in connection with the provision of instruction or training;

(c)   where the child is disabled.

The provisions of the Child Support Act 1991 are complex and the practitioner is referred to a specialist book on the subject for further detail.

15 Procedure for ancillary relief applications

1 THE COST OF THE APPLICATION

1.1 Legal aid cases

The solicitor will no doubt have assessed whether his client is eligible for legal advice and assistance under the green form scheme when first consulted by his client in relation to the divorce. He can give preliminary advice on ancillary matters under the green form scheme. However, it will be necessary for him to make an application on his client's behalf for a full legal aid certificate to cover ancillary relief proceedings (see Chapter 2). He should explain the potential impact of the Legal Aid Board's statutory charge to the client when making the application.

1.2 Private cases

If the client is not eligible for legal aid, the solicitor should attempt to give him some estimate of the potential cost of the ancillary relief proceedings or, if this is not possible, he should at least warn the client that they may be very expensive. He should consider whether he needs to take a payment on account. Whether he insists on this will depend on the normal practice of the firm and his knowledge of the individual client.

2 PROTECTING THE APPLICANT PENDING THE MAKING OF AN ORDER

One of the first matters that the solicitor should consider is whether the client's interests are adequately protected pending the making of an ancillary relief order. Could the other spouse sell the matrimonial home over his client's head, for instance? Will his client's assets pass by will or on intestacy to the respondent if she dies before everything is sorted out? Where the solicitor does not feel his client's interests are sufficiently secure, he should consider steps such as severing the joint tenancy or registering a charge or notice under the Matrimonial Homes Act 1983 or a pending land action. Reference should be made to Chapter 22 where these matters are dealt with more fully.

3 MAKING THE ANCILLARY RELIEF APPLICATION

3.1 Section 26, Matrimonial Causes Act 1973

Section 26 provides that where a petition for divorce, nullity or judicial separation has been presented, then, subject to any rules of court concerning the making of applications, proceedings for maintenance pending suit, for a financial provision order or for a property adjustment order may be begun at any time after the presentation of the petition.

This wide provision has been considerably circumscribed by the Family Proceedings Rules 1991 as the following paragraphs show.

3.2 Petitioner's application

Rule 2.53(1) of the Family Proceedings Rules 1991 provides that any application by a petitioner for:

(a)   an order for maintenance pending suit;
(b)   a financial provision order;
(c)   a property adjustment order

(i.e. all the main forms of ancillary relief except an order for sale under s. 24A, Matrimonial Causes Act 1973) shall be made in the petition.

3.3 Respondent's application

3.3.1 *Respondent filing an answer*
Rule 2.53(1) also applies to a respondent who files an answer, save that, of course, it is in his answer that he must make his ancillary relief claims.

3.3.2 *Respondent not filing an answer*
A respondent who does not file an answer may make his application for ancillary relief by notice in Form M11 (Family Proceedings Rules 1991, r. 2.53(3)).

There are no particular requirements as to when Form M11 should be filed. In theory, therefore, a respondent can file Form M11 months and even years after a decree has been granted. However, delay in filing Form M11 can prejudice a respondent's ancillary relief claims — in particular the client may fall into the remarriage trap (see paragraph 3.4.1 below) or may find the court reluctant to grant relief if the lapse of time has led the petitioner to believe that no claim will be made. It is therefore suggested that the solicitor should make it his practice to file Form M11 claiming the full range of ancillary relief as a matter of course in the early stages of the main suit and certainly before decree absolute. Note that indicating in the acknowledgment of service that the respondent intends to claim ancillary relief does not count as making a formal ancillary relief claim (*Hargood v Jenkins* [1978] Fam 148, [1978] 3 All ER 1001).

3.4 The importance of making a comprehensive claim for ancillary relief

3.4.1 *Generally*
It is usually advisable to make the fullest possible claim for ancillary relief in the petition/answer or Form M11 (despite the fact that it may seem inappropriate at the time to claim, for example, periodic payments from a spouse who is unemployed or a lump sum from a spouse with no capital assets) for the following reasons:

(a)   Circumstances can change between the initiation of the application and the hearing and the spouse who was impecunious when ancillary relief was originally claimed in the petition may, by the date of the hearing, have obtained a lucrative job or won the pools. It is obviously in the interests of all concerned that the court should have the fullest possible powers to resolve the case at the hearing.

(b) The client must be prevented from falling into the remarriage trap. Section 28(3) provides that if a party to a marriage remarries after a decree of divorce or nullity, that party shall not be entitled to apply for a financial provision order or for a property adjustment order in her favour against the other party to the former marriage. A party who may want to remarry can, however, preserve her claim for lump sum and property adjustment orders by making them before remarriage in which case she will be able to pursue the claims after remarriage. Nothing can be done, of course, to preserve a claim for periodical payments which will always cease on remarriage in any event (s. 28(1) and (2), Matrimonial Causes Act 1973).

(c) The petitioner/respondent who later wishes to make a claim for ancillary relief that should have been made in her petition/answer in accordance with r. 2.53 will, in most cases, need leave of the court to make the claim (see paragraph 3.4.2 below).

3.4.2 *Procedure for making claim omitted from petition/answer*

The procedure for making a claim omitted from the petition/answer depends on the attitude of the other party:

(a) If the parties are agreed upon the terms of the proposed ancillary relief order, the petitioner/respondent may make her claim without leave by notice in Form M11 (Family Proceedings Rules 1991, r. 2.53(2)).

(b) If the parties are not agreed, however, one of the following courses must be adopted:

(i) If no decree has yet been pronounced, the appropriate course will usually be for the petitioner/respondent to amend her petition/answer to add the claim in question. If the petition/answer has already been served, leave to amend will be necessary (see Chapter 9). There should not normally be any difficulty in obtaining leave to amend.

(ii) If a decree has been pronounced, the appropriate course will usually be for the petitioner/respondent to seek leave to file notice in Form M11 (Family Proceedings Rules 1991, r. 2.53(2)).

3.5 The need for Form M13

3.5.1 *Form M13 required where application in petition/answer*

The formal application in the petition/answer must be activated by filing Form M13 when the petitioner/respondent wishes to proceed with it. Form M13 gives notice that the petitioner/respondent intends to proceed with her claim for ancillary relief made in her petition/answer (Family Proceedings Rules 1991, r. 2.58(1)). Form M13 can be filed at any stage after the petition/answer is filed. If it is clear that there is going to be a dispute over ancillary relief, it will usually be advisable to file Form M13 at an early stage so that formal application for the hearing (filing of affidavits, etc.) can begin. By so doing, it should be possible to minimise the delay after decree nisi before final ancillary relief orders can be made.

3.5.2   No form M13 where application in Form M11

Where the formal application has been made in Form M11 no further steps are necessary to activate it — Form M11 is sufficient by itself.

3.6   The mechanics of filing and serving Form M11 and Form M13

Note that hereafter the party making the application is referred to as the applicant and the other spouse as the respondent.

3.6.1   Filing

The following documents should be taken to court (normally the divorce county court where the divorce proceedings were commenced) to be issued/filed:

(a)   Form M11/M13 in duplicate (a copy for the court and a copy to be stamped and handed back for service on the other party, i.e. 'issued'). Note that where there is a property adjustment application relating to land, the notice in Form M11/M13 must identify the land and state whether the title is registered or unregistered and, if registered, the Land Registry title number (if the applicant's solicitor does not know whether the land is registered, he should first ask the other side's solicitor for the relevant information and, if this is not forthcoming, search the Index Map) and give particulars, so far as known to the applicant, of any mortgage of the land or any interest therein (r. 2.59(2)).

(b)   An affidavit in support of the ancillary relief application (see paragraph 4.1).

(c)   Where legal aid has been granted in relation to the ancillary matters:

   (i)   the legal aid certificate;
   (ii)   notice of issue of the certificate.

(d)   Notice of acting if the solicitor is not already on the record (if the divorce has been handled on the green form so far, he will not be on the record).

(e)   A copy of any magistrates' court maintenance order currently in force in respect of a spouse or child (although note that, if a copy is not available when Form M11/M13 is filed, it will be sufficient to file a copy on or before the hearing of the application (Family Proceedings Rules 1991, r. 2.56).

(f)   If possible, an estimate of time (which can be given by letter or endorsed on the notice in Form M11/M13).

A fee (currently £20) is payable on issue of Form M11/M13. No one is exempt from the fee but, if the client is legally aided, the fee will be a disbursement covered by legal aid.

Whether the court gives a date for a hearing of the application at this stage will depend on the practice of the individual court. At this point in the case it will rarely be possible to predict accurately when the matter will be ready for a final hearing and how long it is likely to take. Therefore it is only very occasionally that a final hearing date will be arranged at this stage. In the Divorce Registry, no date will normally be given at all. In a divorce county court, a short appointment may be fixed for a preliminary consideration of the case.

Note that although the court will only require one copy of documents (b) to (d) to be filed, the solicitor will, in fact, need further copies for service on the other spouse and on trustees, etc. (see paragraph 3.6.2).

3.6.2   Service

3.6.2.1   Service on the other spouse   A copy of Form M11/M13 must be served on the other spouse within four days of issue (Family Proceedings Rules 1991, rr. 2.55 and 2.58(1)). The following must also be served on the other spouse if applicable:

(a)   a copy of the affidavit that the applicant has filed in support of the ancillary relief application (Family Proceedings Rules 1991, r. 2.58(2));
(b)   notice of issue of the legal aid certificate (if legal aid has been granted) (see Chapter 2 for details of the solicitor's obligations where legal aid is granted);
(c)   a copy of any notice of acting.

Unlike the divorce petition which is normally served through the court, it is the solicitor's responsibility to serve Form M11/M13 and the accompanying documents on the other spouse. Service will usually be carried out by post. If a solicitor is acting for the other spouse, the documents will normally be served by sending them to the solicitor's address.

3.6.2.2   On other persons   Family Proceedings Rules 1991, r. 2.59(3) and (4) provides that, in certain cases, a copy of Form M11/M13 (and in some cases also a copy of the supporting affidavit) must be served on other persons in addition to the other spouse; for example, if an application is made for the variation of a settlement, the trustees of the settlement and the settlor (if living) should be served.

The obligation to serve third parties most commonly arises where an application is made for a property adjustment order in relation to land (usually the matrimonial home) which is subject to a mortgage. In such a case, a copy of Form M11/M13 must be served on any mortgagee mentioned in Form M11/M13 and the mortgagee can apply to the court for a copy of the applicant's affidavit (r. 2.59(4)). The mortgagee may file an affidavit in answer to the application (r. 2.59(5)) though he will rarely do so.

4   AFFIDAVITS OF SPOUSES

Note that all affidavits filed (whether the deponent is a spouse or not) must also, of course, be served on the other party to the application (Family Proceedings Rules 1991, r. 2.60(1)).

4.1   Contents of and order of filing affidavits

(a)   Affidavit in support of application: except in the case of an application for a consent order for financial relief (to which Family Proceedings Rules 1991, r. 2.61 applies, see paragraph 11 below), unless otherwise directed, where an application is made for ancillary relief, the notice in Form M11/M13 must be supported by an affidavit by the applicant containing full particulars of his property and income, and stating the facts relied on in support of the application (Family Proceedings Rules 1991, r. 2.58(2)). Where there is an application for a property adjustment order, the affidavit must also contain, so far as known to the applicant, full particulars as follows:

(i)   Where the application is for a transfer or settlement of property: particulars of the property in respect of which the application is made, *and* particulars of the property to which the party against whom the application is made is entitled either in possession or reversion.

(ii)   Where the application is for an order for a variation of settlement: particulars of all settlements, whether ante-nuptial or post-nuptial, made on the spouses, *and*
particulars of the funds brought into settlement by each spouse (Family Proceedings Rules 1991, r. 2.59(1)).

(b)   Affidavit in answer: the other spouse must file an affidavit in answer containing particulars of his property and income within 28 days after the service of the applicant's affidavit or within such other time as the court may fix (Family Proceedings Rules 1991, r. 2.58(3)).

4.2   Drafting a spouse's affidavit

Each party's affidavit should deal with such of the matters listed below as are relevant. Note that there is a standard form of affidavit of means available. It is in question and answer form and can be used in any case. However, whilst the form is a convenient reminder of the type of matters that should be covered in the client's affidavit and can be used as a basis for taking instructions, the solicitor may find in some cases that he cannot do his client's case justice by simply filing a completed standard form affidavit of means and that it is more efficient to draft a full affidavit from scratch. It is convenient if, in this case, he drafts the affidavit covering matters in the same order as is used in the standard form if possible.

When drafting an affidavit, it is important to try to give all figures for the same period of time. For example, if the client receives a monthly wage, the solicitor should try to reduce all his other income and his outgoings to a monthly figure so that his financial position is readily apparent.

(a)   *Income*   Particulars of the client's income from all sources should be given. His major source of income will usually be from his job. Where the client is employed, the solicitor should be able to obtain the relevant details from his latest wage slip. If the client's earnings vary from week to week, this should be pointed out and explained and, if appropriate, an average weekly figure for gross earnings given. If the client is self-employed, his earnings will have to be ascertained from his accounts. It is usual to look at the last three years' accounts to discover the client's true position. It is often convenient to make copies of the accounts exhibits to the affidavit. If the client is in receipt of state benefit (for example, income support, state pension, family credit) as many details as possible of this should be given. Examples of other income that will be relevant include child benefit, pensions or annuities, interest on bank and building society accounts, and dividends from shares. Wherever possible, the gross amount of the income concerned should be given. If the client is currently receiving income by way of maintenance payments from the other spouse this should be stated — if the payments are made under a court order, details should be given.

(b)   *Fringe benefits*   Details should be given of any benefits in kind that the client receives, for example, a car with the job, free accommodation, cheap loans, discount goods.

(c) *Outgoings* Each one of the client's outgoings should be mentioned specifically in his affidavit. The following list may help jog the memory — obviously it is far from comprehensive:

National Insurance contributions
expenses of travelling to work
food at work
union dues and other expenses associated with work
rent/mortgage
community charge (council tax from 1993), water rates and sewerage charges
insurance
school fees/school dinners/school buses
milk
food
clothes
clubs
loan repayments
TV rental and licence
motoring expenses
gas and electricity

The client's present tax position should be dealt with in so far as this is possible. Where he can, the client should also give details of his income tax liability for the last complete tax year or (where his income fluctuates) for a longer period of time.

(d) *Assets* Full details should be given of the client's assets (owned by himself solely or jointly with the other spouse or with third parties). Many clients will have no assets other than the matrimonial home, its contents and perhaps a car. Others will have money in the bank, a building society account, premium bonds, shares, antiques, paintings, valuable jewellery and so on.

Details should also be given of the other spouse's assets in so far as the client knows about them.

In the case of valuable assets such as the house, the solicitor should consider giving a brief history of how the asset was acquired. This may be relevant when the court comes to determine its orders (for example, if the wife has worked throughout the marriage and earnings have been pooled to buy the matrimonial home, she may well be entitled to a more generous order in relation to it than she would if she had never made any financial contribution towards it). The solicitor should normally, however, resist the temptation to go into detail about run of the mill contents of the house and other minor items. The court is not likely to want to get involved in the detailed history of the acquisition of the souvenir donkey from Benidorm.

The value of the matrimonial home should be given if known, together with details of the outstanding mortgage, if any, and of any endowment policies linked with it.

(e) *Future rights* The client's pension rights and any other rights that he may have in the future (for example, under a settlement or an insurance policy) should be disclosed.

(f) *Argument*   It is often helpful for the solicitor to give advance consideration to how he will put his client's case before the district judge and to draft his client's affidavit so that it fits in with the argument. This is not, of course, to say that he can decide on his approach and miss out all the details that are not helpful or that he can incorporate legal argument in the affidavit. What he *can* do, is, for example, to make a preliminary decision with the client as to the order that she will be seeking (for example, she may decide she would be content with an order that the other spouse transfer his share in the matrimonial home to her in return for which the balance of her claims are dismissed). If the client has pretty definite and realistic requirements, the desired order can be set out in the affidavit and the facts of the case marshalled to justify why it is appropriate. In the case of a respondent to an application, his best offer can be stated in the affidavit in much the same way. Where the solicitor is brave enough to do this, it may have a positive advantage not only in that it makes it easier for him to argue his case to the district judge, but also in that it will be relevant to the question of costs. It shows that the party filing the affidavit has been willing to settle on those terms at least from the date of the affidavit and, if the order ultimately made accords with the proposed order/offer set out in the affidavit, the district judge may be inclined to order the other party to pay the costs occasioned by not agreeing to it earlier in the proceedings. The solitor should, of course, be careful not to commit his client to a proposal in his affidavit before he has obtained sufficient information about the other party's situation to form a judgment as to whether it is realistic.

(g) *Remarriage*   The question of remarriage will be relevant where the remarriage has actually taken place or is definitely planned (see Chapter 16 paragraph 3.3). Where this is the case, details should be disclosed in the client's affidavit. If the client is cohabiting with someone, this should be disclosed together with details of how it affects his or her financial position.

(h) *Conduct*   The conduct of the other party is generally irrelevant to the court's decision on ancillary matters and should be left out of the client's affidavit. However, if the conduct is so serious that it may affect the court's order (see Chapter 16 paragraph 3.5), it should be carefully detailed. Where any substantial contested allegations of conduct arise in proceedings where periodical payments, a lump sum or property are in issue, the court must consider whether the complexity, difficulty or gravity of the issues are such that they ought to be tried in the High Court (Practice Direction [1988] 2 All ER 103, [1988] 1 FLR 540). Note that if an affidavit filed in connection with an ancillary relief application contains an allegation of adultery or of an improper association with a named person, Family Proceedings Rules 1991, r. 2.60(1) requires that that person be served with a copy of the affidavit (or such part of it as the court may direct) endorsed with a notice in Form M14 and that person shall be entitled to intervene in the proceedings.

(i) *Comments on the other party's affidavit*   If the other party has already filed his affidavit, the client's affidavit should comment on that affidavit, showing what facts are in dispute and dealing with any offers or arguments put forward.

4.3   Further affidavits

Although it is obviously in no one's interest to have a profusion of affidavits, subject to any directions the district judge may give, either spouse is free to file more than one affidavit if it is necessary to do so in the particular case.

Example. The applicant files an affidavit in support of her claim for a property adjustment order. The other spouse files an affidavit in answer setting out his means. He raises various points concerning the application which it is necessary for the applicant to answer. She files a further affidavit to deal with these points.

5 EVIDENCE OF OTHER PERSONS

Either spouse is free to file affidavits from other persons supporting his or her case although, in routine application, the evidence is normally confined to an affidavit from each party as there is no further relevant evidence.

It does not seem that the court can order anyone other than a party to file an affidavit or to produce documents prior to the court hearing (see *Wynne* v *Wynne and Jeffers* [1980] 3 All ER 659, [1981] 1 WLR 69). Thus, for example, a mistress of the respondent cannot be ordered to file an affidavit disclosing her means or to produce her wages slips. However, the respondent in such a case can be ordered to file an affidavit disclosing his mistress's means so far as he knows them. It would appear that even if a third party is served with the petitioner's notice of application in accordance with the Family Proceedings Rules 1991, r. 2.59, it does not mean that the party served becomes a party to the proceedings (*Re T (Financial Provision)* [1990] 1 FLR 1, [1989] Fam Law 438). Furthermore, even if a person intervenes and thus becomes a party, it does not necessarily mean that discovery can be obtained against him, since it depends upon what is relevant to the issue being tried (*S* v *X (Intervenors)* [1990] 2 FLR 187, [1990] Fam Law 96).

The Family Proceedings Rules 1991, r. 2.62(4), empower the district judge, either before or during an ancillary relief hearing, to order the attendance of any person for examination or cross-examination and to order the discovery and production of any document or require further affidavits. Furthermore, r. 2.62(7), enables any party to apply to the court for an order that *any person* should attend a 'production appointment' before the court and produce documents specified or described in the order, if the court takes the view that such production is necessary to fairly dispose of the application for ancillary relief or to save costs. However, an important caveat is that no one may be compelled to produce any document at a 'production appointment' which he could not be compelled to produce at the hearing of an application for ancillary relief (r. 2.62(8)). A person attending a production appointment may be legally represented (r. 2.62(9)).

6 OBTAINING FURTHER INFORMATION

6.1 Where the other party does not file an affidavit at all

6.1.1 Seeking a direction from the district judge

Clearly, the court needs evidence of the financial situations of both parties before it can decide on an appropriate order. Where the other party has not filed an affidavit at all, application can be made to the district judge for an order that he should do so. Under Family Proceedings Rules 1991, r. 2.62(5) the district judge can give directions at any stage of the proceedings as to the filing and service of pleadings and as to the further conduct of the proceedings. In order to safeguard the client's position on costs, it is suggested that the other party's solicitor be informed of any intended application in advance and given a fixed period (say 7 or 14 days) in which to stave it off by filing the required affidavit. The district judge should be asked to indorse the order to file an affidavit with a penal notice to facilitate enforcement.

Where a direction has already been given requiring the party to file an affidavit but is not endorsed with a penal notice (for example, as part of the automatic directions that some courts issue in relation to ancillary relief applications; see paragraph 8 below), application should be made to the district judge for the direction to be endorsed with a penal notice so that steps can be taken to enforce it against the spouse if he still fails to comply.

In the event of continued non-compliance with an order endorsed with a penal notice, application can be made for the party concerned to be committed to prison.

6.1.2   Seeking an interim order

Another way to force the other party to disclose his means is to seek an interim order (almost invariably for periodical payments) against him. The court is entitled to draw adverse inferences from a party's failure to provide information about his situation (see, for example *Ette* v *Ette* [1965] 1 All ER 341, [1964] 1 WLR 1433). The idea of seeking an interim order is that the court makes an oppressive order for maintenance on the basis that, in the absence of any hard facts to the contrary, he must be assumed to be a wealthy man. It is hoped that, when he learns of the order, the party concerned will be only too anxious to disclose his limited means in order to ensure that the order will not be confirmed in the long term.

There is no reason why this tactic should not be adopted in addition to making an application to the district judge for a direction that the respondent file an affidavit.

6.2   Where the other party's affidavit is inadequate

6.2.1   Requesting more information by letter

Family Proceedings Rules 1991, r. 2.63 provides that any party to an application for ancillary relief may write to any other party requiring him to give further information concerning any matter contained in any affidavit filed by or on behalf of that party or any other relevant matter. This is the matrimonial equivalent of seeking further and better particulars of a pleading.

Note that the written request can be made simply in a letter or more formally by preparing a form of questionnaire for the other party to answer.

6.2.2   Seeking an order from the district judge in the event of non-compliance

If the other party fails to comply with the request for further information (whether because he fails to reply at all or replies inadequately), an application can be made to the district judge for directions; for example, the district judge could direct that the party concerned should file a further affidavit dealing with the matters set out in the letter requesting further particulars.

6.3 Examining documents to find out the relevant details

It is not desirable to rely wholly on the other party for information about his means. The solicitor should ensure that the fullest possible disclosure of documents takes place so that he has sight of any documents which may help him to ascertain what the true position is. The position as to discovery and inspection is set out in paragraph 7 below.

7 DISCOVERY AND INSPECTION

7.1 Automatic discovery and inspection

Once both spouses have filed affidavits, the next step is discovery. The importance of obtaining as much documentary evidence as possible from the other side is stressed in paragraph 6.3 above. Mutual discovery should take place 14 days after the last affidavit has been filed and, unless some other period is agreed, inspection should take place 7 days later (Practice Direction [1981] 2 All ER 642, [1981] 1 WLR 1010).

7.2 How does discovery take place?

Each solicitor must prepare a list of all the documents which are or have been in the possession, custody or power of his client relating to any matter in question in the case. There is a standard form of list which can be used. Documents are listed under three headings:

(a)   documents in the party's possession, custody or power which he is willing to produce for inspection.

(b)   documents in the party's possession, custody or power which he objects to producing (for example, correspondence passing between the party and his solicitor which is privileged);

(c)   documents which have been in the party's possession, custody or power but are no longer.

7.3 Inspection

When he receives the other party's list, the solicitor will decide which documents he wishes to inspect. Arrangements will normally be made between solicitors for inspection. This may be at the offices of the solicitor for the party having possession of the documents if there are a lot of documents or they are particularly bulky. In other cases, if there are only a few documents, his solicitor will be prepared to photocopy the documents and forward them on the other side agreeing to reimburse the photocopying costs.

7.4 Where sufficient discovery does not take place automatically

If the other party does not furnish a list of documents automatically or offer facilities for inspection, the appropriate course is for the solicitor first to write a letter requiring him to do so (Family Proceedings Rules 1991, r. 2.63). If the other party does not comply with this written request, application can be made to the district judge for directions (a standard direction might be, for example, that a list be served within 14 days and inspection take place 7 days thereafter).

The solicitor will know roughly what documents to expect the other party to disclose although the documents available will vary from case to case. If he has reason to believe that there are other documents that should have been disclosed he can ask for a specific order for discovery and production of particular documents (Family Proceedings Rules 1991, r. 2.63) and see, for example, *B* v *B* [1978] Fam 181, [1979] 1 All ER 801).

The following are suggestions of documents which may already exist or could be requested:

(a)   accounts (it is normally reasonable to expect disclosure of the last three years' accounts);

(b)   bank statements, building society pass books, post office books, etc. (to go back three years is traditional but may be a bit excessive in some cases — the solicitor should exercise his own judgment as to what to require, depending on what he hopes to find out from the statements);

(c)   share certificates and details of other investments;

(d)   wages slips or a letter from the party's employers setting out his earnings (depending on how variable the earnings are, details of at least the past year's earnings can be expected together with the most recent pay slip);

(e)   documentary evidence of bank loans and the purpose for which they were taken out;

(f)   documentary evidence of pension entitlement (for example, the employer's handbook and a letter from the employer setting out the particular employee's entitlement) and of entitlement under insurance policies (life insurance, etc.).

8   DIRECTIONS

Practice varies around the country as to whether the ancillary relief hearing will be preceded by a preliminary hearing for the giving of directions or not. Some courts automatically send out standard written directions soon after Form M11/M13 is filed and leave it to the parties to make a special application if they require other directions. Other courts routinely fix a short directions hearing which is attended by the parties' legal advisers so that they and the district judge can sort out the directions necessary in that particular case. Others may allocate a date for a full hearing and then leave it entirely up to the parties to seek directions if they need them. If the court fixes an appointment for the full hearing of the application and one of the parties intends to apply only for directions on that day, he must file and serve on the other party a notice to that effect (r. 2.62(6)).

The district judge has a broad power to give directions at any stage as to the filing and serving of pleadings and as to the further conduct of the proceedings (r. 2.62(5)). The areas that are commonly covered include:

(a)   Filing and service of affidavits by the parties and supporting witnesses and their attendance at the hearing for examination/cross-examination.

(b)   Discovery and inspection (the district judge is often asked to order that specific documentation be produced, for example, bank statements and accounts; see paragraph 7.4 above).

(c)   Valuation of any land. (When he determines the ancillary relief application, the district judge will need to know the value of any land involved. Therefore unless the parties can agree the value of the property, it will have to be professionally valued. The usual course is for a valuer to be instructed jointly by the parties, each party being responsible for half the valuer's charges. If this has not already been done before the directions appointment, a common direction is for the property to be valued by an agreed valuer or, in default of agreement, evidence of valuation to be restricted to one expert witness each side).

(d)   The fixing of the hearing date (the district judge may be asked to allocate a hearing date there and then or he may give a direction that the application be heard on a day to be fixed, usually on one or both parties certifying compliance with the directions and readiness for trial and giving an estimate of the time required for the hearing).

(e)   Interim periodical payments/maintenance pending suit can be ordered if appropriate.

(f)   Both parties are usually given liberty to apply for further directions if necessary.

(g)   The costs of the directions hearing are usually costs in the cause.

In addition, the directions hearing can be used to deal with any specific problems that have cropped up over the preparation of the particular case.

Note that the Family Proceedings Rules 1991, r. 2.62(7) to (9) enable the district judge to order *any* person to attend a 'production appointment' before the court and to produce specific documents which appear to the court to be necessary for disposing fairly of the application for ancillary relief and for saving costs. Such a person may be legally represented at the production appointment if he so wishes.

9   THE HEARING

9.1   Preparation

It is suggested that the following matters should be covered:

(a)   The solicitor should spend some time isolating the issues in the case and ensuring that he can prove any disputed factual matters that may have a bearing on the district judge's decision and is not wasting his own and the court's time and incurring expense in proving matters that are accepted by the other side. There is no point in calling evidence to show that the respondent has three cars and a large ocean-going yacht if the respondent admits that he has; on the other hand, it would be unfortunate not to call the evidence if the respondent is not prepared to admit this and is alleging that he is as poor as a church mouse.

(b)   A bundle of documents (preferably a joint bundle prepared with the other side) should be compiled for the use of the district judge including pay slips, P 60 forms, bank statements, hire-purchase agreements, valuer's report, etc. The documents should be paginated for easy reference. Too many ancillary relief applications founder in a mass of loose pay slips, pass books and loan agreements produced for the first time like rabbits from a hat at the hearing.

(c)   A calculation of both parties' tax positions should be prepared with copies for the other side and the district judge. The form of this calculation varies but it should show the impact of taxation on both parties and, normally, the net effect on both parties of a one-third order (see Chapter 16 paragraph 6.1) and of any other order proposed on the client's behalf or by the other side. In some areas of the country, district judges issue standard directions about tax calculations, for example, that a tax calculation should be agreed by the parties before the hearing and made available to the court.

(d)   An estimate of the client's likely costs of the hearing and of the divorce generally should be prepared (Practice Direction [1988] 2 All ER 63, [1988] 1 FLR 452; *Singer (former Sharegin)* v *Sharegin* [1984] FLR 114, [1984] Fam Law 58; *Atkinson* v *Atkinson* [1984] FLR 524, [1984] Fam Law 305). The purpose of this is to enable the district judge to know how each party will be affected by costs (either in the form of the Legal Aid Board's charge in legal aid cases or in the shape of the solicitor's bill in private cases). This can affect not only the order as to the costs of the ancillary relief proceedings but also the substantive ancillary relief order that the district judge decides to make.

(e)   Consideration should be given to sending a Calderbank letter to preserve the client's position in relation to the costs of the hearing. Calderbank letters are explained at paragraph 10 below.

(f)   At the risk of stating the obvious, it must be stressed that the practitioner should think out in *advance* what matters are covered adequately in his client's affidavit and what further evidence he will need to elicit from her at the hearing. It is helpful if a written list of the client's current outgoings can be provided for the other side and the district judge, if these have changed since the affidavit was filed, to save everyone having to note them down laboriously whilst the client gives oral evidence. Similarly, thought must be given to cross-examination. Long, repetitive or discourteous cross-examination is likely to antagonise the district judge — the art is putting telling questions pleasantly and in knowing what not to ask and when to stop. This is easier if a brief list has been made in advance of the points that need to be put to the witness.

(g)   Negotiations should be carried on right up to the last minute. The client may be saved a substantial sum in costs if a contested hearing can be averted.

9.2   The hearing itself

The hearing will almost always be before a district judge (though the district judge does have power to refer the application to a judge; r. 2.65). It will be held in the district judge's chambers and will be private. In theory, the procedure should follow the normal pattern (applicant opens the case and calls evidence, respondent calls evidence, respondent addresses the district judge, applicant addresses the district judge). Many district judges do require proceedings to be run in this traditional manner. Others are prepared/prefer to adopt a much more informal approach. It is not unknown for the district judge to start off the proceedings by letting the parties know what he has in mind having read their affidavits and inviting comment and discussion before going on to hear evidence and argument. Sometimes this produces agreement between parties without a fully contested hearing. Even if it does not, it is often valuable to the advocate in giving him an idea as to how the district judge's mind is working — it helps to know what aspects of the client's case do not appeal to the district judge and what points are particularly troubling him.

The question of examination and cross-examination of witnesses is dealt with in paragraph 9.1. The important thing to remember is to cover all relevant points but concisely. Often evidence is one of the least important parts of the case as the district judge knows much of what he needs to know already from the affidavits if they have been drafted properly. Some points should, however, be made here on addressing the district judge, which may be a good deal more important.

The applicant's advocate must be prepared to open the case formally, outlining to the district judge the history of the matter (although often he will have gleaned this from his preliminary reading of the papers) and explaining what order it is that his client wants. It is a help to get matters clear in one's own mind before the hearing by preparing a timetable of the case so far (date of marriage, birth of children, separation, petition, etc.). It may be convenient to put in any agreed bundles of documents, tax calculations, etc. in the opening.

When it comes to addressing the district judge in closing the case, it is not often very useful to indulge in a review of the evidence that the district judge has just heard although important points can be brought out if necessary. It can, however, be a great help to put to the district judge the types of order that the advocate submits may be appropriate, outlining how his suggestions (and any suggestions made by the other side) would work in practice, for example, what effect they would have on the parties' tax positions, on income support entitlement and on the legal aid charge. Where maintenance is concerned, it is also helpful to draw to the district judge's attention how the proposed order would (or would not) enable both parties to meet their reasonable outgoings. From time to time it may be necessary to cite authorities on a legal point, but on the whole ancillary relief cases depend upon their own facts and authorities are not therefore particularly useful.

The district judge may make a bald announcement of his decision or he may give a short judgment. A careful note should be taken of what he says as it can be important if an appeal is made against his order or if an application is made for a variation of the order at a later stage.

9.3 Other important matters

There are a number of most important matters that must not be overlooked at the end of the hearing:

(a) Back-dating an order for periodical payments: there is power to back-date periodical payments orders to the date of the making of the application (see Chapter 14). If an order is back-dated, the payer is instantly in arrears in respect of the payments due prior to the hearing. For this reason, the court will be reluctant to back-date unless the payer has actually been making voluntary periodical payments in the run-up to the hearing which can be offset against the arrears. In orders applied for prior to 15 March 1988 and made before 30 June 1988 it could have been to the advantage of the payer to have the order back-dated so as to enable him to get tax relief for payments he had already made. However, the payer will no longer be entitled to tax relief on any orders applied for after 15 March 1988, save to a very limited extent. The only way in which payments of maintenance will be eligible for tax relief in future is that a spouse paying maintenance will be able to claim a further tax allowance in addition to his normal personal allowance. The extra tax allowance for 1992/93 is £1,720. Although it is now no longer possible, for income tax purposes, to back-date an order to enable tax relief to be claimed for payments that have been made prior to the order, tax relief *may* still be claimed for maintenance which is back-dated in an agreement or order provided that payment of the arrears is made *after* the date of the agreement or order. The practitioner will find this especially important in relation to the year of separation; for that year a husband can claim, in addition to the married couple's allowance, a maintenance deduction of £1,720 (for 1992/93), provided that he has paid maintenance of at least that amount under a legally enforceable written agreement or court order. An example may help to clarify the position:

> **Example.** Sally and Ken separate on 1 November 1991. Ken pays no maintenance. On 1 January 1992 he makes a written agreement under which he is to pay Sally maintenance of £100 per month, payable on the first day of every month and backdated to 1 November 1991. On 2 January 1992 Ken pays Sally £300 (January instalment £100 + arrears accruing since November £200). He pays £100 in each of the months February, March and April 1992. For 1991/92 Ken can claim a maintenance deduction of £600 as his total qualifying maintenance payments for the tax year are less than the maximum deduction of £1,720.

If, however, in the above example, Ken had made *voluntary* payments of maintenance to Sally from November 1991, then the payments between November 1991 and December 1991 could not become tax deductible by back-dating the 1 January written agreement. In that case Ken's maintenance deduction for the tax year 1991/92 would be limited to £400 reflecting the payments made in January, February, March and April 1992. The payer's advocate should be in a position to inform the district judge of the payments already made, so that credit can be given for them.

(b)   Registration of periodical payments order in magistrates' court: application can be made for leave to register a periodical payments order in the magistrates' court (Part I, Maintenance Orders Act 1958). This means that the order will be paid and enforced through the magistrates' court and that any application for a variation will have to be made to that court. It also means that the diversion procedure can be used with regard to social security benefits (see Chapter 35 paragraph 12). An application for registration should certainly be considered where it appears that payment under the order may be erratic.

(c)   Costs: when the district judge has announced his decision, the question of costs must be considered. It is traditional in civil cases for the party who has 'won' to claim (and get) his or her costs. However, this general rule goes by the board in most ancillary relief cases for a variety of reasons. Firstly, it is not always easy to decide who *has* won in an ancillary relief case — both parties often go away partially dissatisfied. Secondly, one or both parties are usually on legal aid and there are restrictions on making costs orders against legally aided litigants (see Chapter 2 paragraph 16.6). Thirdly, the district judge may well already have taken the incidence of costs into account in making his order (but see *Collins* v *Collins* [1987] 1 FLR 226 where it was held that a lump sum order may not be increased to compensate a spouse for the operation of the statutory charge even though her costs were increased by her husband's conduct of the proceedings). As a result, it is quite common for district judge's to order 'no order as to costs', i.e. each party bears his/her own costs unless there is clear evidence that one party has been offering an appropriate settlement all along and the other has been unreasonably sticking out against it (Calderbank letters and open offers made in a party's affidavit can be useful in establishing that this is the case).

(d)   Certificate for counsel: if counsel appears, he should ask the district judge to certify the case fit for counsel. If no certificate is obtained, the cost of instructing counsel will not be recoverable from the other party (where he is ordered to pay the costs) or from the legal aid fund (where the client's costs are borne by the fund).

(e)   Legal aid taxation direction: where a party is legally aided, a legal aid taxation direction should be requested to enable costs to be recovered from the legal aid fund.

10   CALDERBANK OFFERS

A party who wishes to make an offer in settlement of an ancillary relief claim can do so in at least three ways:

(a)   He (or more usually his solicitor) can send an open letter to the other side setting out the offer. The letter can be referred to at the hearing both on the question of costs and on the question of what substantive relief should be granted.

(b)   He can incorporate his offer in his affidavit so that it is plain for the court to see at all stages of the hearing.

(c)   He (or again, more usually his solicitor) can make an offer, preferably in writing, expressed to be 'without prejudice but reserving the right to refer to the offer on the issue of costs'. This is called a 'Calderbank offer' (referring to the case of *Calderbank* v *Calderbank* [1976] Fam 93, [1975] 3 All ER 333) and is the matrimonial equivalent of paying into court. No reference can be made to the offer when the question of ancillary relief is being decided because it was made without prejudice. However, if at the hearing, the district judge orders no more than the amount offered, the offeror can refer to the letter and ask for it to be taken into account on the question of costs, urging, for example, that he should have his costs from the date the offer was made or, at the very least, that he should not have to pay the other side's costs from that date on.

11   CONSENT ORDERS

The importance of attempting to settle ancillary relief disputes without incurring the costs of a contested hearing cannot be stressed too heavily. There is no point in fighting over £750 if a costs bill of £1,000 is run up in the process. Furthermore, a continuing battle over ancillary relief does nothing to help the parties get over the breakdown of their marriage and resolve other difficulties, for example, over children.

Just as each party has a duty to make full disclosure of all material facts to the court hearing an ancillary relief application, each party has a duty to make full and frank disclosure of all material facts to the other party during negotiations which may lead to a consent order (see the case of *Livesey* v *Jenkins* [1985] 2 WLR 47, [1985] 1 All ER 106 where the House of Lords found a consent order to be invalid on the basis that the wife had not disclosed to the husband the material fact that she had become engaged to be married).

The solicitor should not be frightened therefore to seek from the other party all the information that he considers to be necessary in order to advise his client whether a proposed settlement is acceptable.

Rule 2.61 of the Family Proceedings Rules 1991 should go some way to ensuring that relevant facts are disclosed. This rule deals with the procedure for seeking a consent order for financial relief. The procedure where agreement is reached before the hearing date of the ancillary relief applications should now therefore be as follows:

(a)   If agreement is reached before either party has filed a notice in Form M11/M13, application should be made by one or the other party in Form M11/M13 for an order in the agreed terms and, in accordance with r. 2.61(1), there should be lodged with the application minutes of the order in terms sought, indorsed with a statement signed by the respondent signifying his agreement. Presumably, if agreement is reached after Form M11/M13 has been filed, the applicant should simply lodge the indorsed minutes with the court requesting that the district judge should make an order in these terms.

(b)   Section 33A, Matrimonial Causes Act 1973 (as added by the Matrimonial and Family Proceedings Act 1984) provides that, on an application for a consent order for financial relief the court may, unless it has reason to think that there are other circumstances into which it ought to inquire, make an order in the terms agreed on the basis only of the prescribed information furnished with the application. Rule 2.61 prescribes the information that must be furnished. It requires that there shall be lodged with the application a statement of information relied on in support of the application. Matters that must normally be incorporated include an estimate in summary form of the approximate amount or value of the capital and income resources of each party and, where relevant, of any minor child of the family; details of what is intended with regard to the occupation or disposal of the matrimonial home and what is intended with regard to accommodation of both parties and minor children; whether either party has remarried or presently intends to remarry or cohabit; any other especially significant circumstances (see r. 2.61(1)). The statement of information can be provided in more than one document. No doubt affidavits already filed in relation to the application may be sufficient to provide the court with some of the information required.

Where agreement is reached only at the door of the court, r. 2.61(3) enables the court to dispense with the lodging of minutes and a statement of information and to give directions for the order to be drawn and the information that would otherwise be required in the statement of information to be given in such manner as it sees fit.

It is incumbent upon the practitioner to make sure that the order is carefully drafted so as to embody what the parties have agreed upon comprehensively, leaving no room for future doubt (*Sandford* v *Sandford* [1986] 1 FLR 412; *Dinch* v *Dinch* [1987] 1 WLR 252).

12   APPEAL

Where an order is made after a contested hearing in front of the district judge, either party may appeal if dissatisfied to a judge in chambers. Note that the appeal period is 14 days from the date of the district judge's order (see Family Proceedings Rules 1991, r. 8.1(4)). Rule 8.1(2) of the Family Proceedings Rules 1991, makes it clear that any order or decision granting, varying, or refusing to vary an order on an application for ancillary relief is to be treated as a 'final' order for the purposes of the County Court Rules 1981, Ord. 37, r. 6. Furthermore, the appellant must now set out in his notice of appeal the *grounds* of the appeal. It would appear that such an appeal will no longer be conducted by way of a re-hearing. The parties will usually present the appeal on the basis of legal submissions; only in 'exceptional circumstances' will leave be given for fresh evidence to be adduced in the course of the appeal (see *Merrit* v *Merrit, The Independent*, 10 February 1992).

As the case of *Livesey* v *Jenkins* (supra) illustrates, a consent order can also be set aside. The court would be justified in so doing, if it could be shown that the parties' agreement was reached on the basis of a serious mistake by one of the parties or as a result of fraud, or serious misrepresentation, or in circumstances where one party had not disclosed all the material facts to the other and that this had led the court to make an order substantially different from that which would otherwise have been made. The proper procedure to be adopted when challenging a consent order made by a district judge was clarified in the case of *B-T* v *B-T (Divorce Procedure)* [1990] 2 FLR 1. It would appear that the appellant could either appeal against the order to the judge and obtain a hearing *de novo*, or he could make a fresh application to the district judge for a re-hearing (in the proper form under County Court Rules 1981, Ord. 37).

13   FAMILY LAW BAR ASSOCIATION CONCILIATION BOARD

The Family Law Bar Association has set up the Family Law Bar Association Conciliation Board. Where both parties are represented by solicitors, they can (by agreement) submit disputed questions of ancillary relief to an adjudicator selected by the association from a panel of senior barristers. The adjudicator considers the papers submitted to him and makes a recommendation as to the resolution of the dispute. It is for the parties themselves to agree whether the adjudicator's recommendation will be binding on them subject, of course, to the approval of the court where it is intended to obtain a court order embodying the terms of the recommendation. Further details of the scheme and the fees payable for the service can be obtained from the clerk to the Family Law Bar Association.

16 Factors to be considered on ancillary relief applications

1 INTRODUCTION

The court has a very wide discretion as to what orders to make on an application for ancillary relief. Section 25 of the Matrimonial Causes Act 1973 directs that all the circumstances of the case should be taken into account and it has been stressed by the courts that every case has to be dealt with individually on its own facts. This means that decisions in past cases are not normally precedents in the strict sense of the word. As Ormrod LJ pointed out in *Martin* v *Martin* [1978] Fam 12, [1977] 3 All ER 762, they can never be better than guidelines. It follows, as he comfortingly acknowledged, that advising a client on the likely outcome of his ancillary relief application is 'a matter of trial and error and imagination'.

This chapter sets out the s. 25 considerations that must be taken into account and explains a number of the principles (such as the one-third rule) that provide further guidance in ancillary relief matters. New ancillary relief decisions are always being reported. This chapter makes no pretence of citing them all — in fact, the number of authorities cited has been deliberately kept to a minimum on the basis that most decisions are examples only, not precedents. If further authority for a proposition is required, it is suggested that reference should be made to a standard textbook on matrimonial law and, for recent decisions, to the publication *Family Law*.

2 THE S. 25 FACTORS

2.1 General duty

The court's general duty on all ancillary relief applications is set out in s. 25(1) as follows:

> It shall be the duty of the court in deciding whether to exercise its powers under section 23, 24 or 24A above and, if so, in what manner, to have regard to all the circumstances of the case, first consideration being given to the welfare while a minor of any child of the family who has not attained the age of eighteen.

In *Suter* v *Suter* [1987] 2 FLR 232, [1987] 3 WLR 9, [1987] 2 All ER 336, the Court of Appeal underlined that the welfare of the children was to be given first consideration but was not the overriding consideration. Thus the task for the court was to consider all the circumstances, always bearing in mind the important first consideration of the welfare of the children, and then to try to attain a financial result that was just between husband and wife.

2.2   Specific matters to consider on application for provision for a spouse

Section 25(2) directs the court in particular to have regard to the following matters when dealing with an application for ancillary relief for a party to the marriage:

(a)   the income, earning capacity, property and other financial resources which each of the parties to the marriage has or is likely to have in the foreseeable future, including in the case of earning capacity any increase in that capacity which it would in the opinion of the court be reasonable to expect a party to the marriage to take steps to acquire;

(b)   the financial needs, obligations and responsibilities which each of the parties to the marriage has or is likely to have in the foreseeable future;

(c)   the standard of living enjoyed by the family before the breakdown of the marriage;

(d)   the age of each party to the marriage and the duration of the marriage;

(e)   any physical or mental disability of either of the parties to the marriage;

(f)   the contributions which each of the parties has made or is likely in the foreseeable future to make to the welfare of the family including any contribution by looking after the home or caring for the family;

(g)   the conduct of each of the parties, if that conduct is such that it would in the opinion of the court be inequitable to disregard it;

(h)   in the case of proceedings for divorce or nullity of marriage, the value to each of the parties to the marriage of any benefit (for example, a pension) which, by reason of the dissolution or annulment of the marriage, that party will lose the chance of acquiring.

2.3   Specific matters to consider on application for provision for a child

Section 25(3) directs the court to have regard in particular to the following matters when dealing with an application for ancillary relief for a child of the family:

(a)   the financial needs of the child;

(b)   the income, earning capacity (if any), property and other financial resources of the child;

(c)   any physical or mental disability of the child;

(d)   the manner in which he was being and in which the parties to the marriage expected him to be educated or trained;

(e)   the considerations mentioned in relation to the parties to the marriage in paragraphs (a), (b), (c) and (e) of subsection (2) above.

Furthermore, where the application relates to a child of the family who is not the child of the party against whom an order is sought, the court must also have regard:

(a)   to whether that party assumed any responsibility for the child's maintenance, and, if so, to the extent to which, and the basis upon which, that party assumed such responsibility and to the length of time for which that party discharged such responsibility;

(b)   to whether in assuming and discharging such responsibility that party did so knowing that the child was not his or her own;

(c)   to the liability of any other person to maintain the child (s. 25(4)).

2.4   The clean-break approach

The Matrimonial and Family Proceedings Act 1984 added a new section, s. 25A, to the Matrimonial Causes Act 1973.

Section 25A(1) obliges the court, when exercising its ancillary relief powers in relation to a spouse on or after divorce or nullity, to consider whether it would be appropriate to exercise those powers so as to achieve a clean break between the parties as soon after the decree as the court thinks just and reasonable.

Section 25A(2) applies to cases where the court decides to make a periodical payments or secured periodical payments order in favour of a spouse on or after divorce or nullity. It obliges the court to consider, in particular, whether it would be appropriate to make an order for a fixed term only of sufficient length to enable the spouse in whose favour the order is made to adjust without undue hardship to being financially independent of the other party.

Section 25A(3) enables the court to impose a clean break between the parties when it considers that no continuing obligation to make or secure periodical payments should be imposed on either spouse in favour of the other. In such a case, the court can dismiss an application for periodical payments or secured periodical payments without the consent of the applicant and, to put the matter beyond doubt, direct that the applicant shall not be entitled to make any further application in relation to that marriage for a periodical payments or secured periodical payments order.

2.5   Section 24A(6), Matrimonial Causes Act 1973

Section 24A(6) was added to the Matrimonial Causes Act 1973 with the s. 24A power of sale by the Matrimonial Homes and Property Act 1981. It was, at that time, known as s. 25(4). It has been reshuffled by the Matrimonial and Family Proceedings Act 1984 and now appears as s. 24A(6) of the Matrimonial Causes Act 1973.

It ensures that, before an order for sale is made in respect of property owned by a spouse jointly with a third party, the third party will be allowed an opportunity to make representations with respect to the order. Anything that the third party has to say on the subject will be taken into account as one of the circumstances to which the court has to have regard under s. 25(1) when deciding what order to make.

3   THE S. 25 FACTORS IN MORE DETAIL

Certain of the s. 25 factors need no further commentary. Those that do require further explanation are dealt with below.

3.1   Income and earning capacity

Income and earning capacity can be relevant not only in deciding whether periodical payments should be ordered and if so at what rate but also in deciding on lump sum and property adjustment orders.

For example, a lump sum may be ordered not only where a party has capital from which to pay but also where his income is sufficient to meet the repayments on a loan raised for that purpose. Furthermore, in deciding what is to happen to the matrimonial home, it is crucial to know whether there is sufficient income available to pay the mortgage and outgoings — if not, the only realistic course is to order a sale. When it comes to sharing out the equity, again income and earning capacity are important; for instance, a wife may need less from the proceeds of sale if she has an earning capacity and can obtain a mortgage than if she has no income of her own and needs to buy accommodation outright.

Where a spouse is in work, there is normally evidence of his earnings in the form of wage slips or accounts. Benefits in kind such as the use of a company car and free meals must be taken into account as well as cash payments. The court will look at earnings before deduction of tax but normally giving credit for the expenses of working such as travelling to work, union dues, national insurance and superannuation contributions.

The court can take into account not only what a spouse actually *is* earning but also what he or she could reasonably be expected to earn. Thus it is possible for a periodical payments order to be made against a man who is unemployed on the basis that there is work that he could do if he tried. However, in these times of high unemployment, district judges will normally be reluctant to make such an order unless there is very clear evidence that the spouse concerned is shirking. The court can be asked to proceed on the basis that a spouse who is already earning could be earning more, for instance, because he is not working full-time when he could be.

A wife who is not working, for example, because she gave up work on marriage or to look after children, may be expected to get a job. However, the court is unlikely to take the view that she should be working unless any children are, at the very least, of school age and unless there appears to be work available that she could do. If there is evidence that, at the date of the hearing, there is work available to her that would fit in with her domestic commitments, the court can reduce her maintenance, or (if it appears that she can be expected to be self-sufficient in the long term) dismiss her claim entirely. If the evidence is only that she should be able to go back to work in the future (for instance, when the children are rather older or when she has re-trained), the court may consider making a fixed term periodical payments order allowing her a period to adjust to her financial independence or may make a normal open-ended order leaving the onus on the husband to seek a variation when the wife gets a job or when he feels she should be making efforts to seek employment.

3.2 Property and other financial resources

Assets of all sorts can be taken into account, and not only assets that each spouse has at the date of the hearing, but also assets which he or she is likely to have in the foreseeable future.

Thus, for example, money or property that a spouse is likely to inherit under a will can be taken into account. Obviously, wills can be changed right up to death and this element of uncertainty is borne in mind in assessing how valuable the spouse's prospects really are, with the result that the courts tend to be very reluctant to set much store by possible inheritances. One further difficulty is in obtaining evidence of what the inheritance is likely to be. A subpoena directed at the wife's ailing father under whose will the wife was likely to benefit was set aside in *Morgan* v *Morgan* [1977] Fam 122, [1977] 2 All ER 515, on the basis that his privacy should not be invaded in this way.

Entitlements under an insurance policy that could be surrendered or is likely to mature anyway in the foreseeable future can be taken into account. Pension and lump sum entitlement on retirement can be considered.

In *Ibbetson* v *Ibbetson* [1984] FLR 545, the court took into account that the wife's new cohabitee intended to convey his house into their joint names.

The court will pay attention to the fact that not all assets are readily realisable. A businessman, for example, may not be able to draw substantial capital sums out of his business without affecting its liquidity, indeed, he may not even be able to withdraw his entire income entitlement each year as profits may need to be ploughed back as working capital. The court would not make an order that would cause a spouse to lose his livelihood, for example, by forcing him to sell his business. If the other spouse's contribution to a business should be recognised, this will have to be done in some other way, for example, by giving her a greater share in the family's other assets such as the matrimonial home or by ordering a lump sum payment to her to be made by instalments, the instalments being at such a level that the husband can afford to pay them from income without prejudicing his business interests.

Account can be taken of property and income of a cohabitee or new spouse (see paragraph 3.3 below).

Note that where there is doubt as to a party's future prospects, it may be worth considering seeking an adjournment until such time as the position becomes clearer if it appears that this will not delay matters unduly or prejudice either side. However, it has been held that it would be wrong to adjourn an application for a lump sum payment for more than four or five years (*Roberts* v *Roberts* [1986] 2 All ER 483, [1986] 1 WLR 437).

3.3   Needs, obligations and responsibilities

Needs and obligations vary from household to household. Invariably, however, both spouses will need a roof over their heads and the spouse who has a residence order in respect of the children will have a particularly pressing need for a home for the family. This factor is likely to be of great importance in the court's decision. The court will also look at each party's regular outgoings (fuel bills, rent, community charge (council tax from 1993), water rate, mortgage, food, hire-purchase debts, etc.) and take into account such as are reasonable for a person in his circumstances. What is reasonable will obviously vary from case to case — someone travelling a mile to work each day may be expected to use a bicycle or walk if money for the family is tight whereas a person who travels many miles in the course of his job can fairly expect to do so in a relatively comfortable car. The court's approach to each party's regular expenditure will have to be realistic — it may be wholly unreasonable for one party to be purchasing a video recorder on hire-purchase where the other party does not even have enough money for food, but, once the party has entered into the commitment, there is very little that can be done about it and the continuing obligation to pay will have to be taken into account.

Although the abstract prospect of remarriage is not relevant, where one or the other party has actually remarried or formed a new relationship, this will have to be taken into account as it will obviously have an effect on his needs and obligations and possibily also on his resources. He may be in a better position than if he had remained single (for example, where the new partner has substantial means), or the new relationship may burden him with more responsibilities, particularly if there is a child of the new family. Where the new partner is earning or has resources, the proper course is to take these into account not as a figure to add to the spouse's own income and resources but on the basis that the partner's resources release the spouse from obligations he would otherwise have had towards her (and in some cases also from expenditure on himself) and therefore free a greater part of his income or property for distribution by way of ancillary relief. Where the new partner is a liability (for instance, where she is a widow with young children who is not working), the needs for the second family have to be taken into account in assessing financial relief for the first family.

3.4 Age of parties and duration of marriage

Age can have an important bearing on the court's decision. Where the parties are young when the marriage breaks down, it may well be reasonable to impose a clean break between them immediately if there are no children, or to expect the wife to make her way on her own within a period of time (granting her a periodical payments order for a fixed term, for instance) where she is looking after children. Furthermore, young spouses are likely to have a greater capacity to borrow money than those in their fifties or over. This can be taken into account when deciding what is to be done about lump sum and transfer of property orders. Thus where the parties are young it may be possible, for instance, to transfer the matrimonial home to the wife who is looking after young children and to expect the husband to raise capital on mortgage to purchase alternative accommodation for himself; in contrast the older husband with no prospect of obtaining a mortgage will need some capital to rehouse himself.

The court is less likely to expect a wife in her late forties or fifties to go out and get a job (particularly if she has not worked since getting married or having children) than a younger wife brought up in the tradition of working wives and mothers. It can also be taken into consideration that parties who are nearing retirement are likely to need to preserve their capital for when they stop work and will therefore be less able to transfer assets or make lump sum payments than younger people who have time to build up provision for their retirement over the course of their working lives.

The length of the marriage is also an important factor — the longer the marriage, the more each party is likely to have contributed to it and the harder it will be for them to achieve independence again when it breaks down. Where there is a very short marriage with no children, as a general rule each party can expect to withdraw from the marriage only what he or she put into it in terms of money and effort; property rights may be expected to play a larger part than normal and periodical payments may well be inappropriate. There may, of course, be cases where it would be right to make rather more generous provision for one of the parties to a short marriage, for example, where one of them has given up a lot to get married (for instance, a good job with prospects of promotion, a house, etc.). Furthermore, where there are children of a short marriage, the shortness of the marriage may well be less significant than the fact that the children will almost certainly hamper the parent with whom they are living in achieving financial independence. In such a case, the shortness of the marriage may make little difference to the outcome of the case.

3.5 Conduct

Conduct is a vexed question in ancillary relief applications. The provisions of s. 25 as to conduct have been changed by the Matrimonial and Family Proceedings Act 1984 but this does not seem to have made any appreciable difference to the approach adopted by the courts to the problem.

The new provision seems to give conduct more prominence than the former s. 25 (under which conduct was given a passing reference, not listed as one of the factors for specific consideration). However, in practice the courts appear to treat the issues of conduct as they have always done so that it will be taken into account only if it is 'obvious and gross' (a phrase derived from *Wachtel* v *Wachtel* [1973] Fam 72, [1973] 1 All ER 829, and interpreted in *West* v *West*, see example (c) below, as meaning 'of the greatest importance'). Thus in the majority of cases the court will continue to take the view that a certain amount of unpleasant behaviour can be anticipated on both sides when a marriage is breaking down, including a certain amount of violence, and that such matters should not affect the outcome of ancillary relief applications.

From time to time the conduct of one or the other party will stand out in some way and demand consideration. Examples of conduct which has been thought relevant in past cases are given below. Standards change, however, and the facts of cases are always different, so examples should be used simply to get a feel of the attitude of the courts, not as precedents dictating what is and is not relevant conduct.

Examples.   (a)   *Cuzner* v *Underdown* [1974] 2 All ER 351, [1974] 1 WLR 641: wife who allowed her husband to transfer the house from his name into their joint names whilst she was having an adulterous affair was ordered to transfer her share to the husband.

(b)   *Jones* v *Jones* [1976] Fam 8, [1975] 2 All ER 12: wife seriously attacked by husband after decree absolute with a razor causing continuing disability rendering her virtually unemployable; whole house transferred to her from joint names.

(c)   *West* v *West* [1978] Fam 1, [1977] 2 All ER 705: short marriage, wife refused to join husband in the home he had provided and lived at her parents' home instead. Wife's conduct found obvious and gross and, despite the fact there were two children of the marriage living with her, her financial provision was substantially reduced.

(d)   *Kyte* v *Kyte* [1987] 3 All ER 1041: husband was a manic depressive and wife connived at his suicide attempts with a view to gaining as much of the husband's assets as possible. Wife's conduct found to be gross and obvious so that it would be inequitable to ignore it, and accordingly her financial provision was reduced.

(e)   *K* v *K (conduct)* [1990] 2 FLR 225: marriage broke down largely as a result of the husband's excessive drinking. That behaviour, together with his refusal to obtain employment had led to neglect of the house and ultimately forced a sale of the property. The court found that it would be inequitable to disregard the husband's conduct and accordingly refused to make an order that the wife make periodical payments in his favour. The husband was awarded a lump sum just sufficient to re-house himself.

The point is often taken by a husband that it is unreasonable to expect him to make provision for his wife when she has committed adultery or formed a continuing relationship with another man. Unless it takes place in particularly aggravated circumstances (for example, having an affair with the husband's father, see *Bailey* v *Tolliday* (1982) 4 FLR 542), the simple fact that the wife has committed adultery will not generally affect her entitlement to ancillary relief. However, if the wife forms a continuing relationship with another man and starts to cohabit with him or derives financial support from him, this *will* affect her entitlement to ancillary relief. Periodical payments do not automatically cease in this situation as they do on remarriage, but if the wife's boyfriend is or should be expected to contribute towards her maintenance, this will clearly reduce the obligations of the husband towards her, often to nil. Whether the court will see fit to dismiss the wife's periodical payments claim in such a case, thus debarring her from claiming maintenance from her husband for all time, will depend on all the circumstances of the case. The alternative is, of course, for the court to reduce her periodical payments to a small or nominal amount leaving her with the right to seek a variation should her relationship come to an end. Capital provision for the wife may or may not be affected by her new relationship/cohabitation depending on all the circumstances of the case.

Note that where allegations of conduct are made, the case may be transferred for hearing by a High Court judge (see Practice Direction [1988] 2 All ER 103, [1988] 1 FLR 540).

4 THE CLEAN BREAK: S. 25A

Even before the addition of s. 25A to the Matrimonial Causes Act 1973 by the Matrimonial and Family Proceedings Act 1984, the courts had a healthy respect for the 'clean break', i.e. a once and for all settlement with no continuing provision for either party by way of periodical payments enabling the parties to avoid bitterness and to put the past behind them and begin a new life not overshadowed by the relationship that has broken down. The virtues of such a solution were extolled by the House of Lords in *Minton* v *Minton* [1979] AC 593, [1979] 1 All ER 79, although, at that time, it was not possible for the court to *impose* a clean break on the parties — the consent of the party seeking periodical payments had to be obtained before her application could be finally dismissed.

What s. 25A has done is to oblige the courts to give thought to achieving a clean break between the parties in every case of divorce or nullity whether the parties suggest it or not, and to give the court the power to dictate a clean break by dismissing a party's application for periodical payments without his or her consent if appropriate.

It is not possible to achieve a completely clean break where there are children as applications in relation to the children cannot be finally dismissed. However, there is no reason why the dependence of the *wife* on the husband (or vice versa of course) should not be ended in such a case if she can be expected to be self-supporting despite the children.

However, the 'clean break' principle appears to be suffering some considerable erosion at the hands of s. 8, Social Security Act 1990, which (on 15 October 1990) inserted sections 24A and 24B into the Social Security Act 1986. This, when taken in conjunction with the new Income Support (Liable Relatives) Regulations 1990, makes it doubtful whether the divorce court can realistically give effect to a 'clean break' order where, for example, the wife is given the house in return for the dismissal of her periodical payments, or in return for her periodical payments being fixed in amount, limited in duration, and with her right to apply to have their duration extended being excluded. There has long been a residual power in the Department of Social Security where a person is in receipt of State Benefits to recover from a liable relative a contribution towards the benefit being paid for a spouse or child, but the liability would end when the claimant was no longer a spouse, that is to say upon decree absolute. Under the new regulations, however, the liability will continue even after decree absolute (although it should be noted that a liable relative will not be required to contribute towards a child of whom he or she is not the natural parent). Although the magistrates' courts when considering liability under the new legislation are required to have regard to all the relevant facts, which would include any previous matrimonial decision, they will not be bound by any previously-made 'clean break' order.

Section 25A(2) draws attention to the power that the court has always had to make periodical payments orders for a fixed period to terminate after the recipient should have had sufficient time to adjust to being self-supporting — thus a clean break can be set up for some time in the future. This may be appropriate where, for example, there are young children but the wife is trained or experienced or plans to acquire a skill and can be expected to go back to work when the children are old enough, or where a wife who has been working part-time through choice needs time to arrange to work full-time and adjust to the prospect.

Note that if there is to be a clean break between the parties, it will usually be appropriate to ask the court to direct that neither party shall have any right to apply for provision out of the other's estate under the Inheritance (Provision for Family and Dependants) Act 1975 (s. 15 ibid.).

5   OTHER CIRCUMSTANCES NOT SPECIFICALLY REFERRED TO IN S. 25

Section 25 is not an exhaustive catalogue of the circumstances that are to be taken into account on an ancillary relief application. This paragraph lists additional matters which, amongst others, may be relevant.

5.1   Delay in applying

In some cases, ancillary relief claims are made years after the parties actually separated (for instance, where the divorce does not take place until many years later or where a claim for ancillary relief initiated in divorce proceedings soon after the breakdown of the marriage is allowed to go to sleep with no action being taken for a considerable time). As a general rule, the longer the period that elapses between separation and a party actively doing anything about getting ancillary relief, the less likely the court is to make any or any significant provision.

There are a variety of reasons for this, for instance, the passage of time demonstrates the ability of a spouse to manage on his or her own and also lulls the other spouse into a sense of security which may well lead him to arrange his financial affairs on the basis that he will have no obligations arising out of his marriage. Thus, for example, in the extreme cases of *Krystman* v *Krystman* [1973] 3 All ER 247, [1973] 1 WLR 927 (actually an application under what is now s. 10(2), Matrimonial Causes Act 1973, see Chapter 11, but the principles are the same), a wife was entitled to no provision after a marriage of two weeks followed by 26 years' separation before she made an application for financial relief.

5.2   Agreements as to ancillary relief

It can happen that, on or after the breakdown of the marriage, the parties reach an agreement on property and finance and make it a term of the agreement that no claims will be made thereafter for any further or different ancillary provision.

> **Example.** Soon after separating, husband and wife agree that the wife will be allowed to remain in the matrimonial home until the children are grown up and that it will thereafter be sold and the proceeds divided equally between them. The wife agrees never to make any claim for periodical payments for herself and the husband agrees to maintain the children at the rate of £10 per week per child, the figure to be increased periodically to keep pace with inflation.
>
> The wife changes her mind about the agreement and wants to seek a transfer of the house into her name and/or periodical payments for herself after decree nisi of divorce is granted.

Whilst a party cannot be bound by a promise not to apply to the court (see Chapter 33 paragraph 9.2), the court *can* take into account the making of the agreement as part of the conduct of the parties under s. 25 (see *Dean* v *Dean* [1978] Fam 161, [1978] 3 All ER 758; *Edgar* v *Edgar* [1980] 3 All ER 887, [1980] 1 WLR 1410; *Camm* v *Camm* [1983] 4 FLR 577, 13 Fam Law 112). As the Court of Appeal pointed out in *Edgar*, the district judge will decide what weight to give to the agreement by considering the circumstances surrounding the making of it (for example, was there undue pressure on one side, bad legal advice, inadequate knowledge?), the conduct of both parties in consequence of it and any important change of circumstances unforeseen or overlooked at the time of making the agreement. In *Edgar*, the wife was held to her agreement over ancillary relief and the court pointed out the importance of formal agreements, properly and fairly arrived at with competent advice, being upheld unless there are good and substantial grounds for concluding that injustice will be done. In contrast, in *Camm* the wife was allowed to go back on her agreement not to seek further provision and obtained an order for periodical payments. There are no cases of which the writers are aware concerning agreements over provision for children — no doubt this is because it is acknowledged by all concerned that no agreement or order concerning a child is ever final and that the court will never hesitate to intervene and make different provision if it feels that the provision agreed by the parties for a child is inadequate.

5.3   Costs

It may seem foolish to refer to the costs of and associated with the divorce as one of the factors in determining an ancillary relief claim but costs are undoubtedly a major factor these days. When it is considered that the bill for a fairly straightforward divorce (including contested ancillary relief and perhaps one or two difficulties over the children) is likely to be upwards of £1,000, it is not surprising that this is so. Even where one or both of the parties are legally aided, they may well have to bear their own costs out of any property they recover or preserve in the ancillary relief proceedings (see Chapter 2 paragraph 17 et seq. as to the statutory charge with regard to legal aid).

The court will therefore need to know the likely costs of the whole divorce proceedings and how they will affect each party. Each side must be able to inform the district judge what his own bill is likely to be (see Practice Direction [1988] 2 All ER 63, [1988] 1 FLR 452), whether the party is legally aided, whether he or she has already paid a contribution that will cover the costs, whether the legal aid charge is likely to bite immediately (for instance, where there is a lump sum payment) or only on sale of the matrimonial home, etc. Note, however, the case of *Collins* v *Collins* [1987] 1 FLR 226 to which reference is made in Chapter 15 paragraph 9.3(c).

5.4   The tax implications of orders

The tax implications of a proposed order may be important. For example, the court will need to know if the husband will have to bear a considerable amount of capital gains tax in selling assets to raise a lump sum — it may reduce the lump sum payable to take account of this or choose to make a different order with less severe tax consequences. In relation to orders for periodical payments applied for prior to 15 March 1988 and made before 30 June 1988 the district judge was usually prepared to tinker with the order to make it as tax efficient as possible for both parties, for example, stepping up the payments direct to the children slightly at the expense of the wife's maintenance in order to take advantage of the children's tax allowances. However, for orders applied for after 15 March 1988 the payer will no longer be entitled to tax relief, save to a very limited extent: the only way in which payments of maintenance will be eligible for tax relief in future is that a spouse paying maintenance will be able to claim a further tax allowance in addition to his normal personal allowance. The extra tax allowance for 1992/93 is £1,720. See Chapter 20 for a full explanation. The payer will make a payment of the gross amount, and that gross payment will not be taxable in the hands of the recipient.

5.5   The availability of state benefits

The court is not generally entitled to take into account the fact that the applicant for ancillary relief is on income support and that she is therefore unlikely to derive any real advantage from the order that can be made in her favour (see, for example, *Peacock* v *Peacock* [1984] 1 All ER 1069, [1984] 1 WLR 532), except where the available financial resources are very limited and an order would result in the husband being left with a sum that would be inadequate to meet his own financial commitments (see, for example, *Barnes* v *Barnes* [1972] 3 All ER 872; *Stockford* v *Stockford* (1981) 3 FLR 58; *Delaney* v *Delaney* [1990] 2 FLR 457).

In practice the writers have noted a fairly widespread natural inclination among district judges to depress the level of periodical payments orders made where the wife will be remaining on benefit in any event and only the DSS will benefit from the husband's payments.

6   GUIDELINES IN FIXING THE APPROPRIATE ORDER

The courts have evolved a number of standard approaches to assist them in applying the terms of s. 25 and arriving at the appropriate orders in particular cases.

6.1   The one-third approach

6.1.1   When applicable

The one-third approach is well known. It is traditionally traced back to the case of *Wachtel* v *Wachtel* [1973] Fam 72, [1973] 1 All ER 829, and is often referred to as the 'one-third rule', although to call it a rule is something of a misnomer — it has never been more than a rule of thumb, a starting point.

The one-third approach has been in and out of favour with the courts since *Wachtel* (see, for example: *Furniss* v *Furniss* (1981) 3 FLR 46; *Stockford* v *Stockford* (1981) 3 FLR 58, both in the Court of Appeal, generally disapproving of the approach; and *Slater* v *Slater* (1982) 3 FLR 364, *Potter* v *Potter* [1982] 1 WLR 1255, [1982] 3 All ER 321, (1983) 4 FLR 331, both also in the Court of Appeal, reaffirming its usefulness in certain cases). Nevertheless, it is still in widespread current use, probably in default of anything better.

It is important to bear in mind that there are many cases in which the approach most certainly cannot be applied. It has no relevance in calculating provision for children, only for spouses; nor is it applicable where the parties are very wealthy (in which case the results would be over-generous) or very poor (in which case the approach would leave the payer with too little for his own needs).

As regards other cases, the position seems to be this:

(a)   The one-third rule is still undoubtedly helpful in straightforward applications solely for periodical payments where there is no capital to be shared out.

(b)   Whereas the one-third rule was originally applied in determining both capital and income provision and dictated that the starting point for an order for a wife in an average family would be one third of the parties' joint capital plus periodical payments to bring her income up to one third of their joint income, the one-third approach is now rarely appropriate with regard to the redistribution of capital. No doubt the reason for this is that family life has changed since the early 1970s when the rule was laid down — for example, there is generally more equality between the sexes, it is accepted that women work and often contribute financially to the acquisition of family property as well as by caring for the family and many couples buying a house these days expect the matrimonial home to be put into joint names. The result is that orders for an equal division of family property have become more common, particularly as the idea of a clean break between husband and wife has found favour. If the wife is to fend for herself and no longer be a drain on the husband's income, she can expect to share the family capital equally with him. The one-third approach is not, however, an improper one when determining capital orders (see, for example, *Bullock* v *Bullock* [1986] 1 FLR 372 and can be a useful guide to capital redistribution if taken in conjunction with s. 25 itself (see, for example, *Dew* v *Dew* [1986] 2 FLR 341).

(c)   Although, in theory, the one-third rule is not to be used to produce a guide to the appropriate rate for periodical payments if redistribution of capital is involved in the case as well, in practice it is often still used in such cases to produce a very rough starting point for maintenance which is then substantially adjusted to do justice in all the circumstances of the case. Thus, for example, if the applicant gets more than the one-third of the capital that the rule originally dictated went with one-third of the income, the court will be inclined to reduce the starting figure for maintenance accordingly.

6.1.2   How it works
A one-third calculation goes as follows:

(a)   The gross income of each party is calculated (as long as the whole calculation is carried out on the same basis, it really does not matter whether one takes each party's gross income for the year or his average weekly or monthly gross income). Income from all sources save state benefits (income support, child benefit, one-parent benefit) is relevant — thus pension payments, rent from investment property, interest, etc. are included.

(b)   From each party's gross income are deducted allowable expenses, i.e. (normally) the expenses of coming by the income, such as national insurance contributions, expenses of travelling to work, union dues, probably child-minding expenses, etc.

(c)   The parties' gross income less appropriate deductions are added together and the resulting figure is divided by three.

(d)   The gross income less deductions of the party seeking maintenance is compared with the figure of one third of the parties' joint incomes.

(e)   If her income is already as much as or more than one third of the joint incomes, according to the one-third calculation she should receive no mainten-ance. If her present income is less, it should be made up to one third by maintenance payments from the other party.

Example. The husband's gross income after allowable deductions is £159 per week. The wife's gross income from her part-time job after allowable deductions is £30 per week.

	£ per week
Total of both parties' gross incomes less deductions	189
One third joint incomes	63
Less wife's present income	30
Starting point for maintenance	33

6.1.3   Tailoring the one-third to fit the facts
Once the one-third starting point has been worked out, a calculation must be done to see how both parties would actually be placed if maintenance were ordered in accordance with the rule. Can the husband afford to pay at this rate? Will the wife have enough if he does? This is sometimes called the 'net effect method' and is covered in paragraph 6.2 below.

6.2   The net method

It is very helpful to the court to work out how a proposed order (be it a one-third order or an order arrived at on a different basis) would work in practice.

To do this it is necessary to calculate each party's tax liability on the basis of the proposed order. From the payer's gross income is then deducted the tax he would have to pay, and his expenses of earning it. What is left is his spendable income — is it enough to enable him to meet his reasonable expenses? If not, the proposed order may well be too high. If he would have a significant sum over after meeting his expenses, the order may be too low. The position of the payee must also be considered. From her gross income, including the proposed maintenance, child benefit and one-parent benefit, must be deducted tax and her earning expenses. Is her spendable income sufficient for her reasonable expenses?

The net effect approach can be a very valuable way of showing up inequalities between the parties that might not otherwise be apparent; for instance, if the proposed order leaves the husband with £200 a month to spend and the wife with minus £10, the proposed order will obviously have to be adjusted so that the husband pays more. It may well be, however, that *both* parties are left with too little to cover their expenses — an all too common situation following the breakdown of a marriage. In such a case there is no possibility of carrying out a fine balancing exercise to distribute surplus income — the court must do the best it can and may have to work on the basis that one or the other party (or both) will require state benefits.

6.3 The subsistence level approach

In general, the court will not make an order that will depress the husband below subsistence level (i.e. the amount which the DSS would find the husband needed for the normal, additional and housing requirements of his assessment unit if he were on supplementary benefit together with whatever he would receive by way of housing benefit; see Chapter 35). This limitation is of particular importance in low income families (see *Allen* v *Allen* [1986] 2 FLR 265).

Another yardstick which is sometimes used as the level below which the husband's income should not be reduced is the amount of income which the DSS will allow a liable relative to retain when seeking a contribution from him (see Chapter 35). This is slightly higher than subsistence level as the DSS will allow a liable relative to keep, in addition to what he would get on income support and by way of housing benefit, £5 or one quarter of his net earnings (whichever is more) before requiring him to contribute.

7 SPECIAL CONSIDERATIONS WITH REGARD TO PARTICULAR TYPES OF ORDER

7.1 Orders in relation to the matrimonial home

7.1.1 *Matrimonial home owned by one or both parties*

7.1.1.1 Common orders The home is often the only substantial asset that the parties have and is therefore generally the focus of ancillary relief disputes. Although the court has the power to resolve the question of the home in whatever manner it thinks appropriate, in practice there are several types of order which frequently crop up:

(a) immediate sale and division of proceeds;

(b)   transfer of the house into the sole name of one spouse, with or without a charge in favour of the other spouse or an immediate payment of a lump sum in his favour in respect of his interest;

(c)   sale of house postponed, proceeds to be divided between the spouses on sale.

7.1.1.2   Importance of securing homes for all concerned   What will normally be at the forefront of the district judge's mind is the question of homes for both parties and particularly for the children. This consideration is likely to override all others and in particular will undoubtedly take precedence over strict property rights.

7.1.1.3   When will immediate sale be appropriate?   The following are illustrations of the sorts of situation in which the court may be prepared to order immediate sale of the matrimonial home:

(a)   Where the equity in the matrimonial home is sufficiently large to be divided between the parties and to enable them both to buy somewhere new, not necessarily of the same size and standard as the matrimonial home but with adequate accommodation for their needs. In working out what the equity is and whether it is sufficient, account must be taken not only of any outstanding mortgage on the property, but also of the estate agent's and conveyancing fees that will arise on a sale and new purchase and of removal costs. Furthermore, in the case of a legally aided client, the effect of the legal aid statutory charge must be borne in mind (see Chapter 2 paragraph 17 et seq.); if the Legal Aid Board has (or will have when the proceedings are over) a charge over a party's house, that charge *may* be repayable on sale of the property thus reducing the sum available to that party.

On the plus side, the court will take into account the availability of loans and mortgages to assist the parties in their new purchases.

Example 1. Husband and wife live in a five-bedroomed house which they bought 20 years ago in their joint names. The children have all grown up and left home. The wife is living in the property on her own whilst the husband is in rented accommodation. The house is worth £85,000 and there is an outstanding mortgage of £2,000. The equity in the property is therefore £83,000 less the costs of sale. To be on the safe side, these are estimated at £5,000 and the available equity is taken to be £78,000. The court takes the view that this would be sufficient to enable both parties to purchase suitable accommodation for one person with enough room for the children and their families to come to stay and in the same locality as the matrimonial home. The sale of the matrimonial home is ordered, with equal division of the net proceeds.

Example 2. Husband and wife are both in their thirties. There are two children. The husband is a businessman with a healthy income. The wife works part-time as a receptionist to fit in with the children. The matrimonial home is in joint names. It is worth £90,000 but there is a substantial mortgage of £40,000. The wife is to have a residence order in respect of the children. The equity in the house will be in the region of £45,000 after repayment of the mortgage and payment of expenses. The Legal Aid Board will have a statutory charge over the wife's share in the property for her legal aid costs of £1,000 but it is anticipated that they would agree to the charge being transferred to another house. The wife is unable to obtain a mortgage. Equal division of the equity would give her only £22,500 and, as she shows to the court by bringing estate agents' particulars to the hearing, this would not be enough to enable her to buy a three-bedroomed property in the area where the children go to school. She estimates that she requires £35,000 to buy a suitable property. The husband, on the other hand, can obtain a mortgage of up to £30,000. The court therefore orders that the house should be sold and that the husband should receive one fifth of the proceeds (£9,000, which should be enough, together with a mortgage, to enable him to purchase a house for himself) and the wife four fifths (£36,000). Because the wife is doing rather well out of the house, the level of her maintenance payments is reduced considerably from what she would otherwise have been granted. This is possible because she can buy a property outright and will therefore have no mortgage or rent.

(b)   Where one party has already got suitable alternative accommodation and the house can be sold and the proceeds divided enabling her to realise some capital from it but leaving the other spouse with sufficient to purchase accommodation.

Example. After the breakdown of the marriage the wife goes to live with another man in his four-bedroomed detached house taking with her the two children of the family. The husband has continued to reside in the matrimonial home; sale would free approximately £10,000. The wife would like the property to be sold so that she can buy furniture and furnishings for her new home which her cohabitee has allowed to run to seed since his wife died. The court orders that the matrimonial home be sold and the proceeds divided equally. The wife's share of £5,000 would not be enough to enable her to purchase alternative accommodation but she has, of course, no need to do so because she looks upon her cohabitation as a long-term venture. £5,000 is enough to enable the husband to pay a deposit on a new house for himself. He can raise the balance of the purchase price on mortgage. The wife's claim to periodical payments for herself is dismissed in view of her cohabitation with the other man who is in a good job.

(c)   Where there is not enough money to pay for the mortgage and other outgoings on the matrimonial home. In this situation, there is no choice but to sell the home even if this means one or the other party seeking council or other rented accommodation when they have been accustomed to owning their own home.

Example. Both husband and wife are working, taking home about £100 per week each. The husband is living with his parents, while the wife has continued to live in the matrimonial home since the separation but she cannot afford to run it or to make the mortgage repayments on it — neither could the husband. There is very little equity in the house (only about £1,500 before the expenses of sale, etc. are deducted). There is no alternative to a sale of the house which will produce hardly anything for division between the parties. What this means in practice is that the husband will have to go on living with his parents and the wife will have to move into rented accommodation.

Note that where one party wants a sale and the other does not, the party who wants to stay can attempt to raise capital to buy the other spouse out. The court can make an order to this effect by requiring the house to be transferred into the sole name of one spouse in return for the payment of a lump sum, amount stipulated, to the other spouse (see paragraph 7.1.1.4 below). This will only be possible, of course, where the spouse has borrowing power or can lay his hands on realisable assets.

7.1.1.4   Transfer into name of one spouse   There are infinite variations of the orders of this type that can be made. What is usually involved is that the house is transferred into the name of the spouse who is living there either:

(a)   on immediate payment of a lump sum to the other spouse as compensation for losing his interest; *or*

(b)   on the other spouse being given a charge over the property for a proportion of the proceeds of sale realisable when the owner chooses to sell the property (a charge for a fixed sum of money is normally undesirable as it will be whittled away by inflation); *or*

(c)   outright with no charge or lump sum (although in such cases, it is usual for the transferring spouse to be compensated in some other way for the loss of his interest, for example, by his maintenance liability for his spouse being wiped out).

Whether an immediate lump sum can be ordered depends on the ability of the spouse who will be staying on to raise the necessary capital. Whether a charge is feasible depends on whether the transferor can afford to wait to realise his capital interest in the home (does he, for instance, need money now to buy somewhere to live or has he already obtained alternative accommodation?) and also, whether, after the charge is ultimately paid off, the transferee will still have enough to buy a new home. It is possible for the charge to be made realisable not only on the sale of the home but also on the happening of other events such as the remarriage of the transferee or her cohabitation for more than six months. Where this is done, the order will operate very much like a Mesher order described in paragraph 7.1.1.5 below.

Outright transfer with no capital compensation may seem harsh but the idea of, for example, shaking off continuing liability for maintaining a spouse in return for a transfer can appeal, particularly where the transferring spouse has already secured accommodation for himself or has sufficient capital from other sources or borrowing power to buy somewhere else. In particular circumstances, it may even be appropriate to deprive one spouse of his interest in the matrimonial home with little or no reduction in maintenance payments or other compensation — it is really a question of who needs what.

Example 1. Husband is living with his new girlfriend in her house. Wife and the two young children continue to live in the matrimonial home, a two-bedroomed bungalow with an equity of approximately £7,000. The mortgage repayments on the bungalow are £100 per month. The wife works part-time but does not earn much. The court orders that the bungalow should be transferred into the sole name of the wife. The husband is ordered to pay the wife maintenance for herself fixed at a rate sufficient to cover the mortgage repayments and water rate on the matrimonial home and periodical payments for the children at the normal rate.

Example 2. Husband goes to live temporarily with his parents. Wife continues to live in the matrimonial home which is subject to a very small mortgage. Both parties are earning but the wife earns considerably less than the husband. The building society are happy for the wife to take over the existing mortgage repayments and for the husband to be released from his covenants in relation to the mortgage. They are also prepared to lend the wife a further £5,000. The court orders that the home should be transferred to the wife and that she should pay the husband £5,000 in respect of his interest therein (in fact, £5,000 representing about one quarter of the equity in the property). This will provide the husband with a deposit and he can obtain a mortgage for the balance of the purchase price of another property. The wife's claim to periodical payments is dismissed.

7.1.1.5 Mesher type order An order preserving both parties' interests in the matrimonial home but postponing sale until certain specified events, has come to be called a 'Mesher order' after the case of *Mesher* v *Mesher and Hall* decided in 1973 but reported at [1980] 1 All ER 126. For example:

Order that:
The former matrimonial home known as 10 Acacia Avenue continue to be held by the parties upon trust for sale on the following trusts:

(i)   that the petitioner shall have the sole right to occupy the property until sale;

(ii)   that the trust for sale shall not be enforced until the petitioner dies, remarries or voluntarily leaves the said property or until the youngest child of the family, Julie Jones, shall attain the age of 18 years or until further order;

(iii)   that upon sale, the net proceeds thereof after redemption of the mortgage on the said property and discharging the costs of and incidental to the sale shall be divided equally between the petitioner and the respondent.

The beauty of the Mesher order is that it enables the court to escape from a difficult situation — it does not force the wife and children (if there are any) on to the street immediately nor does it totally deprive the husband of his capital asset. Because of this it was seized upon as the ideal answer and such orders were widespread in the mid-1970s.

In 1978, however, (see for instance *Martin* v *Martin* [1978] Fam 12, [1977] 3 All ER 762, and *Hanlon* v *Hanlon* [1978] 1 WLR 592), the Court of Appeal voiced disapproval of the universal use of Mesher orders. It was pointed out that this type of order simply stores up trouble for the future. Families do not, of course, split up when the youngest child leaves school and a family home is often needed for considerably longer. Even when the children have grown up, the wife will need somewhere to live. What the Mesher order does in putting off the evil day is to force the wife into the property market to look for another house when she is least able, probably in her forties with poor employment prospects, (particularly if she has not worked for some time), and possibly vulnerable emotionally because her children are growing up and need her less.

In *Clutton* v *Clutton* [1991] 1 All ER 340, the Court of Appeal (Lloyd LJ) decreed that where there is doubt as to the wife's ability to rehouse herself, on the statutory charge taking effect, then a Mesher order should not be made. However, such an order did provide the best solution:

'where the family assets are amply sufficient to provide both parties with a roof over their heads if the matrimonial home were sold, but nevertheless the interests of the children require that they remain in the matrimonial home. In such a case it may be just and sensible to postpone the sale until the children have left home, since, *ex hypothesi*, the proceeds of sale will then be sufficient to enable the wife to rehouse herself. In such a case the wife is relatively secure.'

7.1.2   Rented homes

7.1.2.1   Transfer under s. 24   Most tenancies are 'property' for the purposes of s. 24, Matrimonial Causes Act 1973 and the court can therefore make an order that one spouse should transfer the tenancy to the other (*Hale* v *Hale* [1975] 1 WLR 931, [1975] 2 All ER 1090 (private sector tenancy); *Thompson* v *Thompson* [1976] Fam 25, [1975] 2 All ER 208 (council tenancy)). It does not matter whether the tenancy is for a fixed term or periodic (for example, weekly). Transfer of a protected or secure tenancy can be ordered and, whereas normally assignment of a secure tenancy would cause it to cease to be a secure tenancy, assignment pursuant to an order under s. 24 does not have this effect (s. 91, Housing Act 1985).

The court is only likely to order a transfer of a tenancy under s. 24 if there is no prohibition against assignment or the landlord agrees to the transfer.

Statutory tenancies are *not* property within s. 24 and no order can therefore be made for such a tenancy to be transferred. However, statutory tenancies are covered by sch. 1, Matrimonial Homes Act 1983 (see paragraph 7.1.2.2 below).

7.1.2.2   Transfer under sch. 1, Matrimonial Homes Act 1983   Quite apart from the power under s. 24 to order the transfer of tenancies, sch. 1, Matrimonial Homes Act 1983 empowers the court, on granting a decree of divorce, nullity or judicial separation or at any time thereafter, to order the transfer of a protected, secure or assured tenancy (under the Housing Act 1988) from one spouse to the other (or from joint names into one spouse's sole name) and to order that a statutory tenant shall cease to be entitled to occupy and the other spouse shall be deemed to be the statutory tenant. The landlord must be given the opportunity to be heard before the court makes an order under the schedule.

There would seem to be a certain amount of overlap between the schedule and the powers under s. 24.

7.2   Provision for children

7.2.1   Periodical payments

Whereas the one-third rule can be a useful starting point for calculating maintenance for a spouse, it has no application with children. Nor is it always easy to work out what is needed to maintain a particular child as his needs are often indistinguishable from those of the rest of the household. Some district judges have adopted their own rules of thumb for assessing children's mainten-ance. For instance, it has been said that a child should have £1 per week per year of his age (e.g. for a 10-year-old child, £10 per week). However, as this rule of thumb has been around for a number of years, provision calculated on this basis must surely now be becoming rather mean. Other district judges seem to have a bracket within which the periodical payments orders that they make for children will normally fall given an average family situation. The writers' experience suggest that the present bracket within which most routine orders for children fall is about £15-£25 per week per child. Obviously, where a family is better off than average (or poorer) or where a child has a particular need (such as private school fees) the district judge's order will have to be tailored to the individual circumstances. The practitioner should note the figures produced by the

National Foster Care Association which show the cost to the average family in London and the provinces of bringing up children. Those figures may have some relevance to the practitioner when making submissions as to quantum of maintenance in certain cases. They are, however, intended for use by local authorities in quantifying fostering allowances. On this basis they can only be used as a rough guide in ancillary relief cases.

7.2.2 *Other provision for children*

It is not common for orders other than periodical payments orders to be made for children (for instance, transfers of property to them or lump sums). No doubt the reason for this is that there is enough difficulty sharing the parties' capital between the two of them without trying to cut the cake into even smaller slices for the children as well. Nevertheless, where there is money to spare, or the children have special needs, it may be appropriate for the court to make a lump sum order or property adjustment order in their favour.

7.3 Payment of expenses

It must be noted that the court does not have power in ancillary relief proceedings to order a spouse to make payments to third parties (except for the benefit of the children). However, it is usually possible to find a way round this. For example, the court cannot order a husband to make the mortgage repayments on the former matrimonial home but it can step up the maintenance that he has to pay for the wife to include an element to cover the mortgage repayments. Nor can the court order a husband or wife to take out an insurance policy to make provision for the other spouse in the event of his or her death but it could, for example, order him or her to provide a lump sum that the spouse could use to make his or her own provision. Nor can the court order a spouse to pay the parties' joint debts or repay a loan from the other spouse's parents but it could order him to pay a lump sum to the other spouse to cover the parties' debts so that she can pay off the debts herself if he is not to be trusted to do so voluntarily.

An alternative method of ensuring that the other spouse will pay money to third parties is to accept an undertaking from him to that effect if he is prepared to give it. The undertaking is set out as a preamble to the order. If the spouse breaches the undertaking, the ultimate sanction is committal to prison. A further alternative is that the order recites that it is made on the basis that the party will be responsible for certain debts. If he fails to pay it is not possible to seek to enforce the payment of the debts but variation of the original order can be sought and his non-payment will be clear evidence of a change in circumstances since it was made. Note that arrangements of this kind are not always tax-efficient. The payer will not get tax relief for paying the gas bill direct whereas he will get tax relief for the increased maintenance if he gives his wife more each month to pay the bill herself (N.B. the current tax allowance being £1,720 (for 1992/93)). One exception to this is where the payer is paying mortgage interest; he may then be entitled to mortgage interest relief on the payments (see Chapter 20 paragraph 7). However, he may prejudice his own chances of obtaining another mortgage for himself if he continues to be liable on the mortgage relating to the property in which his wife lives.

8   MAINTENANCE PENDING SUIT

The court is not directed to take the s. 25 factors into account on an application for maintenance pending suit, simply to make such order as it thinks reasonable (s. 22, Matrimonial Causes Act 1973). The court's calculation will, of necessity, be rather rough and ready. The district judge will not normally have the advantage of a very full hearing nor will all the income and outgoings of each party necessarily be ascertained by that stage. What the district judge has to do therefore is to take into account the income, outgoings and needs of each party as they appear at the time and make an order that will tide the applicant over until the final hearing without causing undue hardship to the respondent. It is quite likely that the sum ordered as maintenance pending suit will be rather less than the applicant can ultimately expect by way of a full periodical payments order.

17 Preventing and setting aside dispositions under s. 37, Matrimonial Causes Act 1973

1 INTRODUCTION

The powers of the court under the Matrimonial Causes Act 1973 to make orders in favour of a spouse in relation to finance and property would be seriously diminished if it were open to the other spouse to wriggle out of his obligations by simply divesting himself of property and income to a suitable accomplice or by transferring it out of the country beyond the reach of the courts before an order was made or before the order could be enforced.

Therefore, under s. 37 the court has power where financial relief proceedings are brought by one spouse to prevent the other spouse from making a disposition or to order him to set aside a disposition that he has made.

In this chapter the spouse making the application for financial relief is referred to as the applicant and the other spouse as the respondent.

2 REQUIREMENT OF FINANCIAL RELIEF PROCEEDINGS

In order to qualify for an order under s. 37 the applicant must have brought proceedings for financial relief against the respondent.

The following applications are classed as financial relief proceedings:

(a) for maintenance pending suit;
(b) for any financial provision order for a spouse or a child of the family;
(c) for any property adjustment order for a spouse or a child of the family;
(d) for an order under s. 27, Matrimonial Causes Act 1973 (neglect to maintain) for a spouse or a child of the family;
(e) for most forms of variation of financial orders under s. 31, Matrimonial Causes Act 1973;
(f) for alteration of a maintenance agreement under s. 35, Matrimonial Causes Act 1973.

3 ORDERS THAT CAN BE MADE

3.1 Preventing a disposition

If the court is satisfied that the respondent is about to make any disposition or to transfer out of the jurisdiction or otherwise deal with any property with the intention of defeating a claim for financial relief, it may make such order as it thinks fit to restrain him from so doing or otherwise for protecting the claim (s. 37(2)(a)).

Example. Mrs Watson has petitioned for divorce. Her petition includes a comprehensive prayer for ancillary relief. She learns that her husband intends to transfer all the funds that he has in his bank account with Lloyds Bank in Grimsby to a bank account in his new girlfriend's name in Switzerland. Mrs Watson may apply for an order freezing her husband's bank account.

3.2 Setting aside a disposition

3.2.1 Disposition to defeat claim
If the court is satisfied:

(a) that the respondent has made a reviewable disposition with the intention of defeating the claim for financial relief; *and*
(b) that if the disposition were set aside financial relief or different financial relief would be granted to the applicant,

it may make an order setting aside the disposition (s. 37(2)(b)).

Example. Before the ancillary relief hearing, Mrs Watson also discovers that her husband has transferred his valuable shareholdings in two companies to his girlfriend. She can apply to have the transfer set aside if she can show that this will make a difference to her ancillary relief claim.

3.2.2 Disposition to prevent enforcement
Section 37(2)(b) copes with the situation where the respondent has disposed of assets *before* the applicant's application for financial relief is dealt with. Even if the respondent waits until *after* the court has made a financial relief order before attempting to put his assets out of reach, he will find himself caught. By virtue of s. 37(2)(c), in a case where a financial relief order has already been made against the respondent, if the court is satisfied that he has made a reviewable disposition with the intention of defeating the order, that disposition may be set aside.

Example. Mr Hepworth is ordered to pay his wife a lump sum of £50,000 under s. 23, Matrimonial Causes Act 1973. In an attempt to prevent his wife from enforcing the order against him, Mr Hepworth transfers all his assets to his cohabitee. Mrs Hepworth can seek an order under s. 37(2)(c) setting aside the transfers to the cohabitee so that she can enforce the lump sum order by means of a charging order, warrant of execution, etc. against Mr Hepworth's goods.

3.3 Consequential directions

Unscrambling a disposition that has already been made is rarely straightforward so the court is given power by s. 37(3) to make such consequential directions as it thinks fit in conjunction with an order under s. 37(2)(b) or (c).

Example. The court makes an order setting aside a conveyance of 10, Acacia Avenue, made by the respondent to his brother who was fully aware of the applicant's claims and of the respondent's intention to prevent the applicant from obtaining any share in the matrimonial home by the sale. The brother paid £10,000 for the property. The court can direct that this sum should be repaid to him.

4   DEFINITIONS

Various terms used in s. 37 require further definition

4.1   'Defeating' the applicant's claim

Any reference in s. 37 to 'defeating' a person's claim for financial relief is a reference to:

(a)   preventing financial relief from being granted to that person or to that person for the benefit of a child of the family; *or*

(b)   reducing the amount of any financial relief which might be granted; *or*

(c)   frustrating or impeding the enforcement of any order which might be or has been made by way of financial relief (s. 37(1)).

4.2   Presumption of intention (s. 37(5))

Section 37 is concerned with respondents who *intend* to defeat financial relief claims and orders. Clearly it is not always easy to prove the intention behind a disposition or intended disposition. Section 37(5) therefore provides that in certain circumstances, the respondent will be presumed to intend to defeat the applicant's claim for ancillary relief. Thus where:

(a)   the disposition or other dealing in question:

(i)   is about to take place; *or*

(ii)   took place less than three years before the date of the application under s. 37; *and*

(b)   the court is satisfied that the disposition would have the consequence or has had the consequence of defeating the applicant's claim;

it is presumed that the respondent has made or is about to make the disposition with the intention of defeating the applicant's claim for financial relief.

If the presumption arises it is then up to the respondent to prove that he did *not* intend to defeat the applicant's claim. If the presumption does not arise, the burden of proving intention will be on the applicant.

4.3   'Disposition'

Section 37(6) provides that the term 'disposition' includes any conveyance, assurance or gift of property of any description by instrument or otherwise except any provision contained in a will or codicil. Examples would include selling or mortgaging a house, giving away assets and squandering money.

4.4   'Reviewable disposition'

A disposition that has already been made will only be set aside if it is a reviewable disposition. 'Reviewable disposition' is defined in s. 37(4) to comprise *any* disposition made by the respondent *unless* it was made:

(a) for valuable consideration other than marriage; *and*

(b) to a person who, at the time of the disposition, acted in relation to it in good faith and without notice of any intention on the part of the respondent to defeat the applicant's claim for financial relief.

Thus a sale to a purchaser who paid good money and had no idea of the respondent's intention to defeat his wife's claim could not be set aside.

18 Collection and enforcement of ancillary relief orders

This chapter deals with the means of enforcing ancillary relief orders in outline only. The practitioner is referred to standard textbooks for further details. It is assumed throughout the chapter that it is the wife who seeks to enforce an order against the husband, but the principles would be no different were the roles reversed.

The practitioner should note that the Child Support Act 1991 will come into force early in 1993 over a phased three-year period. It will transfer to the Child Support Agency the responsibility for assessing, collecting and enforcing child maintenance payments in most cases. In certain circumstances the court will still retain jurisdiction (see Chapter 14 paragraph 7 for a more detailed discussion of the changes which will be implemented by the Act).

A more imminent piece of legislation is the Maintenance Enforcement Act 1991 which came into force on 1 April 1992. It provides for the High Court and the county court to specify that payments of maintenance be made by standing order or some other method, or by the attachment of earnings. It provides that the magistrates' court must specify that payments be made directly from debtor to creditor, through the court, by standing order or some similar method, or by attachment of earnings. Under the old law there was no provision for the courts to order payment of maintenance by standing order, and an attachment of earnings order could only be made if the debtor consented or if he had defaulted on the payments by wilful refusal to pay or by culpable neglect. The Maintenance Enforcement Act 1991 is, to a large extent, an interim measure to improve the mechanics of maintenance collection and enforcement pending the coming into force of the Child Support Act 1991. However, it will continue to be of use after the Child Support Act 1991 comes into force since it deals with all maintenance payments and not simply child maintenance payments.

1 ENFORCING ORDERS FOR THE PAYMENT OF MONEY

There are the following considerations where the wife seeks to enforce an order for the payment of money (usually an order for periodical payments or for the payment of a lump sum):

(a) Payments made direct between the parties: unless the court directs that the periodical payments order should be registered in the magistrates' court, maintenance payments under the order will be made direct between the parties and not through the court. Lump sums will also be paid between the parties directly. It is therefore up to both parties to keep a record of payments directly. It is therefore up to both parties to keep a record of payments made/received in case there are problems in the future. One of the most convenient ways of ensuring that there is a record of payment and guarding against default is for the payments to be made through the bank by cheque in the case of a lump sum and by standing order in the case of periodical payments.

(b)   Affidavit required by r. 7.1(1): before any process is issued to enforce an order made in matrimonial proceedings for the payments of money, it is necessary to file an affidavit verifying the amount due under the order (i.e., the arrears in the case of periodical payments or the unpaid portion of the lump sum) and showing how that amount is calculated (Family Proceedings Rules 1991, r. 7.1(1)).

(c)   Leave required to enforce arrears more than 12 months old: where a party wishes to enforce arrears that are more than 12 months old, leave to enforce the arrears must be sought (s. 32, Matrimonial Causes Act 1973).

(d)   Application for oral examination: where there is uncertainty about the husband's financial position (and therefore how to approach the question of the outstanding money), an application can be made for him to be orally examined as to his means. If the district judge agrees to the application he will order him to produce documents to verify or support his evidence. The aim of the examination is to find out exactly what assets and income the husband has and what his liabilities are. Once the true picture is available, it will be possible for the wife's solicitor to decide what is the best way of enforcing payment of the arrears/outstanding lump sum.

(e)   Methods of enforcement available: the methods of enforcement available include the following:

(i)   Judgment summons (Family Proceedings Rules 1991, r. 7.4) — the wife applies for a judgment summons which requires the husband to attend before a judge to be examined as to his means. At the hearing the judge will make such order as he thinks fit in relation to the arrears/outstanding lump sum. There is power to commit the husband to prison for non-payment but any committal order made will normally be suspended on condition that the husband pays the amount due by a specified date or by specified instalments.

(ii)   Attachment of earnings (Attachment of Earnings Act 1971) — where an attachment of earnings order is made, the husband's employer will be ordered to deduct a specified sum each week or month from his pay and forward it to the court to be used to pay off the arrears (and in the case of a maintenance order, to cover future payments also (see further Chapter 31 paragraph 12.2).

(iii)   Warrant of execution — a warrant of execution enables goods and chattels of the husband to be seized to be sold to pay off the debt.

(iv)   Charging order — an order can be made charging the husband's land or his interest in land with the outstanding sum. Certain securities can also be charged. The charge is enforced by making an application for an order for sale of the charged property.

(v)   Garnishee order — a garnishee order enables the wife to obtain payment of the sum owing to her direct from a third party who is indebted to her husband (for example, a garnishee order can be obtained in relation to money standing to the husband's credit in his bank account).

(vi)   Section 24A sale order — if she is seeking to enforce a lump sum order, the wife can consider seeking an order for sale of property under s. 24A, Matrimonial Causes Act 1973 (with a consequential direction that the proceeds of sale or part of them should be paid to her) (see further Chapter 14 paragraph 3).

2   REGISTRATION OF PERIODICAL PAYMENTS ORDER IN THE MAGISTRATES' COURT

On or at any time after making a periodical payments order, the High Court or county court may direct that it shall be registered in a magistrates' court with the result that it will be paid and enforced throughout that court (see further Chapter 15 paragraph 9.3).

3   ENFORCEMENT OF PROPERTY ADJUSTMENT ORDERS

Property adjustment orders are most commonly made in relation to the matrimonial home. Let us take as an example an order that the husband should transfer the matrimonial home (which is in his name) to the wife. In order that the necessary conveyance or transfer can be effected, the husband's cooperation will be required. What if he refuses to execute the required documents? The answer is simple. The wife can apply to the court for an order that unless he does so within a specified time, the document be executed by a district judge of the court instead (s. 39, Supreme Court Act 1981 in the High Court and s. 38, County Courts Act 1984 in the county court).

If it is anticipated that there may be a problem over the drafting of the necessary documents (rather than over execution of them), the court can direct that the matter be referred to one of the conveyancing counsel of the court for him to settle the proper instrument to be executed by all necessary parties. Where the order is made in proceedings for divorce, nullity or judicial separation, the court may also, if it thinks fit, defer the grant of the decree in question until the instrument has been duly executed (s. 30 Matrimonial Causes Act 1973).

19 *Variation of ancillary relief orders*

The law on variation of ancillary relief orders is set out in s. 31, Matrimonial Causes Act 1973. Note that the Child Support Act 1991 will come into force in early 1993 over a phased three year period. It will transfer to the Child Support Agency the responsibility for assessing, collecting and enforcing child maintenance in most cases. See Chapter 14 paragraph 7 for further details of the changes which this Act will implement.

1 THE SCOPE OF S. 31

1.1 Orders that can be varied

By virtue of s. 31(2), s. 31 applies to the following orders:

    (a)   any order for maintenance pending suit or interim maintenance;
    (b)   any periodical payments or secured periodical payments order (though see paragraph 1.2 below with regard to fixed term orders);
    (c)   any order providing for the payment of a lump sum by instalments;
    (d)   any order for a settlement of property or for a variation of settlement which was made on or after a decree of judicial separation (such an order can, however, only be varied where application is made in proceedings for the rescission of a decree of judicial separation or in subsequent divorce proceedings; s. 31(4));
    (e)   any order for sale of property made under s. 24A(1), Matrimonial Causes Act 1973.

Note that it makes no difference to the court's powers of variation that the original order was made by consent.

Although this chapter deals with the variation of orders made in ancillary relief proceedings, an order made on a s. 27, Matrimonial Causes Act 1973 application (failure to provide reasonable maintenance; see Chapter 32) for periodical payments or for interim maintenance or for the payment of a lump sum by instalments is equally variable.

1.2 Orders that cannot be varied

There is no power to vary an order for the transfer of property made under s. 24(1)(a), Matrimonial Causes Act 1973, nor, except in limited circumstances where the order has been made on judicial separation, an order under s. 24(1)(b), (c) or (d) for the settlement of property or varying an ante-nuptial or post-nutial settlement or extinguishing the interest of either party to the marriage in such a settlement.

There is no power to vary the amount of a lump sum payment (made under s. 27 or s. 23). The most that the court can do is to adjust the arrangements for paying the lump sum if it has been ordered to be paid by instalments.

Where the court has, in connection with divorce or nullity, granted periodical payments for a fixed term in favour of a party to the marriage, it may specify that that party shall not be entitled to apply under s. 31 for an extension of the fixed term (s. 28(1A), Matrimonial Causes Act 1973 as added by the Matrimonial and Family Proceedings Act 1984).

2 WHAT CAN THE COURT DO ON A VARIATION APPLICATION?

On a variation application the court has power to vary or discharge the order concerned or to suspend any provision of the order temporarily and to revive any provision so suspended (s. 31(1)). The most common applications for variation are by the recipients of periodical payments who seek to have their payments increased and by payers who seek to have their payments reduced.

Where the court has made an order for maintenance of some kind (maintenance pending suit, interim maintenance, and periodical payments, secured or unsecured), it has power to remit arrears due under the order in whole or in part (s. 31(2A)).

No property adjustment order can be made on an application for variation of a periodical payments or secured periodical payments order made for a spouse or a child under s. 23, Matrimonial Causes Act 1973 (s. 31(5)).

No lump sum can be ordered on an application for the variation of a periodical payments or secured periodical payments order in favour of a party to a marriage (s. 31(5)). However, a lump sum *can* be ordered on a variation application of this sort that relates to a child. The case of *S* v *S* [1986] Fam 189, [1986] 3 All ER 566, [1986] 3 WLR 518, [1987] 1 FLR 71, shows how the court can get round the provisions of s. 31(5) with regard to a spouse to a limited extent. In that case Waite J held that the new s. 31(7) which (*inter alia*) directs the court to consider terminating periodical payments (see paragraph 3 below) enabled the court to consider imposing a termination on the payee if the payer was prepared to pay a lump sum order on an application to vary periodical payments, merely inviting the payer to agree to pay a sum that would justify a clean break, and nothing in his judgment suggests that there is any power in the court to *order* a lump sum on a variation application in any circumstances. If the payer agreed to pay a lump sum as invited, his agreement could be embodied in an undertaking, the court ordering that periodical payments should cease on the sum being paid in accordance with the undertaking. (Although this case was considered by the Court of Appeal in relation to another point there was no appeal against Waite J's order that the court had jurisdiction under s. 31 to commute the periodical payments into a lump sum: see [1987] 2 All ER 312). This approach was recently endorsed in the case of *Peacock* v *Peacock* [1991] 1 FLR 324, in which Thorpe J held that where the parties had arrived at an agreement for commutation of periodical payments but the party who was to pay the capital sum subsequently reneged, then the court was precluded by s. 31(5) from fixing the fair level of capital commutation and from making an order accordingly. In the absence of commutation the wife's cross-application for the increase of her periodical payments was granted.

3   FACTORS TO BE TAKEN INTO ACCOUNT ON VARIATION APPLICATION

In exercising its powers to vary, etc. under s. 31, the court is directed by s. 31(7) (as amended by the Matrimonial and Family Proceedings Act 1984) to have regard to all the circumstances of the case, first consideration being given to the welfare while a minor of any child of the family under 18. The circumstances of the case include any change in any of the matters to which the court was required to have regard when making the order to which the application relates (i.e., the s. 25, Matrimonial Causes Act 1973 factors; see Chapter 16) and, in a case where the party against whom the order was made has died (a situation that normally only arises on an application for variation of secured periodical payments), the circumstances of the case shall also include the changed circumstances resulting from his or her death. As well as having power to bring periodical payments to an end immediately, the court has power, on a variation application, to limit the future term of the periodical payments or secured periodical payments order to such term as will be sufficient to enable the payee to adjust to the termination of the payments without undue hardship and must always give consideration to exercising this power in all variation applications concerning periodical payment orders (secured and unsecured) made on or after a decree of divorce or nullity. It should be noted that if maintenance is paid by way of a court order applied for prior to 15 March 1988 and made before 30 June 1988 and attracts tax relief, then any subsequent variation of that order will continue to attract tax relief. However, any increase in those payments will fall within the new rules so that the increase is made out of taxed income and is tax-free in the hands of the recipient. (See Chapter 20 paragraph 2.6 for further details.)

PART IV
TAXATION

20 Tax considerations

Solicitors and barristers tend, all too often, to look upon taxation as solely the province of the accountant. This tendency is particularly dangerous when the solicitor is being consulted in connection with the breakdown of a marriage. It is not possible to advise a client properly on arrangements in relation to property and finance on separation or divorce without considering how tax is likely to affect him or her.

An understanding of the principles of taxation will enable the practitioner to see to it that the family's affairs are arranged in the most tax-efficient way. As we shall see, this may simply improve one party's cash flow situation or it may actually produce a saving of tax so that there is more money to go round. Furthermore, should the court have to consider the question of finance and property, it will expect the parties' legal advisers to have worked out the tax effects of the proposals that they are urging on the court so that the actual results for the parties can be clearly seen and the court can make an informed decision (see, for example, the remarks of the Court of Appeal in *S* v *S* [1977] Fam 127, [1977] 1 All ER 56). In a complicated case, the solicitor should consider seeking the expert assistance of an accountant or tax consultant in working out the best solution (see, for example, the remarks of Ormrod LJ in *Preston* v *Preston* [1982] 1 All ER 41 at 50).

A certain amount of the ground rules on taxation are set out in this chapter but, on the whole, it has been assumed that the reader already has a working knowledge of taxation and attention has therefore been directed specifically to the implications of taxation on the family. For a more detailed analysis of taxation, the reader is referred to specialist textbooks such as *Mayson on Revenue Law* and *Simon's Taxes*. When dealing with the tax consequences of separation and divorce, the chapter works on the basis that any payments of money or transfers of property are being made by the husband to the wife or children. The same principles would, however, apply if the wife were to be the provider.

Important reforms in relation to the taxation of spouses were announced by the Chancellor in his Budget speech of 15 March 1988. In summary the changes are as follows:

(a) As from 6 April 1990 a married woman's income is taxed separately from that of her husband. On that date s. 279 ICTA 1988 ceased to apply, and was replaced by ss. 257, 257A and 257B which were inserted by s. 33 FA 1988.

(b)   As from 15 March 1988 the taxation of new maintenance payments was removed from Schedule D Case III, so that income tax relief is no longer available upon such payments, save to a very limited extent (ss. 347A and 347B ICTA 1988 as inserted by s. 36(1) FA 1988).

(c)   For the years 1988/89 onwards a wife's capital gains are taxed at the husband's marginal rate of income tax.

(d)   For the years 1990/91 onwards a wife's capital gains are assessed to tax separately from those of her husband, and she has her own allowance to set against her capital gains.

(e)   As from 15 March 1988 most non-charitable covenants made by individuals (and hence those to adult children) ceased to attract tax relief (s. 347A ICTA 1988 as inserted by s. 36 FA 1988). The new rules do not apply to existing obligations (as defined in s. 36(4) and (5) FA 1988) under such covenants (see s. 36(3) FA 1988).

Note that the figures used in the examples are chosen to produce convenient tax calculations. They do not necessarily give any indication of the appropriate maintenance or other payments in a particular case.

A: INCOME TAX

The Income and Corporation Taxes Act 1988 is referred to throughout as ICTA 1988. The Finance Act 1988 is referred to as FA 1988.

1   GENERAL RULES

1.1   Present rates and bands of tax

For the tax year 1992/93, the rates and bands of tax are as follows:

	£
Lower rate band (20% tax)	1–2,000
Basic rate band (25% tax)	2,000–23,700
Higher rate band (40% tax)	Over 23,700

1.2   Personal allowances

The amounts for the tax year 1992/93 are as follows:

	£
Personal allowance	3,445
Married couple's allowance	1,720
Addition for child if claimant single or wife totally incapacitated ('single parent's allowance')	1,720

The personal allowance and the married couple's allowance are increased if the individual (or one of the married couple) is over 65, and further increased at the age of 75.

Entitlement to the various allowances arises as follows:

(a)   Personal allowance (s. 257 ICTA 1988): Everyone (including a married woman) is entitled to a personal allowance which can be set against all types of income.

(b)   Married couple's allowance (s. 257A ICTA 1988): This is allocated to the husband provided that he can prove that for the whole or any part of the year of assessment he is married and is living with his wife. If he has insufficient income to use the allowance fully himself then the surplus can be transferred to his wife for her use. N.B. From 6 April 1993 a couple will be able to choose to allocate the whole allowance to the wife or to split it equally between them.

(c)   Single parent's allowance (ss. 259 and 260 ICTA 1988): broadly speaking this is a relief available to parents caring for their children on their own because of the death of their spouse or by virtue of separation or divorce. It bolsters up the personal allowance (which is all that would normally be available to such a parent) so that the total relief available to the taxpayer is equivalent in value to the married couple's allowance. The relief is variously described. In this book it is referred to as a 'single parent's allowance'; in ICTA 1988 it is called 'additional relief in respect of children'. The rules are detailed. In summary, their effect is that a single parent's allowance can be claimed by a taxpayer who:

(i)   is not living with his spouse (therefore it is not available to either spouse whilst they are living together, even if they have elected for separate taxation); *and*

(ii)   is not entitled to the married couple's allowance (therefore it is not available to the husband in the year of separation or if he wholly maintains his wife by voluntary payments thereafter); *and*

(iii)   has at least one qualifying child resident with him for the whole or part of the tax year.

A qualifying child is one who satisfies the following conditions:

(i)   age — the child must be either: under 16 at the beginning of the tax year (or born during the tax year); or, if over 16, receiving full-time instruction at any university, college, school or other educational establishment (which includes undergoing training for any trade, profession or vocation in such circumstances that the child is required to devote the whole of his time to the training for a period of not less than two years); *and*

(ii)   relationship with the taxpayer — the child must be either: the tax-payer's child (including a step-child, an illegitimate child of his if he has married the other parent after the birth, and any child he has adopted under the age of 18); or, if not a child of the taxpayer, a child who is under 18 at the start of the tax year (or born during the tax year) and whom he has maintained at his own expense for the whole or part of the year.

A taxpayer can never claim more than one single parent's allowance however many qualifying children he may have living with him. If there is only one qualifying child, only one single parent's allowance will be given no matter how many people may claim to satisfy the conditions for the allowance. Therefore, if both parents do satisfy the conditions (because the child has lived for some part of the year with each parent, for example, under an arrangement whereby one parent has a residence order but the other has a contact order allowing the child to stay with him for significant periods during the school holidays), the allowance will have to be split between them. They can agree as to how the allowance will be divided or, in default of agreement, the Inland Revenue will apportion it between them. If there is more than one qualifying child in the family, it can be possible for both parents to claim a full single parent's allowance if residence of the children is split between the parents (father having a residence order in respect of a child or children and mother of the other child or children) or if, although one parent has a residence order in respect of all the children, at least one of them lives for part of the year with the other parent (for example, substantial staying contact during school holidays).

Note that remarriage will affect entitlement to the single parent's allowance.

For the years 1988/89 onwards s. 259(4A) ICTA 1988 as inserted by s. 30 FA 1988 will come into effect. This means that if either the husband or wife is living with (but not necessarily married to) another person who also has a residence order in respect of a child from a previous marriage then the couple can no longer both claim single parent's allowance as has been the case in the past. The allowance is given to the one with the youngest child.

1.2.1 Year of marriage

In the year of marriage the husband and wife will each be entitled to the personal allowance. They will also be entitled to the married couple's allowance but it will be reduced in the year of marriage by 1/12th for each tax month in the tax year before the date of marriage (s. 257A(6) ICTA 1988).

1.2.2 Year of separation

In the year of separation the husband and wife will each be entitled to the personal allowance. The husband will be entitled to the married couple's allowance for the year during any part of which the wife was living with him (s. 257A(1) ICTA 1988). After that he will only be able to claim the allowance if they separated before 6 April 1990 and since the separation he has wholly maintained her and he has not been entitled to any deduction for sums paid (i.e. they were voluntary payments and not payments made under an agreement or court order): s. 257F ICTA 1988.

1.2.3 Year of divorce

In the year of divorce the husband and wife will each be entitled to a personal allowance. If it is also the year of separation the husband will also be able to claim the married couple's allowance.

1.3 Separate taxation for husbands and wives from 6 April 1990 onwards

As a result of FA 1988, the system of aggregating the wife's income with the husband's was abolished. As from 6 April 1990, the husband and wife are taxed separately on their earned and investment income. Each has their own allowance and independent rates of taxation. The husband receives a married couple's allowance in addition to the personal allowance, and the wife receives a personal allowance (see ss. 32 and 35 and sch. 3 FA 1988).

This is a fundamental reform in the system of computing income tax for spouses, and ends many years of discontent with the old policy of taxing the husband and wife as one unit.

2   TAX ON MAINTENANCE ORDERS

There are three ways in which a husband can find himself paying maintenance to his wife or children:

(a)   He can do so voluntarily.
(b)   He can enter into a binding agreement to pay maintenance.
(c)   He can be obliged to pay maintenance by a court order.

Each possibility has different tax consequences.

Voluntary maintenance payments have never attracted income tax relief, and that position will continue unaltered. However, if maintenance is paid under a binding agreement or court order, then those agreements or orders made before 15 March 1988 will continue to attract income tax relief, whilst those made after that date will cease to do so, save to a very limited extent.

The taxation of new maintenance payments is removed from Schedule D Case III by virtue of s. 347 ICTA 1988 as inserted by s. 36 FA 1988, so that such payments will be made gross, and will be payable out of, and receivable as, net income. However, on new maintenance payments a limited tax allowance is available to the husband (see s. 347B ICTA 1988 as inserted by s. 36 FA 1988); this allowance is currently £1,720 for 1992/93.

This fundamental change to the system of taxing maintenance payments means that there will be a 'transitional' period whilst maintenance orders and agreements already in existence prior to 15 March 1988 run their course, and special rules will apply to such orders. In order to apply those special 'transitional' rules it is necessary to have a thorough working knowledge of the old system of taxation, since the old rules will continue to apply to certain 'existing obligations'. Therefore, the details of the old system whereby tax relief was available will now be set out in some detail. The new rules will be set out later in paragraph 2.5 below.

It should be noted that maintenance payments have no relevance for capital gains tax and it is very unlikely that they will give rise to any liability to inheritance tax as paragraph 5 below shows.

2.1   Voluntary maintenance for a spouse or child

Maintenance is paid voluntarily if it is not paid under any legally binding agreement or under a court order. Determining whether there is a court order for periodical payments is no problem. Even where there is no court order, the status of the payments is often clear as the following examples show:

Example 1. Husband and wife separate. Prior to the separation the husband was paying the wife £20 per week housekeeping. Far from reaching an agreement on money when they separate, the parties never even discuss it. After the separation the husband continues to make payments of £20 per week to the wife. This is clearly voluntary maintenance.

Example 2. Husband and wife separate. They both consult solicitors and agreement is reached that the husband will pay the wife £20 per week maintenance. Their agreement about this and other matters arising from the separation is embodied in a deed. The husband's maintenance payments are clearly not voluntary.

However, where there has been discussion or correspondence between the parties (or their solicitors) which has not resulted in a formal written agreement or deed, it can sometimes be difficult to tell whether there is a legally binding agreement. Normal contractual principles apply so that, provided there is offer and acceptance, sufficient intention to create legal relations and consideration, such discussions or correspondence can amount to a legally binding agreement to pay maintenance.

From a tax point of view, the payment of voluntary maintenance (whether for a child or for a spouse) is very like the payment of housekeeping. Save as set out in (c) below, it has no tax consequence whatsoever. Thus:

(a)   The husband makes the payment in full from taxed income. He gets no tax relief in respect of his payments.

(b)   The payments are not treated as part of the wife's (or child's) income for tax purposes. She does not therefore have to pay tax on the money she receives.

(c)   However, in the tax years before 1990/91 if the husband could establish that he was *wholly* maintaining his wife on a voluntary basis, instead of losing his married man's allowance after the year of separation he continued to be entitled to it until decree absolute of divorce. From 1990/91 onwards he can only claim such an allowance if he was able to claim it in that way for the preceding tax year.

2.2   Maintenance for a spouse paid under a binding obligation: maintenance orders and agreements made before 15 March 1988

2.2.1   The old rules
Under the old rules, obligatory maintenance payments made under an agreement or court order were normally annual payments within Schedule D Case III ICTA 1988. Broadly speaking, this means that they are viewed as the income of the recipient rather than the payer for income tax purposes. As from 15 March 1988 maintenance payments will only be subject to Schedule D Case III taxation if they are paid under 'existing obligations' (s. 51B ICTA 1988). An 'existing obligation' is one which arises:

(a)   under an order made by the court before 15 March 1988;

(b)   under a deed executed, or a written agreement made before 15 March 1988, and received by the inspector of taxes before 30 June 1988;

(c)   under an oral agreement made before 15 March 1988, written particulars of which have been received by the inspector of taxes before 30 June 1988; or

(d)   under a court order or written agreement made on or after 15 March 1988, where the order or agreement replaces, varies or supplements an order within (a), (b) or (c) above.

However, under the old rules the following consequences ensued:

2.2.1.1   The payer's position   The payer is entitled to tax relief from all rates of tax for the gross amount of the payment. The way in which he gets his tax relief is dictated by statute, in particular by s. 348 ICTA 1988. This is what happens in practice:

(a) The basic rate taxpayer (tax relief entirely self-administered):

(i) The payer is taxed on his income as normal, irrespective of the fact that a portion of it is now marked out for maintenance.

(ii) In accordance with s. 348 ICTA 1988 he gives himself tax relief for the maintenance he pays by deducting basic rate tax from the maintenance payments he would otherwise make to the recipient and handing over only the net amount. He keeps the money he has deducted for himself.

(iii) He must give the wife a certificate showing the amount of tax he has deducted from her payments.

(b) The higher rate taxpayer (tax relief partially self-administered):

(i) Section 348 is equally applicable to the higher rate taxpayer. He therefore makes his maintenance payments net of basic tax just as the basic rate taxpayer does (thus giving himself tax relief at basic rate) and provides a certificate of the tax deducted for the wife.

(ii) However, he is also entitled to further tax relief from the higher rates of tax to which he is subject. He receives the balance of the tax relief to which he is entitled (over and above relief from tax at basic rate) by a reduction in the amount of tax which he pays on his own income. This is accomplished by means of an adjustment of his PAYE coding or, if this is not appropriate, by means of a reduction in his tax bill at the end of the year.

If the husband fails to make the appropriate deduction under s. 348, he forfeits basic rate tax relief on his maintenance payments unless the Revenue are prepared to grant it (in whole or in part) as a concession.

2.2.1.2 The recipient's position The wife receives the maintenance payments net of basic rate tax. The gross amount of the maintenance payments is treated as her income and is subject to income tax under Schedule D Case III. However, the basic rate tax deducted by the husband is treated as income tax already paid by the wife on her maintenance payments. How this affects the recipient depends on the rate at which maintenance is being paid and on the income she receives in addition to it:

(a) If the wife is, in fact, liable to basic rate tax on the whole of her maintenance, the deduction of tax by the payer discharges her liability to tax on the payments without more ado.

(b) If her overall tax liability is *less* than the tax deducted from her maintenance payments, she will be able to claim repayment of the excess tax paid.

(c) If she is liable to *higher* rates of tax on the maintenance payment, she will have to pay the difference between basic rate and higher rate tax on the payments.

If the recipient is entitled to a rebate of tax deducted from her maintenance, she claims this from the Revenue, usually at the end of the tax year. She proves that tax has been deducted by the payer by producing the certificate of tax deducted with which he provides her. It can cause difficulties for a recipient with not much money to be deprived of 25% of her maintenance, albeit that the loss of the money is only temporary until she can obtain a rebate at the end of the tax year. The Revenue recognise this and it is possible to arrange for rebates to be paid more frequently during the tax year.

2.2.2 Exceptions to the normal rules

2.2.2.1 Section 349(1)ICTA 1988 By far the majority of maintenance payments will be covered by s. 348 which applies whenever the payment is payable wholly out of profits or gains brought in to charge to income tax. Broadly speaking, therefore, it is applicable provided that the payer has enough income over and above his personal allowances to cover the gross maintenance payments.

However, s. 349(1) applies when the payment is *not* wholly payable out of profits or gains brought in to charge to income tax. Under s. 349(1), the payer still deducts basic rate tax before making the maintenance payments (s. 349(1) *obliges* him to do so). The difference is that, instead of being allowed to keep the money as he would be under s. 348, he must hand it over to the Revenue.

Example. In the year 1989/90 Mr Ayres earns £2,785. He agrees to pay £200 per annum by way of maintenance to his wife.

	£
Gross earnings	2,785
Less: Single person's allowance	2,785

He therefore has no income subject to tax from which to make the maintenance payments. Section 349(1) applies. He pays his wife £150, keeping back basic rate tax of £50. He must hand over the £50 to the Revenue.

2.2.2.2 Small maintenance payments (s. 351(1) ICTA 1988) Where a maintenance payment to or for the benefit of a spouse (which included a party to a marriage which had been dissolved or annulled) was paid *under a court order* (for example under Matrimonial Causes Act 1973 or Domestic Proceedings and Magistrates' Courts Act 1978) and was for an amount not exceeding £48 per week/£208 per month, the payment was classed as a small maintenance payment. Small maintenance payments were outside the scope of ss. 348 and 349(1) so the payer was not entitled to give himself tax relief for the payments by deducting basic rate tax and had to hand over the full gross amount of the payment to his wife. He was, nevertheless, entitled to tax relief for the payment and the gross amount of the payment was a deduction in computing his income for tax. In practice, he actually received the full amount of his tax relief by an adjustment of his PAYE coding if he paid tax by PAYE or, if not, by a reduction in his tax bill which was calculated after the end of the tax year when he had submitted his personal tax return giving details of the maintenance payments he had made.

As far as the recipient was concerned, the gross amount of the payments formed part of her income (just as it did when payment was made under s. 348) and was subject to tax under Schedule D Case III. The advantage of receiving small maintenance payments gross, however, was that the wife need only pay the tax actually found to be due — there was no automatic deduction of basic rate tax on the whole amount of the maintenance on her behalf. This was an enormous relief to the wife as having to reclaim tax overpaid on maintenance from the Revenue could be a burden to her in a number of ways. She may not have been accustomed to dealing with paperwork at all, she may have had to chase up the necessary certificates of tax deducted repeatedly from the payer before she could make her claim, and, above all, she was deprived of a portion of her maintenance for several months at least.

It is most important to note that the provisions for small maintenance payments were *repealed completely* as from 6 April 1989 by virtue of sch. 10 FA 1988. However, existing small maintenance payments on orders made before 15 March 1988 will continue to attract tax relief for 1989/90 and following years by virtue of s. 38 FA 1988. For the year 1988/89 they will be treated as previously if they were made directly to the child, or if made to the spouse (including orders to the spouse for the benefit of the child) — see s. 37 FA 1988. Under the new rules small maintenance payments are not distinguished from other maintenance payments so that all are treated in the same way.

2.2.2.3 Section 660 ICTA 1988 Section 660 provides that income payable under a disposition to or for the benefit of another person is treated as the income of the payer rather than the payee if the sums are payable for a period which cannot exceed six years. Disposition is defined to include any trust, covenant, agreement or arrangement; there must be an element of bounty as dispositions made for valuable and sufficient consideration are excluded.

At first sight it looks as though payments under an agreement and possibly even under a court order could be caught by s. 660. In practice, s. 660 is unlikely to cause any real difficulty. For a start, most agreements and orders relating to maintenance are open-ended and do not therefore fall foul of the six-year rule. Secondly, even where the term of the maintenance is not capable of exceeding six years, it can always be argued that the disposition is excepted from s. 660 on the basis that it was made for valuable and sufficient consideration. Court orders are not caught by s. 660 because there is no element of bounty and therefore there is no settlement; thus the payment is, in effect, not voluntary.

2.3 Maintenance to or for a child paid under a binding obligation: maintenance orders made before 15 March 1988

2.3.1 Income tax on children generally

If a child has an income, he will be subject to income tax in just the same way as an adult. He will, however, be entitled to receive a certain amount of income tax-free by virtue of his entitlement to a normal personal allowance. Most children have no independent income and, during the continuance of the marriage, their personal allowance is unused. In relation to orders made on divorce or separation prior to 15 March 1988, it was usual to arrange for sufficient of the family income to be attributed to the child to ensure that his personal allowance would be fully used. This could only be done with full effect if maintenance for the child was paid under a court order.

It will be seen later in paragraph 2.5.2 that for orders applied for after 15 March 1988 there is no tax relief available to the payer in relation to an order for maintenance 'to' children. Therefore it is better for orders applied for after 15 March to allocate maintenance to a wife first in order to utilise the new allowance referred to in paragraph 2.5 below. Payments 'to' children made after 15 March 1988 are made out of the payer's taxed income, and received tax-free by the child.

2.3.2 Children under 18

By virtue of s. 663(1) ICTA 1988, where any income is paid under a settlement to or for the benefit of an unmarried, minor child of the settlor, the income is treated for income tax purposes as the settlor's income rather than the child's.

Section 663(1) does not simply catch the conventional type of settlement where property is transferred to trustees on trust for beneficiaries. Payments of maintenance by a parent under a maintenance agreement or covenant direct to his minor, unmarried child or to a third person (such as the wife) for the benefit of or in trust for the child are also caught (see, for example, *Harvey* v *Sivyer* [1986] 1 FLR 72). The result is that the taxman views the situation as if the money had never left the parent. Thus:

(a) the paying parent gets no tax relief on the payments; *and*
(b) the maintenance payments are not counted as income of the child.

It follows that the husband cannot improve his tax position by entering into a binding agreement to pay maintenance expressly to or for the benefit of minor children as he can with maintenance for a spouse.

In relation to agreements applied for prior to 15 March 1988 and made before 30 June 1988, tax relief on children's maintenance is, however, secured where, instead of agreeing to pay maintenance expressly to or for the benefit of the children, the husband enters into a binding agreement to pay the wife a sum that actually includes maintenance for the children but with no part of the sum in fact being earmarked for them in the agreement.

Example. For the year 1987/88 the husband, instead of agreeing to pay the wife £15 per week for her own maintenance and to pay £10 per week to each of the two children, simply agrees to pay the wife £35 per week. This means that the husband gets full tax relief on the £35 payment (whereas he would only have got tax relief on the £15 relating to the wife if he had paid the balance specifically for the children). On the other hand, it means that the full £35 per week is part of the wife's income for tax. Thus she has a yearly income of £1,820 from maintenance. If she has no other income this is very efficient as the maintenance is amply covered by her personal allowances and she will have no tax to pay on it. However, if she has got other income (say £3,015 from her own earnings), she will have tax to pay on the maintenance as her income exceeds her personal allowance of £3,795 (single person plus single parent). Had her income only been her earnings plus her own maintenance, i.e., £3,015 + £780 = £3,795, she would have had no tax to pay — her tax bill arises purely and simply because the children's maintenance is attributed to her.

It can be seen from the example that before adopting this solution in relation to orders applied for prior to 15 March 1988 and made before 30 June 1988, it was necessary to work out whether it was more efficient that the maintenance was treated as the wife's income in this way or whether it would be cheaper if it remained the husband's income (i.e. if he were to continue to pay the children's maintenance voluntarily or to agree to make payments expressly to or for the children). This depended on the respective incomes of husband and wife.

The best way round s. 663(1) in relation to orders applied for prior to 15 March 1988 and made before 30 June 1988 was for the maintenance payments to children to be embodied in a court order. That way, the payer received full tax relief for the payments and advantage was taken of the children's personal allowances. In contrast to the position with agreements, the Revenue take the view that a court order for periodical payments direct to an infant, unmarried child does not create a settlement. This means that s. 663(1) does not apply and, subject to the small maintenance provisions, the s. 348 regime will operate in the same way as it does in relation to maintenance for a spouse. The provisions of

s. 348 are dealt with fully at paragraph 2.2.1 above but in summary, as they relate to child maintenance, they mean that the husband hands over the child's periodical payments after deduction of basic rate tax (thus giving himself basic rate tax relief for the payments, higher rate relief being given through his PAYE coding or by adjustment of his tax bill) and the gross maintenance payment becomes the income of the child. As few children have any other income, the gross amount of maintenance is normally absorbed or largely absorbed by the child's personal allowance with the result that all or most of the tax retained by the husband can be reclaimed from the Revenue for the child. Care should have been taken to ensure that the order was for payment *direct* to the child (which does not prevent the parent with whom the child resides from actually receiving the money on the child's behalf). If periodical payments are ordered to be made to the wife for the child, the income will be treated as the wife's and, although the husband will get tax relief on the payment in the normal way, the wife will be subject to tax on it and the child's personal allowance will be wasted.

The small maintenance system applied to maintenance payments ordered by the court to or for a child under 21 for his own benefit, maintenance or education. A payment direct to a child was classed as a small maintenance payment if it did not exceed £48 per week/£208 per month (under the levels fixed for the year 1988/89). A payment to another person for the benefit of the child was classed as a small maintenance payment if it did not exceed £25 per week/£108 per month. As paragraph 2.2.2.2 above shows, small maintenance payments were made in full without deduction of basic rate tax. The gross amount of the payment was subject to income tax in the hands of the recipient child save in so far as it was covered by his personal allowances; the payer received tax relief for the full gross amount through PAYE or by a reduction in his yearly tax bill.

It is important to note that the provisions for small maintenance orders were *repealed completely* as from 6 April 1989 by virtue of sch. 10 FA 1988. However, existing small maintenance payments to children continue to be given tax relief under s. 38 FA 1988 for the years 1989/90 onwards in the same way as other existing maintenance payments, i.e. a deduction of up to the amount of the 1988/89 payments will be allowed against the husband's income, and the child is subject to tax as before (the husband is not entitled to a deduction under s. 37(5) and (6) FA 1988 of the tax allowance currently standing at £1,720 for 1992/93 because direct payments to children are excluded).

For the year 1988/89 small maintenance payments to children were not disallowed by s. 347A ICTA 1988, which removed most annual payments (including maintenance) from ss. 348 and 349. This is because they were existing obligations under s. 36(3) and (4) FA 1988 and they were not within the transitional provisions of s. 37 FA 1988, which did not include direct payments to children, and therefore the old rules applied for the year 1988/89.

Payments for a child made other than by court order should always be for a period capable of exceeding six years in order to avoid falling foul of s. 660 ICTA 1988 (see paragraph 2.2.2.3 above).

2.3.3   Children over 18

Where the child for whom maintenance is to be paid is 18 or over, s. 663(1) does not operate. The payer could therefore obtain tax relief *at basic rate* by paying the child's maintenance under an agreement or covenant (provided, of course, the covenant escaped s. 660; paragraph 2.2.2.3 above). Section 348 or 349(1) applies (see paragraph 2.2.1 above).

However, s. 347A ICTA 1988 removes from Schedule D Case III virtually all annual payments made by an individual (including maintenance payments) unless those payments are made under an existing obligation. 'Existing obligations' cover court orders and agreements (including covenants) made before 15 March 1988 as long as details of any agreement are delivered to the Revenue by 30 June 1988 (or a court order made before that date following an application made before 15 March 1988).

Ordinary (non-maintenance) covenants applied for prior to 15 March 1988 and made before 30 June 1988 continue to be subject to the old rules and will simply run out in due course.

For the year 1988/89, maintenance payments to children over 18 continued under the old rules (they were not within s. 37 FA 1988).

For the year 1989/90, s. 38 FA 1988 applied to maintenance payments to children over 18. This meant that the husband could deduct payments only to the amount of the 1988/89 level (see s. 38(2) and (3) FA 1988). The payment was treated as the income of the payee at the 1988/89 level. The payment was made by the husband without the deduction of tax (see s. 38(7)). Therefore, the position was essentially unchanged for existing covenants in that the husband obtained tax relief and the covenant was taxed as the income of the recipient. However, the payment was made gross, not net, and the tax reliefs were at the 1988/89 level.

For the years 1990/91 onwards the same rules apply as to the year 1989/90, except that the personal reliefs and tax allowance have increased.

As will be seen in the following paragraph, this must have an effect upon payments of school fees because any *increase* of payments will fall within the new rules, i.e., the payment is out of taxed income and is tax-free in the hands of the recipient.

2.3.4 School fees

In maintenance orders applied for prior to 15 March 1988 and made before 30 June 1988 which included an element for school fees it was possible for that element to be paid direct to the school. This meant that the school fees would be treated as part of the child's personal income for tax purposes, so that the child's personal allowance could be set against them. The most tax-effective way of paying school fees was under a court order applied for prior to 15 March 1988 and made before 30 June 1988. In *Sherdley* v *Sherdley* [1987] 2 WLR 1071, [1987] 2 All ER 54 it was held that it was even open to a custodial parent to apply for such an order against himself in order to attain the best possible tax position.

Where a court order was not feasible, the amount of the school fees could be incorporated as part of the wife's maintenance payable under an agreement; this ensured that the husband obtained tax relief on the payments. However, the whole amount received by the wife was her income for tax purposes, and whether this was efficient depended upon the level of the wife's income from other sources. An agreement to pay the amount of the school fees as maintenance to or for the child had no effect for tax purposes because of s. 663(1) ICTA 1988. The income continued to be that of the husband.

For any maintenance orders applied for after 15 March 1988 there is no longer any tax advantage in formulating the order as outlined above (save to the extent that they may be part of the maintenance paid by one spouse to the other) since any maintenance paid to or for the child is not taxable in the child's hands.

Orders in relation to school fees which were applied for prior to 15 March 1988 and made before 30 June 1988 will continue to be tax-effective until they have run their full course. However, any increase in those payments will fall within the new rules, so that the payment is made out of taxed income and is tax-free in the hands of the recipient.

2.4   Example

The following are examples of the *old* rules in action. They are retained merely to ensure that the reader has a thorough understanding of how the old rules worked in order that he may properly deal with cases involving 'existing obligations'.

The example given in this paragraph relates to the tax year 1987/88 and therefore illustrates the old rules in force that year. The figures have been kept simple for the take of clarity. The method of calculation will, however, hold good whatever the situations of the parties, even where the wife is working and one or both parties are higher rate taxpayers.

Husband earns £12,000 per annum. Wife earns nothing. The parties separated several years ago but are not yet divorced. Wife looks after the child of the family, who is four.

The rate of maintenance for the wife is to be £3,000 per annum and £20 per week (£1,040 per annum) is to be paid for the child. There were the following ways of arranging this:

(a)   Husband voluntarily pays the maintenance for his wife and child. He gets no tax relief for doing so — all the income is still treated as his. However, he does retain his married man's allowance.

Tax calculation: husband	£	£
Gross earnings		12,000
Less: Married man's allowance		3,795
Taxable income		8,205
Tax at 27%		2,215.35

Net effect: husband		
Income		12,000
Less: Tax	2,215.35	
Maintenance payments	3,000	
	1,040	6,255.35
Spendable income		5,744.65

Tax calculation: wife		
Income		nil
Tax		nil

Net effect: wife		
Income		3,000
Less: Tax		nil
Spendable income		3,000

Tax calculation: child		
Income		nil
Tax		nil

Net effect: child		
Income		1,040
Less: Tax		nil
Spendable income		1,040

Family's spendable income:
£5,744.65 + £3,000 + £1,040 = £9,784.65

(b)   Husband pays his wife's maintenance under a maintenance agreement in which he also agrees to pay the child's maintenance direct to the child. The husband will lose his married man's allowance but will receive tax relief for his wife's maintenance. However, the agreement with regard to the child is classed as a settlement and the child's maintenance therefore remains his income, no tax relief being given.

Tax calculation: husband	£	£
Gross earnings		12,000
Less: Gross maintenance for wife		3,000
		9,000
Less: Single person's allowance		2,425
Taxable income		6,575
Tax at 27% on £6,575		1,775.25
Tax deducted under s. 52 on wife's maintenance (27% × £3,000)		810
Tax due		2,585.25

Net effect: husband		
Gross earnings		12,000
Less: Tax	2,585.25	
Net maintenance for wife	2,190	
Gross maintenance for child	1,040	5,815.25
Spendable income		6,184.75

Tax calculation: wife		
Gross maintenance		3,000
Less: Single person's allowance	2,425	
Single parent's allowance	1,370	3,795
Taxable income		nil
Tax credit on maintenance (tax withheld by husband		810
Tax refund due		810

Net effect: wife		
Net maintenance		2,190
Tax refund		810
Spendable income		3,000

Tax calculation: child		
Income		nil
Tax		nil

Net effect: child		
Gross maintenance		1,040
Less: Tax		nil
Spendable income		1,040

Family's spendable income
£6,184.75 + £3,000 + £1,040 = £10,224.75

The family's income has increased by £440.10 because the husband has undertaken a binding obligation to pay the wife's maintenance. From the wife's point of view this is at the cost of having to wait for part of her maintenance until she can reclaim overpaid tax from the Revenue. Perhaps her maintenance should be increased to compensate in view of the tax saved for the husband?

(c)   Husband makes binding agreement to pay the wife £4,040 per annum (her own and the child's maintenance), no part of the agreed sum being earmarked for the child in the agreement. The husband will get tax relief on the whole sum (thus he is getting tax relief for the child's maintenance). Wife will be taxed on the whole sum.

Tax calculation: husband	£	£
Gross earnings		12,000
Less: Gross maintenance		4,040
		7,960
Less: Single person's allowance		2,425
Taxable income		5,535
Tax at 27% on £5,535		1,494.45
Tax deducted under s. 52 on maintenance (£4,040 × 27%)		1,090.80
Tax due		2,585.25

Net effect: husband		
Gross earnings		12,000
Less: Tax	2,585.25	
Net maintenance	2,949.20	5,534.45
Spendable income		6,465.55

Tax calculation: wife		
Gross maintenance		4,040
Less: Single person's allowance	2,425	
Single parent's allowance	1,370	3,795
Taxable income		245
Tax at 27%		66.15
Tax credit on maintenance		1,090.80
Tax refund due		1,024.65

Net effect: wife		
Net maintenance		2,949.20
Tax refund		1,024.65
Spendable income		3,973.85

Tax calculation: child		
Income		nil
Tax		nil

Net effect: child		
Maintenance		nil
Spendable income		nil

Family's spendable income:
£6,465.55 + £3,973.85 + nil = £10,439.40

The family's income has further increased by £214.65 by the husband paying both the wife's and child's maintenance under a binding obligation as maintenance for the wife. However, again this is at the expense of the wife waiting for part of her maintenance until she can reclaim overpaid tax from the Revenue. Furthermore, although there is an overall tax saving, it is the husband only who benefits. The wife and child actually have less spendable income because the wife has to pay tax on the maintenance. Again, perhaps she should be receiving slightly more maintenance to compensate?

(d)   Husband pays wife's and child's maintenance under a court order. The order stipulates periodical payments direct to the child. The husband gets full tax relief for all the maintenance. The wife's maintenance is her income. The child's maintenance is his income (thus advantage is taken of his personal allowance). The child's maintenance is a small maintenance payment and is paid gross.

Tax calculation: husband	£	£
Gross earnings		12,000
Less: Gross maintenance for wife	3,000	
Gross maintenance for child	1,040	4,040
		7,960
Less: Single person's allowance		2,425
Taxable income		5,535
Tax at 27% on £5,535		1,494.45
Tax deducted under s. 52 on wife's maintenance (£3,000 × 27%)		810
Tax due		2,304.45
Net effect: husband		
Gross earnings		12,000
Less: Tax		2,304.45
Net maintenance for wife	2,190	
Gross maintenance for child	1,040	5,534.45
Spendable income		6,465.55
Tax calculation: wife		
Gross maintenance		3,000
Less: Single person's allowance	2,425	
Single parent's allowance	1,370	3,795
Taxable income		nil
Tax credit on maintenance (tax withheld by husband)		810
Tax refund due		810
Net effect: wife		
Net maintenance		2,190
Tax refund		810
Spendable income		3,000
Tax calculation: child		
Gross maintenance		1,040
Less: Single person's allowance		2,425
Taxable income		nil

Net effect: child
Gross maintenance	<u>1,040</u>
Less: Tax	<u>nil</u>
Spendable income	1,040

Family's spendable income:
£6,465.55 + £3,000 + £1,040 = £10,505.55

The family's income has further increased by £66.15 because the court order enables advantage to be taken of the child's personal allowance. The wife no longer has to pay tax on the child's maintenance so the position on her side of the family has improved. She still has to wait for a tax refund in relation to her own maintenance but at least the child's maintenance is paid in full, being a small maintenance payment.

2.5 Maintenance orders made after 15 March 1988 — paid to spouses and to or for children under a binding agreement

On 15 March 1988 the Chancellor in his Budget speech announced a fundamental reform of the system for taxing maintenance payments.

The new rules have made radical changes to the availability of tax relief upon maintenance payments where they are paid:

(a)   under a court order for which application was made to the courts after 15 March 1988, or

(b)   under a maintenance agreement made on or after 15 March 1988.

Under the new rules (see s. 347A ICTA 1988 as inserted by s. 36 FA 1988) maintenance payments will be made gross and they will be payable out of, and receivable as, *net* income. Therefore, the wife will not be taxed on maintenance received and the husband will no longer be entitled to tax relief on payments in the same way as before.

However, if the husband makes a 'qualifying maintenance payment' he will still be able to make a deduction in computing his taxable income. The amount allowable will be equivalent to the maintenance being paid, up to a maximum allowance, which currently stands at £1,720; as from 1990/91 the amount is the equivalent of the new married couple's allowance. It should be noted that even in these circumstances the wife still receives a net sum. If one person happens to be paying maintenance to more than one ex-spouse, then the £1,720 is a global limit, not an allowance for each recipient.

2.5.1 *Qualifying maintenance payments (s. 347B(1) ICTA 1988 as inserted by s. 36 FA 1988)*

A 'qualifying maintenance payment' is a periodical payment which is made, under a court order or by virtue of a written agreement, by a party to a marriage (whether that marriage be subsisting or dissolved) to or for the benefit of the other party for his or her maintenance, or for the maintenance of a child of the family. In deciding whether or not the payment amounts to a 'qualifying maintenance payment' the following points should be borne in mind:

(a)   The parties must not be living together and the wife/payee must not have remarried.

(b)   Orders 'to' children are not within the definition. Therefore it will no longer be tax-efficient for the court to make such an order. The best way of proceeding is to allocate maintenance to the wife first in order to utilise the new allowance. Payments 'to' children are made out of taxed income, and received tax-free. The only way of obtaining tax relief in relation to maintenance payments for children is to make payments to the wife but express them to be 'for the benefit of the children'; in this case the payer may obtain tax relief up to the maximum of £1,720. Any such payments would exhaust the payer's relief upon payments to his former wife; he cannot claim £1,720 in respect of his former wife as well as £1,720 in respect of payments to her for the benefit of the children.

Payments which do not count towards the £1,720 limit include:

(a)   voluntary payments;
(b)   capital payments or instalments of a lump sum payment.

2.5.2   Interaction with married couple's allowance

In the year of separation the husband and wife will each be entitled to the personal allowance. The husband will be entitled to the married couple's allowance for the year during any part of which the wife was living with him (s. 257A(1) ICTA 1988). After that he will only be able to claim the allowance if they separated before 6 April 1990 and since the separation he has wholly maintained her and he has not been entitled to any deduction for sums paid (i.e. they were voluntary payments and not payments made under an agreement or court order): s. 257F ICTA 1988. On remarriage, a divorced man will be able to claim the married couple's allowance as well as maintenance relief up to the £1,720 limit for payments to his ex-wife.

2.6   Transitional provisions: existing obligations

It is still necessary to be familiar with the old rules upon tax relief as they will continue to apply where there are 'existing obligations'.

'Existing obligations' are obligations existing under court orders made before 15 March 1988, or before 30 June 1988 where the application was made before 15 March 1988. 'Existing obligations' also include variations made after 15 March 1988 (see s. 36(4)(d) FA 1988).

During the year 1988/89, payments under existing court orders and maintenance agreements, including payments to children, were subject to the old rules, save that the first £1,590 (the current rate for that tax year) received by a divorced or separated spouse (but not a child) was exempt from tax (see s. 37(2) FA 1988). This improved the position of the wife. To qualify as 'existing' an agreement must have been presented to the Inspector of Taxes by 30 June 1988.

The old rules also apply in respect of court orders applied for on or before 15 March 1988 and made by 30 June 1988.

The old rules apply to court orders and agreements varying or replacing arrangements made before 15 March 1988.

For 1989/90 and subsequent years, further complications arise. All payments made on or after 6 April 1989 are paid gross, without deduction of tax. It should be noted that this includes small maintenance payments. The husband obtains tax relief up to an amount not exceeding that obtained for 1988/89. (Therefore, if an order is increased after the end of the tax year 1988/89, by way of a variation, it will operate net of tax under the new rules.) The first £1,720 (1992/93 level) received by a divorced or separated wife will continue to be exempt from tax, and she will only be taxable on an amount not exceeding that which was taxable in 1988/89 (see s. 38 FA 1988).

2.6.1 Examples

Note that the figures used in the following examples have been kept simple deliberately. Therefore, tax rates and allowances may not accurately reflect those in force for the tax year in question.

Example 1. Order made in 1987 – tax effect in 1988/89. Husband ordered to pay £4,000 under court order.

Tax calculation: husband

	£
(a) husband's taxable income	
Gross earnings	12,000
Less: Personal allowance	2,605
Annual payment	4,000
Taxable income	5,395
Tax @ 25% on £5,395	1,348

(b) husband's net income	
Income	12,000
Less: Tax	1,348
Annual payment (of which £3,000 goes to the wife and £1,000 to the Revenue)	4,000
	6,652

Tax calculation: wife

	£
(a) wife's taxable income	
Income	4,000
Less: extra allowance (special transitional rules for 1988/89: s. 37(2) ICTA 1988)	1,590
	2,410
Less: Single person's allowance and single parent allowance	4,095
Taxable income	Nil

(b) wife's net income	
Tax already paid	1,000
Therefore repayment due from Revenue	1,000

Example 2. Order made in 1987 – tax effect in 1989/90. Same husband as in Example 1 above ordered to pay £5,000 under court order (i.e. in 1989 the order was increased by way of variation from £4,000 to £5,000).

	£
Tax calculation: husband	
(a) husband's taxable income	
Gross earnings	12,000
Less: Personal allowance	2,785
Annual payment (tax relief pegged at 1988/89 levels – see Example 1 above)	4,000
	5,215
Tax @ 25% on £5,215	1,303

(b)   husband's net income   £
Income   12,000
Less: Tax   1,303
    Annual payment (now paid gross without deduction of basic rate
    income tax)   5,000
                                     5,697

Tax calculation: wife
(a)   wife's taxable income
Income (N.B. she is taxed on £4,000 rather than £5,000 because only
so much of the payment as is a charge on income in the payer's hands
is treated as income in the hands of the recipient.)   4,000
Less: extra tax allowance   1,590
                                     2,410
Less: Single person's allowance and single parent allowance   4,375
Taxable income   Nil

(b)   wife's net income   5,000
No tax paid by husband, therefore no repayment due from Revenue

2.6.2   Years 1990/91 onwards

For the years 1990/91 onwards the same rules will apply as set out above. However, note that the old single person's allowance is now the 'personal allowance' and the rates of all allowances have increased.

The payer may elect to have all his existing maintenance payments dealt with under the new scheme (note that if he has more than one payment, all or none must be within the election). An election to be taxed under the new system is more likely to become advantageous as time goes by since the extra tax allowance is likely to increase whereas the level of relief claimed under the old system is fixed at that claimed in 1988/89.

2.7   Retrospective court orders

The Inland Revenue will accept that payments made prior to the date of a court order are taken into account for tax purposes provided that certain conditions are met, and this practice will continue to apply to court orders made or varied up to 30 June 1988.

For orders made after 30 June 1988 it is no longer possible, for income tax purposes, to back-date the order to enable tax relief to be claimed for payments that *have been made prior* to the order. However, tax relief *may* still be claimed for maintenance which is back-dated in an agreement or order provided that payment of the *arrears* is made *after* the date of the agreement or order. The practitioner will find this especially important in relation to the year of separation; for that year a husband can claim, in addition to the married couple's allowance, a maintenance deduction of £1,720 (for 1992/93), provided that he has paid maintenance of at least that amount under a legally enforceable written agreement or court order. An example may help to clarify the position.

Example. Sally and Ken separate on 1 November 1991. Ken pays no maintenance. On 1 January 1992 he makes a written agreement under which he is to pay Sally maintenance of £100 per month, payable on the first day of every month and back-dated to 1 November 1991. On 2 January 1992 Ken pays Sally £300 (January instalment £100

+ arrears accruing since November £200). He pays £100 in each of the months February, March and April 1992. For 1991/92 Ken can claim a maintenance deduction of £600, as his total qualifying maintenance payments for the tax year are less than the maximum deduction of £1,720.

If, however, in the above example, Ken had made *voluntary* payments of maintenance to Sally from November 1991, then the payments between November 1991 and December 1991 could *not* become tax deductible by back-dating the 1 January written agreement. In that case Ken's maintenance deduction for the tax year 1991/92 would be limited to £400 reflecting the payments made in January, February, March and April 1992.

2.8   Computation of maintenance under the new rules

Maintenance should now be calculated on the net, and not the gross, incomes of the parties. The Law Society's Family Law Committee has suggested that, for the purpose of calculating maintenance, the following sums should be deducted from the gross income of each spouse:

(a)   the tax they are liable to pay;
(b)   the national insurance they are liable to pay;
(c)   their travel costs to work;
(d)   pension or superannuation payments;
(e)   mortgage interest;
(f)   rent;
(g)   community charge (council tax from 1993) and water rate.

2.9   Example of new rules in operation

The following is a simple example of how the new system of taxation of maintenance works. It should be compared with the examples of the operation of the old system as set out in paragraphs 2.4 and 2.6, above.

By a court order made in June 1991 the husband is ordered to pay maintenance to his wife at £3,000 a year, and to his child at £1,000 a year. The husband earns £12,000 a year, and the wife and child have no other income.

The husband must make the payments gross for the tax year 1991/92, costing him £4,000 in all. These payments will not be deductible for tax purposes.

The husband will be fully taxable on his income of £12,000, less his personal allowance of £3,295, and the extra allowance of £1,720 because of the qualifying maintenance payments.

	£
Income	12,000
Personal allowance	3,295
Allowable maintenance payments	1,720
Taxable income	6,955

Tax on £6,955 @ 25% = £1,738.
The money available for the husband to spend will be:

Income	12,000
Less maintenance	4,000
Less tax	1,738
	6,262

The wife's tax position for 1991/92 will be a total income of £3,000 which is not taxable in her hands.

The child's tax position in 1991/92 will be total sum available for his benefit of £1,000. This is not taxable in his hands, but neither is any tax reclaim available.

Therefore the total money available for the benefit of the wife and child is £4,000.

3   MORTGAGE INTEREST RELIEF: SECTION 355(1) ICTA 1988

It is important to be familiar with the mortgage interest relief provisions when advising clients on marriage breakdown. All sorts of questions crop up. For example, the client may need to know whether he can still get tax relief if his wife goes on living in the matrimonial home but he continues to pay the mortgage or whether he can have tax relief on two mortgages.

3.1   Entitlement

Certain payments of interest on loans are deductible in computing the income of the payer for tax purposes (s. 353(1) ICTA 1988). In order for the interest to be eligible for relief the loan must be for a qualifying purpose. One such purpose is the purchase or improvement of the borrower's home (s. 354(1) ICTA 1988). The relief on interest payments on such loans is commonly referred to as 'mortgage interest relief' because, in practice, a loan of this type will usually be secured by a mortgage of the property. However, the existence of a mortgage is not essential for tax relief.

The rules as to entitlement to mortgage interest relief can be somewhat complex. What follows is a summary of the more important provisions and their practical effect.

If the interest paid on a loan is to qualify for relief, the following conditions must be satisfied:

(a)   The borrower must own an estate or interest in land.

(b)   The money loaned to him must have been used for one of the following purposes:

(i)   In purchasing that estate or interest (be it to purchase the whole interest in the house or a part share in it or to buy someone else out).

Example 1. Miss Smith purchases a terrace property for herself to live in with the aid of a mortgage of £10,000. The interest payments on the loan will be eligible for tax relief.

(ii)   In improving or developing the land or buildings on it (otherwise than by the erection of a new building which is not part of an existing residence) or in making good dilapidation that had occurred before he purchased his estate or interest in the land. However, the interest on loans for this purpose will only attract tax relief if the loan was made before 6 April 1988, and for loans made after that date the relief is abolished (see s. 355(2B) ICTA 1988 as inserted by s. 43 FA 1988).

Example 2. Miss Smith can afford to buy a terrace property outright but it needs to have a lot of work done to it to make it habitable. In January 1988 she borrows £7,000 on mortgage to have the roof repaired, to have a bathroom and kitchen put in and to have the house rewired and redecorated. The interest on the loan will be eligible for tax relief.

If she had taken out the mortgage after 6 April 1988 she would not have been entitled to claim the tax relief because it is a 'home improvement' loan.

(iii)   In paying off another loan on which interest would have been eligible for relief.

Example 3. Miss Smith buys a house with the assistance of a mortgage from the Scunthorpe and Grimethorpe Building Society in January 1986. Two years later she finds that the terms offered by the Welsh National Bank would be more favourable and she arranges to change her mortgage to them in January 1988. The interest she pays on the mortgage from the bank will be eligible for tax relief. Even if she had taken out the replacement mortgage with the bank after 6 April 1988, she would still have been entitled to tax relief upon the interest.

(c)   The general rule is that, at the time the interest is paid, the land must be used as the only or main residence of the borrower. (If the loan was taken out before 6 April 1988 tax relief is also available if the land is used as the only main residence of a dependent relative or former or separated spouse of the borrower (see s. 44FA 1988).) This provision prevents tax relief on interest on loans to buy holiday homes. It is worth noting, however, that if the borrower starts paying interest before he moves in to occupy the property as his home, that interest will still be eligible for relief provided he takes up residence within 12 months after the loan was made. This covers, for example, people who live in temporary accommodation whilst their new home is being done up.

Interest is only eligible for tax relief to the extent that the loan or loans on which it is payable do not exceed £30,000. This means that if the loan or loans total £30,000 or less, tax relief will be given on the whole amount of the interest but, if the loan or loans total more than £30,000, tax relief will only be given on a proportion of the interest.

Example. Mr Smith has £10,000 of his own money to invest in a home for himself and his wife. With the aid of a £40,000 mortgage he purchases a house for £50,000. He will be entitled to tax relief on three quarters of the mortgage interest paid. This is the proportion that the permitted maximum loan of £30,000 bears to the sum of £40,000 actually borrowed.

Where bridging finance is used, however, (so that the taxpayer is paying interest on two loans at the same time — one on his old house and one on his new house, e.g., if Mr Smith is moving house but cannot sell his old house for a time), he will effectively be given tax relief on both loans (up to a maximum of £30,000 each) but only for 12 months from the date of the second loan (see s. 354(5) ICTA 1988).

For loans taken out before 6 April 1988 it was possible for a taxpayer to claim tax relief on two separate houses if both loans fulfilled the conditions for relief.

Example. In January 1988 Mr and Mrs Williams separated. Mr Williams remained in the matrimonial home and continued to make the repayments on the outstanding mortgage of £20,000 on that house. In February 1988 he took a further loan of £10,000 to buy a house for his wife to live in which was conveyed into their joint names. Mr Williams can claim tax relief on the interest paid in relation to both debts. If the loan of £10,000 had been taken out after 6 April 1988 he would not have been able to claim tax relief in relation to that loan because of s. 44 FA 1988.

For the purposes of mortgage interest relief a husband and wife living together are treated as one taxpayer. Thus they have only one £30,000 limit between them; they cannot both take a loan of £30,000 and claim tax relief on the interest payments made on it. However, if the husband and wife are separated, they each have a £30,000 limit.

Formerly, mortgage interest relief was available to the individual taxpayer, so that one or more people could join together to purchase a property and claim relief for a loan of up to £30,000 each. However, as from 1 August 1988 the limit of £30,000 relates to the property. This means that an overall limit of £30,000 will apply even if there is more than one purchaser (s. 356A ICTA 1988 as inserted by s. 42 FA 1988). Loans made to joint borrowers before 1 August 1988 continue to attract relief from income tax for each of the borrowers, but only for so long as the same loan continues.

The new 'residence loans' did not affect the relief available to married couples until 6 April 1990 when the independent taxation rules came into effect. From that date, each spouse became entitled to an equal share in the limit applying at that time, or they could jointly elect to have the relief allocated in whatever proportions they wished on a year-by-year basis (see sch. 3, para. 14, FA 1988). This election was, in certain circumstances, available to couples who had a wife's earnings election in force for 1988/89 and 1989/90 (see s. 356B(4) to (7) ICTA 1988 as inserted by s. 42 FA 1988).

3.2 Method of giving relief

Before April 1983 mortgage interest relief was given either by the Inland Revenue adjusting the borrower's PAYE code to take account of his interest payments or, if he was not subject to the PAYE system, the interest paid would be entered on his yearly tax return and his tax bill would be reduced accordingly.

On most loans, relief from basic rate tax is now given under the MIRAS system, under which interest payments are made net of tax at basic rate. For example, if the mortgagor's monthly interest payments are £100, he will actually have to pay £75 (i.e., £100 less tax at 25% basic rate). It makes no difference that the mortgagor is not liable to any tax — in this case he still pays net. However, he may be given relief against unused personal allowance in his code (see s. 369(4) ICTA 1988).

Section 27 and sch. 6 of the Finance Act 1991 abolished mortgage interest relief in respect of the higher rate of tax for any payments of interest made after 6 April 1991 (even if the liability to make the payment had accrued before then). This means that the relief only applies to the basic rate of tax. However, there are two exceptions whereby relief will still be given against higher rate tax, provided that the loans were made before 6 April 1991:

(a)   for interest payments made under bridging loans; and

(b)   for interest payments made in respect of second loans within s. 371 ICTA 1988 (i.e. only within 12 months of the making of the second loan).

3.3 Paying the mortgage on separation or divorce

If a couple separated prior to 6 April 1988 and the wife continued to live in the matrimonial home, and if the husband continued to pay the mortgage on that house to the building society, he was given mortgage interest relief up to the £30,000 limit provided that he continued to own an estate or interest in the house, since it was the only or main residence of his former or separated spouse. However, s. 44 FA 1988 abolished any relief from mortgage interest in respect of the only or main residence of the borrower's dependent relative or separated or former spouse where the loan was taken out after 6 April 1988. Even if the loan was made before 6 April 1988 and the spouses separated after 6 April 1988, s. 44(2) and (3) FA 1988 would disallow the interest.

4 OTHER EXPENSES

No tax relief is available where one party pays the expenses of the other party (such as gas, electricity, water rate) direct to the creditors, whether under a binding agreement or not. If, by way of a court order or binding agreement applied for prior to 15 March 1988 and made prior to 30 June 1988, the husband pays maintenance or increased maintenance to the wife at a rate sufficient to enable her to pay the expenses herself, he will get tax relief from all rates of tax on the maintenance payments. However, if such an agreement or court order was only applied for after 15 March 1988 no tax relief is available to the husband in respect of maintenance payments, save up to the amount of the new allowance, which currently stands at £1,720 (for 1992/93).

B: INHERITANCE TAX AND CAPITAL GAINS TAX

As a general rule, transfers of assets between husband and wife during their marriage do not give rise to any liability for inheritance tax or capital gains tax (CGT). If the spouses separate or divorce, however, the incidence of these two taxes must be considered when deciding what is to be done with their assets. It is on this aspect of inheritance tax and CGT that this chapter concentrates.

Inheritance tax replaced capital transfer tax in 1986 but is on much the same lines. The Capital Transfer Tax Act 1984 remains with amendments and will be referred to in this chapter by its new title, the Inheritance Tax Act 1984 (IHTA 1984). The Capital Gains Tax Act 1979 has been repealed by the Taxation of Chargeable Gains Act 1992 (referred to as TCGA 1992). The TCGA 1992 came into force on 6 April 1992 and it consolidates the pre-existing pieces of legislation relating to the taxation of chargeable gains, thus bringing them within one statute. The TCGA 1992 makes only very minor amendments to the IHTA 1984.

5 INHERITANCE TAX

5.1 During the marriage

Transfers of value between spouses during the marriage are exempt from inheritance tax (s. 18 IHTA 1984). The spouse exemption continues right up to decree absolute of divorce or nullity regardless of whether the spouses separate before the decree comes through.

5.2 After divorce or nullity

It is often not possible to sort out finances and property before decree absolute. In particular, if it is necessary to refer matters to the court for resolution under ss. 23 and 24, Matrimonial Causes Act 1973, the court's order does not become effective until after decree absolute. Nevertheless, transfers made after decree absolute will usually continue to escape inheritance tax. The reason for this is two-fold:

(a) The transfer will normally be covered by s. 10 IHTA 1984. This provides that a disposition is not a transfer of value (and therefore has no consequence for inheritance tax) if it is shown:

(i) that the transfer was either made in a transaction at arm's length between persons not connected with each other or if made between connected persons, was such as might be expected to be made in a transaction at arm's length between persons not connected with each other; *and*

(ii) that the transfer was not intended to confer gratuitous benefit on any person.

Husband and wife are no longer connected persons after divorce (s. 270 IHTA 1984 and s. 286 TCGA 1992). Transfers between them pursuant to an order of the court in consequence of a decree of divorce or nullity will generally be regarded as transactions at arm's length not intended to confer any gratuitous benefit (see the statement issued by the Senior Registrar of the Family Division in 1975 with the agreement of the Revenue (1975) 119 SJ 596) and therefore within s. 10. It would appear that transfers to children pursuant to a court order will also normally escape inheritance tax on this basis as will periodical payments made under a court order. It is recognised, however, that exceptionally a transfer made pursuant to a court order will not simply be made in order to fulfil legal obligations to provide for wife and children but will be intended to confer gratuitous benefit on them. In such circumstances, s. 10 will not apply and inheritance tax may be payable.

Although the Registrar's statement does not refer specifically to transfers of money or property made pursuant to an agreement or voluntarily rather than under a court order, there would seem to be no reason why such payments should not be covered by s. 10 provided they are along the same lines as the order a court could have been expected to make (at least with regard to payments to ex-spouses though *Harvey* v *Sivyer* [1986] 1 FLR 72 raises some doubts where payments to a child are concerned).

(b) Even if s. 10 does not assist, s. 11 IHTA 1984 may. This provides that a dispositon is not a transfer of value if made by one party to a marriage in favour of the other party or of a child of either party for the maintenance of the party to the marriage or the maintenance, education or training of the child whilst he is under 18 or in full-time education or training. A disposition made on the occasion of the dissolution or annulment of a marriage in favour of the former spouse is within s. 11 (s. 11(6)). Although it is not easy to interpret how s. 11 applies on marriage breakdown, it does seem that it will ensure that no inheritance tax arises by virtue of periodical payments to a spouse or infant children after divorce or, indeed, to an infant child during the marriage (provided the amount is not so excessive that it cannot be said to be for maintenance, education, etc.) or presumably by virtue of any lump sum which can be described as maintenance (for example, capitalised periodical payments). Transfers of some assets may also be said to be for maintenance and covered by the section (arguably, for instance, a transfer of the matrimonial home). Dispositions *varying* provision made on the occasion of divorce or nullity are covered by s. 11 (s. 11(6)). One outstanding query, however, is whether a disposition for a former spouse will still fall within the section if delayed unduly after the divorce — can it still be described as made 'on the occasion of the dissolution'?

In the rare cases where the transfer is not protected by ss. 10 and 11 IHTA 1984, the normal inheritance tax rules still provide further opportunities for exemption from charge, for example, the transfer may be covered by the transferor's annual exemption (currently £3,000 for 1992/93; s. 19 IHTA 1984), or by the exemption for small gifts (£250 per person per year; s. 20 IHTA 1984) or as normal expenditure out of income (s. 21 IHTA 1984) or it may, if a gift, qualify as a potentially exempt transfer (s. 3A IHTA 1984).

There will further be no inheritance tax liability if the disposition falls within the transferor's nil band, which is currently £148,000 for disposals on or after 6 April 1992, but which may well increase to £150,000 for disposals on or after 10 March 1992 if the proposals contained in the March 1992 budget are implemented. This is not a one-off limit but is available every seven years (s. 7(1)(a) IHTA 1984). Each gift drops out of account after seven years and it works on a gift-by-gift basis, so that one looks back from the date of the proposed transfer to see if gifts totalling £148,000 (soon to be £150,000 in all probability) have been made in the past seven years.

6 CAPITAL GAINS TAX

6.1 During the marriage

As the law stands at present a husband and wife living together are basically treated as one person for CGT purposes. Any disposal of a chargeable asset by one to the other is treated as if the consideration were such that neither a gain nor a loss would accrue to the disponor (s. 58 TCGA 1992). Broadly speaking this means that the disponee (let us say the wife) steps into the disponor's shoes (so that, for example, when the asset is finally disposed of outside the marriage, the chargeable gain or loss will be traced back to the time when the asset was first acquired by the husband). Where this rule applies, no CGT can arise on the disposal between the spouses.

However, as a result of FA 1988 there were two major changes in the taxation of capital gains for spouses:

(a) From 1988/89 adding the wife's capital gains to those of the husband meant that they were taxed at the husband's marginal rate of tax. This could prove better or worse than the position for 1987/88. Under the 1987/88 system a flat 30% rate was applied to the total gains of husband and wife. Under the 1988/89 system, if the husband was taxed at 40% the couple were worse off; if at 25% they were better off.

(b) From 1989/90 onwards a wife's gains are assessed to tax separately from those of her husband. This means that both spouses will be separately taxable upon their own gains and will have their own allowances (currently standing at £5,800 for 1992/93) to reduce the amount of their taxable gains each year.

Therefore each spouse will be taxed at his or her own marginal rate. N.B. The new 20% lower rate for income tax will apply to capital gains made by individuals who have not made full use of the lower rate band.

6.2   After separation

It is separation, not divorce, that is important for CGT purposes. If the spouses are no longer living together they start to be treated as separate individuals for CGT again. Thus, for example, each has an annual exemption for gains (currently £5,800 for 1992/93) and the inter-spouse disposal rule ceases to operate (although, in practice, it seems that the Revenue regard the inter-spouse rule as continuing to apply until the end of the tax year in which separation occurs).

6.2.1   Potential charge to CGT after separation

What the rules mean in the context of marriage breakdown is that transfers of assets from one spouse to the other after the year of separation can give rise to CGT. Furthermore, although there is no CGT on a disposal of cash and therefore lump sum payments (and of course periodical payments) have no CGT implications, it must be borne in mind that if the payer has to dispose of assets to raise the lump sum, there may be CGT to pay on that disposal if he makes a chargeable gain.

Before jumping to the conclusion that there has been a disposal of an asset between spouses and that CGT may arise, the position as to ownership of the asset in question must be checked. If a spouse already owns an asset or a share in a particular asset, there cannot be a disposal of that asset/share to her.

Example. Husband and wife purchase a painting from their joint savings. They own the painting in equal shares. The painting is now valuable and, after divorce, it is decided that the wife will keep it. This arrangement amounts to a disposal by the husband of his half share in the painting. There is no disposal of the wife's half share — she simply keeps what she already owns. Only half the gain on the painting is potentially liable to CGT.

It follows that orders of the court under s. 17, Married Women's Property Act 1882 can never give rise to any CGT as the court's only power under that Act is to declare existing property rights. Under s. 24, Matrimonial Causes Act 1973 the court has a wide discretion to redistribute property between the parties. As the court rarely makes any finding as to what the parties' property rights were before the s. 24 order, the CGT implications of the order will depend on whether it is possible to persuade the Revenue that all or part of the asset made the subject of the order already belonged to the transferee. The same is true of arrangements made by the parties in relation to property without a court order.

6.3   Lines of defence against CGT

6.3.1   Non-chargeable assets, exemptions, etc.

Certain disposals cannot give rise to a CGT liability. These include disposals of cars, of tangible movable property which is a wasting asset (i.e. predictable useful life of 50 years or less), of tangible movable property where the consideration/ deemed consideration of the disposal is £6,000 or less (marginal relief is given where tangible movable property is disposed of for more than £6,000), and of the individual's home (see paragraph 6.3.3.1 below). Most disposals on the occasion of marriage breakdown should be covered by these provisions and there should therefore be no question of CGT liability. If, however, a chargeable gain arises, it may be covered by the annual exemption of the spouse concerned. Failing that, it may be possible to hold over the gain (see paragraph 6.3.2 below).

6.3.2 Hold-over relief (s. 79, Finance Act 1980)

Section 79 applies to disposals by an individual to an individual otherwise than by a bargain at arm's length. Where both parties to the transaction elect to use the relief, the effect is that any chargeable gain which would otherwise accrue on the disposal and the amount of the consideration deemed to have been given by the transferee (see below at paragraph 6.4) will both be reduced by an amount equal to the held-over gain. The held-over gain is the gain that would have accrued on the disposal apart from s. 79. In simplistic terms, what this means is that the disponee takes over the disponor's gain and has a potential future liability to CGT in respect of it but that no tax is payable at the time of the disposal.

There is considerable uncertainty as to whether s. 79 applies to transactions between spouses in connection with separation and divorce. It would certainly appear that hold-over relief is available for disposals made prior to decree absolute as the spouses remain connected persons until decree absolute (s. 286 TCGA 1992) and disposals between connected persons are automatically treated as bargains not at arm's length (s. 18 TCGA 1992), although it has been questioned whether the relief does apply in this situation. There is a more justifiable question mark over disposals after divorce, particularly where they are made pursuant to a court order. It will be remembered that the Revenue treat transfers under a court order as made at arm's length for Inheritance Tax (see paragraph 5.2 above). If the same attitude prevails for CGT (and there is no reason really why it should not), then such disposals must be outside the scope of s. 79 and it must follow that no hold-over relief can be claimed.

6.3.3 Particular points on the matrimonial home

Often the parties' only major capital asset is the matrimonial home. Is there any CGT liability on a transfer of one spouse's interest in the home to the other spouse or on a sale of the property on the open market? In dealing with this question in this paragraph it is assumed that the wife stays on in the home and the husband leaves and that any transfer between them is from husband to wife.

6.3.3.1 Most disposals covered by private residence exemption Most disposals of the matrimonial home following marriage breakdown (whether between spouses or on the open market) are covered by the private residence exemption.

Any gain accruing to an individual on a disposal of a dwelling house which is or has at any time in his period of ownership been his only or main residence will be wholly or partially exempt from CGT by virtue of the private residence exemption provided by ss. 222 and 223 TCGA 1992. Where the individual has occupied the house as his home throughout the whole of his period of ownership, the whole of the gain will be exempt. Where the house has only been his home for part of his period of ownership, the gain will be apportioned and the part attributable to the time when he was not in residence will be chargeable to CGT. Note, however, that the individual will be treated as having been in residence during the final 24 months of his ownership whether he actually was or not. How this operates in practice can best be shown by examples of common situations.

Example 1. Husband and wife own the matrimonial home jointly. When the marriage breaks down, the husband moves out leaving the wife to occupy the home on her own. After divorce, the husband agrees to transfer his half share in the house to the wife. Provided he does so within two years of having left home, any gain he is taken to have made on the disposal will be exempt from CGT under the private residence exemption.

Example 2. The facts are as in Example 1 but the court orders that the house should be sold. Provided the sale takes place within two years of the husband moving out, his gain is exempt as before. The wife's gain is exempt, also on the basis of the private residence exemption, as she is actually resident right up to the time of sale.

6.3.3.2 Extra-statutory concession D6 Suppose that by that time the husband transfers his share in the matrimonial home, he has been out of occupation for more than two years. Does this mean he will have to pay capital gains tax on the gain that has accrued during the excess period?

If extra-statutory concession D6 applies, the answer is no. Concession D6 provides that if one spouse transfers an interest in the matrimonial home to the other spouse as part of a financial settlement on divorce or separation, *and*

(a)   the other spouse continues to occupy the home as her only or main residence, *and*

(b)   the transferring spouse has not elected to treat any other property as his only or main residence,

the transferring spouse is deemed to continue in occupation of the home until the date of the transfer, however long it is since he actually left.

Example. The facts are as in Example 1 above save that the husband does not transfer his interest in the home to the wife until he has been away for over five years. Up to this point the husband has been living in rented accommodation so he has not elected to treat any other property as his only main residence; the wife has lived in the home throughout. The transfer takes place as part of a settlement following the parties' divorce on the basis of five years' separation. Concession D6 applies.

6.3.3.3 Cases of absence for more than two years where concession D6 does not apply Where the husband has been absent from the home for more than two years before he transfers or sells his interest in it and where concession D6 does not apply (for instance, where the husband has bought another house and elected to have that as his main residence or where the disposal in question is not a transfer to the wife but a sale on the open market), capital gains tax will, prima facie, be payable not on the gain made whilst he was living in the house or during the two years immediately thereafter, but on any gain accruing to him after the two-year period elapsed. There are a number of reasons why this may not be as bad as it seems:

(a)   It is not the gain for the whole period of ownership that is being taxed, only for the period whilst the husband has been out of occupation less two years.

(b)   Indexation may reduce the amount of the gain so that the husband is not paying tax on gains arising purely by virtue of inflation (at least, that is, inflation since March 1982).

(c)   Any gain that there is may be covered by the husband's annual exemption.

(d)   It may be possible to hold over any gain under s. 79, Finance Act 1980 so that tax is not immediately payable (see paragraph 6.3.2 above).

6.3.4.   Settlements and postponed sales of the matrimonial home

The reader should be aware that certain court orders may create settlements for CGT purposes (for example, where there is an order that the house be held on trust for the wife for life or until remarriage or until she ceases to reside there and thereafter for husband and wife in equal shares). There are special rules governing the incidence of CGT on the creation of, during and at the end of a settlement. They are fairly detailed and the reader is referred to a specialist book on matrimonial taxation such as *Tax on Marriage Breakdown* by Peter White for the provisions. Mesher orders (see Chapter 16 paragraph 7.1.1.5) do not appear to create a CGT settlement but also require special consideration.

6.4.   Calculating the gain

Where it is necessary to calculate the chargeable gain, this is done by deducting the acquisition cost of the asset from the consideration received or deemed to be received on the disposal. Where an asset is sold on the open market, the consideration will normally be the price actually received. When one spouse transfers an asset or a share in an asset to the other, the Revenue will usually deem the consideration for the transfer to have been market value on the basis that it is made between connected persons (spouses are connected until decree absolute) or that the disposal is made otherwise than by way of a bargain at arm's length or for a consideration that cannot be valued (s. 17 TCGA 1992).

However, as a result of the FA 1988, provision is made for 'rebasing' the cost of a disposal for the purposes of calculating a chargeable gain for capital gains tax. By s. 96 FA 1988 on the disposal after 6 April 1988 of an asset held on 31 March 1982 by the person making the disposal, the base cost of that disposal for calculating purposes will be the value of the asset on 31 March 1982. This means that all of the gains accrued before that date are now wiped out.

PART V
INJUNCTIONS AND FAMILY PROTECTION ORDERS

21 Injunctions and family protection orders

This chapter is written on the basis that it is the wife/female cohabitee who is seeking protection against her partner. However, although by far the majority of applications for injunctions and family protection oders are made by women, men are equally entitled to protection and the same principles apply.

A: GENERAL MATTERS

1 INTRODUCTION

The solicitor will regularly find himself called upon to take action, often in a hurry, to protect his client from violent or anti-social behaviour on the part of her husband or cohabitee. After sorting out the question of legal advice and assistance and legal aid if appropriate (see Chapter 2), the solicitor's first task is to take a full statement from the client covering the matters set out in the checklist below. Naturally, if the client is an existing client (for example, in relation to divorce proceedings) this job will be easier as the solicitor will have a good deal of the information on the file already.

Once he has an idea of the problem, the solicitor has to decide what steps to take to deal with it. Occasionally he will have to advise the client that she is being unreasonable and really has very little cause to complain. Sometimes the client does have a legitimate grievance but a letter to her husband or cohabitee asking him to desist from his anti-social behaviour is sufficient. Not infrequently, however, matters have gone beyond the letter stage and it will be necessary to seek the intervention of the courts. The various ways in which the courts can help are set out in outline in paragraph 2 below.

Checklist: points to be covered at initial interview

1. Married?
2. Is client living with spouse/partner or has one of them moved out?
3. Details of the home (who owns it/who is the tenant, how many rooms, etc.).

4. Are there any children of the relationship or any other children living with either party (if so, how old are they and who is responsible for them)?
5. What behaviour does the client complain of and what effect is it having on her and any children?
6. Any particular reason to be concerned about the future, e.g. has her partner issued threats?
7. Has either party got alternative accommodation? If not, can either obtain it?
8. Are there any other relevant proceedings continuing (e.g. divorce proceedings)?

2   SUMMARY OF ORDERS AVAILABLE

2.1   The principal orders

The orders that the courts can make fall basically into two categories: orders designed to protect the applicant and/or children personally; and orders dealing with the occupation of the family home. Application can be made to the magistrates' courts, the county court and the High Court. However, as applications are only infrequently made to the High Court, for the most part this chapter omits High Court proceedings.

2.1.1   Section 16, Domestic Proceedings and Magistrates' Courts Act 1978 (DPMCA 1978)
Orders available:

(a)   personal protection orders (to prevent violence or threats of violence);
(b)   exclusion orders (to regulate the occupation of the matrimonial home).

Application: to a magistrates' court,
            by a party to a marriage.

2.1.2   Section 1, Domestic Violence and Matrimonial Proceedings Act 1976 (DVMPA 1976)
Orders available:
(a)   non-molestation injunctions (to prevent violence, threats of violence and other anti-social behaviour);
(b)   exclusion/ouster injunctions (to regulate occupation of the home and, in some cases, to prevent a spouse or cohabitee from approaching within a specified distance of it).

Application: to the county court,
            by a spouse or cohabitee

2.1.3   Application ancillary to petition for divorce, nullity or judicial separation
Orders available:

Theoretically there is jurisdiction to make whatever order is necessary. In practice, since the case of *Richards* v *Richards* [1984] AC 174, [1983] 2 All ER

807, [1983] 3 WLR 173, normally only non-molestation injunctions will be granted ancillary to the main suit. Exclusion injunctions should be sought under MHA 1983 (or DVMPA 1976) where it applies.

Application: to the county court in which main suit is pending/is to be commenced (or to the High Court if the suit is pending there), by petitioner or respondent in the main suit.

2.1.4 Matrimonial Homes Act 1983 (MHA 1983)
Orders available:

orders regulating occupation of the home.

Application: to the county court (or the High Court)
    by a spouse.

Note that, although children cannot seek orders for their own protection under the above provisions, on an application by a spouse or cohabitee an order can usually be granted to protect the children.

2.1.5 Orders for the protection of children
Orders available:

(a) non-molestation orders in the county court or High Court in favour of a person who has the care of a child who is the subject of Children Act 1989 proceedings or is the subject of an order made under the Children Act 1989;

(b) prohibited steps order against 'any person' to prevent him from 'taking any step which could be taken by a parent in meeting his parental responsibility for a child ... without the consent of the court' (s. 8, Children Act 1989) – within the jurisdiction of the magistrates' court, county court or High Court;

(c) injunction made by the High Court in wardship or in the exercise of its inherent jurisdiction to prohibit interference with a child, both against a person who is a party and against a person who is not a party to the proceedings.

2.2 Urgent cases

In cases of urgency, an order giving personal protection to a spouse or cohabitee or her children can be obtained within a very short time.

In the magistrates' courts, application should be for an *expedited personal protection order* (or, if appropriate, an *ex parte* prohibited steps order).

In the county court (or High Court), application should be for an *ex parte non-molestation injunction* (or, if appropriate, an *ex parte* prohibited steps order).

In contrast, orders in relation to the home can only be made after proper steps have been taken to give the other party an opportunity to be heard.

2.3 Power of arrest

All courts have power, in certain circumstances, to reinforce their orders by attaching a power of arrest. This enables the police to arrest the person against whom the order has been made without further ado if they reasonably suspect that the order has been broken by reason of violence or entry into a particular area.

B: THE LAW

3   SECTION 16, DPMCA 1978

3.1   Principal orders available

3.1.1   Personal protection order

The court may make an order that the respondent shall not use, or threaten to use, violence against the person of the applicant and/or of a child of the family (s. 16(2)).

By virtue of s. 88 DPMCA 1978, 'child of the family' has the same meaning as it does in divorce proceedings (see Chapter 7 paragraph 3.7).

3.1.2   Exclusion order

The court may make an order:

    (a)   requiring the respondent to leave the matrimonial home; *and/or*
    (b)   prohibiting the respondent from entering the matrimonial home (s. 16(3)).

Where the court makes an exclusion order under s. 16(3) it may, if it thinks fit, make a further order requiring the respondent to permit the applicant to enter and remain in the matrimonial home (s. 16(4)). Such an order could be requested, for example, where it appears that the respondent is likely to comply with the exclusion order by moving out of the property but may react spitefully by having the locks changed before he goes so that the applicant cannot get back in.

3.2   Application by party to marriage

Application can be made by either party to a marriage (s. 16(1)). The Act offers no assistance to those who are already divorced or who are simply cohabiting (application to the county court would have to be considered on behalf of such clients, see paragraphs 4 to 6 below).

Note that an application under s. 16 need not be linked to an application under the Act for financial relief (s. 16(1)). Although protection is given in respect of children of the family, a child cannot make his own application; application must be made by a spouse.

3.3   Conditions for granting of s. 16 orders

3.3.1   General

The magistrates' courts can only make orders under s. 16 if the respondent has used violence to the applicant or a child of the family or threatened such violence. The detailed requirements as to what must be proved are set out in paragraphs 3.3.2 and 3.3.3. The magistrates cannot intervene to prevent other anti-social behaviour, such as verbal abuse, pestering (for example, by constant telephone calls or by following the applicant around), or violent behaviour directed at property (for example, smashing the windows of the matrimonial home). If such behaviour is a problem, the solicitor should consider an application to the county court rather than the magistrates' court.

3.3.2 Personal protection order

The court can only make a personal protection order if it is satisfied:

(a) that the respondent has used violence or threatened to use violence against the person of the applicant or a child of the family; and

(b) that an order is necessary for the protection of the applicant or a child of the family.

Whether the respondent has used or threatened violence will usually be simply a question of fact. If the respondent denies the alleged behaviour, the magistrates will have to hear evidence and make up their own minds.

No guidance is given in the Act as to how the magistrates should reach their decision as to what is necessary for the protection of the applicant and the children. The case of *McCartney* v *McCartney* [1981] 1 All ER 597, decided that, when considering the granting of an exclusion order, the magistrates should assess the parties' situation objectively (see paragraph 3.3.3 below). No doubt they must use the same standard when considering applications for personal protection orders. Therefore it will not be sufficient for the complainant to tell the magistrates that she feels an order is necessary; the magistrates must look at all the circumstances of the case (including what the other spouse has to say if he gives evidence) and form their own view as to what is necessary.

Example 1. Mr Logan regularly returns home drunk on Friday nights and behaves violently towards his wife, punching her, pushing her about, etc. Last Friday he threw his supper at her and the plate hit her on her cheekbone causing a cut which required stitching.

Mrs Logan should be able to obtain a personal protection order on the basis that the respondent has used violence against her person and an order is necessary for her protection.

Example 2. Mr Green has always disliked Belinda (his wife's child by an earlier marriage) who is a child of the family. Recently he has threatened violence towards Belinda and Mrs Green is concerned that he will carry out his threats.

On Mrs Green's application the magistrates would be able to make a personal protection order on the basis of Mr Green's threats of violence towards Belinda if they felt an order was necessary to protect her.

When a personal protection order is made, the court can include a provision that the respondent shall not incite or assist any other person (for instance, one of his relatives or friends) to use or threaten to use violence against the applicant or child of the family (s. 16(10)).

3.3.3 Exclusion order

The court can only make an exclusion order if it is satisfied:

(a) *either*:

(i) that the respondent has used violence against the person of the applicant or a child of the family; *or*

(ii) that the respondent has threatened to use violence against the person of the applicant or a child of the family and has used violence against some other person; *or*

(iii)   that the respondent has, in contravention of a personal protection order, threatened to use violence against the person of the applicant or a child of the family; *and*

(b)   that the applicant or a child of the family is in danger of being physically injured by the respondent or would be if the applicant or child were to enter the matrimonial home.

In the case of *McCartney* v *McCartney* supra, the Divisional Court held that the danger of physical injury need not be immediate. However, it was stressed that it is not enough that the applicant thinks there is a danger. The magistrates must look at the evidence objectively taking into account what the respondent has to say about the matter and all the other circumstances of the case and only grant an order if *they* are satisfied that a danger exists.

> **Example 3.** The facts are as in Example 1 above. Mrs Logan could apply to have her husband excluded from the matrimonial home on the basis of his violence to her. She should have no difficulty in satisfying the magistrates that she is in danger of being physically injured by the respondent.

> **Example 4.** The facts are as in Example 2 above. If it can be established that Mr Green has used physical violence against someone (for example, if Mrs Green can establish that he had been convicted of assaulting a police constable), the magistrates will have power to make an exclusion order against Mr Green if they feel that Mrs Green, Belinda or any other child of the family is in danger of physical injury from him.

> **Example 5.** The facts are as in Example 2 above. Mrs Green cannot establish that Mr Green has actually been violent towards anyone. The most she can show is that he has issued threats towards Belinda. The magistrates make a personal protection order that Mr Green shall not use or threaten violence towards Belinda. However, Mr Green disregards the order. He continues to threaten Belinda and begins to threaten Mrs Green as well. Mrs Green can take steps to enforce the personal protection order and, in addition, if the magistrates are satisfied that she or Belinda is in danger of being physically injured by Mr Green, she will be entitled to an exclusion order on the basis that, by his threats, Mr Green has contravened the personal protection order.

3.4   Order subject to exceptions or conditions

The court can make a personal protection order or exclusion order subject to exceptions or conditions (s. 16(9)). It would seem more likely that exceptions or conditions will be attached to exclusion orders than to personal protection orders.

> **Example 1.** The court makes an order requiring the respondent to leave the matrimonial home but permitting him to visit once a week to pick up the children for access visits.

> **Example 2.** The parties live in a very large house with a separate, unoccupied 'granny wing'. The court makes an order excluding the respondent from the house except for the 'granny wing'.

3.5   Duration of order

The court has a discretion as to the duration of an exclusion or personal protection order (s. 16(9)).

The normal time-limit on exclusion injunctions in the county court is three months (see paragraph 5.1.4 below) and the magistrates also usually observe this time-limit.

Where an exclusion order is made against a respondent who is living in the home at the time, it is usual for the magistrates to allow him a period of time, say 7 or 14 days, to arrange alternative accommodation and move out.

3.6 Exclusion orders have no effect on title

An exclusion order does not affect the estate or interest that the respondent or anyone else has in the matrimonial home, except that it will obviously suspend or restrict the respondent's right to occupy the home in the immediate future (s. 17(4) DPMCA 1978). However, although an exclusion order will have no direct effect on property rights, it can give the applicant a tactical advantage when it comes to reaching a more permanent resolution of problems over the home.

> **Example.** Mr and Mrs Smales are joint tenants of a council house. Mr Smales behaves violently towards his wife and she obtains an exclusion order against him. She takes a copy of the order to the council to support her application that the tenancy should be transferred into her sole name.

If a long-term solution is sought and the couple have no plans to seek a divorce or judicial separation in the near future, an application under s. 17, Married Women's Property Act 1882 will have to be considered (see Chapter 34). Of course, if a divorce or judicial separation is planned, the court will have ample power to deal with long-term property rights in ancillary relief proceedings (see Chapter 14 et seq.).

3.7 Power of arrest

3.7.1 Power to grant power of arrest
Where the court:

(a) makes an order under s. 16 which provides that the respondent:

  (i)   shall not use violence against the person of the applicant; *or*
  (ii) shall not use violence against a child of the family; *or*
  (iii) shall not enter the matrimonial home; *and*

(b) is satisfied that the respondent has physically injured the applicant or a child of the family; and
(c) considers that he is likely to do so again;

the court may attach a power of arrest to the order (s. 18(1)). It must follow from the case of *McCartney* v *McCartney* (see paragraphs 3.3.2 and 3.3.3 above) that the magistrates must apply an objective test when determining whether the respondent is likely to injure the applicant or a child of the family again — the applicant's say-so is not enough.

> **Example.** The court makes a personal protection order that the respondent shall not use violence against the applicant. The court is satisfied that the respondent has regularly hit the applicant over the head with various implements, pushed and shoved her, punched her, etc., and that on occasions she has been injured by his conduct. The

magistrates consider that he is likely to injure the applicant again. A power of arrest is attached to the personal protection order.

A power of arrest will not be attached routinely (*Widdowson* v *Widdowson* (1982) 12 Fam Law 153 and see the comments at paragraph 8.2 below). When the magistrates do attach a power of arrest to an order, they should state why they consider it necessary to do so (ibid.).

3.7.2   Effect of power of arrest
See paragraph 14 below.

3.8   Expedited orders

3.8.1   The need for an expedited order
Obviously it will take a little time to arrange a full hearing of a s. 16 application. In some cases, the applicant or the children of the family are in need of immediate protection and cannot wait even a matter of days. In such circumstances, the solicitor should consider seeking an expedited order to tide them over until the full hearing takes place.

3.8.2   The conditions for an expedited order
Only a personal protection order can be expedited. There is no power to make expedited exclusion orders.

Where the court is satisfied of the normal conditions for a personal protection order (see paragraph 3.3.2 above) *and also* that there is imminent danger of physical injury to the applicant or a child of the family, it can grant an expedited personal protection order (s. 16(6)).

A power of arrest can be attached to an expedited personal protection order (s. 18) (see paragraph 14 for the subsequent procedure where this is done).

3.8.3   The advantages of an expedited order
The primary advantage of an expedited order is speed. The normal requirements as to service of the application (see paragraph 11.1.1(e) below) are dispensed with. The court can make the order even though the summons has not been served on the respondent or, though it has been served, has not been served a reasonable time before the hearing or has given him notice to attend at another time/place (s. 16(6)). Furthermore, a single magistrate can deal with the application (s. 16(7)), whereas with a normal application there are special rules as to the composition of the bench (for example, it should normally be composed of three magistrates including a man and a woman).

Another advantage of an expedited order is that it can be used in cases where the applicant is afraid that the respondent will explode into violence against her upon hearing of her application for a court order. An expedited order can be obtained before the respondent learns of the application so that the applicant is protected against a violent reaction.

3.8.4   Duration of expedited order
An expedited order will come into force as soon as a copy of it is served on the respondent (see paragraph 11.2(c) below) and will cease to have effect either:

(a)   when the court commences the full hearing of the application; or, if earlier

(b) on the expiry of 28 days beginning with the date of the making of the order (s. 16(8)).

4 NON-MOLESTATION INJUNCTIONS IN THE COUNTY COURT

4.1 The power

The county court has power to grant a non-molestation injunction either under s. 1 DVMPA 1976 or ancillary to a petition for divorce, nullity or judicial separation. Which power is used will depend upon the circumstances of the particular case. The solicitor should refer to paragraph 9 below for guidance as to how to frame his application in particular circumstances. Whether the court is asked to exercise its power under DVMPA 1976 or ancillary to a matrimonial suit, the principles that it will apply are virtually the same.

4.2 The nature of a non-molestation injunction

A non-molestation injunction can be granted for the protection of a spouse/cohabitee and/or children living with her. The wording of non-molestation injunctions varies. The terms of the injunction are likely to be along these lines:

IT IS HEREBY ORDERED THAT:
1. The respondent be forbidden to use violence towards the petitioner or the children of the family Alice Brown and Bertrand Brown.
2. The respondent be forbidden to molest in any way and further be forbidden to cause or encourage any other person to molest in any way the petitioner or the said children of the family.

Whereas the powers of the magistrates' courts are limited to dealing with personal violence or threats thereof, the county court has a much wider power to restrain any type of molestation. 'Molestation' includes any conduct which can properly be regarded as such a degree of harassment as to call for the intervention of the court (*Horner* v *Horner* [1982] Fam 90, [1982] 2 All ER 495). In colloquial terms, it means 'pestering' (*Vaughan* v *Vaughan* [1973] 3 All ER 449, [1973] 1 WLR 1159).

Example. (The facts of *Vaughan* v *Vaughan*.) Although the husband had behaved violently towards the wife in the past and had been committed to prison, after his release he was no longer violent towards her. However, he did pester her by trying to persuade her to go out with him and to see him and speak to him. He called at her house late at night and early in the morning, called at her place of work and generally made a perfect nuisance of himself the whole time. His wife was frightened of him and his pestering had an adverse effect on her health. The Court of Appeal found the pestering to be molestation.

4.3 General principles as to granting of non-molestation injunctions

Unlike the position in the magistrates' courts, there are no statutory conditions to be satisfied before a non-molestation injunction can be granted. However, it is clear that the court will only grant an injunction if:

(a) there is evidence that there has been molestation (*Spindlow* v *Spindlow* [1979] Fam 52, [1979] 1 All ER 169); *and*

(b)   the court considers that it is necessary to grant an injunction to protect the applicant or a child living with her.

Example 1. Mrs Jones seeks a non-molestation injunction against her husband. He admits that, whilst their marriage was breaking down, he was violent towards her. However, since he moved out of the matrimonial home two months ago, his behaviour towards his wife has been beyond criticism. The court may well decide that it is unnecessary to grant an injunction.

Example 2. Miss Smith and Mr Brown live together as man and wife. Mr Brown is an aggressive man and, in the last few weeks, he has destroyed much of the property in their house in anger. On one occasion Miss Smith was nearly hit by a shovel which Mr Brown had thrown at the wall. Mr Brown repeatedly threatens to beat Miss Smith up and, in view of his past record, she is afraid that he will. She has a good case for a non-molestation injunction.

4.4   Who may apply?

4.4.1   Under DVMPA 1976
Either a spouse or a cohabitee can seek a non-molestation injunction under s. 1 DVMPA 1976.

A person will be counted as a cohabitee if she and her partner are living together in the same household as husband and wife (s. 1(2)).

A cohabitee is not automatically disqualified from obtaining an injunction under DVMPA 1976 because she has ceased to live with her partner before making application; however, the conduct on which the application is based must have occurred whilst the parties were living together (*O'Neill* v *Williams* (1983) 127 SJ 595). If the applicant can satisfy this requirement, the court has jurisdiction to hear her application although she has subsequently separated from her partner. Whether she will actually get her injunction will depend on how long has elapsed since the date of separation and the other circumstances of the case. The longer the time that has elapsed, the less likely the applicant is to get her remedy (see *Harrison and Another* v *Lewis: R* v *S* [1988] 2 FLR 339).

Example 1. (The facts of *McLean* v *Nugent* (1979) 123 SJ 521.) The parties had lived together for three months. The respondent was violent and they parted. A few months later, the applicant obtained an injunction under DVMPA 1976. The Court of Appeal upheld the injunction.

Example 2. (The facts of *O'Neill* v *Williams* supra.) The parties lived together in a flat which was in their joint names. They had no children. The applicant left at the end of August after the respondent allegedly assaulted her. She went to live with her parents and did not consult solicitors until October because she hoped for a reconciliation. Her application for emergency legal aid was turned down and she finally got a legal aid certificate the following February. She sought an order under DVMPA 1976 excluding the respondent from the flat. The Court of Appeal held that there was jurisdiction to make the order as the parties were living together when the conduct on which the application was based occurred but that, after six months, it was not appropriate to grant the applicant relief under the 1976 Act.

4.4.2   Ancillary to matrimonial suit
Either spouse can apply for an injunction ancillary to proceedings for divorce, nullity or judicial separation.

4.5 Duration of injunction

The duration of a non-molestation injunction is often left open. In such circumstances, it would appear that it will last indefinitely (even after the parties are divorced) unless the respondent applies to have it discharged. He may be well advised to do this if, for example, the parties are reconciled. If he does not do so, the injunction will continue to hang over him and there is a danger that, should the reconciliation subsequently break down, the applicant will bring him back to court for breach.

4.6 Ex parte injunctions

4.6.1 When will an ex parte injunction be granted?

In an emergency the court can grant a non-molestation injunction ex parte (i.e., the normal requirements as to service of the application are dispensed with and the respondent does not have an opportunity to give his side of the story; see paragraph 12.2 below). Whilst there are no statutory provisions defining when an ex parte injunction will be granted, in the case of *Ansah* v *Ansah* [1977] Fam 138, [1977] 2 All ER 638, the Court of Appeal stressed that ex parte injunctions would only be granted in an emergency where the interests of justice or the protection of the applicant or a child clearly demanded the court's immediate intervention. The view of the Court of Appeal was reinforced by a Practice Note issued in 1978 ([1978] 2 All ER 919, [1978] 1 WLR 925), stating that an ex parte application should not be made or granted unless there is a real immediate danger of serious injury or irreparable damage. This approach was further endorsed by the Court of Appeal in the case of *G* v *G* *(Ouster: Ex Parte Application)* [1990] 1 FLR 395.

The solicitor should therefore be sure that an ex parte application is merited before he makes it. An ex parte application is only likely to be justified where there has been violence and, even where this is the case, the solicitor should remember that the notice period for non-molestation injunction applications is very short (two or four days depending on whether the application is made ancillary to a matrimonial suit or under the DVMPA 1976) and the client should wait for a hearing on notice if at all possible. The solicitor should be particularly reluctant to apply ex parte when the last incident of violence was some time ago.

Example 1. (The facts of *Ansah* v *Ansah* supra.) The marriage was stormy. The wife left the husband and, by consent, obtained an injunction restraining the husband from molesting her and the children. Subsequently the husband sought an ex parte non-molestation injunction against the wife, filing evidence in support to the effect that the wife had threatened to burn his clothes, had broken glass in the front door and had abused him. The Court of Appeal held that this evidence fell far short of justifying an ex parte injunction.

Example 2. Mrs Asquith's marriage is breaking down. She and her husband are still living together and, over the course of the last week, her husband has come home drunk each evening and assaulted her. Yesterday, he struck her on her arm with the poker causing severe bruising. He then pushed her against the door where she hit her head. The resulting cut requires four stitches. Mrs Asquith has nowhere else to live and she is afraid that her husband's violent behaviour will continue. She would be justified in seeking an ex parte non-molestation injunction.

4.6.2   Duration of ex parte injunction

An ex parte injunction is a temporary measure. It must specify the date on which it is to expire. This date is usually the date fixed for a hearing of the application on notice so the injunction will normally last only for a matter of days.

> **Example.** Mrs Bruce is subjected to serious violence by her husband against whom she is seeking a divorce. She applies ancillary to the divorce proceedings for a non-molestation injunction and, in the first instance, her application is heard ex parte. The court hears her application on the Monday and decides to grant an ex parte injunction. The notice period where proceedings are brought ancillary to divorce proceedings is two clear days. The judge therefore specifies that the injunction shall last until the Friday by which time the respondent should have been given proper notice. On the Friday, if the respondent has been served, the court will consider whether to make a longer-term injunction. If it has not been possible to serve the respondent for some reason (for example, he cannot be found), Mrs Bruce can ask the court to extend the period of the ex parte injunction so that further attempts at service can be made.

5   EXCLUSION INJUNCTIONS/ORDERS IN THE COUNTY COURT

An application to exclude the respondent from the home must be made either under the DVMPA 1976 or under the Matrimonial Homes Act 1983. Such applications are often made in conjunction with an application for a non-molestation injunction. See paragraph 9 below for guidance as to which jurisdiction to invoke.

5.1   Exclusion injunctions under DVMPA 1976

5.1.1   Orders that can be made

On an application under DVMPA 1976, the court can grant an injunction:

    (a)   excluding the other party from the home or part of it or from a specified area in which the home is included; *and/or*

    (b)   requiring the other party to permit the applicant to enter and remain in the matrimonial home or a part of it (s. 1(1)(c) and (d)).

As with non-molestation injunctions, the terms of an exclusion injunction can be varied to suit the circumstances of the case.

> **Example 1.** Miss Peach and Mr Pear live together as man and wife. Mr Pear has been violent to Miss Peach repeatedly and, last week, hit her with a shoe causing her a black eye and a cut which needed stitching. The couple have an 18-month-old child. Miss Peach has nowhere to live except the council flat which the couple share. She seeks an exclusion injunction. Mr Pear threatens that, if she gets her injunction, he will smply hang around in the street outside the flat until she agrees to have him back. The court grants an injunction in the following terms:
>
> IT IS HEREBY ORDERED THAT:
> 1.   After 12 noon on the next day after this Order is served on him the respondent shall not reside at 14A Grove Road, Maidenhead, Berkshire without the permission of the applicant nor shall he enter or remain in the said matrimonial home or any part of it without her permission.
> 2.   After 12 noon on the next day after the day on which this Order is served on him the respondent shall not be within 100 yards of 14A Grove Road, Maidenhead,

Berkshire except for the purpose of visiting 14A Grove Road with the previous permission of the applicant.

3. This order shall remain in force until the . . . day of . . . 1992 unless sooner varied or cancelled by the court.

Miss Peach is also granted a non-molestation injunction under s. 1 DVMPA 1976.

Example 2. Miss Cole has been driven out of the house she shared with Mr Bray by his violent behaviour. She has taken their two children with her. She seeks a non-molestation injunction and an exclusion injunction. Mr Bray has said that he will move out of the house but he will change all the locks before he does so to prevent Miss Cole from getting back in. The court grants an injunction excluding Mr Bray from the house and ordering him to permit Miss Cole and the children to enter and remain there. Miss Cole is also granted a non-molestation injunction.

5.1.2 Who may apply?

Either a spouse or a cohabitee may apply for an exclusion injunction under s. 1 DVMPA 1976. As to who is counted as a cohabitee, see paragraph 4.4.1 above.

Note that it is not necessary for the applicant to have any property rights in relation to the home. For example, an application can be made by one party in relation to a council house where the other party is the sole council tenant.

5.1.3 Principles on which exclusion injunctions are granted

Although there are no criteria laid down in DVMPA 1976 as to when the court will grant an exclusion injunction, it would appear that the court must take into account the same criteria as those laid down in s. 1(3) MHA 1983 for consideration in applications under that Act irrespective of whether the parties are married (*Richards* v *Richards* [1984] AC 174, [1983] 2 All ER 807, [1983] 3 WLR 173). The provisions of s. 1(3) are dealt with at paragraph 5.2.3 below.

5.1.4 Duration of exclusion injunctions

The DVMPA 1976 does not give any time-limit for exclusion injunctions. However, such injunctions are essentially a short-term remedy. It will therefore normally be appropriate for the injunction to be limited to a specific period, long enough to enable the applicant to make other arrangements for her accommodation or to take steps to have property rights in relation to the home sorted out (for example by petitioning for divorce and seeking a transfer of property order or by seeking a declaration under s. 17, Married Women's Property Act 1882). In most cases, a period of three months should suffice, at least in the first instance (*Hopper* v *Hopper* [1979] 1 All ER 181, [1978] 1 WLR 1342 and Practice Note [1978] 2 All ER 1056, [1978] 1 WLR 1123).

The respondent can apply to have the injunction discharged before the specified time is up if circumstances change and it is no longer necessary (for example, if there is a reconciliation, see paragraph 4.5 above). On the other side of the coin, the applicant is free to seek an extension of the period if she needs further protection (for example, if she has been unable to sort out alternative accommodation).

There will be cases where the court is justified in granting an exclusion order for a longer period than three months or for an unspecified period, particularly where the couple are simply cohabiting and the applicant is the legal owner of the home.

Example. The applicant and respondent have been cohabiting but their relationship has broken down because of the respondent's violent behaviour. The house where they have been living belongs to the applicant. She seeks an injunction excluding the respondent from the house. The court grants an exclusion expressed to be until further order. Unless the respondent makes a successful application to have the injunction discharged, it will be permanent.

5.2   MHA 1983

5.2.1   Ambit of the Act

The Act applies only to:

(a)   spouses,
(b)   the matrimonial home; that is a dwelling house (which includes a flat, of course) which is or has been occupied by the spouses as a matrimonial home (s. 1(10)).

5.2.2   Applications in relation to occupation of the home

The court has very wide powers under the Act to adjust the rights of the spouses to occupy the home itself. For the most part these powers are as wide as the court's powers under DVMPA 1976 and, in some respects, they are wider.

It matters very little who is the legal owner of the house. If the house is owned or rented in joint names, either spouse may apply to the court during the marriage for an order prohibiting, suspending or restricting the exercise by the other spouse of his right to occupy the house or requiring the other to permit the applicant to occupy the house (s. 9(1)).

Example. Mr and Mrs Vickers own their matrimonial home jointly, subject only to a mortgage in favour of the building society. In law, therefore, they are both entitled to occupy the house. Their marriage founders and there are constant rows which are affecting the children. Mrs Vickers applies for an order prohibiting Mr Vickers from exercising his right to occupy the house. The court grants the order which is, of course, the equivalent of an exclusion injunction made under DVMPA 1976.

If only one of the spouses holds the legal estate in the house or the tenancy in relation to it, the other spouse will have rights of occupation in the property under s. 1(1) of the Act (see Chapter 22 paragraph 3.2 for a fuller account of these rights). Either spouse will be able to apply under s. 1(2) for an order:

(a)   declaring, enforcing, restricting or terminating the rights of occupation (i.e. the rights arising under s. 1(1) of the Act); or
(b)   prohibiting, suspending or restricting the exercise by either spouse of the right to occupy the house (i.e. the right arising by virtue of his title to the property or tenancy of it); or
(c)   requiring either spouse to permit the exercise by the other of the right to occupy the house.

Example. Mr and Mrs Jogson live in a flat which is in Mr Jogson's sole name. Mrs Jogson automatically has rights of occupation in relation to the flat by virtue of s. 1(1) MHA 1983. Mr Jogson has been violent to her over a period of time and it is no longer possible for them to go on living in the same household. Mrs Jogson can seek an order under s. 1(2) MHA 1983 prohibiting Mr Jogson from exercising his legal rights to occupy the flat, i.e. excluding him from it.

The effect of ss. 1(2) and 9 is that, whichever spouse is entitled to live in the house as a matter of strict law, either spouse can apply to the court and the court can give directions as to the future occupation of it.

Section 1(3) makes it clear that the court's powers do not stop at ordering a spouse out of the house or prohibiting him from re-entering it. Thus:

(a)   The court can exclude a spouse from part of the house only.

Example. Mr Bloom works from home. He sees clients in his study. His wife has been disrupting his business by bursting in on his interviews at frequent intervals. The court makes an order under MHA 1983 excluding Mrs Bloom from her husband's study.

(b)   The court may order a spouse occupying a dwelling house or any part thereof by virtue of s. 1 to pay occupation rent to the other spouse.

(c)   The court may impose on either spouse obligations as to the repair and maintenance of the dwelling house or the discharge of liabilities in respect of it (for example, rent, water rate, the mortgage instalments).

Note that the Act does seem to be narrower than DVMPA 1976 in one respect. Although a spouse can be excluded from the matrimonial home and any yard, garden, garage or outhouse that goes with it (s. 10(1)), it does not seem possible for the court to make an order under MHA 1983 excluding a spouse from the vicinity in which the home is situated. If this protection is needed, an application under DVMPA 1976 will have to be considered.

5.2.3   Principles on which court determines applications

The principles on which the court should determine applications under MHA 1983 are set out in s. 1(3). The court may make such order as it thinks just and reasonable having regard to:

(a)   the conduct of the spouses in relation to each other and otherwise;
(b)   their respective needs and financial resources;
(c)   the needs of any children;
(d)   all the circumstances of the case.

The leading case is *Richards* v *Richards* supra. Indeed, prior to that case, applications were rarely made under MHA 1983 for orders regulating occupation of the matrimonial home. The House of Lords made clear in the *Richards* case that s. 1(3) does not dictate that any one factor should be regarded as more important than any other. The weight to be given to each matter depends on the facts of the particular case.

The following general observations can be made in relation to the factors:

(a)   *Conduct*   The applicant's case will be stronger if she can show that the respondent has been violent towards her or towards one of the children. However, it is not a foregone conclusion that if there has been violence an order will be made excluding the other spouse. Other matters have to be taken into consideration, for example, the conduct of the applicant herself. Has she provoked the attacks upon her or given as good as she has got? If so, her chances of obtaining an order are much reduced.

Although violence is not a prerequisite of an exclusion order, the applicant is unlikely to succeed if the only conduct she can point to on the part of the respondent is trivial. The court will look carefully at her reasons for refusing to live under the same roof as the respondent and, if it appears that she is being unreasonable, her application is likely to fail.

Example. (The facts of *Richards* v *Richards*.) The wife petitioned for divorce based on her husband's behaviour. Her allegations were extremely flimsy and amounted to little more than that she had become disenchanted with her husband. Eventually the wife left home with the children and lived temporarily with a friend. Each weekend and during her holidays she brought the children back to the matrimonial home where the husband looked after them. She had to leave her friend's house and tried to find other accommodation for herself and the children but could only find temporary unsuitable accommodation in a caravan. She sought an order excluding the husband from the matrimonial home so she could go back to live there with the children. The judge found that she had no reasonable ground for refusing to go back to live in the same house as the husband but he felt constrained to grant an exclusion injunction because the children needed to live in the house and they were living with the wife. The House of Lords held that the evidence did not justify the making of an exclusion order against the husband.

It is not only the conduct of one spouse towards the other spouse that is relevant. In the *Richards* case, the House of Lords felt it relevant that the husband was a good, affectionate and loved father.

(b) *Needs and resources*   The court will pay attention to who is to look after the children. Obviously, the need of a spouse and children for accommodation is harder to satisfy than the need of the other spouse, and so a spouse who is caring for children will have a better chance of obtaining an exclusion order than one who is not. However, the court will scrutinise carefully whether the spouses can be expected to live together, bearing in mind that an exclusion order is a drastic and Draconian remedy (see *Wiseman* v *Simpson* [1988] 1 WLR 35). An obvious example of such a case is *Richards* v *Richards*. There, the wife was looking after the children most of the time and yet was refused an order excluding the husband from the home. The judge found that the wife's assertion that she could not go back to live with him in the house was untrue, and the husband's behaviour was beyond criticism. In contrast, a spouse whose claim that she cannot live in the same house as her husband is held to be reasonable, and who has no satisfactory accommodation for herself and the children, is likely to obtain an exclusion order.

The court will also take into account the husband's need for accommodation. If he can obtain suitable accommodation elsewhere, the court is likely to be more disposed to exclude him than if he will be turned on to the street. However, if the circumstances merit it, the court *will* turn a husband out even if he has nowhere to go, although in such a situation the court could be expected to give him a longer period than normal to vacate the house.

The availability of council accommodation will be relevant but it may well be that for the immediate future both parties are equally badly off in this respect. The council are unlikely to be able, in the foreseeable future, to help a man without children and, with the present state of waiting lists, although they may offer a wife with children a roof over her head, the council may be equally unable to offer her *suitable* accommodation for some considerable time.

(c) *Needs of the children*   Until the case of *Richards*, the needs of the children had assumed a paramount importance in exclusion cases. If the children needed the home and the situation in the home was tense and explosive or the parent looking after the children would not live in the home with the other parent, out went the non-custodial parent without further ado. In *Richards*, the House of Lords stressed that the needs of the children should not automatically be given priority over all the other circumstances of the case. Despite this, it seems likely that the court will not hesitate to exclude a spouse if it *is* truly necessary for the emotional or physical well-being of the children and, in an appropriate case, the court will hear an application under the Children Act 1989 at the same time as an application for an ouster injunction (see *Re T (a minor); T v T (ouster order)* [1987] 1 FLR 181).

(d)   *All the circumstances of the case*   This is a general sweeping-up provision which allows the court to take into account anything else it thinks fit.

6   ORDERS FOR THE PROTECTION OF CHILDREN

A principle developed under the law prior to the Children Act 1989 whereby non-molestation injunctions and ouster injunctions could be issued for the protection of a child and the adult with whom he was living (*Re W (a minor)* [1981] 3 All ER 401): a non-molestation order could be granted in support of a custody order under the Guardianship of Minors Act 1971; *Ainsbury* v *Millington* [1986] 4 All ER 73; *T* v *T* [1987] 1 FLR 181.

The authors assume that the court has the power to grant a non-molestation injunction in favour of a person who has the care of a child who is the subject of Children Act 1989 proceedings or of an order made under s. 8, Children Act 1989. Such an injunction could be made against any party to the proceedings. The county court's power to grant an injunction derives from the County Courts Act 1984, s. 38 (as substituted by the Courts and Legal Services Act 1990, s. 3), which gives a county court judge power in 'any proceedings in a county court' to make any order which could be made by the High Court if the proceedings were in the High Court, save for the exceptions set out in s. 38(3). The Supreme Court Act 1981, s. 37(1) gives the High Court power to grant an injunction 'in all cases in which it appears to the court to be just and convenient to do so'. The relevant sections of the County Courts Act 1984 have been amended to enable district judges to grant injunctions (see also the Lord Chancellor's Family Proceedings (Allocation to Judiciary) Directions 1991, [1991] 2 FLR 463). Thus, it would seem to follow that if an unmarried mother wished to obtain an injunction to restrain the father from being violent to her at a time when they were no longer cohabiting (in which case she could neither apply under the Domestic Violence and Matrimonial Proceedings Act 1976 nor, obviously, in the course of divorce proceedings), she should apply to the county court for a residence order pursuant to s. 8, Children Act 1989 and for a non-molestation injunction ancillary to those proceedings. Such an injunction, since it is in the course of family proceedings (as defined in s. 8(4) of the Children Act 1989), could forbid the father from assaulting, molesting or otherwise interfering with the mother and from entering or attempting to enter her home, save in accordance with arrangements for contact with the children. If necessary, there would appear to be no reason why such an injunction should not also extend to protect the children themselves; this would be an exercise of the inherent jurisdiction of the High Court, under the powers derived through s. 38, County Courts Act 1984 (see *Re W (A Minor)* [1981] 3 All ER 401 and *Ainsbury* v *Millington* [1986] 1 FLR 331. The reader is further referred to a most helpful article giving a general review of injunctions and undertakings in county courts; the author is His Honour Judge Nigel Fricker QC and the reference is [1992] Family Law 10.

It would appear that an injunctive order can be made even against a person who is not a party to the proceedings. Pursuant to s. 8(1), Children Act 1989 the court is empowered to make a 'prohibited steps' order, which provides for an order that 'no step which could be taken by a parent in meeting his parental responsibility for a child . . . shall be taken by *any person* without the consent of the court'. However, the scope of this order is limited in that it cannot be used to prevent a person from doing something which cannot possibly be described as 'meeting his parental responsibility'. (*Quaere*: does this mean that it could not be used to prevent a father from using violence to the mother if that violence in no way affected the children? Only the evolution of caselaw under the Children Act 1989 will solve this question.)

Finally, the High Court, in wardship proceedings or under its inherent jurisdiction, can grant an injunction to prohibit interference with a child, both against a person who *is* a party and against a person who is *not* a party to the proceedings (*Attorney-General* v *Newspaper Publishing plc* [1987] 3 All ER 276).

7   POST-DECREE INJUNCTIONS AND ORDERS

The time when the intervention of the court is usually required is before divorce, nullity or judicial separation. Occasionally a couple continue to have trouble even after decree absolute is granted.

No order can be made under DVMPA 1976 after decree absolute (unless, of course, the spouses have continued to cohabit or resumed cohabitation), nor can an order be made under MHA 1983 (as the parties are no longer married). The court may, however, grant an ouster injunction in the exercise of its inherent jurisdiction to ensure the protection of children (see *Quinn* v *Quinn* (1983) 4 FLR 394, followed in *Wilde* v *Wilde* [1988] 2 FLR 83). The court also has jurisdiction to grant a non-molestation order after decree absolute (see *Webb* v *Webb* [1986] 1 FLR 541).

8   POWERS OF ARREST IN THE COUNTY COURT

8.1   When can a power of arrest be attached in theory?

By virtue of s. 2 DVMPA 1976, a power of arrest can be attached to an injunction where:

(a)   the injunction contains a provision

(i)   restraining the respondent from using violence against the applicant or against a child living with her; *or*
(ii)   excluding the respondent from the matrimonial home or from a specified area in which the matrimonial home is included; *and*

(b)   the judge is satisfied that the respondent has caused actual bodily harm to the applicant or the child concerned in the injunction; *and*

(c)   the judge considers that the respondent is likely to cause actual bodily harm to the applicant/child again.

It is worth noting that although the terms of s. 2 differ slightly from those of s. 18 DPMCA 1978 (see paragraph 3.7 above), its practical effect is the same. It is a pity that the draftsmen of the two Acts did not use the same terminology.

It is of no consequence whether the injunction was granted under DVMPA 1976 or ancillary to divorce; a power of arrest can be attached to any injunction granted by a High Court or county court judge provided it satisfies the conditions of s. 2 (*Lewis* v *Lewis* [1978] Fam 60, [1978] 1 All ER 729, [1978] 2 WLR 644). Note that a power of arrest cannot be attached to an undertaking from the respondent (see *McConnell* v *McConnell* (1980) 10 Fam. Law 214 and *Carpenter* v *Carpenter* [1988] 1 FLR 121; [1988] Fam. Law 56) and see paragraph 12.1.2 below as to undertakings.

8.2   When will a power of arrest be attached in practice?

It is not routine for a power of arrest to be attached even where the conditions of s. 2 can be made out. The Court of Appeal stressed in *Lewis* v *Lewis* supra, that the power should only be exercised where the circumstances are exceptional, for example, where the respondent has persistently disobeyed injunctions and been a nuisance to the applicant and others concerned. It is far more likely that a power of arrest will be attached where the applicant is complaining of recent personal violence than where her complaints centre predominantly on other forms or harassment and the last incident of violence was some time ago.

> **Example.** Mrs Blades has repeatedly been assaulted by her husband in the past. The police have been called to the house many times and, on one occasion, Mr Blades was prosecuted for and convicted of an assault occasioning actual bodily harm on his wife. Recently, Mr Blades' violent behaviour towards his wife has been particularly bad. She seeks a non-molestation injunction and, at a hearing on notice, the court grants an injunction restraining Mr Blades from assaulting or otherwise molesting his wife. The judge has no difficulty in finding that Mr Blades has caused actual bodily harm to his wife and is likely to do so again and, in view of Mr Blades' repeated violence, attaches a power of arrest to the injunction.

Only those parts of the injunction in relation to which a power of arrest can be exercised under s. 2(3) DVMPA 1976 must be recited in the power of arrest form (see CCR Ord. 47, r. 8). It is good practice, therefore, to ensure that when the original injunction is drafted the clauses forbidding violence, molestation and exclusion from the matrimonial home or a prescribed area around the matrimonial home are set out in three separate clauses. This will facilitate the attachment of a power of arrest if subsequently that becomes necessary. Where a power of arrest is in fact attached to such an order then the Family Proceedings Rules 1991, r. 3.9(6)(a) *requires* that the relevant provisions be set out in separate clauses and that those clauses should not refer to any form of molestation which would not entitle a constable to arrest the respondent under s. 2(3). In theory, a power of arrest can be attached to an ex parte injunction; however, the circumstances would have to be particularly exceptional for this to be justified in practice.

8.3   Effect of power of arrest

See paragraph 14 below.

C: CHOICE OF PROCEEDINGS

9   DECIDING WHICH PROCEEDINGS

The solicitor should have little difficulty in deciding whether his client's problem merits an application to court. What may trouble him more is what form the application should take.

9.1   The unmarried client

Where the client is unmarried, the decision should be straightforward as the choice of proceedings is very limited. The first point to determine is whether the client qualifies as a cohabitee or not (see paragraph 4.4.1 above).

(i)   If the client is a cohabitee, proceedings for a non-molestation and/or exclusion injunction should be brought under DVMPA 1976. The DPMCA 1978 and MHA 1983 do not apply to unmarried couples and, clearly, there can be no matrimonial proceedings for divorce, etc. on which to hang an ancillary application for an injunction.

(ii)   If the client is not a cohabitee, the only possibility of relief is by way of an action under the normal law of contract, tort, property, etc. (for example, by means of an action for possession or trespass, either to land or to the person). However, if the client has the care of a child then she may well be able to obtain an order in one of the ways set out in paragraph 6 above.

9.2   The married client

The decision as to which application should be brought on behalf of a married client depends firstly on what is to happen in relation to the marriage.

(i)   If divorce, nullity or judicial separation proceedings are pending (whether commenced by the client herself or by her husband), or she intends to commence proceedings in the immediate future, the client should seek personal protection for herself and any children by means of an application for a non-molestation injunction ancillary to the main suit. If no petition has yet been filed, at the hearing of the injunction application, the solicitor should give an undertaking to file a petition forthwith. The occupation of the matrimonial home should normally be regulated by means of an application under MHA 1983.

(ii)   If no petition for divorce, nullity or judicial separation is either pending or intended, there may be a choice of proceedings, i.e. magistrates' court proceedings under DPMCA 1978 or county court proceedings under DVMPA 1976 and/or MHA 1983.

In these circumstances, the solicitor should consider whether the client can satisfy the stringent requirements of s. 16 DPMCA as to violence/threats of violence. If she cannot, magistrates' court proceedings are clearly out.

If the client can satisfy the requirements of s. 16, the solicitor should consider whether she would be able to obtain the relief she requires under DPMCA 1978 (for example, the magistrates cannot exclude the respondent from the area in which the matrimonial home is situated). If not, again magistrates' court proceedings are out. If it looks as if the client should be able to obtain a suitable remedy in the magistrates' court, DMPCA 1978 proceedings should normally be used. It is likely that this will be the cheapest way of obtaining relief and it may also be considerably more convenient for the client (and her solicitor) to visit the local magistrates' court than to traipse further afield to the county court. Furthermore, if the client wishes to rely upon legal aid, she may well have no choice but to use DPMCA 1978, as an application for full legal aid for the county court would be likely to be turned down on the basis that assistance by way of representation for the magistrates' court would be more economical and should be granted instead.

If the solicitor decides that the client will not be sufficiently protected by an application to the magistrates' court, he must make an application to the county court. If he is seeking a non-molestation injunction he will have to do so under DVMPA 1976. However, if (alternatively or as well) he is seeking an order regulating the occupation of the matrimonial home it appears that he again has a choice as to whether to seek the order under MHA 1983 or under DVMPA 1976. Whichever jurisdiction he chooses to rely on, the same factors will apply in deciding whether the respondent should be excluded (see s. 1(3) MHA 1983). However, there are differences between the two procedures in other respects. If the solicitor chooses MHA 1983, the notice period will be 21 days unless abridged but the court's powers will, in some respects, be greater than under DVMPA 1976 (for example, the respondent can be ordered to pay the outgoings of the home, see paragraph 5.2.2 above), whereas if he chooses DVMPA 1976, the notice period will only be four days but the court will not be able to make any peripheral orders as to outgoings, occupation, rent, etc.

10   COMPARISON OF THE REMEDIES AVAILABLE

The following is a summary of the main differences between the various jurisdictions of the courts to make orders against molestation and in relation to the home.

(a) DPMCA 1978:

(i)   likely to be cheapest, quickest and possibly most convenient remedy;
(ii) only applies to spouses;
(iii) stringent conditions as to violence/threats thereof must be satisfied before remedy available;
(iv) court can only protect against personal violence or threats thereof and can only exclude respondent from home itself, not surrounding area;
(v) only children of the family are protected, not other children living with applicant.

(b) DVMPA 1976:

(i)   offers protection to cohabitees;

(ii)   no requirement of violence or threats thereof before remedy can be granted;

(iii)   respondent can be restrained from all manner of conduct;

(iv)   respondent can be excluded not only from house but also from surrounding area;

(v)   no power to make orders re occupation rent, payment of outgoings, etc. (although, with spouses, separate maintenance application can be made to cover these);

(vi)   protection offered to any child living with applicant.

(c)   Ancillary to divorce, etc:

(i)   only applies to petitioner or respondent in main suit;

(ii)   generally only non-molestation injunctions made ancillary to main suit, not exclusion injunctions;

(iii)   power to grant injunction in whatever terms necessary;

(iv)   no requirement of violence or threats thereof before remedy can be granted;

(v)   protection offered to any child in need of it as a result of the breakdown of the marriage.

(d)   MHA 1983:

(i)   applies only to spouses;

(ii)   power not only to regulate occupation of home but also to order occupation rent, payment of outgoings, etc.;

(iii)   no power to exclude from area in which home situated;

(iv)   no power to make non-molestation injunction but can be coupled with application for non-molestation ancillary to divorce or under DVMPA 1976;

(v)   no requirement of violence or threat thereof before remedy can be granted;

(vi)   long notice period unless abridged.

(e)   Orders for the protection of children:

(i)   the county court offers protection to a person with the care of a child whether or not they are married or cohabiting: s. 8, Children Act 1989, as derived from s. 38, County Courts Act 1984. There is power to:

(aa)   grant a non-molestation injunction;

(bb)   prevent respondent from molesting or otherwise interfering with applicant;

(cc)   prevent respondent from entering or attempting to enter applicant's home, save for agreed contact with the child;

(dd)   grant an injunction to protect the child himself.

(ii)   the magistrates' court, county court or High Court can grant a prohibited steps order (ex parte if necessary) to restrain any person from taking any step which could be taken by a person in meeting his parental responsibility for a child (s. 8, Children Act 1989);

(iii)   the High Court in wardship, or in the exercise of its inherent jurisdiction can grant injunctions to prohibit interference with a child against any one, whether they are a party or not.

D: PROCEDURE

11 DPMCA 1978

11.1 Normal procedure

(a) Application should be made to the magistrates' court for the commission area where either the applicant or respondent normally reside (s. 30(1) DPMCA 1978) or for the commission area where the parties last ordinarily resided together as man and wife (Magistrates' Courts (Matrimonial Proceedings) Rules 1980, r. 11).

(b) Application is by complaint (s. 30(2) DPMCA 1978). Normally a written complaint should be prepared on a complaint form, signed by the applicant and presented at the court office. It is possible for a complaint to be made orally by an applicant in person (for example, in an emergency), in which case the applicant will tell her story to a magistrate or a magistrates' clerk and it will be recorded on a complaint form by the clerk. When she lays her complaint, the applicant should provide the magistrates' clerk with all the information she can about the whereabouts of the respondent so that, once a summons has been prepared, the clerk can arrange for it to be served on the respondent.

(c) If the applicant is seeking an expedited order to tide her over until the full hearing of her application (see paragraph 3.8 above and paragraph 11.2 below), the clerk will arrange for the question of the expedited order to be considered by a magistrate as soon as possible. The fact that there is an expedited hearing does not affect the normal preparation for a full hearing which goes on regardless as described in the following sub-paragraphs.

(d) After the complaint is laid, a magistrate or magistrates' clerk will issue a summons provided there is nothing obviously wrong with the complaint (for example, it is not asking for an order that the magistrates' court has no power to make) (s. 51, Magistrates' Courts Act 1980). The summons informs the respondent of the brief details of the complaint made against him and the orders sought, gives him notice of the date, time and venue of the hearing of the complaint and summons him to appear on that day. If the applicant is seeking an exclusion order, the day fixed for the hearing must be as soon as practicable and in any event not later than 14 days after the issue of the summons (Magistrates' Courts (Matrimonial Proceedings) Rules 1980, r. 13(2)).

(e) The magistrates' clerk will then arrange for the summons to be served on the respondent. A notice telling the respondent of the orders that can be made under s. 16 (personal protection and exclusion orders) and s. 18 (power of arrest) of DPMCA 1978 must be served with the summons (Magistrates' Courts (Matrimonial Proceedings) Rules 1980, r. 10). Service can be personal or by leaving the documents for the respondent with someone at his last known address or usual place of abode or, usually, by sending the documents to him by post (Magistrates' Courts (Matrimonial Proceedings) Rules 1980, r. 20 and Magistrates' Courts Rules 1981, r. 99(1)). The respondent must be given reasonable notice of the hearing (s. 55(3), Magistrates' Courts Act 1980).

(f) On the day fixed, the magistrates' court will consider the case. As the proceedings are domestic proceedings, they are not open to the public (s. 69,

Magistrates' Courts Act 1980). The applicant should attend to give evidence in support of her complaint. The normal procedure is for her case to be outlined to the court. She then gives evidence followed by any witnesses in support of her case; the respondent has the opportunity to cross-examine the applicant and each witness. Thereafter, the respondent will give evidence himself and call his witnesses and the applicant will have the opportunity to cross-examine. The respondent will then address the court. The magistrates will consider the evidence and decide whether to grant the applicant the orders requested.

(g)   If an order is made it will be immediately effective (subject, of course, to the fact that the magistrates are likely to give the respondent a period of time in which to arrange to vacate the home if an exclusion order is made). It is usual for the court to arrange for a copy of the order to be served on the respondent after the hearing to ensure that, in the event of a breach of the order, the court has full powers to deal with him.

(h)   It is not unusual for the respondent to fail to turn up for the hearing. If this happens, the court can proceed with the hearing in his absence if it is satisfied that the summons was served on him a reasonable time before the hearing or that he has appeared on a previous occasion to answer to the complaint (s. 55(1), Magistrates' Courts Act 1980). Alternatively, it can adjourn the case for the respondent to be served (or if he has been served, to give him another chance to attend). In certain cases, the magistrates have power to issue a warrant for the arrest of the respondent when adjourning to ensure that he attends on the adjourned hearing (s. 55(2) Magistrates' Courts Act 1980). If the court adjourns the case, it may be prepared to grant an expedited order to protect the applicant during the interim period if she can show that she or a child of the family is in imminent danger of physical injury from the respondent (see paragraph 3.8 above and paragraph 11.2 below).

11.1.1   *Where the respondent does not oppose the making of an order*
In the county court, if the respondent attends the hearing and does not oppose the making of the injunction sought, there is no need for the court to hear any evidence at all – the judge can simply accept an undertaking from the respondent along the lines of the proposed injunction (see paragraph 12.1.2 below).

The magistrates' court, in contrast, cannot deal with the case without first hearing at least brief evidence in support of the applicant's case, whatever the attitude of the respondent. The applicant will therefore have to outline the circumstances of the case to the court and the respondent will be asked to confirm that he has no objection to the making of the order sought.

11.2   Procedure for seeking expedited order

(a)   A complaint is first made in the normal way. At the same time, the applicant must make a statement to the clerk of the court (orally or in writing) that there is imminent danger of physical injury to herself or a child of the family (Magistrates' Courts (Matrimonial Proceedings) Rules 1980, r. 13). It is not uncommon for the clerk to require this statement to be made on oath.

(b)   The clerk must then ensure that, as soon as practicable, the court considers whether to grant an expedited order. The applicant should attend court to give evidence in support of her application. The respondent does not have to have notice of the hearing (see paragraph 3.8.3 above) and will therefore not normally be present.

(c) If an expedited order is made, it will not take effect until it has been served on the respondent (s. 16(8) DPMCA 1978). It is the responsibility of the clerk to arrange for delivery of a copy of the order to the respondent. The order must be delivered personally unless a magistrate is satisfied that prompt personal service on the respondent is impracticable in which case he may allow service to be effected by leaving a copy of the order for the respondent with someone at his last known or usual place of abode or by sending it to him there by post (Magistrates' Courts (Matrimonial Proceedings) Rules 1980, r. 19(1)).

12 PROCEDURE IN THE COUNTY COURT

12.1 Normal procedure

12.1.1 Getting the matter before the court

The bare bones of the procedure for getting the matter before the court initially are basically the same whatever the jurisdiction under which the order is sought. A written application giving the respondent notice of the proceedings must be prepared, supported by an affidavit from the applicant. Both documents are filed at the court office and copies are served on the respondent prior to the hearing.

The nature of the written application varies according to the circumstances of the case:

(i) application for non-molestation injunction and/or MHA 1983 order where divorce, nullity or judical separation proceedings are pending: *a notice of application* in the matrimonial proceedings is used. The notice states briefly the order for which the applicant is applying and gives the date and place of the hearing. For a time after *Richards* v *Richards* it was thought that it would be necessary to use an originating application to claim relief under MHA 1983 which, if the client was seeking a non-molestation injunction ancillary to divorce, etc. *and* an order under MHA 1983, meant filing both a notice of application and an originating application on her behalf. The Family Proceedings Rules 1991, r. 3.8(3) provide, however, that where matrimonial proceedings are pending, application under MHA 1983 shall be made by notice of application in those proceedings. One single notice of application can therefore be used to seek both a non-molestation injunction and an MHA 1983 order.The Family Proceedings (Allocation to Judiciary) Directions 1991 give district judges jurisdiction to grant non-molestation injunctions in pending family proceedings and in applications under the DVMPA 1976 or the MHA 1983 (see also Family Proceedings Rules 1991, r. 3.8(4)). In considering such applications the district judge is empowered by s. 10(1)(b), Children Act 1989 to make, of the court's own motion, a s. 8 order if he considers such a course to be neccssary to safeguard the welfare of any children concerned, even though no application has been made for such an order.

Note that if no divorce, nullity or judicial separation proceedings have yet been commenced but such proceedings are imminent, it should be possible to make an application by notice of application ancillary to the *proposed* proceedings. A copy of the proposed petition should be made available to the court at or before the injunction hearing if possible and the applicant's solicitor will be required at the hearing to give an undertaking to commence proceedings within a specified period.

(ii)   DVMPA 1976: an *originating application* is required unless other matrimonial proceedings under Part III of the Family Proceedings Rules 1991 are pending. If other proceedings are pending then the application under s. 1 of the DVMPA 1976 may be made as an application in those proceedings (Family Proceedings Rules 1991, r. 3.9(3)). The application states briefly the order sought and is accompanied by a notice prepared by the court giving the date and place of the hearing (Family Proceedings Rules 1991, r. 3.9(2)).

(iii)   MHA 1983 application where no matrimonial proceedings pending: where no matrimonial proceedings are pending, application under MHA 1983 must be by *originating application* (Family Proceedings Rules 1991, r. 3.8(2) and r. 3.6(1)).

(iv)   Children Act 1989: a simple application is required stating briefly the order which is sought within the Children Act 1989 proceedings and the nature of the injunction which is applied for ancillary to those proceedings (e.g. a s. 8 residence order with a non-molestation injunction ancillary to it; or, a s. 8 prohibited steps order). For a full description of the proceedure for making applications under the Children Act 1989, see Chapters 25 and 26.

The applicant's supporting affidavit should set out clearly the facts which she alleges entitle her to the order(s) she seeks (for example, the incidents of violence on which she relies, details of the situation in the home and how it is affecting the children etc.).

Wherever possible, the solicitor should also prepare a draft of the order he is seeking in such a form that it can simply be signed by the judge if the judge finds it acceptable. A penal notice (warning the respondent that he can be imprisoned for breach of the order) should be endorsed on the draft order to ensure that there are full powers of enforcement should there be trouble in the future.

In addition to filing at the court office the notice of application/originating application (and a copy for service on the respondent), the supporting affidavit and draft order, the following documents may also be needed:

(i)   legal aid certificate if appropriate;
(ii)   copy notice of issue of legal aid certificate;
(iii)   notice of acting if the solicitor is not already on the record.

If the application is made by originating application (i.e., under the DVMPA 1976 or MHA 1983) there will be a fee to pay (which will be covered as a disbursement on legal aid). There is no fee to pay where the application is by notice of application.

The solicitor will be given a hearing date for the application which will be inserted on the copy of the notice of application/written onto a notice which will be affixed to the originating application for service on the respondent. The solicitor must see to it himself that the requisite documents (i.e., application, affidavit and where appropriate, notice of issue and notice of acting) are served on the respondent at the appropriate time before the hearing. The notice periods vary according to the jurisdiction relied on and are as follows:

(i) ancillary to main suit, including MHA 1983 applications where matrimonial proceedings are pending: *2 clear days* (County Court Rules 1981, Ord. 13, r. 1(2)). This is the shortest of the notice periods. The reason must be that, in such a case the respondent is already geared up to the legal proceedings and can therefore be expected to be ready for a hearing of the application relatively quickly.

(ii) DVMPA 1976: *2 clear days* (Family Proceedings Rules 1991, r. 3.9(5)).

(iii) MHA 1983 where no matrimonial proceedings pending: normally *21 clear days* (CCR 1981, Ord. 7, r. 10(5)) save that there is power to abridge the 21 day notice period on the application of the applicant (CCR 1981, Ord. 13, r. 4). If the situation in relation to the home is urgent, abrigement of the notice period should be sought.

(iv) Children Act 1989: usually 21 days, but the court has power to abridge the notice period (FPR 1991, r. 4.14(2)(b)). The procedure for ex parte applications is set out in FPR 1991, r. 4.4(4). For full details of Children Act 1989 procedure, see Chapters 25 and 26.

It is normal to arrange for personal service on the respondent, often by an enquiry agent. An affidavit setting out the date on which the papers were served on the respondent and the way in which the server identified him (for example, by his photograph provided by the applicant or by prior knowledge of him) should be filed as a matter of course. If the respondent then fails to turn up at the hearing, as not uncommonly happens, the applicant will be in a position to prove service and to ask the court to proceed to make an order in his absence. If the respondent fails to turn up and service cannot be proved, the most the court will do is to grant an ex parte non-molestation injunction. The main application will be adjourned for further efforts to be made to effect/prove service.

The solicitor should arrange for the applicant to attend court for the hearing to give evidence in support of her application. He should also consider the question of witnesses in support of the applicant's case. The applicant's witnesses should swear affidavits which should be filed with the court. Copies should be served on the other side. The witnesses should attend court to be cross-examined. It is not uncommon for a letter from the applicant's doctor to be handed in to the court setting out injuries he has seen on her body. Such a document is only admissible if the other side agree (as they usually will). If they do not agree, the only way in which the evidence contained in the letter can be introduced is by calling the doctor as a witness.

12.1.2 The hearing

The hearing is in chambers. The applicant's solicitor or counsel will explain the nature of her case to the judge or district judge and check that he has had the opportunity to see all the affidavits. The applicant will be called to give evidence. She is unlikely to need to say much in examination in chief as her case should be covered in her affidavit. The respondent, if he is present, will have an opportunity to cross-examine her. The applicant's witnesses will then give evidence and be cross-examined. The respondent and his witnesses will give evidence and be cross-examined. Both parties will then have an opportunity to address the court. The judge or district judge will decide on the appropriate order. The hearing can go ahead in the respondent's absence if service can be proved (see paragraph 12.1.1 above).

If the respondent does not object to the making of the injunction or order requested, he can give an undertaking, i.e. a promise to the court in the terms of the proposed injunction (for example, he can undertake to vacate the matrimonial home within seven days and not to molest the applicant). The respondent's solicitor should ensure that he is fully aware of what the undertaking means before he gives it. Although no finding of fact is made in relation to the respondent's conduct where an undertaking is given, the effect of the undertaking is precisely the same as that of an injunction (save that no power of arrest can be attached to it). A breach of the undertaking is punishable by committal to prison.

12.2   Ex parte applications

If an ex parte application is necessary, an affidavit (or a sworn statement if the application is for an injunction ancillary to Children Act 1989 proceedings) by the applicant setting out the situation should be prepared and sworn. If there is time, a draft order should also be drawn up. The solicitor should take the affidavit (and draft order) to the court office and request the court to arrange for the matter to be heard by a judge or district judge. An appointment can usually be arranged the same day. The applicant should attend the appointment to give further evidence in support of her application if necessary. Indeed, in an emergency, if there is no time to prepare an affidavit, the judge or district judge may grant an ex parte injunction on the basis of the applicant's oral evidence alone.

If the ex parte application is made ancillary to *proposed* matrimonial proceedings, the judge or district judge will require the solicitor to give an undertaking to commence the proceedings within a specified time (see paragraph 12.1.1 above).

Note that, in a dire emergency, a judge or district judge can normally be found even though it is outside the court hours; in some cases, he may be prepared to grant an injunction over the telephone.

In whatever circumstances it is granted, an ex parte injunction is a temporary measure only. It will be expressly limited in duration (see paragraph 4.6.2 above). Quite apart from seeking the ex parte injunction, the solicitor must therefore press on with the normal arrangements for the hearing of the application on notice (see paragraph 12.1 above).

The procedure for making ex parte applications for prohibited steps orders under s. 8, Children Act 1989 is set out in the FPR 1991, r. 4.4(4) and FPC (CA 1989) R 1991, r. 4(4). For further details of procedures to be adopted in Children Act 1989 proceedings see Chapters 25 and 26.

12.3   The order

If the court makes an order in favour of the applicant, either ex parte or on notice, the order will be effective immediately. However, in order to ensure that the court has full powers to enforce the order by committal in the event of a breach, the solicitor must arrange for the order to be served on the respondent personally as soon as possible. A copy of the order for service can be collected from the court office after the hearing.

The respondent's solicitor must explain the order to his client very carefully and should ensure that the respondent is aware of the fact that a breach of the order can be punished by imprisonment.

E: ENFORCEMENT

13 ENFORCEMENT OF ORDERS

13.1 General

An order is no good if the respondent can breach it with impunity. It is most important that the applicant's solicitor tells her how her particular order can be enforced. If there is a power of arrest attached, he will tell her to contact the police in the event of trouble. If there is no power of arrest he should stress that she should contact him if the respondent does not comply with the order so that he can take steps to enforce the order.

13.2 In the magistrates' courts

13.2.1 Bringing the respondent back before the court

(a) *Power of arrest* Where there is a power of arrest attached to the court's order, the respondent will be arrested and brought back before the court by the police in the event of a breach (see paragraph 14 for the procedure).

(b) *Warrant for arrest* Where the court has made a personal protection or exclusion order but has not attached a power of arrest, the obligation is on the applicant to apply to a magistrate for a warrant for the respondent's arrest if she considers that he has disobeyed the order. The magistrate can issue a warrant if:

(i) the application for a warrant is substantiated on oath, i.e. the applicant must give sworn evidence to support her allegation that the respondent is in breach of the order; *and*

(ii) the magistrate has reasonable grounds for believing that the respondent has disobeyed the order (s. 18(4) DPMCA 1978).

13.2.2 Penalties for disobedience (s. 63(3), Magistrates' Courts Act 1980)

(a) *Fine* The court can order the respondent to pay a fine of up to £2,000.

(b) *Imprisonment* Alternatively, the court can commit the respondent to prison for a period not exceeding two months.

13.3 In the county court

13.3.1 Bringing the respondent back before the court

(a) *Power of arrest* Just as in the magistrates' courts, where there is a power of arrest attached to the court's order the respondent will be arrested and brought back before the court by the police in the event of a breach (see paragraph 14 for procedure).

(b) *No power of arrest* Where there is no power of arrest, it is up to the applicant to apply for an order committing the respondent to prison for breach of the injunction. It is most important that the procedure for seeking committal is followed to the letter by the applicant and by the county court. If this is not done, either the court will refuse to make an order or, if an order is made, the order will be invalid (see, for example, *Nguyen* v *Phung* [1985] Fam Law 54 and *Williams* v *Fawcett* [1986] QB 604, [1985] 1 WLR 501, [1985] 1 All ER 787, *Tabone* v *Seguna* [1986] 1 FLR 591 and *Parra* v *Rones* [1986] Fam Law 262). Note, however, the case of *Linnett* v *Coles* [1987] QB 555, [1986] 3 All ER 652, [1986] 3 WLR 843, where the Court of Appeal rectified a defect in a committal order by substituting its own order in the proper form.

The procedure for seeking a committal order is set out in Ord. 29, r. 1, County Court Rules 1981, and is as follows:

(a)   Generally speaking, the court will not make a committal order unless a copy of the injunction endorsed with a penal notice has been personally served on the respondent. The solicitor should therefore check that:

(i)   a copy of the injunction has been served personally on the respondent (Ord. 29, r. 1(2)(a)); *and*

(ii)   that the copy of the injunction served on the respondent was endorsed with a penal notice informing him that disobedience to the order would constitute contempt of court and render him liable to be committed to prison (Ord. 29, r. 1(3)).

However, it may be possible to obtain a committal order despite the fact that the injunction has not been served yet if: *either*

(i)   the judge is satisfied that, pending such service, the respondent has had notice of the injunction either by being present when it was made or by being informed of its terms by telephone, telegram or otherwise (Ord. 29, r. 1(6)); *or*

(ii)   the court dispenses with service (which it can do if it thinks it just to do so) (Ord. 29, r. 1(7)).

(b)   The applicant should ask the court to issue a notice to the respondent to show cause why a committal order should not be made against him (Form N78 of the County Court Forms). The applicant's solicitor prepares three copies of the notice himself and files them in the court office. The notice states that the applicant is seeking an order that the respondent be committed to prison and requires his attendance at the hearing of the application; it must state precisely the alleged breaches of the injunction. The court fixes the date of the hearing, endorses it on the notice and seals the notice (Ord. 29, r. 1(4)).

(c)   The notice to show cause must be served on the respondent personally at least two clear days before the hearing of the application (CCR 1981, Ord. 13, r. 1(2)). The court will therefore return two copies of the notice to the applicant — one for personal service on the respondent and one for the file. The judge does have power to dispense with service of the notice but will only do so in exceptional circumstances (Ord. 29, r. 1(7)). The notice should be supported by an affidavit setting out fully the grounds on which the committal is sought. A copy of the affidavit should be served with the notice.

13.3.2   Power of the court to deal with the respondent for breach
Whether the respondent is brought back to court by virtue of a power of arrest or as a result of the applicant's application for a committal order, the hearing will take place in open court in front of a judge. (N.B. Although district judges

have power to make non-molestation and ouster injunctions they cannot hear applications to commit the respondent for breach of those orders. Committal proceedings must be heard by a judge.) The applicant and her witnesses will give evidence in the normal way detailing the alleged breaches of the injunction followed by the respondent and any witnesses he may have.

If the judge is satisfied that there has been a breach of the injunction (or undertaking) he may make a committal order for a fixed period not exceeding two years. The order will be for the issue of a warrant of committal (Form N80) (Ord. 29, r. 1(5)). The warrant will be enforced by the court bailiff.

However, it is extremely unlikely that the judge will make an order for immediate committal on the first occasion on which the respondent is brought before him for breach. In the case of *Ansah* v *Ansah* [1977] Fam 138, [1977] 2 WLR 760, [1977] 2 All ER 638, the Court of Appeal stressed that a committal order is a remedy of last resort in a family case and should only be made where every other effort to bring the situation under control has failed or is likely to fail. The real purpose of bringing the respondent back to court is to make sure the respondent complies with the injunction in the future rather than to punish him for what has already happened. There are the following alternatives to consider:

(a) If the injunction does not already have a power of arrest attached to it, the applicant should consider asking the court to attach a power of arrest so that the police can intervene if the respondent causes trouble again.

(b) The applicant should consider whether, in the light of the events since the making of the injunction, any amendment of the injunction is necessry.

Example. The original injunction excluded the respondent from the matrimonial home. He moved out but returned, in breach of the injunction, and let himself in one night whilst the applicant was out. When she returned, he hit her. He has also taken to hanging around the neighbourhood of the property hurling abuse at the applicant and the children whenever they venture out of the house. No power of arrest was attached to the injunction so the applicant brings the respondent back to court herself by means of a notice to show cause why he should not be committed for breach of the injunction. At the hearing, she acknowledges that the judge is unlikely to commit the respondent for this first breach but asks that a power of arrest should now be attached to the injunction and that the injunction should be extended to prevent the respondent from coming into the road in which the house is situated.

(c) The respondent can be fined but this is rarely a useful way of dealing with a breach.

(d) The application to commit can be adjourned *sine die*. If this is done, the applicant can restore the matter for hearing immediately should there be another breach by the respondent and, in the light of his repeated disobedience, will have a strong case for committal.

(e) A suspended committal order can be made, i.e. the court can make an order that the respondent should be committed to prison but suspend its execution on whatever terms it thinks fit. The usual suspended order is for committal to be suspended provided that the respondent does not breach the injunction again. However, the Court of Appeal in *Ansah* (supra) warned that it could be dangerous to make suspended committal orders where the respondent could be committed simply on the applicant alleging that there had been another breach as, in such cases, the respondent could be removed to prison with no opportunity to challenge the applicant's evidence.

It is open to the court to deal with an application for committal in the absence of the alleged contemnor where there is sufficient urgency, but if a power to arrest is attached to the court order the better alternative is to request the police to secure the attendance of the contemnor at the committal hearing. The full facts can then be investigated by the court before rather than after sentence is passed (*Benesch* v *Newman* [1987] 1 FLR 262).

14   OPERATION OF POWERS OF ARREST

14.1   Procedure in magistrates' courts and county courts

Whether the power of arrest is attached to an order of the magistrates' court or to an order of the county court, it operates in virtually the same way. For the detailed provisions in relation to magistrates' courts' powers of arrest, reference should be made to s. 18 DMPCA 1978 and the Magistrates' Courts (Matrimonial Proceedings) Rules 1980, and for county court powers of arrest to s. 2 DVMPA 1976. For the procedure to be adopted when an arrest has been made under a power of arrest pursuant to s. 2 DVMPA 1976 see the President's Direction at [1991] 1 FLR 304.

14.2   What happens

(a)   Once an injunction/order has been made with a power of arrest attached, the court will arrange for a copy to be forwarded to the applicant's local police station. Note that, in the magistrates' courts, where the order to which the power of arrest is attached is an *expedited* order, a copy will not be sent to the police station until the order has been served.

(b)   If the respondent breaks the injunction, the applicant should telephone her local police station. A constable can arrest without a warrant a person whom he has reasonable cause to suspect of being in breach of the injunction by reason of his use of violence or by reason of the fact that he has entered any premises or (in the case of a county court injunction) any area which is forbidden to him.

(c)   The arrested person must be brought before a judge (in the case of county court orders) or a magistrate (in the case of magistrates' court orders) within 24 hours. He cannot be released within the 24-hour period except on the direction of the judge/magistrate. It is up to the police to seek the directions of the county court/magistrates' court as to when and where the arrested person should be brought before the court.

(d)   The police will inform the applicant of the time when the arrested person is to be brought before the court. The police will bring the arrested person to court but, thereafter, they normally drop out of the matter and the applicant will be expected to present the case to the court and prove the breach of the injunction/order herself. The county court is not given an express power to remand the arrested person in custody pending a full investigation of the case. It would therefore seem that, unless the court decides within the 24-hour period that he is to be committed to prison, he will have to be released although he can still be required to attend at an adjourned hearing to decide what is to happen in relation to his breach of the injunction. The magistrates' court, on the other hand, may remand the arrested person in custody or on bail pending a hearing.

(e)   If the court finds that there has been a breach of the injunction order it has the powers described in paragraph 13.2.2 above (magistrates' courts) or paragraph 13.3.2 above (county courts).

PART VI
GENERAL MATTERS CONCERNING THE HOME AND OTHER PROPERTY

22 The home: preventing a sale or mortgage

1 THE PROBLEM

The major asset owned by the parties to a marriage is usually their home. For each spouse, this represents both a roof over his or her head and a capital investment. Whilst the marriage is satisfactory they are likely to discuss and agree any step that is to be taken in relation to the home, such as selling it or mortgaging it. However, once the marriage begins to founder, the danger arises that without consulting the other party to the marriage, one spouse will engage in dealings in relation to the house which will jeopardise either the roof over the other spouse's head or his or her financial interest in the property.

Example 1. The parties purchase a house in 1964 with the aid of a mortgage. It is conveyed into the husband's sole name. By 1987 the marriage is on the rocks and the wife petitions for divorce making a comprehensive claim for ancillary relief. She is living in the house but she goes away for two months to see her sister in Australia. Whilst she is away, the husband puts the property on the market and sells it. By the time the wife returns the proceeds of sale have been dissipated. She has lost both the roof over her head and any prospect of having the home transferred to her in ancillary relief proceedings under s. 24, Matrimonial Causes Act 1973 or of receiving under s. 23 a lump sum payment of a share in the proceeds.

Example 2. Instead of selling the house, the husband makes a second mortgage of it to a bank as security for a substantial loan. Provided he keeps up the repayments on both mortgages, this does not prejudice the wife's occupation of the property but it clearly does affect her financial interest in the house. Not only the first but also the second mortgage will have to be discharged from the proceeds of sale if the house is sold before the mortgagees have been fully repaid, thus substantially reducing the equity in the house available for distribution between the parties.

If the husband falls behind with the mortgage instalments, the wife's occupation of the house may also be endangered if the mortgagees seek to enforce their rights in relation to the property.

This chapter sets out what can be done to prevent problems of this sort arising. It is assumed that the solicitor acts for a wife who wishes to prevent her husband from dealing with the property. The same principles would apply if the roles were reversed.

2 HOUSE IN JOINT NAMES

2.1 Protection against sale or mortgage by one spouse

If the house is in the joint names of both spouses the wife will automatically be protected against the husband selling the property without her consent. As she is a joint tenant of the legal estate, the property cannot be conveyed or transferred unless she joins in the conveyance or transfer.

In theory it might be possible for the husband to use the house as security for a loan without the consent of the wife. In practice, however, it would be hard for him to find anyone willing to lend on this basis because the security provided by such arrangements would be inadequate. Thus the wife is unlikely to have anything to fear from this quarter either.

2.2 Providing for the possibility of death before divorce

2.2.1 Generally

The solicitor must give some thought as to what will happen to the wife's share in the property should she die before the parties are divorced and questions of ancillary relief resolved. If husband and wife are joint tenants in equity, the wife's interest will pass to her husband on her death by virtue of the right of survivorship. If they are tenants in common, the husband will still probably obtain the wife's share, perhaps under a will made by the wife in his favour at a time when the marriage was running smoothly, or otherwise under the statutory provisions governing intestacy (see Part IV of the Administration of Estates Act 1925, as amended). This may be perfectly accepable to some clients; others are so embittered by the breakdown of the marriage that they wish to prevent their spouse from benefiting in any way from their death. The matter must therefore be discussed with the client and, if she does not wish her property to pass to her husband, the solicitor must consider:

(a)   whether there is or may be a beneficial joint tenancy, in which case he should consider serving notice of severance; *and*

(b)   whether it is necessary to advise the client to make a will/a new will.

The question of a beneficial joint tenancy is dealt with at 2.2.2 below; the question of making a will is dealt with in Chapter 24.

2.2.2 Severance of the joint tenancy to avoid right of survivorship

The basic principles as to joint tenancies are as follows:

(a)   Where property is conveyed into the names of more than one person, there is always a joint tenancy of the legal estate. The equitable interests in the property may be held on a joint tenancy or as tenants in common.

(b)   If a joint tenancy exists in equity as well as in law, on the death of one joint tenant the other joint tenant will automatically become entitled to his beneficial interest in the property by virtue of the right of survivorship.

(c)   If the equitable interests are held as tenants in common, there is no right of survivorship and the equitable interest of the deceased tenant in common will pass in accordance with his will or according to the intestacy provisions if he has not made one.

One of the difficulties facing the solicitor in a matrimonial case is how to determine whether or not there is a joint tenancy in equity. If:

(a) the conveyance or transfer to the parties expressly provides that they are to hold the equitable interest as tenants in common; *or*

(b) a separate declaration of trust has been made to this effect; *or*

(c) a note or memorandum of severance is endorsed on or annexed to the conveyance to the parties or an appropriate restriction entered on the proprietorship register,

this is conclusive evidence that there is an equitable tenancy in common and therefore no right of survivorship — once a tenancy in common, always a tenancy in common. In such circumstances, there is no need to serve a notice of severance but the solicitor should not forget to consider whether it is necessary to make a will /new will for the client. There is no point in going to the trouble of checking up on the right of survivorship only to overlook the fact that the client's spouse will be entitled to the property anyway under her will or by virtue of the intestacy provisions.

The solicitor will not always be in a position to find out about the equitable interest in the house (for example, a building society may hold the title deeds and may not be prepared to release them without the consent of the other party). If he is unable to find out what the position is or finds that there was originally an equitable joint tenancy which has apparently not been severed, the only safe course is to consider serving a notice of severance (see s. 36(2) Law of Property Act 1925). When considering whether to sever, however, it must be borne in mind that not only will severance of the joint tenancy prevent the client's share in the property passing to her spouse on her death, it will also prevent her becoming automatically entitled by survivorship to his share in the property on his death. This disadvantage must be weighed against the advantages of severance.

If the solicitor decides, in consultation with the client, that it would be appropriate to serve notice of severance, care should be taken over the wording of the notice. Service of an unconditional notice of severance could be taken as an admission by the client that there *is* an equitable joint tenancy and that the parties are entitled to the equitable estate in equal shares. An admission of this nature could be prejudicial (for example in s. 17, Married Women's Property Act 1882 proceedings or when the operation of the Legal Aid Board's statutory charge came to be considered). Therefore, if there is any doubt at all as to whether there is an equitable joint tenancy, the notice of severance should be drafted in such a way that it is clear that no admission is made that there is a joint tenancy, but that if there is one the intention is to sever it. Again it is important that the solicitor should not stop at service of notice of severance — he must then consider whether there is any need to make a will/new will.

Note that while the issue and service of a summons and affidavit under s. 17 Married Women's Property Act 1882 will automatically sever an equitable joint tenancy (*Re Draper's Conveyance* [1969] 1 Ch 486), issue and service of a divorce petition containing a prayer for property adjustment will not (*Harris* v *Goddard* [1983] 1 WLR 1203, [1983] 3 All ER 242).

3   HOUSE IN SOLE NAME OF ONE SPOUSE

3.1   The powers of the spouse who is the legal owner to sell, mortgage, etc.

Theoretically the spouse who is the legal owner (whom we are assuming to be the husband) has the power to deal as he pleases with the property. However, although the husband may feel that he is sitting pretty because he is the sole legal owner, that is not, of course, the end of the story. The wife may well have rights in relation to the property; in particular:

(a)   she will have a right of occupation by virtue of the Matrimonial Homes Act 1983; *and*

(b)   she may have a beneficial interest in the property, normally arising because she has made a contribution to the purchase price.

If the appropriate steps are taken on the wife's behalf, these rights can afford her a substantial measure of protection against her husband selling or mortgaging the property.

3.2   Statutory rights of occupation (s. 1, Matrimonial Homes Act 1983)

3.2.1   When the rights arise

By virtue of s. 1(1), where one spouse is entitled to occupy a dwelling house by virtue of an estate or interest or contract or by virtue of any enactment giving him or her the right to remain in occupation, and the other spouse is not so entitled, the spouse not so entitled has 'rights of occupation' in relation to the house.

These rights only arise if the property is or has been at one time the matrimonial home (s. 1(10)). A spouse has no statutory rights of occupation of, for example, a holiday cottage owned by the other spouse.

> **Example.** The matrimonial home is in the sole name of the husband. His wife has never worked and has made no contribution towards the purchase of the house. The husband is entitled to occupy it by virtue of his legal interest. The wife has neither a legal nor an equitable interest in the property that entitles her to occupy it. However, she does have rights of occupation under s. 1(1).

Section 1(11) provides that, for the purpose only of determining whether he or she has rights of occupation under s. 1, a spouse who has an equitable interest in a dwelling house or in the proceeds of sale thereof, not being a spouse in whom is vested (solely or as a joint tenant) a legal estate or legal term of years absolute in the house, is to be treated as not being entitled to occupy the house by virtue of that equitable interest.

> **Example.** A dwelling house is purchased partly from the savings of a husband, partly from his wife's savings and partly on mortgage. It is conveyed into the sole name of the husband. Both spouses move in and live in the property as their matrimonial home. The husband is entitled to occupy the house because he owns it. The wife has almost certainly got an equitable interest in the property by virtue of her initial contribution to the purchase price. Nevertheless, because she has no legal estate, s. 1(11) means that she is treated as if she is not entitled to occupy the house by virtue of her equitable interest. The situation therefore falls within s. 1(1) and she is entitled to statutory rights of occupation.

3.2.2   What the statutory rights of occupation are

Where the spouse with rights of occupation is in occupation of the house already, her rights of occupation amount to a right not to be evicted or excluded from the house or any part of it by the other spouse except with leave of the court (s. 1(1)(a)).

If she is not in occupation, her rights of occupation amount to a right with the leave of the court to enter into and occupy the house (s. 1(1)(b)).

3.2.3   Termination of rights of occupation

Normally rights of occupation are brought to an end by:

(a)   the death of the other spouse; *or*
(b)   the termination (other than on death) of the marriage.

However, where there is a matrimonial dispute or the parties are estranged, the court has power to direct that the rights of occupation should continue despite either of these events occurring (s. 2(4)). The order to this effect will be made under s. 1. It is important to bear in mind that the order must be made *before* the event which it is intended to override occurs, that is, during the subsistence of the marriage. Application must therefore be made to the court in good time.

In fact, the court has a very wide power under s. 1 to deal with the question of occupation of the matrimonial home on the application of either spouse during the marriage (for instance, the court can not only order the continuation of rights of occupation post-decree, it can also terminate or suspend the right of either spouse to occupy the house during the marriage). Applications under s. 1 are dealt with fully in Chapter 21 at paragraph 5.2

3.2.4   How do rights of occupation protect a wife against sale or mortgage?

It is all very well for a wife to have the benefit of rights of occupation under the Matrimonial Homes Act 1983; how do these rights protect her if her husband attempts to sell or mortgage the house over her head? The answer is very little unless her rights are registered as a charge against the property. It is therefore the solicitor's duty to take the necessary steps to register his client's rights of occupation as soon as he is consulted in relation to her matrimonial problems.

The rules are as follows:

(a)   The wife's rights of occupation are a charge on the husband's estate or interest in the property concerned (s. 2(1) MHA 1983).
(b)   They should be protected as follows:

(i)   in case of unregistered land, by the registration of a Class F land charge against the name of the husband in the register of land charges (s. 2, Land Charges Act 1972);
(ii)   in the case of registered land, by the entry of a notice in the Charges Register under the Land Registration Act 1925 (s. 2(8)(a) MHA 1983). Note that there is no need to produce the land certificate when applying to register such a notice. This is an exception to the general rule and emanates from s. 4(1), Matrimonial Homes and Property Act 1981 which amended s. 64 of the Land Registration Act 1925. It is no longer possible to register a caution to protect rights of occupation (s. 2(9) MHA 1983).

Once the wife's rights have been properly registered, what protection is she given? Although registering her rights of occupation will constitute actual notice of those rights to purchasers of the matrimonial home (see s. 198(1), Law of Property Act 1925), it does not follow that the wife will be able to continue to occupy for as long as she wishes. The purchaser may apply to the court for an order determining the wife's rights of occupation, and on such an application the court has a wide discretion, having to consider not only the circumstances of the wife (and any children residing with her) but the circumstances of the purchaser as well (s. 1(3) MHA, as explained in *Kashmir Kaur* v *Gill* [1988] Fam 110; [1988] 2 All ER 288.

> **Example.** (The facts of *Kashmir Kaur* v *Gill*.) The matrimonial home was in the husband's sole name. The wife, driven out of the house by her husband's conduct, registered her rights of occupation by way of a notice. The registration did not come to the actual notice of the purchaser, who purchased the house from the husband, until after completion. The wife then sought an order of the court under s. 1(2) MHA declaring that she had the right to occupy and prohibiting the purchaser from exercising any rights over it.
>
> The Court of Appeal held that, in hearing the wife's application, the court had to consider all of the circumstances of the case (s. 1(3) MHA), which included the circumstances of the purchaser. The purchaser was blind and had bought the house with his special needs in mind. The judge's decision that the wife should lose her right to occupy was therefore upheld ás being a proper exercise of his discretion.

However, generally the registration of rights of occupation provides more effective protection than this. The prospective purchaser or mortgagee will carry out a search prior to completion and will uncover the wife's rights at that stage if he has not learnt of them before. He will immediately go back to the vendor to find out how he proposes to deal with the problem. If the wife will not agree to her charge or notice being cancelled, the vendor will be in breach of contract and the purchaser will withdraw from the deal, leaving the wife to enjoy her rights of occupation in peace.

3.3 The wife with a beneficial interest

It is not uncommon for a wife to have a beneficial interest in the matrimonial home even though she is not on the title deeds (see Chapter 34). The usual reason for such a beneficial interest is that the spouse concerned has contributed to the purchase price of the house directly (for example by providing part of the deposit or making mortgage repayments). A wife with a beneficial interest in the home can register her rights of occupation in the normal way and should be able to protect both her financial interest and her occupation of the home by thus preventing a sale/mortgage of the property except on her terms. But what if she omits to register her rights of occupation? Has she any independent rights arising from her beneficial interest?

3.3.1 *Overreaching provisions*
Where property is held by the husband on trust for both himself and his wife (or for his wife alone), a trust for sale will automatically be imposed.

Where property subject to a trust for sale is sold, the purchaser, if he knows of the trust for sale, will insist that the purchase money is paid to two trustees because in this way he can ensure that the conveyance overreaches all the equitable interests under the trust for sale, leaving him with the property free of obligation. Where the wife's interest is recognised on the deeds or in a separate declaration of trust, the overreaching provisions should therefore ensure that she will get the money that represents her beneficial interest (because, unless her husband has the second trustee in his pocket, her share will be paid to her by the trustees), even if she has omitted to register her rights of occupation and thus cannot prevent the sale itself or insist on living in the property after it is sold. The overreaching provisions apply whether the property is registered or unregistered (see *City of London Building Society* v *Flegg* [1988] AC 54, [1987] 3 All ER 435).

Where the wife's beneficial interest arises under an implied, resulting or constructive trust (for instance, where she has made payments of mortgage instalments), a prospective purchaser or mortgagee may know nothing about this, as her rights are unlikely to appear on the deeds. In such a case it is quite possible that the purchase or mortgage money will simply be paid to the husband and there is nothing to prevent him disappearing with it or spending it and there can be no question of the wife's interest being overreached. The protection she may have in these circumstances will differ according to whether the land is registered or unregistered.

3.3.2 Beneficial interest in registered land as an overriding interest

A wife with a beneficial interest in registered land whose interest is not overreached (see paragraph 3.3.1 above) has the prospect of full protection against a sale or mortgage quite independently of the question of registration of her rights of occupation. If she is in actual occupation of the property (i.e. physically present there), whether or not her husband is also living there, her beneficial interest can constitute an *overriding interest* under s. 70(1)(g), Land Registration Act 1925. This was established by the House of Lords in the case of *Williams and Glyn's Bank Ltd* v *Boland* [1981] AC 487, [1980] 2 All ER 408. The only proviso is that there will be no overriding interest if enquiry is made of the wife and her rights are not disclosed.

A sale or mortgage of registered land takes effect subject to any overriding interest existing at the time of completion of the transaction in question, whether or not the purchaser or mortgagee has notice of the overriding interest.

In the context of a sale or mortgage by a party whose spouse has an overriding interest under s. 70(1)(g), as the *Williams and Glyn's* case illustrates, this means that the purchaser or mortgagee will be bound by the wife's equitable interest in the property which is not only a financial burden on the property but also gives her a right to possession.

Example. (The facts of *Williams and Glyn's Bank Ltd* v *Boland*.) The husband was the registered proprietor of the matrimonial home. Both he and the wife had contributed to the purchase price of the property and they were therefore equitable tenants in common. Both spouses lived in the matrimonial home. Without the wife's knowledge, the husband mortgaged the house to the bank under a legal mortgage. The bank did not enquire of the husband or the wife before taking the mortgage whether the wife had any interest in the property. The husband defaulted on the mortgage and the bank took proceedings for a possession order which initially they obtained. The wife appealed to the Court of Appeal and the possession order was discharged on the basis that the wife, being in actual occupation of the property, had an overriding interest within s. 70(1)(g). The Court of Appeal held that the bank had taken the mortgage subject to the overriding interest and the wife was entitled to remain in possession against them. The bank's appeal to the House of Lords was dismissed.

Note that, before agreeing to lend in respect of a property, banks and building societies now tend to ask all those who are occupying or are going to occupy the property to sign a document under seal stating that any rights they have or may acquire in relation to the property are postponed to those of the bank or building society. If the wife has entered into such an agreement it may adversely affect her rights as against the bank or building society.

3.3.3   Beneficial interest in unregistered land and notice

The wife with a beneficial interest in unregistered land has no prospect of establishing an overriding interest since the concept is peculiar to registered land. Her rights depend instead upon the doctrine of notice. Unless the purchaser or mortgagee has actual or constructive notice of the wife's equitable interest at the time of the disposition, he will not be bound by it (*Caunce* v *Caunce* [1969] 1 WLR 286, [1969] 1 All ER 722). In *Caunce* v *Caunce* the court took the view that the mere fact that the wife is resident in the property with the husband does not fix the purchaser/mortgageee with notice. However, this view is now seriously outmoded. Whether a purchaser/mortgagee has actual or constructive notice of the wife's interest is a question of fact in each case (*Kingsnorth Finance Co. Ltd* v *Tizard* [1986] 1 WLR 783; [1986] 2 All ER 54). Where the purchaser/mortgagee is held to have notice, the wife may be able to enforce her rights in the property against him.

3.4   Registration of pending land action

Where proceedings are begun in relation to the matrimonial home (for example under s. 17, Married Women's Property Act 1882 or under s. 24, Matrimonial Causes Act 1973), a pending land action can be registered in the case of unregistered land. This protects the wife's interest in the property in much the same way as the registration of a Class F land charge save that, whereas the wife would normally have to agree to a Class F land charge being cancelled once decree absolute comes through, the registration of a pending land action will protect her until the dispute in relation to the property is settled.

Note also that a pending land action can be registered in relation to a property that has never been the matrimonial home — a situation in which no Class F land charge can be registered. In the case of registered land, the appropriate way to prevent dealings with the land where an action is pending would appear to be by lodging a caution in the Proprietorship Register.

4   BANKRUPTCY AND THE MATRIMONIAL HOME

The security of the matrimonial home will be threatened in the event of either spouse (we shall assume, here, the husband) being declared bankrupt. The question will then arise whether the wife (and children) can continue to live in the home, or whether the property should be sold to pay off the landlord's creditors.

The husband's property will vest in his 'trustee in bankruptcy'. However, his wife's right of occupation (under the Matrimonial Homes Act 1983) will bind the trustee and the creditors if they are duly registered, as will any rights the wife has by reason of her having a legal or beneficial interest in the home. However, the trustee will be able to apply for an order for sale of the property (under s. 1, Matrimonial Homes Act 1983 or s. 30, Law of Property Act 1925) in the bankruptcy proceedings. The court may make such order as it thinks just and reasonable having regard to the creditors' interests, the conduct of the wife (so far as contributing to the bankruptcy), the wife's needs and financial resources, the needs of any children, and all the circumstances of the case other than the needs of the bankrupt husband (Insolvency Act 1986, s. 336(4)). Where one year has elapsed from the date the trustee took office, then the court must assume, unless the circumstances are exceptional, that the interests of the bankrupt's creditors outweigh all other considerations (Insolvency Act 1986, s. 336(5)). In applications for sale of the matrimonial home by a trustee in bankruptcy, the interests of the creditors do generally prevail (see, most recently, *Re Citro* [1990] 3 WLR 880, [1990] 3 All ER 953).

23   Keeping up with the mortgage or rent

1   GENERAL

The importance of keeping up with the mortgage repayments or rent on the matrimonial home in spite of the breakdown of the marriage need hardly be stressed. If arrears are allowed to accumulate, there is a danger that the mortgagee or landlord will take action which could ultimately lead to the parties losing their home.

> **Example.** Husband and wife are joint owners of the matrimonial home. There is a mortgage in favour of a building society. Repayments are £100 per month and have always been made by the husband as the wife is not working. The marriage fails and the husband leaves to live with another woman. He ceases to pay the mortgage instalments. The wife cannot pay the instalments herself as she has no income. No payments are made for six months. The building society become concerned and press for payment. They threaten to bring proceedings for possession in order to sell the property if payments are not resumed together with some payment each month off the arrears.

2   STEPS THAT CAN BE TAKEN

2.1   Contacting the mortgagee/landlord

Where the client is in difficulties with mortgage instalments or rent, it is often a good idea to contact the mortgagee/landlord straight away to explain the position and to outline what the client proposes to do to alleviate it (for example, she may be intending to make application for maintenance from her husband or to seek state benefits). Provided that it appears that the problem is capable of solution within a reasonable period of time, most building societies and banks are prepared to be patient, as are some landlords.

2.2   Seeking financial help

2.2.1   State benefits

It is possible for rent or the interest repayments on a mortgage to be met by state benefits (see Chapter 35). The solicitor should consider whether his client is likely to be entitled to any benefit and, if so, advise her how to go about making a claim. The claim should be made as soon as possible — the situation will be harder to deal with if arrears have been allowed to build up.

Where mortgage interest is to be covered by state benefits, arrangements will have to be made in relation to the capital repayments. The mortgagee may be prepared to agree to these being suspended temporarily; if not, the client will have to scrimp and save on other outgoings in order to be able to discharge the payments.

2.2.2   Maintenance

An application for maintenance from the client's spouse should be considered. If the client is to continue to discharge the mortgage payments herself, she can ask the court to take this into account in fixing the amount of her maintenance. Applications for maintenance can be made in the magistrates' court under the Domestic Proceedings and Magistrates' Courts Act 1978 (see Chapter 31) and in the county court under the Matrimonial Causes Act 1973 ancillary to proceedings for divorce, nullity or judicial separation or under s. 27 (see Chapters 14 et seq. and 32).

2.3   Submitting to a possession action

The client may, in fact, be prepared to leave her home if she can be rehoused by the local authority. If she moves out voluntarily, she will have to take her normal turn in the queue for council houses. If, on the other hand, she is turned out of the house as a result of a possession order made by the court, the council are more likely to rehouse her straight away. For this reason it may be necessary for the client to allow the mortgagee/landlord to take proceedings for possession and to submit to the making of a possession order.

3   SPECIAL PROVISIONS OF MATRIMONIAL HOMES ACT 1983

3.1   Payment of other spouse's outgoings

Where a spouse has rights of occupation in relation to a dwelling house or any part of it, any payment that that spouse makes towards the other spouse's liability for the rent, rates or mortgage payments or other outgoings affecting the house is as good as if the other spouse had made the payment himself (s. 1(5)).

> **Example.** Mr Simpkins is the tenant of a flat where he lives with his wife. The marriage breaks down and Mr Simpkins walks out and stops paying the rent. His wife pays the rent instead. Her payment is as good as payment from Mr Simpkins would have been. The landlord cannot refuse Mrs Simpkins' payments and use the tenant's non-payment of rent as the ground for possession proceedings.

It is only necessary to rely on s. 1(5) where the spouse is not herself a tenant or an owner with a right to tender payment.

3.2   Where a mortgagee takes action to enforce his security

Section 8 ensures that the wife will be protected where her husband has defaulted on the mortgage and the mortgagees are seeking possession.

3.2.1   Notice of enforcement action

Where a spouse has registered a Class F land charge or notice, a mortgagee bringing an action for enforcement of his security must serve notice of action on that spouse if she is not a party to the action (s. 8(3)).

3.2.2   Joinder of spouse as party

A spouse who is enabled by s. 1(5) to meet the mortgagor's liabilities under the mortgage (see paragraph 3.1 supra) can apply to the court to be made a party to an action brought by the mortgagee to enforce his security and will be entitled to be a party if the court:

(a)   does not see any special reason against it; *and*
(b)   is satisfied that she is likely to be able to contribute sufficient towards the mortgage to affect the outcome of the possession proceedings (s. 8(2)).

Example. Mr Michaels is the sole owner of the matrimonial home which is subject to a mortgage in favour of a building society. He leaves his wife and goes abroad where he cannot be traced. He ceases to make any mortgage repayments. Although s. 1(5) enables his wife to make the payments, Mrs Michaels cannot afford to do so immediately after the separation as she is not working. She refuses to seek state benefits on principle. The building society are informed of the position and allow the arrears to mount for six months. Thereafter they press for payment and ultimately take proceedings for possession to enable them to exercise their power to sell the property to recoup the mortgage debt. Mrs Michaels has registered a Class F land charge and therefore is entitled to receive notice of the proceedings by virtue of s. 8(3). She may apply to the court to be joined as a party to the action. The court orders that she should be a party as she has just obtained a sufficiently well-paid job to enable her to meet the normal mortgage repayments and pay off a small amount from the arrears each month, in which circumstances the court would be unlikely to grant immediate possession.

3.3   Security of tenure with rented property

Under the Rent Act 1977 and the Housing Act 1985 and the Housing Act 1988, a tenant's security of tenure is dependent on his remaining in possession or occupation of the property. Section 1(6) MHA 1983 ensures that security of tenure will not be prejudiced when the tenant moves out, provided his spouse continues to live in the property. Her possession or occupation will be treated as his, thus protecting not only his rights in relation to the home but also hers (which are dependent on his).

1 THE NEED TO CONSIDER WHAT WILL HAPPEN ON CLIENT'S DEATH

When the solicitor is consulted by a client who is experiencing matrimonial difficulties or (in the case of the unmarried client) problems with her cohabitee, it is most important for the solicitor to consider with her what is to happen to her property should she die.

The first matter to investigate is what the present position would be were she to die today. If the client and her spouse/partner own land (for example, the home) as joint tenants, the spouse/partner would be entitled to the whole of the property on the client's death by virtue of the right of survivorship. In the case of a married client, the chances are that her spouse would also end up with a good deal of her remaining estate by virtue of her will if she has made one and otherwise by virtue of the intestacy provisions. What would happen to the balance of the estate in the case of a cohabitee would depend on whether she had made a will benefiting her partner. If so, the partner would clearly benefit in accordance with the terms of the will; if not, property would pass in accordance with the intestacy provisions under which the partner would have no entitlement.

Having ascertained what would happen to the client's property under the present arrangements, the solicitor should find out whether this is what the client wants. Some people are content for their spouse/cohabitee to continue to benefit after their death despite the breakdown of the relationship, for example, for the sake of the children or because they have no one else to whom they wish to leave their property. Others wish to take all possible steps to deprive their partner of any benefit, for example, because they now wish to benefit a new girlfriend/boyfriend or child or because they are embittered over the breakdown of the marriage/relationship.

2 THE EFFECT OF MARRIAGE ON A WILL

Before considering the effect of marital breakdown on existing testamentary documents, it is important to realise the effect which marriage itself may have had on an earlier will. By s. 18, Wills Act 1837, a will is revoked by the marriage of the testator. This rule does not apply, however, to invalidate dispositions in the will in exercise of a power of appointment (see s. 18(2), unless the property appointed would, in default of appointment, pass to the testator's personal representative), or (more significantly) where it appears from a will that at the time it was made the testator was expecting to be married to a particular person *and* that he intended that the will should not be revoked by the marriage (s. 18(3), as applied to wills made on or after 1 January 1983).

3 THE EFFECT OF DIVORCE, JUDICIAL SEPARATION AND NULLITY ON SUCCESSION

Certain events, such as divorce, automatically affect existing wills and entitlement on intestacy. The rules are set out in the following paragraphs and they should be borne in mind when considering the position with the client.

3.1 The effect of divorce or nullity on a will

Section 18A, Wills Act 1837 (as inserted by the Administration of Justice Act 1982) provides that, unless the contrary intention appears in the will, the granting of a decree absolute of divorce or nullity will have the following effects on the will of either spouse:

(a)   Any appointment in the will of the testator's former spouse as executor or as executor and trustee of the will is ignored.
(b)   Any devise or bequest to the former spouse automatically lapses.

The property that would have passed to the former spouse will either become part of the residue and pass to whoever is entitled to the residuary estate or, if the gift to the former spouse is a residuary gift, will pass according to the intestacy provisions. If it is intended to rely simply on s. 18A, the solicitor must be careful to check with the client that the result will fit in with her wishes. It may be, for example, that she was originally very happy for the Society for the Assistance of Beleaguered Budgerigars to benefit from her residuary estate when it was likely to be in the region of £250. She is not likely to be anxious to endow the Society with her entire estate worth £50,000.

Note that divorce and nullity have no effect on the right of survivorship. Thus any property which, at the time of her death, the deceased still holds as a joint tenant with her former spouse will pass automatically to her former spouse by survivorship despite the termination of the marriage. This underlines the necessity to consider serving a notice of severance where a joint tenancy exists or may exist (see Chapter 22 paragraph 2.2.2).

Note also that a decree of judicial separation has no effect on a will.

3.2 The effect of divorce or nullity on intestacy

Where a marriage is void or has been annulled or dissolved by decree absolute of nullity or divorce, on the death intestate of either party to the marriage, the other party will have no right to any part of the estate under the intestacy provisions. This is because he or she no longer qualifies as a surviving spouse. However, the former spouse (who has not married someone else) may be able to make a claim for family provision against the estate pursuant to the Inheritance (Provision for Family and Dependants) Act 1975, s. 1(1)(b).

3.3 The effect of judicial separation on intestacy

Whilst a decree of judicial separation is in force and the separation is continuing, if either party dies intestate his or her real and personal estate will devolve as if the other party had been dead (s. 18(2), Matrimonial Causes Act 1973).

4   STEPS TO BE TAKEN

In the light of the client's instructions, either or both of the following steps may be necessary;

    (a)   service of notice of severance of joint tenancy (see Chapter 22 paragraph 2.2.2);

    (b)   drafting of will/new will.

If the will/new will is drafted before a decree of divorce or nullity is granted and contains a provision benefiting the client's spouse or appointing him executor or executor and trustee, the solicitor should take care to make it clear in the will (if it be the case) that the provisions are intended to be effective even after divorce/nullity. If this is not done, s. 18A, Wills Act 1837 will obviously nullify the provisions relating to the spouse.

5   INHERITANCE (PROVISION FOR FAMILY AND DEPENDANTS) ACT 1975

If the client's instructions are to take steps to deprive her spouse/cohabitee of substantial benefit from her estate, she should be warned that, whatever steps are taken, her spouse/cohabitee may ultimately be able to secure a share in her estate by means of an application under the Inheritance (Provision for Family and Dependants) Act 1975.

    Applications under the Act are made on the ground that the disposition of the deceased's estate effected by her will or by the intestacy rules (or by a combination of both) is not such as to make reasonable financial provision for the applicant. In some cases, the client may be well advised, despite her feelings, to make some limited provision for her spouse herself in her will in an attempt to rule out the possibility of him subsequently applying to the court under the Act for provision. At least this way she may be able to dictate her own terms rather than leaving the matter at large for the court to sort out after her death.

    Note that a former spouse may still apply under the 1975 Act, provided that he or she has not remarried. However, it is possible to preclude such an application during the course of ancillary relief proceedings (see Chapter 16, paragraph 4).

6   IMPORTANCE OF CONSIDERING SUCCESSION

The importance of considering succession can be illustrated by an example.

Example. Mr and Mrs Heap are joint tenants of the matrimonial home 'Inglefield'. Mr Heap makes a will leaving £50,000 to his wife and the residue of his estate (which he anticipates will be small) to his old school. Mrs Heap does not make a will. There are no children.

    The marriage runs into difficulties. Mrs Heap petitions for divorce but no decree has yet been pronounced. If Mr Heap died today, his share in Inglefield would pass to Mrs Heap by survivorship. The balance of his estate excluding Inglefield would be worth £25,000 and this would pass to Mrs Heap by his will.

If Mrs Heap died today, her share in Inglefield would pass to Mr Heap by survivorship and the rest of her estate (worth £10,000) would pass to him under the intestacy provisions.

If nothing is done to alter the present position, decree absolute of divorce will automatically produce the following results:

(a)   On Mr Heap predeceasing Mrs Heap:

(i)   his share in Inglefield will still pass to Mrs Heap by survivorship;
(ii)   the gift to Mrs Heap in the will will lapse and the balance of his estate (£25,000) will therefore pass to his old school.

(b)   On Mrs Heap predeceasing Mr Heap:

(i)   her share in Inglefield will still pass to Mr Heap by survivorship;
(ii)   the balance of her estate (£10,000) would still pass under the intestacy provisions but *not* to Mr Heap who would no longer qualify as a spouse. If she has a surviving parent or parents, they would be the ones to benefit. If not, other relatives would inherit her estate.

Neither Mr nor Mrs Heap wishes the other to benefit by his/her death before or after the divorce. Mr Heap wishes to leave a slightly larger sum to his old school and the balance of his estate to his girlfriend, Miss Maybury. Mrs Heap wishes to leave her estate to her sister. The following steps should be taken by their solicitors:

(a)   The joint tenancy in relation to Inglefield should be severed with the effect that, on the death of either party, his or her interest in the property will pass with his or her estate.
(b)   A new will should be made for Mr Heap.
(c)   A will should be made for Mrs Heap.

When the new wills are being drafted, each party's solicitor should consider with him or her whether a will leaving nothing to his or her spouse would be reasonable or whether it would be a good idea to make some limited provision for the spouse in an attempt to rule out the possibility of future litigation under the Inheritance (Provision for Family and Dependants) Act 1975. This consideration is likely to be more important for Mr Heap, who has a considerably larger estate than Mrs Heap.

If either party does decide to leave money or property to his or her spouse and the will is to become effective before decree absolute, care should be taken to express in the will the intention that the provision concerning the spouse will continue after the decree is granted.

7   APPOINTING A GUARDIAN FOR CHILDREN

The solicitor should consider with the client whether it is appropriate to make provision in the will for the appointment of a guardian for her minor children. Section 5, Children Act 1989 enables parents and guardians to appoint guardians to take their place after their death. Such an appointment will not take effect until there is no surviving parent with parental responsibility, or unless the child was living with the appointor by virtue of a residence order at the time of his or her death. Such appointments will be valid if made in writing and signed. This is a departure from the old rules whereby such appointments were only valid if made by deed or will. For further discussion about guardianship see Chapter 25, paragraph 4.

PART VII
CHILDREN

25 The Children Act 1989 – General principles and procedures

1 INTRODUCTION

1.1 The Children Act 1989 - an overview

The Children Act 1989 came into force on 14 October 1991 and brought with it sweeping changes in the law relating to children. It repealed eight statutes in their entirety:

(a)   the Nurseries and Childminders Regulation Act 1948;
(b)   the Guardianship of Minors Act 1971;
(c)   the Guardianship Act 1973;
(d)   the Children Act 1975;
(e)   the Child Care Act 1980;
(f)   the Foster Children Act 1980;
(g)   the Children's Homes Act 1982;
(h)   the Children and Young Persons (Amendment) Act 1986.

The Children Act 1989 also limits other statutes (most notably the Children and Young Persons Act 1969) to purely criminal provisions.

For the first time the public law (e.g. care orders, supervision orders, emergency protection orders) and the private law (e.g. residence orders, contact orders, prohibited steps orders, specific issue orders) relating to children are contained in the same statute. The law is streamlined and simplified.

The Act provides a clear and consistent code for the whole of child law and avoids the problems caused by conflicting powers in public and private law. It also aims to protect families from unwarranted State interference and to promote the basic principle that parents and local authorities should be free to work together in 'voluntary partnership' for the benefit of the children concerned. It is no longer possible for a court to commit a child to care without a formal application by the local authority or the NSPCC.

The Act is divided into 12 parts:

Part I reasserts the basic principle, which applies across both private and public law, that the child's welfare is paramount. It introduces the concept of 'parental responsibility' to replace the old 'parental rights and duties'. It delineates the circumstances in which parental responsibility is acquired and lost. It also restructures the law of guardianship.

Part II deals primarily with the private law of children and creates an entirely new system of court orders which will mainly apply to disputes between parents. Custody and access orders are replaced by orders for 'residence' and 'contact'. 'Specific issue' and 'prohibited steps' orders are new orders created as an alternative to the use of wardship. 'Family assistance orders' replace supervision orders in family proceedings. The provisions governing financial relief for children, formerly found in several statutes, are consolidated, with minor amendments, in schedule 1.

Parts III to IV form the nub of the provisions governing the public law affecting children. Part III redefines the general powers and duties of local authorities in relation to children. Part IV deals principally with care proceedings, which will no longer be conducted exclusively in the magistrates' court. The grounds for making a care order are simplified, streamlined and extended. There are no longer any alternative routes by which a local authority may acquire the care of a child: criminal courts and the High Court in wardship are no longer free to make care orders. Local authorities are under a duty to endeavour to promote contact between children looked after by them and a wide range of family members and friends (sch. 2, para. 15). Care orders will automatically contain provisions allowing the child reasonable contact with parents, guardians etc. Part IV also states the principles applicable to supervision orders and creates new 'education supervision orders' to deal with poor school attenders.

Part V radically reforms the system dealing with the emergency protection of children. Place of safety orders are replaced by 'emergency protection orders'. These last for eight days, can be extended for seven days, and are subject to review after 72 hours. Where an emergency protection order appears too Draconian, but the court considers that enquiries into the welfare of the child are necessary, the 'half way house' of 'child assessment orders' is now available.

Parts VI to X deal with the regimes for children in community homes, voluntary homes, registered children's homes, private fostering, child minding and day care for young children.

Parts XI and XII detail the supervisory functions of the Secretary of State, and enact various 'miscellaneous and general' provisions. Of particular importance are the 'restrictions on the use of the wardship jurisdiction by local authorities (s. 100): in future local authorities will need leave to make an application.

The *Schedules* to the Act contain important provisions. The *transitional provisions* set out in *sch. 14* mean that existing private law orders will continue to have effect subject to modification and non-custodial parents will have parental responsibility: certain existing public law orders or resolutions will be deemed to be care orders. There are also extensive reforms of the law of adoption and a new legal regime for child minders and providers of 'day care' for children.

The foundations of a new structure for dealing with cases under this Act and the Adoption Act 1976 are put in place. The 'domestic court' is renamed the 'family proceedings court' and will be able to handle most cases. Care cases will usually start in that court but rules of court give power to transfer cases to specified county courts or the High Court. Appeals in care cases will be heard in the High Court (s. 94).

1.2 The rules made under the Children Act 1989

Many of the procedural rules and relevant forms for making applications under the Children Act 1989 will be found:

(a) for the High Court and county court — in the Family Proceedings Rules 1991;

(b) for the magistrates' court — in the Family Proceedings (Children Act 1989) Rules 1991.

In order to avoid confusion any reference to the rules will be to the Family Proceedings Rules 1991 unless specifically stated to be otherwise. However, the practitioner will find the substance and layout of the two sets of rules to be largely the same, save for necessary adjustments to take account of the procedural differences between the magistrates' court and the other courts. The main substance of the rules is discussed at paragraphs 5 and 6 below.

1.3 The transitional provisions

This book contains only the new law relating to children. However, the practitioner will also need to be familiar with the old law in order to deal with those cases which span the transition between the old and the new law. The transitional provisions will be found mainly in s. 91 and sch. 14 of the Children Act 1989; they inform the practitioner about the steps to be taken in respect of proceedings under the old law which were already pending on 14 October 1991 ('pending proceedings'). However, there will be future legislation which amends and adds to the transitional provisions as and when it becomes necessary. Further provisions, for example, will be found in the Courts and Legal Services Act 1990, sch. 16, and in the schedule to the Children Act 1989 (Commencement and Transitional Provisions) Order 1991.

2 GENERAL PRINCIPLES

There are certain general principles contained in the Children Act 1989 which apply both to private law and public law proceedings alike. Those principles will be set out in this chapter. Chapters 26 and 27 will deal in detail with private law and public law proceedings respectively.

2.1 The paramountcy of welfare

Section 1(1), Children Act 1989 states that 'when a court determines any question with respect to:

(a) the upbringing of a child; or

(b) the administration of a child's property or the application of any income arising from it,

the child's welfare shall be the court's paramount consideration'.

In practical terms the 'welfare principle' will have the same effect as the equivalent provision in the old Guardianship of Minors Act 1971.

The welfare principle will not apply to the determination of other questions which are outside the ambit of s. 1(1) even though they indirectly affect the child e.g. whether the court should make an ouster injunction pursuant to the Matrimonial Homes Act 1983, s. 1(3): see *Richards* v *Richards* [1984] AC 174; or whether blood tests should be taken in an attempt to ascertain paternity (*S* v *McC* [1972] AC 24). The principle will not apply in adoption proceedings where different statutory criteria prevail (Adoption Act 1976, s. 6). Furthermore, maintenance is excluded from the definition of 'upbringing' in the Act (see s. 105(1)) and orders relating to maintenance after divorce are not subject to the welfare test in s. 1(1) but to the requirement in s. 25(1) of the Matrimonial Causes Act 1973 to give 'first consideration' to the welfare of the child.

'*Child*' is defined as anyone under the age of 18 (Children Act 1989, s. 105), but the court's power to make 'section 8 orders' is restricted to children under 16 unless the case is exceptional (Children Act 1989, s. 9(7)). Likewise, the court may not make a care or supervision order in respect of a child who has reached the age of seventeen (or sixteen if the child is married): Children Act 1989, s. 31(3).

'*Paramount*' does not mean 'first and paramount' as it was expressed in the Guardianship of Minors Act 1971. In the past the old wording led some courts to balance other considerations against the child's welfare rather than to consider what light they shed upon it. The new wording means that 'the welfare of the child should come before and above any other consideration in deciding whether to make an order' (Hansard, HL, vol 502, col. 1167). There is no provision which indicates how the court should approach cases involving more than one child where the welfare of each conflicts.

'*Welfare*' is not defined by the Children Act 1989. However, the checklist set out in s. 1(3) indicates some of the issues which might be relevant.

2.2 The statutory checklist

Section 1(3), Children Act 1989 requires the court to have regard to a 'statutory checklist' of factors whenever it is considering the following matters:

(a) whether to make, vary or discharge a section 8 order, and the making, variation or discharge of the order is opposed by any party to the proceedings (s. 1(4)(a)); or

(b) whether to make, vary or discharge an order under Part IV of the Children Act 1989, i.e. a care or supervision order (s. 1(4)(b)). (N.B. the use of the list is not mandatory where the court is considering an emergency protection order.)

There would be nothing to prevent a court from referring to the statutory checklist for guidance in any other type of case. Its use is only *mandatory* for the categories of proceedings in (a) and (b) above.

The checklist consists of the following factors, which are not listed by the statute in any order of importance:

(a) the ascertainable wishes and feelings of the child concerned (in the light of his age and understanding);

(b) his physical, emotional and educational needs;

(c) the likely effect on him of any change in his circumstances;

(d)   his age, sex, background and any characteristics of his which the court considers relevant;

(e)   any harm which he has suffered or is at risk of suffering;

(f)   how capable each of his parents, and any other person in relation to whom the court considers the question to be relevant, is of meeting his needs;

(g)   the range of powers available to the court under the Children Act 1989 in the proceedings in question.

The list aims to guide the court and to achieve consistency across the country as well as informing legal advisers and helping parties to concentrate on the issues that affect their children.

In reaching decisions in respect of applications for orders under the Children Act 1989 it is highly likely that the court will still take into account case law decided under the old legislation, provided that the principles thereby decided are still relevant to the factors which the court is now required to consider.

2.2.1   The wishes and feelings of the child (s. 1(3)(a))

Where a child expresses a wish to reside with a particular parent or to have contact with a parent then the court must give due weight to that factor. The court will consider the age and maturity of the child when deciding how much weight to attach to such wishes. The court will be aware that the child is likely to be influenced, consciously or not, by the views of the parent with whom he resides. He may be afraid to voice (or even to form) his own opinion for fear of hurting one or the other parent. Even if he obviously does have strong wishes of his own, they may not be in his own interests.

The child's wishes may become known to the court in a variety of ways (for example, by the parents giving evidence of what he has said to them). The best evidence of a child's wishes is through the welfare report and from the judge's personal assessment of the child if he meets him. The court welfare officer will normally mention in his report anything that the child has said to him about his wishes; with older children, he may actually ask the child what he feels about the case. The judge can see the child in private during the hearing if he thinks it desirable. Whether he will do so will depend on his own practice and, in particular, on the age of the child. It is highly unlikely that the judge will see a child of less than eight. The older a child is the more likely it is that the judge will see him and the more likely it is that his wishes will be given some weight.

Neither the Children Act 1989 nor the rules made thereunder make any provision for magistrates to interview children. Under the old law the rule was that magistrates should not interview children in private (*Re T (a minor)* (1974) 4 Fam Law 48).

2.2.2   The child's physical, emotional and educational needs (s. 1(3)(b))

The fact that one parent has greater material prosperity or offers more pleasant surroundings than the other carries very little weight in a dispute as to where a child is to live. In any event, the courts are often able to go some way towards equalising the differences between parents in this respect by making a maintenance order or, where there is a decree of divorce, nullity or judicial separation, by means of ancillary relief orders.

If, however, there is evidence that the accommodation offered by a parent is undesirable in some way, this will have a bearing on the decision as to where the child lives. The court needs to know if the accommodation is cramped, dirty, in a bad area, etc. This information will be provided by the welfare report although both parents are also likely to have some comments to make on the question when giving evidence. Naturally, the court will be reluctant to entrust the care of a child to a parent who is presently in unsatisfactory accommodation and has no definite plans about obtaining something better.

Another factor that will be taken into account is whether a move is proposed in the foreseeable future. Even if the accommodation presently offered is acceptable and there is no doubt that the parent will replace it with something of equal standard, the court may hesitate before transferring the care of the children to that parent if he is shortly to move areas and the children will therefore have the upheaval of changing schools, making new friends, etc. all over again. Where a move is likely in the foreseeable future, the parent concerned should do his best to provide the court with information about his proposals and should make sure that he investigates the sort of property he could afford in the new area, the schools available, etc. If he is awaiting council accommodation, he should be in a position to tell the court how he is placed on the waiting list (preferably by providing a letter from the council).

What is likely to be more important than accommodation is the standard of day-to-day care the parents offer. It is rare that one finds a parent against whom no criticism can be levelled. The court will not therefore go into all the minor grumbles that one parent has about the other's care of the children (for example, they do not go to bed until 8 o'clock and they should be in bed at 7, or they are allowed to get down from the meal-table before everyone has finished). However, if there is evidence, for example, that the children are often dirty, or hungry, or unsupervised or that the parent does not or cannot exercise discipline, this will be relevant to the issue as to where the child is to live.

Another factor which the court will consider is the need of a child for regular medical treatment. It may be that one of the parents lives in an area where the provision of treatment is significantly better. In those circumstances the 'physical needs' of the child might be a deciding factor in determining where the child is to live. Where the child has special needs (for example, because of a physical or mental handicap), the court will take this into account and will look to see who is best equipped to deal with the child in terms of accommodation, experience, patience, motivation and so forth.

In considering the child's emotional needs the court will place weight upon the closeness of the child's ties with one or other of his parents, or with his brothers and sisters, and the trauma consequent upon a breaking of those ties. The court is reluctant to split brothers and sisters (*C* v *C (Minors: Custody* [1988] 2 FLR 291). However, there are, very occasionally, special cases where such an order is justified.

Example. Gemma is 7 and her brother, Adam, is 15. The children have never been close in view of the difference in their ages and they have grown further apart since Adam went away to school two years ago. Adam has expressed the view that he wants to live with his father and Gemma has told the court welfare officer that she wants to live with her mother. The court feels that the circumstances justify making a residence order in respect of Gemma in favour of her mother and a residence order in respect of Adam in favour of his father, particularly since both parents envisage that there should be generous contact arrangements.

There is no general rule that a mother should have the children living with her (see *Re A (a minor) (custody)* [1991] 2 FLR 394 and *Re S (a minor) (custody)* [1991] 2 FLR 388). However, in practice, a mother does have a better chance than a father of obtaining a residence order, particularly in respect of young children and babies (see, for example, *A v A (custody appeal: role of appellate court)* [1988] 1 FLR 193).

Where one parent (usually the father) is working and the other is not, the parent who can be at home full-time for the children has a considerable advantage. This is especially the case where the children are below school age. As they get older and spend time at school and with their own friends, the question of work becomes less decisive providing the arrangements proposed by the working parent for after school, school holidays and illnesses are satisfactory.

Sometimes the father proposes to give up work or to remain unemployed in order to look after the children. The fact that he will be voluntarily unemployed and relying on the state for income is a factor to be taken into consideration in a dispute as to where the child should live. However, it is not sufficient on its own to justify the court in refusing to grant him a residence order (*B v B (custody)* [1985] Fam Law 29).

In the past there have been few cases where the *educational* needs of the child have proved decisive. In its widest sense 'educational needs' could cover almost anything to do with the upbringing of the child. However, education in the sense of 'schooling' may still be a significant factor, particularly if one parent is moving away from the area at a time which is especially important (for example, when the child is just about to take his GCSE). In those circumstances the parent who will continue to live in proximity to the child's current school may well be at an advantage in any dispute over residence. The younger the child is the less weight is likely to be attached to a temporary disruption of his schooling whilst he moves from his old home to the new one. If the child needs a special school for some reason then this will be an important factor, whatever the age of the child.

2.2.3　The likely effect on the child of a change in circumstances (s. 1(3)(c))

The court is always very reluctant to remove a child from his present home unless there is a strong reason to do so. It follows that the parent who is looking after the child at the time of a dispute as to where the child is to live starts with a considerable advantage over anyone else. The longer that situation continues, the greater the advantage will become. This is commonly referred to as the 'status quo' argument. For example, faced with two parents of equal merit, one of whom has been caring for the child for a considerable time already, the court will almost inevitably grant a residence order to that parent.

2.2.4　The child's age, sex, background and any relevant characteristics (s. 1(3)(d))

The *age* of a child will often be an important factor in deciding what is in his best interests. For example, a young baby's needs will usually be best satisfied by living with his mother, whereas a 15 year-old will generally be considered sufficiently mature to make up his own mind as to where he would like to live. The age and maturity of the child will be important when the court decides what weight to attach to the child's wishes, as already discussed in paragraph 2.2.1 above.

The *sex* of the child is another factor to be placed in the balance. For example, importance is often attached to the need of a teenage girl for the assistance of her mother whilst negotiating the years of puberty.

The child's *background* can cover a multitude of different factors, for example, his religious upbringing, his family environment and so forth.

Likewise, the child's relevant characteristics could cover a broad spectrum of matters, for example, a disability or a severe illness. It could also cover religious, sporting or intellectual factors.

Where the child's parents have a different culture, the court may be asked to take into account the attitudes and habits prevalent in that culture in deciding with whom the child is to live.

Example. Mother and father are both Muslims. There are two children, a boy aged 12 and a girl aged 3. The mother seeks a residence order in respect of both children and the father of the boy only. There is evidence on behalf of the mother that in the parties' Muslim community a mother is ostracised if she does not obtain the care of all her children. The court feels that the mother must have a residence order in respect of the little girl. Although, in the particular circumstances of the case, the judge is prepared to contemplate splitting the children, he takes into account that both children will be affected if their mother is ostracised and decides that custody of both children should be awarded to her.

Where a child is of mixed race, the court will take into account the differences between the parent's cultures and look to see how the child has been brought up so far. If he has been brought up, for example, in the mother's English way of life, the court will be reluctant to grant a residence order to the father who is now living the Indian way of life in an Indian community. However, the court will be inclined to require generous contact in such cases in order that the child should be able to maintain his links with the cultures of both parents.

Disputes over the care of children do not often centre around the child's religious upbringing these days. However, from time to time a parent is particularly concerned about the child's religious welfare and argues that it is necessary for him to have a residence order in order that he can be responsible for the child's proper religious education. Whilst the court will take into account the parent's views, it is unlikely that consideration of religion will determine the outcome of the case.

Example. Mr Harris is a Catholic and his wife is an Anglican. They have two children who have been brought up in the Catholic faith. They are now three and five. The parties separate and the children live with Mrs Harris. Mr Harris does not question the fact that they are very happy with her and she cares for them satisfactorily. However, he is concerned that Mrs Harris and the children do not attend the Catholic church. On the few occasions when Mrs Harris has been to church since the separation, she and the children have attended the local Church of England. She envisages that the children should attend Sunday School there and, in due course be confirmed into the Church of England. Mr Harris seeks a residence order in order that he can bring up the children as Catholics. The court refuses his application. However, Mr Harris could ask the court to give directions as to the religious education of the children and, if the court orders that the children should receive Catholic religious instruction, Mrs Harris would have to comply with this.

If the child is old enough (see paragraph 2.2.1), the court can consider his wishes as to religion.

The court can use contact arrangements to ensure that the child benefits from the religions of both parents. For example, if the court grants a residence order to a parent who is a Jehovah's Witness and refuses to celebrate Christmas, it can order that the other parent (a Methodist) have contact over the Christmas period so that the child can enjoy some of the Christmas festivities and services with him.

2.2.5   Any harm which the child has suffered or is at risk of suffering (s. 1(3)(e))
The word 'harm' is a deliberately wide-ranging term. It covers both physical injury and psychological trauma.

2.2.6   How capable are the parents and any other relevant person of meeting the child's needs (s. 1(3)(f))
The court will have to assess the capability for child care of the persons who apply to look after children. If the dispute is between two parents who are equally committed and able to care for the child then the deciding factor may be that one works full-time whereas the other is available all day.

It goes without saying that if a parent has ill-treated the child in the past, this will be a very important factor in the dispute as to with whom the child should live. His claim will also be prejudiced if he has ill-treated another child.

Other matters that may be taken into account include:

(a)   The sexual proclivities of a parent – the court will take into account the fact that the mother is a lesbian or the father a homosexual if this is likely to affect the children (for example, because the mother openly lives with another woman and the children may suffer embarrassment or ostracism at school and in their neighbourhood because of this).

(b)   The criminal record/criminal conduct of a parent – to what extent criminal conduct will affect the outcome of a dispute over the care of a child depends very much on the particular circumstances of the case. If both parents have been regularly involved in crime, it is unlikely that the application of either will be affected by this factor (although it must be remembered that the court does have power to commit the child to local authority care if it feels that it is undesirable for him to be in the care of either parent or any other individual). On the other hand, if one parent is a law-abiding citizen and the other has a criminal record or is known to commit criminal offences, this will prejudice that parent's application for the care of the child. The court will be particularly reluctant to place the child in an environment where he will be subjected to bad influences in his day-to-day life (for example, where there is evidence that a parent takes drugs, regularly commits offences of dishonesty, etc.). Furthermore, the court will have to take account of the fact that a parent who commits criminal offences jeopardises the stability of the home he offers in that he is at risk of being imprisoned, in which case other arrangements would have to be made for the care of his child.

(c)   Mental and physical illness – the mental illness of a parent is relevant to a dispute over the care of a child. However, whether it will have any bearing on the outcome of the case depends on the nature of the mental illness. If there is evidence that the illness causes the parent concerned to behave in a way that may be harmful to the children's physical or mental state, or if the parent is likely to need regular in-patient treatment in hospital for the condition, obviously this will be an important consideration. If the question of mental illness is raised and the parent concerned feels that he or she is, in fact, perfectly well or has been treated successfully, it would be advisable to obtain medical evidence to this effect. Physical illness will only have a bearing on the case if it prevents the parent from looking after the children properly, for example because he or she is bed-ridden or handicapped or has to return for prolonged stays in hospital.

(d)   Religious views – the religious views of a parent are rarely of much importance in a case relating to the care of children. However, the court is likely to be reluctant to grant the care of a child to a parent who belongs to an extreme religious sect if there is evidence that the influence of this sect may be harmful to the child. It is worth bearing in mind that the court has wide powers to attach conditions to section 8 orders and it may be possible in this way to ensure that the child is not exposed to harmful aspects of the parent's faith. For example, when granting a residence order to a parent who belongs to a sect that is against blood transfusions, the court may be able to impose a condition that the child should be allowed to have a transfusion if it becomes necessary for his health or life.

The court is also enjoined to consider the capability 'of any other person in relation to whom the court considers the question to be relevant'. This would include, for example, the new partner of one of the spouses, the child's grandparents or other members of the child's family, child minders, nannies and nurseries.

Not infrequently the child will be in regular contact with someone other than the parent with care of the child. For example, either parent may be sharing accommodation with relatives for the foreseeable future, or may propose that the child is cared for by a nanny or by a relative whilst he is out at work, or may have formed a relationship with a new partner or intend to remarry. In these circumstances it is most important that the court should be informed about anyone else who will be in regular contact with the child and should hear oral evidence from anyone who will be closely involved with the care of the child as their personality, character and so on will have a bearing on the outcome of the case.

Example 1. Both parents work. The mother proposes that the child should be cared for whilst she is at work by her nanny who has been looking after her for six months. The father proposes that his mother should look after the child whilst he is at work. The court will need to hear oral evidence from both the nanny and the grandmother.

Example 2. After the parties separate, the mother returns to live with her own father and mother. She is available full-time to look after the child. However, she does not dispute that of her three brothers who also live in the family home, two are regularly in trouble with the police and one is a glue-sniffer. The father lives with his sister who has two young children and proposes that, whilst he is at work, his sister will look after the

302 The Children Act 1989 – General principles and procedures

children. The court hears from the mother and her own father and from the father and his sister. A residence order is awarded to the father in view of the undesirable family circumstances of the mother.

2.2.7 The range of powers available to the court (s. 1(3)(g))

It is of particular importance for the practitioner to note the factor in s. 1(3)(g) which requires the court to have regard to the range of powers available to it in the relevant proceedings. Thus the court is able to choose the appropriate order for a case, even where nobody has made an application for that particular order. It allows the court to direct matters to a greater extent than it was able to do under the old law. For example, the court can grant *anyone* a section 8 order, even without a formal application having been made to the court (s. 10(1)(b), Children Act 1989); this might happen, for example, where it becomes clear in the course of a hearing that a grandparent, rather than either of the parents, would be the most appropriate person to care for the child whose residence is in dispute. Another example might arise where a parent makes an application for a residence order but during the course of the hearing the court considers that a care or supervision order may be appropriate. In that situation the court has power to adjourn the case and to direct the local authority to investigate the circumstances of the child with a view to deciding whether it would be appropriate for them to apply for an order (s. 37(1), Children Act 1989).

The court also has power to prevent further applications being made to the court for any type of order under the Children Act 1989, for example, for parental responsibility (s. 4), guardianship (s. 5) and section 8 orders without leave (s. 91(14)).

2.3 Presumption of no order

Section 1(5), Children Act 1989 provides that 'where a court is considering whether or not to make one or more orders under this Act with respect to a child, it shall not make the order or any of the orders unless it considers that doing so would be better for the child than making no order at all'.

The importance of this principle to the practitioner cannot be too greatly stressed. Increasingly, the courts are showing a tendency, where parties meet at court and reach a compromise in what was until then a dispute about their children, to make no order at all. If the court takes the view that the parties are now agreed as to what should happen then it may well decide that it would be better for the child for those agreed arrangements to prevail between the parties rather than embodying them in a court order. Such a solution may well prevent a parent from feeling bitter that he has had arrangements imposed upon him by the court (albeit in a consent order). The less bitter the parents feel about the arrangements made for the children the easier it is likely to be for them to cooperate with each other in future, with the consequence that the children will suffer less upset as a result. It is a principle running throughout the Children Act 1989 that wherever possible the courts should not interfere with the arrangements made by parents in respect of their children unless it is necessary in the interests of the children to do so.

Of course, it may happen that the agreed arrangements break down in any event with the result that the case has to return to court and an order has to be made. However, at least the parties will have had every possible opportunity to achieve a solution without the interference of the court.

2.4 The delay principle

Section 1(2), Children Act 1989 requires the court 'in any proceedings in which any question with respect to the upbringing of the child arises' to have regard 'to the general principle that any delay in determining the question is likely to prejudice the welfare of the child'.

Once again, this provision is of great importance. The practitioner must be very aware of the court's desire to hear applications in respect of children as soon as possible. In order to put the provision into proper effect s. 11 (in relation to section 8 orders) and s. 32 (in relation to care and supervision orders) of the Children Act 1989 require the court to draw up a timetable for the progress of the case with a view to eliminating undue delay in the proceedings.

The practical procedure for arranging the timing of proceedings is contained in the Family Proceedings Rules 1991, r. 4.15 (High Court and county court) and in the Family Proceedings Courts (Children Act 1989) Rules 1991, r. 15 (magistrates' court). Experience already shows that the courts expect the timetable to be adhered to and will take steps to enforce adherence to it. This may sometimes mean, for example, that the court will proceed to hear a case without a welfare report if it decides that the advantage to the child of a speedy hearing outweighs the disadvantage to him of proceeding without a welfare report.

3 PARENTAL RESPONSIBILITY

Parental responsibility is a new concept introduced by the Children Act 1989. The Children Act 1975 referred to 'parental rights and duties' and phrases used in other statutes referred to 'powers and duties' or 'rights and authority' in respect of children. The new wording is an attempt to give statutory recognition to the change in emphasis from rights *over* children to responsibility *for* children.

The concept of parental responsibility is defined in s. 3(1), Children Act 1989 as 'all the rights, duties, powers, responsibilities and authority which by law a parent of a child has in relation to the child and his property'. However, no further definition is attempted since the Law Commission took the view that the list would be changing constantly 'to meet differing needs and circumstances' (Law Com. No. 172, 2.6).

A person with parental responsibility may not surrender or transfer any part of that responsibility (Children Act 1989, s. 2(9)). However, he may arrange for some part, or all, of that responsibility to be met by one or more other persons e.g. schools, local authorities, churches etc. The exercise of parental responsibility will often be qualified in some way by agreement between the parents or by order of the court. For example, the father of a child may agree that the child should live with the mother, in which case the mother has a greater degree of day to day 'parental responsibility' than does the father. He agrees to his parental responsibility being curtailed so that his ability to exercise it is subject to his agreement with the mother (or, in default of agreement, subject to the order of the court).

3.1 Who has parental responsibility?

Under the Children Act 1989 there is a wide variety of people who may acquire parental responsibility for a child in different ways. The following are just some examples:

(a) guardians will acquire parental responsibility for children, so that they are equated with natural parents (s. 5(6));

(b) local authorities may acquire parental responsibility, for example, on the making of a care order (s. 33(3));

(c) a person who has been granted an emergency protection order will acquire parental responsibility for the duration of the order (s. 44(4));

(d) a person who has been granted a residence order will automatically have parental responsibility for the duration of the order (s. 12(1) and (2));

(e) 'unmarried fathers' (i.e. fathers who were not married to the mother at the time of the child's birth) may acquire parental responsibility by agreement with the mother or by order of the court (s. 4), or by obtaining a residence order (s. 12(1));

(f) when a child becomes a ward of court then the court itself will acquire parental responsibility.

There is no limit on the number of people who can have parental responsibility for a child at any one time, and a person does not lose parental responsibility merely because someone else acquires it. Although on the making of a care order a local authority obtains parental responsibility for a child the parents will not lose it and it will be 'shared'.

3.1.1 Meaning of 'father' and 'mother'

It is to be assumed that references in the Children Act 1989 to 'father' and 'mother' are intended to denote the natural parents of the child. Unmarried fathers are now included within the definition of 'father'. The problem of who is the real mother of a child born as a result of *in vitro* fertilization is resolved by s. 27(1), Human Fertilization and Embryology Act 1990 which states that 'the woman who is carrying or has carried a child as a result of the placing in her of an embryo or of sperm and eggs, and no other woman is to be treated as the mother of the child'. Where a child is born to a married woman as a result of her having been artificially inseminated with the sperm of a man other than her husband, then the latter rather than anyone else is to be treated as the father of the child unless it is shown that he did not consent to his wife's insemination. The same rule applies where the birth of the child is the result of the placement of embryo or sperm and eggs in the married woman and the sperm donor is not the husband (s. 28, Human Fertilization and Embryology Act 1990).

3.1.2 Automatic parental responsibility

Parental responsibility is conferred automatically on the mother of a child irrespective of her marital status. Whether the father also has parental responsibility depends on whether he was married to the mother at the time of the child's birth (s. 2(1)). If he was so married then he will also have automatic parental responsibility. Even if the father was not lawfully married to the mother at the time of the birth he may still be treated as so married in particular circumstances (s. 2(3), importing the Family Law Reform Act 1987, s. 1), e.g. if the child is subsequently legitimated. It would appear that the only way in which a parent can be divested of 'automatic' parental responsibility is upon the child being adopted.

3.1.3 Unmarried fathers

If the father was not married to the mother at the time of the child's birth and does not come within the extensions to this concept then *prima facie* he will not have parental responsibility for the child. However, he may acquire parental responsibility in one of several ways:

(a)   by applying for and obtaining a residence order, using Form CHA 10 to make the application (s. 12(1)), in which case parental responsibility will last for as long as the residence order is in existence (s. 12(2));

(b)   by applying to the court for a parental responsibility order, using Form CHA 1 to make the application (s. 4(1)(a)), in which case the order will last until discharged by the court (s. 4(3));

(c)   by making a 'parental responsibility agreement' with the mother in the 'prescribed form' (s. 4(1)(b)), which will last until discharged by the court (s. 4(3)). The form which such an agreement must take is prescribed by the Parental Responsibility Agreement Regulations 1991;

(d)   by being appointed the child's guardian by the court, using Form CHA 3 to make the application (s. 5(1));

(e)   by being appointed the child's guardian by the mother or by another guardian (s. 5).

When considering an application by an unmarried father under s. 4, Children Act 1989 the court will have to consider whether it is in the child's best interests for the father to have parental responsibility. The meaning of 'welfare' in this context is not defined. It will be necessary to satisfy the court (on the balance of probabilities) that the applicant is the father of the child before an order granting him parental responsibility can be made.

The unmarried father who does not seek parental responsibility will still remain liable to maintain his child (Children Act 1989, s. 3(4)).

3.1.3.1 Termination of parental responsibility agreements and orders   A

parental responsibility order or agreement will automatically end upon the child attaining the age of 18 (Children Act 1989, s. 91(7) and (8)). The order or agreement could be discharged by the court before the child attains 18 if the court is satisfied on the 'welfare' test contained in s. 1(1) of the Children Act 1989 that it would be better for the child if the court were to discharge it rather than refuse to do so (s. 4(3)). Any person with parental responsibility may apply to discharge the order or agreement, as indeed may the child himself if he is of sufficient age and understanding (Children Act 1989, s. 4(3)(b) and (4)). However, parental responsibility cannot be removed from a father in whose favour a residence order exists (Children Act 1989, s. 12(4)). Indeed, where a residence order has been made in favour of a person who is not a parent or guardian of the child, that person must also continue to have parental responsibility whilst the residence order remains in force (Children Act 1989, s. 12(2)).

3.1.4 Step-parents

Step-parents may acquire parental responsibility in the same way as any other person who is not a natural parent of the child, that is to say:

(a) by the making of a residence order in his favour, parental responsibility being retained for as long as the order remains in force (s. 12(2)). However, the rights enjoyed by natural parents in relation to adoption and guardianship will not apply to him (s. 12(3));

(b) by the making of an adoption order in his favour.

A step-parent will be responsible for the maintenance of a child in so far as the step-parent is a party to the marriage (whether or not subsisting) in relation to which the child concerned is a child of the family (sch. 1, para. 16, Children Act 1989). (For a definition of 'child of the family' see s. 105(1), Children Act 1989.) This will be the case irrespective of whether the step-parent has 'parental responsibility' or not (s. 3(4)(a)).

A step-parent who has care of a child may do what is reasonable in all the circumstances of the case for the purpose of safeguarding or promoting the child's welfare (s. 3(5)).

3.1.5 Person with de facto care of child

Where a person has *de facto* care of a child but no parental responsibility for him then that person may do whatever is reasonable to safeguard and promote the child's welfare.

3.1.6 Transitional provisions

The Children Act 1989, sch. 14, provides for persons having custody or care and control under an 'existing order' (for meaning of 'existing order' see sch. 14, para. 5(1) and (2) in force on 14 October 1991) to be deemed to have parental responsibility for the child in question. If an unmarried father has 'parental rights and duties' under the Family Law Reform Act 1987, or custody, care and control, immediately prior to 14 October 1991 then he automatically has parental responsibility after that date.

4 GUARDIANSHIP

Central to the new role of guardians under the Children Act 1989 is the conferment upon them of parental responsibility for the child in question (Children Act 1989, s. 5(6)). There will no longer be different 'levels' of guardianship. Under the old law there was a distinction between guardians of the child's estate and guardians of the child's person. This will no longer be the case, save for transitional circumstances (see Children Act 1989, sch. 14, paras. 12 to 14). In future a guardian of the child's estate may only be appointed in accordance with the rules (Children Act 1989, s. 5(11) and (12)).

4.1 Appointment of a guardian

A guardian may be appointed for a child under 18 in the following ways:

(a) by the court in family proceedings, with or without an application:

(i) where the child has no parent with parental responsibility for him (s. 5(1)(a)); or

(ii)   where a residence order has been made with respect to the child in favour of a parent or guardian of his who has died while the order was in force (s. 5(1)(b));

(b)   by a parent with parental responsibility (s. 5(3));
(c)   by an existing guardian (s. 5(4)).

When a court decides whether or not to appoint a guardian it must apply the 'welfare' principle set out in s. 1(1), Children Act 1989. It is not mandatory for the court to use the statutory checklist of factors in s. 1(3), Children Act 1989 unless it is making the decision in the course of hearing a contested application for a section 8 order, care order or supervision order. However, in practice the court is likely to refer to the checklist in any event, and in addition to consider the relationship between the child in question and the proposed guardian, the recorded wishes of the deceased parent, the wishes of the child's nearest relative and other such matters.

A parent who has parental responsibility, or a guardian, may appoint a guardian to assume parental responsibility on the death of the appointor (s. 5(3) and (4)). Two or more persons may join together to make such an appointment (s. 5(10)). Any such appointment need not be made by will nor by deed. It was felt that such formalities may deter people from making an appointment. Instead, it will be sufficient for the appointment to be in writing, dated and signed at the direction of the person making the appointment in his presence and in the presence of two witnesses. Unmarried fathers will be able to make appointments if they have obtained parental responsibility or been appointed as guardians.

4.2   Revocation of guardianship

Revocation of guardianship can be achieved in the following ways:

(a)   by a later appointment of a guardian (unless it is clear that the later appointment is of an *additional* guardian (s. 6(1));
(b)   by a written, signed and dated instrument revoking the appointment (s. 6(2));
(c)   by the destruction of the document in question with the intent of revoking the appointment, except in the case of a will or codicil (s. 6(3));
(d)   by the revocation of the will or codicil that contains the appointment (s. 6(4)).

Where the initial appointment of a guardian was by way of court order then the court retains jurisdiction to terminate the appointment at any time in the following ways (s. 6(7)):

(a)   on the application of anyone with parental responsibility for the child;
(b)   on the application of the child himself;
(c)   by the court's own motion in the course of any family proceedings if the court considers it should be brought to an end even though no application has been made.

If the appointment is not terminated earlier it will end on the child reaching the age of 18, as will any court order made under s. 5(1): see s. 91(7) and (8).

4.3   Disclaimer of guardianship

A guardian appointed other than by way of a court order may disclaim his appointment by making an instrument in writing to this effect, provided that he does so within a reasonable time of first knowing that the appointment has taken effect (s. 6(5) and (6)).

4.4   Transitional provisions

When the Children Act 1989 came into effect on 14 October 1991 an existing guardian whose appointment took effect pursuant to any previous statute was deemed to have been appointed under s. 5 of the Children Act 1989 (sch. 14, para. 12 et seq.). From that date onwards he has parental responsibility for the child and will be able to appoint someone to succeed him in the event of his death.

5   THE COURTS — JURISDICTION AND ALLOCATION OF PROCEEDINGS

In addition to streamlining and codifying the law relating to children the Children Act 1989 creates a unified structure of the High Court, county courts and magistrates' courts. The structure is as follows:

(a)   High Court tier: staffed by Family Division judges;
(b)   county court tier: staffed by selected circuit judges sitting at designated trial centres. There are three classes of county court:

    (i)   divorce county courts;
    (ii)   family hearing centres;
    (iii)   care centres.

(c)   magistrates' tier: staffed by the family proceedings court.

The criteria which will govern which court is the most appropriate venue are contained in the Children (Allocation of Proceedings) Order 1991. After considering the important guiding principle in s. 1(2) of the Children Act 1989, which establishes the presumption that delay in the conduct of proceedings is prejudicial to the interests of the child, the basic factors to be taken into account (as set out in art. 7(2) of the Allocation Order 1991), are:

(a)   the length, importance and complexity of the case;
(b)   the urgency of the case;
(c)   the need to consolidate the case with other proceedings that are pending.

In *J* v *Berkshire CC, The Times*, 10 March 1992 (sub nom *L* v *Berkshire CC, The Independent*, 16 March 1992), the President indicated that cases requiring a lengthy hearing (in this instance eight days) should be transferred to a district judge, thus avoiding the difficulty of having to assemble the magistrates on a number of days. This would appear to be an example of proceedings that are 'exceptionally grave, important or complex'.

5.1 Commencement of proceedings

5.1.1 *Proceedings to be commenced in magistrates' court*

Proceedings with a public law element will, generally speaking, commence in the family proceedings court. However, there is provision for them to move horizontally within the same tier of courts or vertically up and down from one tier to another. Therefore, criteria have been created to ensure that cases are allocated to the most appropriate venue for the hearing. Those criteria are contained in the Children (Allocation of Proceedings) Order 1991. Article 3 of that Order sets out those proceedings which *shall* be commenced in the magistrates' court:

(a) s. 25 (use of accommodation for restricting liberty);
(b) s. 31 (care and supervision orders);
(c) s. 33(7) (leave to change name of or remove from United Kingdom child in care);
(d) s. 34 (parental contact with children in care);
(e) s. 36 (education supervision orders);
(f) s. 43 (child assessment orders);
(g) s. 44 (emergency protection orders);
(h) s. 45 (duration of emergency protection orders etc.);
(i) s. 46(7) (application for emergency protection order by police officer);
(j) s. 48 (powers to assist discovery of children etc.);
(k) s. 50 (recovery orders);
(l) s.75 (protection of children in an emergency);
(m) s. 77(6) (appeal against steps taken under s. 77(1));
(n) s. 102 (powers of constable to assist etc.);
(o) para. 19 of sch. 2 (approval of arrangements to assist child to live abroad);
(p) para. 23 of sch. 2 (contribution orders);
(q) para. 8 of sch. 8 (certain appeals);
(r) s. 21, Adoption Act 1976.

However, the practitioner should note that there are two exceptions to the general rule that the above proceedings should commence in a magistrates' court:

(i) where proceedings within (b), (c), (f), (g), (i) or (j) above arise as a result of the High Court or county court directing that a local authority should investigate the child's circumstances, then the proceedings must be commenced in the court which directed that investigation, provided that it is the High Court or a county court 'care centre'. If it is not, then the court which directed the investigation must choose a care centre. The reason for this is that the court directing the investigation did so with a view to the possibility of the local authority instigating care or supervision proceedings;

(ii) where proceedings are of the type in (a)-(k), (n) or (o) *and* there are proceedings of the same kind pending in another court, then that *other* court is the appropriate court for *all* of the proceedings. The proceedings should be consolidated and heard together.

5.1.2   Extension, variation or discharge of an order

Article 4 of the Children (Allocation of Proceedings) Order 1991 provides that, generally speaking, proceedings under the Children Act 1989 or under the Adoption Act 1976:

(a)   to extend, vary or discharge an order, or
(b)   the determination of which may have the effect of varying or discharging an order

shall be made to the court which made the order. However, there are two exceptions to that rule:

(i)   an application for a s. 8 order which would have the effect of varying or discharging a s. 8 order which was made by a county court of its own motion (i.e. under s. 10(1)(b), Children Act 1989) must be made to a *divorce county court* (Article 4(2));
(ii)   an application to extend, vary or discharge an interim care order or interim supervision order made by a county court under s. 38, Children Act 1989, or for an order which would have the effect of extending, varying or discharging of such an interim order must be made to a *care centre* (Article 4(3)).

5.2   Transfer of proceedings

The transfer of proceedings horizontally or vertically is largely governed by the Children (Allocation of Proceedings) Order 1991 (the 'Allocation Order 1991'). However, those provisions are supplemented by the Family Proceedings Rules 1991 (the 'FPR 1991' – for High Court and county court) and the Family Proceedings Courts (Children Act 1989) Rules 1991 (the 'FPC(CA 1989)R 1991' – for magistrates' courts).

There are complex provisions governing the following matters and the authors do not propose to expand upon the details here. Instead the appropriate references to the relevant provisions for each type of transfer are set out below.

(a)   transfer from one magistrates' court to another — (see Article 6 of the Allocation Order 1991 and r. 6 of the FPC(CA 1989)R 1991);
(b)   transfer from magistrates' court to county court by magistrates' court (see Article 7 of the Allocation Order 1991 and r. 6 of the FPC(CA 1989)R 1991). See also Chapter 29, paragraph 2.8.2;
(c)   transfer from magistrates' court following refusal of magistrates' court to transfer (see Article 9 and FPR 1991 r. 4.6);
(d)   transfer from one county court to another (see Articles 10 and 14–20 of the Allocation Order 1991);
(e)   transfer from county court to magistrates' court by county court (see Article 11 of the Allocation Order 1991);
(f)   transfer from county court to High Court by county court (see Article 12 of the Allocation Order 1991);
(g)   transfer from High Court to county court (see Article 13 of the Allocation Order 1991).

5.3 Public law applications in the county court

If an application under Parts III, IV or V of the Children Act 1989 (i.e. for an order with a public law element) is to be heard in a county court, then that county court must also be a designated *care centre* (see Article 18 of the Allocation Order 1991).

5.4 Private law proceedings

Private law proceedings will be largely self-allocating, since they will usually arise in the course of divorce proceedings and so will be heard in the appropriate county court.

6 PROCEDURE

The procedure to be adopted in proceedings under the Children Act 1989 is set out in the Family Proceedings Rules 1991 ('FPR 1991' for the High Court and county court) and in the Family Proceedings Courts (Children Act 1989) Rules ('FPC(CA 1989)R 1991' for the magistrates' court). The substance and order of the two sets of rules are largely the same, in accordance with the intention of Parliament to unify and streamline the law and procedure in proceedings relating to children.

It is noticeable that the court is encouraged to take a much more inquisitorial role than formerly, in an effort to play down the adversarial nature of the proceedings. The court is expected to take control of the timetable for hearings, to make directions as to the evidence to be filed, to make directions as to the conduct of the proceedings generally and to call for welfare reports where necessary. There is now much more emphasis on written material and on disclosure by each party of its evidence in advance of the hearing so that the real issues involved in the case are clear. It is hoped that this will help to avoid the all-too-familiar scenario whereby advocates waste time during a hearing in following unproductive lines of examination and cross-examination which do not go to the heart of the issues between the parties.

6.1 Allocation of functions within the courts

Which type of case will be heard by a judge, district judge, magistrate(s) or justices' clerk?

6.1.1 County court care centres
Care centres will be staffed by:

    (a) designated family judges;
    (b) nominated care judges;
    (c) nominated care district judges.

They will hear the following types of cases:

    (a) transferred/issued public law cases;
    (b) contested matrimonial applications;
    (c) adoptions;
    (d) injunctions.

6.1.2 County court family hearing centres

Family hearing centres will be staffed by:

(a) nominated family judges;
(b) all district judges.

They will be able to hear the following cases:

(a) contested matrimonial and s. 8 applications;
(b) adoptions;
(c) injunctions.

6.1.3 Divorce county courts

Divorce county courts will be staffed by:

(a) non-nominated circuit judges;
(b) all district judges.

They will have 'district judge jurisdiction' only.

6.1.4 County courts

Ordinary county courts will be staffed by:

(a) non-nominated circuit judges;
(b) all district judges.

They will have no involvement in Children Act 1989 proceedings save for applications for injunctions.

6.1.5 Magistrates' courts

Magistrates' courts hearing Children Act 1989 applications will be staffed by family proceedings panels of magistrates. They will hear the following types of cases:

(a) public law cases;
(b) private family proceedings (outside divorce).

There are certain types of cases in which a *single justice* may sit as the family proceedings court (see r. 2 of the FPC(CA 1989)R 1991). These are as follows:

(a) ex parte applications for:

   (i) prohibited steps orders;
  (ii) specific issue orders;
 (iii) emergency protection orders;
  (iv) warrant under s. 48(9);
   (v) recovery orders;
  (vi) orders under s. 75;
 (vii) search warrant under s. 102(1);

(b) interim orders;
(c) specified provisions of the Children Act 1989;
(d) transfer of proceedings under the Allocation Order 1991;
(e) rules 3–8, 10–19, 21, 22 or 27 of the FPC(CA 1989)R 1991.

There are certain functions which the justices' clerk may perform on his own, without any magistrates at all. These include the power to give, vary or revoke directions as to:

(a)   timetable;
(b)   variation of time allowed by Rules;
(c)   attendance of child;
(d)   appointment of guardian ad litem or solicitor;
(e)   service of documents;
(f)   submission of evidence, including experts' reports;
(g)   preparation of welfare reports;
(h)   transfer from magistrates' court vertically or horizontally;
(i)   consolidation of cases.

6.1.6   District judges

6.1.6.1   Nominated care district judges   Nominated care district judges will be able to hear the following matters in relation to *public law* cases:

(a)   review of transfer decision by justices' clerk;
(b)   allocation between High Court and county court;
(c)   interlocutory applications, including applications for uncontested interim orders;
(d)   emergency protection orders within transferred proceedings;
(e)   minor substantive applications.

They will be able to hear the following *private law* matters:

(a)   matrimonial applications;
(b)   s. 41 consideration of arrangements for the children;
(c)   pronouncement of decrees nisi;
(d)   directions in adoption cases;
(e)   applications for injunctions, but they have no powers to commit for breach of injunctions (committals must be heard by a judge).

6.1.6.2   All other district judges   All other district judges (i.e. those who are not 'nominated care district judges') will have no jurisdiction at all in *public law* cases. They will, however, have the same jurisdiction in *private law* cases as the nominated care district judges (see paragraph 6.1.6.1, above).

6.2   Forms of Application

Both the FPR 1991, r. 4.4 and the FPC(CA 1989)R 1991, r. 4 make provision for applications under the Children Act 1989 to be made by way of a simple application. Gone are the days when one had to choose amongst all the different types of originating process, e.g. motion, summons, writ. From now on there are prescribed forms for each type of application. Those forms will be found in Appendix 1 of the FPR 1991 and sch. 1 of the FPC(CA 1989)R 1991. The forms are designed to extract the essential information from the applicant at an early stage. They also provide litigants with essential information about the conduct of their case, for example, as to the importance of obtaining legal advice and as to the right to file an answer to an application.

6.3   Withdrawal of an application

Once an application has been made it may only be withdrawn with the leave of the court (FPR 1991, r. 4.5(1) and FPC(CA 1989)R 1991, r. 5(1)). An application for leave can be made orally to the court, provided that the parties and either the guardian ad litem or court welfare officer are present. Otherwise there must be a written request setting out the reasons for the request. It must be served on all parties. The court can grant the request provided that the parties consent, the guardian ad litem (if there is one) has had an opportunity to make representations and the court thinks fit. Instead of granting the request, the court may direct that a date be fixed for the hearing of the request.

6.4   Requests for leave to bring proceedings

In some circumstances the Children Act 1989 requires a person to obtain leave before commencing proceedings, e.g. applications by grandparents for s. 8 orders. Both the FPR 1991, r. 4.3 and the FPC(CA 1989)R 1991, r. 3 require such a person to file:

(a)   a written request for leave setting out the reasons for the application, and
(b)   a draft of the application for the making of which leave is sought.

Note that there is no prescribed form for making a written request for leave, and it is to be presumed that a simple letter would suffice. The draft application, however, must be in the prescribed form as set out in Appendix I of the FPR 1991 and sch. I of the FPC(CA 1989)R 1991 respectively. If there is no prescribed form then the application should be in writing. From that point onwards the procedure for considering the request is the same as that described in paragraph 6.3 above in relation to an application for the withdrawal of an application.

6.5   Parties

The joinder of parties to proceedings is governed by the FPR 1991, r. 4.7, and the FPC(CA 1989)R 1991, r. 7. Those persons who are to be made respondents to particular applications made under the Children Act 1989, and those who are to be given notice of such proceedings are set out in user-friendly columns in Appendix 3 of the FPR 1991 and sch. 2 of the FPC(CA 1989)R 1991! The two sets of rules do differ slightly in this respect and the practitioner is warned to study the respective provisions carefully when he makes an application.

The respective rules provide that, in any 'relevant proceedings' (i.e. any proceedings brought under the Children Act 1989, under any statutory instrument made under the Children Act 1989 or under any amendment to the Children Act 1989) a person (i.e. *any* person) may make a written request that he be joined as a party or that he cease to be a party. A request for joinder *may* be granted by the court without a hearing. Otherwise the court will order that a date be fixed for a hearing to consider the request or else it will invite the parties to make written representations, within a specific period, as to whether the request should be granted.

The exception to the general rule is that where a person with parental responsibility requests that he be joined as a party the court *must* accede to his application (FPR 1991, r. 4.7(4) and FPC(CA 1989)R 1991, r. 7(4)).

6.6 Service

The rules governing the service of documents are to be found in the FPR 1991, r. 4.8 and in the FPC(CA 1989)R 1991, r. 8.

6.7 Answers

Each respondent to an application for a s. 8 order, or to an application for financial provision for children under sch. 1, Children Act 1989, is now required to serve an answer in the prescribed form within 14 days of being served with the application (FPR 1991, r. 4.9 and FPC(CA 1989)R 1991, r. 9). The prescribed forms for the respective answers will be found in Appendix I of the FPR 1991 and sch. 1 of the FPC(CA 1989)R 1991. The requirement for the making of an answer is new to the magistrates' courts' procedure and brings it more into line with that already existing in the higher courts in relation to private law proceedings. Respondents to other types of application *may*, if the application is in the High Court or county court, file an answer if they so wish but there is no obligation to do so.

6.8 Appointment of guardian ad litem

Section 41(1), Children Act 1989 requires the court in any 'specified proceedings' (i.e. proceedings of a public nature – care orders, supervision orders, emergency protection orders etc.) to appoint a guardian ad litem for the child concerned *unless* it is satisfied that it is not necessary to do so in order to safeguard his interests. By s. 41(2), Children Act 1989 the appointment of and duties of the guardian ad litem are to be regulated by rules of court. The appropriate rules will be found in the FPR 1991, rr. 4.10 and 4.11 and in the FPC(CA 1989)R 1991, rr. 10 and 11.

Both sets of rules require that in carrying out his duties the guardian ad litem shall have regard to the 'delay principle' set out in s. 1(2), Children Act 1989, i.e. that there is a presumption that delay in hearing a case will be prejudicial to the welfare of the child concerned. This emphasises the need for the guardian ad litem to complete as quickly as possible any necessary inquiries and reports. Furthermore, the guardian ad litem is enjoined to have regard to the 'checklist' of 'welfare factors' set out in s. 1(3), Children Act 1989 when carrying out his duties.

The obligations of the guardian ad litem are extensive and include the following:

(a) to appoint a solicitor to represent the child (unless this has already been done) and to instruct that solicitor, unless the child is of sufficient age and understanding to instruct a solicitor himself;

(b) to advise the court whether any person might have an interest in becoming a party to the proceedings or in making representations to the court;

(c) to attend all hearings (including directions hearings);

(d) to advise whether the child is of sufficient understanding for such purposes as the service of documents, refusal to submit to a medical or psychiatric examination or assessment, attendance at court etc.;

(e) to advise the court of the wishes of the child in respect of any relevant matter;

(f)　to advise as to the appropriate forum for, and timing of, the proceedings;

(g)　to advise as to the options available to the court and as to the suitability of each option;

(h)　to deliver interim and final written reports as directed by the court. As a rule final reports should be served on the parties at least seven days before the date fixed for the final hearing.

The rules provide for the inspection by the guardian ad litem of local authority records as allowed by s. 42, Children Act 1989. The rules also allow the guardian ad litem, either of his own motion or at the direction of the court, to obtain such professional assistance as he thinks appropriate.

It is generally expected that a guardian ad litem will be appointed in *most* of the cases to which s. 41, Children Act 1989 applies (i.e. in 'specified proceedings' as set out in s. 41(6), Children Act 1989). In this context 'specified proceedings' include any proceedings:

(a)　in relation to an application for a care order or a supervision order;

(b)　in which the court has given a direction under s. 37(1), Children Act 1989 and has made, or is considering whether to make, an interim care order or supervision order;

(c)　on an application for the discharge of a care order or the variation or discharge of a supervision order;

(d)　in which the court is considering whether to make a residence order with respect to a child who is the subject of a care order;

(e)　with respect to contact between a child who is the subject of a care order and any other person;

(f)　in which the court is considering making an order under Part V of the Children Act 1989, e.g. emergency protection order, child assessment order, education supervision order etc.;

(g)　on an appeal against the orders at (a) to (f) above.

6.9　Solicitor for the child

The rules require the guardian ad litem to appoint a solicitor for the child unless an appointment has already been made. In that event the solicitor is required to represent the child 'in accordance with instructions received from the guardian ad litem' (FPR 1991, r. 4.12 (1) (a) and FPC(CA 1989)R 1991, r. 12(1) (a)).

However, as was true under the old law, provision is made for the solicitor to receive instructions from the child personally. This will take place if the solicitor considers, having taken into account the views of the guardian ad litem, that:

(a)　the child wishes to give instructions which conflict with those of the guardian ad litem, and

(b)　that he is able, having regard to the degree of his understanding, to give such instructions on his own behalf.

In such cases the guardian ad litem will continue to participate in the proceedings to advocate what he believes to be in the child' s best interests as a sort of 'amicus curiae', subject to any directions which the court may make.

See Chapter 29, paragraph 2.8.1 for further discussion of the appointment of a solicitor for a child in proceedings for a care or supervision order.

6.10 Directions appointments

The provisions governing directions appointments will be found in r. 4.14 FPR 1991 and in r. 14 FPC(CA 1989)R 1991. They make provision for a preliminary hearing at which the court can give directions for the subsequent conduct of the proceedings. There can be several directions appointments. They can take place of the court's own motion or as a result of a request made by one of the parties. The period of notice required for such hearings will usually be two days, although in urgent cases a request for directions can (with leave) be made orally or without notice to the other parties, or both (r. 4.14(4) FPR 1991 and r. 14(6) FPC(CA 1989)R 1991). The matters which can be dealt with include:

(a) timetable for the proceedings;
(b) varying time limits;
(c) service of documents;
(d) joinder of parties;
(e) preparation of welfare reports;
(f) submission of evidence, including experts' reports;
(g) appointment of guardian ad litem/solicitor;
(h) attendance of child;
(i) transfer of case to another court;
(j) consolidation with other proceedings.

The aim of directions appointments is to simplify the interlocutory stages of proceedings.

6.11 Timing

A recurring theme of the Children Act 1989 is the avoidance of delay in proceedings wherever possible. Thus, where the rules provide for a period of time within which, or by which, a certain act is to be performed then that period may not be extended except by direction of the court/justices' clerk (r. 4.15 FPR 1991 and r. 15(4) FPC(CA 1989)R 1991). There is also a mandatory requirement that whenever proceedings are adjourned the court *must* fix a date for reconvening (r. 4.15(2) FPR 1991 and r. 15(5) FPC(CA 1989)R 1991). The aim of these provisions is to prevent the proceedings from lying dormant through the delay of the parties or their advisers. Both sets of rules regulate the minimum period which must generally elapse between the commencement of the proceedings and the first hearing. Those periods have been kept short deliberately in order to reduce delays so far as possible. The appropriate minimum periods for the various types of proceedings will be found in tabular form in Appendix 3 of the FPR 1991 and sch. 2 of the FPC(CA 1989)R 1991.

6.12 Attendance at hearing/directions appointment

All parties, including the child, *must* attend a directions appointment of which they have had notice unless the court directs otherwise (r. 4.16 FPR 1991 and r. 16 FPC(CA 1989)R 1991).

Where the child is a party then proceedings *may* take place in his absence if:

(a) the court considers it to be in the interests of the child, having regard to the matters to be discussed or the evidence likely to be given at the hearing or directions appointment, and

(b)   the child is represented by a guardian ad litem or solicitor.

The court must not begin a case in the absence of a respondent unless:

(a)   it is proved that he had reasonable notice of the hearing, or
(b)   the circumstances of the case justify proceeding.

If the respondent appears but the applicant does not then the court can refuse the application, or, if it has sufficient evidence, it can proceed in the absence of the applicant.

If neither the applicant nor the respondent appear then the court may refuse the application.

In the High Court and county court most hearings and directions appointments will take place in chambers. In the magistrates' court there is provision for hearings and directions appointments to take place in private.

6.13   Documentary evidence

Great emphasis is placed upon the need for advance disclosure of evidence in proceedings under the Children Act 1989 (see r. 4.17 FPR 1991 and r. 17 FPC(CA 1989)R 1991). Each party is required to file and serve not only written statements of the oral evidence he intends to adduce at the hearing, but also copies of any documents upon which he intends to rely. The rules are very clear upon the requirement that at a hearing a party *may not adduce* evidence or seek to rely upon a document which has not been disclosed in advance to the other parties, except with the leave of the court. Statements of witnesses must be dated and signed by the person making the statement and must contain a declaration that the maker believes the statement to be true.

'In advance' means by such time as the court/justices' clerk directs, or in the absence of such a direction, before the hearing.

The practitioner should note that in s. 8 proceedings a party must file no document other than as required or authorised by the rules without leave of the court (r. 4.17(4) FPR 1991 and r. 17(4) FPC(CA 1989)R 1991). The aim of this rule is to prevent information being set down in writing which may only serve to inflame the situation between the parties and thus prevent a sensible settlement of the matter. If it becomes clear at a later stage that the matter is not going to be settled then the court can direct that further evidence be filed in readiness for a contested hearing.

6.14   Expert evidence – examination of child

No person may cause a child to be medically or psychiatrically examined or otherwise assessed for the purpose of the preparation of expert evidence for use in proceedings, *except* with the leave of the court (see r. 4.18 FPR 1991 and r. 18 FPC(CA 1989)R 1991). If such an examination or assessment is made without the leave of the court then that evidence cannot be adduced in the proceedings without the leave of the court.

6.15   Amendment

If a document has been filed or served in proceedings then it cannot be amended without leave of the court (r. 4.19 FPR 1991 and r. 19 FPC(CA 1989)R 1991).

6.16 Oral evidence

The court, proper officer or justices' clerk must keep a note of the substance of any oral evidence given at a hearing or directions appointment (r. 4.20 FPR 1991 and r. 20 FPC(CA 1989)R 1991).

6.17 Hearing

In the family proceedings court the rules now require the justices to read all of the documents which have been filed in respect of the hearing (r. 21(1) FPC(CA 1989)R 1991). Thus the procedure in the family proceedings court now reflects that in the higher courts. Rule 4.21 of the FPR 1991 and r. 21 of the FPC(CA 1989)R 1991 provide that:

(a)   the court may give directions as to the order of evidence and speeches;

(b)   unless the court directs otherwise, the parties and guardian ad litem should usually adduce evidence in the following order:

  (i)   applicant;
  (ii)   any party with parental responsibility for the child;
  (iii) other respondents;
  (iv)   guardian ad litem;
  (v)   the child, if he is a party and there is no guardian ad litem.

(c)   after the final hearing the court must make its decision 'as soon as practicable';

(d)   when making an order or refusing an application the court must indicate both its findings of fact and the reasons for its decision.

6.18 Appeals

An appeal against the making of an order by a magistrates' court, or against the refusal of the magistrates to make an order will lie directly to the High Court (s. 94(1), Children Act 1989) and will usually be heard by a single judge (r. 4.22(8) FPR 1991). However, an application to withdraw such an appeal, or to have it dismissed with consent of all the parties, or to amend the grounds of appeal, may be heard by a district judge (r. 4.22(7) FPR 1991).

An appeal against the decision of a district judge will usually be made to the judge of the court in which the decision was made (r. 8.1 FPR 1991). Note that an appeal from the district judge to the judge will *not* be conducted by way of rehearing. Furthermore, fresh evidence in respect of the appeal may not be adduced unless there are exceptional circumstances (see *Merrit* v *Merrit, The Independent*, 10 February 1992). Appeals against the decision of a county court or the High Court will be directly to the Court of Appeal.

The procedure for conducting appeals is set out in r. 4.22 of the FPR 1991. The appellant must file and serve on the parties and on the guardian ad litem the following documents:

(a)   a written notice of appeal, setting out the grounds upon which he relies;

(b)   a copy of the summons or application and of the order appealed against and any order staying its execution;

(c)   a copy of any notes of evidence;
(d)   a copy of any reasons given for the decision.

6.18.1   Time limits
The time limits for filing and serving notice of appeal are:

(a)   generally, within 14 days after the determination against which the appeal is brought;
(b)   however, for appeals against interim care orders or interim supervision orders the time limit is seven days;
(c)   otherwise, such other time as the court may direct.

6.18.2   Respondents to appeals
A respondent who wishes to contend:

(a)   that the decision of the court below should be varied, or
(b)   that the decision of the court below should be affirmed on grounds other than those relied upon by that court, or
(c)   by way of cross-appeal that the decision of the court below was wrong in whole or in part,

must, within 14 days of receipt of notice of the appeal, file and serve on all other parties to the appeal a notice in writing, setting out the grounds upon which he relies.

6.19   Confidentiality of documents

Rule 4.23 of the FPR 1991 and r. 23 of the FPC(CA 1989)R 1991 state that no document relating to Children Act 1989 proceedings which is *held* by the court, other than a record of an order may, without leave of the judge or district judge, be disclosed to anyone, save for the following persons/authorities:

(a)   a party;
(b)   the legal representative of a party;
(c)   the guardian ad litem;
(d)   the Legal Aid Board;
(e)   a welfare officer.

Note that the duty of confidentiality appears to apply only to documents *held* by the court (i.e., those already filed). On the face of it, therefore, it would seem that no such duty applies to documents which are only in their preparatory stages prior to being filed. This is probably not what Parliament intended, and it is to be hoped that no one will take advantage of this lacuna by disclosing documents which are clearly intended to be confidential at all times.

6.20   Welfare reports

Section 7, Children Act 1989 extends the court's power to call for a welfare report so that it can do so when considering any question with respect to a child under the Act. For the first time this includes cases where, for example, the court is considering the appointment of guardians, or the granting of parental responsibility to unmarried fathers (s. 7(1)). Because the court may make a s. 8 order in any 'family proceedings' (s. 8(3) and (4)), the court may now call for a welfare report, inter alia, in an injunction case.

The probation service and local authorities will be under a duty to provide reports as requested (s. 7(5)), but a local authority may delegate the task to someone who is not a member of its staff (s. 7(1)) e.g. a guardian ad litem. The court may consider reports and evidence given about matters in reports regardless of the hearsay rule, provided that it is relevant to the question that the court is considering (s. 7(4)).

There is no duty upon the court to request a welfare report, even if the case is contested. When considering whether to request a report the court must give paramount consideration to the child's welfare and have regard to the problems caused by delay (s. 1). Sometimes the benefit to the child of a speedy hearing will outweigh the disadvantage of the court proceeding without the benefit of a welfare report, particularly as the preparation of welfare reports can take three or four months.

The welfare officer is required to attend at any hearing in respect of which his report has been made or in the course of which his report is due to be considered. His report should be filed at least five days before the hearing unless the court has directed a different time limit (r. 4.13 FPR 1991 and r. 13 FPC(CA 1989)R 1991).

6.21 Hearsay evidence

Hearsay evidence is now admissible in civil proceedings before the High Court, county court and magistrates' court when given in connection with the upbringing, maintenance or welfare of a child (see the Children (Admissibility of Hearsay Evidence) Order 1990). However, the weight to be given to such evidence will be in the discretion of the judge. The Order allows hearsay evidence to be admissible in respect of the following statements:

(a) statements by children;

(b) statements against interest by those with control, or concerned with the control, of the child;

(c) statements contained in reports submitted by a guardian ad litem or local authority.

6.22 Legal aid

The availability of legal aid for Children Act 1989 proceedings is fully set out in Chapter 2, paragraph 23.

26 Orders in family proceedings

1 INTRODUCTION

The Children Act 1989 has made enormous changes to the private law relating to children and ss. 8, 9 and 10, Children Act 1989 form the heart of the new statutory scheme in this respect. The old scheme of custody and access orders encouraged the parent who succeeded in obtaining an order to take the view that he had 'won' his case once and for all. The intention of the new legislation is to move away from the concept of final orders in children's cases and towards a more flexible method of resolving disputes about, for example, where children should live, with whom they should have contact and how they should be brought up. The needs and circumstances of children are constantly changing and therefore it is right that the orders that regulate the arrangements for their upbringing are sufficiently flexible to reflect those changes as and when it becomes necessary.

The new orders available under the Children Act 1989 also highlight the efforts of the new legislation to move away from the tendency of parents to feel that they have *rights over* children towards an acknowledgment by them of their *responsibilities for* their children. The principle of 'parental responsibility' under the Children Act 1989 has already been discussed in Chapter 25 at paragraph 3.

A further aim of the Children Act 1989 is to ensure that wherever possible orders relating to the upbringing of children can be made in the course of existing proceedings in respect of the same family, so as to avoid the necessity for several sets of proceedings to run concurrently. For example, where the occupation of the matrimonial home is in dispute the needs of the children are frequently an important factor in determining the relief sought. The new provisions allow the court, at the same time as making an order excluding the father from the house, to make, for instance, a residence order in favour of the mother who remains there and a contact order in favour of the father.

The court will be able to make a s. 8 order in the course of any 'family proceedings'. For the purposes of the Children Act 1989 'family proceedings' are defined in s. 8(3) and (4) as any proceedings under:

    (a)   the inherent jurisdiction of the High Court in relation to children;
    (b)   Parts I, II and IV of the Children Act 1989;
    (c)   the Matrimonial Causes Act 1973;
    (d)   the Domestic Violence and Matrimonial Proceedings Act 1976;
    (e)   the Adoption Act 1976;
    (f)   the Domestic Proceedings and Magistrates' Courts Act 1978;

(g)   ss. 1 and 9, Matrimonial Homes Act 1983;

(h)   Part III of the Matrimonial and Family Proceedings Act 1984.

1.1   Jurisdiction to make s. 8 orders under the Family Law Act 1986

1.1.1   Meaning of 'Part I order'

The Family Law Act 1986 (as amended by the Children Act 1989, sch. 13, paras. 62 to 71) sets out the circumstances in which a court in England and Wales will have jurisdiction to make an order under Part I of the Family Law Act 1986 (i.e. a 'Part I order'). A court in England and Wales may make two types of Part I order:

(a)   a s. 8 order, other than one varying or discharging a s. 8 order (Family Law Act 1986, s. 1(1)(a)); and

(b)   an order made in the exercise of the inherent jurisdiction of the High Court with respect to children:

(i)   in so far as it gives the care of a child to any person or provides for contact with or the education of a child, but

(ii)   excluding an order varying or discharging such and order (Family Law Act 1986, s. 1(1)(d)).

The rules as to jurisdiction in relation to s. 8 orders are different for matrimonial and non-matrimonial proceedings.

1.1.2   Matrimonial proceedings

A court in England and Wales will only have jurisdiction to make a s. 8 order within proceedings for divorce, nullity or judicial separation which are still continuing. If the proceedings have been dismissed then the s. 8 order must be made forthwith, or the application for the order must have been made on or before the dismissal (Family Law Act 1986, s. 2A(1)). If the court considers that it would be more appropriate for the Part I matters to be determined outside England and Wales then the court can direct that no s. 8 order be made in the matrimonial proceedings (Family Law Act 1986, s. 2A(4)).

1.1.3   Non-matrimonial proceedings

A court in England and Wales will only have jurisdiction to make s. 8 orders in non-matrimonial proceedings where the child is either:

(a)   habitually resident in England and Wales, or

(b)   is present in England and Wales and is not habitually resident in any part of the United Kingdom on the relevant date (i.e, on the date of the application, or, if there is no application, on the date when the court is considering whether to make the orders), and

(c)   in the case of either (a) or (b) above the court's jurisdiction is not excluded.

The jurisdiction of the court will be *excluded* if, on the relevant date, matrimonial proceedings are continuing in Scotland or Northern Ireland in relation to the marriage of the child's parents, *unless* that court has made an order waiving its jurisdiction or staying proceedings so as to allow the Part I order proceedings to take place in England and Wales (Family Law Act 1986, s. 3).

2   SECTION 8 ORDERS

Section 8 of the Children Act 1989 creates the following orders:

(a)   a residence order: this settles the arrangements to be made as to the person with whom a child is to live;

(b)   a contact order: this requires the person with whom a child lives to allow the child to visit or stay with the person named in the order, or for that person and the child otherwise to have contact with each other;

(c)   a prohibited steps order: this orders that no step which could be taken by a parent in meeting his parental responsibility for a child, and which is of a kind specified in the order, shall be taken by any person without the consent of the court;

(d)   a specific issue order: this gives directions for the determination of a specific question which has arisen, or which may arise, in connection with any aspect of parental responsibility for a child.

Any reference to 'a s. 8 order' means any of the above orders and any order varying or discharging such an order (s. 8(2)).

When a court is hearing *contested* proceedings in relation to a s. 8 order it *must* have regard to the following:

(a)   the principle that the child's welfare is the paramount consideration (s. 1(1));

(b)   the statutory checklist of factors (s. 1(3));

(c)   the principle that it must not make any order unless it considers that doing so would be better for the child than making no order at all (s. 1(5)).

See Chapter 25, paragraphs 2.2 to 2.4 for a detailed discussion of these principles.

2.1   Who can apply for section 8 orders?

The court can make s. 8 orders in two ways:

(a)   in the course of existing family proceedings (s. 10(1)): 'family proceedings' are defined in s. 8(3) (N.B. They include care proceedings);

(b)   as a result of a specific self-contained application to the court for a s. 8 order (s. 10(2)).

In each case certain persons are 'entitled to apply' for s. 8 orders as of right whilst anyone else may only do so with leave of the court.

2.1.1   *Persons 'entitled to apply' for section 8 orders*
There is a distinction between those entitled to apply:

(a)   for a residence or contact order, and

(b)   for a specific issue or prohibited steps order.

The class of persons entitled to apply for the orders in (a) is wider than the class of those who are entitled to apply for the orders in (b).

The following are the class of persons who can apply for *any* s. 8 order:

(a)   any parent or guardian of the child (s. 10(4));

(b)   any person in whose favour a residence order is in force with respect to the child (s. 10(4));

(c)   any person who has custody or care and control of the child under an 'existing order' (sch. 14, paras. 5 and 7(3)(b)).

The persons who are entitled to apply to the court for a residence or contact order are *extended* by s. 10(5) to include:

(a)   any party to the marriage (whether or not subsisting) in relation to whom a child is a child of the family (as defined in s. 105(1));

(b)   any person with whom the child has lived for at least three years (not necessarily a continuous period, but must not have begun more than five years before, nor ended more than three months before, the making of the application);

(c)   any person who, in any case where a residence order is in force with respect to the child (or an 'existing order' under sch. 14, para. 5 is in force conferring care and control: sch. 14, para. 8(3)), has the consent of each of the persons in whose favour the order was made;

(d)   any person who, in any case where the child is in the care of the local authority by virtue of a care order, has the consent of that authority;

(e)   any person who, in any other case, has the consent of each of those (if any) who have parental responsibility for the child.

Note that this list is *in addition* to those persons set out in s. 10(4), and that it may be further extended by rules of court (s. 10(7)).

2.1.2   Obtaining leave of the court

Any person who does not fall within the categories set out in paragraph 2.1.1. above must apply to the court for leave to make a s. 8 application. If the child himself applies for leave then the court may only grant leave if it is satisfied that the child has sufficient understanding to make the proposed application (s. 10(8)). If the person applying for leave is someone other than the child then the court must consider the specific matters set out in s. 10(9) when making its decision, that is to say:

(a)   the nature of the proposed application for the s. 8 order;

(b)   the applicant's connection with the child;

(c)   any risk there might be of that proposed application disrupting the child's life to such an extent that he would be harmed by it; and

(d)   where the child is being looked after by a local authority:

(i)   the authority's plans for the child's future; and

(ii)   the wishes and feelings of the child's parents.

The 'welfare principle' in s. 1(1), Children Act 1989 applies to applications for leave just as it does in relation to substantive applications.

2.1.3   Foster parents

Section 9(3), Children Act 1989 purports to restrict local authority foster parents from applying for leave to apply for s. 8 orders without the consent of the local authority if the child has lived with them for less than three years. The position appears to be as follows:

(a)   if the child has lived with the foster parents for less than three years and is in the care of the local authority by virtue of a *care order*, then the foster parents can apply for a residence or contact order as of right if they have the consent of the local authority (s. 10(5)(c)(ii));

(b)   if the child has lived with the foster parents for less than three years but is merely being *accommodated* by the local authority (pursuant to its duties under s. 20, Children Act 1989), then the foster parents must obtain *both* the consent of the local authority *and* the leave of the court before making an application for the order itself (s. 9(3)).

The position is different in relation to applications for prohibited steps and specific issue orders: if the child has lived with the foster parents for less than three years then they will need *both* local authority consent *and* leave of the court, since s. 10(5) only applies to residence and contact orders.

When the child has lived with the foster parents for *at least* three years they will be entitled to apply for a residence or contact order irrespective of the local authority's consent (s. 10(5)(b)). If they wish to apply for a specific issue order or a prohibited steps order they need the leave of the court but *not* the consent of the local authority.

2.2   Duration of section 8 orders

The main provisions which govern the duration of s. 8 orders are as follows:

(a)   as a general rule s. 8 orders will continue unless discharged by the court or otherwise, until the child reaches the age of 16 (s. 91(10));

(b)   the court must not make a s. 8 order which is to have effect for a period which will end after the child has reached 16, unless it is satisfied that the circumstances of the case are exceptional (s. 9(6));

(c)   the court must not make a s. 8 order, other than one varying or discharging a s. 8 order, once the child has reached 16, unless it is satisfied that there are exceptional circumstances (s. 9(7));

(d)   if an order is extended beyond, or made after, the child reached 16, then it comes to an end when he reaches 18 (s. 91(11));

(e)   the making of a care order will discharge all current s. 8 orders (s. 91(2)), as will the making of certain orders in adoption proceedings.

3   RESIDENCE ORDERS

Residence orders settle the arrangements to be made as to the person with whom the child lives. They aim to cater for a wider range of situations than a custody order was able to do. A residence order is not a 'once and for all' order as the old custody order often appeared to be. A custody order usually meant that the custodial parent had the right to the everyday care and control of the child, together with the power to make most routine and some major decisions about the child's life. Although custody orders could always be altered, the court would require highly convincing evidence before it could be persuaded that a transfer of custody from one parent to another was justified.

A residence order, on the other hand, does not have any effect on the parental responsibility of either parent; it is intended to settle the child's living arrangements and no more. A residence order can be made in favour of more than one person. If those people are not living together then the order may specify the periods to be spent in each household (s. 11(4)).

Example 1. Mr and Mrs Green divorce. They have two children, Sophie, aged 10, and Jason, aged 8. Each of the parents wishes the two children to live with them and each is willing to work part-time in order to create a home for the children. However, they cannot agree upon the arrangements and therefore both of them apply for residence orders in respect of the children. During the course of the hearing it becomes apparent to the judge that Mr Green can work from Monday to Wednesday each week and that Mrs Green can work from Thursday to Saturday each week. Therefore the judge decides to make a 'split residence order' whereby the children reside with Mr Green from Wednesday at 6 pm until noon on Sunday and with Mrs Green from noon on Sunday until Wednesday at 6 pm each week.

Example 2. Mr and Mrs Brown divorce. The two children of the family, Tom, aged 10, and Maisie, aged 8, are at school in Brighton where their mother continues to live. Mr Brown moves to Liverpool after the divorce. Each of the parents wishes the children to live with them and applies for a residence order. At the hearing the judge takes the view on the evidence that the children should remain at school in Brighton and should live with their mother during term time but that their relationship with their father is so good that they should spend six weeks with him during the summer holidays as well as one week at Easter and one week at Christmas. As the periods of 'contact' with Mr Brown are so substantial the judge decides that it is more realistic to define the arrangement as a 'split residence order' and specifies it as such in the order itself.

3.1 Restriction on change of name

Section 13(1) of the Children Act 1989 states that where a residence order is in force with respect to a child then no person may cause the child to be known by a new surname without first obtaining either:

(a) the written consent of every person with parental responsibility for the child; or
(b) the leave of the court.

Note that it is not only a change of name by deed poll that is prevented; the person with the residence order is equally prohibited from taking less formal steps to change the name the child is known by (for example, instructing the child's school that he should be called by a different surname).

If a person with a residence order does wish to change the child's surname then he should first contact the other persons who have parental responsibility to see if they will consent in writing to the change. If so, the change of name can go ahead as planned. If no consent is forthcoming then the court's leave will be necessary. An application for leave should be made using Form CHA11.

In the case of *W* v *A (child: surname)* [1981] Fam 14, [1981] 1 All ER 100, the Court of Appeal stressed that changing a child's name is viewed as a matter of importance and the parent seeking leave will have to show that it is in the child's best interests for his name to be changed. Whether leave is granted is a matter for the discretion of the judge hearing the case, seeing the parents and possibly seeing the children. The judge will take into account all the circumstances of the case including, where appropriate, any embarrassment which may be caused to the child by not changing his name and, on the other hand, the long-term interests of the child, the importance of maintaining the child's links with his paternal family, and (where the mother seeks leave because she has remarried) the stability or otherwise of the mother's new marriage.

> **Example.** (The facts of *W* v *A supra*.) There were two children of the marriage. The parties divorced and both remarried. They had joint custody of the children with care and control being granted to the mother and reasonable access to the father. The mother's second husband was an Australian and wished to return to Australia with her and the children. The mother wanted the children (aged 12 and 14) to use her new husband's surname and the children, who saw the judge in his room, also wanted to use his name. The judge ruled that the children were to continue to use the father's surname. He paid little regard to the children's view on the matter as he felt that it reflected that of the mother. The Court of Appeal upheld his decision.

3.2   Restriction on removal from the jurisdiction

Section 13(1), Children Act 1989 also dictates that where a residence order is in force with respect to a child then no person may remove him from the United Kingdom without either:

(a)   the written consent of every person with parental responsibility for the child; or
(b)   the leave of the court.

However, the person with the residence order is permitted to remove the child from the jurisdiction for a period of less than one month without having to comply with the two requirements set out above. The idea is to allow for short holiday trips. However, there is no restriction on the number of trips that may be taken. Note that the prohibition covers not only trips to Europe and further afield but also trips to Scotland and Ireland.

Furthermore, the court can give a general direction at the time it makes the residence order to allow the removal of the child from the jurisdiction generally or for specified purposes. This can be in favour of the person with the residence order or any other person. This can be very useful in that it avoids repeated minor applications to the court. For instance, where the non-residential parent (say, the father) lives abroad and it is envisaged that the child will visit him regularly twice each year the court can make a direction that the father have leave to remove the child from the jurisdiction twice each year.

If a person with a residence order (say, the mother) finds that the consent of the other people with parental responsibility is not forthcoming in respect of the proposed temporary removal from the jurisdiction then she must apply to the court for leave using Form CHA 11A. In deciding whether to give leave the guiding consideration is the welfare of the children. As a general rule it should not be difficult to persuade a court to give leave unless there are grounds to suspect that the proposed holiday is really a cover for an unauthorised permanent removal of the children from the jurisdiction.

If it is proposed that the children should emigrate permanently but the other persons with parental responsibility refuse to consent then the leave of the court must be sought. In considering whether to give leave to take a child out of the jurisdiction permanently, the welfare of the child is the first and paramount consideration. However, the current view is that leave should not be withheld unless there is a compelling reason to do so where the decision of the person with the residence order to emigrate is reasonable. The danger that must be taken into account is that there will be frustration and bitterness in the family if the court interferes with the decision of the person with the residence order and that this will rebound on the children (*Chamberlain* v *De La Mare* (1983) 4 FLR 434; *Lonslow* v *Hennig* [1986] 2 FLR 378).

3.3 Residence orders and parental responsibility

The granting of a residence order in favour of anyone automatically gives them parental responsibility for the child (s. 12(2)). Where a father who does not have parental responsibility applies for a residence order and the court grants one in his favour, then the court must make an order under s. 4 giving the father parental responsibility (s. 12(1)). The s. 4 order must last for the duration of the residence order and can only be ended by an order of the court (ss. 12(4) and 4(3)). However, s. 12(3) prevents those with residence orders who are not parents or guardians from giving consent to adoption, freeing for adoption and appointing a guardian for the child.

3.4 Restriction on local authorities applying for residence orders

A local authority may not apply for a residence order nor have one made in its favour s. 9(2)). However, a residence order may be made in favour of any child, even one subject to a care order (s. 9(1)), although in such a case the residence order will have the effect of discharging the care order (s. 91(1)).

3.5 Enforcement of residence orders

One of the methods by which a residence order may be enforced is set out in s. 14, Children Act 1989. If a person is in breach of the arrangements settled by the residence order (whether it be the person in whose favour the order has been made or some other person who is in breach), then the person with the residence order can enforce it under s. 63(3) of the Magistrates' Courts Act 1980 as if it were an order requiring the other person to produce the child to him. In order to enforce the order he must first serve a copy of the residence order upon the other person. The use of this remedy does not prevent the person with the residence order from pursuing any other remedy that may be open to him.

Another way in which a residence (or indeed a contact) order may be enforced is by using s. 34 of the Family Law Act 1986. The object of s. 34 of the Family Law Act 1986 is to give effect to the decision of the court that a child should be given up into the care of a person in accordance with the residence order (or that a child be given up to a person for a period of contact). The Family Law Act 1986 refers to the enforcement of 'custody' and 'access' orders. However, the Children Act 1989, sch. 13, para. 62 makes provision for s. 34, Family Law Act 1986 to apply to residence and contact orders too.

3.6 Discharge of residence orders

(a) A residence order will usually end upon the child in question attaining the age of 16 (s. 91(10)).

(b)   If a residence order is made in favour of parents, each of whom have parental responsibility for the child, it will cease to have effect if they live together for a continuous period of more than six months (s. 11(5)).

(c)   If a care order is made in respect of a child, then any residence order (together with any other s. 8 orders) will be discharged automatically (s. 91(2)). Conversely, if a child in care is made the subject of a residence order then the care order will be discharged automatically (s. 91(1)).

4   CONTACT ORDERS

Contact orders replace the old access order. They require the person with whom the child is living to allow the child to visit or stay with the person named in the order, or for that person and the child otherwise to have contact with each other. Where the parties are unable to agree over the degree of contact which the non-residential parent should have with the child either party may ask the court to determine the contact arrangements. This is called making an application for 'defined contact'. Application is usually made by the non-residential parent who is not being allowed to see the child as much as he would like. However, where a defined contact order has already been made, the residential parent can apply to have contact redefined, or even stopped, if she feels that it is having a bad effect on the children. Normally applications are for definition of regular contact visits but, even where the normal contact visits are working satisfactorily, the court can be asked to resolve a particular issue over contact (for example, whether there should be contact on Christmas Day).

The usual form of order will be for 'reasonable contact', and if for some reason it is not appropriate or practicable for the child to visit the named person then it is open to the court to order other forms of contact, e.g. telephone calls, letters or visits by the named person *to* the child. It is a growing principle of recent case law that contact should not be refused between parent and child unless absolutely necessary in the child's interests (see *Re B (minors: access)* [1992] 1 FLR 140 and *Re H (minors: access)* [1992] 1 FLR 148). However, the relevance of a blood tie in contact disputes has been recently explored in *Re C* [1992] 1 FLR 306. The applicant for access was not the child's father, although the child had believed him to be her father at one time. The mother had formed a relationship with another man (who was not the child's father either). The recorder refused the application on the basis that in the long term it would be disruptive to the child and contrary to her welfare. The Court of Appeal upheld the decision, rejecting the applicant's claim that because he had lived with the child for a period of time as her father there must be a compelling reason to justify denying him access. The Court of Appeal held that the existence of a blood tie was an important factor because children, as they grow up, are likely to want to get to know their natural parents. Thus in such a case although the short term prognosis of contact might indicate that it would not be beneficial the long term considerations might prevail. These long term considerations were not present where there was no blood relationship and therefore its absence was a significant factor to be examined when assessing the course most appropriate for the welfare of the child. The observations in this case are likely to be relevant to cases concerning contact by non-parents generally. Such cases are likely to become more common as a result of the Children Act 1989 which makes it possible for all interested parties to seek s. 8 orders (with the leave of the court where appropriate).

4.1 What may a person with a contact order do to safeguard the welfare of the child while he is in his care?

If the child visits or stays with someone with parental responsibility for him (e.g. a parent, guardian or someone with a residence order) then that person may exercise his parental responsibility in so far as it is not incompatible with any order under the Children Act 1989 (s. 2(8)). If the child visits or stays with someone without parental responsibility (e.g. a grandparent) then that person may take such action as is reasonable to safeguard or promote the child's welfare (s. 3(5)).

4.2 Contact order or split residence order?

There will be occasions when it is not clear whether the appropriate order will be for a residence order in favour of one party with generous contact to the other, or for a split residence order. For example, if a child spends each weekday with one parent and every weekend with the other then a split residence order may be more suitable. If, however, the child lives with one parent for the majority of the time and only sees the other every third weekend then a residence order and contact order will probably be made.

4.3 Restrictions on the making of contact orders

(a) The court must not make a contact order in respect of a child who has reached the age of 16 unless there are exceptional circumstances (s. 9(7)).

(b) Contact orders cannot be made in respect of children who are in local authority care by virtue of a care order, and local authorities may not apply for contact orders nor have them made in their favour (s. 9(2)). However, s. 34, Children Act 1989 does provide a special scheme whereby orders can be made allowing or refusing contact with children in care (see Chapter 29, paragraph 2.7).

(c) A contact order requiring one parent to allow the child to visit the other will lapse automatically if the parents live together for a continuous period of more than six months (s. 11(6)).

(d) The making of a care order will discharge a contact order (and any other s. 8 order): s. 91(2).

4.4 Enforcement of contact orders

The enforcement of contact orders can most easily be dealt with by using s. 34 of the Family Law Act 1986. This remedy is the same as that described for residence orders at paragraph 2.3.5 above. It is a growing principle that contact should not be ended unless absolutely necessary in the interests of the child (*Re B (minors: access)* [1992] 1 FLR 140; *Re H (minors: access)* [1992] 1 FLR 148). Contempt proceedings are not really suitable for enforcing a contact order, and should only be used as the very last resort when the parent with whom the child resides unreasonably refuses contact (*Re N (a minor) (access: penal notices)* [1992] 1 FLR 134).

5 PROHIBITED STEPS ORDERS

A prohibited steps order directs that no step which could be taken by a parent in meeting his parental responsibility for a child, and which is of a kind specified in the order, must be taken by a person without the consent of the court. It aims to incorporate one of the most valuable features of the wardship jurisdiction into proceedings under the Children Act 1989. When a child is made a ward of court it is an automatic consequence that *no* important step may be taken in his life without the leave of the court. Prohibited steps orders differ from wardship in that they require that the actions that are prohibited or the areas over which control is lost to the court must be specified in the order. It is hoped that the availability of this order, together with the new specific issue order, will obviate the need to resort to wardship in many cases. The order can be made either on its own or together with a residence or contact order. It might be used, for example, in a case where no residence order is in force, to restrain one parent from removing the child of the family from the jurisdiction without the consent of the other parent. So far there is, as yet, very little case law in respect of prohibited steps orders. However, one case very recently decided gives a useful illustration of the ways in which such orders will and will not be considered appropriate. *Croydon LBC* v *A* (1992) 136 SJ (LB) 69 (FS) concerned a case where the local authority had removed children from their home under an emergency protection order because the father had sexually abused one of them. The children were placed with foster parents and the local authority applied to the magistrates for an iterim care order. The magistrates refused the interim care order and instead made two prohibited steps orders, the first one preventing the father from seeing the children and the second prohibiting him from having contact with the mother. The authority appealed and Hollings J held that the second order was beyond the scope of the Children Act 1989 because the act of the father in contacting the mother did not fall within the statutory definition of a 'step which could be taken by a parent in meeting his parental responsibility for a child'. In the circumstances, Hollings J found that since the parents were in continuous contact with one another the proposed orders would not protect the children in any event. Therefore, the authority's appeal was allowed and an interim care order was made instead.

5.1 Restrictions on the use of prohibited steps orders

(a) A prohibited steps order may not be made in respect of children over the age of 16, save in exceptional circumstances (s. 9(7)).

(b) A prohibited steps order can only relate to an action which is within the power of a parent and does not (unlike wardship) appear to bind the child or give the court control over the decisions which the child is entitled to take for himself.

(c) A prohibited steps order cannot be made in respect of a child in the care of a local authority pursuant to a care order (s. 9(1)).

(d) A prohibited steps order cannot be used as a 'back-door' method of achieving a result which could have been achieved by the making of a residence or contact order (s. 9(5)(a)).

(e) A prohibited steps order cannot be used in any way which is denied to the High Court by s. 100(2) in the exercise of its inherent jurisdiction with respect to children eg. to commit a child to care, to require a local authority to accommodate a child or to give the local authority power to make decisions about children. The order could not be used to prevent the child's removal from care where there is no care order, but it could be used to prevent someone from visiting the child in a foster home in such circumstances (see ss. 100(2) and 9(5)(b)).

(f) The making of a care order will discharge a prohibited steps order (s. 91(2)).

6 SPECIFIC ISSUE ORDERS

Specific issue orders, like prohibited steps orders, are designed to be made either on their own or together with a residence or contact order. It enables the court to give directions to determine a specific issue which has arisen, or which may arise, in connection with any aspect of parental responsibility for a child, e.g. the decision to change the child's surname, choice of schools, religious upbringing, medical treatment.

This new provision extends to disputes involving non-parents, including some involving local authorities, e.g. sterilization or abortion in relation to a child in care. The court could either take the relevant decision itself or direct that it should be determined by others, e.g. that a child be treated as a specified doctor deems appropriate.

6.1 Restrictions on the making of specific issue orders

The restrictions are the same as those described for prohibited steps orders at paragraph 5.1 above.

7 INTERIM ORDERS AND SUPPLEMENTARY PROVISIONS

The supplementary provisions set out in s. 11(3) and (7) of the Children Act 1989 are intended to preserve the greatest possible flexibility of the court's powers in relation to s. 8 orders so that the court can make interim orders, delay implementation of orders or attach other special conditions to orders where the circumstances call for it. The court can, for example, direct that the order be made to have effect for a specified period, or contain provisions which are to have effect for a specified period.

7.1 When will an interim application be appropriate?

Section 11(3), Children Act 1989 states that where the court has power to make a s. 8 order, it may do so at any time during the course of the proceedings in question even though it is not in a position to dispose finally of those proceedings.

The solicitor should always consider applying for an interim order where the parties are unable to agree about residence or contact. The longer the period that elapses during which the client does not have residence/contact, the more damage is done to his long-term application and an interim application should therefore be made if it is felt that it will secure residence/contact for the client in advance of the full hearing. However, it should be stressed that the normal approach of the court on an interim residence hearing is to maintain the status quo unless there are strong reasons against this. Thus where one party has in fact had the child residing with him for some time (even if not by virtue of a court order), the court is unlikely to order the child to be transferred to the other party pending the full hearing.

Example 1. Mr and Mrs Jones separate. They are in the process of a divorce. The children remain in the matrimonial home with Mrs Jones. Six months later Mr Jones manages to secure a house for himself and wishes the children to live with him. He intends to make an application for a residence order and wishes to seek an interim residence order meanwhile. His application will almost certainly fail.

Example 2. The facts are as in Example 1. Fed up with waiting, Mr Jones fails to return the children after a contact visit and keeps them at his flat. Mrs Jones makes an application for an interim residence order in respect of the children. The court takes the view that the children should be returned to Mrs Jones pending a final hearing as this was the status quo before the snatch. She is therefore granted an interim residence order.

The court is more likely to make an interim order defining contact than transferring the residence of the children. If a parent who wishes to seek a long-term order for residence or contact is being denied any, or any regular contact, with the children, application should usually be made for interim contact in order to ensure that his full application will not be prejudiced because he has lost touch with the children.

Example 3. The facts are as in Example 1 above. Mr Jones is being refused any access to the children. Although Mr Jones is unlikely to be granted an interim residence order in respect of the children, he should apply for interim contact in an attempt to preserve close contact with the children. Depending on the reasons that Mrs Jones puts forward for her attitude, the chances are that an interim contact order will be made.

It can also be very valuable for the court hearing a final contact application if a few interim visits have taken place during the run-up to the case in order that their effect can be assessed. If there is real concern as to the children's attitude to access, the court may order these visits to be supervised by a welfare officer who can then report to the court.

If a parent with a residence order in respect of the children has been ordered to afford reasonable contact or defined contact to the other parent, she should not thereafter stop contact visits of her own accord. If she does so she will be in breach of the contact order and liable to be brought before the court with a view to committal for contempt (although other methods of enforcing orders are preferred to committal proceedings except as a last resort). The proper course if she is worried about contact continuing is for her to make an application to have contact stopped and, in the meanwhile, to seek an interim order to this effect. In practice, a parent who is genuinely worried about the effect of contact on the children will normally simply refuse to let the children go, leaving it up to the other party to decide whether to take the matter back to court to obtain an order for defined contract or to enforce the existing defined contact arrangements. A parent who has stopped access or is contemplating doing so must, however, be warned that it will weigh heavily against her in any applications concerning the children if it is found that she has done so without good reason.

7.2 Use of other supplementary provisions

The court can use its powers under s. 11(7) in other ways:

> **Example 1.** Mr and Mrs Jones are divorcing. Mr Jones has moved to Coventry. Each of them applies for a residence order in respect of their son, Tom, aged 12. Tom is presently at school near to the former matrimonial home in Exeter where Mrs Jones still lives. The court hears the dispute in May 1992 and decides that Tom should move to live with his father. Tom is just about to take his school examinations. Therefore the court *delays implementation* of the order to allow Tom to finish the school term at his present school. The court directs that the residence order will take effect on 1 August 1992.

The court could also use the supplementary provisions to order a gradual build-up of contact in circumstances where a child had not seen the person concerned for a long time.

7.3 Procedure for an interim application

(a) Legal aid: the question of costs must be sorted out before embarking on an interim application . If the matter is truly urgent, application can be made for an emergency certificate to cover the interim application. However, the solicitor may find the legal aid authorities reluctant to grant such a certificate unless there are very special circumstances (for example, where the other party has snatched the child from the *de facto* care of the client and refuses to return him). If no emergency certificate is forthcoming, the solicitor will have to await the granting of a full legal aid certificate before taking action.

(b) The normal method of application for an interim order will be by filing the appropriate application form and asking the court for an early hearing date before a nominated family judge. The hearing itself will be in chambers and is likely to be brief. It follows the normal pattern but any evidence given by the parties and witnesses is likely to be short. As well as announcing his decision as to who should have a residence/contact order pending the final hearing, the court will usually order a welfare report. Other directions can be requested if they are required (for example, a direction that the parties should file sworn statements within a certain period).

(c) Note that the FPR 1991 and the FPC(CA 1989)R 1991 do not appear to provide for applications for residence and contact orders to be made ex parte, whereas ex parte applications for prohibited steps and specific issue orders are expressly permitted (see r. 4.4 FPR 1991 and r. 4 FPC(CA 1989)R 1991). However, the FPR 1991, rr. 4.14 and 4.15 and the FPC(CA 1989)R 1991, rr. 14 and 15 do permit the court to vary time limits and deal with urgent cases. Those provisions may allow the time for service of applications for residence and contact orders to be abridged, but as yet the precise position is not clear.

8 SETTLING RESIDENCE AND CONTACT DISPUTES

It is of the utmost importance that the parties should be encouraged to resolve their differences over residence and contact. Bitter disputes between parents cause a great deal of distress to children, particularly if a full court hearing has to be held to delve into all the issues. The Family Mediation Service, which is affiliated to the National Family Conciliation Council, is located at:

43 New Cavendish Street
London WlM 7RG

Telephone: 071 935 1651

This can be a valuable service to help parents negotiate a proper parenting relationship after divorce.

Furthermore, the practitioner should be aware of the availability of conciliation meetings held before the district judge, usually with the welfare officer in attendance. The contents of such meetings are confidential and privileged. They may well assist in a settlement of the issues and avoid the necessity for a contested hearing. The procedure is contained in a Practice Direction set out at [1992] 1 FLR 228.

It should be remembered at all times that one of the fundamental principles of the Children Act 1989 is that the court should make no order at all unless it considers that to make an order would be better for the child than making no order at all (s. 1(5)). If, therefore, the parties do reach a compromise and the court takes the view that there is a realistic possibility of it working then the court may well be reluctant to embody the agreement in any form of court order, whether by consent or otherwise.

9 VARIATION OF SECTION 8 ORDERS

The court has power to make new s. 8 orders from time to time and to vary or discharge existing orders. A party who seeks to vary an existing order must file the appropriate application form and apply for a hearing. Naturally the court will not make a new order if nothing has changed since the original order was made.

10 FAMILY ASSISTANCE ORDERS

The Children Act 1989 introduces the new 'family assistance order' which is designed to involve a probation officer (or officer of the local authority) for a *short period* in helping a family at a time of marital breakdown. Under the old law the court was able to make the more powerful 'supervision order' in custody proceedings, but such orders will no longer be available to the court in Children Act 1989 proceedings unless the statutory care grounds in s. 31 of the Act have been proved (i.e. that the child is suffering, or is likely to suffer, significant harm etc.)

Family assistance orders may only be made in *exceptional circumstances* and with the *agreement* of all those involved (except the child): s. 16(3) and (7). There is no need for the court to make a s. 8 order as a prerequisite to granting a family assistance order (s. 16(1)), but the supervisor may refer the matter back to the court if there is a s. 8 order in force (s. 16(6)). However, he may only refer back to issues relating to existing s. 8 orders and cannot therefore take steps for the child's committal to care. Where the case is referred back to court then the court may make any s. 8 order (s. 10(1)(b)), subject to the restrictions contained in

s. 9, Children Act 1989; the officer would not need to make an application. When the officer is concerned about the child's well-being he should refer the case to the local authority for investigation under s. 47(1)(b), Children Act 1989.

11   PROCEDURE FOR SECTION 8 ORDERS

The court has power to make s. 8 orders either:

(a)   in the course of any 'family proceedings' (as defined by s. 8(3): s. 10(1)); or
(b)   on a free-standing application: s. 10(2).

Where a question as to a child's welfare arises as part of s. 8 proceedings the court has power to make a s. 8 order of its own motion in spite of the fact that no application has been made for such an order (s. 10(1)(b)).

The general outline of procedures to be adopted in Children Act 1989 proceedings will be found in Chapter 25, paragraph 6. The authors intend here only to highlight the most important points as they relate to s. 8 proceedings.

11.1   Applications within divorce proceedings

Where one or both parties to divorce proceedings decide to apply for a residence order (or any other s. 8 orders) then they should (each) make an application by using form CHA 10D. Note that if there is more than one child then a separate form must be used for each child. The matter will then be heard within the current divorce proceedings and dealt with by the appropriate county court judge.

If the petitioner (say, the wife) knows that the respondent will not agree to the children continuing to live with her then she should seek a residence order in the prayer of her petition. However, that will not be sufficient to put her application into effect. She must then go on to file a full application in Form CHA 10D. If there is more than one child then a separate form must be used for each child. If the respondent wishes to make an application in his own right for a s. 8 order then he is quite at liberty to file a Form CHA 10D too, setting out his alternative proposals for the child(ren).

The divorce will then be processed by the district judge, who will be relieved of the burden of considering the arrangements for the children pursuant to s. 41, Matrimonial Causes Act 1973 (see Chapter 8, paragraph 13). The contested s. 8 orders will then be referred to the county court judge for hearing.

11.2   Free-standing applications for residence orders

A person who wishes to make a free-standing application for a residence order (or any other s. 8 order) should do so by completing Form CHA 10. The rules for service of the application will be found in r. 4.8 of the FPR 1991 and r. 8 of the FPC(CA 1989)R 1991. The application may be made to the magistrates' court, county court or High Court. If the applicant is in receipt of legal aid then his certificate will usually contain a restriction that the proceedings should be commenced in the magistrates' court since that will normally be the cheapest route. However, if there are any other proceedings already afoot in relation to the relevant children then the new proceedings should be consolidated with them so that all matters are heard together. Note that if there is more than one child a separate form must be used for each child.

11.3   Applicants

The categories of persons who can apply automatically for s. 8 orders, and those who may only apply with leave are set out fully in paragraph 2.1, above.

11.4   Respondents

Those persons who must be made respondents to an application are set out in tabular form in the FPR 1991, Appendix 1 and FPC(CA 1989)R 1991, sch. 2. They are as follows:

(a)   every person whom the applicant believes to have parental responsibility for the child;
(b)   where the child is the subject of a care order, every person whom the applicant believes to have had parental responsibility immediately prior to the making of the care order;
(c)   if the application is to extend, vary or discharge an order, the parties to the proceedings leading to the original order which the applicant seeks to have extended, varied or discharged.

11.5   Service

The applicant must serve a copy of the application, endorsed with the date, time and place for a hearing or directions appointment on each respondent at least 21 days before the hearing or directions appointment (FPR 1991, r. 4.4(1) and FPC(CA 1989)R 1991, r. 4(1)). The rules for service will be found at FPR 1991, r. 4.8 and FPC(CA 1989)R 1991, r. 8.

11.6   Persons who must be given written notice

At the same time as effecting service of the application on the relevant respondents the applicant must give written notice of the application and of the date, time and place of the hearing or directions appointment to those persons set out in FPR 1991, Appendix 3 and FPC(CA 1989)R 1991, sch. 2. They are as follows:

(a)   the local authority providing accommodation for the child;
(b)   persons who are caring for the child at the time when the proceedings are commenced;
(c)   if the child is in a refuge, then the person providing the refuge;
(d)   every person whom the applicant believes:

(i)   to be named in a current court order with respect to the child, (unless the applicant believes the order is not relevant to the present application);
(ii)   to be a party in pending proceedings in respect of the child (unless the applicant believes the pending proceedings not to be relevant to the present application);
(iii)   to be a person with whom the child has lived for a period of at least three years prior to the application.

11.7   Answer to application

Each respondent must file and serve on the parties an answer to the application within 14 days of being served with it. He must file his answer on Form CHA 10A (FPR 1991, r. 4.9 and FPC(CA 1989)R 1991, r. 9).

11.8 Withdrawal of an application

The general rules apply. See Chapter 25, paragraph 6.3.

11.9 Transfer of proceedings

Section 8 proceedings are 'relevant proceedings' for the purpose of the transfer of proceedings from one court to another vertically or horizontally. The general rules apply. See Chapter 25, paragraph 5.2

11.10 Directions

The court can give such directions as are necessary for the conduct of the proceedings, e.g. timing, service of documents, joinder of parties, preparation of welfare reports, submission of evidence, appointment of guardian ad litem/ solicitor, attendance of the child, transfer of proceedings and consolidation of proceedings. For a full discussion of the procedure to be adopted and the matters upon which the court may issue directions, see Chapter 25, paragraph 6.10 and 6.12.

11.11 Timetable

The court will bear in mind at all times the general principles of the Children Act 1989, and in particular the principle that any delay in proceedings is likely to be prejudicial to the welfare of the child. Section 11(1), Children Act 1989 requires the court to draw up a timetable for the conduct of s. 8 proceedings with a view to obviating any unnecessary delay. It is also empowered to give such directions as are necessary to ensure that the timetable is adhered to (for further details as to timing see Chapter 25, paragraph 6.11).

11.12 Documentary evidence

For a general discussion as to the provisions for documentary evidence made by the Children Act 1989 see Chapter 25, paragraph 6.13. For details of the rules relating to expert evidence of a medical or psychiatric examination of the child see Chapter 25, paragraph 6.14.

Note that r. 4.17 of the FPR 1991 and r. 17 of the FPC(CA 1989)R 1991 require that in proceedings for s. 8 orders a party must file *no* document *other* than as required or authorised by the rules without leave of the court. This aims to prevent information being set down in writing which may only serve to inflame an already volatile situation and thus may prevent a sensible settlement of the matter. If, however, it becomes clear that a contested hearing is inevitable then the court will make directions that allow further evidence to be filed, e.g. witness statements.

As and when it becomes necessary for further evidence to be filed then it would be advisable for the party applying for the residence (or other s. 8 order) to file a sworn statement dealing not only with the merits of his own application but also with any matters raised by the other party in his application/statement.

Great care must be taken over the preparation of a party's statements. The court will read them before it hears the application and they will therefore colour the court's initial approach to the case. For this reason it is important that statements are reasonably comprehensive and read clearly. The following matters should be covered if possible:

(a)   The proposed living arrangements for the child (where he will live, who else will be living there, who will look after him when the parent is not available, etc.). If the parent proposes to move in the foreseeable future, his proposed new arrangements should also be covered. The more definite they are, the better. Indeed, if the parent can actually be installed in the new accommodation before the hearing it will be helpful as the welfare officer may then have an opportunity to visit the accommodation and report on it to the court. It is particularly important that a parent should investigate and, if possible, try to arrange alternative accommodation if his present circumstances are unsuitable for the children. If he is awaiting council accommodation he should be in a position to produce to the court a letter from the council dealing with his place on the waiting list and his prospects of obtaining housing.

(b)   The proposed arrangements for school. If the parent is seeking a transfer of residence to him, he should point out if the child can stay at the same school or, if this is not possible, he should state what alternative arrangements are available. This will mean him doing some homework himself in visiting the schools in his area, checking whether they can take the child, etc. If he does make this effort, it will help to give the impression that he is a conscientious and caring parent and really does wish to have the child living with him. If the child is below school age, opportunities for nursery education, playgroups, etc. in the parent's area should be investigated.

(c)   Where the parent lives with or has a close relationship with a new partner, the statement should inform the court how the child gets on with the new partner.

(d)   If there are any problems over the child's health, these should be outlined in the statement and, if possible, a medical report should be exhibited.

(e)   The parent's attitude to contact and also that of the child should be dealt with. For example, it will clearly help a parent's application for a residence order if he has had frequent regular contact with the child for prolonged periods and the child has enjoyed it. It will also be in his favour if he is prepared to facilitate generous contact between the child and the other parent if he obtains a residence order. The courts are disapproving of parents who try to turn the child against the other parent or to disrupt contact arrangements.

(f)   Any views that the child has expressed about residence and contact. Obviously, what is said on this score will be viewed cautiously by the court, particularly if the child is young. However, it is worth mentioning in the statement if the child has made more than a throw-away remark.

(g)   Any worries that the parent has about the care the other parent is giving/would give to the child. It must be emphasised that it is advisable to avoid an endless catalogue of minor grumbles about the other parent's standard of care. In particular it is not generally appropriate to go into the question of who is to blame for the breakdown of the marriage or to detail the circumstances in which the marriage broke down. Throwing mud at the other parent only encourages mud-slinging in return and simply irritates the court. However, if there are *genuine* worries that really do relate to the children and not to the unfortunate situation between the parents, these must be set out fully in the statement.

(h)   If the other party's statement has already been served, the statement should incorporate comments on the matters contained in it if the deponent has any to make.

The most important statements in a dispute over residence or contact are obviously from the parties themselves. However, each side is free to file and serve other statements if appropriate (see paragraph 11.14 below).

11.13 Welfare officer's report

A welfare officer's report will usually be ordered where there are to be contested s. 8 proceedings. The court may refer the case of its own motion to a welfare officer for investigation (s. 7(1)). Where a welfare report is ordered then the report should be filed at least five days before the hearing for which it has been commissioned. Furthermore, there is a presumption that the welfare officer must attend each directions appointment and hearing unless the court has ordered otherwise (FPR 1991, r. 4.13 and FPC(CA 1989)R 1991, r. 13).

If a welfare report is not ordered automatically then one of the parties should request the district judge or justices' clerk, by way of a directions hearing, to refer the matter for a report (see Chapter 25, paragraph 6.20). This must be done early on in the proceedings since it normally takes several weeks (or even months) for a report to be prepared. The party wishing for the report may find that if he delays his request for a report for too long the court may take the view that the advantages to the court of having the report for the hearing are outweighed by the disadvantages to the child of having to wait for too long for a resolution of the case; in that case the court would refuse the request for the report, in the interests of the child.

The welfare officer will be able to inspect the court file relating to the case on which there will, of course, be copies of all the statements filed in relation to the dispute. He will therefore be aware of what the issues between parties are. He will see both parties (often on several occasions) preferably in their homes and with and without the children present. The impression that the welfare officer forms of a parent is vital and the client must therefore be warned to cooperate with the welfare officer fully and make him or her welcome. The welfare officer will also see the children on their own if they are old enough for this to be of benefit. In addition he will make whatever other enquiries seem to be appropriate in the particular case. For example, he may well visit the children's school as problems at home are often reflected in behaviour at school; he may see other relations; he will contact any social workers who have been involved with the family, etc. Having carried out his investigations, the welfare officer will prepare what is usually a lengthy report for the court setting out the investigations he has made and the conclusions he has reached. The report may make a recommendation as to who should have a residence order.

It will be noted that welfare reports often contain a lot of what would traditionally be classed as hearsay evidence (for example, 'I spoke to the child's form-teacher who told me that she is often distressed at school the day after a contact visit with her father . . .'). The court will receive such evidence in children's cases and attach to it whatever weight it thinks fit (see Chapter 25, paragraph 6.21). The parties' solicitors should be fortunate enough to receive copies of the report prior to the hearing so that they can take instructions from their clients on it and review the witnesses that they were intending to call in the light of the investigations the welfare officer has made. It may be necessary to cross-examine the officer if, for example, the officer has misreported conversations with the client or has made a clear recommendation in favour of the other party on grounds which the solicitor feels to be unsound. If the welfare officer does make recommendations which are in favour of the other party, the solicitor should consider seriously with the client whether he wishes to proceed with his application. Looking at things realistically, it is almost always an uphill battle to obtain a residence order if the welfare officer is against you.

If the report is not available before the hearing, it will certainly be disclosed on the day and practitioners should ensure that they ask for sufficient time to go through it thoroughly with their client before embarking on the hearing.

11.14   Other evidence

The solicitor should consider in good time whether any evidence other than that of the party should be obtained for the hearing. For example, where someone other than the parent (for example, a new spouse or a grandparent) is going to assist in the care of the child, there must be evidence from that person. If a parent is concerned about the standard of care that the other party would provide or about his or her lifestyle, consideration should be given to obtaining evidence from independent witnesses on these points. For example, the child's school might be approached in a case where it is alleged that the child is not properly fed, clothed and kept clean. However, in determining whether to call further witnesses, it must be borne in mind that the welfare officer's report is likely to deal with a number of the matters that are of concern and it may be possible to rely simply on this without calling further evidence. A final decision as to this can only be taken once the welfare officer's report has been seen.

Generally speaking it is not a good tactical move to call a string of witnesses unless their evidence really does further the client's case. The solicitor will have the advantage of seeing the potential witnesses and evaluating their evidence for himself. A statement should be prepared for each of those who are to give evidence and should preferably be filed at court and served on the other side before the hearing. In addition, unless the other side indicate that they accept the evidence of the witness, the witness should be warned to attend the hearing. In particular it is vital that (whatever the attitude of the other side to her evidence) anyone who is to help in looking after the child is present at court to give oral evidence. If there is a last-minute witness, it may be possible to call oral evidence at the hearing without having filed and served a statement previously provided that the court gives leave.

Sometimes a potential witness may be reluctant to get involved. The solicitor should be wary of such witnesses – their evidence can often turn out to be less valuable than the client expects.

11.15   Attendance of parties

For the general rules as to the attendance of parties at hearings and directions appointments see Chapter 25, paragraph 6.12.

11.16   The hearing

For the general rules as to how the hearing will be conducted see Chapter 25, paragraph 6.17. However, it should be noted that a hearing before the High Court or a county court will be in chambers (FPR 1991, r. 4.16(7)), and a hearing before the magistrates' court may be held in private (FPC(CA 1989)R 1991, r. 16(7)).

The various factors which the court must consider in relation to the case are set out extensively in Chapter 25, paragraph 2. In general, the court must bear in mind that the child's welfare is paramount. When hearing contested s. 8 proceedings the court must apply the statutory checklist of 'welfare factors' contained in s. 1(3). Furthermore, it must have regard to the general principle that any delay in deciding the case is likely to be prejudicial to the welfare of the child (s. 1(2)). Finally, the court must have regard to the whole range of orders available to it (not just the order specifically applied for), but must not make any order unless satisfied that to make an order would be better for the child than making no order at all (s. 1(5)).

11.17 Oral evidence

The court, proper officer or justices' clerk must keep a note of the substance of any oral evidence given at a hearing or directions appointment (FPR 1991, r. 4.20 and FPC(CA 1989)R 1991, r. 20).

11.18 Hearsay evidence

Hearsay evidence is now admissible in civil proceedings before the High Court, county court or magistrates' court when given in connection with the upbringing, maintenance or welfare of a child. See Chapter 25, paragraph 6.21 for further details.

11.19 The decision

After the final hearing the court must make its decision 'as soon as practicable' (FPR 1991, r. 4.21(3) and FPC(CA 1989)R 1991, r. 21(4)). When making an order or refusing an application the court must state any findings of fact and the reasons for the court's decision (FPR 1991, r. 4.21(4) and FPC(CA 1989)R 1991, r. 21(6)). If a s. 8 order is made, it must be recorded in the appropriate Form and as soon as possible the justices' clerk or the proper officer of the court must serve a copy of the order on the parties and on any person with whom the child is living (FPR 1991, r. 4.21(5) and (6) and FPC(CA 1989)R 1991, r. 21(7)).

11.20 Power of court to direct investigation by local authority

If, during the course of hearing proceedings for a s. 8 order (or, indeed, in the course of any family proceedings, as defined by s. 8(3)), it becomes apparent to the court that the circumstances of the child may merit the making of a care or supervision order, then the court has power to direct the local authority to investigate (s. 37(1)). Where the court decides to give that direction then the local authority must carry out the appropriate inquiries in respect of the child and must consider whether they should do one of the following:

(a) apply for a care or supervision order;
(b) provide services or assistance for the child or his family; or
(c) take any other action with respect to the child (s. 37(2)).

If, in due course, the authority decide not to apply for a care or supervision order in respect of the child they must, within a period of eight weeks of the direction being made, inform the court of the following matters:

(a) the reasons for their decision;
(b) any service or assistance they have provided, or intend to provide, for the child or his family;
(c) any other action they have taken, or propose to take, with respect to the child (s. 37(3)).

In the event that the authority decide *not* to apply for a care or supervision order they must consider whether it would be appropriate to review the case at a later date, and if so, when (s. 37(6)).

11.21 Appeals

The question of appeals is dealt with fully in Chapter 25 at paragraph 6.18.

12 TRANSITIONAL PROVISIONS

The general rule is that 'existing orders' (as defined in sch. 14, para. 5(1), Children Act 1989: NB they do not include care orders) will continue despite the new legislation, save where a successful application is made to the court for:

(a) a residence order or a care order, or
(b) discharge of the order in question.

Proceedings which are already pending at the date when the Children Act 1989 came into force (i.e. 14 October 1991) will continue under the old legislation and old-style orders will be made in respect of them (sch. 14, para. 1(1)).

The court will not be prevented from making an order under Part II of the Children Act 1989 even though there is an 'existing order' in force (sch. 14, para. 11(2)), e.g. if the mother has obtained a custody order in relation to the child under the old legislation there would be nothing to stop the father from applying for a contact order after 14 October 1991. The old custody order and the new contact order can happily run side by side.

The court also has power to discharge existing orders where the welfare of the child so demands (sch. 14, para. 11(3) to (6)). For example, if the mother has obtained a custody order in relation to the child under the old legislation, then the father could apply for a residence order after 14 October 1991. If the court decided to grant his application it could discharge the 'existing custody order' and replace it with the new residence order.

If there is an 'existing access order' under the old legislation but one of the parties, after 14 October 1991 wishes to vary it, then the appropriate course is to apply for a contact order (i.e. not for a variation of the old access order).

13 FINANCIAL PROVISION AND PROPERTY ADJUSTMENT FOR CHILDREN

Section 15, Children Act 1989, together with sch. 1 of the Act, set out the provisions whereby the court can order financial provision for children. The new provisions do not replace those in the Matrimonial Causes Act 1973 or the Domestic Proceedings and Magistrates' Courts Act 1978. They mainly incorporate those provisions which were formerly contained in the Guardianship of Minors Act 1971, the Guardianship Act 1973 and the Children Act 1975 (all of which are now repealed).

13.1 'Financial provision' comes within definition of 'family proceedings'

An application for financial provision comes within the definition of 'family proceedings' for the purposes of the Children Act 1989. Therefore, a court hearing such an application may make residence or contact orders (or any other s. 8 order) if it considers such orders should be made (s. 10(1)).

13.2 Who is under an obligation to pay?

The obligation to pay lies only upon parents and step-parents.

'Parents' include the child's natural mother and father and also any party to a marriage (whether or not subsisting) in relation to whom the child concerned is a child of the family (sch. 1, para. 16(2)).

'Child' includes a child over 18 where an application is made under sch. 1, para. 2 or 6 (sch. 1, para. 16(1)).

'Child of the family' is defined in s. 105(1) as being, in relation to the parties to a marriage:

(a)   a child of both those parties;

(b)   any other child, not being a child who is placed with those parties as foster parents by a local authority or voluntary organization, who has been treated by both of those parties as a child of their family.

When deciding whether or not to exercise its powers against a person who is not the mother or father of the child, the court must have regard to:

(a)   whether that person had assumed responsibility for the maintenance of the child and, if so, the extent to which and basis on which he assumed that responsibility and the length of period during which he assumed that responsibility and the length of the period during which he met that responsibility;

(b)   whether he did so knowing that the child was not his child;

(c)   the liability of any other person to maintain the child.

13.3 Who can apply for payment?

Parents, including unmarried mothers, unmarried fathers without parental responsibility, guardians and people with a residence order will be able to apply for a range of orders in relation to children (sch. 1, para. 1(1)).

13.4 What orders are available?

An application can be made on behalf of a child to *any* court for periodical payments and/or a lump sum. However, applications on behalf of a child for secured periodical payments, settlements and property transfer orders can only be made to the High Court or county court (sch. 1, para. 1(1) and (2)). It is not possible for repeated applications for settlements and property transfer orders to be made by the same person in relation to the same child; only one such order may be made (sch. 1, para. 1(5)(b)).

As a general rule orders for financial provision will end upon the child attaining the age of 17. However, provision can be made for orders to extend until the child reaches 18 or beyond (sch. 1, paras. 2 and 3).

13.5 What matters will the court consider when making an order for financial provision?

The list of factors to which the court must have regard in considering whether or not to order financial provision for a child are set out in sch. 1, para. 4. The factors include the income, earning capacity, property and other financial resources of the parents, the applicant and any other person in whose favour the court proposes to make the order, together with their financial needs, obligations and responsibilities; the financial needs of the child; the income, earning capacity, property and other financial resources of the child; any physical or mental disability of the child;. the manner in which the child was being, or was expected to be, educated or trained.

13.6 Variation of orders for financial relief

The provisions for variation of periodical payments are contained in sch. 1, para. 6.

13.7 Interim orders

The court has power to make interim orders for financial provision in respect of a child and the relevant provisions are to be found in sch. 1, para. 9. There are no time-limits imposed by the statute upon interim orders and provision is made for orders to be renewed from time to time. This reflects the principle that all orders are really interim because the needs and circumstances of children are always changing. The court is given power to make further orders for periodical payments and lump sums after the original application has been determined. However, property adjustment orders remain a 'once and for all' provision.

14 LEGAL AID

The availability of legal aid for Children Act 1989 proceedings is fully set out in Chapter 2, paragraph 23.

27 Wardship

1 WHAT DOES WARDSHIP MEAN?

The wardship jurisdiction of the court is used to protect the interests of children. Parental responsibility for a child who is a ward vests in the court. Day-to-day care and control of the ward will be given to an individual (often one of the child's parents) or to a local authority, but no important step can be taken in the child's life without the court's consent and, if necessary, the court can give particular directions during the wardship to safeguard the welfare of the child.

Wardship proceedings are 'family proceedings' within the Children Act 1989 since they are part of the inherent jurisdiction of the High Court (s. 8(3)(a)). Therefore, when the court is hearing wardship proceedings it may make any of the orders available to it under the Children Act 1989, save for those which it is prohibited from making by the Act itself. Therefore, provided that the child is not in the care of a local authority by virtue of a care order the court in wardship may make the following:

(a)   a residence order;
(b)   a contact order;
(c)   a prohibited steps order;
(d)   a specific issue order;
(e)   it may appoint a guardian where a child has no parent with parental responsibility for him, or a parent or guardian with a residence order died while the order was in force;
(f)   a family assistance order where the circumstances of the Children Act 1989, s. 16 are satisfied;
(g)   a care or supervision order on the application of a local authority (or other qualified applicant), provided that the statutory criteria in s. 31 are satisfied (N.B. upon the making of such a care order the child will cease to be a ward);
(h)   an order for financial provision in respect of the child whether or not any application has been made for it (see Children Act 1989, s. 15(1) as amended by the Courts and Legal Services Act 1990, sch. 16, para. 10, and sch. 20 repealing the Family Law Reform Act 1969, s. 6).

2 IMPACT OF THE CHILDREN ACT 1989 ON WARDSHIP

The Children Act 1989 has had a significant impact upon the inherent jurisdiction of the High Court. By introducing a flexible range of s. 8 orders, i.e. residence, contact, prohibited steps and specific issue orders, the Children Act

1989 has incorporated the most valuable features of the wardship jurisdiction within its own proceedings. The likely result of this is that there will be very few cases in which it will still be necessary to resort to the wardship jurisdiction. The Children Act 1989 procedure is generally cheaper, quicker and simpler than that for wardship proceedings.

2.1   Wardship and private law proceedings

In private law proceedings the Children Act 1989 makes no restriction on the use of wardship in private disputes not involving local authorities. However, the wide availability of s. 8 orders should largely obviate the need for the use of wardship in private law proceedings. It may still be useful in certain circumstances, for example, to bypass the requirement for leave to commence a s. 8 application, to gain immediate access to the High Court or to cater for the situation where there is a need for the court to have continuing control over a child's upbringing.

2.2   Wardship and local authorities

2.2.1   *Local authorities must not use the inherent jurisdiction as a method of committing a child into their care or placing him under their supervision*

The Children Act 1989 has severely curtailed the rights of local authorities to use the wardship jurisdiction. Section 100(2), Children Act 1989 prohibits local authorities from resorting to the inherent jurisdiction in general, and the wardship jurisdiction in particular, in order to achieve the admission of a child into their care. It also imposes substantial restrictions on the freedom of local authorities to use wardship for other purposes. As a result of the Children Act 1989 the only way in which a child may be committed into the care, or placed under the supervision, of a local authority is by satisfying the statutory 'threshold' criteria set out in s. 31 of the Act. This reflects one of the main principles behind the Children Act 1989 whereby it is intended that state interference with the upbringing of children should be kept to a minimum wherever possible. Thus, s. 100(1), Children Act 1989 specifically states that s. 7, Family Law Reform Act 1969 (which gave the High Court power to place a ward in the care, or under the supervision, of a local authority) ceases to have effect.

2.2.2   *Inherent jurisdiction must not be used to make a child who is subject to a care order a ward of court*

In pursuance of the same policy, s. 100(2)(c), Children Act 1989 directs that the inherent jurisdiction of the High Court must not be used so as to make a child who is the subject of a care order a ward of court. Formerly, the wardship jurisdiction could be invoked in respect of a child who was in the compulsory care of the local authority, provided that the local authority agreed to it. Their agreement was only bypassed if the ward was committed to care under s. 7(2), Family Law Reform Act 1969; in those circumstances the court retained power to give directions to the local authority on the application of others, e.g. the child's parents. The disadvantage of this was obvious; both the local authority and the court shared responsibility for the child's care and it was never clear exactly what were the local authority's powers in that situation since the authority could not take any major step in the child's life without prior reference to the court. The Children Act 1989 makes wardship and care incompatible. The current position is as follows:

(a)   when a ward is committed to the care of the local authority the wardship ceases to have effect (s. 91(4));
(b)   while a child is in care he cannot be made a ward of court (s. 100(2) and s. 41, Supreme Court Act 1981 as amended by the Children Act 1989, sch. 13, para. 45).

2.2.3   Inherent jurisdiction may not be used to confer on local authority power to determine any question relating to parental responsibility
Section 100(2)(d), Children Act 1989 prohibits the use of the High Court's inherent jurisdiction for the purpose of conferring on any local authority the power to determine any question which has arisen, or which may arise, in connection with any aspect of parental responsibility for a child. This means that, in making an order under its inherent jurisdiction the court cannot confer on the local authority any degree of parental responsibility it does not already have.

2.2.4   Transitional arrangements
The transitional arrangements as they affect wardship and children in the care of local authorities are contained in the Children Act 1989, sch. 14, para. 15 (as amended by the Courts and Legal Services Act 1990, sch. 16, para. 33). Upon the Children Act 1989 coming into force on 14 October 1991 the following consequences ensued.

(a)   Any orders made committing wards into local authority care under:
    (i)   s. 7(2), Family Law Reform Act 1969, or
    (ii)   in the exercise of the High Court's inherent jurisdiction
were *deemed* to be care orders made under the Children Act 1989.
(b)   Where a child is in care as a result of an order made by the High Court in the exercise of its inherent jurisdiction, he *ceased to be a ward* on 14 October 1991 (Children Act 1989, sch. 14, as amended by para. 33(4) of sch. 16, Courts and Legal Services Act 1990 by inserting a new paragraph 16A).
(c)   Where, before 14 October 1991, a child is in care as a result of an order under s. 7(2), Family Law Reform Act 1969 or made in the exercise of the High Court's inherent jurisdiction and continues to be in the care of a local authority and was made a ward of court, he *ceased to be a ward* after 14 October 1991 (Children Act 1989, sch. 14, as amended by the schedule to the Children Act 1989 (Commencement and Transitional Provisions) Order 1991).

However, any *directions* made in the course of such a wardship prior to the commencement of the Children Act 1989 will continue in force until varied or discharged by the court (Children Act 1989, sch. 14, para. 16, as amended by para. 33(3) of sch. 16 of the Courts and Legal Services Act 1990).

If a child is a ward and is in care on 14 October 1991 by virtue of an interim care order made by the High Court in the exercise of its inherent jurisdiction then, whether or not those proceedings could be regarded as pending, they will be deemed to cease to be pending on 14 October 1992. If no final decision has been made about the child on that date then the child will become the subject of a full

Children Act 1989 care order and the wardship will lapse. If a final care order is made by 14 October 1992 then that care order will 'convert' into a Children Act 1989 care order and the wardship will lapse.

2.2.5   When can the local authority use the inherent jurisdiction of the High Court?
The local authority will still be able to resort to the use of the inherent jurisdiction of the High Court for limited purposes, provided that they first seek the leave of the court to do so (s. 100(3)). Leave may only be granted if the court is satisfied that:

(a)   the result which the local authority wish to achieve could not be achieved by the making of any other type of order which the local authority might be entitled to apply for under the statutory code (s. 100(4)(a) and (5)); and

(b)   there is reasonable cause to believe that if the court's inherent jurisdiction is not exercised with respect to the child he is likely to suffer significant harm (s. 100(4)(b)).

The local authority is likely to use the inherent jurisdiction when it seeks the resolution of a specific issue concerning the future of a child in its care. Examples of this might be where they wish to overrule the child (see *Re R, The Times,* 31 July 1991, CA); in sterilisation cases; for injunctions which do not relate to the exercise of parental responsibility; to restrain publicity about the child; for wardship, if only the immediate effects of warding are required.

Where a child is in the care of a local authority the court is prevented from making any s. 8 order in respect of the child, save for a residence order (s. 9(1)). This means that the local authority cannot apply for a prohibited steps or specific issue order in respect of a child in its care. If, however, the child is not in the local authority's care under a care order (e.g. where the child is simply being accommodated by the authority) then the authority could apply for leave to make a specific issue or prohibited steps order in respect of the child. Such an order may be available if the action which the authority wishes to take or prevent falls within the scope of parental responsibility, in which case the authority would not be able to invoke the inherent jurisdiction under s. 100.

3   WHEN SHOULD WARDSHIP BE USED?

3.1   Suitable applicants

No particular relationship is required between the minor and the applicant. Wardship proceedings are therefore open not only to parents of the child concerned but also to other relatives of the child, prospective adopters, people with whom the child has had his home such as foster parents and step-parents, local authorities and their officers, etc. Even the child himself can apply, by his next friend, to be made a ward of court. However, the court will not entertain applications which are an abuse of the process of the court. The applicant is required to state his relationship to or interest in the ward in the originating summons; see paragraph 4.3.2.2 below. Once the originating summons has been issued, particulars of the originating summons will be recorded in the register of wards at the principal registry. If the recording officer is in any doubt as to whether the application is proper, the matter will be referred immediately to the appropriate district judge who, if he considers the application for wardship is an abuse of the process of the court, may dismiss the originating summons forthwith or refer the point to the judge (Practice Direction of 28 February 1967 [1967] 1 All ER 828, [1967] 1 WLR 623).

Example. (The facts of *Re Dunhill* (1967) 111 SJ 113.) A night-club owner made a 20-year-old model a ward, mainly for publicity purposes. The summons was struck out as being frivolous, vexatious and an abuse of the process of the court and the night-club owner was held liable for costs.

3.2   In what type of case?

3.2.1   Kidnapping cases

In the past, wardship proceedings were extremely useful in cases where it was feared that a parent, or indeed some other person, was about to remove a child from England and Wales without the consent of the parent or other person with whom the child was residing. The implementation of the Child Abduction Act 1984 and the new port alert system introduced in 1986 (see Chapter 28) will no doubt reduce the importance of wardship in this area although it may remain important in certain cases, for example, in relation to children of 16 and over.

3.2.2   Wardship as a means of intervening in relation to proposed medical treatment

Wardship can be used as a means of influencing the medical treatment proposed for a child.

Example 1. *(Re D (a minor) (wardship: sterilisation)* [1976] Fam 185, [1976] 1 All ER 326.) D was born with mental and physical handicaps. Her mother was concerned that she might, in the future, give birth to a handicapped child. When she was 11 arrangements were made for her to be sterilised. An educational psychologist attached to her local authority applied to make her a ward of court in order that the operation should be prevented. The court ordered the wardship to continue and did not consent to the operation which could therefore not be carried out (contrast *Re B (a minor) (wardship: sterilisation)* [1987] 2 WLR 1213 where sterilisation of Jeanette, a mentally handicapped 17 year old, was permitted).

Example 2. *(Re B (a minor) (wardship: medical treatment)* [1981] 1 WLR 1421.) A local authority made a child suffering from Down's syndrome a ward of court in order to obtain the court's consent to an operation to save the child's life to which the child's parents were not prepared to consent. The court took the view that it was in the child's best interests for the operation to be performed and authorised it.

3.2.3   Wardship and adoption

The court's wardship jurisdiction is not excluded by the making of an adoption order. The following paragraphs give examples of situations in which wardship jurisdiction may still be invoked. However, it will be seen that there has to be something special about the case to persuade the court to interfere with the normal course of events after the making or refusing of an adoption order. Wardship cannot be used simply to re-open old issues in relation to the adoption of the child.

3.2.3.1   Wardship application by natural parent in attempt to displace normal effect of an adoption order   The natural parent of a child who has been adopted can take wardship proceedings in an attempt to override the effects of the adoption order and to maintain contact with her child. However, the court will not necessarily be prepared to review the effects of the adoption order at a full hearing. The principles applicable are set out in *Re O (a minor) (wardship: adopted child)* [1978] Fam 196, [1978] 2 All ER 27. Whether the court will let the case proceed to a full hearing will depend on whether or not it is in the best interests of the child that there should be a full investigation or whether his interests would be better served if the wardship proceedings were dismissed at the outset so that the adoption order would take its normal course. In an ordinary case where the natural parents have parted with the child and not seen him at all and the adoptive parents have assumed the parental role, there will be a very heavy burden on a natural parent seeking to persuade the court to look into the merits of the case in wardship proceedings; the wardship proceedings would normally be dismissed in the initial stages.

There follows an example of the sort of case in which the court might be prepared to exercise its wardship jurisdiction.

Example. (The facts of *Re O* supra.) When the child was adopted by Mr O'B, it was intended that the child would still be cared for by his natural mother after the adoption. The adoptive father then attempted to deny the mother contact with the child. The mother made the child a ward of court. The court held that the circumstances should be fully investigated in the wardship proceedings.

3.2.3.2   Application by prospective adopters whose application for an adoption order has failed   Wardship has been used successfully by prospective adopters whose adoption application has failed, to retain care and control of the child concerned where this was in the best interests of the child (*Re E (an infant)* [1963] 3 All ER 874, [1964] 1 WLR 51). However, it would seem that the court will be reluctant to exercise its wardship jurisdiction to hear the merits of the case if the prospective adopters have not pursued to the full their rights of appeal against the adoption order (*Re S (a minor)* (1978) 122 SJ 759).

Wardship can be used to obtain an order granting care and control to prospective adopters after a failed adoption application, to maintain the status quo pending an adoption appeal (*Re C (MA) (an infant)* [1966] 1 All ER 838, [1966] 1 WLR 646).

3.2.4   As a means of preventing undesirable associations
Wardship can be used to prevent a child forming an undesirable association. For example, the court can grant an injunction preventing a third party from associating with the ward where the ward proposes to make an independent marriage or has formed a relationship with an undesirable person of the same sex. The court can also intervene to prevent the ward joining an undesirable religious sect.

3.2.5   Where there is no subsisting residence order
Wardship can be used as a means of resolving a dispute as to who should have care and control of a child. Thus, where there is no subsisting residence order,

the solicitor will (at least in theory) have the choice whether to start ordinary section 8 proceedings or to embark on wardship proceedings.

In practice, in the vast majority of cases, ordinary section 8 proceedings will be the appropriate choice. As a general rule, only if the case requires relief that cannot conveniently be obtained in ordinary proceedings should wardship proceedings be commenced. This is particularly so in view of the potentially high cost of wardship proceedings and also in view of the fact that an inevitable part of wardship is the continuing intervention of the court in relation to important decisions in the child's life. This can mean repeated applications to the court for directions even when the child's parents are able to reach agreement between themselves on a particular matter concerning the child and is likely to be seen by some parents as annoying interference rather than paternal protection by the court.

4 PROCEDURE

4.1 Costs

Wardship can be a very expensive procedure and the solicitor must therefore ensure that the question of cost is fully discussed with the client and, where appropriate, a green form completed and a legal aid application sent off (see Chapter 2).

4.2 Jurisdiction

Jurisdiction in wardship cases depends upon the basis upon which the jurisdiction is exercisd. The Family Law Act 1986 sets out grounds upon which the wardship jurisdiction may be exercised for the purpose of making an order to which Part I of the Family Law Act 1986 applies (for full meaning of 'Part I order' see Chapter 26, paragraph 1.1). However, the Family Law Act 1986 does not affect the wardship jurisdiction in so far as it is exercised otherwise than for the purpose of making a 'Part I order'.

4.2.1 Jurisdiction to make a Part I order under the Family Law Act 1986
A Part I order in relation to the exercise of the inherent jurisdiction, including wardship, means an order made by a court of England and Wales in the exercise of the inherent jurisdiction of the High Court with respect to children:

(a)   in so far as it gives the care of a child to any person or provides for contact with or the education of a child, but
(b)   excluding an order varying or discharging such an order (Family Law Act 1986, s. 1(1)(d)).

Furthermore, the court would only have jurisdiction to make one of the above orders if on the relevant date (i.e. the date of the application, or, if there is no application, the date on which the court is considering whether or not to make the order), the child is:

(a)   habitually resident in England and Wales, or
(b)   present in England and Wales and is not habitually resident in any part of the United Kingdom, or

(c) present in England and Wales on the relevant date and in need of emergency protection (Family Law Act 1986, s. 2(3)(b)).

There will be no jurisdiction in relation to (a) and (b) above if there are proceedings for divorce, nullity or judicial separation continuing in a court in Scotland or Northern Ireland in respect of the child's parents, *unless* that court has waived its jurisdiction to deal with the Part I matters or has stayed its proceedings to enable the English court to deal with them.

4.2.2 *Jurisdiction to make an order other than a Part I order under the Family Law Act 1986*
The court has power to exercise its inherent wardship jurisdiction other than in respect of a Part I order under the Family Law Act 1986 over any child who is:

(a) under 18, and
(b) a British subject.

Such jurisdiction can be exercised whether or not the child is physically present within the jurisdiction and regardless of his place of birth, domicile, habitual residence or ordinary residence. The case would have to be very exceptional, however, for the court to be persuaded to exercise its inherent jurisdiction in relation to a child who was neither born nor is resident within the jurisdiction.

The court may not, in any circumstances, exercise its wardship jurisdiction over any child who:

(a) is in the care of the local authority by virtue of a care order, or
(b) is entitled to diplomatic immunity.

4.3 Commencing proceedings

4.3.1 *Originating summons*
Wardship proceedings are commenced in the Family Division of the High Court by originating summons issued out of the principal registry or out of a district registry (FPR 1991, r. 5.1(1)).

The original originating summons will be required together with a copy for each defendant and there is a fee to pay.

4.3.2 *Notes on drafting originating summons*

4.3.2.1 Who should be made defendant? The basic principle is that any person (or body) against whom an order is sought should be made defendant.

Example. Mr and Mrs Grant have separated. Mrs Grant is looking after their son, Peter. One day Mr Grant collects Peter from school without his wife's consent. Mrs Grant is afraid that he will take Peter out of the country to America where he has relations. Mrs Grant therefore consults her solicitor who advises that wardship proceedings should be commenced. Mr Grant should be made the defendant to the originating summons.

However, note the following points:

(a) The minor himself should not be made a defendant to the originating summons unless the district judge has given leave (FPR 1991, r. 5.1(3)).

(b)   Where the wardship proceedings are taken to prevent the minor from forming or continuing an undesirable association with a third party, the third party should not be made a defendant to the originating summons (Practice Direction of 16 June 1983 [1983] 1 WLR 790, [1983] 2 All ER 672).

(c)   Sometimes there is no one other than the minor himself who is a suitable defendant (notably in cases of the kind referred to at (b) above where the minor's parents are seeking to put an end to an undesirable relationship). In such a case an application should be made to the district judge for leave to issue either an originating summons with the child as defendant or an ex parte originating summons (FPR 1991, r. 5.1(3)). The district judge will then decide whether it is appropriate to make the minor a defendant. The Practice Direction of 8 December 1981 [1982] 1 WLR 118, [1982] 1 All ER 319, makes it clear that the minor should only be joined as a party in exceptional cases. If the minor is joined, the Official Solicitor will be asked to consent to act as guardian *ad litem* for him.

4.3.2.2   Contents of originating summons   The originating summons is in the normal form (see Form No. 8, Appendix 1 to the Rules of the Supreme Court), tailored to suit a wardship case. In particular, it must:

(a)   name the minor concerned;

(b)   set out the orders that the plaintiff claims (primarily, of course, an order that the minor be made a ward of court);

(c)   state briefly the relationship of each party to the minor or his interest in the minor (FPR 1991, r. 5.1(6));

(d)   contain a notice to the defendant informing him of his obligations under FPR 1991, r. 5.1(8) and (9) (see below at paragraph 4.5.2); and, unless otherwise directed,

(e)   state the date of birth of the minor (FPR 1991, r. 5.1(5)); and

(f)   state the minor's present whereabouts (or state that the plaintiff is unaware of his whereabouts if that is the case) (FPR 1991, r. 5.1(7)).

4.3.3   Further documentation required to issue proceedings
The plaintiff's solicitor will also require:

(a)   A certified copy of the minor's birth certificate. This must be filed in the registry on issuing the originating summons or before or at the first appointment in the wardship proceedings (FPR 1991, r. 5.1(5)).

(b)   In legal aid cases, a copy of the legal aid certificate. This must be filed as soon as it becomes available together with a notice of issue of the legal aid certificate and a copy notice of issue.

(c)   A certificate by the solicitor as to whether there are presently any other proceedings in relation to the minor. This must be filed when the originating summons is issued.

4.3.4   Issuing the originating summons
The originating summons, the fee and the documents referred to in paragraph 4.3.3 above should be taken to the appropriate registry to be issued. A stamped copy of the originating summons for each defendant will be returned to the plaintiff with:

(a)   A slip showing the court file number allocated to the proceedings which must be endorsed on all documents filed in the registry.

(b)   A notice of wardship: this is a notice stating that the minor has become a ward of court (this happens automatically on issuing the summons, see paragraph 4.4 below), that he may not marry or go outside England and Wales without leave of the court and that no material change should be made in the arrangements for his welfare, care and control or education without leave. It also advises the ward (who may be served with a copy of the notice, see paragraph 4.3.5 below) that he may approach the Official Solicitor if he is in doubt what to do.

(c)   A blank form of acknowledgment of service of originating summons for each defendant.

4.3.5   Serving the papers

(a)   On the defendant   The solicitor must arrange to have the stamped copy of the originating summons served on the defendant together with a copy of the notice of wardship. The original notice of wardship must be produced at the time of service. Although Ord. 10, Rules of the Supreme Court 1981 would seem to authorise service of the originating summons by first-class post or by insertion through the defendant's letter-box, in view of the requirement that the original notice of wardship must be produced at the time of service it would appear that strictly speaking personal service should be arranged (normally by an enquiry agent). If the minor himself is a defendant to the proceedings, he should not automatically be served with the documents himself. In such a case, the Official Solicitor should be contacted for advice; he may be prepared to accept service on behalf of the minor even if he has not yet formally consented to act.

(b)   *On other people*   A copy of the notice of wardship may also be served on anyone else who should be made aware that the minor has been made a ward (for example, it may be appropriate to serve a copy of the notice of wardship on the ward himself if he is old enough to understand its meaning and the circumstances are such that he may be in need of independent advice, on a third party with whom the ward is associating and/or on the person with whom the ward is living if that person is not already a party to the proceedings). However, care must be taken that the originating summons (or indeed, in most cases, any of the other papers connected with the wardship), is not served on anyone who is not a party.

4.4   Wardship immediately effective; need to seek appointment within 21 days

The minor automatically becomes a ward as soon as the originating summons is issued (s. 41(2), Supreme Court Act 1981). He will then remain a ward for at least 21 days.

If the plaintiff wishes the minor to remain a ward for a longer period, he must make sure that he follows up the originating summons by making an application within 21 days after the issue of the originating summons for a hearing of the originating summons.

If no application is made within the 21-day period, the wardship will cease to be effective after the 21 days have elapsed. The originating summons will, however, continue to be effective and the court can be asked to order that the child become a ward again but the automatic protection enjoyed during the first 21 days will have been forfeited (FPR 1991, r. 5.3(1)(a)).

On the other hand, if an application for an appointment is made during the first 21 days, unless the court orders otherwise, the minor will continue automatically to be a ward until the court hears the full wardship application and, of course, also thereafter if the court confirms the wardship at the full hearing (FPR 1991, r. 5.3(1)(b)).

Note that it is not necessary for the first hearing of the originating summons actually to take place within the 21-day period, only that application should be made for an appointment for a first hearing.

4.5 Defendant's obligations when served with originating summons

4.5.1 To acknowledge service

The defendant must acknowledge service within 14 days of service of the originating summons. He must do this by completing the acknowledgment of service form and returning it by post or by hand to reach the registry from which the originating summons was issued before the expiry of the 14-day period (RSC 1981, Ord. 12).

4.5.2 To inform court and plaintiff of his own and minor's address

The defendant (other than the minor if he is the defendant) must also:

(a) lodge in the registry from which the originating summons was issued a notice stating:

(i) his own address; *and*

(ii) the whereabouts of the minor (or that he is unaware of the minor's whereabouts if this is the case) (FPR 1991, r. 5.1(8)); *and*

(b) serve a copy of this notice on the plaintiff unless the court otherwise directs (FPR 1991, r. 5.1(8)); *and*

(c) if he then changes his address or becomes aware that the minor has changed his address, unless the court otherwise directs, he must lodge notice of the change in the appropriate registry and serve a copy of the notice on every other party (FPR 1991, r. 5.1(9)).

4.6 The first appointment

The full hearing of the originating summons (at which it will be decided whether the minor should remain a ward of court in the long term and, if so, what arrangements should be made for his care and control, etc.), normally takes place before a judge. Such a hearing cannot usually be arranged for several months. One reason for this is that the court lists are very busy and the case will therefore have to wait its turn until sufficient court time is available for a full hearing. Another reason is that all parties require time to prepare their cases. Preparation for a full wardship hearing is not unlike preparation for a contested residence dispute; there will therefore be witnesses to interview and affidavits to prepare, etc., and time will be required for a welfare officer's report to be prepared and considered.

It is usual, therefore, for the first appointment in relation to the originating summons to be before a district judge. This opportunity can be used to deal with a wide variety of interim matters, for example:

(a) The district judge will give directions as to the filing and giving of evidence for the final hearing.

(b) He can consider whether it is desirable that other people should be added as parties.

(c) He can consider whether the Official Solicitor should be appointed (to look after the interests of the ward).

(d) He may (and usually will) direct that a court welfare report be prepared (i.e. an independent objective report on the child and his background prepared by a court welfare officer after an investigation of the case).

Unless further directions are likely to be needed at a later stage, the district judge will then normally adjourn the case to the judge for a full hearing.

4.7 The full hearing

4.7.1. *Venue*
The full hearing will normally take place in front of a High Court judge sitting in chambers. The court does, however, have power to adjourn the application to open court. It might do this, for example, in the case of a missing ward if it were felt that publicity might help in tracing the ward (see Chapter 28).

Note that s. 38, Matrimonial and Family Proceedings Act 1984 (as amended by the Children Act 1989, sch. 13, para. 51) gives the High Court power to transfer wardship applications to the county court, except applications that a minor be made or cease to be a ward of court. This means that the county court can deal with matters such as the appointment of a person to have day-to-day care and control of the ward, the making of maintenance orders in relation to the ward, etc. but reference should be made to Practice Direction [1988] 2 All ER 103, [1988] 1 FLR 540, for guidance as to the distribution of business between the High Court and the county courts.

4.7.2 *The form of the hearing*
The wardship hearing is likely to take much the same form as a contested residence hearing. The parties are usually represented by counsel. Evidence is given by affidavit and the court may well hear oral evidence as well. It is usual for a welfare officer's report to be available and the welfare officer may be asked questions about it. If the Official Solicitor is involved in the case, he will place before the court any evidence which he considers to be material on the ward's behalf. He will usually prepare a report based on his enquiries into the case. The report will set out his investigations (interviews with the ward, with parents and other relevant persons, reports obtained from doctors, schools, etc.), analyse the issues in the case and the courses open to the court and set out his submissions, if they can be formulated at this stage.

4.7.3 *The court's orders*
The court will decide whether or not to confirm the wardship in the long term. This will depend on whether the court feels that it is necessary for it to continue to exercise control over the arrangements for the child or whether, once the initial crisis has been resolved, it would be more appropriate to entrust the care of the child to an individual in the normal way.

If the wardship is confirmed, the court itself will have parental responsibility for the child but it will make an order as to who should have care and control. Whoever is awarded care and control, the court has power to make any of the orders set out in paragraph 1 above, since wardship proceedings are 'family proceedings' within the Children Act 1989, s. 8(3).

Whether the court makes any further orders will depend on the circumstances of the case. There is power to make maintenance orders against either or both of the ward's parents (sch. 1, paragraph 1, Children Act 1989) and the court can give whatever directions are necessary as to other aspects of the ward's life such as education, religious upbringing, medical treatment, etc.

In deciding any question relating to the parental responsibility for or upbringing of a minor or to his property, s. 1, Children Act 1989 dictates that the court shall regard the welfare of the minor as the first and paramount consideration (see Chapter 25 paragraph 2.1). This principle applies to wardship cases just as it does to any other case concerning the upbringing of a child. As Lord Scarman pointed out giving the decision of the House of Lords in *Re E (SA) (a minor) (wardship)* [1984] 1 WLR 156, [1984] 1 All ER 289, the court's particular duty in a wardship case is to act in the way best suited in its judgment to serve the true interest and welfare of the ward. A fundamental feature of wardship jurisdiction is that it is not adversarial; in other words, the court's duty is not limited to the dispute between the parties. The court takes over ultimate responsibility for the child and it can look beyond the submissions of the parties and, if necessary, take a course not advocated by any party to the proceedings.

Note that it may well be appropriate for a wardship application to be coupled with an application under the Children Act 1989 for s. 8 orders to enable the court to deal with the question of residence, contact, prohibited steps or specific issue orders should it decide to discontinue the wardship.

5 THE FUTURE OF THE WARD

Whoever is awarded care and control of the ward should be reminded that no important step can be taken in the ward's life without the leave of the court.

The way this restraint is most likely to be felt is in relation to trips outside the jurisdiction. The ward cannot go or be taken outside England and Wales, even for a holiday, without leave. Clients do not always appreciate that this restriction includes holidays in Scotland. However, the court may be prepared to grant general leave for the ward to be taken for *temporary* visits outside England and Wales. In this case there is no need for the person to whom leave is granted to seek the court's approval before each proposed trip, but certain formalities must still be complied with by the person in whose favour leave has been granted, i.e. he must lodge at the registry at least seven days before the proposed departure:

(a) a written consent from the other party or parties to the ward leaving the jurisdiction for the proposed period;

(b) a written statement giving the date of departure, the period of absence and the whereabouts of the ward during that absence; and

(c) unless otherwise directed, a written undertaking to return the ward to England and Wales at the end of the period.

Provided these formalities are complied with, a certificate for production to the immigration authorities stating that the conditions of the general leave have been complied with, may be obtained from the registry, Practice Direction [1973] 1 WLR 690, [1973] 2 All ER 512. If general leave is not granted, a separate application for leave will have to be made each time it is proposed to take the ward temporarily outside England and Wales and the applicant will be required to give a written undertaking to the court to return the ward after the visit.

If it is desired to take the ward out of England and Wales *permanently*, special leave must be obtained from the court. If leave is granted, the court may or may not order that the wardship should be discontinued. If the wardship is to continue, the applicant will be asked to give an undertaking to return the child if ever ordered to do so by the court (see *Re F (a ward) (leave to remove ward out of the jurisdiction)* [1988] 2 FLR 116).

In considering any application for leave, the court will be concerned as to whether it is in the child's interests to go outside England and Wales and as to whether the child will be returned to the jurisdiction at the end of his visit abroad or, if leave is given for him to leave the jurisdiction indefinitely, should the court ever order his return (see *Re F (a ward) (leave to remove ward out of the jurisdiction)* [1988] 2 FLR 116).

Other matters which must be referred to the court for approval include medical treatment/examination other than normal emergency or day to day treatment (for example, if it is proposed that the ward should be examined by a psychiatrist with a view to a report being prepared to be put in evidence, or should have an abortion), proposals for the adoption of the ward, and any proposed marriage of the ward.

6 INJUNCTIONS

6.1 General

Although the very fact that a child has been made ward means that he will automatically be protected by the court in many respects, this is not always sufficient to ensure his welfare. Thus the court also has extensive powers to grant injunctions whenever it is necessary to safeguard the interests of the ward, for example preventing him from associating with a third party who is considered to be undesirable.

The plaintiff is free to ask the court to make a long-term injunction at the full hearing of the case but in many wardship cases this will not be soon enough — the damage will already have been done by that time. In such cases it will be necessary to seek an interlocutory injunction before the full hearing. If the circumstances warrant it, such an application can be made (ex parte, if necessary) even before the originating summons has been issued commencing the wardship proceedings. Indeed, it is possible to obtain an injunction within hours of first taking instructions from the client if necessary. Furthermore, the fact that the courts are closed at the relevant time is no obstacle in an emergency.

6.2 The normal procedure for seeking an interlocutory injunction (RSC Ord. 29, r. 1)

(a)   The normal procedure for seeking an interlocutory injunction is for the plaintiff, after the originating summons has been issued, to apply by *summons* to a judge in chambers. Notice must be given to the other party to the summons; RSC Ord. 32, r. 3, requires that the period of notice should be not less than two clear days before the day specified for the hearing in the summons.

(b) Thus the solicitor must prepare:

(i) a summons (in the general form) with sufficient copies for service on all parties to the summons;

(ii) an affidavit in support of the summons with sufficient copies for service;

(iii) a draft injunction which should include a penal notice informing the defendant that disobedience to the terms of the injunction is a contempt of court and will make him liable to be committed to prison.

(c) These documents should be taken to the court office where the summons will be issued and the copies for service returned to the plaintiff's solicitor. The supporting affidavit and draft injunction should be filed with the court.

(d) The solicitor should then arrange for a copy of the summons and the supporting affidavit to be served on the other party or parties to the summons. If there is a solicitor acting for the party to be served, the documents may be served on him. If not, the documents can be posted to the party himself (see RSC Ord. 65).

(e) All parties should attend the hearing which will be before a judge in chambers. If there is time, the defendant to the summons is entitled to file an affidavit in answer to that of the plaintiff. It may be necessary for the judge to hear some oral evidence. He can be asked to grant the injunction in the terms of the draft prepared by the plaintiff's solicitor. It is not uncommon for the judge to make amendments to the draft to ensure that the injunction deals properly with the circumstances of the case as they appear at the interlocutory hearing. The injunction may be expressed to last until the full hearing of the originating summons or for a shorter period if the judge thinks fit.

(f) The injunction should be served on those parties against whom it is effective.

6.3 Ex parte applications (RSC Ord. 29, r. 1)

In an urgent case when there is insufficient time for notice to be given or it is desirable for some reason that notice should not be given, the court can grant an ex parte injunction.

The following example illustrates the sort of situation in which an ex parte injunction might be appropriate and also the procedure involved in obtaining one. The procedure is more fully described in the rest of this paragraph.

Example. Mrs Smith consults her solicitor on Monday 10 February because she is concerned about a relationship her son Eric has formed with a man in his forties (Mr Jones) who has convictions for indecency with boys. Her son is at boarding school but she has received a letter from him saying that he has been in touch with the man who is coming to pick him up from school on Wednesday 12 February when half-term begins. The solicitor issues an originating summons on Monday 10 February commencing wardship proceedings. Eric is thus automatically a ward of court. However, this does not prevent Mr Jones and Eric from associating with each other. An injunction is therefore required to prevent Mr Jones from associating with Eric, visiting the school, etc. There is not time to serve Mr Jones with notice of an injunction hearing, therefore the court is asked for an appointment with the judge to request an ex parte injunction. At the same time, the solicitor issues at the court office a summons for an 'inter partes' injunction hearing. He is given a hearing date of the following Tuesday 18 February. An affidavit by Mrs Smith is sworn setting out the circumstances of the case and the reasons why it is urgent and a draft injunction is drawn up. The solicitor arranges for the summons and the supporting affidavit to be served personally on Mr Jones. On Tuesday 11 February, Mrs Smith and her solicitor attend before the judge who grants an ex parte injunction in the terms requested to last until the following Tuesday (which is the date fixed for the hearing of the injunction summons). On Tuesday 18 February an inter partes hearing takes place and the injunction is renewed until the full hearing of the originating summons.

The procedure for seeking an ex parte injunction is as follows:

(a)   Oral evidence will be sufficient in a dire emergency; the plaintiff and his solicitor should attend upon the judge to explain the position and request the injunction. This attendance may be at court or, if there is no judge sitting at court at the time, arrangements may be made for the judge to deal with the matter at his lodgings, at his home or even over the telephone. If the solicitor is not aware of the appropriate way to trace a judge locally, he should contact the Royal Courts of Justice in London where someone is always on duty to advise.

(b)   Except in an extreme emergency application should be by affidavit which should set out the full circumstances of the case and the reasons why the application is made ex parte. The solicitor should prepare a draft injunction. The court should then be asked to arrange an ex parte hearing in front of a judge at which the plaintiff and his solicitor should attend. Although the defendant is not entitled to notice of the hearing, there is no reason why he should not be told that it is taking place as a matter of courtesy if this is appropriate in the circumstances of the case.

(c)   If the judge agrees to grant an ex parte injunction, it will be an interim injunction and will be expressed to last only for a matter of days until an application can be made on notice for it to be renewed until the full hearing of the originating summons. This means that, in addition to arranging the ex parte hearing, the solicitor will have to issue and serve a summons for an injunction in the normal way (see paragraph 6.2 above) giving notice of the inter partes hearing. It is not uncommon for the solicitor to issue this summons at the same time as he seeks an appointment for the ex parte hearing if he has had time to prepare the papers.

(d)   The ex parte injunction must be served personally on the defendant as soon as possible. In very urgent cases, he should be informed of the terms of the injunction over the telephone if possible.

6.4   Injunction required before originating summons issued

In practice, provided that the court office is open, it should be possible to issue an originating summons before making an application for an injunction. However, if this is not possible for any reason, the court does have power to grant an injunction (which will be ex parte) even before proceedings have been commenced by the issue of an originating summons (RSC Ord. 29, r. 1).

The injunction will usually be granted on terms that the originating summons be issued as soon as possible.

Example. Mr and Mrs Rose consult their solicitor on Saturday morning. They have just learnt that their 15-year-old daughter has agreed to take part in a nude modelling session for a local photographer, Mr Briggs, on the Sunday afternoon. Their attempts to dissuade her from participating have failed. They wish to seek an injunction to prevent the photographic session from taking place. No originating summons can be issued to commence wardship proceedings as the court office is closed. The solicitor contacts the Royal Courts of Justice and an appointment is arranged with the duty judge for the Saturday afternoon. There is no time to swear an affidavit. Mr and Mrs Rose and their solicitor therefore attend on the judge who hears oral evidence from Mr Rose and grants an ex parte injunction forbidding Mr Briggs to hold the photographic seesion. The solicitor undertakes to issue an originating summons commencing wardship proceedings when the court office opens on Monday. This he does and a summons is also taken out and served on Mr Briggs giving notice of an application for an injunction to last until the full hearing of the wardship application preventing Mr Briggs from holding any photographic sessions involving Mr Rose's daughter.

28 Preventing the removal of a child from the jurisdiction

1 FAMILY LAW ACT 1986

The Family Law Act 1986 considerably reduces the problems that can arise when a child is taken out of the jurisdiction of the English courts to another part of the United Kingdom. The Family Law Act 1986 has been amended by the Children Act 1989, sch. 13, paras. 62 to 71. The Family Law Act 1986, in its amended form, establishes a procedure whereby a 'Part I order' made in relation to a child under 16 in one part of the United Kingdom will be recognised in any other part of the United Kingdom as having the same effect as if it had been made by a local court. It is now possible to register a 'Part I order' in the appropriate court in another part of the United Kingdom. Once this has been done, one can apply to that court for the order to be enforced as if it were one of the court's own orders (see Chapter V of Part I, Family Law Act 1986). For the meaning of 'Part I order' and for details of the other rules as to jurisdiction to make s. 8 orders under the Family Law Act 1986, see Chapter 26, paragraph 1.1. However, note that Part I orders include s. 8 orders (other than one varying or discharging a s. 8 order) and certain orders made in the exercise of the inherent jurisdiction of the High Court with respect to children.

2 REMOVAL FROM THE UK

2.1 Child Abduction Act 1984

Section 1(1), Child Abduction Act 1984 (CAA 1984), as amended by the Children Act 1989, sch. 12, para. 37, makes it a criminal offence for a person 'connected' with a child under 16 to take or send the child out of the United Kingdom without the appropriate consent.

The following are 'connected' with the child:

(a)   a parent of the child;

(b)   in the case of a child whose parents were not married to each other at the time of his birth, a person who there are reasonable grounds for believing to be the father of the child;

(c)   a guardian of the child;

(d)   a person in whose favour a residence order is in force with respect to the child;

(e)   a person who has custody of the child.

The consent that is needed is from the following:

(1)   (a)   the child's mother;

    (b)   the child's father, if he has parental responsibility for him;
    (c)   any guardian of the child;
    (d)   any person in whose favour a residence order is in force with respect to the child;
    (e)   any person who has custody of the child; or
(2)   the leave of the court granted under or by virtue of any provision of Part II, Children Act 1989; or
(3)   if any person has custody of the child, the leave of the court which awarded custody to him.

A person does *not* commit an offence under CAA 1984 if he takes or sends a child out of the United Kingdom without the appropriate consent *if*:

    (a)   he is a person in whose favour there is a residence order in respect of the child; and
    (b)   he takes or sends the child out of the United Kingdom for a period of less than one month,
unless he does so in breach of the terms of an order made under Part II, Children Act 1989 (CAA 1984, s. 4A).

Section 1(5), CAA 1984 provides that a person does not commit an offence by doing anything without the consent of another person whose consent is technically required if:

    (a)   he does it in the belief that the other person:

      (i)   has consented, or
     (ii)   would consent if he was aware of all the relevant circumstances; or

    (b)   he has taken all reasonable steps to communicate with the other person but has been unable to do so; or
    (c)   the other person has unreasonably refused his consent.

However, (c) above does *not* apply if:

    (a)   the person who refused to consent is a person:

      (i)   in whose favour there is a residence order in force with respect to the child; or
     (ii)   who has custody of the child; or

    (b)   the person so taking or sending the child is doing so in breach of an order made by a court in the United Kingdom.

For the purposes of CAA 1984 the terms 'guardian of a child', 'residence order' and 'parental responsibility' have the same meaning as in the Children Act 1989.

Note that there are special modifications of s. 1. for certain children, for example, those who are in the care of local authorities , detained in a place of safety, remanded to local authority accommodation or the subject of an order relating to adoption (see s. 1(8) and the schedule to CAA 1984).

By virtue of s. 2, CAA 1984, a person who is *not* the parent, guardian, someone with a residence order in respect of the child or someone with custody of the child commits an offence if, without lawful authority or reasonable excuse, he takes or detains a child under 16 so as to:

(a)   to remove him from the lawful control of any person having lawful control of him, or

(b)   to keep him out of the lawful control of any person entitled to lawful control of him.

A person charged under s. 2, CAA 1984 has a defence if he can show that, at the time of the alleged offence:

(a)   he believed that the child was at least 16, or

(b)   in the case of an illegitimate child, he had reasonable grounds for believing he was the child's father.

Although the provisions of CAA 1984 may be a psychological deterrent to anyone contemplating abducting a child and taking him abroad, the Act itself does not establish any practical safeguards to prevent the removal of the child. What it has done, however, is to prompt the setting up of a 'port alert' system which does offer more concrete help.

2.2   The port alert system

2.2.1   General

The port alert system is described fully in Practice Direction [1986] 1 All ER 983, [1986] 1 WLR 475. It is operated by the police and replaces the former Home Office procedure for preventing the unauthorised removal of children from England and Wales.

The police provide a 24-hour service and, in conjunction with immigration officers at the ports, will attempt to prevent the unlawful removal of a child from the country.

2.2.2   Eligibility for assistance under the system

Before they will institute a port alert for a child, the police will need to be satisfied:

(a)   That there is a real and imminent danger of the child being removed. 'Imminent' means within 24 to 48 hours and 'real' means that the port alert is not just being sought as an insurance.

(b)   That:

(i)   the child is under 16, or

(ii)   the child is a ward (the police should be shown evidence of this, for example, confirming the wardship, an injunction or, in an urgent case, a sealed copy of the originating summons in wardship), or

(iii)   in the case of a child of 16 or over who is not a ward of court, there is in force a residence order relating to the child or an order restricting or restraining his removal from the jurisdiction.

2.2.3   Means of seeking police help

An application for assistance in preventing a child's removal from the jurisdiction must be made by the applicant or his legal representative to a police station. Application should normally be made to the applicant's local police station but, in urgent cases, any police station will do. The police require quite a lot of detail to be given when assistance is requested, for example, likely travel details and information about the child, the applicant and the person likely to remove the child from the jurisdiction. Reference should be made to the 1986 Practice Direction for a complete list of the details that should be given if possible. Where a court order has been obtained in relation to the child, it should be produced to the police even where the child is under 16 and a court order is not strictly required.

2.2.4 How the system works

If the police are satisfied that the port alert system should be used, the child's name will be entered on a stop list for four weeks. The ports will be notified directly, and police and immigration officers will attempt to identify the child and prevent his removal from the country. After four weeks the child's name will automatically be removed from the stop list unless a further application is made.

2.3 Passports

An interested party may give notice in writing to the Passport Department at the Home Office that passport facilities should not be provided in respect of a minor either without leave of the court or, in cases other than wardship, the consent of the other parent, guardian or person to whom a residence order or care and control has been granted, or the consent of the mother where the child is illegitimate (Practice Direction [1986] 1 All ER 983, [1986] 1 WLR 475).

If the child has not already got passport facilities, notification given to the Passport Department should be effective to prevent his unlawful removal from the country. However, it does not assist where the child already has his own passport or is mentioned on the passport of a parent who it is feared will remove him from the country. The courts (even the magistrates' courts, it would appear — see *Stone's Justices' Manual* 1991, para. 4–1831) can order the surrender of the child's passport or of a passport containing particulars of the child. The court informs the Passport Office if this is done, to prevent the issue of a new passport (Practice Direction [1983] 2 All ER 253, [1983] 1 WLR 558).

The law on the surrender of passports is statutory now that s. 37, Family Law Act 1986 has come into force. Section 37 provides that where there is in force an order prohibiting or restricting the removal of a child from the United Kingdom or from any part of it, the court that made the order and appropriate courts in other parts of the United Kingdom may require any person to surrender any United Kingdom passport which has been issued to or contains particulars of the child.

3 TRACING A LOST CHILD

If a ward is missing, the court has power to permit the publication of information regarding the wardship to enable him to be traced. If it is felt that publicity would help, the judge should therefore be asked to lift reporting restrictions to enable the publication of information about the child (his description and a photograph if possible, a description of the adult thought to be accompanying the child, details concerning his disappearance and anything known about where he may be). (See further, Practice Note [1980] 2 All ER 806 and, for example, *Re R (MJ) (a minor) (publication of transcript)* [1975] Fam 89, [1975] 2 All ER 749.)

There are also formal procedures for tracing a missing ward through the police, DSS records, etc.

Now that s. 33, Family Law Act 1986 (as amended by the Children Act 1989, sch. 13, para. 62), has come into force, all courts will have power in proceedings for or relating to an order under s. 8 of the Children Act 1989 to require any person whom they have reason to believe may have information relevant to where a child is to disclose that information to the court.

29 *Children in local authority care*

1 INTRODUCTION — CHILDREN AND LOCAL AUTHORITIES

1.1 Only one route into care

As a result of the coming into force on 14 October 1991 of the Children Act 1989 there is now only one method of committing children into the care of a local authority: that is by satisfying the statutory 'threshold' criteria set out in s. 31(2) of the Act. All other forms of committing children into care are abolished. The Children Act 1989 repeals the whole of the Child Care Act 1980, much of the Children and Young Persons Act 1969 and the numerous family proceedings which formerly enabled the courts to make care orders. Those are all replaced with one single composite ground. See also Chapter 25 for the general principles to be applied in *all* proceedings brought under the Children Act 1989, whether they be for private law or public law orders.

1.2 The general duty

Local authorities are placed under a general duty to:

(a) safeguard and promote the welfare of children within their area who are in need, and

(b) so far as it is consistent with that duty, to promote the upbringing of children by their families

by providing a range and level of services appropriate to those children's needs (s. 17(1)).

Thus, the Children Act 1989 emphasises that the prime responsibility for the upbringing of children lies with their parents. The intention is that the State should be ready to help parents to discharge that responsibility, especially if it lessens the risk of family breakdown. Services to families in need of help should be arranged in voluntary partnership with parents, so far as possible. If those services include looking after the child away from home then the underlying principle is that close contact should be maintained between the child and his family and, if appropriate, the family should be reunited as soon as possible.

A child is taken to be 'in need' if he is unlikely to achieve or maintain, or to have the opportunity of achieving or maintaining, a reasonable standard of health or development without the provision for him of services by a local authority under Part III of the Children Act 1989 (s. 17(10)).

'Family', in relation to a child in need, includes any person who has parental responsibility for the child and any other person with whom he has been living (s. 17(10)).

'Development' means physical, intellectual, emotional, social or behavioural development (s. 17(11)).

'Health' means physical and mental health (s. 17(11)).

The specific duties placed on local authorities are set out in the Children Act 1989, sch. 2, Part I and lack of space means that the authors do not propose to explore them in this book.

1.3 Duty to accommodate children in need

The system of 'voluntary care' has been abolished and, instead, a duty is imposed on local authorities to accommodate children in need in the following circumstances:

(a)   where there is no person with parental responsibility for him;

(b)   where he is lost or has been abandoned; or

(c)   where the person who has been caring for him is prevented (whether or not permanently, and for whatever reason) from providing him with suitable accommodation or care (s. 20).

The former power to assume 'parental rights' over children in voluntary care by administrative resolution has been abolished. From now on a child 'accommodated' by the local authority (but not the subject of a care order) may be removed by his parents at any time. The only way in which a local authority can assume 'parental responsibility' for a child is by applying for, and being granted, a care order. This reflects the aim of Parliament that the transfer to a local authority of the legal powers and responsibilities of caring for a child should only be done by a full court hearing following due legal process. Thus, the application of emergency powers to remove a child at serious risk (e.g. by way of an emergency protection order), which necessarily cannot be preceded by a full court hearing, should be of short duration and subject to court review.

1.3.1 The child's view

The Children Act 1989 stipulates that wherever possible the local authority should consider the wishes of the child before providing him with accommodation. They should give due consideration to such wishes as they have been able to ascertain (having regard to his age and understanding) (s. 20(6)).

If the child is over 16 then the Children Act 1989 effectively gives the child complete autonomy in that he may consent to being provided with accommodation by the local authority even though:

(a)   the person(s) with parental responsibility for him object (s. 20(11)), and

(b)   the person with parental responsibility is able to provide the child with accommodation (s. 20(4)).

1.3.2 Parental removal

Once a child is accommodated by a local authority, then any person with parental responsibility may *at any time* remove the child from the local authority accommodation (s. 20(8)). There are only two exceptions:

(a)   where a person in whose favour a residence order has been made in respect of a child, or who has care and control of the child by virtue of an order made in the exercise of the inherent jurisdiction of the High Court (s. 20(9)) or by virtue of an existing order (sch. 14, para. 8(4)) *agrees* to the child being looked after by the local authority (s. 20(9)). If there are two such persons then *both* must agree (s. 20(10));

(b)   where the child has reached 16 and *agrees* to being so accommodated (s. 20(11)).

If the local authority wish to prevent the child from being removed from local authority accommodation they now have only two choices:

(a)   to apply to the court for a care order, by satisfying the s. 31(2) statutory grounds; or

(b)   to apply to the court for an emergency protection order under s. 44(1) of the Children Act 1989; this will be suitable only where the case is urgent.

1.4   Duties of local authorities in relation to children 'looked after' by them

A child is 'looked after' by a local authority for the purposes of the Children Act 1989 if he is:

(a)   in local authority care by virtue of a care order; or

(b)   provided with accommodation by the local authority (for a continuous period of more than 24 hours) under a voluntary arrangement (ss. 22(1) and 105(4)).

1.4.1   General duties

When a local authority 'look after' a child, s. 22(3), Children Act 1989 places upon that authority a general duty:

(a)   to safeguard and promote his welfare; and

(b)   to make such use of services available for children cared for by their own parents as appears to the authority reasonable in his case.

The local authority must act as a 'good parent'. *Before* making decisions about the child the authority are required by s. 22(4), Children Act 1989 to ascertain the wishes and feelings of the following persons:

(a)   the child;

(b)   the child's parents;

(c)   any person who is not a parent of the child but has parental responsibility for him.

Once the local authority actually engage in the process of *making* the decision, s. 22(5), Children Act 1989 require them to give consideration:

(a)   to the wishes and feelings of those persons listed above; and

(b)   to the child's religious persuasion, racial origin and cultural and linguistic background.

1.4.2   Provision of accommodation and maintenance

Once the local authority are 'looking after' a child they are under a duty to provide him with accommodation and to maintain him (s. 23(1) and (2)).

There is a statutory *presumption* that an authority 'looking after' a child must make arrangements enabling him to live with one of the following:

(a)   a parent;
(b)   a person who is not a parent but has parental responsibility;
(c)   a person in whose favour a residence order was in force immediately before a care order was made; or
(d)   a relative, friend or other person connected with him,

unless those solutions would not be reasonably practicable or consistent with his welfare (s. 23(6)).

Once the child is the subject of a care order that presumption is reversed.

1.4.3   Contact between the child and his family

Once a local authority are 'looking after' a child they must endeavour, so far as is practicable and consistent with the child's welfare, to promote contact between the child and the following persons:

(a)   his parents;
(b)   any person who is not a parent but has parental responsibility for him;
(c)   any other person connected with him (sch. 2, para. 15(1)).

For further discussion of parental contact with children in care see paragraph 2.7 below.

1.4.4   Advice and assistance for certain children

Where a child is being 'looked after' by a local authority the authority are under a duty to 'advise, assist and befriend him' with a view to promoting his welfare when he ceases to be looked after by them (s. 24(1)).

1.5   Review of cases

The Children Act 1989 requires local authorities to conduct at regular intervals a general review of the progress of each child who is being looked after or provided with accommodation by them in accordance with the Review of Children's Cases Regulations 1991.

The Children Act 1989 also requires local authorities to provide a review procedure, with an independent element, to resolve disputes and complaints raised when a child, his parents, anybody with parental responsibility for him or a local authority foster-parent is unhappy with the arrangements made for the child's care (s. 26(3)). See the Representations Procedure (Children) Regulations 1991.

2   CARE AND SUPERVISION ORDERS

The Children Act 1989 has streamlined the law to the extent that there is now only one method of committing a child to the care of, or placing him under the supervision of, a local authority. A summary of the main points is as follows:

(a)   The court may only make a care order if it is satisfied that:

(i)   the statutory criteria in s. 31(2) have been met; and
(ii)   the child's welfare demands that a care order be made.

(b)   Care orders may be made on specific application or in the course of 'family proceedings'.

(c) Wardship is no longer available to local authorities as a method of committing children into their care where they are unable to prove the statutory grounds.

(d) The magistrates' court, county court and High Court all have jurisdiction to make care orders. However, most care proceedings will commence in the magistrates' court. For further details as to the allocation of work between the courts see Chapter 25, paragraphs 5.1 to 5.3.

(e) The local authority assume parental responsibility for the child on the making of a care order and any existing s. 8 orders terminate. However, other persons having parental responsibility for the child will not be divested of it. They will 'share' parental responsibility with the local authority.

(f) There is a statutory presumption that the authority will allow the child in care to have contact with his parents and other specified persons. Section 34, Children Act 1989 contains the mechanisms for determining and enforcing the existence and levels of such contact.

(g) The court has power to make supervision orders in the course of care proceedings.

2.1 Who can apply for a care or supervision order?

The application for a care order may be made by:

(a) any local authority, or
(b) an authorised person (s. 31(1)).

So far the only 'authorised person' is the NSPCC. However, there is provision for the Secretary of State to name others in due course.

Nobody else may initiate care proceedings. The court itself may not make a care or supervision order without an application having been made by the local authority. If the court is concerned about a child's circumstances then the most it can do is to direct the local authority to investigate pursuant to s. 37(1), Children Act 1989. If the authority investigate but choose not to make an application then the court has no power to make a care/supervision order. If a parent is unable to control his child and wishes the local authority to take care proceedings then he cannot compel a reluctant authority to do so other than by way of judicial review.

A care order may only be made where the child is under the age of 17 (or under 16 if the child is married): s. 31(3).

2.2 What must the local authority or authorised person do before making an application?

Where a local authority or authorised person suspect that a child in their area has suffered significant harm or is likely to do so then they must fully investigate the circumstances of the child so that they can decide whether any action should be taken to 'safeguard or promote the child's welfare' (s. 47(1)). *Before* making a decision the authority must (so far as is reasonably practicable) ascertain the wishes and feelings of the child, his parents, anyone else with parental responsibility (e.g. a guardian) and any other person whose wishes and feelings the authority consider to be relevant (s. 22(4)). The duty to consult could be waived on the basis that it was not 'reasonably practicable' if the circumstances of the child required urgent action which might be prejudiced by such consultation. For example, where the parents are likely to run away with the child if they are informed in advance that an application for a care order is to be made.

If the authority conclude that they should take action then they must do so 'so far as it is both within their power and reasonably practicable for them to do so'.

2.3   Who are the respondents in care proceedings?

The persons who must be made respondents to an application for a care or supervision order are defined in the Family Proceedings Rules 1991, r. 4.7 and Appendix 3 and in the Family Proceedings Courts (Children Act 1989) Rules 1991, r. 7 and Schedule 2. They are as follows:

(a)   every person whom the applicant believes to have parental responsibility for the child;

(b)   where the child is the subject of a care order (i.e. in the course of an application for a supervision order), every person whom the applicant believes to have parental responsibility immediately prior to the making of the care order;

(c)   in the case of an application to extend, vary or discharge an order, the parties to the proceedings leading to the order which it is sought to have extended, varied or discharged;

(d)   the child.

2.4   Who may be a party to care proceedings?

Anybody can make a written request that he be joined as a party, or cease to be a party to care proceedings (FPR 1991, r. 4.7(2) and FPC(CA 1989)R 1991, r. 7(2)). However, if a person with parental responsibility for the child requests to be made a party the court must grant the request (FPR 1991, r. 4.7(4) and FPC(CA 1989)R 1991, r. 7(4)). In the case of anyone else making such a request the court must follow the procedure set out in FPR 1991, r. 4.7(3) and FPC(CA 1989)R 1991, r. 7(3). A request for joinder may be granted by the court without a hearing. Otherwise, the court will order that a date be fixed for a hearing to consider the request or else it will invite the parties to make written representations, within a specific period, as to whether the request should be granted.

The court has a discretion to direct that a person who would not otherwise be a respondent be joined as a party to the proceedings or that a party to the proceedings ceases to be a party (FPR 1991, r. 4.7(5) and FPC(CA 1989)R 1991, r. 7(5)).

2.5   The statutory grounds

Section 31, Children Act 1989 sets out new provisions in relation to care and supervision orders. It eliminates the complicated grounds that formerly existed under the old law and replaces them with one composite ground. A court may *only* make a care or supervision order if it is satisfied that:

(a)   the child is suffering, or likely to suffer, significant harm; *and*

(b)   the harm, or likelihood of harm, is attributable to:

(i)   the care given to the child, or likely to be given to him if the order is not made, not being what it would be reasonable to expect a parent to give to him; or

(ii)   the child's being beyond parental control.

Grounds (a) and (b) are cumulative. Both must be satisfied, although (b) may be satisfied by either of its sub-paragraphs. Once the grounds have been made out then the court moves on to the second limb of its decision-making exercise. Before completing its determination of the case the court must abide by the dictates of s. 1, Children Act 1989, that is to say:

(a)   the child's welfare is the paramount consideration (s. 1(1)); and

(b)   in considering the welfare of the child the court must apply the statutory checklist of factors set out in s. 1(3); and

(c)   the court must bear in mind the general principle in s. 1(2) that there is a presumption that any delay in determining the matter is likely to prejudice the welfare of the child; and

(d)   the court must not make an order unless it considers that making it would be better for the child than making no order at all (s. 1(5)).

2.5.1   Definition of terms used in s. 31(2)

For the purposes of the Children Act 1989 the following terms used in s. 31(2) are defined in s. 31(9) as follows:

'Harm' means ill-treatment or the impairment of health and development.

'Development' means physical, intellectual, emotional, social or behavioural development.

'Health' means physical or mental health.

'Ill-treatment' includes sexual abuse and forms of ill-treatment which are not physical.

'Significant' is not defined in the Children Act 1989, but it will obviously be construed by the lawyer with reference to the *de minimis* principle. The layman should be warned not to equate 'significant' with ' substantial'. Where the question of whether the harm suffered by the child is 'significant' or not turns upon the child's health or development, then his health or development is to be compared with that which could reasonably be expected of a similar child (s. 31(10)). Thus, a subjective stance is to be adopted in relation to the particular characteristics and disabilities of this particular child. Thereafter, an objective test is to be applied as to whether the standard of his health and development is a standard which could reasonably be expected of a child with similar characteristics.

There is very little case law, as yet, upon the new statutory grounds. However, in the recent case of *Re O, The Times*, 6 March (1992) (FD), Ewbank J held that truancy was a basis for a care order where it resulted in the child's intellectual and social development being impaired. This would occur either because of a failure by the parents to give reasonable care or because the child was beyond their control. The judge found that usually in this type of case an education supervision order under s. 36 of the Children Act 1989 should be tried before a care order was sought. However, in this case the local authority was correct to argue that an education supervision order would not have permitted them to do anything that they had not already tried without success.

2.5.2   Meaning of present and future harm

Ground (a) refers both to *present* harm and to *future* harm. The requirement that the child *is suffering* significant harm does not mean that the court must look only at the position of the child at the exact moment in time when it is deciding whether or not to make a care or supervision order. It means:

> a situation over a period, not now at this precise moment but over a period of time sufficiently proximate to the date of inquiry to indicate that it is the present, not history and not the days to come. It is a description of a continuing set of circumstances which may not obtain on the particular day on which the matter is being considered but represents a category which the description of the child fits (per Bush J in *M* v *Westminster City Council* [1985] FLR 325, at p. 340, considering the use of the present tense in the old grounds under the Children and Young Persons Act 1969).

The inclusion of *future* harm in the new grounds is of vital importance. In the past local authorities were able to resort to the use of wardship to deal with cases in which the harm was anticipated rather than actual. Now that this avenue is denied to them it is crucial that they be able to bring cases of 'likely harm' within Children Act 1989 proceedings. The magistrates' courts did not have power to deal with cases of future harm under the old legislation. The availability to them of this new power is an important extension of their jurisdiction and one to which they may well find that it takes some time to become accustomed.

The meaning of 'likely harm' was referred to by *The Law on Child Care and Family Services* (Cm 62, 1987, paragraph 60) as follows:

> It is intended that 'likely harm' should cover all cases of unacceptable risk in which it may be necessary to balance the chance of harm occurring against the magnitude of that harm if it does occur . . . the court will have to judge whether there is a risk and what the nature of the risk is.

Clearly, therefore, the authority will have to show that the likelihood of harm is something more than mere surmise on their part, and that on the balance of probabilities it is likely to occur in the future if steps are not taken to prevent it.

2.5.3   Cause of the harm, or likely harm

Ground (b), in its alternatives, requires the court to find the cause for the harm, or likely harm. In relation to ground (b)(i), i.e. that the care being given to the child is not that which one would expect a reasonable parent to give him, the court must look to the standard of care which the child obtains, or is likely to obtain if the care order is *not* made. It must evaluate that standard of care and then ask the following question: is that standard below that which it would be reasonable to expect the parent of *such* a child to give him? The intention is that the court should focus upon the characteristics of the particular child and that the child's *needs* be assessed subjectively. However, the standard to be applied to the care being given to that particular child is an objective one.

In relation to ground (b)(ii) the relevant question for the court is this: is the child beyond parental control? The parent may not necessarily be at fault for this ground to be satisfied. For example, the parent may have tried to discipline the child only to find that the child will not accept it. A parent in such a position cannot force the local authority to bring proceedings in respect of the child. If he informally requests the authority to do so and they refuse then his only remedy is by way of judicial review.

2.6 Effect of care orders

2.6.1 Local authority obtains parental responsibility under a care order

While a care order is in force with respect to a child, the local authority have parental responsibility for him (s. 33(3)). However, parents do *not lose* their parental responsibility as a result of a care order being made (s. 2(5)). The parents share parental responsibility with the local authority, although the authority have the power to determine, largely, the extent to which a parent or guardian of the child may meet his parental responsibility for the child (s. 33(3)(b)). However, s. 33(4) directs that the local authority should not limit the extent to which the parent exercises his parental responsibility for the child *unless* they are satisfied that it is necessary to do so in order to safeguard or promote the child's welfare. Furthermore, s. 33(5), Children Act 1989 states that where a parent has *de facto* care of the child then he may do what is reasonable in all the circumstances to safeguard or promote the child's welfare (see also s. 3(5)).

However, there are certain things which the local authority have no right to do even if they have a care order in respect of a child, since those matters remain the prerogative of the parents. The authority may not:

(a) bring the child up in a different religion from that in which he would have been brought up if the order had not been made (s. 33(6)(a)). However, the child could choose to practise a different religion if he was of sufficient age and understanding, since he is entitled to be consulted by the authority about such matters (s. 22(4) and (5));

(b) consent to or refuse the making of an application freeing the child for adoption (s. 33(6)(b)(i));

(c) agree or refuse to agree to the making of an adoption order in respect of the child (s. 36(b)(ii));

(d) appoint a guardian for the child (s. 33(6)(b)(iii)).

2.6.2 Care order discharges all existing s. 8 orders

A care order has the effect of discharging all existing s. 8 orders (i.e. residence, contact, prohibited steps and specific issue orders). There is a separate scheme under s. 34, Children Act 1989 which provides for parental contact with children in care (see paragraph 2.7, below).

2.6.3 Restriction of change of name and removal from the jurisdiction

While a care order is in force s. 33(7), Children Act 1989 provides that no person may:

(a) cause the child to be known by a new surname; or
(b) remove him from the United Kingdom,

without *either*:

(i)   the written consent of every person who has parental responsibility for the child; or

(ii) the leave of the court.

However, the above consent is not necessary if the authority wish to remove the child from the jurisdiction for periods of less than one month (s. 33(8)(a)).

2.6.4   Local authority power to place child with his parents
Section 23(4), (5) and (6) gives the local authority power to place a child in their care with one or both of his parents. See the Placement of Children with Parents etc. Regulations 1991.

2.6.5   Duties of local authority towards a child in their care
The duties of local authorities in relation to children 'looked after' by them apply equally to a child in their care by virtue of a care order. Those duties have already been discussed earlier in this chapter at paragraph 1.4.

2.7   Parental contact with children in care

Schedule 2, para. 15, Children Act 1989 places a duty upon local authorities to 'endeavour to promote contact' between any child they are 'looking after' (N.B. 'looking after' includes children being looked after by virtue of a care order) and the following persons:

(a)   his parents;

(b)   those who have parental responsibility for him (e.g. guardians); and

(c)   any relatives, friends or other persons connected with him.

This duty applies in all cases *unless* contact is not reasonably practicable or is not consistent with the child's welfare.

The court has no power to make a s. 8 order (other than a residence order) whilst a child is in the care of a local authority (s. 9(1)). However, the Children Act 1989 sets out a special scheme in s. 34 which enables the court to make orders directing or refusing contact with children in care.

Where the child is the subject of a care order s. 34(1) imposes a statutory presumption that the local authority must allow the child to have reasonable contact with:

(a)   his parents;

(b)   any guardian of his;

(c)   where there was a residence order in force with respect to the child immediately before the care order was made, the person in whose favour the residence order was made; and

(d)   where, immediately before the care order was made, a person had care of the child by virtue of an order made in the exercise of the High Court's inherent jurisdiction, that person.

Section 34 of the Children Act 1989 makes the duty enforceable in the courts.

2.7.1   When may a s. 34 contact order be made?
A s. 34 contact order may be made at the same time as the care order itself or later (s. 34(10)). Before making the care order the court must consider the arrangements which the authority have made, or propose to make, for arranging

contact between the child and the persons to whom s. 34 applies (s. 34(11)). Therefore, in the course of care proceedings all parties should be prepared to present evidence and make submissions about contact.

2.7.2 Who may apply for contact under s. 34?

The following persons may make an application under s. 34 that the court make such order as it considers appropriate with respect to the contact which is to be allowed between the child and the *person named in the order*:

(a)   the local authority (s. 34(2));
(b)   the child (s. 34(2));

The following persons may make an application under s. 34 that the court make such order as it considers appropriate with respect to the contact which is to be allowed between the child and *that person*:

(a)   any of the persons listed in paragraph 2.7 (a) to (d) above (s. 34(3)(a));
(b)   anyone else who has first obtained the leave of the court to make an application (s. 34(3)(b)), for example, grandparents and siblings may well wish to retain contact with the child in care.

2.7.3 Power of the court to attach conditions to a s. 34 order

Section 34(7) of the Children Act 1989 makes provision for the court to attach to a s. 34 contact order such conditions as it considers appropriate. It is open to the court to specify the timing, nature and duration of the contact, if necessary.

2.7.4 Prohibition of contact with a child in care

If the local authority or the child wish to apply to the court to prohibit contact between the child and the persons set out in paragraph 2.7(a) to (d) above then the appropriate section for them to use is s. 34(4), for example, to prevent contact between a child and a parent who has sexually abused him. It is not open to anyone other than the local authority or the child to apply for such a *prohibition* on contact. For example, if a mother took the view that the child's father should not have contact with the child while he is in care then she could not apply for an order under s. 34(4); she would have to rely upon the authority sharing her anxieties about contact and making the application in their own right.

The authority may refuse to allow contact that would otherwise be required by virtue of s. 34(1) or by an order under s. 34 if:

(a)   they are satisfied that it is necessary to do so to promote the child's welfare; and
(b)   the refusal:

   (i)   is decided upon as a matter of urgency; *and*
   (ii)   does not last for more than *seven* days (s. 34(6)).

Where the authority exercise their power to refuse to allow contact with a child in care then they must adopt the procedure set out in the Contact with Children Regulations 1991. Those regulations require that the authority notify the following persons, in writing, of their decision:

(a)   those listed in s. 34(1);
(b)   the child, if he is of sufficient understanding; and

(c)   any other person whose wishes and feelings the authority consider to be relevant.

In the notification the authority should give their reasons for the decision, its date, its duration and the remedies available in case of dissatisfaction.

The same principles apply where:

(a)   the authority decide to depart from the terms of any agreement as to contact made with the person in relation to whom the s. 34 order was made; or

(b)   the authority intend to vary or suspend arrangements made, *other than under a s. 34 order*, with a view to affording any person contact with a child in care.

The practitioner is referred to the regulations themselves for the precise details of the steps which the authority is required to take in the circumstances outlined above.

2.7.5   *Variation and discharge of s. 34 contact orders*

The court may vary or discharge any s. 34 order on the application of:

(a)   the person named in the order;
(b)   the authority; or
(c)   the child concerned (s. 34(9)).

Where a person other than a local authority has made a s. 34 application and that application has been refused, then that person may not make a similar application in respect of the *same* child until at least *six months* have elapsed since the refusal, unless he has first obtained the leave of the court (s. 91(17)).

A s. 34 contact order must be discharged if the care order to which it relates is discharged. A s. 8 contact order could be made instead in the course of the proceedings dealing with the discharge of the care order (s. 10).

2.8   Care/supervision order procedure

As to procedure generally, see Chapter 25 paragraph 6. However, the aspects which specifically affect public law proceedings are set out below.

2.8.1   *Representation of the child*

The court is under a duty to appoint a guardian ad litem for a child for the purpose of 'specified proceedings' *unless* it is satisfied that it is not necessary to do so in order to safeguard the child's interests (s. 41(1)). 'Specified proceedings' are defined in s. 41(6) of the Children Act 1989 and they include:

(a)   applications for care and supervision orders;
(b)   proceedings in which the court has given a direction under s. 37(1) and has made, or is considering whether to make, an interim care order;
(c)   applications to discharge care or supervision orders;
(d)   appeals against care or supervision orders.

The above are just *some* of the relevant categories of proceedings to which the duty applies. The practitioner is referred to s. 41(6) itself for the remainder of the list.

The method of appointing a guardian ad litem is set out in Chapter 25, paragraph 6.8, together with a description of his role and duties towards the child. The appropriate rules of court are FPR 1991, rr. 4.10 and 4.11 and the FPC(CA 1989)R 1991, rr. 10 and 11.

The court may appoint a solicitor to represent the child provided that:

(a)   he is not already represented by one; and

(b)   one of the conditions in s. 4l(4) is satisfied: (s. 41(3)). The conditions are that no guardian ad litem has been appointed for the child, that the child has sufficient understanding to appoint a solicitor and wishes to do so, or that it appears to be in the child's best interests for him to be represented by a solicitor.

Once appointed the solicitor must represent the child in accordance with the rules of court. The relevant rules are to be found in FPR 1991, r. 4.12 and FPC(CA 1989)R 1991, r. 12.

There is also provision for a guardian ad litem to appoint a solicitor for the child. This topic is further discussed in Chapter 25 at paragraph 6.9.

2.8.2   Jurisdiction and procedure

Proceedings with a public law element (e.g. applications for care orders, supervision orders, s. 34 contact orders, emergency protection orders) will generally commence in the 'family proceedings court', i.e. the magistrates' court. For a full list of the applications which will begin in the family proceedings court see Chapter 25, paragraph 5.1 et seq. However, the magistrates' court, county court and High Court all have concurrent jurisdiction, and are all capable of hearing public law cases in appropriate circumstances (N.B. only 'nominated care judges' may hear cases with a public law element in the county court).

Initially, the clerk to the justices (or the justices themselves) will make a decision as to the level of court at which the matter is to be tried. The criteria for transferring the proceedings vertically upwards to the county court or High Court are set out in the Children (Allocation of Proceedings) Order 1991, Article 7 and FPC(CA 1989)R 1991, r. 6. The criteria for transferring the case include factors such as the forensic or legal complexity of the case, the number of parties involved and the involvement of a question of general public interest. For an outline on the topic of the transfer of proceedings see Chapter 25, paragraph 5.2.

If a party is dissatisfied with the decision reached by the magistrates' court as to the level of court at which the matter is to be tried, then he may *apply* for a transfer before the district judge of the relevant county court (FPR 1991, r. 4.6 and FPC(CA 1989)R 1991, r. 6(4)). Note that this is by way of *application* only; it is not by way of appeal from the magistrates' decision. The district judge may then make his own decision as to the level of court before which the case is to be heard.

For a general outline of the procedure to be adopted in Children Act 1989 proceedings see chapter 25 paragraph 6. The authors now intend to highlight some of the most important points of procedure as they relate to care and supervision proceedings.

2.8.3   The application

An applicant for a care or supervision order must:

(a)   file an application in respect of each child in Form CHA 19; and

(b)   serve a copy of the application on each respondent a minimum of three days before the hearing or directions appointment; and

(c)   at the same time as effecting service, give written notice of the proceedings to, inter alia:

(i)   the local authority providing accommodation for the child;

(ii)   persons caring for the child at the time when the proceedings are commenced;

(iii)   every person whom the applicant believes to be a party to pending proceedings in respect of the same child; and

(iv)   every person whom the applicant believes to be a parent without parental responsibility for the child.

The general procedure for applications is to be found in FPR 1991, r. 4.4 and FPC(CA 1989)R 1991, r. 4. The persons who are to be made respondents to proceedings and the persons who are to be notified of proceedings are set out in tabular form in the FPR 1991, Appendix 3 and the FPC(CA 1989)R 1991, sch. 2. The rules for service are set out in FPR 1991, r. 4.8 and FPC(CA 1989)R 1991, r. 8.

2.8.4   Withdrawal of an application
The general rules apply. See Chapter 25, paragraph 6.3.

2.8.5   Answer to application
In the county court and High Court following service of the application upon him the respondent should file a written answer and serve a copy on the other parties. However, there is no equivalent provision for an answer to be filed in public law proceedings in the magistrates' court (although there is provision for answers to be filed in s. 8 and sch. 1 proceedings in the magistrates' court).

2.8.6   Directions appointment
A directions appointment may be held by the justices' clerk, a single justice or the full court *at any time* during the proceedings in order to make directions as to the conduct of the proceedings. The magistrates' court may choose to hold the directions appointment in private (FPC(CA 1989)R 1991, r. 16(7)). However, the county court or High Court *must* hold such appointments in chambers unless the court directs otherwise (FPR 1991, r. 4.16(7)).

For further discussion of the procedure to be adopted as to such appointments and the matters upon which the court may issue directions see Chapter 25, paragraph 6.10.

2.8.7   Timetable
Section 32, Children Act 1989 reflects the general principle of the Act that delay in proceedings is likely to be prejudicial to the child's welfare. It requires the court hearing applications under Part IV of the Children Act 1989 to draw up a timetable with a view to disposing of the application without delay. It also enables the court to give directions to ensure that the timetable is adhered to. The relevant rules of court which deal with the timing of proceedings are to be found in FPR 1991, r. 4.15 and FPC(CA 1989)R 1991, r. 15. The aim of these provisions is to prevent the proceedings from lying dormant through the delay of the parties

and their advisers. For further discussion of the general rules as to timing see Chapter 25, paragraph 6.11.

2.8.8   The hearing

For the general rules as to the conduct of hearings see Chapter 25, paragraph 6.17. However, a hearing before the High Court or county court will be in chambers (FPR 1991, r. 4.16(7)) and a hearing before the magistrates' court may be held in private (FPC(CA 1989)R 1991, r. 16(7)).

2.8.8.1   Attendance of parties   For the general rules as to the attendance of parties at hearings or directions appointments see Chapter 25, paragraph 6.12. In the course of hearing any application made under Part IV or V of the Children Act 1989 (e.g. for a care order, supervision order, s. 34 contact order, emergency protection order etc.), the court has a discretion to order the attendance of the child at any stage in the proceedings (s. 95(1)). Where it believes that such an order will not be, or has not been, complied with the court may authorise a constable or other named person to enter and search premises in order to take charge of the child and to bring him to court (s. 95(4)(a)). Furthermore, the court may order anyone who it believes to be in a position to bring the child to court to do so, or to order a person with information as to the whereabouts of the child to disclose it to the court (s. 95(4)(b)).

2.8.8.2   Factors to be considered by the court   The various factors which the court must consider when hearing contested proceedings of this nature are set out fully in Chapter 25, paragraph 2. In general, the court must bear in mind that the child's welfare is paramount. In doing so, it must apply the statutory checklist of factors contained in s. 1(3), and must have regard to the principle that any delay in deciding the case is likely to be prejudicial to the welfare of the child. Finally, the court must have regard to the whole range or orders available to it (and not just the one applied for), but must not make any order unless satisfied that to make an order would be better for the child than making no order at all (s. 1(5)).

2.8.8.3   Documentary evidence   The general rules as to the need for the advance disclosure of documentary evidence are discussed in Chapter 25, paragraph 6.13.

2.8.8.4   Oral evidence   The court, proper officer or justices' clerk must keep a note of the substance of any oral evidence given at a hearing or directions appointment (FPR 1991, r. 4.20 and FPC(CA 1989)R 1991, r. 20). In the course of any proceedings under Parts IV or V of the Children Act 1989 (e.g. applications for care orders, supervision orders, s. 34 contact orders, emergency protection orders etc.) no-one is excused from giving evidence on any matter, or answering any question put to him in the course of giving his evidence, on the ground that doing so might incriminate him or his spouse of an offence. However, any statement or admission made in such proceedings is not admissible in proceedings for an offence other than perjury (see ss. 98 and 48(2), Children Act 1989).

2.8.8.5   Welfare reports   The question of welfare reports is dealt with fully in Chapter 25, paragraph 6.20.

2.8.8.6   The decision   After the final hearing the court must make its decision 'as soon as practicable'. Furthermore, when making an order or refusing an application the court must indicate both its findings of fact and the reasons for its decision (FPR 1991, r. 4.21 and FPC(CA 1989)R 1991, r. 21). If a care or supervision order is made then it must be recorded by the court in Form CHA 20. A copy of the order must be served by the justices' clerk as soon as practicable on the parties and on any person with whom the child is living (FPR 1991, r. 4.21(5) and (6) and FPC(CA 1989)R 1991, r. 21(7)).

2.9   Interim orders

Despite the presumption that delay in proceedings is likely to prejudice the welfare of the child concerned, there will be occasions when an adjournment of care proceedings is unavoidable. For example, the parties may need time in which to prepare their cases properly, or the guardian ad litem may need time in which to investigate and report on the child's circumstances. The effect of an interim care order is the same as a full order (for example, the authority obtains parental responsibility and there is a presumption that they will allow reasonable contact between the child and his parents), except where express provision is made to the contrary. The two main differences between full and interim orders are in respect of their duration (see paragraph 2.9.1 below) and in respect of the directions which the court may make in respect of them (see paragraph 2.9.2 below).

The court has power to make an interim care or interim supervision order where:

(a)   proceedings are adjourned on an application for a care or supervision order; or

(b)   the court gives a direction under s. 37(1) (i.e. that the local authority investigate the child's circumstances).

The power to make an interim order must not be exercised unless the court is satisfied that there are *reasonable grounds for believing* that the statutory criteria in s. 31(2), Children Act 1989 are satisfied with respect to the child concerned. The court does not have to be satisfied that the s. 31(2) grounds *exist*, since that would defeat the purpose of an adjournment and require the authority to prove their case on the first hearing. In effect, the authority have to show a *prima facie* case. In addition, the court must consider the three fundamental dictates contained in s. 1, Children Act 1989 before making an interim order, that is to say:

(a)   the child's welfare is the paramount consideration (s. 1(1));

(b)   any delay in determining the proceedings is likely to prejudice the welfare of the child (s. 1(2)); and

(c)   the court must not make any order unless it considers that making an order would be better than making no order at all (s. 1(5)).

There is, as yet, very little case law in respect of interim care orders. However, one case, very recently decided, gives a useful illustration of the ways in which such orders will and will not be considered appropriate. *Croydon LBC* v *A* (1992) 136 SJ (LB) 69 (FS) concerned a case where the local authority had removed children from their home under an emergency protection order because the father had sexually abused one of them. The children were placed with foster parents and the local authority applied to the magistrates for an interim care order. The magistrates refused the interim care order and instead made two prohibited steps orders, the first preventing the father from seeing the children and the second prohibiting him from having contact with the mother. The authority appealed and Hollings J held that the second order was beyond the scope of the Children Act 1989, because the act of the father in contacting the mother did not fall within the statutory definition of a 'step which could be taken by a parent in meeting his parental responsibility for a child'. In the circumstances, Hollings J found that since the parents were in continuous contact with one another the proposed orders would not protect the children in any event. Therefore, the authority's appeal was allowed and an interim care order was made instead. The case shows the way in which the possibility of using s. 8 orders in care proceedings may be used, albeit that Hollings J found them to be inappropriate in these particular circumstances. It illustrates the principle running through the Children Act 1989 that all orders are available in all cases.

If the court is hearing an application for a care or supervision order but decides, instead, to make a residence order, then the court *must* make an interim supervision order as well *unless* it is satisfied that the child's welfare will be satisfactorily safeguarded without an interim supervision order (s. 38(3)).

2.9.1   Duration of interim orders
An interim care or supervision order will last for an initial period of eight weeks (s. 38(4)). The court may extend the order for a further period of four weeks (s. 38(5)), and there appears to be nothing to prevent further extensions at four-weekly intervals. The rules about extension of time are complex and the practitioner is advised to study them in detail. In any event, the court must draw up a timetable with a view to disposing of the case without delay, and it is to be hoped that the duration of interim orders will thus be kept as short as possible. In fixing the period of the interim order the court can take into account whether any party opposed to the order was in a position to argue his case in full (s. 38(10)).

2.9.2   Directions made under an interim order
When a court makes a full care order it has no jurisdiction to give directions as to the child's welfare and upbringing. However, when it makes an *interim* care or supervision order it may give directions as to the medical or psychiatric examination or other assessment of the child (s. 38(6)); such a direction can be to the effect that no such examination or assessment is to take place (s. 38(7)). If the child is of sufficient understanding to make an informed decision he may refuse to submit to such an examination or assessment (s. 38(6)).

A direction may be varied at any time on the application of a qualified applicant, but it cannot be appealed (s. 38(8) and FPR 1991, r. 4.2(1) and FPC(CA 1989)R 1991, r. 2(1)).

2.10   Discharge of care orders

A care order, other than an interim care order, will remain in force until the child reaches 18 unless determined earlier (s. 91(12)). The other ways in which it might be terminated or discharged are as follows:

(a)   when the court makes a residence order in respect of a child in care the care order will be discharged automatically (s. 91(1));

(b)   when the court makes an adoption order the care order will be discharged automatically (Adoption Act 1976, s. 12(3) as substituted by the Children Act 1989, sch. 10, para. 3);

(c)   when a successful application is made under s. 39(1) to discharge the order. Such an application may be made by:

(i)   any person with parental responsibility for the child; or
(ii)   the child; or
(iii) the local authority.

When the court considers whether or not to discharge a care order it simply applies the welfare criteria set out in s. 1, Children Act 1989. There are no additional criteria to be considered as there are when the court considers whether or not to *make* a care order.

Upon an application to discharge a care order the court can consider an application to substitute the care order with a supervision order (s. 39(4)). When it considers such an application the court is relieved of the exercise of deciding whether or not the s. 31(2) grounds are made out (s. 39(5)).

When an unsuccessful application has been made for the discharge of a care order or for its substitution with a supervision order, then no repeat applications may be made for a period of six months following that disposal of the matter, except with the leave of the court (s. 91(15)).

2.11   Supervision orders

Up until now only passing mention has been made of supervision orders. It is now proposed to examine them in more detail.

2.11.1   *When may a supervision order be made?*
The court may make an order placing a child under the supervision of a local authority or a probation officer pursuant to s. 31(1) provided that:

(a)   the court is satisfied that the statutory grounds in s. 31(2) are made out in relation to the child concerned; and

(b)   the making of the supervision order is for the welfare of the child (s. 1).

Many of the rules relating to care orders apply equally to supervision orders:

(a)   an application can only be made if the child is under 17 (or under 16, if married): s. 31(3);

(b)   any delay in the determination of the application will be presumed to prejudice the welfare of the child, and therefore a timetable should be drawn up for the speedy disposal of the proceedings (s. 32);

(c)   the court may take the initiative and direct the local authority to investigate the circumstances of the child pursuant to s. 37(1), Children Act 1989, in order that the authority might decide whether or not to make an application for a supervision (or care) order;

(d)   interim supervision orders may be made on the same principles as interim care orders (see paragraph 2.9 above);

(e)   the provisions relating to guardians ad litem apply equally to proceedings for a supervision order as they do to care order proceedings (s. 41(1);

(f)   the same rules apply to the variation and discharge of supervision orders as for care orders (s. 39 and see paragraph 2.10 above).

2.11.2   *Effect of supervision order*

(a)   The supervising officer does not acquire parental responsibility for the child.

(b)   The supervisor's duties are set out in s. 35(1). His main duties are to advise, assist and befriend the supervised child and to take such steps as are reasonably necessary to give effect to the order. Where the supervision order is not wholly complied with or the supervisor considers that it may no longer be necessary then he may consider whether or not to apply to the court for the variation or discharge of the order (s. 35(1)(c)).

(c)   The making of a supervision order brings to an end any earlier care or supervision order made in respect of that child which would otherwise continue in force (Children Act 1989, sch. 3, para. 10).

2.11.3   *Duration of supervision order*

A supervision order will last for an initial period of one year, but the supervisor may apply to the court to have it extended for a period of up to three years beginning with the date on which the order was first made (Children Act 1989, sch. 3, para. 6). If the authority take the view, towards the end of the three year period, that the supervision order is still necessary then they will have to apply to the court again and prove that the s. 31(2) grounds are still in existence.

2.11.4   *Power to give directions to supervised child*

A supervision order may (pursuant to the Children Act 1989, sch. 3, para. 2) require the supervised child to comply with directions given by the supervisor to:

(a)   live at a particular place for a particular period of time;
(b)   present himself to specified persons at specified times and places;
(c)   participate in specified activities at specified times.

However, the child may only be required to comply with such directions for a total of 90 days (sch. 3, para. 7).

The supervisor has no power to give directions in respect of any medical or psychiatric treatment for the child (sch. 3, para. 2(3)). Such directions can only be given by the court (sch. 3, para. 4 and see paragraph 2.11.6 below).

2.11.5   *Imposition of obligations on responsible persons*

The Children Act 1989 enables obligations to be imposed upon 'responsible persons' (sch. 3, para. 1), provided that:

(a)   the person concerned *consents* to those obligations; and
(b)   the total numbers of days in respect of which the person can be required to comply does not exceed 90 (sch. 3, para. 7).

A 'responsible person' in relation to a supervised child means:

(a)   any person with parental responsibility for the child; and
(b)   any other person with whom the child is living (e.g. step-parents).

The obligations can be to take all reasonable steps to:

(a)   ensure that the child complies with his supervisor's directions; and
(b)   ensure that the child complies with any requirements in the supervision
order, for example, to attend for medical and psychiatric treatment.

The parent can apply to the court to have any requirement affecting him varied
(s. 39(2) and (3)).

2.11.6   Psychiatric and medical examination
A supervision order may require a child to submit to a medical or psychiatric
examination, or to do so from time to time as directed by his supervisor, provided
that:

(a)   the child *consents* to it (where he is of sufficient understanding to do so)
(sch. 3, para. 4(4)(a)) ; and
(b)   satisfactory arrangements have been made for the examination (sch. 3,
para. 4(4)(b)); and
(c)   the order must require that the examination be conducted by a specified
medical practitioner at a specific place (sch. 3, para. 4(2)).

2.11.7   Psychiatric and medical treatment
When a court makes or varies a supervision order it may include a requirement
that the child shall submit to psychiatric or medical treatment by a registered
medical practitioner at a specific place (sch. 3, para. 5). Before including such a
requirement the court must be satisfied:

(a)   on the evidence of an appropriate medical practitioner that the treatment
is justified; and
(b)   that the child consents to it (where he is of sufficient understanding to do
so); and
(c)   that satisfactory arrangements have been made for the treatment.

The medical practitioner may seek a variation of the requirement (for example,
where he feels that the treatment should continue for longer than the specified
period) by submitting a written report to the supervisor to that effect. Thereupon,
the supervisor must refer the report to the court and the court can make an order
cancelling or varying the requirement (sch. 3, para. 5(7)).

2.12   Care and supervision orders at the instigation of the court

It may happen that whilst the court is engaged in hearing family proceedings (for
example, an application for a s. 8 order), it becomes apparent that a care or
supervision order may be necessary. In those circumstances the court may direct
the local authority, pursuant to s. 37(1), to investigate the circumstances of the
child. Thereupon, the court will normally adjourn the matter in hand (and
perhaps make an interim care or supervision order in the meantime: see

paragraph 2.9 above) whilst the authority conduct their investigation and compile a report.

If the authority, in due course, decide *not* to apply for a care or supervision order they must inform the court of the reasons for their decision. They must also tell the court of any services or assistance they have provided, or intend to provide, for the child and his family, and of any other action they have taken, or will take (s. 37(3)). Furthermore, they must consider whether it would be appropriate to review the case at a later date (s. 37(6)).

It cannot be stressed too often that the court no longer has any power to commit a child into the care of, or place him under the supervision of, a local authority unless the authority concerned have made an express application.

2.13 Transitional provisions – care and supervision orders

Schedule 14, Children Act 1989 contains the vast majority of the transitional provisions relating to care and supervision orders. The main points are these:

(a)   Existing care orders made under old legislation were converted on 14 October 1991 into 'new style' care orders under the Children Act 1989 and the new law in Part IV of the Children Act 1989 will apply to them (sch. 14, para. 15(2)).

(b)   If the child in care was placed under the care and control of his parent or guardian on or before 14 October 1991, then after that date the provisions of the Children Act 1989 apply as if the child had been placed with that person under s. 23(5), Children Act 1989 (sch. 14, para. 17(2)).

(c)   If the child was in voluntary care prior to 14 October 1991 then after that date he is treated as if he is merely 'provided with accommodation' by the local authority under Part III of the Children Act 1989 (sch. 14, para. 17(2)).

(d)   Where, on 14 October 1991, an 'access' order was in force (under the Child Care Act 1980, s. 12C), then it has effect after that date as a 'contact' order under s. 34, Children Act 1989 (sch. 14, para. 18).

(e)   A supervision order made under the Children and Young Persons Act 1969 prior to 14 October 1991 is deemed after that date to be a supervision order made under the Children Act 1989 and its duration is governed by sch. 14, para. 25.

(f)   A supervision order made prior to 14 October 1991 under legislation *other* than the Children and Young Persons Act 1969 is *not* thereafter to be treated as a supervision order under the Children Act 1989. However, it will continue in force for a maximum of one year after the Children Act 1989 comes into force (i.e. not beyond 14 October 1992): sch. 14, para. 26.

(g)   Parental rights resolutions made by local authorities prior to 14 October 1991 continue to have effect for six months after that date (i.e. until 14 April 1992): sch. 14, para. 31.

(h)   A criminal care order in force prior to 14 October 1991 will continue to have effect for 6 months after that date (i.e. until 14 April 1992): sch. 14, para. 36.

3 LEGAL AID

The availability of legal aid for Children Act 1989 proceedings is dealt with fully in Chapter 2 at paragraph 23.

4 APPEALS

The question of appeals is dealt with fully in Chapter 25 at paragraph 6.18. However, note that the family proceedings court has no inherent power to grant a stay of execution pending an appeal to the High Court. If a stay is required then an application to the High Court is necessary (*Re O, The Times*, 6 March 1992 (FD)).

30 *Emergency protection of children*

1 INTRODUCTION

Part V of the Children Act 1989 introduces a new code for the protection of children. It aims to ensure that proper protective action can be taken in respect of children whilst providing proper procedures to enable parents and others connected with the child to challenge such action before the court. The main orders now available under the new statutory scheme are as follows:

(a)   Local authorities are placed under a positive duty to investigate cases of suspected child abuse and to decide upon the appropriate action to take (s. 47 and sch. 2, para. 4).

(b)   If parents refuse to cooperate with the local authority's assessment of a child whom they have reasonable cause to suspect is suffering, or is likely to suffer, significant harm then a 'child assessment order' is now available to enable the authority to complete its inquiries (s. 43).

(c)   The Children Act 1989 introduces 'emergency protection orders' to provide for the emergency protection of children; they replace the old 'place of safety order'. The grounds upon which they may be granted are more tightly defined than those relating to place of safety orders. Furthermore, parents and others will be able to challenge the making of an emergency protection order if they are present at the hearing; if they are not, then they will be able to seek a discharge of the order from the court after 72 hours (ss. 44 and 45).

(d)   'Police protection': powers are available to enable the police to detain a child for the purpose of protecting him (s. 46).

(e)   'Recovery orders' are available to facilitate the recovery of children who have been abducted whilst the subject of a care, emergency protection or recovery order (s. 50).

2. CHILD ASSESSMENT ORDERS

The 'half-way house' of a child assessment order is available to cover the situation where the local authority suspect that the child may be at risk of significant harm, but not at immediate risk requiring his removal or retention (e.g. in a hospital) under an emergency protection order, and his parents or others responsible for him refuse to cooperate with the authority's attempts to make an assessment of the child (s. 43). The order aims to allow the authority to complete their assessment so that they can decide whether or not to take further action in respect of the child. Where the court hears an application for a child assessment order it may, instead, make an emergency protection order if it is satisfied that the circumstances of the case warrant it (s. 43(4)).

2.1 The application

Only a local authority or 'authorised person' may apply for a child assessment order. The court may only make an order if it is satisfied that:

(a) the applicant has reasonable cause to suspect that the child is suffering, or is likely to suffer, significant harm;

(b) an assessment of the state of the child's health or development, or of the way in which he is being treated, is required to enable the applicant to establish whether or not the child is suffering, or is likely to suffer, significant harm; and

(c) it is unlikely that the assessment will be made, or be satisfactory, without a child assessment order.

Before making a child assessment order the court must also have regard to the 'welfare' and 'presumption of no order' principles set out in s. 1, Children Act 1989 (see Chapter 25, paragraph 2).

The application should always be made on notice at a full hearing in which the parties are able to participate, so that it can be challenged at that stage.

The court has power to prevent a further application being made by particular persons (including a local authority) without the court's leave, or to refuse to allow a further application within six months without leave (s. 91(14) and (15)).

2.2 Parties

An application can be made in respect of a child under the age of 18 (N.B. it is not subject to the age 17 limit applicable to care and supervision orders). Those who must be respondents to child assessment order proceedings and those who must be notified of the proceedings are set out in the FPR 1991, Appendix 3 and the FPC(CA 1989)R 1991, schedule 2.

The persons who must be made respondents are:

(a) every person the applicant believes to have parental responsibility for the child;

(b) where the child is the subject of a care order, every person the applicant believes to have had parental responsibility immediately prior to the making of the care order;

(c) where the application is to extend, vary or discharge an order, the parties to the original proceedings when the order was made;

(d) the child;

(e) any other person *may* be made a respondent, provided that he has first obtained leave of the court (FPR 1991, r. 4.7 and FPC(CA 1989)R 1991, r. 7).

2.3 Commencement and duration

The court may allow up to seven days for the assessment, and the order must specify the date by which the assessment is to begin (s. 43(5)).

2.4 Effect of child assessment order

The main effects of a child assessment order are as follows:

(a) Parental responsibility does not vest in the applicant by virtue of an order being made.

(b) The order requires the person in a position to do so to produce the child to the person named in the order so that the assessment may take place, and requires him to comply with any other directions contained in the order (s. 43(6)).

(c) The order authorises the carrying out of the assessment in accordance with the terms of the order (s. 43(7)).

(d) The child to whom the order relates may refuse to consent to the assessment if he is of sufficient understanding to do so (s. 43(8)).

(e) Child assessment orders may run alongside s. 8 orders (but will not be required where a care, supervision or emergency protection order is in force).

2.5 Directions

The court is empowered to attach directions to the child assessment order. For example, the court may wish to limit the extent of the assessment to a medical examination; it may wish to direct that a particular medical practitioner conduct the examination; it may wish to direct that specific persons be present during an examination and so forth. Furthermore, where it is necessary for the child to be kept away from home for the purposes of the assessment (e.g. in hospital), then tight conditions are imposed as to the circumstances in which this may be done and provision is made for contact between the child and persons connected with him during that time (s. 43(9) and (10)).

2.6 Variation and discharge of child assessment orders

Provision is made for an application to the court for a child assessment order to be varied or discharged (see s. 43(12)). Those who may apply include:

(a) the child;
(b) his parents;
(c) any other person with parental responsibility for him;
(d) any other person caring for him;
(e) any person in whose favour a contact order is in force with respect to the child;
(f) any person allowed to have contact with the child under a s. 34 contact order.

The circumstances in which such an application may be made, and additionally qualified applicants, are prescribed by rules of court (see FPR 1991, rr. 4.1(2)(c) and 4.2(3); FPC(CA 1989)R 1991, r. 2(3)).

2.7 Appeals

The provisions for appealing from a child assessment order are the same as those for appealing any order made under the Children Act 1989 (see Chapter 25, paragraph 6.18).

3   EMERGENCY PROTECTION ORDERS

3.1   Who may apply – and on what grounds?

There are three categories of applicants and different grounds apply to each category:

(a) 'Any person' may apply for an emergency protection order under s. 44(1)(a). The court may only grant the order under this ground if it is satisfied that there is reasonable cause to believe that the child is likely to suffer significant harm if either:

(i)   he is not removed to accommodation provided by or on behalf of the applicant; or

(ii) he does not remain in the place where he is then being accommodated.

(b) A local authority may apply on the ground set out in (a) above *or* they may, instead, rely on the ground set out in s. 44(1)(b), that is to say:

(i)   inquiries are being made with respect to the child under s. 47(1)(b); and

(ii) those inquiries are being frustrated by access to the child being unreasonably refused to a person authorised to seek access *and* that the applicant has reasonable cause to believe that access to the child is required as a matter of *urgency*.

(c) An 'authorised person' (the meaning of which is the same as for the purposes of s. 31, i.e. at the moment only the NSPCC have this status) may apply on the ground set out in s. 44(1)(c) if he can show that:

(i)   he has reasonable cause to believe that a child is suffering, or is likely to suffer, significant harm;

(ii) he is making inquiries with respect to the child's welfare; and

(iii) those inquiries are being frustrated by access to the child being unreasonably refused to a person authorised to seek access *and* the applicant has reasonable cause to believe that access to the child is required as a matter of *urgency*.

'Harm' and 'significant harm' are defined in s. 31(9) and (10) and have already been discussed in Chapter 29, paragraph 2.5.1.

A 'person authorised to seek access' is defined in s. 44(2)(b) as:

(a) in the case of a local authority – an officer of the authority or a person authorised by them to act on their behalf in connection with their inquiries;

(b) in the case of an 'authorised person' that person.

3.2   Effects of an emergency protection order

The effects of an emergency protection order are as follows:

(a) the court can direct any person who is in a position to do so to comply with any request to produce the child to the applicant (s. 44(4)(a));

(b) the court can authorise:

(i)   the removal of the child at any time to accommodation provided by or on behalf of the applicant; or

(ii)   the prevention of the child's removal from any hospital, or other place, in which he was being accommodated immediately before the making of the order (s. 44(4)(b)).

(c)   the emergency protection order gives the applicant parental responsibility for the child for the duration of the order (s. 44(4)(c)). The applicant should only take such action in meeting his parental responsibility as is reasonably required to safeguard or promote the welfare of the child (having particular regard to the duration of the order): s. 44(5);

(d)   the court has power under s. 44(6) to make directions as to:

(i)   the contact which is, or is not, to be allowed between the child and any named person; and

(ii)   the medical, psychiatric or other assessment of the child.

3.3   Duration of emergency protection order

An emergency protection order may have effect in the first instance for a maximum of eight days (s. 45(1)). The court may extend the order once only for a period of up to seven days (s. 45(6)), but *only* if the applicant has parental responsibility for the child as a result of the emergency protection order *and* is entitled to apply for a care order with respect to the child (i.e. only local authorities and the NSPCC at the moment). The extension should only be granted if the court has reasonable cause to believe that the child is likely to suffer significant harm if the order is not extended (s. 45(4), (5) and (6)).

3.4   Who should be informed?

The FPR 1991, Appendix 3 and the FPC(CA 1989)R 1991, schedule 2 set out those persons who should be informed of an application for an emergency protection order.

3.5   Parental contact

The court may give directions as to the contact which is, or is not, to be allowed between the child and any named person (s. 44(6)(a).

Furthermore, the applicant is under a duty, while the emergency protection order is in force, to allow the child reasonable contact (subject to any direction of the court under s. 44(6)) with the following persons:

(a)   his parents;

(b)   any person who is not a parent but has parental responsibility for him;

(c)   any person with whom he was living immediately before the making of the order;

(d)   any person in whose favour a contact order is in force with respect to him;

(e)   any person who is allowed to have contact with the child by virtue of an order under s. 34; and

(f)   any person acting on behalf of any of those persons.

The contact provisions may not be challenged (s. 45(10)).

3.6 Challenging an emergency protection order

An emergency protection order may be challenged by any of the following persons (s. 45(8)):

(a) the child;

(b) any parent of his;

(c) any person who is not a parent of his but who has parental responsibility for him;

(d) any person with whom he was living immediately before the making of the order.

Any application for the order to be discharged, may only be made after a period of 72 hours has expired. The 72 hours is calculated from the time when the order was made (s. 45(9)). The right of challenge is not available where the prospective challenger was given notice of the hearing at which the order was made and was present at that hearing (or at a hearing as a result of which the period of the order was extended): s. 45(11). The reason for this is that no challenge should be allowed if it could have been made at the time of the application for the order.

There is no right to appeal against the making of, or refusal to make, an emergency protection order, or against any direction given by the court in connection with such an order (s. 45(10)).

3.7 Returning the child

The applicant has a discretion to return the child if it appears to him that it is safe for the child to be returned or that it is safe for the child to be allowed to be removed from the place in question (s. 44(10) and (11)). However, the applicant may remove the child again under the same order, provided that the time of the original order is still running and it appears to him that a change in the circumstances of the case makes it necessary for him to do so (s. 44(10) and (12)).

4 POLICE PROTECTION

The police have important powers under s. 46, Children Act 1989. Where a constable has reasonable cause to believe that a child would otherwise be likely to suffer significant harm, he may:

(a) remove the child to suitable accommodation and keep him there; or

(b) take reasonable steps to prevent the removal of the child from any hospital, or other place, in which he is then being accommodated.

4.1 Duration of police protection

A child may not be kept in police protection for a period of more than 72 hours (s. 46(6)). As soon as practicable after taking the child into police protection the constable must ensure that the appropriate inquiries into the case are undertaken by the police officer designated for this purpose. After completing his inquiries the designated officer must release the child unless there is still reasonable cause to believe that the child would be likely to suffer significant harm if released (s. 46(3)(e) and (5)). The constable who initially took the child into police protection has a duty to inform various persons, including the local authority, the child, the child's parents and persons with parental responsibility for the child, of, *inter alia,* the steps that have been taken and the reasons for them. The full extent of those duties are set out in s. 46(3) and (4).

4.2 Parental responsibility

Neither the constable concerned nor the designated officer acquire parental responsibility for the child whilst he is in police protection. However, the designated officer must do what is reasonable to promote the child's welfare, bearing in mind the short duration of the period of police protection (s. 46(9) and s. 3(5)).

4.3 Contact with the child

The designated officer must allow the following persons to have contact with the child during the period of police protection, provided that *in his opinion* it is both reasonable and in the child's best interests:

(a) the child's parents;
(b) anyone else who has parental responsibility for the child;
(c) anyone with whom the child was living immediately before he was taken into police protection;
(d) a person who has a contact order in his favour relating to the child;
(e) anyone acting on behalf of the persons listed in (a) to (d) above.

5 RECOVERY ORDERS

A court may make a 'recovery order' in respect of a child, pursuant to s. 50, Children Act 1989, where:

(a) the child is in care, in police protection or is the subject of an emergency protection order (ss. 50(2) and 49(2)); and
(b) there is reason to believe that the child:

(i) has been unlawfully taken away, or is being unlawfully kept away from the 'responsible person'; or
(ii) has run away or is staying away from the 'responsible person'; or
(iii) is missing.

5.1 Who can apply?

The court may make a recovery order only on the application of the following persons:

(a) a person with parental responsibility for the child by virtue of a care order or emergency protection order; or
(b) where the child is in police protection, the designated officer (s. 50(4)).

5.2 Effect of recovery order

A recovery order will have the following effects (s. 50(3)):

(a)   it operates as a direction to any person who is in a position to do so to produce the child on request to any authorised person;

(b)   it authorises the removal of the child by any authorised person;

(c)   it requires any person who has information as to the child's whereabouts to disclose that information, if asked to do so, to a constable or an officer of the court;

(d)   it authorises a constable to enter any premises specified in the order and search for the child, using reasonable force if necessary.

PART VIII
FINANCIAL PROVISION AND PROPERTY DURING MARRIAGE

31   Financial provision in the magistrates' courts

1   INTRODUCTION

The following statutes empower magistrates' courts to grant financial provision for spouses and children:

(a)   Domestic Proceedings and Magistrates' Courts Act 1978 (DPMCA 1978) — financial provision can be made for a spouse or a child of the family.

(b)   Children Act 1989 – financial provision can be made for legitimate and illegitimate children (see Chapter 26, paragraph 13).

The practitioner should note that the Child Support Act 1991 is due to come into force over a phased three-year period, commencing in 1993. It will introduce a formula for the calculation of children's maintenance based upon Income Support rates, and will implement a system for the collection and enforcement of such payments. A Child Support Agency will be set up within the DSS and will take over from the courts the responsibility for the calculation of most claims for children's maintenance. Where the agency has been involved in the assessment of the level of children's maintenance it will also take over from the courts the responsibilities of collection and enforcement of the payments. It would appear that there is going to be an appeals system, to be part of the Social Security Appeals Tribunals and Medical Appeals Tribunals run by the Lord Chancellor's Department, but, if the functioning of the SSATs is anything to go by, the appeals tribunals will be so hedged in by regulations prescribed by statutory instrument as to make an appeal against quantum of little value.

Furthermore, the Maintenance Enforcement Act 1991 came into force on 1 April 1991. It provides new methods whereby the courts can attempt to enforce maintenance orders: at the same time it improves the efficiency of existing methods of enforcement.

This chapter deals with the provisions of the Domestic Proceedings and Magistrates' Courts Act 1978.

2   SUMMARY OF MAIN FINANCIAL SECTIONS

Part I of DPMCA 1978 deals with matrimonial proceedings in the magistrates' courts. The main sections enabling the court to make financial orders are as follows:

Section 2 — empowers the court to make periodical payments and lump sum orders for a party to the marriage or a child of the family if one of the grounds set out in s. 1 is made out (failure to provide reasonable maintenance, behaviour and desertion).

Section 6 — empowers the court to make agreed orders as to periodical payments and lump sums for a party to the marriage or a child of the family.

Section 7 — empowers the court to make an order for periodical payments for a party to the marriage or a child of the family where the parties have been living apart for three months and one of the parties has actually been making periodical payments for the other party or for a child of the family.

3   JURISDICTION UNDER PART I DPMCA 1978

Clarity is unfortunately not a feature of the jurisdiction provisions of Part I, DPMCA 1978. However the essential rules are set out in paragraphs 3.1 and 3.2 below.

3.1   Is the matter one that the English courts can hear?

The effect of s. 30, DPMCA 1978 seems to be that a magistrates' court in England and Wales will have jurisdiction to hear an application for an order under Part I of the Act if, at the date of the making of the application:

(a)   both parties to the marriage are resident in England and Wales; *or*

(b)   the applicant is resident in England and Wales and the parties last ordinarily resided together as man and wife in England and Wales but the respondent resides in Scotland or Northern Ireland; *or*

(c)   the respondent is resident in England and Wales and the applicant resides in Scotland or Northern Ireland, irrespective of where the parties last cohabited (s. 30(1) and (3)).

Example 1. The solicitor is consulted by Mrs Smith who wishes to seek an order for periodical payments for herself under s. 2, DPMCA 1978 on the ground of her husband's behaviour. She and her husband both live in Grimsby — indeed, they have done so all their lives. A magistrates' court in England and Wales will clearly have jurisdiction (see (a) above).

Example 2. The facts are the same as in Example 1 except that when the parties separated Mr Smith went to live in Scotland with his mother. A magistrates' court in England and Wales will have jurisdiction on the basis that the applicant is resident in England and Wales and the parties last ordinarily resided together in England and Wales. The fact that Mr Smith now lives in Scotland does not preclude jurisdiction.

Example 3. Mr and Mrs O'Brian's last matrimonial home was in Northern Ireland. When they separated, Mr O'Brian remained in Northern Ireland and Mrs O'Brian came back to live with her family in England. The English magistrates' courts will not have jurisdiction to hear a complaint by Mrs O'Brian; the only possible ground for jurisdiction would have been (b) above but this is not made out because the parties last resided together as man and wife outside England and Wales.

Example 4. The situation is as in Example 3, save that it is Mr O'Brian not Mrs O'Brian who comes to England to live after the separation. A magistrates' court in England and Wales would have jurisdiction under (c) above to hear a complaint by Mrs O'Brian since, where the respondent is resident in England and Wales, it is immaterial where the parties last cohabited.

Example 5. Mr and Mrs Gonzalez have lived in England during their married life. When they separate, Mr Gonzalez goes back to live in Spain, his home country. Mrs Gonzalez wishes to seek an order for periodical payments under s. 1, DPMCA 1978. Because the respondent now lives abroad, the English magistrates' courts have no jurisdiction.

Proceedings for variation or revocation of periodical payments orders under s. 20, DPMCA 1978 are an exception to these rules. Section 24 applies in substitution for s. 30(3). The effect of s. 24 combined with s. 30(1) (which does still apply to these proceedings) is that a magistrates' court in England and Wales has jurisdiction to hear the proceedings provided that one party is ordinarily resident in England and Wales despite the fact that the other party to the proceedings resides outside England and Wales (whether he resides in another part of the British Isles or overseas).

3.2 Which magistrates' court?

A particular magistrates' court has jurisdiction to hear an application under Part I of the 1978 Act if, at the date of the making of the application, either the applicant or the respondent ordinarily resides within the commission area for which the court is appointed (s. 30(1)).

In the case of applications for orders under ss. 2, 6 and 7 DPMCA 1978, the court also has jurisdiction if the applicant and respondent last ordinarily resided together as man and wife within the commission area for which the court is appointed (Magistrates' Courts (Matrimonial Proceedings) Rules 1980, r. 11).

4 WHO MAY APPLY FOR AN ORDER UNDER SS. 2, 6 AND 7?

Only a party to a marriage may apply for an order under ss. 2, 6 and 7, DPMCA 1978 (see ss. 1, 6(1) and 7(1) respectively).

A child of the family is not entitled to make an application for an order for himself although, of course, if a party to the marriage makes an application, the court will have power to make financial provision for the child as well as, or instead of, for the party to the marriage.

5 DEFINITION OF 'PARTY TO A MARRIAGE' AND 'CHILD OF THE FAMILY'

'Party to a marriage' is not defined in the Act but means a party to a subsisting marriage. Therefore applications cannot be made by a divorced spouse or a spouse whose marriage has been annulled. Applications by cohabitees are clearly out of the question.

'Child of the family' is defined in s. 88 DPMCA 1978 in exactly the same way as it is defined for the purposes of the Matrimonial Causes Act 1973 (see Chapter 7 paragraph 3.7). However, where there is a child of the family under 18 years of age the court may not dismiss an application made by a party to the marriage under ss. 2, 6 or 7, DPMCA 1978, nor may it make a final order in respect of it until it has decided whether or not to exercise any of its powers under the Children Act 1989 with respect to the child concerned (DPMCA 1978, s. 8, as substituted by the Children Act 1989, s. 108(5), sch. 13 para. 36 – and see Chapter 26 for a discussion of the powers of the court under the Children Act 1989). Note that proceedings under the DMPCA 1978 come within the definition of 'family proceedings' set out in ss. 3 and 4 of the Children Act 1989. This enables a court hearing DMPCA 1978 proceedings to make orders under the Children Act 1989 where appropriate.

6   ORDERS UNDER S. 2

6.1   Grounds for an order (s. 1)

Either party to a marriage may apply for an order under s. 2 on the ground that the other party to the marriage:

(a)   has failed to provide reasonable maintenance for the applicant; or
(b)   has failed to provide, or to make proper contribution towards, reasonable maintenance for any child of the family; *or*
(c)   has behaved in such a way that the applicant cannot reasonably be expected to live with him; *or*
(d)   has deserted the applicant.

6.1.1   Failure to provide reasonable maintenance (s. 1(a) and (b))
DPMCA 1978 gives no guidance as to how to determine whether or not the respondent has been providing reasonable maintenance for the applicant or has been providing or making proper contribution towards reasonable maintenance for any child of the family. This is a question of fact.

A court determining the same question under s. 27, Matrimonial Causes Act 1973 is required to have regard to all the circumstances of the case including the matters referred to in s. 25 of that Act (i.e. the matters to which the court is directed to have regard when determining ancillary relief applications; see Chapter 32, paragraph 4). It would seem common sense for a magistrates' court to adopt the same approach and to make reference to the factors set out in s. 3 DPMCA 1978 (see 6.3 below, i.e. the matters to which the court is to have regard in exercising its powers to make financial orders under s. 2, which are virtually identical to the s. 25, Matrimonial Causes Act 1973 factors).

Thus a proper approach to the question of reasonable maintenance by the magistrates' court might be as follows:

(a)   To determine what order it would have made under s. 2 for the maintenance of the applicant and/or any child of the family concerned in the application, bearing in mind all the factors set out in s. 3. This will mean taking into account financial needs and resources, etc.

(b)   To determine what the respondent is actually paying and compare it with what the court would have ordered.

(c)   If the amount the respondent is paying is significantly less than the amount that the court would have ordered, this is a strong indication that the respondent is not making reasonable provision.

There is no need to prove that the respondent's failure to provide is morally reprehensible, i.e. that he has intentionally or negligently kept the applicant or a child of the family short of money. He can be held to have failed to provide reasonable maintenance where he has been totally unaware that the applicant or a child was in need. Indeed, even a wife who is in desertion may successfully establish a case on the ground of failure to provide reasonable maintenance; *Robinson* v *Robinson* [1983] Fam 42, [1983] 1 All ER 391, appears to be such a case.

> **Example.** Mr and Mrs Brown live apart by consent. Mrs Brown does not work full-time because she has to look after the three young children. Before the separation, she used to work two evenings a week in the local pub in York for which she earned £20. However, she gave this up the week after Mr Brown and she separated because she could not get a baby-sitter. She has never told Mr Brown that she has had to give up work. Mr Brown is a sales representative earning £14,000 per annum. He is currently working in the South East and has been paying Mrs Brown £40 per week by standing order to cover the maintenance of herself and the children. Mr and Mrs Brown have no contact and Mrs Brown has never told her husband that she finds it difficult to manage.
>
> Mrs Brown makes a complaint to the magistrates' court based on s. 1(a) and (b). Taking into account all the circumstances, the magistrates decide that it would be appropriate for Mr Brown to pay £15 per week for each child and £60 per week for Mrs Brown, a total of £105 per week. The maintenance he has been paying falls considerably short of this figure and the magistrates therefore find Mrs Brown's complaint proved, despite the fact that Mr Brown was unaware that his wife was in difficulty. They make an order that he should pay £15 per week for each child and £60 per week for his wife.

It has been suggested that the court will only be able to make an order on the basis of failure to maintain if the respondent is still failing to make reasonable provision at the time of the hearing of the complaint (by analogy with the case of *Irvin* v *Irvin* [1968] 1 All ER 271, [1968] 1 WLR 464 which may be applicable to desertion cases; see paragraph 6.1.3 below). There has been no decision on the point. However, it would seem somewhat unrealistic if the respondent were to be able to escape liability under s. 1(a) and (b) simply by starting to make reasonable payments a short time before the hearing. Surely the period before the hearing must be taken as a whole and a decision reached as to whether, taking good weeks with bad weeks, the respondent's record of payment can be said to amount to reasonable provision or not.

6.1.2   Behaviour (s. 1(c))
This ground is identical to the behaviour fact set out in s. 1(2)(b), Matrimonial Causes Act 1973 in relation to divorce and judicial separation proceedings. The test for behaviour is therefore exactly the same (*Bergin* v *Bergin* [1983] 1 All ER 905, [1983] 1 WLR 279). The law as to behaviour is set out in Chapter 3 paragraph 5. Note, however:

(a)   Adultery is not relied upon as behaviour under s. 1(2)(b), Matrimonial Causes Act 1973 as there is a separate adultery fact (s. 1(2)(a), Matrimonial Causes Act 1973). Section 1 DPMCA 1978 does not include an adultery ground. It is therefore suggested that adultery may well amount to behaviour for the purposes of s. 1 DPMCA 1978.

(b)   The provisions of s. 2, Matrimonial Causes Act 1973 as to cohabitation after the last incident of behaviour do not apply to behaviour under s. 1 DPMCA 1978. Presumably, therefore, the court has a free hand to take into account the fact that the applicant *has* gone on living with the respondent when determining whether she *can reasonably be expected* to go on living with him. However, the mere fact that the applicant has gone on living with the respondent will not automatically prevent her from relying on behaviour; the court will look at her reason for doing so (see *Bradley* v *Bradley* [1973] 3 All ER 750, [1973] 1 WLR 1291 and Chapter 3 paragraph 10.2.2).

(c)   There is, however, a time-limit on complaints of behaviour in the magistrates' courts. Section 127, Magistrates' Courts Act 1980 provides that a complaint must be made within six months of the time when the matter of complaint arose. If the behaviour complained of is continuing, s. 127 will cause no problem. However, if the last incident of behaviour occurred more than six months before a complaint is made, the magistrates' court will not be able to hear the complaint. Section 127 also applies to s. 1(a) and (b) DPMCA 1978 but, as these are continuing matters of complaint, should be of no practical significance in relation to these grounds.

6.1.3   Desertion (s. 1(d))
The same principles must be applied to determine whether the respondent has deserted the applicant as are applicable to determine whether there has been desertion in divorce and judicial separation cases based on s. 1(2)(c), Matrimonial Causes Act 1973 (see Chapter 3 paragraph 7). However, whereas desertion must have continued for a minimum of two years for divorce or judicial separation purposes, there is no minimum period for desertion under s. 1 DPMCA 1978.

The case of *Irvin* v *Irvin* [1968] 1 All ER 271, [1968] 1 WLR 464 decided, in relation to desertion under Matrimonial Proceedings (Magistrates' Courts) Act 1960 (the predecessor of DPMCA 1978), that the desertion must be continuing at the time of the hearing of the complaint. It may be that the same principle applies to a complaint under s. 1(d) DPMCA 1978.

6.2   Orders which can be made (s. 2)

6.2.1   General
Where the applicant satisfies the court of any of the grounds mentioned in s. 1, the court may make any one or more of the following orders:

(a)   An order that the respondent shall make to the applicant such periodical payments, and for such term, as may be specified in the order.

(b)   An order that the respondent shall pay to the applicant such lump sum not exceeding £1,000 as may be so specified.

(c)   An order that the respondent shall make to the applicant for the benefit of a child of the family to whom the application relates, or to such a child, such periodical payments, and for such term, as may be so specified.

(d)   An order that the respondent shall pay to the applicant for the benefit of a child of the family to whom the application relates, or to such a child, such lump sum as may be so specified.

6.2.2   Special provisions as to lump sums ordered under s. 2

(a)   £1,000 limit: s. 2(3) provides that the amount of any lump sum required to be paid shall not exceed £1,000 (or such larger amount as the Secretary of State may from time to time fix). Whilst each person can thus only receive £1,000 by way of lump sum in the first instance, there is no reason why, for example, a lump sum of £1,000 should not be given to each child of the family in addition to a lump sum of £1,000 for the applicant if this seems appropriate in the circumstances (*Burridge* v *Burridge* [1982] 3 All ER 80, [1982] 3 WLR 552, [1983] Fam 9).

(b)   The court must take into account the matters set out in s. 3 DPMCA 1978 (see paragraph 6.3 below) in deciding whether to order a lump sum and if so of what amount. There may be all sorts of circumstances warranting a lump sum payment but it is expressly provided by s. 2(2) that, inter alia, a lump sum may be ordered for the purpose of enabling any liability or expenses reasonably incurred in maintaining the applicant, or any child of the family to whom the application relates, before the making of the order to be met. Note that another way of dealing with the problem of accrued expenses would be for the court to make a back-dated periodical payments order (see paragraph 9.2). This would avoid using up any part of the permitted £1,000 lump sum and such a lump sum could therefore be made as well if the circumstances merited it.

Example. (A suitable case for a lump sum order.) Mrs Wilkinson establishes the behaviour ground under s. 1(c). She and her husband are living apart. Her husband is earning £9,000 per annum as a postman. She does not work as there are two children of the family under five for whom she cares. Before Mrs Wilkinson stopped work, she and her husband each used to contribute to the family budget and then each put away the balance of their earnings in their own savings account. Mrs Wilkinson had £1,100 in her account before the separation; however, the money has been used up whilst the parties have been living apart paying household bills, buying clothes and food for the children and taking them on holiday to Filey. Mr Wilkinson still has a substantial amount in his savings account. The court makes an order for periodical payments to Mrs Wilkinson and the two children and also orders Mr Wilkinson to pay a lump sum of £1,000 to his wife.

The case of *Burridge* v *Burridge* supra, established that a lump sum can be ordered even where the respondent has no capital resources provided the court takes into account the respondent's capacity to pay.

The court in *Burridge* also approved the making of lump sum orders for children although the respondent was impecunious. Lump sums would rarely be ordered for children by a divorce court unless the respondent was a man of some means (see Chapter 16 paragraph 7.2.2). However, it must be borne in mind that the making of lump sums for children in the magistrates' court is a way round the £1,000 limit on lump sum orders for an applicant. Therefore where, as in the *Burridge* case, expenses of over £1,000 have been incurred, partly on behalf of the children, it may be appropriate to reimburse the applicant indirectly by orders to the children.

Example. (The facts of *Burridge v* Burridge supra.) The applicant wife and respondent husband had separated. The wife looked after the two children and, when the husband failed to maintain the family, the wife incurred substantial debts in maintaining herself and the children. She applied for an order under s. 2 on the basis of the husband's failure to provide reasonable maintenance for herself and the children. The husband was unemployed and had no capital. He told the magistrates that he was confident he could obtain employment within six weeks. The magistrates ordered him to pay £500 lump sum (N.B. the limit for lump sum orders at that time was £500) for the wife and £125 for each child payable by weekly instalments, the first instalment to be payable six weeks from the order. The husband failed to find work and appealed against the order. The order was upheld although the case was remitted to the magistrates for further enquiry into the husband's resources to see if he was now working with a view to putting forward the date of the first instalment payment if he was not.

It is difficult to see why the magistrates in *Burridge* chose to make what is, in effect, a periodical payments order, in this round-about way. It may be that they did make a periodical payments order as well which is not mentioned in the report. If not, one wonders whether it would not have been more appropriate, for example, for them to have adjourned the wife's complaint after finding it proved to see whether the husband's confidence about his job was justified (in which case they could have made an appropriate order on the adjourned hearing) or to have made a periodical payments order forthwith to commence in six weeks' time on the basis that the husband would by then have a job. If this latter course had been taken, the husband could have sought a variation if work was not forthcoming.

(c)   The magistrates can order payment of the lump sum by instalments or simply give time for payment (s. 75, Magistrates' Courts Act 1980). Where payment by instalments is ordered, application can be made subsequently by the payer or the payee to the magistrates' court under s. 22 DPMCA 1978 for a variation in the number of instalments or the dates for payment or the amount of any instalment.

(d)   On an application under s. 20 to vary or revoke the periodical payments order made under s. 2(1)(a) or (c), the court is not limited to attending to the periodical payments order. It can also make an order under s. 2(1)(b) or (d) for the payment of a lump sum not exceeding £1,000. Strangely, this provision would seem to mean that, if there is a variation application, the court may end up having made more than one £1,000 lump sum in favour of the same person. Section 20(7) expressly provides that a lump sum can be ordered notwithstanding that the payer was required to pay a lump sum by a previous order under Part I of the Act. Nowhere is it expressly stated that there is power to order a second (or even subsequent) lump sum where a lump sum has already been ordered *for the same person* but this seems to be implicit in the legislation. Variation is dealt with more fully at paragraph 14 below.

6.3   Matters to which the court has regard in exercising its powers under s.2 (s.3 as amended by the Matrimonial and Family Proceedings Act 1984)

6.3.1   Provisions in line with s. 25, Matrimonial Causes Act 1973
The provisions of s. 3 DPMCA 1978 are virtually the same as the provisions of s. 25, Matrimonial Causes Act 1973 which sets out the matters to which the court

is to have regard in deciding how to exercise its powers in relation to financial relief and property adjustment after divorce, nullity or judicial separation. The provisions of s. 3 are given in full below and the minor points of difference between s. 3 and s. 25 are pointed out. However, reference should be made to Chapter 16 for commentary on how the courts apply the principles to determine the appropriate periodical payments order or lump sum. It is worth bearing in mind that, although the magistrates must take virtually the same approach as that of the divorce court district judges in deciding what orders to make (taking into account the same matters, employing the one-third rule where appropriate, looking at the net effect of the proposed order, etc.), it may be found that the orders made by magistrates tend to be rather less generous in amount than those made by district judges. In the case of lump sum orders, this is clearly partly the result of the ceiling of £1,000 on each lump sum the magistrates can order. However, the magistrates are no doubt also influenced in the case of both lump sums and periodical payments by the fact that their experience is gained largely in dealing with parties who are of limited means.

6.3.2   General duty of the court (s. 3(1))
Section 3(1) provides that, where an application is made for an order under s. 2, it shall be the duty of the court, in deciding whether to exercise its powers under that section and, if so, in what manner, to have regard to all the circumstances of the case, first consideration being given to the welfare while a minor of any child of the family who has not attained the age of 18.

6.3.3   Considerations in relation to orders for a party to a marriage (s. 3(2))
Section 3(2) provides that, as regards the exercise of its powers under s. 2(1)(a) and (b) (periodical payments and lump sums for a party to a marriage), the court shall in particular have regard to the following matters:

(a)   The income, earning capacity, property and other financial resources which each of the parties to the marriage has or is likely to have in the foreseeable future, including in the case of earning capacity any increase in that capacity which it would in the opinion of the court be reasonable to expect a party to take steps to acquire.

(b)   The financial needs, obligations and responsibilities which each of the parties to the marriage has or is likely to have in the foreseeable future.

(c)   The standard of living enjoyed by the parties to the marriage before the occurrence of the conduct which is alleged as the ground of the application.

(d)   The age of each party to the marriage and the duration of the marriage.

(e)   Any physical or mental disability of either of the parties to the marriage.

(f)   The contributions which each of the parties had made or is likely in the foreseeable future to make to the welfare of the family, including any contribution by looking after the home or caring for the family.

(g)   The conduct of each of the parties, if that conduct is such that it would in the opinion of the court be inequitable to disregard it.

The following differences between s. 3(2) and s. 25(2) should be noted:

(a)   Section 3(2)(c) directs the court to have regard to the standard of living enjoyed *by the parties to the marriage before the occurrence of the conduct alleged* as a ground for the application. Section 25(2)(c) directs the court to have regard to the standard of living enjoyed *by the family before the breakdown of the marriage*.

(b)   Section 25(2)(h) directs the court to consider the value of any benefit which each of the parties to the marriage will lose the chance of acquiring by reason of the termination of the marriage, for example, lost pension rights. There is no equivalent provision in s. 3(2) for the obvious reason that orders of the magistrates' court do not affect the status of the parties and are therefore not likely to affect their entitlement to any benefit.

Under Matrimonial Proceedings (Magistrates' Courts) Act 1960, the predecessor of DPMCA 1978, certain conduct on the part of the applicant used to constitute an absolute bar to relief, for example, she was not entitled to relief if she had committed adultery. Section 3(2) DPMCA 1978 brings the magistrates' courts into line with the divorce courts on the question of conduct and there are no longer any absolute bars to relief. The case of *Robinson* v *Robinson* [1983] Fam 42, [1983] 1 All ER 391, makes it clear that the magistrates' and the divorce courts should take the same attitude towards conduct. This case was decided before the amendment of ss. 3 and 25 in relation to conduct by the Matrimonial and Family Proceedings Act 1984 but no doubt the principle will hold good under the amended law also. For an authority on conduct in the magistrates' courts, see *Vasey* v *Vasey* [1985] 15 Fam Law 158.

6.3.4   Considerations in relation to orders for a child of the family (s. 3(3) and (4))

Section 3(3) provides that, as regards the exercise of its powers under s. 2(1)(c) and (d), the court shall in particular have regard to the following matters:

(a)   the financial needs of the child;

(b)   the income, earning capacity (if any), property and other financial resources of the child;

(c)   any physical or mental disability of the child;

(d)   the standard of living enjoyed by the family before the occurrence of the conduct which is alleged as the ground of the application;

(e)   the manner in which the child was being and in which the parties to the marriage expected him to be educated or trained;

(f)   the matters mentioned in relation to the parties to the marriage in s. 3(2)(a) and (b) (financial needs and resources).

Section 3(4) provides that, as regards the exercise of its powers under s. 2 in favour of a child of the family who is not the child of the respondent, the court shall also have regard to:

(a)   whether the respondent has assumed any responsibility for the child's maintenance and, if he did, the extent to which, and the basis on which, he assumed that responsibility and to the length of time during which he discharged that responsibility;

(b)   whether in assuming and discharging that responsibility the respondent did so knowing that the child was not his own child;

(c)   the liability of any other person to maintain the child.

The following differences between s. 3(3) and s. 25(3) should be noted:

(a) The standard of living to which the court must have regard under s. 3(3) is the standard of living enjoyed by the family *before the conduct alleged*. Under s. 25(3) it is the standard of living enjoyed *before the breakdown of the marriage* that is relevant.

(b) Section 3(3)(f) directs the court to take into account the financial resources and needs of the parties to the marriage (the matters mentioned in s. 3(2)(a) and (b)). Section 25(3)(e), the corresponding provision under s. 25, directs the court to have regard not only to those additional matters (s. 25(2)(a) and (b)) but also to any physical or mental disability of either of the parties to the marriage (s. 25(2)(e)).

6.4 Substitution of s. 6 application for s. 2 application (s. 6(4))

Where a party to a marriage has applied for an order under s. 2 he may, at any time before the s. 2 application is determined, apply for a s. 6 order. If a s. 6 order is then made, the application under s. 2 will be treated as withdrawn. Any order made under s. 6 instead of s. 2 in this way can be back-dated to the date of the making of the original s. 2 application if the court thinks fit (even though the s. 6 application will actually have been made at some stage after this date and back-dating is normally only permitted to the date of the making of the application concerned) (s. 6(8) as added by Matrimonial and Family Proceedings Act 1984).

If the parties reach a settlement during the run-up to the final hearing of a s. 2 complaint, the appropriate course is therefore for the applicant to make an alternative complaint under s. 6 for an agreed order. The complaint can be made orally to the court if it is not convenient to make a written complaint.

7 AGREED ORDERS UNDER S. 6

7.1 Grounds for an order (s. 6(1))

7.1.1 General

Either party to a marriage may apply to a magistrates' court for an order under s. 6 on the ground that either the party making the application or the other party to the marriage has agreed to make such financial provision as may be specified in the application.

Subject to s. 6(3) (which obliges the court to approve the financial provision agreed for any child of the family before it makes an order; see paragraph 7.3 below), the court may order that the respondent shall make the financial provision specified in the application if:

(a) it is satisfied that the applicant or the respondent, as the case may be, has agreed to make the provision; *and*

(b) it has no reason to think it would be contrary to the interests of justice to exercise its powers under s. 6.

7.1.2 Meaning of financial provision (s. 6(2))

'Financial provision' means any one or more of the following sorts of provision:

(a) the making of periodical payments by one party to the other;

(b)   the payment of a lump sum by one party to the other;

(c)   the making of periodical payments by one party to a child of the family or to the other party for the benefit of such a child;

(d)   the payment by one party of a lump sum to a child of the family or to the other party for the benefit of such a child (s. 6(2)).

7.2   Use of a s. 6 order

In effect s. 6 means that the court can, by consent, make any of the orders that it can make under s. 2 with no restriction on the amount of the lump sum that can be ordered and with no obligation on the applicant to prove any ground other than that the respondent agrees. It is not a rubber-stamping procedure — the court still has duties to consider the suitability of the agreed provision, particularly where children are involved (see paragraphs 7.3 and 7.4 below) and not to make the order if it thinks it would be contrary to justice to do so (see paragraph 7.1.1). Nevertheless, it provides a valuable means whereby either party to the marriage can have their agreement over financial provision embodied in an enforceable court order. The advantages of a s. 6 order over an agreement include the following:

(a)   The terms of the agreement are beyond dispute.

(b)   Neither party can have a change of heart and resile from the agreement unilaterally at a later date — if either party wishes to go back on the agreement he will have to obtain the consent of the other party or ask the court for a variation.

(c)   The payer may become entitled to tax advantages as a result of the order if the order was applied for prior to 15 March 1988 and made before 30 June 1988 (see Chapter 20). There will be no doubt that he is under a binding obligation to make any periodical payments for his spouse specified in the order, thus there can be no dispute by the Inland Revenue that he is entitled to tax relief for the payments (without an order there could be doubt as to the payer's obligation to pay, particularly if the parties reached only a relatively informal oral agreement). Furthermore, the fact that periodical payments for children are made under an order, albeit a consent order, may well take the payments outside the settlement provisions and enable the payer to obtain tax relief for them also (impossible without an order). However, if the order was applied for after 15 March 1988 it will only attract tax relief in very limited circumstances (see Chapter 20).

(d)   Note that the provisions relating to 'small maintenance payments' which enabled the payee to receive her maintenance gross were repealed as from 6 April 1989 (see further Chapter 20 paragraph 2.3.2 for a description of how such payments made prior to 6 April 1989 will be treated under the new tax rules).

Example. (Routine s. 6 order.) Mr and Mrs Simms have separated. They agree that Mr Simms will pay his wife periodical payments of £30 per week and will make her a lump sum payment of £1,000. Mrs Simms wants the matter put on a formal footing so applies to the magistrates' court for an order for periodical payments and a lump sum order under s. 6. The magistrates grant an order in the terms agreed.

7.3   Where provision for children is involved (s. 6(3))

Where the financial provision specified in a s. 6(1) application consists of or includes provision in respect of a child of the family, the court has a duty to consider the suitability of the provision agreed. The court shall not make any order under s. 6(1) unless it considers that the agreed provision provides for or makes a proper contribution towards the financial needs of the child.

7.4 Proposal of alternative provision by the court

As we have seen, there are two obstacles on which an application for agreed provision may founder:

(a)   the court may decide that it would be contrary to the interests of justice to make the agreed order (se 7.1.1 above); *or*

(b)   the court may decide that the provision the agreement makes for a child of the family is not suitable (see 7.3 above).

In the event of the court refusing to make the agreed order on either of these two bases, if the court is of the opinion:

(a)   that it would not be contrary to the interests of justice to make an order for the making of some other financial provision specified by the court; *and*

(b)   that in so far as that other financial provision contains any provisions for a child of the family, it provides for, or makes a proper contribution towards, the financial needs of that child,

and provided that both parties agree, the court may order that either party shall make that other provision (s. 6(5)).

> **Example.** Mr and Mrs Riley have two children aged 10 and 12, Mr Riley is earning a good salary. Mrs Riley also works. Mr and Mrs Riley agree that Mr Riley should pay £10 per week for each child and, in order that Mr Riley should get tax relief for the payments, he applies for an agreed order under s. 6.
>
> In accordance with its obligations under s. 6(3), the court reviews the provisions agreed for the children and decides that £10 per week per child is not a proper contribution towards the financial needs of the children. The court then goes on to consider the possibility of making a higher order under s. 6(5). It decides that it would not be contrary to justice to do so and further decides that £15 per week per child would constitute a proper contribution towards the financial needs of the children. Provided Mr and Mrs Riley agree to such an order, the court can order periodical payments at the higher rate.

8   ORDERS TO CONTINUE PAYMENTS MADE DURING VOLUNTARY SEPARATION (S. 7)

8.1   Use of s. 7

Section 7 enables the court to make periodical payments orders where the parties are living apart but no ground can be made out under s. 1 (i.e., there is no failure to maintain, no desertion and no behaviour) and, although the respondent has actually been paying maintenance, the parties cannot reach sufficient agreement for an application under s. 6.

8.2   Grounds for order (s. 7(1))

Where:

(a)   the parties to a marriage have been living apart for a continuous period exceeding three months (neither party having deserted the other); *and*

(b)   one of the parties has been making periodical payments for the benefit of the other party or of a child of the family,

the other party may apply to a magistrates' court for an order under s. 7.

8.3   Obligation on applicant to specify payments made when applying under s. 7

The applicant must specify in her application the aggregate amount of the payments made by the respondent for the benefit of herself and the children of the family in the three months preceding the date of the making of the application (s. 7(1)).

8.4   Orders that can be made (s. 7(3))

If the court is satisfied the respondent has made the payments specified in the application, it may make one or both of the following orders:

(a)   an order that the respondent shall make to the applicant such periodical payments, and for such term, as may be specified in the order;
(b)   an order that the respondent shall make to the applicant for the benefit of a child of the family to whom the application relates or to such child, such periodical payments and for such term, as may be so specified.

Note that there is no power to order a lump sum payment under s. 7.

8.5   Limitations on the orders made under s. 7

There are a number of limitations on the court's powers under s. 7, which are set out below.

8.5.1   Section 7(3)(a)
Section 7(3)(a) deals with the relationship that there must be between the rate of payment under the order and the rate of payment by the respondent in the three months prior to the application. It provides that the order shall not require the respondent to make payments that exceed in aggregate during any period of three months, the aggregate amount paid by him for the benefit of the applicant or a child of the family during the period of three months immediately preceding the date of the application (see the example at paragraph 8.7 below).

Whilst the court cannot, under this section, order the respondent to pay *more* than he has been paying, there is no reason, however, why it should not order the respondent to pay *less* if it sees fit, i.e., if an order based on what the respondent has been paying would amount to more than the court would have ordered had the application been made under s. 1 (see paragraph 8.5.2).

8.5.2   Section 7(3)(b) and (c)
Section 7(3)(b) and (c) obliges the court to consider what it would have ordered under s. 2 and to ensure that the s. 7 order is in line with this.

Section 7(3)(b) provides that the court shall not require the respondent to make payments to or for the benefit of any person which exceed in amount the payments which the court considers that it would have required the respondent to make to or for the benefit of that person on an application under s. 1 of the Act.

Section 7(3)(c) provides that the court shall not require payments to be made to or for the benefit of a child of the family who is not the respondent's child unless the court considers that it would have made an order in favour of that child on an application under s. 1 of the Act.

8.5.3 Section 7(4)

Section 7(4) provides that the court shall not make an order under s. 7 if it considers that the orders which it has power to make under the section:

(a)   would not provide reasonable maintenance for the applicant; *or*
(b)   if the application relates to a child of the family, would not provide, or make a proper contribution towards reasonable maintenance for that child.

8.6   Considerations in relation to orders

Section 7(5) provides that the provisions of s. 3 DPMCA 1978 (see paragraph 6.3 above) apply to s. 7 applications as they do to applications for s. 2 orders with a minor modification. This is that under s. 3(2)(c) the court is directed to have regard to the standard of living enjoyed by the parties before they began to live apart, rather than their standard of living before the conduct alleged as the ground of the application, as is the case on an application for a s. 2 order.

> **Example.** Mr and Mrs Swift have been living apart for six months. There are two children of the family who live with Mrs Swift. One child is the natural child of both parties, the other (Andrea) is a child of Mrs Swift by her previous marriage (her former husband died).
>
> Mr Swift has been making periodical payments for the benefit of Mrs Swift and the children since the separation. The payments for Mrs Swift have not been regular or at a uniform rate. Sometimes she receives as much as £150 over the course of a month for herself, sometimes payments for her drop as low as £50 over the course of a month. The payments made for the children have been regular at the rate of £40 per child per month. Mrs Swift decides to apply for an order under s. 7. She calculates that the total of the payments made for herself over the last three months is £300. The payments made for the children over the last three months come to £120 each child. She specifies these figures in her application.
>
> The magistrates' court can order Mr Swift to make periodical payments to Mrs Swift that will not exceed £300 over any three-month period. As they have it in mind to order payments for both Mrs Swift and the children at a regular monthly rate, this means they can order periodical payments of a maximum of £100 per month for Mrs Swift. They can also order periodical payments for each child of the family of up to £40 per month. The court compares these figures with what it would have ordered on an application under s. 1 and decides that they do not exceed the orders it would have made. Furthermore, it considers the position with regard to Andrea and decides that it would have made an order in her favour on an application under s. 1. It decides that orders of £40 per month for each child and £100 per month for Mrs Swift would constitute reasonable provision and therefore makes periodical payments orders in these terms.
>
> Note that if the court had thought the provision made by Mr Swift in the past three months over-generous bearing in mind all the factors set out in s. 3, it could have made periodical payments orders of whatever lesser sum it thought fit.

8.7   Power to treat s. 7 application as application for s. 2 order

Where the court considers that the orders it has power to make would not provide reasonable maintenance, it cannot make an order under s. 7 (see paragraph 8.5.3 above). What the court can do is to treat the application as if it were an application for an order under s. 2 instead. This frees the court from the constraints of the respondent's record of payment over the past three months and also entitles the court to order lump sum payments.

The procedure where the court decides to take this course is set out in r. 5, Magistrates' Courts (Matrimonial Proceedings) Rules 1980.

9 MISCELLANEOUS PROVISIONS RELATING TO PERIODICAL PAYMENTS AND LUMP SUM ORDERS (DURATION, ORDERS FOR CHILDREN, ETC.)

9.1 Frequency of periodical payments

The court may order periodical payments to be paid at weekly or monthly intervals, or indeed, at any other intervals that seem fit.

9.2 Duration of orders for periodical payments for parties to a marriage (s. 4)

Periodical payments for a party to a marriage (whether made under ss. 2, 6 or 7) may be for whatever term the court thinks fit subject to the following limitations:

(a)   The term shall not begin earlier than the date of the making of the application for the order (i.e. the date of the making of the complaint). Back-dated orders are therefore permitted (see Chapter 15 paragraph 9.3 for the matters that should be considered by a court contemplating the making of a back-dated order).

(b)   The term shall not extend beyond the death of either of the parties to the marriage.

(c)   Where the parties' marriage is subsequently dissolved or annulled but the magistrates' order continues in force, the order will cease to have effect on the remarriage of the payee except in relation to arrears already accrued due on that date. The decree of divorce or nullity will not itself have any effect on the magistrates' order.

Note that there is nothing to prevent the court making an order for a limited period, for example to tide the applicant over until the children reach school age and she can work (see, for example, *Robinson* v *Robinson* [1983] Fam 42, [1983] 1 All ER 391 — order for five years only).

9.3 Age limit on orders for children and duration of periodical payments for children

Subject to s. 5(3), no order for periodical payments or a lump sum shall be made in favour of a child who has attained 18 (s. 5(1)).

Section 5(2) as amended by the Matrimonial and Family Proceedings Act 1984 provides that periodical payments orders for children:

(a)   in the first instance shall not extend beyond the child's 17th birthday unless the court considers that in the circumstances of the case the welfare of the child requires that it should extend to a later date; *and*

(b)   shall not in any event extend beyond the child's 18th birthday except in the circumstance set out in s. 5(3).

Section 5(3) permits the court:

(a)   to make a lump sum or periodical payments order in favour of a child who has attained 18; *and*

(b)   to make a periodical payments order for a child under 18 that will extend beyond his 18th birthday *if* it appears to the court:

(i)   that the child is, or will be, or if such an order or provision were made would be, receiving instruction at an educational establishment or undergoing training for a trade, profession or vocation, whether or not he is also, or will also be in gainful employment; *or*

(ii)   that there are special circumstances which justify this course.

Periodical payments orders for children can be back-dated to the date of the complaint (s. 5(2)). They will always cease to have effect on the death of the payer (s. 5(4)).

It will be noted that the rules contained in s. 5 are virtually the same as those contained in s. 29, Matrimonial Causes Act 1973 in relation to provision for children following divorce, nullity or judicial separation (see Chapter 14).

10   EFFECT OF LIVING TOGETHER ON FINANCIAL ORDERS UNDER DPMCA 1978: S. 25 DPMCA 1978

10.1   'Living together'

Living together means living with each other in the same household (s. 88(2)). The concept of living together is dealt with fully in Chapter 3 at paragraph 6.1.

10.2   Effect with regard to s. 7

Section 7 orders cannot be made if the parties are living together.

Jurisdiction under s. 7 is, it will be remembered, dependent on the parties having been living apart for a continuous period exceeding three months (see paragraph 8.2 above).

If a s. 7 order is made whilst the parties are living apart, it will cease to have effect immediately if they resume living with each other (s. 25(3)).

Example. Mr and Mrs Young have been separated for four months. Mr Young has in fact been paying maintenance for his wife and child and she obtains a s. 7 order for periodical payments for herself and the child. A month after the hearing, they are reconciled and start to live together again. Mr Young is not entitled to have the periodical payments he has made so far refunded but the s. 7 order does forthwith cease to be effective for the future.

10.3   Effect on s. 2 and s. 6 orders

Orders under s. 2 and s. 6 can be made where the spouses are living together. Living together will have the following effect on such orders:

(a)   *Orders for periodical payments payable to spouses for self or child*   An order for periodical payments (or interim periodical payments, see paragraph 12.6 below) to be made to a spouse for her own benefit or for the benefit of a child of the family will be enforceable even if:

(i)   the spouses are living together when the order is made; *or*

(ii) although not living together when the order is made, the spouses subsequently resume cohabitation (s. 25(1)).

However, if the spouses live together for a continuous period exceeding six months at any stage after the making of the order, the order *will* cease to have effect (s. 25(1)).

(b) *Orders for periodical payments direct to a child*   Where the court orders a spouse to pay periodical payments or interim periodical payments *direct* to a child (as opposed to a spouse for his benefit), unless the court otherwise directs, the order will continue to be effective and enforceable even though the spouses are living together when it is made or subsequently resume living together, no matter how long the cohabitation lasts (s. 25(2)).

Example. Mr and Mrs Old are living together but their marriage is on the rocks and Mrs Old seeks a periodical payments order under s. 2 for herself and the children in order to obtain a measure of financial independence so that she can move out of the matrimonial home and seek alternative accommodation. A s. 2 order is made for periodical payments to be paid to Mrs Old for herself and to each of the children direct. The order is effective despite the fact that the parties are cohabiting when it is made. A week after the order, Mrs Old and the children move out. However, she and her husband are subsequently reconciled and Mrs Old moves back into the matrimonial home. If she and her husband live together for a continuous period of more than six months, *her* periodical payments order will cease to be effective. The children's orders will continue in force.

11   PROCEDURE

11.1   Legal aid

Assistance by way of representation is available for proceedings for financial orders under DPMCA 1978. The green form should therefore be completed at an early stage and prompt application made for authority to give assistance by way of representation (see Chapter 2 paragraph 10.1).

Legal aid is generally not used in DPMCA 1978 cases but may occasionally be needed where the client's means put him or her outside the financial limits of the green form scheme but not outside the slightly more generous limits of the legal aid scheme. Application is made on Form SJ1 (see Chapter 2 paragraph 10.1.4).

11.2   Proceedings begun by complaint

Proceedings for a financial order under DPMCA 1978 are begun in the normal way by complaint. The procedure is governed by Magistrates' Courts (Matrimonial Proceedings) Rules 1980. The rules contain specimen forms of complaint which can/must be used.

(a) *Complaint for order under s. 2*   The complaint must be in writing and must state the ground or grounds on which the application is made (the applicant can rely on two or more grounds in the alternative) (r. 3(1)). Where the applicant relies on the respondent's behaviour under s. 1(c), she must give brief particulars of the behaviour alleged (r. 3(2)). Form 1 from the rules may be used.

(b) *Complaint for order under s. 6*   The complaint must be in writing and must state the type or types of financial provision agreed to be made, the amount of any payment to be made under the s. 6 order and, in the case of periodical payments, the term for which the payments are to be made. Form 3 may be used. There is one exception to the rule that the complaint must be in writing, i.e. when the applicant wishes to change from an application for a s. 2 order to a s. 6 application where the parties have come to terms (see s. 6(4)).

(c) *Complaint for order under s. 7* Form 6 *must* be used for a complaint for an order under s. 7. The complaint must specify the aggregate of the payments made by the respondent in the preceding three months (see paragraph 8.3 above).

The complaint must be filed at the appropriate magistrates' court (see paragraph 3.2 as to jurisdiction). The applicant will be provided with a notice setting out the court's powers under ss. 8 to 11 DPMCA 1978 in relation to the children of the family (Form 10 of the forms contained in the rules; see r. 8).

11.3 Summons to respondent

A summons will be issued and served on the respondent normally by the court. Rule 20 provides that service may be effected:

(a) by delivering the summons to the respondent; *or*
(b) by leaving it for him with some person at his last known or usual place of abode; *or*
(c) by sending it to him by post in a letter addressed to him at his last known or usual place of abode or at an address given by him for that purpose.

A notice in Form 10 setting out the court's powers in relation to the children of the family will be served on the respondent with the summons (r. 8).

11.4 Hearing

11.4.1 Composition of the court

Proceedings under Part I DPMCA 1978 are domestic proceedings (s. 65, Magistrates' Courts Act 1980). With one or two exceptions, a magistrates' court hearing domestic proceedings must be composed of not more than three magistrates including, so far as practicable, both a man and woman (s. 66, Magistrates' Courts Act 1980). The magistrates must be members of the domestic court panel specially appointed to hear domestic proceedings (s. 67(2), Magistrates' Courts Act 1980).

11.4.2 Restrictions on persons present in court during hearing

Only officers of the court, people directly concerned with the case (parties, witnesses, lawyers, etc.), press and other people given special permission by the court may be present at the hearing (s. 69(2), Magistrates' Courts Act 1980). Normally witnesses remain outside the court until they are called to give evidence and the only people present through the whole hearing are the magistrates, the court clerk and usher, the parties and their lawyers. The press never bother to attend as there are too many restrictions on what they can report to make it worth their while.

11.4.3 Respondent fails to attend

Where the respondent fails to turn up at the hearing, the provisions of s. 55, Magistrates' Courts Act 1980 generally apply, empowering the court to proceed in the respondent's absence in certain cases or alternatively to adjourn, possibly issuing a warrant for the respondent's arrest (see Chapter 21 paragraph 11.1.1(h)).

Note that, where the application is for an order under s. 6 and the respondent is not present or represented by counsel or a solicitor at the hearing, the court shall not make an order unless there is produced to the court a written statement in Form 5 of the Magistrates' Courts (Matrimonial Proceedings) Rules 1980 signed by the respondent in the presence of a magistrate, magistrates' clerk or solicitor (r. 4(3)). Form 5 signifies the respondent's consent to the making of an order under s. 6 either in exactly the terms that the applicant is requesting or in alternative terms which the respondent sets out in the form. The form also requires the respondent to give details of his financial resources. Where the respondent attends the hearing, he can give oral evidence of his consent and his means so there is no need for him to complete Form 5. Where the application relates wholly or partly to financial provision to be made by the applicant in respect of a child of the family, the court will also need Form 5A declaring the financial resources of the child if the respondent is not present or represented.

11.4.4   Order of proceedings

The proceedings will take the normal form. The complaint is first put to the respondent. Even if the respondent admits the complaint, it is normal for the court to hear outline evidence before making an order. The applicant opens the case to the court explaining to the magistrates briefly what it is about and the applicant and her witnesses give evidence and are cross-examined. Note that if either party is not legally represented and seems to be unable to examine or cross-examine a witness effectively, the court is under a duty to help him (s. 73, Magistrates' Courts Act 1980). The respondent has the right (only used in exceptional cases) to submit that there is no case for him to answer at the conclusion of the applicant's case if he feels there is a chance that the magistrates will throw the case out at this point. However, submissions are rarely appropriate in matrimonial cases and it should also be borne in mind that a respondent who makes a submission may be forced to decide whether he wishes the magistrates to consider his submission or whether he wants to give evidence and call witnesses to give his side of the story — he may not be allowed to do both.

After the applicant has closed her case, the respondent may address the magistrates before putting any of his evidence before them (although he will usually choose to wait until the end of the case to do this). He and his witnesses then give evidence. The respondent then addresses the court as of right if he has not already done so. If he addressed the court in opening his case, he may only address them a second time with leave of the court. If he is permitted to make a second speech, the applicant will also have a second turn thereafter. If a question of law has arisen during the case, the applicant's advocate may be given leave to address the magistrates on the legal point irrespective of whether the respondent makes a second speech or not. The respondent will also be allowed to address the court on the legal issue.

The magistrates will then consider whether the case is proved and what order they should make.

Note that the magistrates cannot make a final order until:

(a) they have considered whether to exercise their s. 8 (Children Act 1989) powers in relation to any child of the family under 18 and if so in what manner (see Chapter 26); *and*

(b) where the application is for a s. 2 order, they have considered whether there is any possibility of reconciliation (s. 26 DPMCA 1978).

It may be in some cases that evidence of the parties' means is not relevant to whether the ground for relief is made out; in such cases, the court may choose to hear the evidence only if they find the case proved and are ready to make an order. Unless the applicant expressly makes representations to the court and the court finds that it would be undesirable to do so, the court will direct that payment under the order must be made to the clerk of the court or the clerk of another magistrates' court (s. 59, Magistrates' Courts Act 1980). It may be worth the applicant making representations for direct payments where, for example, the respondent is a good payer and will arrange for payments to be made by standing order. However, there are two distinct advantages of payment through the court; it ensures that an independent record of the respondent's payments will be kept and, should he default, the responsibility for enforcing the order will be that of the clerk of the court, not the applicant (see paragraph 13.7 below).

Once the decision of the court is announced, the court should be asked to deal with the question of costs.

11.5 Evidence

11.5.1 Generally

The applicant's solicitor must ensure that he is familiar with the provisions of the section on which he proposes to rely and has gathered together sufficient evidence to make out a case for an order. This means proving the ground on which the applicant relies and also providing the court with evidence of her means and (where there is a dispute over the respondent's means) in so far as it is possible, with evidence of the respondent's means. The respondent's solicitor must consider whether there is any documentary or witness evidence (other than the evidence of his client) that may help to weaken the applicant's case and arrange for it to be available at court. He too will have to be in a position to provide the court with evidence of the respondent's means (and, as far as possible, the applicant's means if they are disputed).

Note that, even if the respondent has indicated clearly that he does not intend to contest the case, evidence of both parties' means will still be required at the hearing so that the court can determine the appropriate financial orders or decide on whether the orders agreed between the parties are suitable, although the court is unlikely to require *documentary* proof of income and outgoings where the parties are agreed on the order to be made.

11.5.2 Proving means

(a) *Documentary evidence of income and outgoings* It is traditional for a party to be allowed to produce documentary evidence of his income and outgoings even if he has not obtained the consent of the other party to this prior to the hearing (for example, wages slips, letter from employer, supplementary benefits book, copy of hire-purchase agreements, rent book, gas and electricity bills etc.). In the case of evidence of earnings this practice is supported by statute, i.e. s. 100, Magistrates' Courts Act 1980 which provides that evidence of wages can be given by a statement in writing signed by or on behalf of the employer of the person concerned. If it is proposed to introduce documentary evidence of income and outoings, it is good practice to provide the other side with copies of such documents prior to the hearing so that they can consider them and raise any objections in advance.

(b) *Report on means by probation officer*   Once the court has determined all the issues arising in the proceedings other than the amount to be directed to be paid by order of the court and any questions as to the care of and contact arrangements for any children of the family (i.e. once the court has found the complaint proved), it may request a probation officer to investigate the means of the parties and report on them to the court (s. 72, Magistrates' Courts Act 1980 and s. 8(8) DPMCA 1978). The court would usually only think of making such a request where it is not possible to discover the means of the parties by their giving evidence in the normal way.

(c) *Section 6 cases*   Form 5 of the Magistrates' Courts (Matrimonial Proceedings) Rules 1980 contains a section on which a respondent to an application under s. 6 who proposes to consent to the making of an order can give evidence of his financial resources and expenses and thus avoid the need to come to court for the hearing (see paragraph 11.4.3 above).

11.5.3   Other evidential matters

The normal rules of evidence (as to hearsay, etc.) apply in the magistrates' courts as they do in the other courts. However, the provisions of Part I of the Civil Evidence Act 1968 do not apply to the magistrates' courts. Thus the introduction of documentary evidence of witnesses who are dead, ill, abroad, etc. is still governed by the Evidence Act 1938.

Unless the Evidence Act 1938 applies, where a party wishes to rely on documentary evidence in relation to the grounds for the order rather than simply on the question of means, it is imperative that the consent of the other party to the introduction of the documentary evidence should be sought well in advance. Without this, the document will not be admitted in evidence. For example, suppose that, in support of her allegation of behaviour under s. 1(c) the applicant wishes to put in evidence a letter from her general practitioner stating that he has seen bruises on her body, the letter must first be forwarded to the respondent's solicitor asking for consent for it to be put in evidence. If the respondent objects, the letter will not be admissible and the doctor will have to be called to give evidence if the applicant wishes to rely on his testimony.

11.6   Interim orders (s. 19 DPMCA 1978)

Section 19 of DPMCA 1978 empowers the court to make an interim periodical payments order on an application for an order under ss. 2, 6 or 7 at any time before making a final order or dismissing the application. The order can require the respondent to make to the applicant or to any child of the family who is under 18 or to the applicant for the benefit of such a child such periodical payments as the court thinks reasonable (s. 19(1)). If a child of the family under 18 is living with a parent who is not a party to the marriage, the court can make an interim order requiring the respondent to make periodical payments to the parent for the benefit of the child (s. 19(2)). Section 19(3A) (added by the Matrimonial and Family Proceedings Act 1984) provides that where the application has been made under s. 6 by the party to the marriage who has agreed to make the financial provision specified in the application, an interim order can be made under s. 19(1) or (2) against the applicant.

The order can be back-dated to the date of the complaint (s.19(3)). The order will cease to have effect on the earliest of the dates listed below:

(a)   the date specified by the magistrates;
(b)   the expiration of three months after the date of the making of the order;
(c)   when the court finally determines the case (s. 19(5)).

Only one interim order can be made on any s. 2, 6 or 7 application (s. 19(7)). However, where the existing interim order looks as if it will determine before the case is finally disposed of, the magistrates' court can extend the order from time to time subject to the restriction that the order cannot be extended so that it continues for more than three months from the first extension order (s. 19(6)). Therefore, no interim order may remain in force for a period of more than six months in total.

12   ENFORCEMENT OF ORDERS

12.1   The Maintenance Enforcement Act 1991

The Maintenance Enforcement Act 1991 came into force on 1 April 1992. It enables the magistrates' court to specify the method of payment to be made when it makes, varies or enforces a maintenance order requiring periodical payments. Section 2 substitutes the Magistrates' Courts Act 1980, s. 59, and requires the magistrates' court to specify that 'qualifying maintenance payments' be made directly from the debtor to the creditor, through the court, by standing order or by some similar method, or by attachment of earnings. Formerly, there was no provision for courts to order payments by standing order to the creditor, and attachment of earnings could only be made if the debtor consented or if he had defaulted on his payments due to wilful refusal or culpable neglect. Where payment is ordered by standing order (or some similar method) the court may require the debtor to open an account.

The Act is an interim measure to improve the collection and enforcement of maintenance pending the coming into force of the Child Support Act 1991 in 1993 (over a phased three-year period). The Child Support Act 1991 will create a child support agency which will be responsible for the assessment, collection and enforcement of child maintenance. The Maintenance Enforcement Act 1991 will, however, still be relevant to non-child maintenance even after the Child Support Act 1991 comes into force.

12.2   Generally

An order for the payment of money under DPMCA 1978 may be enforced as a magistrates' court maintenance order (s. 32(1) DPMCA 1978). This means that the order may be enforced:

(a)   by attachment of earnings (Attachment of Earnings Act 1971); *or*
(b)   by committal to prison (s. 76, Magistrates' Courts Act 1980); *or*
(c)   by distress (s. 76 ibid); *or*
(d)   the order can be registered in the High Court under the Maintenance Orders Act 1958 for enforcement in that court (rarely appropriate unless the total arrears are large).

12.2   Attachment of earnings (Attachment of Earnings Act 1971)

This is probably the most efficient way of enforcing payment of a periodical payments order. However, it can only be used if the debtor is employed; it is not appropriate if he is self-employed or unemployed.

Application for an attachment of earnings order can be made by the debtor himself or by the person to whom payment should be made (whether direct or through the court) or, where the order is payable through the court (as it usually is), by the clerk of the court if the person entitled to the payments requests him to apply.

Note that an attachment of earnings orders can be made from the outset as a result of s. 2(3)(d) of the Maintenance Enforcement Act 1991. Formerly, it could only be made where the debtor consented or where his failure to pay was due to his wilful refusal or culpable neglect.

If an order is made it will be directed to the debtor's employer and will instruct him to make deductions from the debtor's earnings and send the money to the court. The money can then be used to meet the debtor's liability under the maintenance order in respect of arrears and continuing payments. The court will fix a 'normal deductions rate' which is what the employer will usually deduct and also a 'protected earnings rate', which is the level below which the debtor's take-home pay should not be reduced. If the debtor's earnings for a particular week are not enough for the normal deduction to be made without reducing him below the protected level, the employer deducts less than the normal rate.

12.3   Committal to prison

Committal of the debtor to prison for non-payment is very much a last resort. Before imprisonment can be imposed, the following conditions must be satisfied.

(a)   The court must inquire in the presence of the debtor whether the default was due to his wilful refusal or culpable neglect; only if it is of the opinion that it was so caused can the debtor be imprisoned (s. 93(6), Magistrates' Courts Act 1980).
(b)   Where there is power to impose an attachment of earnings order the court must not impose imprisonment unless it is of the opinion that attachment of earnings would be inappropriate (s. 93(6) ibid).
(c)   The debtor must be present when imprisonment is imposed (s. 93(6) ibid).

The overall maximum period of imprisonment is six weeks (s. 93(7)) but a shorter maximum may apply, depending on the amount of the debt, by virtue of s. 76 and sch. 4, Magistrates' Courts Act 1980.

Payment of the whole outstanding debt together with costs and charges will prevent the imprisonment ordered from taking effect or, if the debtor has been imprisoned, will buy him out of prison. Part-payment reduces the term that has to be served (s. 79, Magistrates' Courts Act 1980).

Whilst the debtor is in prison, no arrears will accrue unless the court otherwise directs (s. 94, Magistrates' Courts Act 1980) and, although the arrears already accrued will not be wiped out by the term served (s. 93(8), Magistrates' Courts Act 1980), the debtor cannot be sent to prison again in respect of the same debt. If he continues to default in the future, he can, of course, be returned to prison in respect of his fresh non-payments.

Note that any debtor in prison or otherwise detained because of non-payment can apply to the court for the committal order to be reviewed and the warrant of commitment cancelled (s. 18(4), Maintenance Orders Act 1958).

The court has power to suspend committal, for example, on condition that the debtor pays the order in future together with something off the arrears each week (s. 77(2), Magistrates' Courts Act 1980). If the debtor fails to observe the condition imposed, he will be notified that a warrant of commitment to prison is going to be issued and given a chance to show cause why this should not happen. If he fails to show cause, the warrant will be issued (s. 18, Maintenance Orders Act 1958).

An alternative to a suspended committal order is for the court simply to adjourn to see how the debtor pays — if he still has a bad payment record by the time of the adjourned hearing, he is in grave danger of being committed to prison.

12.4 Distress

A warrant of distress is an order by the court to the police to seize goods belonging to the debtor and sell them to cover the debt. It is rare for a warrant of distress to be issued though the court has said, in *R* v *Birmingham Justices ex parte Bennett* [1983] 1 WLR 114 that, if there is a reasonable likelihood that the debtor has assets to satisfy the sum he owes, distress should be used rather than committal.

12.5 Order to search debtor

Under s. 80, Magistrates' Courts Act 1980 there is power for a debtor to be searched when the magistrates have ordered enforcement of a maintenance order or he has been arrested or taken to a prison or other place of detention in default of payment. Subject to safeguards to protect the debtor's family, any money found on him will be applied in reducing his debt.

12.6 Remission of arrears

Section 95 of the Magistrates' Courts Act 1980 (as substituted by the Maintenance Enforcement Act 1991, sch. 2, para. 8), gives the magistrates the power to remit the whole or part of the arrears on an application for enforcement (or indeed for revocation, revival, variation or discharge of the order). Arrears which are more than a year old are usually to be remitted. Section 8 of the Maintenance Enforcement Act 1991 inserts a new Magistrates' Courts Act 1980, s. 94A, enabling the Secretary of State to give the magistrates' court the power to order interest to be paid at a specified rate on the whole or any part of arrears of a maintenance payment. The court is to specify the method of payment of the interest.

12.7   Procedure for enforcement

Proceedings are by complaint. As most maintenance orders are payable through the court, it is normally the responsibility of the clerk of the court to bring proceedings for enforcement if requested in writing to do so by the person for whose benefit the order was made (s. 59, Magistrates' Courts Act 1980) although the person entitled can proceed directly himself if he prefers. The court will be able to prove the payer's non-payment as records will have been kept by the court office. Section 3 of the Maintenance Enforcement Act 1991 inserts Magistrates' Courts Act 1980, ss. 59A and 59B. Section 59A makes provision for the justices' clerk to take enforcement proceedings in certain circumstances on behalf of the creditor. It also allows the creditor to give the justices' clerk a standing authority to take enforcement proceedings if payment is made through the court. Section 59B imposes a financial sanction in respect of certain maintenance orders if the debtor fails to make payments by the method specified.

If the order is not payable through the court, the clerk has no responsibility for enforcement and the person entitled will therefore have no choice but to take proceedings himself. It is imperative that the payee herself keeps a clear record of the payments made and missed by the payer in these circumstances so that she can prove non-payment to the court.

The debtor will normally be summoned to attend for the proceedings but a warrant can be issued for his arrest to secure his attendance if necessary (s. 93(5), Magistrates' Courts Act 1980).

12.8   Diversion procedure

Where the payer is a consistently poor payer, arrangements can be made for the payee to receive her full entitlement to state benefit each week irrespective of the maintenance order. She then assigns the payments made under the order to the DSS (see Chapter 35 paragraph 11).

13   VARIATION

13.1   General

The court generally has power to vary or revoke periodical payments and interim periodical payments orders made under Part I DPMCA 1978 (s. 20 ibid). Section 4 of the Maintenance Enforcement Act 1991 substitutes the Magistrates' Courts Act 1980, s. 60, and enables a magistrates' court to specify the method of payment when varying or reviving a maintenance order and to enable the justices' clerk to vary the method of payment to allow payment to be made through the court. Section 5 of the Maintenance Enforcement Act 1991 inserts a new Domestic Proceedings and Magistrates Courts Act 1978, s. 20 ZA, to the same effect.

The power to vary or revoke includes a power to suspend a provision of a periodical payments order temporarily and to revive a suspended provision (s. 20(6)).

13.2   Lump sums on variation applications

In certain cases, lump sums can be ordered on a variation application, i.e.:

(a) *Original order under s. 2 DPMCA 1978* Where the periodical payments order was made under s. 2 DPMCA 1978, the court's power to vary includes a power to make an order under s. 2(1)(b) or (d) for a lump sum for the applicant or a child of the family (s. 20(1)). It appears that it makes no difference to this power that the respondent has already been ordered to pay a lump sum on the original s. 2 application or an earlier variation application (s. 20(7)).

(b) *Original order under s. 6 DPMCA 1978* Where the periodical payments order was made under s. 6 DPMCA 1978, as well as having power to vary the periodical payments order, the court has power to order a lump sum payment to the other party to the marriage or to or for a child of the family by the person originally ordered to pay periodical payments (s. 20(2)).

Any lump sum ordered on a variation application is subject to the £1,000 limit (s. 20(7)) unless the application to vary relates to a s. 6 order and the payer agrees to pay more (s. 20(8)).

Just as s. 7 contains no power to order a lump sum, there is no power to order a lump sum on an application for variation of a s. 7 order.

13.3 Who may apply?

Generally variation applications are made by one of the parties to the marriage. Thus where, for example, the husband is the payer, he may apply for the order to be reduced or the wife may apply because she needs more.

Other beneficiaries of periodical payments orders are entitled to apply in certain circumstances (such as the local authority where the child has been committed to its care). Where the order is for periodical payments to or for a child, the child himself may apply if he is 16 or over (s. 20(12)).

13.4 Factors on variation application

In deciding the variation application, s. 20(11) dictates that the court shall give effect to any agreement between the parties relating to the application so far as it appears just to the court to do so. If there is no agreement or the court decides not to give effect to the parties' agreement, the court must have regard to all the circumstances of the case, first consideration being given to the welfare while a minor of any child of the family who is under 18, and the circumstances of the case shall include any change in any of the matters to which the court was required to have regard when making the original order or, where the application relates to a s. 6 order, to which the court would have been required to have regard if the order had been made under s. 2 (i.e. the factors set out in s. 3 DPMCA 1978). In effect the court is required to consider the case *de novo*.

1 GROUNDS FOR APPLICATION

Applications under s. 27 can be made by either party to a marriage (the applicant) on the ground that the other party (the respondent):

(a) has failed to provide reasonable maintenance for the applicant; *or*

(b) has failed to provide, or to make proper contribution towards, reasonable maintenance for any child of the family (s. 27(1)).

2 JURISDICTION

The court has jurisdiction under s. 27 if:

(a) the applicant or respondent is domiciled in England and Wales at the date of the application; *or*

(b) the applicant has been habitually resident in England and Wales throughout the year ending with the date of the application; *or*

(c) the respondent is resident in England and Wales on the date of the application (s. 27(2)).

(See Chapter 5 for the meaning of domicile, habitual residence, etc.)

3 ORDERS THAT CAN BE MADE

3.1 General

The court can make one or more of the following orders:

(a) an order that the respondent shall make periodical payments or secured periodical payments to the applicant;

(b) an order that the respondent shall pay the applicant a lump sum;

(c) an order that the respondent shall make periodical payments (secured or unsecured) for the benefit of a child to whom the s. 27 application relates, to the child himself or to the applicant or such other person as the court specifies;

(d) an order that the respondent shall pay the child or the applicant or such other person as the court specifies a lump sum for the benefit of the child (s. 27(6)).

Note that these orders are identical to the financial provision orders that can be made under s. 23, Matrimonial Causes Act 1973 after divorce, nullity or judicial separation (see Chapter 14). Just as is the case under s. 23, the amount of any periodical payments or lump sum ordered is within the court's discretion although the court must take into account specified factors (see paragraph 4 below). There is no financial limit on the amount of the lump sum that can be ordered. The court has power to order that the lump sum should be paid by secured or unsecured instalments if it thinks fit (s. 27(7)). The court is also able to specify the duration of any periodical payments order it makes subject to certain limitations which are set out in paragraph 3.2 below.

In contrast to the position on divorce, etc. the court does not have power to make property adjustment orders.

3.2   Limitations on orders relating to children and duration of orders generally

The limitations on the orders that can be made to or for the benefit of children and as to the duration of orders are basically the same as those applicable to financial provision orders under s. 23.

3.2.1   *Limitations on orders relating to children*
The restrictions imposed by s. 29(1) and (3), Matrimonial Causes Act 1973 on the making of financial provision orders in favour of children who have attained the age of 18 apply also to s. 27 (see Chapter 14 paragraph 2.2.2 for the provisions of s. 29(1) and (3)).

3.2.2   *Duration of orders under s. 27*
The provisions of s. 28 and s. 29, Matrimonial Causes Act 1973 relating to the duration of periodical payments orders apply to s. 27 periodical payments orders for spouses and children. These provisions are dealt with in Chapter 14 at paragraph 2.6.

Note that whereas orders for periodical payments made after divorce, etc. can normally date back to the date of the petition, in the case of periodical payments ordered under s. 27, back-dating can be to the date of the originating application for relief under s. 27.

The fact that there is a subsequent decree of divorce, nullity or judicial separation has no effect on the orders made under s. 27.

However, if the marriage is dissolved or annulled and the spouse in whose favour the s. 27 order was made remarries, the s. 27 order will automatically cease to have effect except in relation to any arrears which might have accrued up to the date of the remarriage (s. 28(2)).

4   FACTORS TO BE CONSIDERED ON AN APPLICATION UNDER S. 27

The factors to be considered on a s. 27 application are virtually the same as those to be considered on an application under s. 23.

4.1   In relation to orders for a spouse

In deciding whether the respondent has failed to provide reasonable maintenance for the applicant and what order, if any, to make in her favour, the court shall have regard to all the circumstances of the case including the matters mentioned in s. 25(2), Matrimonial Causes Act 1973 and, where an application is also made under s. 27 in respect of a child of the family who is under 18, first consideration shall be given to the welfare of the child while a minor (s. 27(3) as substituted by

s. 4, Matrimonial and Family Proceedings Act 1984). (For the matters mentioned in s. 25(2), see Chapter 16 paragraph 2.)

Note that there are minor differences between the approach under s. 27 and that under s. 23:

(a)   Under s. 23, first consideration must always be given to the welfare whilst a minor of any child of the family under 18 whether any application is made in respect of the child or not (s. 25(1)). Under s. 27, first consideration is given to the child's welfare only if an application is made in respect of him under s. 27.

(b)   Section 25(2)(c), which provides that the court must take into account the standard of living enjoyed by the family before the breakdown of the marriage is modified so that, in s. 27 cases, the court must take into account the standard of living enjoyed by the family before the failure to provide reasonable maintenance for the applicant (s. 27(3B)).

(c)   Section 25(2)(h) (consideration of benefits lost, such as pensions) is confined to proceedings for divorce or nullity and cannot therefore apply in s. 27 cases.

4.2   In relation to orders for a child

In deciding whether the respondent has failed to provide, or to make proper contribution towards, reasonable maintenance for a child of the family in respect of whom an application under s. 27 has been made and what order, if any, to make under this section in favour of the child, the court shall have regard to all the circumstances of the case including the matters mentioned in s. 25(3)(a) to (e), Matrimonial Causes Act 1973. If the child to whom the application relates is not a child of the respondent, the court must also have regard to the matters mentioned in s. 25(4), Matrimonial Causes Act 1973 (s. 27(3A)). (For the matters mentioned in s. 25(3) and s. 25(4), reference should be made to Chapter 16 paragraph 2.)

There is one minor alteration to the terms of s. 25(3) in order that it should fit the circumstances of a s. 27 application. This is to s. 25(2)(c) which deals with the standard of living enjoyed by the family before the breakdown of the marriage. This must be read as if it referred to the standard of living enjoyed by the family before the failure to provide, or to make proper contribution towards, reasonable maintenance (s. 27(3B)).

4.3   Approach in practice

In practice, what the court is likely to do when faced with a s. 27 application is to decide what order it would have made had it been considering the case under s. 23 after a divorce and then to compare what it would have ordered with what the respondent has actually been paying. If his provision does not measure up, the court can be expected to make an order for periodical payments and/or lump sum payments for the application and any children of the family in substantially the same terms as the order it would have made had the application been for ancillary relief.

4.4   Expenses that can be subject of lump sum orders

The power to order a lump sum is wide enough to enable the court to order a lump sum for any reason whatsoever. It is specifically provided by s. 27(7) that an order may, inter alia, be made for the payment of a lump sum to cover liabilities or expenses reasonably incurred in maintaining the applicant or any child of the family to whom the application relates before the making of the application.

5 PROCEDURE

Application is to a divorce county court by originating application which must be supported by an affidavit from the applicant. The procedure is governed by the Family Proceedings Rules, r. 3.1. Legal aid is available for s. 27 proceedings.

Section 27 applications are usually dealt with by a district judge and the hearing can be expected to be much the same as the hearing of an application for ancillary relief after a divorce.

6 INTERIM ORDERS

Where it appears to the court that the applicant or any child of the family to whom the s. 27 application relates is in immediate need of financial assistance but it is not yet possible to determine what order, if any, should be made on the application, the court can make an interim order for maintenance, i.e. an order requiring the respondent to make to the applicant until the determination of the application such periodical payments as the court thinks reasonable (s. 27(5)). Note that there is no power to order interim periodical payments to be made to the child direct or to any person other than the applicant for the benefit of the child.

7 VARIATION OF S. 27 ORDERS

An order for periodical payments made under s. 27 can be varied under s. 31, Matrimonial Causes Act 1973 as can the instalment element of an order for the payment of a lump sum by instalments (see Chapter 19).

8 SECTION 27 COMPARED WITH DOMESTIC PROCEEDINGS AND MAGISTRATES' COURTS ACT 1978 (DPMCA 1978)

It will have been noted that the grounds for an application under s. 27 are the same as two of the grounds for an application in the magistrates' courts for an order under s. 2 DPMCA 1978, i.e. s. 1(a) (failure to provide reasonable maintenance for the applicant) and s. 1(b) (failure to provide/contribute properly towards reasonable maintenance for a child of the family) (see Chapter 31 paragraph 6.1.1).

It follows that the applicant intending to rely on failure to maintain has a choice whether to proceed in the magistrates' courts under DPMCA 1978 or in the divorce county court under s. 27, Matrimonial Causes Act 1973. In practice, by far the majority of applications appear to be made in the magistrates' courts but the solicitor must consider what is best for his particular client in each case.

The following points must be borne in mind:

(a)   The grounds for an order under s. 27 relate only to failure to maintain whereas the applicant for an order under s. 2 DPMCA 1978 can rely alternatively on behaviour or desertion (s. 1(c) and (d) DPMCA 1978). If, therefore, there is doubt about proving failure to maintain but a possibility of making out one of the other grounds it may well be prudent to apply in the magistrates' court alleging, as an alternative, behaviour or desertion.

(b)   The grounds for jurisdiction are more restricted under DPMCA 1978 (compare Chapter 31 paragraph 3 with paragraph 2 above). This simply means that the solicitor must check that the magistrates' court would have jurisdiction in his particular case. If not, he may still be able to bring the case under s. 27.

(c)   The orders that can be made under s. 2 DPMCA 1978, although basically the same as those available under s. 27 are, in fact, more restricted as follows:

(i)   No secured periodical payments can be ordered under s. 2 DPMCA 1978; they can under s. 27.

(ii)   There is an upper financial limit of £1,000 on a lump sum ordered under s. 2 DPMCA 1978; there is no limit under s. 27.

(d)   The powers under the two Acts to make interim orders differ significantly in the following ways:

(i)   Under s. 19 DPMCA 1978 (the section dealing with interim orders), the magistrates' court has power to make an interim maintenance order requiring the respondent to make periodical payments direct to a child of the family under 18. Under s. 27, interim periodical payments can only be ordered to be made to the applicant herself and, although no doubt they will include a sum for the child's benefit, for orders made prior to 15 March 1988 this could have been a waste of the child's tax relief (see Chapter 20). However, note that any such order applied for after 15 March 1988 will not be recognised for tax relief purposes in any event, save for the fact that the payer will be entitled to an extra tax allowance in addition to his normal personal allowance. The extra allowance is currently £1,720. The magistrates' court also has power to order interim periodical payments for the benefit of the child to be made to his parent even if that parent is not the applicant for the order. Under s. 27, the court is limited to orders to the applicant only.

(ii)   Section 27 is far more generous than s. 19 DPMCA 1978 about the duration of interim orders. Interim orders under s. 27 can go on until the determination of the s. 27 application, however long it takes for that application to be heard. Interim orders under s. 19 DPMCA 1978 can only be made for a period of up to three months in the first instance and, although they can be extended, can only be extended so that they continue for a maximum of three months more (a total of six months in all, maximum). If it takes longer than six months for the case to be heard, the applicant and child will cease to be entitled to any interim payments. It is to be hoped that this will rarely prove a problem in practice as six months should be ample time in most cases for the application to be disposed of by a final order.

In fact, the apparent choice facing the applicant may, in any event, be determined for her by the legal aid authorities if she is reliant upon legal aid. Unless good grounds can be shown for seeking an order under s. 27, it is likely that the applicant will be expected to pursue what will probably be the less expensive course of an application to the magistrates' court and that her legal aid application for s. 27 will be turned down on the basis that she should be seeking assistance by way of representation for the magistrates' courts.

33 Separation and maintenance agreements

1 THE DIFFERENCE BETWEEN SEPARATION AND MAINTENANCE AGREEMENTS

The essence of a separation agreement is that the parties agree to live apart. A separation agreement may, however, include all manner of other terms dealing with maintenance, family property, arrangements for the children, etc.

An agreement which deals with the payment of maintenance by one spouse to or for the benefit of the other and/or the children but not with the separation of the parties is sometimes referred to as a 'maintenance agreement'; there may or may not be other terms in the agreement as well as provision for maintenance. This general use of the term should not be confused with maintenance agreements as defined in s. 34(2), Matrimonial Causes Act 1973. The full s. 34(2) definition is given at paragraph 9.1 below.

2 LIKELY CONTENTS OF SEPARATION AGREEMENTS

There are very few restrictions on the contents of a separation agreement and agreements are therefore likely to vary considerably depending on the circumstances of each case. The following are examples of matters commonly dealt with:

(a) *Agreement to live apart* The agreement of the parties to a marriage to live apart is central to a separation agreement. The spouses frequently also agree not to molest each other.

(b) *Maintenance* The spouses often agree that one spouse (usually the husband) will pay maintenance of a certain amount to or for the benefit of the other spouse and/or the children. Care must be taken in drafting agreements to pay maintenance. In particular, thought must be given as to when the obligation to pay maintenance under the agreement should terminate. It is possible to draft an agreement to pay maintenance that will create an obligation that will continue irrespective of whether the parties start to live together again or get divorced and despite the remarriage or cohabitation of the payee or even the death of the payer. If such an open-ended commitment is what the parties want, all well and good. Generally, however, the payer will be anxious to limit his obligations and the relevant clauses should therefore make clear the events that will bring the duty to pay maintenance to an end.

(c) *Property* The spouses may also reach agreement over what is to become of the family property. This is less common than an agreement over maintenance.

(d) *Arrangements for the children* The agreement may provide for where, and with whom, any children of the family are to live and for any arrangements as to contact.

3 WHAT A SEPARATION AGREEMENT CANNOT DO

A separation agreement must provide for *immediate* separation. Spouses cannot enter into a valid agreement to provide for their legal rights in case they should separate at any stage in the future as this is contrary to public policy.

However, a couple who have already separated but who want to attempt a reconciliation are free to negotiate a reconcilation agreement containing provisions as to what will happen should they separate again in the future. As soon as they separate, the appropriate terms will become effective.

4 THE FORM OF A SEPARATION OR MAINTENANCE AGREEMENT

A separation or maintenance agreement is a contract just like any other contract. It can be made orally or in writing or even by conduct although if the agreement covers more than simple separation it is prudent to record the terms of the agreement in writing so that they are beyond dispute.

The normal contractual rules apply to determine whether a binding agreement exists, i.e. the court will look for offer and acceptance, for an intention to create legal relations, and for consideration (consideration will usually be present in a separation agreement in the form of each party's agreement to forego his right to the consortium of the other party; *Re Weston* [1900] 2 Ch 164). However, consideration may be lacking in a maintenance agreement. An agreement by the payee not to seek further or different provision by making application to the court is void (*Hyman* v *Hyman* [1929] AC 601) and cannot therefore constitute good consideration for a promise to pay maintenance. Unless there are clearly other covenants which *are* binding on the payee, it is therefore recommended that a maintenance agreement should be embodied in a deed to ensure that it is binding.

Note that a separation or maintenance agreement can be void for mistake or fraud and can be set aside on the grounds of misrepresentation, duress or undue influence. In order to preclude future problems of this sort over the validity of the agreement, it is therefore desirable that both parties to the agreement should receive separate legal advice.

5 EFFECT OF A SEPARATION AGREEMENT

Apart from the specific matters upon which agreement is reached, a separation agreement will:

(a) release both spouses from their duty to cohabit with each other thus preventing either of them from alleging that the other is in desertion;

(b) provide evidence that the parties looked upon the marriage as at an end (necessary to prove separation for divorce and judicial separation; see *Santos* v *Santos* [1972] Fam 247, [1972] 2 All ER 246 and Chapter 3 paragraph 6.1) and as to the date of their separation;

(c) if the agreement also makes provision for maintenance and the payer fulfils his obligations in this respect, be rebuttable evidence against a claim on the basis of his failure to provide reasonable maintenance (see Chapters 31 and 32).

6 ADVANTAGES OF A SEPARATION OR MAINTENANCE AGREEMENT

The possibility of a formal separation or maintenance agreement is sometimes overlooked by solicitors who tend only to consider making an application to court for financial provision. Such an agreement does, however, have a number of advantages, for example:

(a) An agreement is flexible — it can include any terms which the parties wish subject to very few limitations.

(b) Financial matters often cause some of the bitterest disputes between couples after marriage breakdown. If its terms are observed, an agreement may serve to take the heat out of the breakdown of the marriage and will enable both parties to know where they stand. It provides a means of resolving financial and other problems formally but without the need to have recourse to court, which can be expensive and can also encourage the parties to draw up battle lines.

(c) Where provision is made for maintenance payments to a spouse, tax relief will become available for the payments (whereas it is not for voluntary payments). This can produce a tax saving in some cases (see Chapter 20, paragraph 2.5).

It should be pointed out, however, that there are disadvantages of a separation order in comparison with a court order, notably:

(a) It will not enable a spouse to obtain tax relief on payments of maintenance made direct to a child whereas tax relief is likely to be available where maintenance payments to a child are ordered by the court (provided that the application was made before 15 March 1988 and order made before 30 June 1988). However, note that no tax relief will be available for maintenance payments made direct to a child by court order if that court order was applied for after 15 March 1988, save in so far as the payments may be part of the maintenance paid by one spouse to the other (in which case an extra allowance may be available to a maximum of £1,720: see Chapter 20).

(b) It is not so easy to enforce (for enforcement of agreements, see paragraph 7 below; for enforcement of court orders see Chapter 18 and Chapter 31, paragraph 12).

(c) It cannot achieve the same degree of finality as a court order. The jurisdiction of the court to entertain future financial and property applications (for example, after divorce) cannot be ousted by an agreement (see paragraphs 8 and 9.2 below).

(d) Whilst variation by the court can be sought if the agreement can be classed as a maintenance agreement within s. 34, Matrimonial Causes Act 1973, if the agreement falls outside the definition, it can only be varied by consent. Court orders for periodical payments are always variable by subsequent order.

7 ENFORCEMENT

A separation or maintenance agreement is enforceable in the same way as any other contract. Thus an action can be brought for damages (for example, if the breach alleged is a failure to pay maintenance, damages equal to the arrears of maintenance could be sought), and the equitable remedies of specific performance and an injunction to prevent a breach of a negative clause of the agreement are also available.

8 IMPACT OF SUBSISTING SEPARATION AGREEMENT OR MAINTENANCE AGREEMENT ON FINANCIAL ARRANGEMENTS AFTER DIVORCE, ETC.

The fact that there is a subsisting maintenance or separation agreement dealing with finance and/or property does not preclude either party making a comprehensive application for ancillary relief in conjunction with divorce, nullity or judicial separation even if that party undertakes in the agreement not to seek further provision from the court (an undertaking which will be void, see paragraph 9.2 below). However, the existence of the agreement will be one of the factors for the court to take into account under s. 25, Matrimonial Causes Act 1973 when it considers the application for ancillary relief (see Chapter 16).

9 THE PROVISIONS OF SS. 34–36, MATRIMONIAL CAUSES ACT 1973 AS TO MAINTENANCE AGREEMENTS

9.1 Definition of maintenance agreements (s. 34(2))

Sections 34–36 apply to maintenance agreements as defined by s. 34(2), i.e. to any agreement in writing made between the parties to a marriage, being:

(a)   an agreement containing financial arrangements, whether made during the continuance or after the dissolution or annulment of the marriage; *or*

(b)   a separation agreement which contains no financial arrangements in a case where no other agreement in writing between the same parties contains such arrangements.

'Financial arrangements' means provisions governing the rights and liabilities towards one another when living separately of the parties to a marriage (including a marriage which has been dissolved or annulled) in respect of the making or securing of payments or the disposition or use of any property, including such rights and liabilities with respect to the maintenance or education of any child, whether or not a child of the family.

9.2 Attempts to oust the court's jurisdiction

Section 34(1) provides that any provision in a maintenance agreement purporting to restrict any right to apply to a court for an order containing financial arrangements is void. However, other financial arrangements contained in the agreement are not thereby rendered void and unenforceable. Therefore, unless the other arrangements are void or unenforceable for some other reason (and subject to the court's power to vary the arrangements under ss. 35 and 36), the parties to the agreement will be bound by them.

Note that a term purporting to oust the jurisdiction of the court in an agreement which is not classed as a maintenance agreement (for example, because it is oral) is still void as it is contrary to public policy. However, in the case of such an agreement, the effect is more dramatic — it renders the whole agreement void (*Sutton* v *Sutton* [1984] 1 All ER 168, [1984] 2 WLR 146).

9.3   Alteration of agreements by the court during the lives of the parties (s. 35)

9.3.1   *Which courts can entertain applications?*
Applications under s. 35 may be made to:

(a)   the High Court or county court (s. 35(1)) – the procedure will be regulated by the Family Proceedings Rules 1991, r. 3.2, which provides that the application must be by way of originating application; or

(b)   the magistrates' court (proceedings in the magistrates' court are 'family proceedings': Magistrates' Courts Act 1980, s. 65(1), as amended by MFPA 1984 and the Children Act 1989, s. 92, sch. 11, para. 10). The procedure will be regulated by the Magistrates' Court Rules 1981, and s. 105 provides that the application must be by way of complaint.

9.3.2   *When can an application be made?*
An application can be made under s. 35 if:

(a)   the maintenance agreement is subsisting; *and*

(b)   in the case of an application to a divorce county court, each of the parties to the agreement is either domiciled or resident in England and Wales, *or* if the application is to be made to a magistrates' court, both parties to the agreement are resident in England and Wales and at least one of them is resident within the commission area of the magistrates' court in question (s. 35(1) and (3)).

9.3.3   *What orders can be made?*
The magistrates have more limited power to alter maintenance agreements than the divorce courts.

The divorce county court can make such alterations in the agreement as may appear just by:

(a)   varying or revoking any financial arrangements contained in the agreement; *or*

(b)   inserting in it financial arrangements for the benefit of one of the parties to the agreement or of a child of the family (s. 35(2)).

The magistrates' court has power only as follows:

(a)   Where the agreement includes no provision for periodical payments by either of the parties, by inserting provision for the making by one of the parties of periodical payments for the maintenance of the other party or of any child of the family. *And*

(b)   Where the agreement includes provision for the making by one of the parties of periodical payments, by increasing or reducing the rate of any of her payments or terminating them (s. 35(3)).

9.3.4   What matters are to be taken into consideration?

The court cannot alter the agreement unless it is satisfied either:

(a)   that by reason of a change in the circumstances in the light of which any financial arrangements contained in the agreement were made or, as the case may be, financial arrangements were omitted from it (including a change foreseen by the parties when making the agreement), the agreement should be altered so as to make different financial arrangements, or as the case may be, so as to contain financial arrangements; *or*

(b)   that the agreement does not contain proper financial arrangements with respect to any child of the family.

When deciding what alterations to make the court must decide what would be just having regard to all the circumstances, including, if relevant, the matters set out in s. 25(3), Matrimonial Causes Act 1973 (i.e. the extent to which the party concerned has assumed responsibility for a child of the family who is not his child, etc.; see Chapter 16 paragraph 2.3).

9.3.5   Effect of order

If the court alters the agreement, the alteration will take effect as if the alteration had been made by agreement between the parties and for valuable consideration (s. 35(2)).

9.3.6   Duration of order

If the court decides to alter the agreement by inserting provision for one party to make periodical payments or secured periodical payments for the other or for a child of the family or by increasing the rate of the periodical payments payable under the agreement by one party for the maintenance of the other or for the maintenance of a child, the term of the payments or additional payments will be such as the court shall specify subject to the following limits (which are in line with the limits on orders made in ancillary relief proceedings):

(a)   *Payments for spouses*:

(i)   unsecured payments — not to extend beyond the death of either of the parties or the remarriage of the payee;

(ii)   secured payments — not to extend beyond remarriage or death of payee; s. 35(4).

(b)   *Payments for children*   The provisions of s. 29(2) and (3) apply (i.e. order not to extend beyond 17th birthday in the first instance and not beyond 18th birthday unless child in full-time education or training or there are special circumstances; see Chapter 14 paragraph 2.6.2).

9.4   Alteration of agreements by the court after the death of one party (s. 36)

Section 36 permits application to be made in certain circumstances to the High Court or a county court for alteration of a maintenance agreement which provides for the continuation of payments after death of the parties. The procedure is governed by the Family Proceedings Rules 1991, r. 3.3.

10   ALTERATION OF MAINTENANCE AGREEMENTS RELATING TO CHILDREN UNDER THE CHILDREN ACT 1989

Schedule 1, para. 10, Children Act 1989 gives the court power to alter certain maintenance agreements during the lifetime of the parties to the agreement. Schedule 1, para. 11 makes provision for alteration following the death of one of the parties.

For the purposes of paragraphs 10 and 11 a 'maintenance agreement' means *any* agreement in writing made *with respect to a child*, whether before or after 14 October 1991, which:

(a)   is or was made between the father and mother of the child; and

(b)   contains provisions with respect to the making or securing of payments, or the disposition or use of any property, for the maintenance or education of the child.

This gives the court power to vary maintenance agreements made between the father and mother of the child *irrespective* of whether they are or have ever been married.

34 Section 17, Married Women's Property Act 1882

1 INTRODUCTION

Section 17 of the Married Women's Property Act 1882 provides a procedure for determining the property rights of spouses, of formerly engaged couples and of certain divorcees without relying on the court's powers to grant ancillary relief after divorce.

In practice, s. 17 is not much used these days as the power of the court under that section is so much more restricted than the powers available under ss. 22 to 24A, Matrimonial Causes Act 1973 that most couples prefer to wait to have their disputes settled under the ancillary relief provisions in conjunction with proceedings for divorce, judicial separation or nullity. Only if neither party contemplates taking any of these proceedings or if, for some other reason, the ancillary relief provisions do not apply (for example, where the couple were only ever engaged and not married, or where a spouse has remarried after divorce without making a claim for ancillary relief and therefore lost his or her rights to lump sum and property adjustment orders), will s. 17 be invoked. Because s. 17 proceedings are relatively rare these days, this chapter does not go into either the law or the procedure in any depth. The reader is referred to the major textbooks on family law, on property law and on trusts for further information.

2 THE BASIC PROVISION

Section 17 provides that, in any question between husband and wife as to the title to or possession of property, either party may apply in a summary way to a High Court or county court judge who may make such order with respect to the property in dispute and as to the costs of the application as he thinks fit.

3 POSSIBLE APPLICANTS

The following can make application under s. 17:

    (a) either party to a marriage during the marriage (s. 17);

    (b) either party to a marriage within three years of the dissolution or annulment of the marriage (s. 39, Matrimonial Proceedings and Property Act 1970);

    (c) engaged couples within three years of the termination of the engagement (s. 2(2), Law Reform (Miscellaneous Provisions) Act 1970).

Note that s. 17 does not assist cohabitees for whom no special procedure exists for determining property disputes. Where a dispute arises between cohabitees, therefore, the only means of resolving it is unfortunately by relying on the general jurisdiction of the county court or High Court. The exact nature of the application that should be made depends on the circumstances of the case but the following forms of relief are not uncommonly sought: an order declaring and enforcing a trust; an order for sale under s. 30, Law of Property Act 1925; an order granting possession of real property; injunctions and damages for wrongful interference with goods (where chattels are in dispute).

4 WHAT PROPERTY IS COVERED?

Application can be made under s. 17 to sort out disputes over all manner of property including, for example, houses and land, money, shares, furniture, jewellery and even items of very little financial value such as holiday souvenirs, garden tools, photograph albums.

Although most disputes concern property which is in the possession of one or the other party, it is not essential for either party to have the property in his possession at the time of the application. By s. 7, Matrimonial Causes (Property and Maintenance) Act 1958, application can be made where it is alleged:

(a)   that the other party has had in his possession or control property to which the applicant was partly or wholly beneficially entitled even though he no longer has the property; *or*

(b)   that the other party has or has had in his possession or control money representing the proceeds of sale of property to which the applicant was wholly or partly entitled.

5 WHAT ORDERS CAN BE MADE?

5.1 Orders declaring parties' property rights

Section 17 is a procedural provision only. It empowers the court to determine in a summary way what the parties' rights in particular property *are* as a matter of strict law and to declare them accordingly. There is no power under s. 17 to make orders *adjusting* property rights such as the court can make under s. 24, Matrimonial Causes Act 1973.

5.2 Order for sale

The court also has power under s. 17 to order a sale of the disputed property (see paragraph 10 below).

6 ORDINARY TRUST PRINCIPLES GENERALLY APPLY IN DETER-MINING DISPUTES

Statutory provision has been made for one or two problems that have arisen frequently in disputes between husband and wife (see paragraph 8 below). However, on the whole the same principles apply in determining property disputes between spouses and others under s. 17 as apply to disputes between total strangers. Thus, the courts will generally apply normal trust principles though with the assistance of numerous authorities in the reports illustrating how these principles have been interpreted in family situations (for example, in disputes between husband and wife under s. 17 or, more commonly these days, between cohabitees in a trust action).

7 DISPUTES OVER LAND

7.1 *Pettitt* v *Pettitt* and *Gissing* v *Gissing*

The present law in relation to disputes over the ownership of land can be traced back to the cases of *Pettitt* v *Pettitt* [1970] AC 777, [1969] 2 All ER 385 and *Gissing* v *Gissing* [1971] AC 886, [1970] 2 All ER 780 in the House of Lords and the principles set out in this paragraph derive largely from these cases.

7.2 Examples of the types of problem that arise

Example 1. The matrimonial home was purchased in the sole name of the husband. The wife claims to have a beneficial interest in the property because she has paid for substantial improvements to be made to the property.

Example 2. Miss James and Mr Harris are engaged. They buy a house to be their home after they are married. The house is conveyed into Mr Harris's sole name but both parties contribute equally to the deposit, legal fees and mortgage instalments. The engagement is broken off. Miss James claims to have a beneficial interest in the property by virtue of her contribution to the purchase price.

Example 3. The matrimonial home was purchased in the joint names of husband and wife. The wife claims that, as she put up the deposit and her earnings have been used to pay the mortgage instalments, the whole beneficial interest in the house belongs to her.

7.3 The need to establish a trust

Where one party claims to be entitled to a greater share in the house than the legal title suggests, he or (more usually) she must establish that the legal estate in the property is held on trust for her to the extent that she alleges she is beneficially entitled. Thus, for example, in Example 2 (paragraph 7.2), Miss James would no doubt argue that Mr Harris holds the legal estate in the house on trust for herself and himself in equal shares and in Example 3, the wife would have to establish that the parties hold the legal estate on trust for her absolutely.

7.4 Existence of trust dependent on common intention

Whether a trust exists depends on the parties' common intention in relation to the beneficial ownership of the property at the time of acquisition.

7.5 Ascertaining the parties' intention

7.5.1 The importance of the title deeds
The first step is to examine the title deeds of the property. The conveyance or transfer will obviously stipulate who is to hold the legal estate. The beneficial interest may or may not be mentioned specifically.

Where the conveyance/transfer deals with the legal estate only and is silent as to the beneficial interests in the property, prima facie the beneficial interest goes with the legal estate. Thus where the conveyance/transfer says, for example, 'To Joe Bloggs in fee simple', Joe Bloggs is prima facie entitled to the whole beneficial interest in the property and where the conveyance/transfer consigns the legal estate to, say, husband and wife jointly, husband and wife are prima facie entitled to equal shares in the beneficial interest. However there is nothing to prevent a claimant arguing that the intention was that the legal estate should be held on trust in different proportions. Mrs Joe Bloggs could therefore argue that her financial contributions to the purchase demonstrate a common intention that she should have a beneficial interest in the property and that Mr Bloggs therefore holds the property on trust for both parties.

On the other hand, if the conveyance/transfer stipulates not only who is to hold the legal estate but also who is entitled to the beneficial interest in the property (for example, 'to Joe Bloggs and Freda Walker as tenants in common in equal shares' or 'to Joe Bloggs and Mildred Bloggs as beneficial joint tenants') that concludes the question of beneficial ownership of the property unless it can be shown that the statement in the conveyance was the result of fraud or a mistake or that there has subsequently been a fresh agreement varying the position in the conveyance/transfer. The same is true where a separate deed of trust has been prepared dealing with the beneficial interest in the property.

Example. The matrimonial home is purchased in the joint names of husband and wife. The conveyance is expressed to be to H and W 'as joint tenants in law and equity'. In fact, the wife has never worked and the whole of the purchase price has been provided by the husband. The husband cannot argue that he is entitled to the whole beneficial interest in the property on the basis that he provided the purchase money (and see *Goodman* v *Gallant* [1986] 1 FLR 513, [1986] Fam 106, [1986] 1 All ER 311).

Note, however, that s. 37, Matrimonial Proceedings and Property Act 1970 (see paragraph 7.5.2.2(c) below) can operate to entitle a spouse to a bigger interest in property by virtue of improvements that he or she has effected to the property subsequently and this *will* override the provisions of the conveyance/transfer.

7.5.2 Ascertaining intention when the title deeds are not conclusive of the beneficial interests and there is no express deed of trust
Where the beneficial interests in the property are not finally determined by the conveyance/transfer/express deed of trust, the parties' intention must be ascertained from what they said and did concerning the house.

7.5.2.1 Express declarations of trust and agreements It is very rare for a couple to discuss their respective entitlements to their home at all, let alone to reach agreement on the subject. Occasionally, however, one party does make a statement which is capable of amounting to an express declaration of trust or the parties do expressly reach agreement as to the ownership of the home. Where this happens it is the clearest indication of their intentions and, subject to s. 53, Law of Property Act 1925 (see paragraph 7.7 below), will be given effect. Note that even if the parties do not go so far as an express declaration of trust or agreement, their conversations can still be taken into account as part of their conduct in determining what was their common intention (see paragraph 7.5.2.2(b) below).

7.5.2.2   No express declaration of trust/agreement   If nothing has been said expressly, the court must ascertain the parties' common intention from their conduct. The following matters are relevant:

(a)   *Contribution to purchase price*   The general rule is that, in the absence of evidence showing that some other arrangement was intended, a contributor to the purchase price will acquire a beneficial interest in the property (this is traditionally called the presumption of resulting trust). The following count as contributions towards the purchase price:

(i)   Outright payment of deposit/purchase price: the most straightforward case is where a claimant has paid all or part of the initial deposit for the property or, where the property is purchased outright without the aid of a mortgage, has paid all or part of the purchase price.

(ii)   Payment of mortgage instalments: where the property is purchased on mortgage (or with other borrowed finance) a share can be acquired by *direct* contribution to the mortgage instalments (at least where the claimant's contributions are substantial, not merely the odd instalment every now and then).

Example.   Miss Smythe and Mr Mead are engaged. They purchase a house to be their matrimonial home. Mr Mead pays the deposit and the house is conveyed into his sole name. However, they arrange that they will pay alternate mortgage instalments, Miss Smythe one month, Mr Mead the next, from their salaries. This arrangement continues for a year before the engagement is called off. A trust may arise in favour of Miss Smythe by virtue of her direct contributions to the mortgage repayments.

(iii)   Payment of household or other expenses referable to purchase of house: a share can be acquired by *indirect* contribution to the mortgage instalments, i.e. by meeting household and other expenses thereby freeing the other party to pay the mortgage instalments. The payment of expenses must be 'referable' to the acquisition of the house. The cases of *Richards* v *Dove* [1974] 1 All ER 888, *Burns* v *Burns* [1984] 1 All ER 244 and *Risch* v *McFee* [1991] 1 FLR 105 illustrate this. In *Richards* v *Dove* a man and mistress had been living together and decided to buy a house. The mistress had been paying for food and other housekeeping expenses and the man for the rent, electricity, rates, etc. whilst they lived in rented accommodation. The mistress continued to contribute in exactly the same way when they bought the new property. Thus her payments could not be said to be referable to the purchase but simply a continuation of their existing financial arrangements. In *Burns* v *Burns* the court found that the purchase by the female cohabitee of domestic items such as sheets, bedcovers, a bed, dishwasher, washing machine, etc. for the house was not referable to the purchase of the house itself and did not indicate a common intention that she should have a beneficial interest in the house (although, in such circumstances, the purchaser of the chattels may well own or part own the chattels themselves). In *Risch* v *McFee* the court found that the loan of £1,700 by the plaintiff to the defendant which enabled him to buy the house was made with the common intention that the plaiintiff shoud have a beneficial interest in the property. Once that had been established the £1,700 could be said to be part of her contribution to the cost of acquiring the property, and an assessment could be made of the size of her beneficial interest in it.

Example.   Mr and Mrs Young have been living in rented accommodation throughout their married life. After the children have left school, Mrs Young decides to get a job. In view of their improved circumstances, the parties decide to buy their own house. It is conveyed into Mr Young's sole name. He pays the mortgage instalments from his salary which he can afford to do because he no longer has to pay housekeeping money to Mrs Young as she uses her own salary to buy food and clothes and pay household bills. There is little doubt that Mrs Young's payments are referable to the purchase of the new house and a trust may well arise in her favour by virtue of them.

The presumption of resulting trust that arises from a contribution to the purchase price can be rebutted by evidence showing that the parties did not intend the contributor to acquire a share in the equity thereby. For example, there may be evidence to show that the money was an outright gift or, at the other end of the scale, was intended simply as a loan. In the past, the presumption of advancement has been important in this respect. In accordance with the presumption of advancement, where a husband puts up the money for the purchase of a house that is conveyed into his wife's name, it is presumed unless the contrary is shown that he intended the property to be a gift to her. (There is no corresponding presumption applicable when a wife puts up the purchase money.) However, the value of the presumption of advancement was questioned in *Pettitt* v *Pettitt* [1970] AC 777, [1969] 2 All ER 385, where the general view was that it is outdated and no longer particularly useful and can therefore be rebutted easily by evidence showing that a gift to the wife was not intended.

   (b)   *Payment of legal costs*   The fact that the claimant pays the legal expenses connected with the purchase may be sufficient to secure her a benficial interest but it may be that this will only be so if the claimant has also contributed to the deposit (see Lord Diplock in *Gissing* v *Gissing* [1971] AC at 910, [1970] 2 All ER at 791). The crucial question must be whether the payment of legal expenses indicates a common intention that the beneficial interest in the home should be shared or not.

   (c)   *Improvements*   Section 37, Matrimonial Proceedings and Property Act 1970 makes it clear that a share in property can be acquired by carrying out, helping with or paying for improvements. It provides that where a husband or wife makes a substantial contribution in money or money's worth to the improvement of real or personal property in which, or in the proceeds of sale of which, either or both of them has or have beneficial interest, the contributor shall, subject to any contrary agreement between them, be treated as having acquired a share or an enlarged share in the beneficial interest by virtue of his or her contribution. The proportion of the share/increased share acquired is dependent on the parties' agreement at the time or, in default of agreement, will be determined by the court as it thinks just in all the circumstances (see *Passee* v *Passee* [1988] 1 FLR 263, [1988] Fam Law 132, and *Thomas* v *Fuller-Brown* [1988] 1 FLR 237, [1988] Fam Law 53, and *Risch* v *McFee* [1991] 1 FLR 105).

   In view of the fact that the claimant must have made a *substantial* improvement, a husband's entitlement will not be affected by the fact that he has done (or paid for) routine do-it-yourself jobs that husbands often do, nor will a wife's share increase because she cleans the walls, works in the garden or helps with the painting and decorating (see Lord Denning MR in *Button* v *Button* [1968] 1 WLR 457, [1968] 1 All ER 1064). On the other hand, it is clear that doing a considerable amount of heavy building work, for example, using a sledge hammer to demolish buildings, working a cement mixer, etc. (such as the mistress did in *Eves* v *Eves* [1975] 1 WLR 1338, [1975] 3 All ER 768 and *Cooke* v *Head* [1972] 1 WLR 518, [1972] 2 All ER 38) will be sufficient to acquire a share and it is suggested that a share will normally also be acquired by paying for a fairly major improvement such as the installation of central heating, or of a new bathroom or the conversion of a loft.

> **Example.** Mr and Mrs Couch are looking for a new home. They find a row of three dilapidated cottages which are suitable for conversion and buy them. Mr Couch puts up the purchase money and the cottages are conveyed into his name. The Couches carry out much of the renovation work themselves. They re-roof the property, Mr Couch going up on the roof and Mrs Couch loading up the tiles on the conveyor at the bottom for him. They knock down several internal walls, both wielding a sledge hammer and wheeling away the stone although there are certain bits that Mr Couch has to lift as his wife is not strong enough. They install new window frames which Mrs Couch paints and glazes whilst Mr Couch installs central heating. Mrs Couch pays for the property to be professionally rewired. There is no doubt that Mrs Couch will acquire a beneficial interest in the property by virtue of her hard work and her payment for the rewiring.

7.6 No share from looking after the family

There have been repeated attempts (in particular by wives and female cohabitees) to establish that a share can be acquired in property simply by looking after the family and bringing up the children. Although the efforts that she has made for the family may lead to the claimant being awarded a greater share in the family assets in ancillary relief proceedings, it is now clearly established that being a good wife will not avail her when it comes to establishing a share in property on the basis of ordinary trust principles under s. 17. A pronouncement to this effect is contained in *Burns* v *Burns* [1984] 1 All ER 244. This was a case between cohabitees but the principle is equally applicable to married couples.

7.7 Section 53, Law of Property Act 1925

It was thought, at one time, that the provisions of s. 53, Law of Property Act 1925 would cause difficulties in matrimonial situations. Section 53(1)(b) provides that a declaration of trust respecting any land or any interest in land must be manifested and proved by writing signed by some person who is able to declare such a trust. Section 53(1)(c) goes further and requires that a disposition of an equitable interest or trust subsisting at the time of the disposition must be in writing signed by the person disposing of it or his agent or by will. However, there are two major exceptions to the provisions of s. 53 as to writing, i.e. the requirements of the section do not affect the creation or operation of resulting, implied or constructive trusts (s. 53(2)) nor do they affect the doctrine of part performance (s. 55(d)). These exceptions have given the courts a way round the strict provisions of s. 53 so that it is rare for a claimant in a family situation to fail to establish a trust simply because there is no written evidence of it (though see *Midland Bank plc* v *Dobson & Dobson* [1986] 1 FLR 171 which makes it clear that it *can* happen).

8   THE OWNERSHIP OF CASH AND ASSETS OTHER THAN LAND

As with land, entitlement to cash and other assets generally depends on the intention of the parties. A number of matters that commonly cause difficulty are dealt with below.

8.1   Housekeeping money

Section 1 of the Married Women's Property Act 1964 provides that if any question arises as to the right of a husband or wife to money derived from any allowance made by the husband for the expenses of the matrimonial home or for similar purposes, or to any property acquired out of such money, the money or property shall, in the absence of any agreement between them to the contrary, be treated as belonging to the husband and the wife in equal shares.

> **Example.** Mr Hill pays his wife £55 housekeeping each week. She manages to save £15 a week and, at the end of the year, buys a Victorian button-back chair with the savings. Nothing is said by either party as to who the savings from the housekeeping or the chair belong to. Section 1 therefore dictates that the chair belongs to the parties equally.

8.2   Joint accounts

The ownership of a joint account and of property purchased from it depends on the intention of the parties.

In some cases, the proper inference is that the parties are pooling their resources and intend that the account and any assets acquired from it shall belong to them jointly (see, for example, *Jones* v *Maynard* [1951] Ch 572, [1951] 1 All ER 802). In other cases, one party provides all the funds and a joint account is only opened as a matter of convenience, in which case the funds in the account and any property bought with them belong to the spouse who put up the money unless there is specific agreement about particular items purchased (see, for example, *Heseltine* v *Heseltine* [1971] 1 WLR 342, [1971] 1 All ER 952). In other cases it may be that assets bought from the joint account belong solely to the spouse making the purchase (see, for example, *Re Bishop* [1965] Ch 450, [1965] 1 All ER 249).

8.3   Wedding presents and other gifts

Naturally each spouse owns the items that were given to him or her personally, for example as birthday presents.

Who owns the wedding presents and other gifts to the parties jointly will depend on the intention of the donor. However, in the absence of other evidence, the court may be inclined to find that wedding presents in particular belong to the spouse whose side of the family donated them (*Samson* v *Samson* [1960] 1 All ER 653, [1960] 1 WLR 190).

8.4   Property purchased before marriage

Property purchased by one of the spouses before the marriage without a view to the marriage will normally belong to that spouse absolutely. It is possible, however, for that spouse subsequently to give the property or a share in it to the other spouse. Again, it is a question of intention.

9 FIXING THE SIZE OF EACH PARTY'S SHARE IN THE DISPUTED PROPERTY

Where it is decided that the claimant does have a share in the property, whatever it may be, the court must determine the size of the share. This is another matter which depends, at least in theory, on the intentions of the parties. In practice exact calculations are not often likely to be possible, although there may be cases where the claimant's share is acquired only by direct financial contributions to the purchase price of the asset where it is possible to compare her contribution with the total purchase price to ascertain her share.

> **Example.** Husband and wife purchase a matrimonial home which is conveyed into the husband's sole name. The price is £15,000 which is paid outright and provided by each of them in equal proportions. There are no further matters such as improvements to be taken into account. The value of the property is now £30,000. The court finds that the husband holds the property on trust for himself and the wife in equal shares.

In other cases, the court will look at the evidence and take a broad approach. If all else fails, the court can fall back on the maxim that 'equality is equity'.

10 ORDERS FOR SALE

The court has power to order a sale of the disputed property. Where there is a dispute over who is to have possession of a jointly owned chattel, the court can therefore order that the item in question be sold and the proceeds divided between the parties in accordance with their shares. The threat of sale of a cherished item (usually, of course, for considerably less than the parties feel that the garden gnomes or whatever the item is, are worth to them) is usually sufficient to introduce a more rational attitude as to who should have what.

The power is more important in relation to the matrimonial home. Where land is held on trust for the parties jointly, a trust for sale is automatically imposed by the Law of Property Act 1925 (*Bull* v *Bull* [1955] 1 QB 234, [1955] 1 All ER 253). Whether a sale will be ordered is a question for the court's discretion but basically depends on whether the underlying purpose of the trust for sale is continuing (*Re Buchanan-Wollaston's Conveyance* [1939] Ch 738, [1939] 2 All ER 302). The court will therefore look to see why the house was bought. The normal purpose is to provide a home. In cases of this type, where there are no children (or no children living at home), the purpose of the trust will come to an end on the breakdown of the relationship and a sale will therefore normally be ordered. In contrast, where the house is still needed to provide a home for the children, the court is unlikely to order a sale.

11 PROCEDURE

Application is to the High Court or county court. In the High Court proceedings are commenced by originating summons and in the county court by originating application. The relevant procedure is set out in the Family Proceedings Rules 1991, rr. 3.6 and 3.7.

12 PRACTICAL IMPORTANCE OF S. 17

Where one of the parties has commenced or contemplates proceedings for divorce, nullity or judicial separation, it is generally a waste of time and money for the court to investigate their strict property rights in an applicaton under s. 17. It is preferable to rely on the wide powers of the court under ss. 23 and 24, Matrimonial Causes Act 1973, which will enable the court to do broad justice between the parties.

There are, however, cases where the strict property rights of the parties have to be determined under s. 17. The following situations are examples:

(a)   Where the parties have only ever been engaged.

(b)   Where the spouses do not want or cannot get a decree of divorce, nullity or judicial separation.

(c)   Where a claim is made on behalf of a spouse who has remarried without making ancillary relief claims and is therefore debarred from relying on the Matrimonial Causes Act 1973).

(d)   Where one spouse is adjudicated bankrupt, his property vests in his trustee in bankruptcy to be administered for the benefit of his creditors. It may be necessary for the other spouse to seek a declaration of the parties' strict property rights under s. 17 in order to prevent the trustee in bankruptcy laying claim to property that is legally hers.

PART IX
WELFARE

35 Welfare benefits

1 INTRODUCTION

This chapter deals with the following welfare benefits:

(a) income support;
(b) family credit;
(c) housing benefit;
(d) child benefit;
(e) one-parent benefit.

The law on benefits is to be found in various statutes and regulations and is immensely detailed. It is not possible to deal with each benefit comprehensively in a book of this sort. The aim of this chapter is to give the practitioner a broad outline of the provisions, firstly so that he can advise his client whether it is worth his while making further enquiries of the local social security office or local authority with a view to making a claim, and secondly so that he will be aware of how maintenance and other payments to the client from his or her spouse or former spouse will affect his or her entitlement to benefit. Should a specific problem arise over the client's benefit, the practitioner can find out more about the rules of entitlement from specialist books on social security and state benefits and from the DSS handbooks on individual benefits. The rates of benefit are raised regularly and care must be taken to find out whether the figures given in this chapter are still applicable at the time of reference. Where examples are given, the figures used are those in force from 6 April 1992 until April 1993.

The Society Security Act 1986 made sweeping changes to welfare law when it came into force in April 1988. It replaced supplementary benefit with 'income support', family income supplement with 'family credit', and made provision for cash help for those with special needs from the 'social fund'. Furthermore, the Act has made substantial alterations to housing benefit.

The Child Support Act 1991 will make significant changes to child mainten-ance. A Child Support Agency will be set up to trace absent parents and will assess, collect and enforce certain maintenance payments. Many of the necessary regulations have not been published yet, but one of the reforms which takes effect from April 1992 is the reduction in the number of qualifying hours for family credit and income support from 24 to 16.

A: INCOME SUPPORT

The law on income support is presently to be found in the Social Security Act 1986, as amended by the Social Security Act 1988, and (*inter alia*) the Income Support (General) Regulations 1987 which tend to be amended annually. It should be noted that in social security law the regulations are extremely important as they set out the fine detail of each benefit. Income support replaces the old system of supplementary benefit. Income support is a cash benefit to help people who do not have enough money to live on. People receiving income support will automatically be entitled to other benefits, e.g., exemption from certain NHS charges, free milk and free school meals.

2 INCOME SUPPORT AND FAMILY CREDIT COMPARED

If the claimant or his or her partner works for more than 16 hours per week neither of them will be entitled to income support, but if the claimant has at least one child then the claimant may be entitled to family credit. There are transitional provisions for those who were claiming income support prior to the reduction in hours from 24 to 16 on 7 April 1992.

3 WHO CAN CLAIM?

Claimants must:

(a)   Be 18 or over. There are some special groups of people under 18 who may be entitled to income support if they do not have enough money to live on, e.g., a single parent looking after a child, a person incapable of work because of disablement. The practitioner should refer to s. 4 of the Social Security Act 1988 and the regulations made thereunder for an exhaustive list.

(b)   Be present in Great Britain.

(c)   Not be engaged in remunerative work for more than 16 hours per week, and not have a partner who is engaged in remunerative work for more than 16 hours per week. A partner is someone to whom the claimant is married, or with whom he or she lives as if married to them.

(d)   Be available for employment and actively seeking work unless exempt from the condition, e.g., lone parents, disabled people, women in an advanced state of pregnancy.

(e)   Not be receiving 'relevant education'. A child or young person is treated as receiving 'relevant education' if he is receiving full-time non-advanced education or, although not receiving such education, is treated as a child for the purposes of child benefit. In certain circumstances a young person who is in relevant education may nevertheless be entitled to income support, e.g., where he is living away from his parents, or is responsible for a child. In such cases he must also satisfy the other conditions of entitlement to income support.

Generally speaking, pupils receiving full-time education up to and including A-level standard cannot claim benefit in their own right. Full-time further and higher education students are not normally regarded as available for employment and therefore cannot claim benefit even during the summer vacation subject to certain exceptions, e.g. lone parents.

4   ENTITLEMENT TO INCOME SUPPORT

In order to be entitled to income support the claimant must satisfy a means test to ensure that his income is not above the level prescribed by law as the amount necessary for a person to live on. The income of the whole family will be taken into account in assessing entitlement. If the claimant is working for 16 hours or more each week, or has a partner who is doing so, then he or she will not normally be entitled to income support. For the purposes of this assessment the 'family' includes a married couple (who are married to each other and are members of the same household) or an unmarried couple (a man and woman who are not married to each other but are living together as husband and wife). For further details of who will be treated as a member of the household for the purposes of income support see Income Support (General) Regulations 1987, r. 16.

4.1   Calculating the claimant's income

For the purposes of establishing entitlement to income support the claimant's weekly income is calculated as follows:

(a)   Take the claimant's net (not gross) weekly income — the practitioner should refer to the regulations for full details, but as a general outline 'income' includes periodical maintenance payments made to the claimant or his or her children (whether made voluntarily or under a court order), lump-sum orders (whether or not payable by instalments), statutory sick pay, statutory maternity payments (if the claimant has not been in receipt of them for 13 weeks or more), housing benefit and any social fund payments.

(b)   Add to it any 'tariff income' the claimant may receive from capital. This arises if the claimant's capital exceeds £3,000; if so, then each complete £250 in excess of £3,000 (but not exceeding £8,000) is treated as a weekly income of £1.

(c)   Certain sums will be disregarded in the calculation of earnings. The rules in relation to this are complex and the practitioner should refer to the appropriate regulations for full details. Examples of sums that will be disregarded include the earnings of a child or young person who is part of the household, and the first £5 per week of the claimant's or his partner's part-time earnings or the first £15 in the case of a lone parent.

4.2   Effect of capital

The claimant will not be entitled to income support if his capital exceeds £8,000. The first £3,000 of capital will be ignored, and capital of between £3,000 and £8,000 will be taken into account by assuming a weekly income for each £250 of capital over the £3,000 level. The rules as to exactly which sums will be treated as capital and which sums will be disregarded for that purpose are complex and the practitioner is referred to the regulations for further details.

5   AMOUNT OF INCOME SUPPORT

If the claimant is entitled to income support, then the following are the amounts to which he is entitled:

(a)   If the claimant has no income, the amount of income support is the 'applicable amount'.

(b)   If the claimant has income, the amount of income support is the difference between the claimant's income and the 'applicable amount'.

Ordinary 'applicable amounts' fall into four categories:

(a)   A 'personal allowance' for the claimant and his partner (if there is a partner), and an allowance for any child or young person that the claimant and his partner look after.

(b)   A 'family premium' if the claimant is a member of a family of which at least one member is a child or young person.

(c)   Special 'premium payments' for groups of people with special expenses.

(d)   'Housing costs payments' to cover certain costs of accommodation not met by housing benefit, e.g., mortgage interest payments and interest on loans for repairs and improvements to the house.

6   RATES OF BENEFIT

The rates of benefit change regularly, and the practitioner should ascertain the appropriate rates at his time of reference.

The rates as at 7 April 1992 are as follows:

(a)   *Personal allowances*

			£
(i)	Single		
		under age 18	25.55/33.60
		aged 18–24	33.60
		aged 25 or over	42.45
(ii)	Lone parent		
		under age 18	25.55/33.60
		aged 18 or over	42.45
(iii)	Couple		
		both under age 18	50.60
		at least one aged 18 or over	66.60
(iv)	Dependent children		
		under age 11	14.55
		aged 11–15	21.40
		aged 16–17	25.55
		aged 18	33.60

(b)   *Premiums*

			£
(i)	Family		9.30
(ii)	Lone parent		4.75
(iii)	Pensioner		
		Single	14.70
		Couple	22.35
(iv)	Enhanced pensioner		
		Single	16.65
		Couple	25.00

(v)	Higher pensioner		
		Single	20.75
		Couple	29.55
(vi)	Disability		
		Single	17.80
		Couple	25.55
(vii)	Severe disability		
		Single	32.55
		Couple (one qualifies)	32.55
		Couple (both qualify)	65.10
(viii)	Disabled child		17.80
(ix)	Carers		11.55

(c)	*Housing costs – deductions for non-dependants*	£
(i)	Aged 18, or over, and in remunerative work	
	Gross income: low income threshold to £99.99	8.00
	Gross income: £100 to £129.99	12.00
	Gross income: £130 or more	18.00
	Others, aged 18, or over, or on income support and over 25	4.00
(ii)	Low earnings threshold	65.00

7 THE SOCIAL FUND

The social fund was set up by s. 32 of the Social Security Act 1986, and replaces the system of single payments under the supplementary benefit scheme. The practitioner will find that the DSS guide to the social fund is a useful reference book. The object of payments from the social fund is to meet special needs which are not catered for by other benefits. The question of whether or not a payment will be made is decided by a social fund officer, who has a wide discretion. The most usual form of payment will be a loan. There are powers to make 'budgeting loans' which are interest-free and help to spread the cost of large one-off expenses over a longer period; 'crisis loans' which are interest-free and are for living expenses or items needed urgently (the applicant does not have to be in receipt of income support in order to qualify for one); and 'community care grants'. Other forms of payment available include a maternity payment to help buy necessities for a baby. Applications for payments from the social fund should be made to the claimant's local social security office.

It is important to note how much more restricted the system of the social fund is as compared with the former system of single payments.

8 HOW TO CLAIM

The income support scheme is run by the DSS. Enquiries about entitlement should be made to the claimant's local social security office. The normal method of applying for benefits is to fill in the appropriate form which should be sent or delivered to the local office. An interview will usually be arranged to determine the claimant's circumstances unless the claimant has claimed income support before. The adjudication officer will then determine whether the claimant is eligible for benefit and, if so, how much.

If the claimant is not required to be available for work, benefit will be paid by a book of weekly orders which can be cashed at a post office. There are provisions for certain of the claimant's expenses to be paid direct if he gets into difficulties (for example, gas and electricity bills). Claimants who are required to be available for work are sent their benefit each fortnight in a girocheque which includes any unemployment benefit to which the claimant is entitled.

9   APPEAL AND REVIEW

If the claimant feels he has been wrongly refused benefit or that benefit has been fixed at too low a level, he should write to the local DSS office asking for a review on the basis that the adjudication officer did not know about or made a mistake about some material fact, or that there has been a change in the circumstances on which the decision was based. If the outcome of the request for a review is still not satisfactory, consideration can be given to appealing to a social security appeal tribunal. There is a right of appeal from any decision of the adjudication officer, be it the original decision whether to grant benefit, or a review decision (including a decision by the adjudication officer to refuse to carry out a review at all). Written notice of appeal must be given within three months of the decision against which appeal is made. There will be a tribunal hearing and the decision will be sent to the claimant.

A further appeal by the claimant or the adjudication officer on a point of law may be possible to the Social Security Commissioners provided leave is granted. The chairman of the tribunal should be asked for leave to appeal and, if he refuses it, an application for leave can be made to a Commissioner.

If there is a point of law involved, the claimant or the Secretary of State may then be able to appeal from the Commissioner to the Court of Appeal. Leave to do this is required. The Commissioner can grant leave and, if he refuses, application for leave can be made to the Court of Appeal.

10   STATUTORY DUTY TO MAINTAIN OTHER MEMBERS OF THE FAMILY

A 'liable relative' is under a statutory obligation to maintain certain members of his family. Thus a man is liable to maintain his wife (up to, but not after, divorce) and children, including any illegitimate child of whom he is the putative father and a woman is liable to maintain her husband and children including her illegitimate children.

If a liable relative fails to fulfil his obligation to maintain and the other person claims income support, the DSS can apply for a court order obliging the liable relative to pay maintenance. They will normally contact the liable relative first to see whether a voluntary arrangement to pay can be sorted out. There is a special formula used by the DSS for calculating the appropriate amount for the liable relative to contribute. The DSS should not put any pressure on a woman to take maintenance proceedings against her husband — the DSS should use their own powers to seek a court order if necessary. However, proposed regulations (issued under the Child Support Act 1991) will change this by requiring a lone parent to cooperate in tracing an absent parent and to pursue maintenance with the risk of benefit deduction in the event of failure to co-operate.

Where a liable relative persistently refuses or neglects to maintain a person for whom he is responsible with the result that income support has to be paid for that person, he commits a criminal offence and can be fined or imprisoned.

11   THE DIVERSION PROCEDURE

Where the amount that will be paid to the family by way of maintenance will not be enough to take them off income support, it can be convenient (particularly if the maintenance payments tend to be erratic) for the family to continue to receive benefit in full and for the maintenance payments to be assigned to the DSS. This is called the 'diversion procedure'.

County court maintenance orders must be registered in the magistrates' courts if the diversion procedure is to be used. The diversion procedure is not usually used where the maintenance order exceeds the income support levels and is therefore enough to take the family off benefit altogether. However, if maintenance is not paid (or not paid in full) in a particular week, the family will be able to claim income support for that week and, if it turns out over a period of time that payments are regularly not made or not made on time, the diversion procedure may prove to be the most convenient way of dealing with the problem.

B: FAMILY CREDIT

The law on family credit is to be found in the Social Security Act 1986 and the Family Credit (General) Regulations 1987. The aim of family credit is to supplement the earnings of low-income families with children. It applies to people who are present in Great Britain. It is a tax-free benefit. Those in receipt of family credit are not entitled to free school meals, but family credit does entitle the claimant to assistance with NHS charges.

12   WHO QUALIFIES?

The claimant or his partner must be engaged in, or normally engaged in, remunerative work, and the claimant or his partner must be responsible for a member of the same household who is a child or young person. For the purposes of assessing entitlement to family credit the 'family' will include a married or an unmarried couple. 'Married couple' means a man and a woman who are married to each other and are members of the same household; 'unmarried couple' means a man and a woman who are not married to each other but who are living together as husband and wife.

12.1   Remunerative work

Remunerative work is work in which the claimant or his partner is engaged for 16 hours a week or more, and which is done for payment or in expectation of payment. If the hours of work fluctuate, the claimant or his partner must be engaged on average for not less than 16 hours a week.

12.2 Responsibility for a child or young person

If the claimant or his partner is treated as 'responsible for' (see Family Credit (General) Regulations 1987, regs. 8 and 9) a child or young person, then that child or young person (and any child of that child or young person) will normally be treated as a member of the claimant's household. A child or young person will not be treated as a member of the household if he has been resident in an institution on account of physical or mental handicap or disease for the 12 weeks immediately preceding the claim and is not in regular contact with the claimant or members of the household; or if he has been boarded out with the claimant or the claimant's partner, even if he has been so boarded out prior to adoption; or if he has been placed for adoption with the claimant or the claimant's partner.

13 ENTITLEMENT TO FAMILY CREDIT

Entitlement to family credit depends upon the claimant's financial resources, and is based upon the claimant's net (not gross) weekly earnings.

13.1 Calculating the claimant's income

For the purposes of establishing entitlement to family credit the claimant's weekly income is calculated as follows:

(a) Take the claimant's net weekly income. The practitioner should refer to the regulations for full details, but as a general outline 'income' includes periodic maintenance payments made to the claimant or to his or her children subject to a disregard of £15 per week from April 1992 (whether paid voluntarily or under a court order); lump sum orders (whether or not payable by instalments); most social security pensions and benefits, but note that the following benefits are disregarded in assessing entitlement to family credit — housing benefit, child benefit, one-parent benefit, income support and various other benefits described fully in the regulations.

(b) Add to it any 'tariff income' the claimant may receive from capital. This arises if the claimant's capital exceeds £3,000; if so, then each complete £250 in excess of £3,000 (but not exceeding £8,000) is treated as a weekly income of £1.

(c) Certain sums will be disregarded in the assessment of entitlement to family credit. The rules are complex and the practitioner should refer to the regulations for full details.

13.2 Effect of capital

The claimant will not be entitled to family credit if his capital exceeds £8,000. The first £3,000 of capital will be disregarded, and capital of between £3,000 and £8,000 will be taken into account by assuming a weekly income for each £250 of capital over the £3,000 level. The rules as to exactly which sums will be treated as capital and which sums will be disregarded for that purpose are complex and the practitioner is referred to the regulations for further details.

14 AMOUNT OF FAMILY CREDIT

The amount of family credit awarded depends upon whether the claimant's income exceeds the 'applicable amount'.

(a) If the claimant's income does not exceed the 'applicable amount' then he will receive the 'maximum appropriate family credit'.

(b) If the claimant's income does exceed the 'applicable amount' then the family credit he receives will be what remains after deducting from the 'appropriate maximum family credit' a 'prescribed percentage' of the excess of the claimant's income over the 'applicable amount'.

15 CURRENT RATES OF FAMILY CREDIT

The rates of benefit change regularly, and the practitioner should ascertain the appropriate rates at his time of reference.

The applicant may be entitled to the maximum amount of family credit if the family's net income is less than £66.60 per week. However, families with much higher incomes may still be entitled to *some* family credit.

As at 7 April 1989 the maximum rate is made up as follows:

	£
Adult credit (amount for 1 or 2 parents)	41.00
plus — for each child aged:	
under 11	10.40
11–15	17.25
16–17	21.45
18	29.90

16 PERIOD FOR WHICH FAMILY CREDIT IS PAYABLE

Family credit is normally payable for a period of 26 weeks. At the end of that period the claimant's entitlement to family credit will be reassessed. This can be a major advantage or disadvantage for the claimant, since changes of circumstances within the 26 weeks are not taken into account until the next assessment.

C: HOUSING BENEFIT

The law on housing benefit is to be found in the Social Security Act 1986 and the Housing Benefit (General) Regulations 1987. The scheme is in the form of rent rebates funded and administered by housing authorities, and rent allowances funded and administered by local authorities. The level of direct subsidy is determined by the Secretary of State in an annual order. Rent rebates affect public sector tenants who rent from a council, and rent allowances affect private sector tenants who rent from a private landlord or a housing association.

17 WHO QUALIFIES?

In order to qualify for housing benefit the claimant must be liable to make payments in respect of a dwelling which he occupies as his home. In general only one home is allowed.

The following people will be treated as if they are 'liable to make payments in respect of a dwelling':

(a)   The person who is liable to make those payments or his partner.

(b)   A person who has to make the payments if he is to continue to live in the home, because the third party who is liable to make the payments is not doing so; in this case the claimant must have been the former partner of the defaulting third party, or some other person whom it is reasonable to treat as liable to make the payments.

Since September 1990 most full-time students have been unable to claim housing benefit.

18   WHAT PAYMENTS WILL BE MADE?

Housing benefit is payable for rent, and the appropriate maximum housing benefit to which the claimant is entitled is calculated by reference to the amount of the claimant's 'eligible rent' – in respect of a rent rebate or rent allowance.

18.1   'Eligible rent'

The amount of the claimant's 'eligible rent' means those periodical payments which the claimant is liable to make in respect of the dwelling which he occupies as his home. Such payments include the following: rent; payments in respect of a licence or permission to occupy the dwelling; mesne profits; payments for use and occupation of the dwelling; service charges which are a condition of the right to occupy the dwelling.

The amount of the claimant's 'eligible rent' is the total rent which the claimant is liable to pay, minus charges for water, sewerage and certain ineligible service charges.

If the rent is registered and the rent which the claimant is liable to pay is limited to the registered rent, then the claimant's 'eligible rent' cannot exceed the amount of the registered rent.

18.2   Reduction of 'eligible rent'

The amount of the claimant's 'eligible rent' may be reduced by an 'appropriate' amount if the assessment officer considers that:

(a)   the claimant is occupying a dwelling that is too large for the requirements of the claimant and those who also occupy that dwelling; or

(b)   the rent payable for the claimant's dwelling is unreasonably high.

In this situation the claimant's maximum housing benefit will be calculated with respect to the 'eligible rent' as reduced by the 'appropriate' amount.

19   AMOUNT OF HOUSING BENEFIT

A payment of housing benefit will be made if:

(a)   the claimant has no income, or

(b)   the claimant's income does not exceed the 'applicable amount'.

19.1 The applicable amount

The applicable amount appropriate for the claimant and his family includes personal allowances and premiums which are almost the same as those used for calculating income support.

19.2 Assessing the claimant's income and capital

Having ascertained the amount of a claimant's 'applicable amount', the next step is to ascertain his income and capital in order to determine whether or not his income exceeds his weekly applicable amount.

Where the claimant is a member of a family, the income and capital of any member of that family will be treated as the income and capital of that person. The capital of a child or young person who is a member of the claimant's family will not be treated as the capital of the claimant, but special rules will apply where the child or young person has capital in excess of £3,000. The practitioner is referred to the regulations for full details.

The claimant's income is assessed as follows:

(a) Calculate the claimant's weekly earnings (the sums that will be counted as part of the claimant's earnings are clearly set out in the regulations and the practitioner is referred to them).

(b) Adding to it any tariff income from capital — where the claimant's capital exceeds £3,000, it will be treated as equivalent to a weekly tariff income of £1 for each complete £250 in excess of £3,000 but not exceeding £16,000.

(c) Certain sums will be disregarded in assessing the claimant's income. The rules in relation to those sums are complex and the practitioner is referred to the regulations for details. It should be noted that where the claimant is in receipt of income support the whole of his income will be disregarded.

19.3 Effect of capital on housing benefit

Where a claimant's capital exceeds £16,000 he will be disqualified from any entitlement to housing benefit. Certain sums will be disregarded in assessing what does and does not amount to capital. The rules in respect of this are complex and the practitioner is referred to the regulations for details.

19.4 Appropriate maximum housing benefit

The appropriate maximum housing benefit consists of 100% of the claimant's eligible rent.

In each case there will be a deduction, where appropriate, in respect of a non-dependent person who resides with the claimant. The rates of the relevant weekly deductions are updated regularly, and the practitioner should ascertain the appropriate rate at his time of reference.

19.5 Where the claimant's income exceeds the applicable amount

If the claimant is entitled to housing benefit but his income exceeds the 'applicable amount', then the amount of housing benefit is what remains after deduction from the appropriate maximum housing benefit of a 'prescribed percentage' of the excess of his income over the applicable amount. The 'prescribed percentage' is 65%.

19.6 Minimum housing benefit

Housing benefit will not be payable if the amount to which the claimant is entitled is less than 50 pence per week.

Community charge benefit operates in a very similar way to housing benefit save that the maximum community charge benefit is 80% of your 'eligible community charge' and the 'prescribed percentage' is 15%.

D: CHILD BENEFIT AND ONE-PARENT BENEFIT

The law on child benefit and one-parent benefit is to be found in the Child Benefit Act 1975 and the various Child Benefit Regulations.

20 CHILD BENEFIT

20.1 General

Child benefit is a standard weekly amount presently £9.65 for the only, elder or eldest child and £7.80 for each subsequent child paid to the person (normally but not necessarily a parent) who is responsible for a child.

20.2 Definition of a child

Child benefit is payable in respect of:

(a) all children under 16;
(b) children of 16 to under 19 who are still in full-time non-advanced (i.e. not above A-level) education.

Child benefit is not paid for children at university, training for professional qualifications, apprenticed, etc. or for children in full-time employment.

When a child under 19 leaves school, child benefit will generally still be payable for him until the start of the new term after he has left, i.e. right through the school holiday, unless he gets a full-time job or a Youth Training place.

20.3 Person responsible

A person is responsible for a child if either:

(a) he has the child living with him; *or*
(b) he contributes to the child's maintenance at a weekly rate of not less than the rate of child benefit.

More than one person may count as responsible for one child but benefit will only be paid to one person. There are rules for determining who should receive the benefit if more than one person claims it. If the child is living with both his parents (whether they are married or not), his mother will be the one entitled to claim the benefit. If the child is not living with both parents, the person with whom he is living (whether a parent or not) will have first claim to the benefit. If the household in which the child is living comprises a parent and a non-parent (for example, his mother and her boyfriend), the parent will naturally have priority over the non-parent.

Example 1. Cedric is 16 and is still at school doing A-levels. He lives with his mother and father, Mr and Mrs Conn. Child benefit will be payable in respect of Cedric. As he is living with both his parents, both parents qualify as responsible for him. His mother is the one who has the prior claim to benefit, although if she wants Mr Conn to receive the benefit, he can apply enclosing her written statement that she does not wish to claim the benefit herself.

Example 2. Dennis is five. His parents, Mr and Mrs Drabble, have split up. Dennis is living with his mother who is cohabiting with Mr Eves. Mr Drabble pays voluntary maintenance for Dennis of £10 per week. Child benefit is payable in respect of Dennis. Mr Drabble, Mrs Drabble and Mr Eves can all claim to be responsible for him (Mrs Drabble and Mr Eves because he is living with them and Mr Drabble because he contributes to Dennis's maintenance). Mrs Drabble and Mr Eves have the prior claim to the benefit over Mr Drabble because Dennis is living with them. As between Mrs Drabble and Mr Eves, Mrs Drabble has the prior claim because she is Dennis's parent.

20.4   Making a claim

A form on which to claim child benefit can be obtained from the local social security office. If the claimant is seeking to have the benefit transferred from someone else who has priority, he will have to provide with the claim form a statement from the person with priority that she does not want to claim the benefit herself. If he is seeking to have the benefit transferred on the basis that he now has priority, three weeks will have to elapse after the claim is made before the transfer can take place.

20.5   Payment of benefit

Benefit is paid once every four weeks. The recipient will receive a book of orders which she can cash at a named post office. Single parents and families on income support or family credit can elect to have the benefit paid weekly. The DSS also have a general power to allow weekly payments in other cases where four-weekly payment causes hardship. It can be credited direct to a bank account. Those entitled before 1982 can draw benefit weekly.

Child benefit is tax-free. It forms part of the recipient's income for the purposes of income support but not for family credit.

21   ONE-PARENT BENEFIT

A person who is bringing up a child alone will be entitled to a further tax-free single weekly payment in addition to her child benefit payments. To qualify, the claimant must:

(a)   not be living with anyone as man and wife; *and*
(b)   either

(i)   never have been married, *or*
(ii)   be divorced, judicially separated or widowed; *or*
(iii)   if still married, be permanently separated from his or her spouse which separation must already have lasted for at least 13 weeks.

The extra sum payable as one-parent benefit is presently £5.85 per week irrespective of the number of children the claimant looks after. Payment will be made at the same time as child benefit is paid.

> **Example.** Mrs Jones separated from her busband six months ago. Although they are not yet divorced, there is no prospect of a reconciliation. Mrs Jones lives on her own and looks after the two children of the family who are aged 5 and 7 and in respect of whom she receives £17.45 per week child benefit (i.e. £9.65 + £7.80). Mrs Jones will qualify for one-parent benefit and will therefore receive an additional £5.85 on top of her £17.45 child benefit. Because she is a single parent, she can apply to have her child benefit and the one-parent benefit paid weekly.

One-parent benefit must be claimed separately from child benefit. There is a standard application form obtainable from the DSS.

E: STATE BENEFITS AND MARRIAGE BREAKDOWN

22 RELEVANCE OF STATE BENEFITS IN DETERMINING APPROPRIATE MAINTENANCE

A spouse cannot normally rely on the fact that his family will be eligible for state benefits as relieving him from his obligation to maintain them. The relevance of state benefits in an application for periodical payments after divorce is discussed in Chapter 16 at paragraph 5.5.

23 MAINTENANCE VERSUS STATE BENEFITS: PROS AND CONS FOR THE RECIPIENT

It quite often happens that one spouse, usually the wife, is on benefit (usually income support) and the other spouse is earning but not at a very high rate. Where it is unlikely that maintenance from the husband will be fixed at a rate significantly more than the wife would be receiving by way of state benefits, it must be remembered that if the wife is taken off benefit she may well lose not only the weekly amount of cash benefit but also the other benefits to which she is automatically entitled by virtue of the fact that she is on income support, for example, housing benefit, free school meals and milk, prescriptions, etc. (Family credit is not 'passport' benefit.) On top of this, she will lose her opportunity to claim payments from the social fund as she could have done had she remained on income support.

It follows that sometimes it may pay the wife to receive slightly less maintenance in order to stay on benefit and this possibility must be kept firmly in mind when advising on the level of maintenance which would be acceptable and in presenting applications for periodical payments to the court.

24 LUMP SUMS AND INCOME SUPPORT

A lump sum payment which is in reality a form of capitalised maintenance will be counted as income of the family for income support purposes and will prevent the family from receiving benefit for a period of time.

There does, however, seem to be some leeway over certain lump sums where what is really happening is that the recipient is realising her interest in a capital asset owned by her solely or by her and her spouse jointly and sold/divided up/retained by the other spouse on the breakdown of the marriage. Thus the following types of lump sum will be regarded as capital and will therefore only put a stop to the family's entitlement to benefit if the family has more than £8,000 capital altogether:

(a)   A lump sum ordered by the court or agreed between the parties as representing the capitalisation of an interest in joint property or property held by the other party solely; for example, £2,000 paid by the husband to the wife representing her interest in the family car and the furniture in the matrimonial home which he has kept.

(b)   A lump sum ordered by the court or agreed between the parties representing the allocation of or division of money held in banks, building societies or similar.

(c)   A sum derived from the proceeds of sale of the matrimonial home or intended to compensate the claimant for her loss of interest in the home (such a sum will not even be counted as capital for at least six months).

(d)   Payments in kind. The court does not have power in ancillary relief proceedings to order one spouse to purchase any item for the other spouse so the most that could be done would be for him to give an undertaking to do so.

36 The local authority and housing

1 THE HOMELESS

Part III of the Housing Act 1985 deals with the provision of accommodation for those who are without a home.

1.1 Who is homeless?

A person is 'homeless' for the purposes of the Act if he has no accommodation. He is treated as having no accommodation if:

(a) There is no accommodation which he, together with any person who normally resides with him as a member of his family or in circumstances in which it is reasonable for that person to reside with him, is entitled to occupy. *Or*

(b) If he has accommodation but he cannot secure entry to it or it is probable that occupation of it will lead to actual violence from some other person living there or to threats of violence from some other person living there who is likely to carry the threats out.

However, a person shall not be treated as having accommodation unless it is accommodation which it would be reasonable for him to continue to occupy.

A person is 'threatened with homelessness' if it is likely that he will become homeless within 28 days (s. 58).

It is those who are homeless or threatened with homelessness who may be able to receive help under the Act. Some claimants have priority over others.

1.2 Priority need for accommodation

A homeless person or a person threatened with homelessness has a priority need for accommodation if:

(a) he has dependent children who are residing with him or might reasonably be expected to reside with him; *or*

(b) he is homeless or threatened with homelessness as a result of an emergency such as a flood, fire or other disaster; *or*

(c) he, or any person who lives with him or might reasonably be expected to do so, is vulnerable as a result of old age, mental illness or handicap or physical disability or other special reason; *or*

(d) she is a pregnant woman or he or she lives with or might reasonably be expected to live with a pregnant woman (s. 59).

1.3 Duties of the housing authority

If a person applies to a housing authority for accommodation or assistance in obtaining accommodation and the authority have reason to believe that he is homeless or threatened with homelessness the authority must make enquiries to satisfy themselves whether the person is homeless or threatened with homelessness and, if so, whether he has a priority need and whether he became homeless or threatened with homelessness intentionally. If the housing authority have reason to believe that the person may be homeless and have a priority need, they must provide him with temporary accommodation pending the outcome of their enquiries (s. 62).

Once they have made their enquiries, if the housing authority are satisfied that the person *is* homeless or threatened with homelessness, they are under a duty towards him. The exact nature of the duty depends on whether he has a priority need and whether he has become homeless or threatened with homelessness intentionally (see paragraph 1.4 below):

(a)   No priority need or (if he has a priority need) homeless or threatened with homelessness intentionally — duty to give him advice and appropriate assistance in any attempts he may make to get accommodation or to prevent himself losing his current accommodation. Where he is *actually* intentionally homeless with a priority need, the authority also have a duty to provide him with temporary accommodaton for such period as they consider will give him a reasonable opportunity of getting himself accommodation.

(b)   Threatened with homelessness with priority need, not intentionally — duty to take reasonable steps to secure that he does not become homeless.

(c)   Homeless with a priority need, not intentionally — duty to rehouse him (ss. 65 and 66).

There are provisions enabling the housing authority to whom application has been made to pass responsibility to another housing authority if the applicant has no local connection with the area in which the application has been made (s. 67).

The accommodation provided may be in council property but applicants may be placed in private housing and temporary accommodation may be in hostels, women's refuges, bed and breakfast establishments, etc.

1.4 'Intentionally homeless'

A person becomes homeless intentionally if he deliberately does or fails to do anything in consequence of which he ceases to occupy accommodation which is available for his occupation and which it would have been reasonable for him to continue to occupy.

A person becomes threatened with homelessness intentionally if he deliberately does or fails to do anything the likely result of which is that he will be forced to leave accommodation which is available for his occupation and which it would have been reasonable for him to continue to occupy.

It would seem that people who have got into genuine financial difficulties and thus put themselves at risk of eviction will not be regarded as intentionally homeless. But if someone deliberately decides to sell his house or give up his tenancy or wilfully refuses to pay his rent so that he is turned out of his house, he will probably be regarded as intentionally homeless. However, the fact that it must be reasonable for the person to continue to live in his house means that

battered wives who leave home because they have been subjected to violence will
not be regarded as intentionally homeless (s. 60).

2   SECURE TENANTS

Council tenants and other tenants classed as secure tenants under the Housing
Act 1985 (see s. 79), enjoy special protection under the Act. In particular, the
tenancy cannot be brought to an end by the landlord unless he obtains a court
order for possession (s. 82). The grounds on which possession can be ordered are
set out in the Act.

Index